C O N T E N T S

CHAPTER ONE

Overview of Computers and Programming

Since the 1940s, the computer has dramatically changed the way we live and how we do business. Today computers provide instructional material in school, print transcripts, prepare bills and paychecks, reserve airline and concert tickets, allow us to bank and shop conveniently, and help us write term papers and even books.

Although we often are led to believe otherwise, computers cannot reason as we do. Basically, computers are devices for performing computations at incredible speeds (more than one million operations per second) and with great accuracy. To accomplish anything useful, however, a computer must be provided with a program, that is, a list of instructions to perform. Programs are usually written in special computer programming languages such as Pascal, which is the subject of this book.

In this chapter, we introduce you to the computer and its components and then present an overview of programming languages. Finally, we describe how to use a particular Pascal system called Turbo Pascal.

1.1 Electronic Computers Then and Now

In our everyday life, we come in contact with computers frequently, some of us using computers for word processing or even having studied programming in high school. But it wasn't always this way. Not so long ago, most people considered computers to be mysterious devices whose secrets were known only by a few computer wizards.

The first electronic computer was designed in the late 1930s by Dr. John Atanasoff at Iowa State University. Atanasoff designed his computer to assist graduate students in nuclear physics with their mathematical computations.

The first large-scale, general-purpose electronic digital computer, called the ENIAC, was completed in 1946 at the University of Pennsylvania with funding from the U.S. Army. Weighing 30 tons and occupying a 30-by-50-foot space, the ENIAC was used to compute ballistics tables, predict the weather, and make atomic energy calculations.

These early computers used vacuum tubes as their basic electronic component. Technological advances in the design and manufacture of electronic components led to new generations of computers that were considerably smaller, faster, and less expensive than previous ones.

computer chip
the electronic component that comprises a computer processor

Using today's technology, a computer processor can be packaged in a single electronic component called a **computer chip,** which is about the size of a postage stamp. Their affordability and small size enable computer chips to be installed in watches, pocket calculators, cameras, home appliances, automobiles, and, of course, computers.

Today, a common sight in offices and homes is a personal computer, which can cost less than $2000 and sit on a desk, and yet has as much computational power as one that 15 years ago cost more than $100,000 and filled a 9-by-12-foot room. Even smaller computers can fit inside a briefcase (Fig. 1.1a) or your hand (Fig. 1.1b).

Modern-day computers are categorized according to their size and performance. *Microcomputers,* shown in Fig. 1.1, are used by a single person at a time. The largest microcomputers are called *workstations* (Fig. 1.1c). Businesses and research laboratories also use larger and faster computers, called *minicomputers* and *mainframes,* which can be used by many people simultaneously. *Supercomputers,* the most powerful mainframe computers, can perform in seconds computations that might take hours or even days on other computers.

Figure 1.1
(a) Notebook Computer. (b) Palmtop Computer. (c) Workstation.

(a)

(b)

(c)

hardware
the actual computer equipment
software
the set of programs associated
with a computer
program
a list of instructions that enable a computer to perform a
specific task
binary number
a number whose digits are 0
and 1

A computer system consists of two major components: hardware and software. **Hardware** is the equipment used to perform the necessary computations and includes the central processing unit (CPU), monitor, keyboard, and
printer. The **software** is the **programs** that enable us to solve problems
with a computer by providing it with lists of instructions to perform.

Programming a computer has undergone significant changes over the
years. Initially, the task was very difficult, requiring programmers to write
their program instructions as long **binary numbers** (sequences of 0s and
1s). Today's programming languages such as Pascal make programming
much easier.

Exercises for Section 1.1

Self-Check

1. Is a computer program a piece of hardware or is it software?
2. Which do you think is the major source of computer errors, faulty com-
    puter hardware or incorrect software?

1.2 Introduction to Computer Hardware

Despite significant variations in cost, size, and capabilities, modern computers resemble one another in many basic ways. Essentially, most consist of
the following components:

▶ Main memory
▶ Secondary memory, which includes storage devices such as hard disks
   and floppy disks
▶ The central processor unit
▶ Input devices, such as keyboards and mouses
▶ Output devices, such as monitors and printers

Figure 1.2 shows how these components interact in a computer, with the
arrows pointing in the direction of information flow. The program must first
be transferred from *secondary memory* to *main memory* before it can be executed. Normally the person using a program (the *program user*) must supply some data to be processed. These data are entered through an *input
device* and are stored in the computer's *main memory,* where they can be
accessed and manipulated by the *central processor unit*. The results of this
manipulation are then stored back in *main memory*. Finally, the information
in main memory can be displayed through an *output device*. In the remainder of this section, we describe these components in more detail.

Memory

Memory is an essential component in any computer. Before discussing the
types of memory—main and secondary—let's look at what it consists of and
how the computer works with it.

Figure 1.2
Components of
a Computer

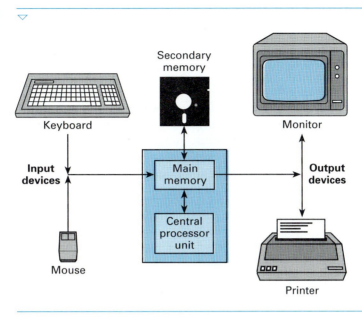

Anatomy of Memory

memory cell
an individual storage location in memory

address of a memory cell
the relative position of a memory cell in the computer's main memory

contents of a memory cell
the information stored in a memory cell, either a program instruction or data

Imagine the memory of a computer as an ordered sequence of storage locations called **memory cells** (see Fig. 1.3). To store and access information, the computer must have some way of identifying the individual memory cells. Therefore each memory cell has a unique **address** that indicates its relative position in memory. Figure 1.3 shows a computer memory consisting of 1000 memory cells with addresses 0 through 999. Most computers, however, have millions of individual memory cells, each with its own address.

The data stored in a memory cell are called the **contents** of the cell. Every memory cell always has some contents, although we may have no idea what they are. In Fig. 1.3, the contents of memory cell 3 are the number −26 and the contents of memory cell 4 are the letter H.

stored program concept
storing program instructions in main memory prior to execution

Although not shown in Fig. 1.3, a memory cell can also contain a program instruction. The ability to store programs as well as data is called the **stored program concept**: A program's instructions must be stored in main memory before they can be executed. We can change the computer's operation by storing a different program in memory.

Bytes and Bits

byte
the amount of storage required to store a single character

A memory cell is actually a grouping of smaller units called bytes. A **byte** is the amount of storage required to store a single character, such as the letter H used in Fig. 1.3. The number of bytes a memory cell can contain varies

Figure 1.3
1000 Memory Cells in
Main Memory

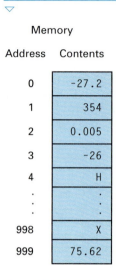

Memory

Address	Contents
0	-27.2
1	354
2	0.005
3	-26
4	H
·	·
·	·
·	·
998	X
999	75.62

bit
a **bi**nary digi**t**; a 0 or a 1

from computer to computer. A byte is composed of even smaller units of storage called bits (see Fig. 1.4). The term **bit**, deriving from the words **bi**nary digi**t**, is the smallest element a computer can deal with. Binary refers to a number system based on two numbers, 0 and 1, and so a bit is either a 0 or a 1. Generally there are eight bits to a byte.

Storage and Retrieval of Information in Memory

data storage
setting the individual bits of a memory cell to 0 or 1, destroying its previous contents
data retrieval
copying the contents of a particular memory cell to another storage area

Each value in memory is represented by a particular pattern of 0s and 1s. A computer can either store a value or retrieve a value. To **store** a value, the computer sets each bit of a selected memory cell to either 0 or 1, destroying the previous contents of the cell in the process. To **retrieve** a value from a memory cell, the computer copies the pattern of 0s and 1s stored in that cell to another storage area for processing; the copy operation does not destroy the contents of the cell whose value is retrieved. This process is the same regardless of the kind of information—character, number, or program instruction—to be stored or retrieved.

Figure 1.4
Relationship Between a
Byte and a Bit

Main Memory

Main memory stores programs, data, and results. Most computers have two types of main memory: **random access memory (RAM)**, which offers temporary storage of programs and data, and **read-only memory (ROM)**, which stores programs or data permanently. RAM temporarily stores programs while they are being executed (carried out) by the computer. It also temporarily stores such data as numbers, names, and even pictures while a program is manipulating them. RAM is usually **volatile memory**, which means that everything in RAM will be lost when the computer is switched off.

ROM, on the other hand, stores information permanently within the computer. The computer can retrieve (or read), but cannot store (or write), information in ROM, hence its name, read-only. Because ROM is not volatile, the data stored there do not disappear when the computer is switched off. ROM stores the instructions needed to get the computer running when you first switch it on. In most computers, RAM memory capacity is much greater than ROM memory and RAM can often be increased (up to a specified maximum), whereas the amount of ROM is usually fixed. When we refer to main memory in this text, we mean RAM because that is the part of main memory that is normally accessible to the Pascal programmer.

Secondary Memory and Secondary Storage Devices

Secondary memory, through secondary storage devices, provides semipermanent data storage capability. A common secondary storage device is a **disk drive**, which stores and retrieves data and programs on a storage medium called a **disk**. A disk is considered semipermanent instead of permanent because its contents can be changed, rather like a cassette tape that contains music that can be played over and over, but that can be erased and recorded over.

There are two kinds of disks: **hard** (also called fixed) and **floppy**. Most computers contain one hard disk that cannot be removed from its disk drive and so provides a storage area to be shared by all users of the computer. Normally the programs that are needed to operate the computer system are stored on its hard disk. Each computer user can have one or more floppy disks that can be inserted into a computer's floppy disk drive. A floppy disk is a plastic sheet with a diameter of 3.5 or 5.25 inches housed in a thin square container. These floppy disks can store an individual user's programs and personal data.

A hard disk can store much more data, and can be accessed by the CPU much more quickly, than can a single floppy disk. Each user, however, can have an unlimited number of floppy disks. Unlike a hard disk, a floppy disk is portable, which means it can be used with many different computers as long as they are all compatible.

Information stored on a disk is organized into separate collections called **files**. One file may contain a Pascal program. Another file may contain the

random access memory (RAM)
the part of main memory that temporarily stores programs, data, and results

read-only memory (ROM)
the part of main memory that permanently stores programs or data

volatile memory
memory whose contents disappear when the computer is switched off

disk drive
a device used to store and retrieve information on a **disk**

hard disk
a disk with drive that is built into the computer and normally cannot be removed

floppy disk
a personal, portable disk that can be used with different computers

file
a collection of related information stored on a disk

data to be processed by that program (a *data file*). A third file could contain the results generated by a program (an *output file*).

An increasingly common secondary storage device is a CD-ROM drive. This drive accesses information stored on plastic disks that resemble the CDs used in a CD player. The ROM in CD-ROM indicates that currently most drives can only read the data stored on a CD and cannot write new information to the CD.

Comparison of Main and Secondary Memory

Because the computer processor can manipulate data only in main memory, data stored in secondary memory, including program instructions, must be transferred into main memory before they can be processed. For this reason, the computer manipulates data and instructions already in main memory much faster than those in secondary memory.

A fixed disk has much more storage capacity than does main memory. On most computers, you can increase the size of main memory by installing additional memory chips. You can also increase the size of secondary memory, by purchasing additional floppy disks or installing another fixed disk. However, main memory is considerably more expensive than secondary memory. Furthermore, data in main memory are volatile and disappear when you switch off the computer, whereas data in secondary memory are semipermanent and do not disappear when the computer is switched off. Therefore store all your programs as files in secondary memory, and transfer a program file into main memory when you want it executed.

Central Processor Unit

central processor unit (CPU)
coordinates all computer operations and performs arithmetic and logical operations on data

The **central processor unit (CPU)** has two roles: coordinating all computer operations and performing arithmetic and logical operations on data. The CPU follows the instructions contained in a computer program to determine which operations should be carried out and in what order. It then transmits coordinating control signals to the other computer components. For example, if the instruction requires reading a data item, the CPU sends the necessary control signals to the input device.

fetching an instruction
retrieving an instruction from main memory

To process a program stored in main memory, the CPU retrieves each instruction in sequence (called **fetching an instruction**), interprets the instruction to determine what should be done, and then retrieves any data needed to carry out that instruction. Next, the CPU performs the actual manipulation, or processing, of the data it retrieved. The CPU stores the results in main memory.

The CPU can perform such arithmetic operations as addition, subtraction, multiplication, and division. The CPU also can compare the contents of two memory cells (for example, Which contains the larger value? Are the values equal?) and make decisions based on the results of that comparison.

Input/Output Devices

We use *input/output (I/O) devices* to communicate with the computer. Specifically, they allow us to enter data for a computation and to observe the results of that computation.

You will be using a *keyboard* (see Fig. 1.5) as an input device and a *monitor* (display screen) as an output device. When you press a letter or digit key on a keyboard, that character is sent to main memory and is also displayed on the monitor at the position of the **cursor**, a moving place marker (normally a blinking underscore symbol). A computer keyboard resembles a typewriter keyboard except for some extra keys for performing special functions. For example, on the computer keyboard shown in Fig. 1.5, the 12 keys in the top row labeled F1 through F12 are **function keys**. The activity performed when you press a function key depends on the program currently being executed; that is, pressing F1 in one program will usually not produce the same results as pressing F1 in another program. Other special keys enable you to delete characters, move the cursor, and "enter" a line of data you typed at the keyboard (see the highlighted parts of Fig. 1.5).

Another common input device is a mouse. A **mouse** is a hand-held device used to select an operation. When you move the mouse around on your desktop, a rubber ball attached to the mouse rotates and simultaneously moves the *mouse cursor* (normally a small rectangle or an arrow) displayed on the monitor's screen. You select an operation by moving the mouse cursor to a word or picture that represents the computer operation you wish to perform and then pressing or clicking a mouse button to activate the operation selected.

cursor
a moving place marker that appears on the monitor

function keys
special keyboard keys used to select a particular operation; the operation selected depends on the program being used

mouse
an input device that moves its cursor on the computer screen to select an operation

Figure 1.5
Keyboard for IBM-Type Computers

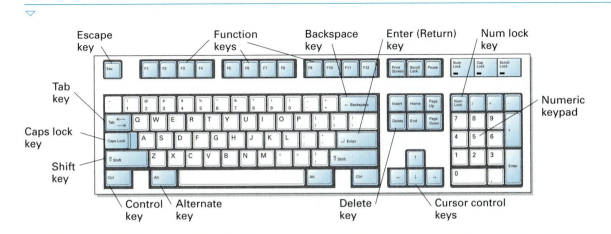

A monitor provides a temporary display of the information that appears on its screen. Once the image disappears from the monitor screen, it is lost. If you want *hard copy* (a printed version) of some information, you must send that information to an output device called a **printer**.

printer
an output device that produces a hard copy of information sent to it

Computer Networks

Until now we have talked about the components of individual computers. Often several computers are interconnected as a **computer network**, so each computer user can access a large hard disk and high-quality printers. The computer that controls access to the shared disk is called the **file server**. Each computer in the network also has its own keyboard, monitor, and disk drives. Many computer laboratories arrange their computer hardware in a network.

computer network
a group of interconnected computers
file server
the computer in a network that controls access to the shared disk

Exercises for Section 1.2   **Self-Check**

1. If a computer were instructed to sum the contents of memory cells 2 and 999 in Fig. 1.3 and store the result in cell 0, what would be the contents of cells 0, 2, and 999?
2. One bit can have two values, 0 or 1. A combination of 2 bits can have 4 values: 00, 01, 10, 11. List all of the values you can form with a combination of 3 bits. Do the same for 4 bits.
3. List the following in order of smallest to largest: byte, bit, main memory, memory cell, secondary memory.

1.3   Problem Solving and Programming

Because it cannot think, a computer requires a program to do any useful work. Computer programming involves much more than simply writing a list of instructions. Problem solving is a crucial component of programming and requires a good deal of preplanning. Before writing a program to solve a particular problem, you must consider carefully all aspects of the problem and then develop and organize its solution.

Like most programming students, you will probably spend a great deal of time entering your programs into the computer. Later you will spend more time removing the errors that inevitably will be present in your programs. So resist the temptation to rush to the computer and start entering your program as soon as you have some idea of how to write it. Instead, think carefully about the problem and its solution before writing any program instructions. When you have a potential solution in mind, plan it out beforehand, using either paper and pencil or a word processor, and modify the solution if necessary before you write the program in a programming language.

desk check
do a step-by-step simulation of a solution plan

You should **desk check** your solution plan by carefully performing each step much as the computer would. To desk check a solution plan, simulate

Figure 1.6
Programming Strategy

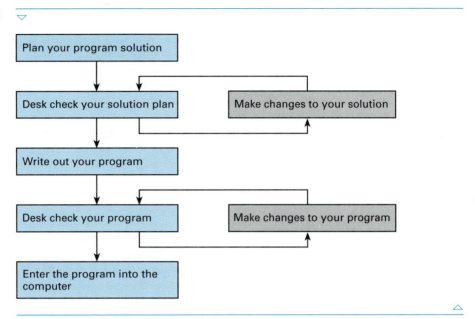

the result of each step using sample data that are easy to manipulate (for example, small whole numbers). Then compare your results with the expected results, and make any necessary corrections to the solution plan.

At this point, you can write your solution plan as a program. You should also desk check your program before you enter it into the computer. A few extra minutes spent evaluating the solution plan and program using the process summarized in Fig. 1.6 often saves hours of frustration later.

In this text, we stress a methodology for problem solving that has proved useful in helping students learn to program. We describe this technique and show you how to apply it in Section 2.1.

Exercise for Section 1.3   **Self-Check**

1. If a computer can execute your program quickly and efficiently, what is the purpose of desk checking the program?

1.4 Overview of Programming Languages

We use programming languages to write computer programs. Although there are many different programming languages, the most commonly used today are called high-level languages. To understand the advantage of high-level languages, we must first understand how a computer communicates.

Machine Language

machine language
a computer's native language
with instructions that are
binary numbers

The native tongue of a computer is **machine language**. Each machine language instruction is a binary string of 0s and 1s that specifies an operation and identifies the memory cells involved in that operation. For example, if we wanted to represent the algebraic formula

cost = price + tax

in a machine language program, we might need a sequence of instructions such as

```
0010 0000 0000 0100
0100 0000 0000 0101
0011 0000 0000 0110
```

In each machine language instruction, the operation to be performed and the address of the data to be manipulated are written as binary numbers. Although the computer would have no difficulty understanding the three preceding machine language instructions, they are unintelligible to most people.

High-Level Languages

high-level language
a programming language
whose instructions resemble
everyday language

When writing programs in a **high-level language**, we use instructions that resemble everyday language. In Pascal, we would use the statement

```
Cost := Price + Tax
```

which closely resembles the original formula. This statement means "Add the value of Price to the value of Tax and store the result as Cost." When writing a program in a high-level language, we can reference data that are stored in memory using descriptive names—for example, Price, Cost, Tax—rather than numeric memory cell addresses. We can also use familiar symbols (such as +) to describe operations we want performed.

language standard
a description of the syntax
and meaning of each high-
level language instruction

A high-level language has a **language standard** that describes the grammatical form (syntax) of the language. Every high-level language instruction must conform to the syntax rules specified in the language standard. These rules are very precise—they make no allowances for instructions that are *almost* correct. Programs that conform to these rules are *portable,* which means that they can be used without modification on many types of computers. A machine language program, on the other hand, can be used on only one type of computer.

application software
programs written for a computer user

system software
programs written for the computer system

Common high-level languages include Pascal, Fortran, BASIC, COBOL, C, and C++. Although each of these languages was designed for a specific purpose (see Table 1.1), all are used to write a variety of **application software**—software that performs tasks for the computer user. The languages C and C++ are frequently used to write **system software**—software that performs tasks required for the operation of the computer system.

Table 1.1
Common High-Level
Languages

High-Level Language	Original Purpose
Pascal	For teaching students to program in a careful, disciplined way
Fortran (**For**mula **tran**slation)	For engineering and scientific applications
BASIC	Simple language intended for student use in schoolwork
COBOL	For performing business data processing
C	For writing system software
C++	Extension of C that supports object-oriented programming

Relationship Between High-Level and Machine Language

source program
the high-level language program being translated

object program
the machine-language translation of a source program

Because a computer understands only programs written in machine language, each instruction in a high-level language program must first be translated into machine language before it can be executed. The original high-level language program is called the **source program**; the machine-language translation is called the **object program**. The next section discusses the steps required to process a high-level language program.

Exercises for Section 1.4

Self-Check

1. What do you think these four high-level language statements mean? Assume that the symbol ; separates the statements.

   ```
   X := A + B + C;   X := Y / Z;   D := C - B + A;   Z := Z + 1
   ```

2. List two reasons why it would be preferable to write a program in Pascal rather than machine language.

1.5 Processing a High-Level Language Program

Before the computer can execute a high-level language program, the programmer must enter the source program into the computer and the computer must store it in executable form in memory. Several system programs assist with this task. We describe the role of these programs next and summarize the process in Fig. 1.7.

Steps for Preparing a Program for Execution

editor
a program used to enter source programs and save source files

1. Use the **editor** program to enter each line of the source program into memory and to save it on disk as a source file.

compiler
a program that translates a high-level language program into machine language

syntax error
an error in the grammatical form of a line in a high-level language program

linker/loader
a program that combines (**links**) an object program with other object files and stores (**loads**) the final machine language program in memory

executable file
a disk file containing a ready-to-execute machine language program

2. Use a **compiler** program to translate the source program into machine language. If there are any **syntax errors** (errors in grammar), the compiler displays these errors on the monitor. Use the editor program to correct the errors by editing and resaving the source program.

3. When the source program is error free, the compiler saves its machine-language translation as an object program.

4. The **linker/loader** program combines your object program with additional object files that may be needed for your program to execute (for example, programs for input and output) and stores the final machine language program in memory, ready for execution. The linker/loader can also save the final machine language program as an **executable file** on disk. Often the linker/loader is written as two separate system programs.

Executing a Program

To execute a machine language program, the CPU must examine each program instruction in memory and send out the command signals required to carry out the instruction. Although the instructions normally are executed in sequence, as we will discuss later, it is possible to have the CPU skip over some instructions or execute some instructions more than once.

During execution, data can be entered into memory and manipulated in some specified way. Special program instructions are used for entering or

Figure 1.7
Preparing a Program for Execution

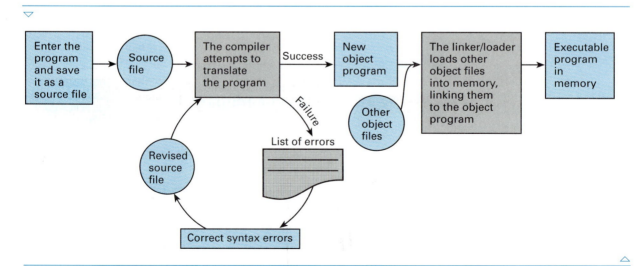

input data
the data values that are read by a program

program output
the lines displayed by a program

reading a program's data (called **input data**) into memory. After the input data have been processed, instructions for displaying or printing values in memory can be executed to display the program results. The lines displayed by a program are called the **program output**.

Let's use the situation described in Fig. 1.8—executing a payroll program stored in memory—as an example. The first step of the program enters into memory data that describe the employee's hours and pay rate. In step 2, the program manipulates the employee data and stores the results of the computations in memory. In the final step, the computational results are displayed as payroll reports or employee payroll checks.

Exercises for Section 1.5   **Self-Check**

1. Would a syntax error be found in a source program or an object program? What system program would find a syntax error if one existed? What system program would you use to correct it?
2. Explain the differences among the source program, the object program, and an executable program. Which do you create, and which does the compiler create? Which does the linker/loader create?

Figure 1.8
Flow of Information During Program Execution

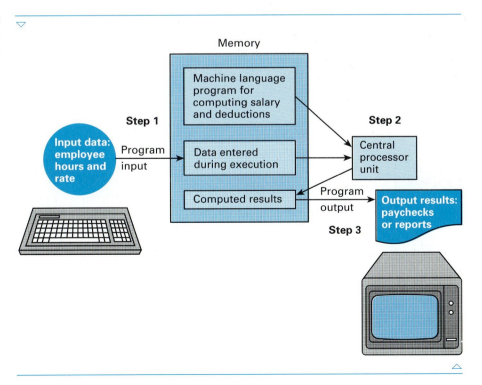

1.6   Using the Turbo Pascal Integrated Environment

The mechanics of entering a program as a source file, translating it to machine language, and executing the machine language program differ on each computer system. In this text, we use an IBM PC (personal computer) or compatible computer and Turbo Pascal version 7.0. Earlier versions of Turbo Pascal may perform differently; your instructor will tell you which version of Turbo Pascal is available to you. Developed by Borland International for IBM PCs, Turbo Pascal provides an **integrated environment**, which means that you will be able to create, edit, compile, link, and load your Pascal programs from within Turbo Pascal.

integrated environment
a coordinated system for editing, compiling, linking, and loading a program

operating system
the program with which the program user interacts in order to specify which application programs and/or system operations the computer should perform

To use a computer, you must interact with a supervisory program, called the **operating system**. Two common operating systems for the IBM PC are MS-DOS® (Microsoft® Disk Operating System) and Microsoft Windows (or Windows). The operating system provides several essential services to the computer user:

▶ Loading and running application programs
▶ Allocating memory and processor time
▶ Providing input and output facilities
▶ Managing files of information

Booting the Computer and Entering Turbo Pascal

booting up
the process of switching a computer on and loading the operating system into memory

When you switch on, or **boot up**, a personal computer, the operating system is loaded into memory from the hard disk (designated as disk drive C) and begins execution. If you are using MS-DOS, the operating system issues the prompt

```
C>
```

to inform you that it is ready for you to type in the next operation. Enter the following commands in color:

```
C>CD \BP\BIN
C>Turbo
```

to enter the Turbo Pascal integrated environment. The first command (CD, for Change Directory) makes the subdirectory \BP\BIN, which contains Turbo Pascal, the active disk directory. This command is installation dependent, so you may need to enter a different subdirectory (for example, \TP\BIN). Typing in Turbo puts you in the Turbo Pascal integrated environment.

If you are using Windows, type in

```
C>Win
```

You will see a screen display that shows icons (pictures) for several applications programs. To enter the Turbo Pascal integrated environment, move the mouse cursor to the Turbo Pascal icon and click the left mouse button twice in rapid succession.

Turbo Pascal Menus

Once in the Turbo Pascal integrated environment, you can create new programs, modify old ones, and compile and run those programs. You can interact with the environment through the **menu screens**. The top line in Fig. 1.9 is Turbo Pascal's Main menu (File, Edit, Search, and so on). If your computer has a mouse, you can select a Main menu item by positioning the mouse cursor on that item and then clicking the left mouse button. Otherwise, you can select a Main menu task by pressing and holding down the Alt key and then pressing the first letter of the task name (for example, Alt-F for File). You can also move from one Main menu task to another by pressing the left and right arrow keys.

The screen in Fig. 1.9 shows what happens when you select File. The list of tasks (New, Open, Save, and so on), all subtasks associated with File, appears on a **pull-down menu**. A different pull-down menu appears for each Main menu task that you select. You can use your mouse to select a subtask from the pull-down menu, or you can move the highlight bar over a particular task (using the up and down arrow keys) and then press Enter. You also can select a task from a pull-down menu by typing in the capitalized letter for that task (for example, N for New) or by pressing the function keys shown on the right of the task (for example, F3 for Open).

menu screen
a screen display showing several options from which you make a selection by using a mouse or pressing keyboard function keys

pull-down menu
a menu screen that appears when you select a particular menu task

Figure 1.9
Turbo Pascal File Menu

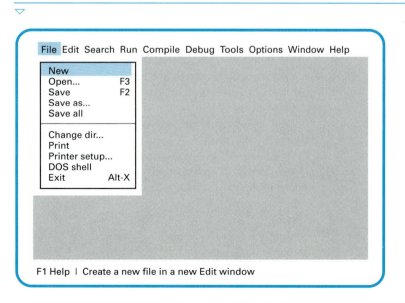

The line at the bottom of the screen describes the task you have highlighted (New—Create a new file . . .) and lists other tasks you can select (for example, Press F1 for Help). The bottom line changes as you move from one portion of the Turbo Pascal environment to another.

The dark area in the middle of Fig. 1.9 is the desktop area, where you will open the various windows used to create and test your Pascal programs.

On-Line Help

Through its on-line Help system, Turbo Pascal provides additional information about any menu task. If you want more information about a particular menu option, highlight that menu option (using your mouse or arrow keys) and then press F1. A Help window will pop up on the screen, displaying descriptive information about this operation. To exit the Help window and return to your current screen, select Cancel or press Esc (Escape).

Creating a New Program

To create a new Pascal program, you must begin with an empty Edit window on the desktop. To open a new window, select the New option from the File menu, as shown in Fig. 1.9. Turbo Pascal 7.0 places you in an Edit window called NONAME00.PAS.

Once Turbo Pascal places you in the empty Edit window, you begin entering your program one line at a time. Press the Enter key after typing each program line, and use the arrow keys on the keyboard to position the blinking cursor anywhere on the screen. Correct typing errors by pressing the backspace key to erase all characters from the current cursor position back to the incorrect character, then entering the correct letters in their place. Figure 1.10 shows a complete (but incorrect) program in the Edit window NONAME00.PAS.

After your program is complete, place a formatted floppy disk (see Appendix A for formatting instructions) in a floppy disk drive and save your program on the disk by selecting Save or by pressing the F2 key. Up until this point, your program has been assigned the name NONAME00.PAS by Turbo Pascal. Before saving your program with this name, Turbo Pascal gives you a chance to use a more meaningful name. For example, if you want to save your program as file HELLO on disk drive A, type A:HELLO.PAS when prompted by Turbo Pascal, as shown in Fig. 1.11. The A: is the computer's disk drive designator, HELLO is the file name, and .PAS is an extension signifying to Turbo Pascal that this file contains Pascal source code. MS-DOS file names (for example, HELLO) may be any combination of no more than eight letters, digits, or some special characters (no periods or spaces are allowed). If you fail to type a file extension, Turbo Pascal automatically adds the file extension .PAS. Now you are ready to save the file and return to the Main menu, which you do by selecting OK.

Figure 1.10
Incorrect Program Hello

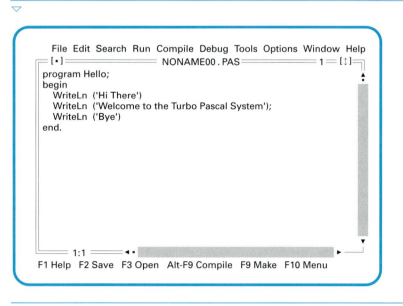

Figure 1.11
Saving Program as
HELLO.PAS

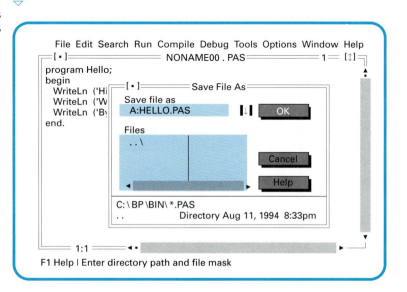

Compiling and Running a Program

To compile a program, select the Compile menu from the Main menu bar. Figure 1.12 shows the choices contained in the Compile menu. Since you wish to compile your program, select the Compile option. Turbo Pascal will begin to compile the program displayed in the Edit window.

If you attempt to compile the program shown in Fig. 1.10, Turbo Pascal will display the syntax error message

```
Error 85: ";" expected
```

and return to the Edit Window. The cursor is positioned at the point in the program where the compilation process stopped (at WriteLn in the fourth line). Error 85 explains that you have forgotten to add a semicolon to the end of the third line of program text. After changing the line to

```
WriteLn ('Hi There');
```

save the revised program to disk by selecting Save. Then exit the Edit window and return to the Main menu. From the Main menu, select the Compile menu again and then select the Compile option. This time there are no errors in the program, and a *Compilation status window* containing the message Compile successful: Press any Key will be displayed (Fig. 1.13). Then press a key on the keyboard.

To run (or execute) the program from the Main menu after it has been compiled, select the Run menu. Figure 1.14 shows the choices contained in the Run menu. Since you want to run the program, select the Run option.

Figure 1.12
Turbo Pascal
Compile Menu

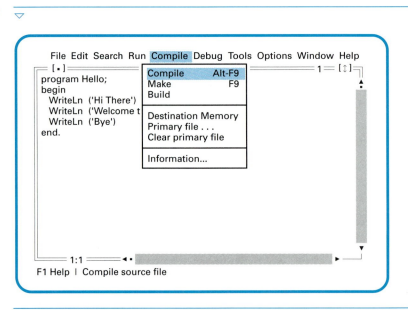

Turbo Pascal begins executing the program. The Main menu is replaced briefly by a user screen containing the program output

```
Hi There
Welcome to the Turbo Pascal System
Bye
```

Figure 1.13
Successful Compilation

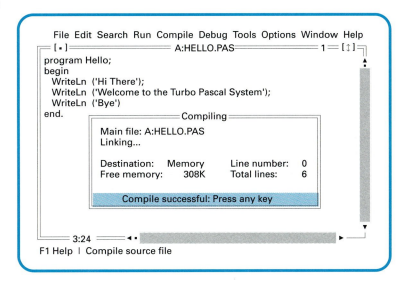

Figure 1.14
Turbo Pascal Run Menu

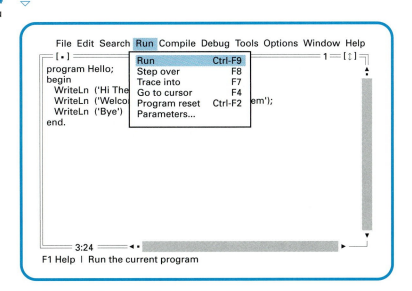

and then the Main menu display returns. To review your program output, type Alt-F5 (that is, press and hold down the Alt key, then press the F5 key). The user screen containing the program output reappears and remains visible until you press any key on the keyboard, which returns you to the Main menu screen.

Viewing Program Output in Windows

When using Windows, you must insert the line

```
uses WinCrt;
```

as the second line of every program you write. This line causes a window with your program output to appear on the screen. Without this line, your program output will not be displayed.

Loading a File

To load a previously saved file into an Edit window, you must get Turbo Pascal to display an *Open a File* dialog box (Fig. 1.15). Do this either through the File menu (select option Open) or by pressing function key F3. When the dialog box appears, either type the name of the file into the bar labeled Name or select the file name from the list shown under the label Files. If you do not have a mouse, press the Tab key to access the list of files, then use the up and down arrow keys to select the desired file.

Exiting Turbo Pascal

The File menu Exit option provides you with a way to leave Turbo Pascal and return to the operating system. If you choose the Exit option and have made changes to your program in the Edit window, but have forgotten to save your revised program, Turbo Pascal gives you one last chance to do so by displaying a dialog box similar to that shown in Fig. 1.16.

If you press the letter Y on the keyboard, your program will be saved before you exit from Turbo Pascal. To leave the File menu and return to the Main menu, press the Esc (Escape) key or F10.

It is good practice to clear your Turbo Pascal desktop before quitting. You do so by selecting Window from the Main menu, then selecting Close all from the pull-down menu to close all open windows and to clear the desktop.

Read Appendix A to learn more about using the Turbo Pascal environment. You can get additional information regarding a Turbo Pascal task by selecting Help (press F1) when the highlight bar is over that task.

Figure 1.15
Loading File HELLO.PAS
from Disk A

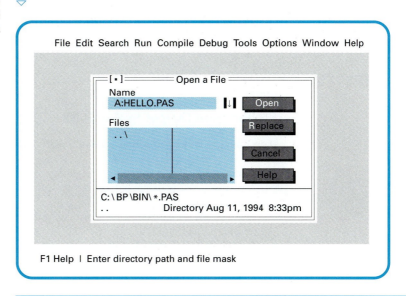

Figure 1.16
Turbo Pascal Information
Dialog Box

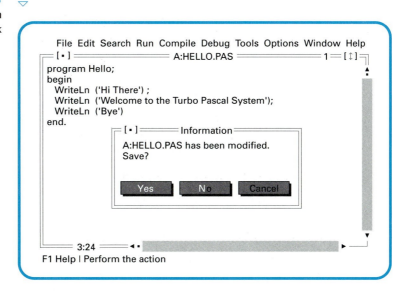

Exercise for Section 1.6   **Self-Check**

1. Modify the `Hello` program to print the message `My name is` <*your name*> rather than `Welcome to the Turbo Pascal System`.

CHAPTER REVIEW

1. The basic components of a computer are main and secondary memory, the CPU, and input and output devices.
2. Main memory is organized into individual storage locations called memory cells.
   - ► Each memory cell has a unique address.
   - ► A memory cell is a collection of bytes; a byte is a collection of 8 bits.
   - ► A memory cell is never empty, but its initial contents may be meaningless to your program.
   - ► The current contents of a memory cell are destroyed whenever new information is stored in that cell.
   - ► Programs *must* be loaded into the memory of the computer before they can be executed.
   - ► Data cannot be manipulated by the computer until they are first stored in memory.
3. Information in secondary memory is organized into files: program files and data files. Secondary memory stores information in semipermanent form and is less expensive than main memory.
4. A computer cannot think for itself; you must use a programming language to instruct it in a precise and unambiguous manner to perform a task.
5. Programming a computer can be fun—if you are patient, organized, and careful.
6. Two categories of programming languages are machine language (meaningful to the computer) and high-level language (meaningful to the programmer). Several system programs are used to prepare a high-level language program for execution, and an editor enters a high-level language program into memory. A compiler translates a high-level language program (the source program) into machine language (the object program). The linker/loader links this object program to other object files, creating an executable program, and loads the executable program into memory.
7. Through the operating system, you can issue commands to the computer and manage files.

Quick-Check Exercises

1. The _____ translates a(n) _____ language program into _____.
2. A(n) _____ provides access to system programs for editing, compiling, and so on.
3. Specify the correct order for these operations: execution, translation, linking/loading.
4. A high-level language program is saved on disk as a(n) _____ file or a(n) _____ file.
5. The _____ finds syntax errors in the _____ file.

6. Before linking, a machine language program is saved on disk as a(n) _____ file.
7. After linking, a machine language program is saved on disk as a(n) _____ file.
8. Computer programs are _____ components of a computer system while a disk drive is _____.
9. In a high-level language, you can reference data using _____ rather than memory cell addresses.
10. Determine whether each of the following characteristics applies to main memory or secondary memory:

   a. Faster to access
   b. Volatile
   c. May be extended without limit
   d. Less expensive
   e. Used to store files
   f. Central processor accesses it to obtain the next machine language instruction for execution
   g. Provides semipermanent data storage

Answers to Quick-Check Exercises

1. compiler, high-level (or source program), machine language (or object program)
2. operating system
3. translation, linking/loading, execution
4. source, program
5. compiler, source program
6. object
7. executable
8. software, hardware
9. descriptive names
10. main (a, b, f), secondary (c, d, e, g)

Review Questions

1. List at least three kinds of information stored in a computer.
2. List two functions of the CPU.
3. List two input devices, two output devices, and two secondary storage devices.
4. Draw the process that should be used to evaluate a proposed solution to a problem.
5. Why are there two categories of programming languages?
6. What is a syntax error?
7. What processes are needed to transform a Pascal program to a machine language program that is ready for execution?
8. Explain the relationship between memory cells, bytes, and bits.
9. Name two operating systems for IBM compatible computers. Which are you using?
10. Name three high-level languages, and describe their original usage.
11. What are the differences between RAM and ROM?

INTERVIEW

▼

David A. Patterson

David A. Patterson is a professor of computer science at the University of California, Berkeley. An author and active consultant, Patterson led the design and implementation of RISC I, a 45,000-transistor microprocessor that was likely the first Reduced Instruction Set Computer. He is currently working on developing input/output systems to match the increasingly higher performance of new processors.

▼ **Looking back on your own experience as a student, what influenced you to choose computer science as a profession? Why computer architecture?**

▲ I was a mathematics major as an undergraduate, and the math class I was planning to take was canceled. I took a computer class instead. I found I loved the reality of the problem solving and the rapid change of ideas in computer science more than the abstraction and stability of higher mathematics. Serendipity played a role in my choice of computer architecture as well. As a graduate research assistant in computer software, I became the father of two sons about the time the research grant ran out. While I finished my Ph.D., my adviser helped get me a job at Hughes Aircraft Company, where we designed computers. Hence I learned software in academia and hardware in industry. My dissertation combined hardware and software, leaving my options open when I got a "real" job. U.C. Berkeley wanted me to work in computer architecture, so my path was set.

▼ **What are your impressions of the state of computer architecture education today? Do you think students majoring in computer science receive enough of a background in architecture?**

▲ Computer architecture education today is in the middle of a revolution—from a more historical or descriptive list of possible problem solutions to a foundation that teaches how to evaluate quantitatively the cost/performance of different options in different situations. I believe this is a transition that all systems fields will need to go through if computer science is to mature as a discipline. Obviously, it is better to learn the quantitative approach.

▼ **Where do you see the exciting research being done in computer architecture today?**

▲ The processor-centric approach to doing research in computer architecture is now reaping the harvest of neglect: computers are becoming input/output bound. Hence I believe the most exciting areas in computer architecture today revolve around I/O, particularly communication and storage. The possibility of using fast networks to allow thousands of desktop computers to act in concert as a supercomputer could change the industry. Taking advantage of the advances in magnetic tape (such as those used in video cameras) or optical disks (like those used in CD players) offers the opportunity to store 1000 times the data we can today. Such a large quantitative change will bring about a qualitative change in our society. For example, all books on a college campus could be stored on-line, requiring the same space and cost as a minicomputer. Imagine what would happen if any student with a TV screen and a telephone could get any book in several seconds!

My thesis is that a factor-of-1000 increase in the storage capacity available on most local area networks will have a much greater impact than a factor-of-1000 increase in processing speed for a gaggle of scientists.

▼ **The complexity of architecture seems to be ever increasing. What do you think fuels the need for more powerful and efficient machines?**

▲ Architecture complexity goes in cycles, and we recently just reset to simplicity as a result of the Reduced Instruction Set Computer (RISC) movement. Complexity comes from the desire to get greater performance from a mature technology. As new technologies emerge, the rewards of simplicity inspire the return to simpler styles of computers.

▼ **Do you think the much discussed international competition (the United States versus Japan, for example) in the creation of supercomputers is overblown?**

▲ The international competition over the lead in traditional supercomputers is, to my way of thinking, like a competition to produce the world's fastest car. Even though it may be possible to build a few exotic cars that go as fast as a slow jet, it is clear that jets offer much greater speed and distance. The jets of computer architecture are parallel computers, with the effective top speed being a function of the number of processors you buy and the parallelism of the problem being stored. This is clearly the important competition, although not everyone may realize it.

The opportunity to become technological heroes is available for people who know their three A's: architecture, algorithms, and applications. These will be the people who can take advantage of the potential of parallel computers to solve problems important to society hundreds or thousands of times faster than today's most expensive computer.

▼ **What major developments do you foresee occurring in architecture in the 1990s?**

▲ Massively parallel computers will be established as the fastest computers in the land in the 1990s, washing away traditional supercomputers built by Cray, Convex, and NEC. For example, I believe we have already crossed the "teraflops threshold." A teraflops computer can calculate 10^{12} ("tera") **fl**oating-point arithmetic **o**perations **p**er **s**econd ("FLOPS"), which is about 1000 times faster than today's supercomputers. Suppose you had an important computation that takes 10^{17} operations today and you have the choice of buying today's supercomputer and dedicating it to that computation or waiting and buying a teraflops machine and then starting the computation. Crossing the "teraflops threshold" means you get your answer sooner if you wait for the teraflops machine than if you started today. My view is that we have already crossed that threshold.

Terabytes (10^{12} bytes) are the flip side of teraflops—computers that will be connected to hundreds of terabytes via high-speed networks. If copyrights and royalties can be resolved to the benefit of authors, publishers, and society, this technology will revolutionize the availability of information in all forms: books, libraries, magazines, mail, newspapers, and so on.

CHAPTER TWO

Problem Solving and Pascal

Programming is a problem-solving activity. If you are a good problem solver, you have the potential to become a good programmer. One goal of this book is to help you improve your problem-solving ability. To this end, we introduce in Section 2.1 a systematic approach to solving programming problems called the software development method and show you how to apply it in Section 2.2.

This chapter introduces Pascal, a high-level programming language developed in 1971 by Nicklaus Wirth of Zurich, Switzerland. Currently, Pascal is the most popular programming language for teaching programming concepts, partly because its syntax is relatively easy to learn. Another reason for Pascal's popularity is the availability of efficient Pascal compilers for most computers.

Pascal facilitates the writing of *structured programs*—programs that are easy to read, understand, and keep in good working order. Pascal is popular in industry because structured programming is standard programming practice. Another good reason for studying Pascal is that it is the basis for the design of the programming language Ada, the official language approved by the Department of Defense for software development.

To ensure that a Pascal program written on one computer executes on another, the coded instructions must conform to the Pascal language standard, which describes all Pascal language constructs and their syntax. The programs in this text are written in Turbo Pascal, a dialect of Pascal developed by Borland International for use on IBM-compatible computers. Turbo Pascal extends standard Pascal and contains features not described in the language standard. We compare Turbo Pascal and standard Pascal whenever we introduce a Turbo Pascal extension.

This chapter describes the sections of a Pascal program and the types of data that can be processed by Turbo Pascal. It also describes Pascal statements for performing computations, for entering data, and for displaying results.

2.1   The Software Development Method

Problem-solving methods are covered in many subject areas. For example, business students learn to solve problems with a *systems approach,* engineering and science students the *engineering and scientific method,* and programmers the *software development method.*

Software Development Method

1. Specify the problem requirements.
2. Analyze the problem.
3. Design the algorithm to solve the problem.
4. Implement the algorithm.
5. Test and verify the completed program.
6. Maintain and update the program.

PROBLEM

Specifying the problem requirements forces you to state the problem clearly and unambiguously and to gain a clear understanding of what is required for its solution. Your objective is to eliminate unimportant aspects and zero in on the root problem. This may not be as easy as it sounds. You may find you need more information from the person who posed the problem.

ANALYSIS ▼

Analyzing the problem involves identifying the problem (a) *inputs,* that is, the data you have to work with; (b) *outputs,* the desired results; and (c) any additional requirements or constraints on the solution. At this stage, you should also determine the required format in which the results should be displayed (for example, as a table with specific column headings) and develop a list of problem variables and their relationships. These relationships may be expressed as formulas.

If steps 1 and 2 are not done properly, you will solve the wrong problem. Read the problem statement carefully, first to obtain a clear idea of the problem and second to determine the inputs and outputs. You may find it helpful to underline phrases in the problem statement that identify the inputs and outputs, as in the following problem statement:

Determine the <u>total cost of apples</u> given the number of <u>pounds of apples purchased</u> and the <u>cost per pound of apples</u>.

Next, summarize the information contained in the underlined phrases:

Problem Inputs

quantity of apples purchased (in pounds)
cost per pound of apples (in dollars per pound)

Problem Output

total cost of apples (in dollars)

Once you know the problem inputs and outputs, develop a list of formulas that specify relationships between them. The general formula

total cost = unit cost × number of units

computes the total cost of any item purchased. Substituting the variables for our particular problem yields the formula

total cost of apples = cost per pound × pounds of apples

In some situations, you may have to make certain assumptions or simplifications to derive these relationships. This process of extracting the essential problem variables and their relationships from the problem statement is called **abstraction.**

abstraction
the process of extracting the essential variables and relationships of a problem

DESIGN ▼

Designing the algorithm to solve the problem requires you to write step-by-step procedures—the **algorithm**—and then verify that the algorithm solves the problem as intended. Writing the algorithm is often the most difficult part of the problem-solving process. Don't attempt to solve every detail of the problem initially; instead, discipline yourself to use top-down design. In

algorithm
a recipe, or list of steps, for solving a problem

top-down design
breaking a problem into its major subproblems and solving it by solving the subproblems

top-down design (also called *divide and conquer*), you first list the major steps, or subproblems, that need to be solved, then solve the original problem by solving each of its subproblems. Most computer algorithms consist of at least the following subproblems.

Algorithm for a Programming Problem

1. Read the data.
2. Perform the computations.
3. Display the results.

Once you know the subproblems, you can attack each one individually. For example, the *perform the computations* step may need to be broken down into a more detailed list of steps called **algorithm refinements**.

algorithm refinement
a detailed list of steps needed to solve a particular step in the original algorithm

You may be familiar with top-down design if you use outlines when writing term papers. Your first step is to create an outline of the major topics, which you then refine by filling in subtopics for each major topic. Once the outline is complete, you begin writing the text for each subtopic.

desk checking
the step-by-step simulation of the computer execution of an algorithm

Desk checking is an important but often overlooked part of algorithm design. To **desk check** an algorithm, carefully perform each algorithm step (or its refinements) just as a computer would and verify that the algorithm works as intended. You'll save time and effort if you locate algorithm errors early in the problem-solving process.

IMPLEMENTATION ▼

Implementing the algorithm (step 4 in the software development method) involves writing it as a program. You must convert each algorithm step into one or more statements in a programming language.

structured program
a program that is easy to read, understand, and maintain

Structured programming is a disciplined approach to programming that results in programs that are easy to read and understand and less likely to contain errors. The emphasis is on following accepted program style guidelines (which will be stressed in this book) to write code that is clear and readable. Obscure tricks and programming shortcuts are strongly discouraged. Government organizations and industry are strong advocates of structured programming because structured programs are much easier to design in the beginning and easier to maintain over the long term.

TESTING ▼

Testing and verifying the program requires testing the completed program to verify that it works as desired. Don't rely on just one test case—run the program several times using different sets of data, making sure that it works correctly for every situation provided for in the algorithm.

MAINTENANCE ▼

Maintaining and updating the program involves modifying a program to remove previously undetected errors and to keep it up to date as government regulations or company policies change. Many organizations maintain a program for five years or more, often after the programmers who originally coded it have left or moved on to other positions.

Exercises for Section 2.1 **Self-Check**

1. List the steps of the software development method.
2. In which phase is the algorithm developed? In which phase do you identify the problem inputs and outputs?

2.2 Applying the Software Development Method

Throughout this book, we use the first five steps of the software development method to solve programming problems. These problems, presented as case studies, begin with a *problem statement*. As part of the problem *analysis,* we identify the data requirements for the problem, indicating the problem inputs and the desired outputs. Next, we *design* and refine the initial algorithm. Finally, we *implement* the algorithm as a Pascal program. We also provide a sample run of the program and discuss how to *test* the program.

We walk you through a sample case study next. This example includes a running commentary on the process that you can apply when solving other problems.

CASE STUDY **Converting Units of Measurement**

PROBLEM ▼

You work in a store that sells imported fabric. Most of the fabric you buy is measured in square meters, but your customers want to know the equivalent amount in square yards. Write a program to perform this conversion.

ANALYSIS ▼

The first step in solving this problem is to determine what you are asked to do. You must convert from one system of measurement to another, but are you supposed to convert from square meters to square yards, or vice versa? The problem states that you buy fabric measured in square meters, so the problem input is *fabric size in square meters.* Your customers want to know the equivalent amount in square yards, so the problem output is *fabric size in square yards.* To write the program, you need to know the relationship between square meters and square yards. Consulting a metric table shows that 1 square meter equals 1.196 square yards.

The data requirements and relevant formulas are listed next. SqMeters identifies the memory cell that will contain the problem input, and SqYards identifies the memory cell that will contain the program result, or the problem output.

Data Requirements

Problem Input

SqMeters {the fabric size in square meters}

Problem Output

SqYards {the fabric size in square yards}

Relevant Formula

1 square meter = 1.196 square yards

DESIGN ▼

Next, formulate the algorithm that solves the problem. Begin by listing the three major steps, or subproblems, of the algorithm.

Algorithm

1. Read the fabric size in square meters.
2. Convert the fabric size to square yards.
3. Display the fabric size in square yards.

Now decide whether any steps of the algorithm need refinement or whether they are perfectly clear as stated. Step 1 (reading data) and step 3 (displaying a value) are basic steps and require no refinement. Step 2 is fairly straightforward, but some detail might help.

Step 2 Refinement

2.1 The fabric size in square yards is 1.196 times the fabric size in square meters.

The complete algorithm with refinements is listed next to show how it all fits together. The algorithm resembles an outline for a term paper. The refinement of step 2 is numbered as step 2.1 and is indented under step 2.

Algorithm with Refinements

1. Read the fabric size in square meters.
2. Convert the fabric size to square yards.
   2.1 The fabric size in square yards is 1.196 times the fabric size in square meters.
3. Display the fabric size in square yards.

Let's desk check the algorithm before going further. If step 1 reads in a fabric size of 2.00 square meters, step 2.1 would convert it to 1.196 × 2.00, or 2.392 square yards. This correct result would be displayed by step 3.

IMPLEMENTATION ▼

To implement the solution, you must write the algorithm as a Pascal program. Begin by telling the Pascal compiler about the problem data requirements, that is, what memory cell names you are using and what kind of data will be stored in each memory cell. Then convert each algorithm step into one or more Pascal statements. If an algorithm step has been refined, you must convert the refinements, not the original step, into Pascal statements.

Figure 2.1 shows the Pascal program along with a sample execution. The program appears in the *Edit window*; the sample execution appears in the *Output window*. For easy identification, the input data typed in by the program user is in color in the *Output window*. Don't worry about understanding the details of this program yet. We explain the program in the next several sections.

TESTING ▼

How do you know the sample run is correct? You should always examine program results carefully to make sure that they make sense. In this run, a

Figure 2.1
Metric Conversion
Program

Edit Window

```pascal
program Metric;
{Converts square meters to square yards.}

  const
    MetersToYards = 1.196; {conversion constant}

  var
    SqMeters,          {input - fabric size in meters}
    SqYards : Real;    {output - fabric size in yards}
begin
  {Read the fabric size in square meters.}
  WriteLn ('Enter the fabric size in square meters >');
  ReadLn (SqMeters);

  {Convert the fabric size to square yards.}
  SqYards := MetersToYards * SqMeters;

  {Display the fabric size in square yards.}
  WriteLn ('The fabric size in square yards is ', SqYards)
end.
```

Output Window

```
Enter the fabric size in square meters >
2.00
The fabric size in square yards is 2.3920000000E+00
```

fabric size of 2.00 square meters is converted to 2.392 square yards, as it should be. To verify that the program works properly, enter a few more test values of square meters. You needn't try more than a few test cases to verify that a simple program like this is correct.

Exercises for Section 2.2   ***Self-Check***

1. Change the algorithm for the metric conversion program to convert fabric size in square yards to fabric size in square meters.
2. List the data requirements, formulas, and algorithm for a program that converts a weight from pounds to kilograms.

2.3   Overview of Pascal, Reserved Words, and Identifiers

One advantage of Pascal is that it lets us write programs that resemble everyday English. Even though you do not yet know how to write your own programs, you can probably read and understand the program in Fig. 2.1. Figure 2.2 repeats Fig. 2.1 with the basic features of Pascal highlighted. We identify them briefly next, and explain them in detail in Sections 2.4 through 2.6.

Figure 2.2

Pascal Language Elements in Metric Conversion Program

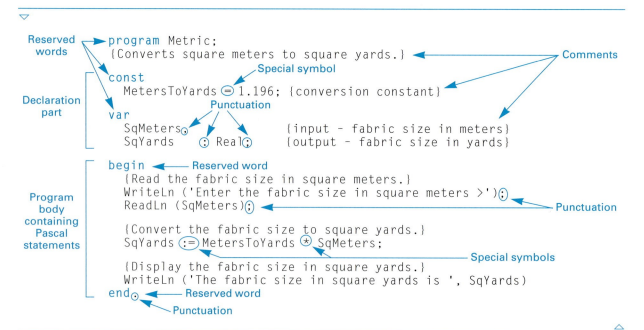

declaration part
the part of a program that tells the compiler the names of memory cells in a program
program body
the executable statements in a program

reserved word
a word that has special meaning in Pascal

A Pascal program has two parts: the declaration part and the program body. The **declaration part** tells the compiler which memory cells are needed in the program. To create this part of the program, the programmer uses the problem data requirements identified during problem analysis. The **program body** begins with the line begin, and the program body contains statements (derived from the algorithm) that are translated into machine language and later executed. Certain words in the program, such as begin and end, are **reserved words**, which have special meaning to the Pascal compiler.

The lines that contain text enclosed in braces are *comments*. Comments provide supplementary information to the person reading the program, but they are ignored by the Pascal compiler.

Finally, the program contains *punctuation* and *special symbols* ($*$, $=$, $:=$). Commas separate items in a list, and a semicolon appears at the end of several lines. The last line ends with a period.

After learning more about each feature, you will be able to write your own simple programs, such as the metric conversion program.

Each line of Fig. 2.2 contains one or more words, some written in all lowercase characters and some written in mixed upper- and lowercase. The words in lowercase are reserved words and have special meaning to the Pascal compiler. Table 2.1 describes the reserved words in Fig. 2.2.

Table 2.1
Reserved Words in Fig. 2.2

Reserved Word	Meaning
program	The first word of a Pascal program
const	Precedes the list of constants
var	Precedes the list of variables
begin	Starts the program body
end	The last word of a Pascal program

Standard Identifiers

standard identifier
a word having special meaning but one that a programmer may redefine

The other words in Fig. 2.2 are identifiers that come in two varieties: standard and user-defined. Like reserved words, **standard identifiers** have special meaning in Pascal. Some standard identifiers represent names of predefined operations (e.g., ReadLn for **Read** a **Lin**e, WriteLn for **Write** a **Lin**e), and others name the predefined data types (e.g., Real for real number). Unlike reserved words, standard identifiers can be redefined and used by the programmer for other purposes—however, we don't recommend this practice. If you redefine a standard identifier, Pascal will no longer be able to use it for its original purpose.

Appendix B lists all of Pascal's reserved words and standard identifiers. If you have a color monitor, Turbo Pascal displays all reserved words and standard identifiers in color for easy identification.

User-Defined Identifiers

We choose our own identifiers (called user-defined identifiers) to name memory cells that will hold data and program results, to name operations that we define (more on this in Chapter 3), and to specify the name of a Pascal program. The first user-defined identifier in Fig. 2.2, `Metric`, specifies the program name and appears in the program heading

```
program Metric;
```

You have some freedom in selecting identifiers. The syntax rules and some valid identifiers follow. Table 2.2 shows some invalid identifiers.

Syntax Rules for Identifiers

1. An identifier must always begin with a letter.
2. An identifier must consist only of a combination of letters and digits.
3. A Pascal reserved word cannot be used as an identifier.
4. In Turbo Pascal, if an identifier is longer than 63 characters, only the first 63 characters are valid.

Valid Identifiers

`Letter1, Letter2, Inches, Cent, CentPerInch, Hello, Variable`

Table 2.2
Invalid Identifiers

Invalid Identifier	Reason Invalid
`1Letter`	Begins with a number
`const`	Reserved word
`var`	Reserved word
`Two*Four`	Character * not allowed
`Joe's`	Character ' not allowed

The identifier `Cent_Per_Inch` is invalid in standard Pascal, but Turbo Pascal does allow the underscore symbol _ in identifiers and would consider `Cent_Per_Inch` to be valid. To enhance program portability, however, we recommend that you avoid using the underscore symbol.

The category of each identifier appearing in Fig. 2.2 is listed in Table 2.3.

Table 2.3
Reserved Words and
Identifiers in Fig. 2.2

Reserved Words	Standard Identifiers	User-Defined Identifiers
program, var, const, begin, end	Real, ReadLn, WriteLn	Metric, MetersToYards, SqMeters, SqYards

Syntax Display for Program Heading

For each new Pascal construct introduced in this book, we provide a syntax display that describes and explains its syntax and shows examples of its use. In the following syntax display, the italicized element, *pname,* is discussed in the interpretation section.

SYNTAX DISPLAY

Program Heading

Form: program *pname*;
     program *pname* (Input, Output);
Example: program Hello;
     program Hello (Input, Output);
Interpretation: The program name is specified by *pname.* Program headings have two forms. The second form indicates that the input data will be read from the system Input (the keyboard); the output results will be written to the system Output (the screen). This second form is the only form of the program heading that is valid in standard Pascal.

Program Style

The Use of Uppercase and Lowercase in Pascal Programs

We discuss program style throughout the text in displays like this one. A program that "looks good" is easier to read and understand than one that is sloppy. Most programs will be examined or studied by someone other than the original programmers. In the real world, only about 25% of the time spent on a particular program is devoted to its original design or coding; the remaining 75% is spent on maintenance (i.e., updating and modifying the program). A program that is neatly stated and whose meaning is clear makes everyone's job simpler.

In the programs in this text, reserved words always appear in lowercase and identifiers are in mixed uppercase and lowercase. The first letter of each identifier is capitalized. If an identifier consists of two or more "words" run on together (e.g., MetersToYards), the first letter of each word is capitalized. We recommend that you follow this convention in your programs to simplify distinguishing reserved words from other identifiers.

The Turbo Pascal compiler does not differentiate between uppercase and lowercase. This means that you could write the reserved word `const` as `CONST` or the standard identifier `ReadLn` as `READLN`. However, according to our convention, `const` and `ReadLn` are the preferred forms.

Because standard identifiers have special meanings just like reserved words, many computer scientists write standard identifiers in the same way as reserved words (i.e., all lowercase). If your instructor prefers this convention, you should write the standard identifier `ReadLn` as `readln`.

Program Style

Choosing Identifier Names

Pick a meaningful name for a user-defined identifier so that its use is easy to understand. For example, the identifier `Salary` would be a good name for a variable used to store a person's salary, whereas the identifier `S` or `Bagel` would be a bad choice.

It is difficult to form meaningful names with fewer than three letters. On the other hand, typing errors become more likely when identifiers are too long. A reasonable rule of thumb is to use names having 3 to 10 characters.

If you mistype an identifier, the compiler detects the mistake as a syntax error and displays an `undefined identifier` error message during program translation. Because mistyped identifiers sometimes resemble other identifiers, avoid picking similar names. Don't choose two names that are identical except for their case, because the compiler will not distinguish between them.

Exercises for Section 2.3   **Self-Check**

1. What are the two parts of a Pascal program?
2. Why shouldn't you use a standard identifier as the name of a memory cell in a program? Can you use a reserved word instead?
3. Which of the following identifiers are (a) Pascal reserved words, (b) standard identifiers, (c) valid identifiers, and (d) invalid identifiers?

```
end        ReadLn         Bill      program    Sue's
Rate       Start          begin     const      XYZ123
123XYZ     ThisIsALongOne Y=Z       Prog#2     'MaxScores'
```

2.4   Data Types and Declarations

declaration part
the program part that communicates to the compiler the identifiers in the program, the usage of each identifier, and the kind of information stored in each identifier (memory cell)

The **declaration part** of a Pascal program communicates to the Pascal compiler the names of all user-defined identifiers that can appear in the program and the usage of each identifier. It also tells the compiler what kind of information will be stored in each memory cell.

Data Types

data type
a set of values and operations that can be performed on those values

How a particular value is represented in memory is determined by the **data type** of that value. In standard Pascal, there are four predefined data types: Real (for real numbers), Integer (for integers), Char (for single character values), and Boolean (for values of True and False). Turbo Pascal provides another data type, string, that is nonstandard and facilitates processing sequences of characters (for example, a person's name). Each data type has its own set of values and operations that can be performed on those values. We introduce these data types in this section and elaborate on them in Chapter 7.

A value can be written within a line of a Pascal program (in-line) or typed in as a data item to be read by the program. A value that appears in-line in a program is called a **literal**.

literal
a value that appears in-line in a program

Integer Data Type

In mathematics, integers are positive or negative whole numbers and a number without a sign is assumed to be positive. The Integer data type is used to represent integers in Pascal.

Because of the finite size of a memory cell, not all integers can be represented. Turbo Pascal can represent integers in the range of values -32768 through 32767. There is a predefined constant named MaxInt whose value represents the largest positive integer. An integer cannot contain a comma. Some valid integers are

```
-10500    435    15    -25
```

We can read and display integers, perform the common arithmetic operations (add, subtract, multiply, and divide), and compare two integers.

Real Data Type

A real number has an integral part and a fractional part and separates them with a decimal point. In Pascal, the Real data type is used to represent real numbers and a Real literal must always begin and end with a digit. Therefore the fraction -.25 and the whole number 64. must be written in Pascal as the real literals -0.25 and 64.0, respectively.

We can use scientific notation to represent very large and very small values. In normal scientific notation, for example, the real number 1.23×10^5 is equivalent to 123000.0 where the exponent 5 means "move the decimal point 5 places to the right." In Pascal scientific notation, we write this number as 1.23E5 or 1.23E+5. If the exponent has a minus sign, the decimal point is moved to the left (e.g., 0.34E-4 is equivalent to 0.000034). Table 2.4 lists some valid and invalid real numbers. The last line shows that we can write a Real literal in Pascal scientific notation without a decimal point.

Table 2.4
Valid and Invalid
Real Literals

Valid Real Literals	Invalid Real Literals
3.14159	150 (no decimal point)
0.005	.12345 (no digit before decimal point)
12345.0	16. (no digit after decimal point)
15.0E-04 (value is 0.0015)	-15E-0.3 (0.3 invalid exponent)
2.345E2 (value is 234.5)	12.5E.3 (.3 invalid exponent)
1.15E-3 (value is 0.00115)	.123E3 (no digit before decimal point)
12E+5 (value is 1200000.0)	

We can read and display real numbers, perform the common arithmetic operations (add, subtract, multiply, and divide), and compare them.

Char Data Type

Data type Char represents an individual character value—a letter, a digit, or a special symbol. Each type Char literal is enclosed in apostrophes (single quotes), as shown here.

```
'A' 'z' '2' '9' '*' ':' '"' ' '
```

The next to last literal represents the character " ; the last literal represents the blank character, which is typed by pressing the apostrophe key, the space bar, and the apostrophe key.

Although a type Char literal in a program requires apostrophes, a type Char data value should not have them. Thus, for example, when entering the letter z as a character data item to be read by a program, press the z key instead of the sequence 'z'.

We cannot perform arithmetic operations on type Char data. This means that '3' + '5' is invalid in Pascal. However, we can compare characters and read and display them.

Boolean Data Type

Unlike the other data types, the Boolean* data type has just two possible values: True and False. We can use this data type to represent conditional values so that a program can make decisions. We can display Boolean data but we cannot read a Boolean data item.

---

*The Boolean data type is named after the English mathematician George Boole (1815–1864), the inventor of a two-valued algebra.

String Data Type

The data types `Real`, `Integer`, `Char`, and `Boolean` are all standard. Turbo Pascal also supports a fifth data type, `string` (a reserved word in Turbo Pascal), which is a sequence of characters enclosed in apostrophes. The next line contains four string literals:

`'ABCDE' '1234' 'True' 'Enter fabric size in square meters >'`

Note that the string `'1234'` is not stored the same way as the integer `1234` and cannot be used with arithmetic operators. The string `'True'` is also stored differently from the Boolean value `True`.

In Turbo Pascal, strings can be read, stored in memory, compared, and displayed. A string value can contain up to 255 characters. When entering a string value to be read by a program, omit the apostrophes, just as for type `Char` data values.

Although standard Pascal does not support the string data type, it does allow the use of string literals. They usually appear in instructions used to display information.

Purpose of Data Types

The use of different data types enables the compiler to know which operations are valid for each memory cell used in a program. If you try to manipulate a value in memory in an incorrect way (for example, add two character values), the Pascal compiler displays an error message telling you that this is an incorrect operation. Similarly, if you try to store the wrong kind of value in a memory cell (for example, a string in a memory cell that is type `Integer`), you get an error message. Detecting these errors keeps the computer from performing operations that make no sense. In the next section, we discuss how to tell the Pascal compiler the data type of each memory cell.

Declarations

We tell the Pascal compiler the names of memory cells used in a program and the kind of information stored in these cells through constant declarations and variable declarations.

Constant Declarations

The constant declaration

```
const
  MetersToYards = 1.196;
```

specifies that the identifier `MetersToYards` is the name of a memory cell that always contains the real number `1.196`; the identifier `MetersToYards` is

constant

a memory cell whose value cannot change

called a **constant**. Pascal determines the data type of MetersToYards (type is Real) from the form of the literal (1.196) it represents. Use constants only to identify data values that never change (e.g., the number of square yards in a square meter is always 1.196). You cannot write instructions that attempt to change the value of a constant.

EXAMPLE 2.1 ▼

The constant declaration

```
const
  MyLargeInteger = 9999;             {value is 9999}
  MySmallInteger = -MyLargeInteger;  {value is -9999}
  Star = '*';                        {value is symbol *}
  FirstMonth = 'January';            {value is string
                                      'January'}
```

declares four constants of different types. The value of the second constant, MySmallInteger, is based on the first constant, MyLargeInteger. The third constant, Star, has a type Char value, and the fourth constant, FirstMonth, has a string value. ▲

SYNTAX DISPLAY

Constant Declaration

Form: const *constant* = *value*;
Example: const MyPi = 3.14159;
Interpretation: The specified *value* is associated with the identifier *constant* and cannot be changed. The *value* can be a literal or a previously defined constant; a numeric *value* can have a sign. More than one constant declaration may follow the word const, with a semicolon appearing at the end of each constant declaration.

Variable Declarations

variable

a memory cell whose value can change

The memory cells used for storing a program's input data and its computational results are called **variables** because the values stored in them can change (and usually do) as the program executes. The variable declaration

```
var
  SqMeters,        {input - fabric size in meters}
  SqYards : Real;  {output - fabric size in yards}
```

in Fig. 2.1 gives the names of two variables (SqMeters, SqYards) used to store real numbers. Note that Pascal ignores the comments in braces describing the usage of each variable.

In a variable declaration, the identifier (e.g., Real) after the symbol : tells the Pascal compiler the type of data (e.g., a real number) stored in a particular variable. You can declare variables for any data type.

SYNTAX DISPLAY

Variable Declaration

Form: `var` *variable list* : *data type*;
Example: `var`

```
        X, Y     : Real;
        Me, You  : Integer;
```

Interpretation: A memory cell is allocated for each variable in the *variable list*. The data type (`Real`, `Integer`, etc.) of each variable is specified between the colon and the semicolon. Commas separate the variables in *variable list*. The word `var` should appear only once, but it can be followed by multiple variable lists and associated data types, each ending with a semicolon.

Exercises for Section 2.4

Self-Check

1. a. Write the following numbers in normal decimal notation:

   `103E-4  1.2345E+6  123.45E+3`

   b. Write the following numbers in Pascal scientific notation:

   `1300  123.45  0.00426`

2. Indicate which of the following literal values are legal in Pascal and which are not. Identify the data type of each valid literal value.

   ```
   15   'XYZ'  '*'  $25.123  15.   -999   .123  'x'
   "X"  '9'   '-5'  True     'True'
   ```

3. Why should the value of pi (3.14159) be stored in a constant?
4. What would be the best variable type for the area of a circle in square inches? How about the number of cars passing through an intersection in an hour? Your name? The first letter of your last name?

Programming

1. Write the program heading and declarations for a program named `Mine` that has the constant `MyPi` (3.14159), variables `Radius`, `Area`, and `Circumf` defined as `Real`, variable `NumCirc` as an `Integer`, and variable `CircName` as a `string`.

2.5 Executable Statements

The executable statements follow the declaration part, after the reserved word `begin`. They are the Pascal statements used to write or code the algorithm and its refinements. The Pascal compiler translates the executable statements into machine language; the computer executes the machine language version of these statements when we run the program.

Programs in Memory

Before examining the executable statements in the metric conversion program (Fig. 2.1), let's see what computer memory looks like before and after that program executes. Figure 2.3(a) shows the program loaded into memory and the program memory area before the program executes. The question marks in memory cells SqMeters and SqYards indicate that the values of these cells are undefined before program execution begins. During program execution, the data value 2.00 is read into the variable SqMeters. After the program executes, the variables are defined as shown in Fig. 2.3(b). We will see why next.

Assignment Statements

assignment statement
an instruction that stores a value or a computational result in a variable

An **assignment statement** stores a value or a computational result in a variable and is used to perform most arithmetic operations in a program. The assignment statement

```
SqYards := MetersToYards * SqMeters
```

in Fig. 2.1 assigns a value to the variable SqYards. The value assigned is the result of the multiplication (* means multiply) of the constant MetersToYards by the variable SqMeters. The memory cells for MetersToYards and SqMeters must both contain valid information (in this case, real numbers) before the assignment statement is executed. Figure 2.4 shows the contents of memory before and after the assignment statement executes; only the value of SqYards is changed. In Pascal the symbol := is the assignment operator. Read it as "becomes," "gets," or "takes the value of" rather than "equals." The : and the = must be adjacent with no intervening space.

SYNTAX DISPLAY

Assignment Statement

Form: *variable* := *expression*
Example: X := Y + Z + 2.0
Interpretation: The *variable* before the assignment operator is assigned the value of the *expression* after it, and in the process, the previous value of *variable* is destroyed. The *expression* can be a variable, a constant, a literal, or a combination of these connected by appropriate operators (for example, +, -, /, and *). The data type of *expression* and *variable* must be the same except that *expression* can be type Integer when *variable* is type Real, or *expression* can be type Char when *variable* is type string.

EXAMPLE 2.2 ▼

In Pascal, you can write assignment statements of the form

```
Sum := Sum + Item
```

where the variable Sum appears on both sides of the assignment operator. This is obviously not an algebraic equation, but it does illustrate a common

Figure 2.3
Memory Before and After
Execution of a Program

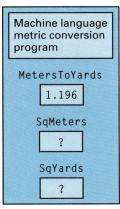

a. Memory Before Execution   b. Memory After Execution

programming practice: This statement instructs the computer to add the current value of Sum to the value of Item; the result is then stored back into Sum. The previous value of Sum is destroyed in the process, as illustrated in Fig. 2.5. The value of Item, however, is unchanged. ▲

EXAMPLE 2.3 ▼

You can also write assignment statements that assign the value of a single variable or constant to a variable. If X and NewX are type Real variables, the statement

```
NewX := X
```

Figure 2.4
Effect of SqYards :=
MetersToYards * SqMeters

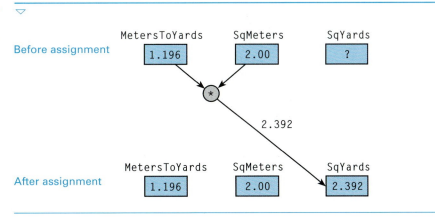

Figure 2.5
Effect of Sum :=
Sum + Item

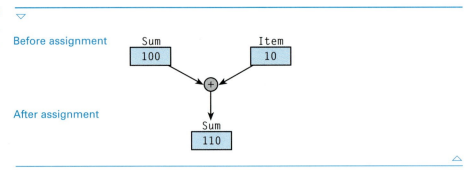

copies the value of variable X into variable NewX. The statement

```
NewX := -X
```

instructs the computer to get the value of X, negate that value, and store the result in NewX. For example, if X is 3.5, NewX is -3.5. Neither of these assignment statements changes the value of X. ▲

Section 2.7 continues the discussion of type Integer and Real expressions and operators. Next, we show some assignment statements involving other data types.

EXAMPLE 2.4 ▼

Assume Ch is type Char, BoolVar is type Boolean, and Name is type string for the following assignment statements, all valid in Pascal. Note that Pascal requires you to insert a semicolon between executable statements.

```
Ch := 'C';
BoolVar := True;
Name := 'Alice'
```

Next, we show memory after these statements execute. Note that the apostrophes are not stored with character or string data and that the Boolean value True is stored in BoolVar, not the string 'True'.

Ch   BoolVar   Name
| C | | True | | Alice |

Because Pascal represents the values of each data type differently, the value being assigned must be *assignment compatible* with the variable receiving it. For now, this means that the variable and value must be the same type, unless the value is type Integer and the variable receiving it is type Real. The following assignment statements are invalid for the reasons given:

```
Ch := 5;         {invalid assignment of integer to type Char
                  variable}
Ch := Name;      {invalid assignment of type string variable to
                  type Char variable}
```

```
Name := True;          {invalid assignment of type Boolean
                         value to type string variable}
BoolVar := 'False'     {invalid assignment of type string
                         literal to type Boolean variable}  ▲
```

Input/Output Operations and Procedures

Data can be stored in memory in three ways: associated with a constant, assigned to a variable, or read into a variable. We have discussed the first two methods. You would use the third method, reading data into a variable, if you wanted a program to manipulate different data each time it executes. Reading data into memory is called an **input operation**. As it executes, a program performs computations and stores the results in memory. These program results can be displayed to the program user by an **output operation**.

All input/output operations in Pascal are performed by special program units called **input/output procedures**. The input/output procedures are supplied as part of the Pascal compiler, and their names are standard identifiers (for example, ReadLn and WriteLn). In Pascal, a **procedure call statement** is used to call or activate a procedure. Calling a procedure is analogous to asking a friend to perform an urgent task. You tell your friend what to do (but not how to do it) and wait for your friend to report back that the task is finished. After hearing from your friend, you can go on and do something else.

input operation
an instruction that reads data into memory
output operation
an instruction that displays information stored in memory
input/output procedure
a Pascal procedure that performs an input or output operation
procedure call statement
an instruction that calls or activates a procedure

The WriteLn Procedure

To see the results of a program execution, we must have a way to specify what variable values should be displayed. In Fig. 2.1 the procedure call statement

```
WriteLn ('The fabric size in square yards is ', SqYards)
```

calls procedure WriteLn to display a line of program output containing two items: the string literal 'The fabric size ... is ' and the value of SqYards. For the string literal, the characters inside the apostrophes are printed but the apostrophes are not. The WriteLn procedure displays the line

```
The fabric size in square yards is 2.3920000000E+00
```

Unless directed otherwise, Pascal scientific notation is used to display a real value (2.3920000000E+00 is 2.392).

WriteLn Without an Output List

The statements

```
WriteLn ('The fabric size in square yards is ', SqYards);
WriteLn;
WriteLn ('Metric conversion completed')
```

would display the lines

```
The fabric size in square yards is 2.3920000000E+00
```

```
Metric conversion completed
```

Because the second `WriteLn` has no output list, the blank line you see in the middle of the program output occurs. Execution of a `WriteLn` always causes the cursor to advance to the next line, creating a blank line if nothing is printed on the current line.

SYNTAX DISPLAY

WriteLn Procedure

Form: `WriteLn (`*output list*`)`
        `WriteLn`
Example: `WriteLn ('My height in inches is ', Height)`
Interpretation: The `WriteLn` procedure displays the value of each variable or constant in the order in which it appears in the *output list* and then advances the cursor to the next line. A string literal is printed without the apostrophes. If there is no *output list,* the cursor advances to the first column of the next line.

The Write Procedure

Pascal provides a second output procedure, `Write`, that is similar to `WriteLn` in all respects except that the cursor does not advance to the start of the next line after the output list is displayed. The statement pair

```
Write ('The fabric size in square yards is ');
WriteLn (SqYards)
```

would display the same output line as the single statement

```
WriteLn ('The fabric size in square yards is ', SqYards)
```

It is generally more convenient to use the latter form.

SYNTAX DISPLAY

Write Procedure

Form: `Write (`*output list*`)`
Example: `Write ('My height in inches is ', Height, ' and my ')`
Interpretation: Displays the value of each variable or constant in its output list. A string literal is displayed without the apostrophes. The cursor does not advance to the next line after the output is displayed.

Program Style

Guidelines for Write Versus WriteLn

Generally, the `WriteLn` procedure is used to display program results, but very long output lists can be split and displayed piecemeal. In this case, use the `Write` procedure to display all but the last part of the output list and use the `WriteLn` procedure to display only the last part of the output list, as shown here:

```
Write ('This line displays ');
Write ('the value of X (', X, ') and ');
WriteLn ('the value of Y (', Y, ').')
```

The output lists for the second and third lines contain a string, a variable, and a string. The three statements generate one line of output that looks like

```
This line displays the value of X (55) and the value of Y (7).
```

The ReadLn Procedure

When input data are needed, use the `Write` procedure to display a prompting message, or prompt, that tells the program user what data to enter. The `Write` statement

```
Write ('Enter the fabric size in square meters >');
ReadLn (SqMeters)
```

displays a prompt for square meters (a numeric value) in the form of a string literal and advances the cursor to the screen position just after the symbol >. The program user can then type in the data value requested, and the `ReadLn` procedure will process the input.

The statement

```
ReadLn (SqMeters)
```

calls procedure `ReadLn` (pronounced "read line") to read data into the variable `SqMeters`. Where does procedure `ReadLn` get the data it stores in the variable `SqMeters`? It reads the data from the standard input device (called `Input` by Pascal). In most cases the standard input device is the keyboard; consequently, the computer will attempt to store in `SqMeters` whatever data the program user types at the keyboard. Since `SqMeters` is declared as type `Real`, the input operation will proceed without error only if the program user types in a number. The effect of the `ReadLn` operation is shown in Fig. 2.6.

Whenever `ReadLn` executes, the program pauses until the required data are entered and the Enter key is pressed. If an incorrect data character is typed, the program user can press the backspace key (←) to edit the data.

Figure 2.6
Effect of ReadLn (SqMeters)

However, once the Enter key is pressed, the data are read exactly as typed in and it is too late to correct any data entry errors.

ReadLn can also read data values for the other predefined data types, except for type Boolean. The number of characters read by the ReadLn procedure depends on the type of variable receiving data. Table 2.5 shows some examples of ReadLn with a single input variable. Assume that the Enter key is pressed after the last character shown in the column labeled "Data Line." Remember, when typing in character or string data in a program, do not enclose those characters in apostrophes.

Table 2.5
Rules for Reading Data

Type of *var*	Effect of ReadLn (*var*)	Example	
		Data Line	**Effect**
Char	Reads next data character.	XYZ	Stores X in *var*.
Integer	Skips leading blanks—reads all characters through next blank, control character, or Enter. Characters read must form an integer value.	35 55	Stores 35 in *var*.
Real	Skips leading blanks—reads all characters through next blank, control character, or Enter. Characters read must form a real or integer value.	1.54	Stores 1.54 in *var*.
string	Reads all characters through Enter.	Sam SBD 55	Stores Sam SBD 55 in *var*.

What happens to the extra data characters in the data lines shown in Table 2.5 (for example, YZ in the first data line and 55 in the second)? These characters are processed by ReadLn but are not stored in memory. Note that all characters on the data line are stored when *var* is type string.

SYNTAX DISPLAY

The ReadLn Procedure

Form: ReadLn (*input list*)
             ReadLn

Example: ReadLn (Age, NumDepend)

Interpretation: The ReadLn procedure reads into memory the data the program user types at the keyboard during program execution. The program user must enter one data item for each variable specified in the *input list* and then press the Enter key. Commas separate the variable names in the *input list.*

The order of the data must correspond to the order of the variables in the *input list.* Insert one or more blank characters between consecutive numeric data items. Do not use commas within or between numeric values. Do not insert any blanks between consecutive character data items unless the blank character is one of the data items to be read and stored. Any extra data characters at the end of the line are processed but ignored (i.e., not stored in memory). If there is no *input list* (second form line), all data characters through the Enter key are processed but ignored.

The Read Procedure

In Chapter 8, we will discuss another way to enter data, the Read procedure. The main difference between Read and ReadLn is that any extra characters on a data line after a Read operation are not read until the next Read or ReadLn operation. A ReadLn operation, in contrast, processes all characters on a data line, ignoring any extra characters at the end of the line.

Reading Multiple Data Items

Most of the time ReadLn will read one data item at a time, although it is possible for a single ReadLn to read multiple data values. This is most often done with type Char variables.

EXAMPLE 2.5 ▼

Assuming Ch1, Ch2, and Ch3 are type Char variables, the statement

```
ReadLn (Ch1, Ch2, Ch3)
```

reads and stores three data characters, storing the first in Ch1, the second in Ch2, and the third in Ch3. Entering the data characters EBK results in

Unless you intend to store a blank data character in memory, do not press the space bar between the data characters, as it would count as one of the three characters read and stored. For example, if you enter E B K, the three characters stored would be E, a blank, and B. The next blank and K would be processed but not stored. ▲

EXAMPLE 2.6 ▼

Assuming `Age` is type `Integer` and `Name` is type `string`, the statement pair

```
WriteLn ('Enter your age and your name >');
ReadLn (Age, Name)
```

reads and stores the first data item (an integer) in `Age` and the second data item in `Name`, as shown in Fig. 2.7. At least one blank must appear after the integer, and Turbo Pascal stores the blank(s), shown as □, in the string.   ▲

Program Style

Avoiding Data Entry Errors with String Data

The program user must enter the data items in the correct sequence when a `ReadLn` statement is reading multiple data items. For example, consider what would happen if the program user typed in the data line

```
Janice 35
```

when `ReadLn (Age, Name)` executes. Because `Age` is the first variable in the input list, `ReadLn` would attempt to read and store the user's name (`Janice`) in the `Integer` variable `Age`. This would cause an `invalid numeric for-mat` error message because the character `J` is not numeric.

You might try to read and store this data line using the following statement:

```
ReadLn (Name, Age)      {invalid attempt to read string first}
```

However, this statement would read and store all characters on the data line (`Janice 35`) in `Name`, then the program would pause until the program user typed in a second data line with a value for `Age`. To avoid these data entry problems, we recommend that you read one data item with each `ReadLn` statement, except when reading character data into type `Char` variables (see Example 2.5).

Figure 2.7
Reading an Integer
and a String

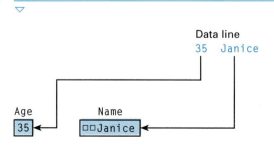

Exercises for Section 2.5   ***Self-Check***

1. Show the output displayed by the following program lines when the data entered are 5 and 7:

```
WriteLn ('Enter two integers> ');
ReadLn (M, N);                    {data line is: 5 7 }
M := M + 5;
N := 3 + N;
WriteLn ('M = ', M);
WriteLn ('N = ', N)
```

2. Show the output displayed by the following lines:

```
Write ('My name is: ');
WriteLn ('Doe, Jane');
WriteLn;
Write ('I live in ');
Write ('Ann Arbor, MI ');
WriteLn ('and my zip code is ', 48109)
```

3. Indicate whether each of the following assignments is valid or invalid and indicate the result of each valid assignment. Assume R is type Real, I is type Integer, B is type Boolean, C is type Char, and S is type string.

   a. R := 3.5 + 5.0   f. S := C
   b. I := 2 * 5   g. C := S
   c. C := 'My name'   h. R := I
   d. S := Your name   i. I := R
   e. B := Boolean   j. R := 10 + I

Programming

1. Write statements that ask the user to enter three numbers and then read the three user responses into First, Second, and Third.
2. a. Write a statement that displays the following line with the value of X at the end:

   ```
   The value of X is _____.
   ```

   b. Assuming Radius and Area are Real variables containing the radius and area of a circle, write a statement that will display this information in the form:

   ```
   The area of a circle with radius _____ is _____.
   ```

3. Write a program that asks the user to enter the radius of a circle and then computes and displays the circle's area. Use the formula

   Area = MyPi × Radius × Radius

   where *MyPi* is the constant 3.14159.

2.6   General Form of a Pascal Program

Now that we have discussed the individual statements that can appear in Pascal programs, we will review the rules for combining them into programs. We will also cover the use of punctuation, spacing, and comments in a program.

As shown in Fig. 2.8, each program begins with a heading that specifies the name of the program. Next comes the declaration part, in which you declare every identifier used in the program except for standard identifiers. All constant declarations follow `const`, and all variable declarations follow `var`. More than one constant may be declared, and there may be more than one variable list. Commas separate identifiers in a variable list; the semicolon terminates each declaration.

In standard Pascal, the reserved words `const` and `var` can appear no more than once and must be in the order shown in Fig. 2.8. In Turbo Pascal, in contrast, the reserved words `const` and `var` may appear more than once and in any order. However, it is good programming practice to follow the standard Pascal rule to ensure portability.

The reserved word `begin` signals the start of the program body. The program body contains statements that are translated into machine language and eventually executed. The statements we have looked at so far perform computations and input/output operations. The last line in a program is `end..`

Figure 2.8
The General Form of a
Pascal Program

```
program Name;
   const
      constant = value;
                 .
                 .
                 .
      constant = value;

   var
      variable list : type;
                 .
                 .
                 .
      variable list : type;

begin
   statement;
        .
        .
        .
   statement
end.
```

Declaration part

Program body

Semicolons separate Pascal statements. Because a semicolon is not needed before the first statement in a sequence or after the last statement, a semicolon should not appear after the reserved word `begin`. Although we don't recommend it, you can type in a semicolon after the last statement in a program. If present, this semicolon has the effect of inserting an "empty statement" between the last actual statement and the program terminator (`end.`).

Pascal ignores line breaks, so a Pascal statement can extend over more than one line. For example, the variable and constant declarations in Fig. 2.1 start on one line and finish on the next. A statement that extends over more than one line cannot be split in the middle of an identifier, a reserved word, or a literal.

Also, we can write more than one statement on a line. For example, the line

```
WriteLn ('Enter two letters >');  ReadLn (Letter1, Letter2)
```

contains a statement that displays a prompt message and a statement that reads the data requested. A semicolon separates the two statements; another semicolon should occur at the end of the line if more statements follow. We recommend that you place only one statement on a line because it improves readability and simplifies program maintenance.

Spaces in Programs

The consistent and careful use of blank spaces can improve the style of a program. A blank space is required between words in a program line.

The compiler ignores extra blanks between words and symbols, but you may insert space to improve the readability and style of a program. You should always leave a blank space after a comma and before and after operators such as `*`, `-`, and `:=`. Remember to indent each line of a program except for the first and last lines and the line `begin` and to write the reserved words `const`, `var`, and `begin` on lines by themselves so they stand out. All lines except the first and last lines of the program and the line `begin` are indented two or more spaces. Finally, use blank lines between sections of the program.

Although stylistic issues have no effect whatever on the meaning of the program as far as the computer is concerned, they can make it easier for people to read and understand the program. Take care, however, not to insert blank spaces where they do not belong. For example, there cannot be a space between the characters `:` and `=` when they form the assignment operator `:=`. Also, an identifier such as `StartSalary` cannot be written as two words, `Start Salary`.

Comments in Programs

program documentation
information (comments) that enhances the readability of a program

Programmers make a program more readable by using comments to describe the purpose of the program, the use of identifiers, and the purpose of each program step. Comments are part of the **program documentation** because they help others read and understand the program. The compiler, however, ignores comments and does not translate them into machine language.

A comment can appear by itself on a program line, at the end of a line following a statement, or embedded in a statement. In the following variable declarations, the first comment is embedded in the declaration, while the second one follows the declaration. We document most variables in this way.

```
var
  SqMeters,               {input - fabric size in meters}
  SqYards    : Real;      {output - fabric size in yards}
```

SYNTAX DISPLAY

Comments

Form: {*comment*}
Example: {This is a comment}
             (* and so is this *)
             {one comment (* inside another *) comment}
Interpretation: A left curly brace indicates the start of a comment; a right curly brace indicates the end of a comment. Also (* and *) can mark the beginning and the end, respectively, of a comment. Comments are listed with the program but are otherwise ignored by the Pascal compiler.
Note: Turbo Pascal (but not standard Pascal) allows comments to be nested inside one another. If the first comment begins with {, the second must begin with (* and vice versa.

Program Style

Using Comments

Each program should begin with a header section that consists of a series of comments specifying

▶ the programmer's name
▶ the date of the current version
▶ a brief description of what the program does

When writing programs for a class assignment, you should also list the class identification and your instructor's name. For example:

```
program Metric;
{
 Programmer: William Bell     Date completed: May 9, 1993
 Instructor: Janet Joseph     Class: CS1
 This program reads a value in square meters and converts it
 to square yards.
}
```

Before implementing each step in the initial algorithm, you should write a comment that summarizes the purpose of the algorithm step. This comment should describe what the step does rather than simply restate the step in English. For example, the comment

```
{Convert the fabric size to square yards}
SqYards := MetersToYards * SqMeters;
```

is more descriptive and hence preferable to

```
{Multiply MetersToYards by SqMeters, save result in SqYards.}
SqYards := MetersToYards * SqMeters;
```

Exercises for Section 2.6

Self-Check

1. Change these comments so they are syntactically correct:

   ```
   {This is a comment?*)
   {How about this one {it seems like a comment} doesn't it}
   ```

2. What is the purpose of a semicolon in the program body?
3. Correct the syntax errors in the following program and rewrite it so it follows our style conventions. What does each statement of your corrected program do? What values are printed?

   ```
   program SMALL  VAR X, Y, X, real;
   BEGIN Y = 15.0
   Z := -Y + 3.5;  Y + z =: x;
   writeln (x; Y; z);  end;
   ```

Programming

1. Write a program that stores the values 'X', 76.1, and 'MyDog' in separate memory cells. Your program should read the values as data items and display them again for the user when done.

2.7 Arithmetic Expressions

To solve most programming problems, you need to write arithmetic expressions that manipulate type Integer and Real data. This section describes the operators used in arithmetic expressions and the rules for writing and evaluating these expressions.

Table 2.6 shows all the arithmetic operators. Each operator manipulates two *operands,* which may be constants, variables, or other arithmetic expressions. The operators +, −, *, and / may be used with type Integer or Real operands. As shown in the last column, for operators +, −, and * the data type of the result is the same as the data type of its operands. The real division operator (/) always yields a real number as its result, so the expression X / 2 always yields a type Real result even when X is type Integer. For example, if X is 4, the value of X / 2 is the real number 2.0. The last two operators, div and mod, can be used only with integers.

Arithmetic Operator	Meaning	Example
+	Addition	5 + 2 is 7 5.0 + 2.0 is 7.0
-	Subtraction	5 - 2 is 3 5.0 - 2.0 is 3.0
*	Multiplication	5 * 2 is 10 5.0 * 2.0 is 10.0
/	Real division	5.0 / 2.0 is 2.5 5 / 2 is 2.5
div	Integer division	5 div 2 is 2
mod	Modulus operator	5 mod 2 is 1

Operators div and mod

The integer division operator, div, computes the integral part of the result of dividing its first operand by its second. For example, the value of 7 / 2 is 3.5, but the value of 7 div 2 is the integral part of this result, or 3. Similarly, the value of 299 / 100 is 2.99, but the value of 299 div 100 is the integral part of this result, or 2. Both operands of div must be integers, and the div operation is undefined when the divisor (the second operand) is zero. Table 2.7 shows some examples of the div operator.

3 div 15 = 0	3 div -15 = 0
15 div 3 = 5	15 div -3 = -5
16 div 3 = 5	16 div -3 = -5
17 div 3 = 5	-17 div 3 = -5
18 div 3 = 6	-18 div 3 = -6

Although mathematically equivalent, the results of the expressions 6 / 2 and 6 div 2 are not the same in Pascal. The value of 6 / 2 is the real number 3.0, but the value of 6 div 2 is the integer 3.

The modulus operator, mod, returns the integer remainder of the result of dividing its first operand by its second. For example, the value of 7 mod 2 is 1 because the integer remainder is 1.

You can use long division to determine the result of a div or mod operation. The following calculation on the left shows the effect of dividing 7 by 2 by long division: We get a quotient of 3 (7 div 2 is 3) and a remainder of 1 (7 mod 2 is 1). The calculation on the right shows that 299 div 100 is 2 (quotient) and that 299 mod 100 is 99 (remainder).

```
7 div 2                        299 div 100
   ↓                                ↓
   3 R1  ← 7 mod 2                  2 R99  ← 299 mod 100
2)7                          100)299
   6                             200
   1                              99
```

The magnitude of M mod N must always be less than the divisor N, so if M is positive, the value of M mod 100 must be between 0 and 99. The mod operation is undefined when N is zero. Table 2.8 shows some examples of the mod operator. By comparing the second and third columns, you can see that -M mod N is equivalent to -(M mod N).

Table 2.8
Examples of the
mod Operator

3 mod 5 = 3	5 mod 3 = 2	-5 mod 3 = -2
4 mod 5 = 4	5 mod 4 = 1	-5 mod 4 = -1
5 mod 5 = 0	15 mod 5 = 0	-15 mod 5 = 0
6 mod 5 = 1	15 mod 6 = 3	-15 mod 6 = -3
7 mod 5 = 2	15 mod 7 = 1	-15 mod -7 = -1
8 mod 5 = 3	15 mod 8 = 7	15 mod 0 is undefined

EXAMPLE 2.7 ▼

If you have P people and B identical boats, the expression

P div B

tells you how many people to put in each boat. Notice that P / B may give the wrong answer. For example, if P is 18 and B is 4, 18 div 4 is 4 (correct), but 18 / 4 is 4.5 (incorrect). The formula

P mod B

tells you how many people would be left over (18 mod 4 is 2). ▲

Data Type of an Arithmetic Expression

We indicated earlier that a type Integer expression could be assigned to a type Real variable, but not vice versa. How does Pascal determine the data type of an arithmetic expression? The following rule applies:

An expression is type Integer if all of its operands are type Integer and none of its operators is /; otherwise, the expression is type Real.

This rule is based on two properties of arithmetic operators:

▶ The operator / always yields a Real result.
▶ If an operator has one Real operand and one Integer operand, the operator yields a Real result (for example, 5 + 2.0 is 7.0, not 7).

mixed-type expression
an expression that has type Real and Integer operands and always evaluates to a Real result

A **mixed-type expression** has both Integer and Real operands. According to the preceding rule, a mixed-type expression must be type Real. It is a good programming practice to avoid writing mixed-type expressions.

Mixed-Type Assignment Statements

When an assignment statement is executed, the expression is first evaluated and then the result is assigned to the variable preceding the assignment operator (:=). Either a type Real or a type Integer expression may be assigned to a type Real variable. Thus, if M and N are type Integer and X and Y are type Real, all the following assignment statements are valid:

```
M := 3;
N := 2;
X := M / N;    {assigns 1.5 to X}
Y := M + N     {assigns 5.0 to Y}
```

In the last statement, the expression M + N evaluates to the integer 5 and this value is converted to its type Real equivalent (5.0) before it is stored in Y. Notice that the type conversion is done after the two integer values are summed, not before (i.e., 3 and 2 are summed, not 3.0 and 2.0). This is an example of a **mixed-type assignment** statement because the variable being assigned and the expression have different data types.

mixed-type assignment
assignment of an expression of one type to a variable of a different type

Pascal does not allow a type Real expression to be assigned to a type Integer variable, because the fractional part of the expression cannot be represented and so will be lost. This means that the following mixed-type assignment statements are invalid if Count is type Integer:

```
Count := 3.5;          {invalid assignment of real value to
                        Integer variable}
Count := Count + 1.0;  {invalid; 1.0 is Real, so result is
                        Real}
Count := Count / 2;    {invalid; result of division is
                        Real}
```

Expressions with Multiple Operators

In our examples so far, most expressions have had a single operator; however, expressions with multiple operators are common. To understand and write expressions with multiple operators, we must know the Pascal rules for evaluating expressions. For example, in the expression 10 + 5 / 2, is + performed before /, or vice versa? In the expression 10 / 5 * 2, is / performed before *, or vice versa? Verify for yourself that the order of evaluation does make a difference. In both expressions, the / operator is evaluated first. The reasons are explained in the Pascal rules for expression evaluation, which are based on familiar algebraic rules.

Rules for Evaluating Expressions

a. *Parentheses rule:* All expressions in parentheses must be evaluated separately. Nested parenthesized expressions must be evaluated from the inside out, with the innermost expression evaluated first.
b. *Operator precedence rule:* Operators in the same expression are evaluated in the following order.

```
*,/,div,mod    first
+,-            last
```

c. *Left associative rule:* Operators in the same expression and at the same precedence level (such as + and -) are evaluated left to right.

These rules will help you understand how Pascal evaluates expressions. Use parentheses as needed to specify the order of evaluation. For complicated expressions, it is a good idea to use extra parentheses to document clearly the order of operator evaluation. For example, the expression

```
X * Y * Z + A / B - C * D
```

can be written in a more readable form using parentheses:

```
(X * Y * Z ) + (A / B) - (C * D)
```

EXAMPLE 2.8 ▼

The formula for the area of a circle

$$a = \pi r^2$$

can be written in Pascal as

```
Area := MyPi * Radius * Radius
```

where `MyPi` is the constant `3.14159`. Figure 2.9 shows the evaluation tree for this formula. In this tree, read from top to bottom, arrows connect each operand with its operator. The order of operator evaluation is shown by the number to the left of each operator; the letter to the right of the operator indicates which evaluation rule applies.   ▲

EXAMPLE 2.9 ▼

The formula for the average velocity, v, of a particle traveling on a line between points p_1 and p_2 in time t_1 to t_2 is

$$v = \frac{p_2 - p_1}{t_2 - t_1}$$

This formula can be written and evaluated in Pascal as shown in Fig. 2.10.   ▲

Figure 2.9
Evaluation Tree for Area :=
MyPi * Radius * Radius

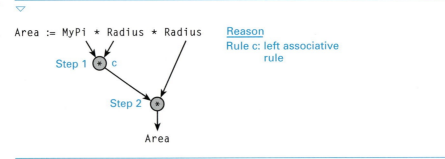

Reason
Rule c: left associative
rule

EXAMPLE 2.10 ▼

Consider the expression

```
Z - (A + B div 2 ) + W * Y
```

containing Integer variables only. The parenthesized expression (A + B div 2) is evaluated first (rule a) beginning with B div 2 (rule b). Once the value of B div 2 is determined, it can be added to A to obtain the value of (A + B div 2). Next, the multiplication operation is performed (rule b) and the value for W * Y is determined. Then, the value of (A + B div 2) is subtracted from Z (rule c). Finally, the result is added to W * Y. The evaluation tree for this expression is shown in Fig. 2.11.   ▲

Writing Mathematical Formulas in Pascal

You may encounter two problems in writing a mathematical formula in Pascal. The first concerns multiplication, which often is implied in a formula by writing the two multiplicands next to each other, for example, *a = bc*. In Pascal, however, you must always use the * operator to indicate multiplication, as in

```
A := B * C
```

Figure 2.10
Evaluation Tree for V :=
(P2 −P1)/(T2 −T1)

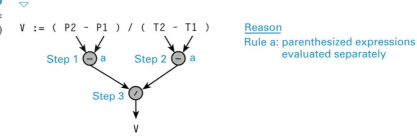

Reason
Rule a: parenthesized expressions
evaluated separately

Figure 2.11
Evaluation Tree for
Z −(A + B div 2) + W * Y

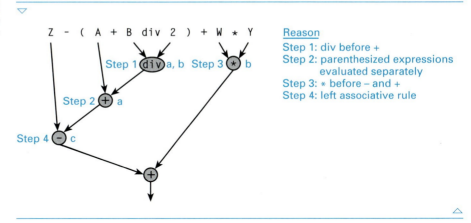

The other difficulty arises in formulas using division, in which we normally write the numerator and the denominator on separate lines:

$$m = \frac{y - b}{x - a}$$

In Pascal, however, the numerator and denominator must be placed on the same line. Consequently, parentheses often are needed to separate the numerator from the denominator and to indicate clearly the order of evaluation of the operators in the expression. Thus the preceding formula would be written in Pascal as

```
M := (Y - B) / (X - A)
```

Table 2.9 gives other examples of mathematical formulas rewritten in Pascal. The points illustrated in Table 2.9 can be summarized as follows:

Table 2.9
Mathematical Formulas as
Pascal Expressions

Mathematical Formula	Pascal Expression
1. $b^2 - 4ac$	B * B - 4 * A * C
2. $a + b - c$	A + B - C
3. $\dfrac{a + b}{c + d}$	(A + B) / (C + D)
4. $\dfrac{1}{1 + x^2}$	1 / (1 + X * X)
5. $a \times -(b + c)$	A * (-(B + C))

▶ Always specify multiplication explicitly by using the operator * where needed (formulas 1 and 4).

▶ Use parentheses when required to control the order of operator evaluation (formulas 3 and 4).

▶ Never write two arithmetic operators in succession; they must be separated by an operand or an open parenthesis (formula 5).

Unary Minus

The fifth Pascal expression in Table 2.9 uses a unary minus to negate the value of (B + C) before performing the multiplication. The unary minus has only one operand and has the same precedence as the subtraction operator.

Mixed-Type Expressions with div and mod

You must be very careful when using div and mod in a mixed-type expression or with the real division operator /. The expression

7 div 2 / 3.0

is valid and evaluates to 1.0 as shown in Fig. 2.12. However, the expression

7 / 2 div 3

is invalid because 7 / 2 is 3.5 (/ yields a Real result) and 3.5 cannot be an operand of div.

The following case study demonstrates the manipulation of type Integer data (using div and mod) and a string data item.

CASE STUDY Evaluating Coins

PROBLEM ▼

Your little sister, who has been saving nickels and pennies, is tired of lugging her piggy bank when she goes shopping. She wants to exchange the

Figure 2.12
Evaluation Tree for
7 div 2 / 3.0

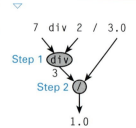

coins for dollar bills and change, so she needs to know the value of her coins in dollars and cents.

ANALYSIS ▼

To solve this problem, you need a count of nickels and a count of pennies in the collection. From those counts, determine the total value of the coins in cents. Once you have that figure, you can do an integer division using 100 as the divisor to get the dollar value; the remainder of this division will be the loose change that she should receive. In the data requirements, list the total value in cents (TotalCents) as a program variable, because it is needed as part of the computation process but is not a required problem output.

Data Requirements

Problem Inputs

```
Name : string      {your sister's name}
Nickels : Integer  {the count of nickels}
Pennies : Integer  {the count of pennies}
```

Problem Outputs

```
Dollars : Integer  {the number of dollars she should receive}
Change : Integer   {the loose change she should receive}
```

Additional Program Variables

```
TotalCents : Integer   {the total number of cents}
```

Relevant Formulas

1 dollar = 100 pennies
1 nickel = 5 pennies

The input variable Name stores the program user's name and helps to personalize the interaction between your sister and the program.

DESIGN ▼

The algorithm is straightforward.

Initial Algorithm

1. Read and display the program user's name.
2. Read in the count of nickels and pennies.
3. Compute the total value in cents.
4. Find the value in dollars and loose change.
5. Display the value in dollars and loose change.

Steps 3 and 4 may need refinement. Their refinements follow.

Step 3 Refinement

3.1 TotalCents is the value of Nickels in cents plus Pennies.

Step 4 Refinement

4.1 Dollars is the integer quotient of TotalCents and 100.
4.2 Change is the integer remainder of TotalCents and 100.

IMPLEMENTATION ▼

The program is shown in Fig. 2.13. The statements

```
Write ('Hello ', Name);
WriteLn ('. Let''s find the value of your coins.');
```

display the first line in the output window. In the second line, the word
Let''s contains an embedded apostrophe indicated by two consecutive
apostrophes. Because single apostrophes begin and end strings, you must
use two apostrophes to denote an apostrophe inside a string. Using just one
would terminate the string prematurely and cause a syntax error.
    The statement

```
TotalCents := 5 * Nickels + Pennies;
```

implements algorithm step 3.1. The statements

```
Dollars := TotalCents div 100;
Change := TotalCents mod 100;
```

use the mod and div operators to implement algorithm steps 4.1 and 4.2.

Figure 2.13
Finding the Value of Coins

Input Window

```
program Coins;
{Determines the value of a coin collection.}

   var
      Name : string;         {input - name of program user}
      Pennies,               {input - count of pennies}
      Nickels,               {input - count of nickels}
      Dollars,               {output - number of dollars}
      Change,                {output - loose change}
      TotalCents : Integer;  {total cents}

begin
   {Read and display the program user's name.}
   Write ('Type in your name and press Enter >');
   ReadLn (Name);
   Write ('Hello ', Name);
   WriteLn ('. Let''s find the value of your coins.');
```

▷ ▷ ▷ ▷ ▷

```
{Read in the count of nickels and pennies.}
Write ('Number of nickels >');
ReadLn (Nickels);
Write ('Number of pennies >');
ReadLn (Pennies);

{Compute the total value in cents.}
TotalCents := 5 * Nickels + Pennies;

{Find the value in dollars and change.}
Dollars := TotalCents div 100;
Change := TotalCents mod 100;

{Display the value in dollars and change.}
WriteLn;
Write ('Your coins are worth ', Dollars, ' dollars');
WriteLn (' and ', Change, ' cents.')
end.
```

Output Window

```
Type in your name and press Enter >Sally
Hello Sally. Let's find the value of your coins.
Number of nickels >30
Number of pennies >77

Your coins are worth 2 dollars and 27 cents.
```

△

TESTING ▼

To test this program, try running it with a combination of nickels and pennies that yields an exact dollar amount with no change left over. For example, 35 nickels and 25 pennies should yield a value of 2 dollars and no cents. Then increase and decrease the amount of pennies by one (26 and 24 pennies) to make sure that these cases are also handled properly.

....

Exercises for Section 2.7   **Self-Check**

1. a. Evaluate the following expressions with 7 and 22 as operands.

    ```
    22 div 7    7 div 22    22 mod 7    7 mod 22
    ```

    Repeat the exercise for these pairs of integers:
    b. 15, 16   c. 3, 23   d. -4, 16

2. Given the declarations

    ```
    const
      MyPi = 3.14159;
      MaxI = 1000;
    ```

```
var
   X, Y : Real;
   A, B, I : Integer;
```

indicate which statements are valid and find the value of each valid statement. Also indicate which statements are invalid and explain why. Assume that A is 3, B is 4, and Y is -1.0.

a. I := A mod B   j. I := (MaxI - 990) div A
b. I := (990 - MaxI) div A   k. X := A / Y
c. I := A mod Y   l. I := MyPi * A
d. X := MyPi * Y   m. X := MyPi div Y
e. I := A / B   n. X := A div B
f. X := A / B   o. I := (MaxI - 990) mod A
g. X := A mod (A / B)   p. I := A mod 0
h. I := B div 0   q. I := A mod (MaxI - 990)
i. I := A mod (990 - MaxI)

3. Draw evaluation trees for the following expressions. What is the value of the last one?

```
1.8 * Celsius + 32.0
(Salary - 5000.00) * 0.20 + 1425.00
10 mod 4 + 1 div 2
```

4. Write an assignment statement to implement the following equation in Pascal:

$$q = \frac{kA(T_1 - T_2)}{L}$$

5. Assume that you have the following variable declarations:

```
var
   Color, Lime, Straw, Red, Orange : Integer;
   White, Green, Blue, Purple, Crayon : Real;
```

Evaluate each of the following statements given these values: Color is 2, Crayon is -1.3, Straw is 1, Red is 3, Purple is 0.2E+1.

a. White := Color * 2.5 / Purple
b. Green := Color / Purple
c. Orange := Color div Red
d. Blue := (Color + Straw) / (Crayon + 0.3)
e. Lime := Red div Color + Red mod Color
f. Purple := Straw / Red * Color

6. Let A, B, C, and X be the names of four type Real variables, and let I, J, and K be the names of three type Integer variables. Each of the following statements contains a violation of the rules for forming arithmetic expressions. Rewrite each statement so it is consistent with the rules.

a. X := 4.0 A * C   d. K := 3(I + J)
b. A := AC   e. X := 5A / BC
c. I := 2 * -J   f. I := 5J3

Programming

1. Extend the program in Fig. 2.13 to handle dimes and quarters as well as nickels and pennies.

2.8   Formatting and Viewing Program Output

Pascal displays all real numbers in scientific notation unless we instruct it to do otherwise. This section explains how to specify the format or appearance of your output.

Formatting Integer Values

It is fairly easy to specify the format of an Integer variable or value displayed by a Pascal program. You simply add the symbols :*fw* after the variable or value, where *fw* specifies the **field width**, or number of digits to be displayed. The lines

field width

the number of characters used to display a value

```
Write ('Your coins are worth ', Dollars :1, ' dollars');
WriteLn (' and ', Change :2, ' cents.')
```

indicate that one digit will be used to display the value of Dollars and two digits will be used to display the value of Change (a number between 0 and 99). If Dollars is 7 and Change is 8, the program output would be

```
Your coins are worth 7 dollars and  8 cents.
```

In this line, notice that there is an extra space before the value of Change (value is 8). The reason is that the format specification :2 allows space for two digits to be displayed. If the value of Change is between 0 and 9, a single digit is displayed right-justified, preceded by one blank space. We can use the format symbols :2 to display any output value between -9 and 99. For negative numbers, you must include the minus sign in the count of digits displayed.

Table 2.10 shows how two integer values are displayed using different format specifications. In this table, the character □ represents a blank character. The next-to-last line shows that Pascal expands the field width if it is too

Table 2.10

Displaying 234 and 2234 Using Different Formats

Value	Format	Displayed Output	Value	Format	Displayed Output
234	:4	□234	-234	:4	-234
234	:5	□□234	-234	:5	□-234
234	:6	□□□234	-234	:6	□□-234
234	:1	234	-234	:1	-234
234	:Len	□□234 (if Len is 5)	-234	:Len	□-234 (if Len is 5)

small for the integer value displayed. You can use the format specification :1 to display any integer value without leading blanks. The last line shows the field width specification may be a variable (or even an expression) that has an integer value.

Formatting Real Values

To describe the format specification for a type Real variable or value, we must indicate both the total *field width* needed and the desired number of *decimal places* after the variable or value (:*fw* :*dp*). The total field width should be large enough to accommodate all digits before and after the decimal point. We should also include a display column for the decimal point and for a minus sign if the number can be negative.

If X is a type Real variable whose value will be between -99.9 and 999.9, we could use the output list item X :5:1 to display the value of X to an accuracy of one decimal place. Table 2.11 shows different values of X displayed using this format specification. The values displayed are rounded to one decimal place, and all values are displayed right-justified in five columns.

Table 2.11
Displaying X Using Format Specification :5 :1

Value of X	Displayed Output	Value of X	Displayed Output
99.42	-99.4	-25.55	-25.6
0.123	□□0.1	99.999	100.0
-9.53	□-9.5	999.43	999.4

Table 2.12 shows some real values displayed using other format specifications. The next-to-last line shows that Pascal expands the field width if it is

Table 2.12
Formatting Real Values

Value	Format	Displayed Output	Value	Format	Displayed Output
3.14159	:5:2	□3.14	3.14159	:4:2	3.14
3.14159	:4:2	3.14	3.14159	:5:1	□□3.1
3.14159	:5:3	3.142	3.14159	:8:5	□3.14159
0.1234	:4:2	0.12	-0.006	:4:2	-0.01
-0.006	:8:3	□□-0.006	-0.006	:8:5	-0.00600
25.876	:3:1	25.9	-124.3123	:4:2	-124.31
-0.006	:9	-6.00E-03	-3.14159	:9	-3.14E+00

too small for the real value displayed. You can use format specifications $3:1$ and $4:2$ to display any real value without leading blanks. The last line shows that you can use a format specification of the form $:n$ for real values. In this case, the real value is displayed in scientific notation using a field width of n.

Program Style

Eliminating Leading Blanks

As shown in Tables 2.10 through 2.12, a number that requires fewer display columns than are specified by the format field width is displayed with leading blanks. To eliminate extra leading blanks, choose a format that will display the smallest value expected. If the actual value requires more display columns, the field width will expand to accommodate it. Thus a format of $:1$ displays any integer value without leading blanks (for example, 29397 $:1$ is displayed as 29397). A format of $:3:1$ displays any real number to an accuracy of one decimal place without leading blanks (for example, 99397.567 $:3:1$ is displayed as 99397.6); similarly, a format of $:4:2$ displays any real number to an accuracy of two decimal places without leading blanks.

Formatting Strings

A string value is always displayed right-justified in its field. Therefore blank spaces will precede a string if the field in which it is displayed is wider than the string. If the field width is too small for a string value, Turbo Pascal expands the field width so that the entire string can be displayed. (In standard Pascal, the number of characters displayed is equal to the field width, so not all characters will be displayed.) Table 2.13 illustrates these points.

Table 2.13
Displaying String Values Using Formats

String	Format	Displayed Output
'*'	:1	*
'*'	:2	□*
'*'	:3	□□*
'ACES'	:1	ACES (A in standard Pascal)
'ACES'	:2	ACES (AC in standard Pascal)
'ACES'	:3	ACES (ACE in standard Pascal)
'ACES'	:4	ACES
'ACES'	:5	□ACES

EXAMPLE 2.11 ▼

The statements

```
Quantity := 15;
Cost := 55.0;
Description := 'Toaster oven';
WriteLn (Quantity :5, '$' :5, Cost :8:2, Description :20)
```

display an integer (value of Quantity), a character ($), a real number (value of Cost), and a string (value of Description). The output line displayed would be

□□□15□□□□$□□55.00□□□□□□□□Toaster□oven

where the symbol □ denotes a blank. The integer 15 is preceded by 3 blanks, the character $ by 4 blanks, the real number 55.00 by 3 blanks, and the string by 8 blanks. You may prefer to remove the spaces between the $ character and the number 55.00. You can accomplish this by changing the third output list item to Cost :5:2 . ▲

Using the Output Window

Normally, Turbo Pascal displays the Edit window while a program is running. Turbo Pascal momentarily switches to the user screen whenever a program pauses for data entry. Typing Alt-F5 (press and hold the Alt key while pressing the F5 key) displays the user screen and allows you to review the program output when your program completes execution. However, some programmers prefer to view a program's output continually while the program is running.

Turbo Pascal allows you to open an Output window and will display it on the screen at the same time as the Edit window. To do this, select the Output option from the Debug menu, as shown in Fig. 2.14. This causes the Output window to appear at the bottom of the screen and selects it as the active window. You can use your mouse or the arrow keys to scroll through the Output window and display any output that does not appear in the Output window. To return to the Edit window and make it the active window, position and click your mouse cursor on the Edit window or press the F6 key. (The F6 key allows you to switch back and forth between the Edit window and the Output window.)

When you return to the Edit window, you will notice that it now covers the Output window. To display both windows at the same time, you can reduce the size of the Edit window and uncover the Output window by using the mouse (click and drag the lower right corner of the Edit window) or by selecting the Size/Move option from the Window menu and using the arrow keys while pressing the Shift key. These operations are described in more detail in the Help screen for Size/Move. Figure 2.15 shows how the screen might look with the Edit window resized and both windows displayed.

Figure 2.14
Turbo Pascal Debug Menu

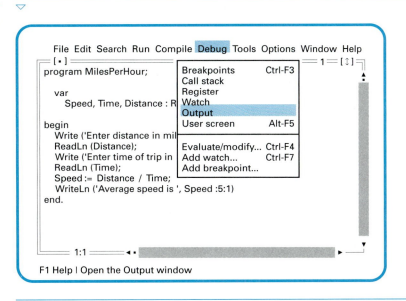

Figure 2.15
Turbo Pascal Edit and
Output Windows

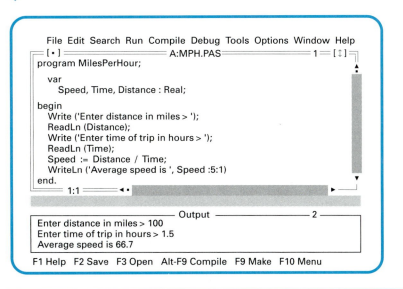

Printing Programs and Output

There are several ways to print your program or its output. The easiest approach is to use the PrintScreen key. First, display the Edit window or user screen on your screen, then press the PrintScreen key to obtain a printed copy of your current screen display.

You also can print a copy of your program file from MS-DOS by using the operating system command

```
TYPE FileName.PAS >PRN
```

This prints file *FileName*.PAS. If you omit the characters >PRN, the file is displayed on the screen.

If your computer has its own printer, you can activate the MS-DOS logging feature, which causes all characters sent to the user screen to go simultaneously to the printer. To activate the logging feature, select DOS shell from the File submenu and press Ctrl-PrintScreen (press and hold down the Ctrl key and then press the PrintScreen key). Type EXIT to return to Turbo Pascal. To deactivate the logging feature, repeat this process.

Exercises for Section 2.8 **Self-Check**

1. Show the output lines for the following statements:

   ```
   Write (-99 :4);
   WriteLn ('Bottles' :8);
   WriteLn (-99 :4, -99 :8)
   ```

2. Show how the value -15.564 (stored in X) would be displayed using these formats:

   ```
   X :8:4    X :8:3    X :8:2    X :8:1    X :8:0    X :8
   ```

3. What is the output of the following sequence of program statements assuming I is an integer? Use the symbol □ to denote a blank space.

   ```
   I := 1;
   WriteLn (I : 5, ' ', I :1, I : 5);
   I := I * 10;
   WriteLn (I : 5, ' ', I :1, I : 5);
   I := I * 10;
   WriteLn (I : 5, ' ', I :1, I : 5);
   I := I * 10;
   WriteLn (I : 5, ' ', I :1, I : 5)
   ```

4. Assuming X (type Real) is 12.335 and I (type Integer) is 100, show the output lines for the following statements:

   ```
   WriteLn ('X is ' :10, X :6:2, 'I is ' :4, I :5);
   Write ('I is ' :10, I :1);
   WriteLn ('X is ' :10, X :2:1)
   ```

Programming

1. A researcher wants to display a table of readings from an experiment. Each line will contain an integer from 1 to 1000, to indicate the reading number (value of `Reading`), and the pressure amount (value of `Pressure`), which is always less than 100 pounds. Give a `WriteLn` statement that will display outputs in the form

   `RRRR□□□□□PP.PPP`

   where each `R` is a digit of the reading value, each `P` is a digit of the pressure value, and each □ is a space.
2. Write a series of statements that will display a three-line heading consisting of your name, your school, and its city and state. Each line should be approximately centered on the computer screen.

2.9 Debugging and Programming Errors

Beginning programmers soon discover that a program rarely runs correctly the first time it executes. Murphy's Law, "If something can go wrong, it will," seems to have been written with the computer program in mind. In fact, errors are so common that they have their own special name—*bugs*—and the process of correcting them is called **debugging** a program. (According to computer folklore, the first hardware error was caused by a large insect found inside a computer component.) To alert you to potential problems, we will provide a section on common programming errors at the end of each chapter.

debugging
removing errors from a program

When Turbo Pascal detects an error, the computer displays an error message indicating that you have made a mistake and what the likely cause of the error might be. You will be placed in the editor with the cursor positioned on the incorrect statement. Unfortunately, error messages are often difficult to interpret and are sometimes misleading. Even the editor cursor position should be regarded only as indicating the approximate position of the error. If you press F1 after an error message is displayed, the Turbo Pascal Help system will provide additional information describing the error. As you gain experience, you will become more proficient at locating and correcting errors.

Three kinds of errors—syntax errors, run-time errors, and logic errors—can occur, as discussed in the following sections.

Syntax Errors

syntax error
a violation of the Pascal grammar rules, detected during program translation

A **syntax error** occurs when your code violates one or more grammar rules of Pascal and is detected and displayed by the compiler as it attempts to translate your program. If a statement has a syntax error, it cannot be translated and your program will not be executed.

The payroll program shown in the Edit window of Fig. 2.16 has two syntax errors. After the first attempt to compile this program, we get an error message that suggests that the problem is an `Invalid subrange base type`. The real problem is that the symbol : was used incorrectly in place of the symbol = in a constant declaration.

Figure 2.17 shows the Edit window after the first error has been corrected and the program recompiled. In this case, the error message indicates that the compiler cannot find a declaration for the identifier `Net`. After you correct this variable declaration error, the program should compile successfully.

Removing syntax errors, one at a time, can be time-consuming. Desk check your program carefully before compiling it the first time. Two common errors made by beginning programmers are forgetting to declare (or misspelling) identifier names and omitting semicolons. Both errors are easily discovered by careful desk checking.

Improper use of a Pascal data type often causes a syntax error. Two examples follow:

▶ Use of arithmetic operators with character or string data
▶ Assigning a value of one type to a variable of another type (exception: an `Integer` value can be assigned to a type `Real` variable)

Improper use of apostrophes with a string also causes a syntax error. Make sure you always use a single quote or apostrophe to begin and end a string; double quotes cannot be used to begin or end a string.

Figure 2.16
Invalid Constant
Declaration

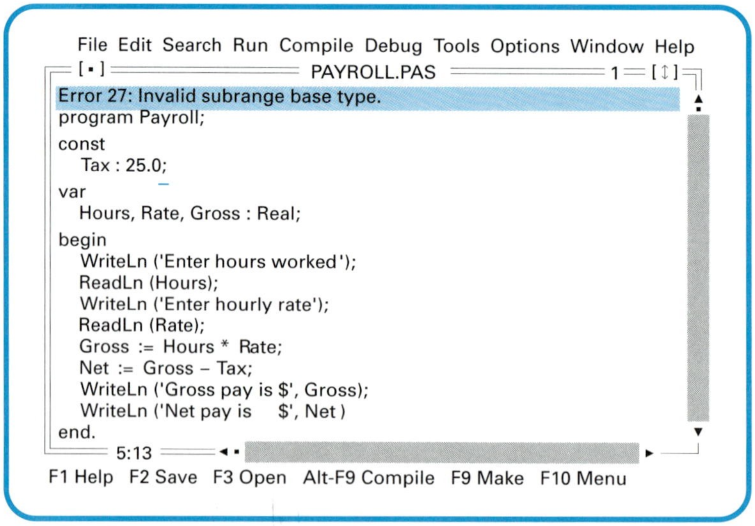

```
   File Edit Search Run Compile Debug Tools Options Window Help
 [•]                       PAYROLL.PAS                      1  [↕]
 Error 27: Invalid subrange base type.
 program Payroll;
 const
    Tax : 25.0;
 var
    Hours, Rate, Gross : Real;
 begin
    WriteLn ('Enter hours worked');
    ReadLn (Hours);
    WriteLn ('Enter hourly rate');
    ReadLn (Rate);
    Gross := Hours * Rate;
    Net := Gross – Tax;
    WriteLn ('Gross pay is $', Gross);
    WriteLn ('Net pay is    $', Net )
 end.
    5:13           ◄ •
 F1 Help  F2 Save  F3 Open  Alt-F9 Compile  F9 Make  F10 Menu
```

Figure 2.17
Unknown Identifier

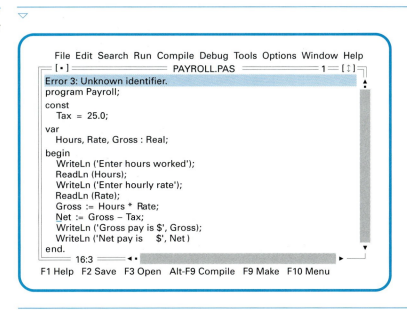

Another common syntax error is a *missing or extra apostrophe in a string.* If the apostrophe at the end of a string is missing, the Turbo Pascal compiler will display the error message `String constant exceeds line`.

Remember to use two consecutive apostrophes to represent an apostrophe within a string:

```
WriteLn ('Enter Joe''s nickname>');
```

Run-Time Errors

run-time error
an attempt to perform an invalid operation, detected during program execution

Run-time errors are detected and displayed by the computer during the execution of a program. A run-time error occurs when the user directs the computer to perform an invalid operation, such as dividing a number by zero or manipulating undefined or invalid data.

The program in Fig. 2.18 compiles successfully but contains no statement assigning a value to the variable X before the assignment statement

```
Z := Y / X;
```

executes, causing a run-time error. The Turbo Pascal compiler assigns the default value `0.0` to X. When the assignment statement executes, the error message

```
Error 200: Division by Zero
```

is displayed, indicating an *attempt to divide by zero,* an invalid operation.

Figure 2.18
Program with a
Run-Time Error

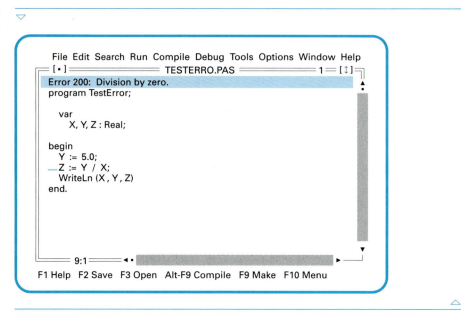

You will be placed in the Turbo Pascal editor with the cursor positioned at the beginning of the assignment statement. Selecting Help causes a window to pop up, showing possible causes of the run-time error. You should insert a statement that assigns a nonzero value to X; it is poor programming practice to allow the compiler to assign default values to your variables.

Data entry errors are common run-time errors caused by reading data of the wrong type into a variable—for example, reading a real number or a character into a type Integer variable. Another common run-time error is **arithmetic overflow**. This error occurs when a program attempts to store a value that is too large in a variable.

arithmetic overflow
a run-time error caused by an attempt to store a value in a variable that is too large

Logic Errors

logic error
an error caused by following a faulty algorithm

Logic errors occur when a program follows a faulty algorithm. Because logic errors usually do not cause run-time errors and do not display error messages, they are very difficult to detect. The only sign of a logic error may be incorrect program output. You can detect logic errors by testing the program thoroughly, comparing its output to calculated results. You can prevent logic errors by carefully desk checking the algorithm and the program before you type it in.

Because debugging can be time-consuming, plan your program solutions carefully and desk check them to eliminate bugs early. If you are unsure of the syntax for a particular statement, look it up in the text or in Appendix E. Following this approach will save time and avoid trouble.

CHAPTER REVIEW

1. Follow the first five steps of the software development method to solve programming problems: (1) specify the problem, (2) analyze the problem, (3) design the algorithm, (4) implement the program, and (5) test and verify the solution. Use structured programming techniques to write error-free code that is easy to read and maintain.

2. Every Pascal program has a declaration part and a program body.

3. Within the declaration part, you must declare each identifier and its use unless the identifier is a standard identifier in which case its meaning is predefined. All identifiers begin with a letter and consist only of letters and digits. A reserved word cannot be used as an identifier.

    ▶ Declare as a constant a memory cell used to store a value that cannot change.

    ▶ Declare as a variable a memory cell used to store a data value or a program result.

4. Pascal's data types enable the compiler to determine how to store a particular value in memory and what operations can be performed on that value. The four standard data types are `Integer`, `Real`, `Char`, and `Boolean`. Turbo Pascal uses a fifth data type, `string`, to store a sequence of characters. The data type of each variable must be declared; Pascal determines the data type of a constant from its value.

5. The program body consists of the executable statements, which are translated into machine language. Assignment statements perform computations and store results in memory, `Write/WriteLn` statements display values stored in memory, and `ReadLn` statements read data values into memory.

Summary of New Pascal Constructs

Construct	Effect
Program Heading	
`program Payroll;`	Identifies `Payroll` as the name of the program.
Constant Declaration	

`const`
`  Tax = 25.00;`
`  Star = '*';`
	Associates the constant `Tax` with the real value `25.00` and the constant `Star` with the type `Char` value `'*'`.

Variable Declaration	

`var`
`  X, Y, Z : Real;`
`  Me, It : Integer;`
	Allocates memory cells named `X`, `Y`, and `Z` for storage of real numbers and `Me` and `It` for storage of integers.

Assignment Statement	
`Distance := Speed * Time`	Assigns the product of `Speed` and `Time` as the value of `Distance`.

Construct	Effect
ReadLn Procedure ReadLn (Hours, Rate)	Enters data into the variables Hours and Rate.
Write Procedure Write ('Net = ', Net :4:2)	Displays the string 'Net = ' followed by the value of Net printed in a field of four columns and rounded to two decimal places.
WriteLn Procedure WriteLn (X, Y)	Prints the values of X and Y and advances the cursor to the next line.

Quick-Check Exercises

1. What value is assigned to X by the following statement?

   X := 25.0 * 3.0 / 2.5

2. What value is assigned to X by the following statement, assuming X is 10.0?

   X := X - 20.0

3. Show the exact form of the output line displayed when X is 3.456 and N is 890:

   WriteLn ('Some numbers are ', X :3:1, '*', X :6:3,
            N : 4, '*', N : 1);

4. In the following expression, what operator will be evaluated first: A + B / C * D?
5. Indicate which data type you would use to represent the following items: number of children at school, a letter grade on an exam, the average number of school days absent each year.
6. In which step of the software development method are the problem inputs and outputs identified?
7. How does WriteLn differ in its effect from Write?
8. If procedure ReadLn is reading two numbers from a data line, what character is typed in after the first number? What is typed in after the second number?
9. In Pascal, begin is a _____ .
10. How does the computer determine how many and what kind of data values to read when a ReadLn operation is performed?
11. What is the syntactic purpose of the semicolon in the body of a Pascal program?

Answers to Quick-Check Exercises

1. 30.0
2. -10.0
3. Some numbers are 3.5* 3.456 890*890
4. /
5. Integer,Character,Real
6. Analysis
7. WriteLn causes subsequent output to be displayed on the next line; Write causes subsequent output to be displayed on the same line.
8. A blank, the Enter key
9. reserved word
10. By the number of variables in the input list and their data types
11. It separates two executable statements.

Review Questions

1. What kind of information should be specified in the comments that appear at the beginning of a program?
2. Check the variables that are syntactically correct:

   Income _____   Two fold _____ Hours*Rate _____   MyProgram _____

   1time _____   C3PO   _____ ReadLn   _____ program   _____

   const _____   Income#1 _____ var   _____ Program   _____

   Tom's _____   item   _____ variable   _____ Pi   _____

3. What is illegal about the following declarations and statement?

   ```
   const
     MyPi = 3.14159;

   var
     C, R : Real;

   begin
     MyPi := C / (2 * R * R)
   ```

4. List and define the rules for order of evaluation of arithmetic expressions.
5. If the average size of a family is 2.8 and this value is stored in the variable FamilySize, provide the Pascal statement to display this fact in a readable way (leave the cursor on the same line).
6. Which of the following expressions evaluate to the same value?
   a. A + B * C   b. (A + B) * C   c. A + (B * C)
7. List five standard data types of Turbo Pascal.
8. Assuming A and B are integer variables, what are the types of the following expressions?
   a. A div B   b. A mod B   c. A * B   d. A / B
9. Differentiate among syntax errors, run-time errors, and logic errors.

Programming Projects

1. Write a program to convert a temperature in degrees Fahrenheit to degrees Celsius.

    Problem input
    ```
    Fahrenheit : Integer {temperature in degrees Fahrenheit}
    ```

    Problem output
    ```
    Celsius : Real {temperature in degrees Celsius}
    ```

    Relevant formula
    ```
    Celsius = (5.0 / 9.0) × (Fahrenheit - 32.0)
    ```

2. Write a program to read two data items and print their sum, difference, product, and quotient.

    Problem inputs
    ```
    X, Y : Integer {two items}
    ```

    Problem outputs
    ```
    Sum : Integer {sum of X and Y}
    Difference : Integer {difference of X and Y}
    Product : Integer {product of X and Y}
    Quotient : Real {quotient of X divided by Y}
    ```

3. Write a program to read in the weight (in pounds) of an object and then compute and print the weight in kilograms and grams. (*Hint:* 1 pound is equal to 0.453592 kilogram and 453.59237 grams.)

4. Write a program that prints your first initial as a block letter. (*Hint:* Use a 6 × 6 grid for the letter and read in six strings, each representing a different row of the grid and consisting of asterisks (symbol *) interspersed with blanks. For example, if E is your first initial, the first string would consist of six asterisks and the second string would begin with one or two asterisks and the rest blanks. After reading the six strings, display them in sequence to show the block letter.

5. Write a program that reads in the name of a dinosaur and the number of years ago that the dinosaur lived and then computes the number of months, days, and seconds ago that the dinosaur lived. (Use 365.25 days per year.) Test your program with Eric, a triceratops that lived 145 million years ago, and Alfred, a brontosaurus that lived 182 million years ago.

6. Write a program that reads in the length and the width of a rectangular yard and the length and the width of a rectangular house situated in the yard. Your program should compute the time required (in minutes) to cut the grass at the rate of 2.3 square meters a second.

7. Arnie likes to jog in the morning. As he jogs, he counts the number of strides he makes during the first minute and during the last minute of his jogging. Arnie then averages these two and calls this the average number of strides he makes in a minute when he jogs. Write a program that accepts these averages and the total time Arnie spends jogging in hours and minutes and then outputs the distance Arnie has jogged in miles. Assume Arnie's stride to be 2.5 feet. (There are 5280 feet in a mile.)

8. Write a program that inputs a number of seconds up to 18,000 (5 hours) and outputs the hours, minutes, and seconds equivalent.

9. The Pythagorean theorem states that the sum of the squares of the sides of a right triangle is equal to the square of the hypotenuse. For example, if two sides of a right triangle have lengths 3 and 4, then the hypotenuse must have a length of 5. The integers 3, 4, and 5 together form a Pythagorean triple. There are an infinite number of such triples. Given two positive integers, *m* and *n,* where *m > n,* a Pythagorean triple can be generated by the following formulas:

    side1 $= m^2 - n^2$

    side2 $= 2m\ n$

    hypotenuse $= m^2 + n^2$

    Write a program that reads in values for *m* and *n* and prints the values of the Pythagorean triple generated by these formulas.

INTERVIEW
▼

Philippe Kahn

Philippe Kahn is chairman, president, and CEO of Borland International, Inc. Kahn holds a doctorate in mathematical sciences and taught at the university level in his native France before setting out with close colleagues to build a compiler based on the Pascal programming language. The result was Turbo Pascal, destined to become the number one programming language in the world. In 1983, Kahn came to the United States and founded Borland International to market this product. Kahn remains closely involved with product development and marketing at Borland today.

▼ **What was the impetus to developing your own software company?**

▲ I was lucky—twice—to be in the right place at the right time: in Zurich to study under Niklaus Wirth, one of the most influential computer scientists of the last decade, and then discovering the Micral and programming on it. The Micral was the first computer I ever used, and it has since been recognized by the Boston Computer Museum as the first personal computer.

I never really planned to start a company. I moved to Silicon Valley to work in high tech, but I couldn't get a legitimate job because I didn't have a green card. It was the decision to market the Pascal we had written that launched Borland. We placed an ad in *Byte* for our first product, Turbo Pascal, and pulled in $500,000 in orders. I was amazed!

▼ **What role has Turbo Pascal taken in helping to redefine the way that people use Pascal? What do you see as major advantages of Turbo Pascal over standard Pascal?**

▲ Back in 1983, Turbo Pascal went beyond what Jensen and Wirth originally defined for the language. Since then, Turbo Pascal has advanced even further, with enhancements for structured and object-oriented programming.

Throughout the eighties, Pascal was the ideal language for learning structured programming. In the nineties, Turbo Pascal has become the standard for learning object-oriented programming. Turbo Pascal's unit feature lets programmers create libraries of reusable procedures and abstract data types. Using it, they can create the reusable objects and truly modular programs that are so important in software engineering today. Whether a student is planning to become a dedicated software engineer or not, Pascal is the perfect training ground for developing object-oriented programming skills.

▼ **How do you explain the success of Turbo Pascal? Where is it primarily used?**

▲ At one time, Pascal was considered to be only a learning language. With over two million users today, however, it has become recognized as an important commercial tool. It is used by corporations throughout the world to create mission-critical applications, and there are more proponents of it every day. Turbo Pascal is used for a wide variety of applications, ranging from commercial and complex business and scientific applications to vertical market applications. Turbo Pascal has always appealed to programmers who want to work smarter, not harder.

Working smarter is possible because Pascal is a structured language that allows you to specify more clearly the code that you write. It allows users to solve problems in a more structured fashion. Turbo Pascal's integrated programming environment also makes it easier to work smarter. Programmers can write, compile, run, and debug programs without exiting to the operating system. This not only saves time, but the environment also gives programmers tools for accomplishing these tasks efficiently.

For the same reasons, Turbo Pascal is a fantastic learning aid for students, too. To program in Pascal, the student must adhere to structured programming methods, and these lessons become lifelong habits.

Whether a student wishes later to become a dedicated programmer or not, the logic and problem-solving skills learned during the process are invaluable.

▼ **Your two biggest language products are Turbo Pascal and C++. How do you see their interrelationship and development in the future?**

▲ Turbo Pascal is an applications programming language, while C is a systems language. That is, they are both modern and powerful languages, but Turbo Pascal is designed for higher-level applications programming—writing programs to solve specific problems. Borland C++ is more frequently used to create the systems within which applications programs run. Both products will continue to be improved. As the leader in language tools, we continually add new features and functionality to our products.

▼ **How do you see the changing role of programmer in the future as application packages such as Paradox and Quattro become more widely used?**

▲ Although prepackaged software is a valuable resource for corporations, companies will always have a need for mission-critical applications that are customized for particular applications. That's where products such as Turbo Pascal and Borland C++ come in.

▼ **Do you have any advice for students who are currently learning Turbo Pascal and/or anyone entering the field of computer science?**

▲ Stick with it! U.S. industry needs more engineering and science majors, and the future of our competitiveness is dependent upon you. You should learn all you can about object-oriented programming—that's the wave of the future.

CHAPTER THREE

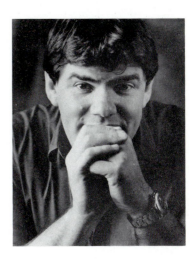

Functions, Procedures, and Graphics

Programmers who use the software development method to solve problems seldom tackle each new program as a unique event. Information contained in the problem statement and amassed during the analysis and design phases helps the programmer plan and complete the program. Programmers also use segments of earlier program solutions as building blocks to construct new programs.

In Section 3.2, we demonstrate how to tap existing information and code in the form of predefined functions to write programs. In addition to using existing information, programmers can use top-down design techniques to simplify the development of algorithms and the structure of the resulting programs. To apply top-down design, the programmer starts with the broadest statement of the problem solution and works down to more detailed subproblems. In Sections 3.3–3.5, we demonstrate top-down design and emphasize the role of modular programming using procedures.

We conclude the chapter with an optional section introducing computer graphics. In advanced forms, computer graphics is used to make science fiction movies and cartoons and to create video games. Our intention is to introduce you to Turbo Pascal's capabilities for doing graphics programming, not to make you graphics experts.

3.1 Building Programs from Existing Information

Programmers seldom start off with a blank slate (or empty screen) when they develop a program. Often some—or all—of the solution can be developed from information that already exists or from the solution to another problem, as we demonstrate for the metric conversion program.

Carefully following the software development method generates important system documentation before you even begin to code a program. Such documentation, consisting of a description of a problem's data requirements (developed during the analysis phase) and its solution algorithm (developed during the design phase), summarizes your intentions and thought processes.

You can use this documentation as a starting point in coding your program. For example, you would begin by duplicating the problem data requirements in the program declaration part (Fig. 3.1), then edit those lines to conform to the Pascal syntax for constant and variable declarations, thereby completing the declaration part of the program (Fig. 3.2). This approach is especially helpful if the documentation was created with a word processor and is in a file that you can edit.

Figure 3.1
The Declaration Part
Before Editing

```
program Metric;
{Converts square meters to square yards}

relevant formula
  1 square meter = 1.196 square yards

problem input
  SqMeters {the fabric size in square meters}

problem output
  SqYards {the fabric size in square yards}

begin

end.
```

Figure 3.2
Using the Refined
Algorithm as the
Program's Framework

```
program Metric;
{Converts square meters to square yards}

  const
    MetersToYards = 1.196; {conversion constant}

  var
    SqMeters,          {input - fabric size in meters}
    SqYards : Real;    {output - fabric size in yards}

begin
  {1.   Read the fabric size in square meters.}

  {2.   Convert the fabric size to square yards.}
     {2.1  Size in sq. yards is 1.196 * size in sq. meters.}

  {3.   Display the fabric size in square yards.}

end.
```

To develop the program body, first use the initial algorithm and its refinements as program comments. The comments describe each algorithm step and provide program documentation that guides your Pascal code. Figure 3.2 shows how the program will look at this point. After the comments are in place in the program body, you can begin to write the Pascal statements. Place the Pascal code for an unrefined step directly under that step. For a refined step, either edit the refinement to convert it from English to Pascal or replace it with Pascal code (Fig. 2.1). We illustrate this entire process in the next case study.

CASE STUDY   **Finding the Area and Circumference of a Circle**

PROBLEM ▼

Read in the radius of a circle and compute and print the circle's area and circumference.

ANALYSIS ▼

Clearly, the problem input is the circle's radius. Two outputs are requested: the circle's area and circumference. These variables should be type `Real` because the inputs and outputs may contain fractional parts. The geometric relationships between a circle's radius and its area and circumference are listed next, along with the data requirements.

Data Requirements

Problem Constant

```
MyPi = 3.14159;
```

Problem Input

```
Radius : Real {radius of a circle}
```

Problem Outputs

```
Area : Real {area of a circle}
Circum : Real {circumference of a circle}
```

Relevant Formulas

area of a circle $= \pi \times radius^2$
circumference of a circle $= 2\pi \times radius$

DESIGN ▼

After identifying the problem inputs and outputs, list the steps necessary to solve the problem. Pay close attention to the order of the steps.

Initial Algorithm

1. Read the circle radius.
2. Find the area.
3. Find the circumference.
4. Print the area and the circumference.

Algorithm Refinements

Next, refine any steps that lack an obvious solution (steps 2 and 3).

Figure 3.3
Outline of Program Circle

```
program Circle;
{Finds and prints the area and circumference of a circle}

   const
     MyPi = 3.14159;

   var
     Radius,           {input - radius of a circle}
     Area,             {output - area of a circle}
     Circum : Real;    {output - circumference of a circle}

begin
  {1.  Read the circle radius.}

  {2.  Find the area.}
      {2.1 Assign MyPi * Radius * Radius to Area.}

  {3.  Find the circumference.}
      {3.1 Assign 2 * MyPi * Radius to Circum.}

  {4.  Print the area and circumference.}

end.
```

Step 2 Refinement

2.1 Assign `MyPi * Radius * Radius` to `Area`.

Step 3 Refinement

3.1 Assign `2 * MyPi * Radius` to `Circum`.

IMPLEMENTATION ▼

Figure 3.3 shows the Pascal program so far. The program body consists of the initial algorithm and its refinements.

To write the final program, convert the refinements (steps 2.1 and 3.1) to Pascal, write Pascal code for the unrefined steps (steps 1 and 4), and delete the step numbers from the comments. Figure 3.4 shows the final program.

Figure 3.4
Finding the Area and
Circumference of a Circle

Edit Window

```pascal
program Circle;
{Finds and prints the area and circumference of a circle}

   const
     MyPi = 3.14159;

   var
     Radius,            {input - radius of a circle}
     Area,              {output - area of a circle}
     Circum : Real;     {output - circumference of a circle}
begin
  {Read the circle radius.}
  Write ('Enter radius> ');
  ReadLn (Radius);

  {Find the area.}
  Area := MyPi * Radius * Radius;

  {Find the circumference.}
  Circum := 2.0 * MyPi * Radius;

  {Print the area and circumference.}
  WriteLn ('The area is ', Area :4:2);
  WriteLn ('The circumference is ', Circum :4:2)
end.
```

Output Window

```
Enter radius> 5.0
The area is 78.54
The circumference is 31.42
```

TESTING ▼

The sample output in Fig. 3.4 provides a good test of the solution because it is relatively easy to compute by hand the area and the circumference for a radius value of 5.0. The radius squared is 25.0 and π is approximately 3, so the value of the area appears to be correct. The circumference should be 10 times π, which is also an easy number to compute by hand.

CASE STUDY   Finding the Most Pizza for Your Money

Another way in which programmers use existing information is by *extending the solution for one problem to solve another*. For example, you can easily solve the next problem by building on the solution to the previous one.

PROBLEM ▼

You and your college roommates frequently order a late-night pizza snack from the many pizzerias in the area that deliver. Since you are on a tight budget, you want to know which pizza is the best value.

ANALYSIS ▼

To find which pizza is the best value, you must be able to compare pizza costs. One way to make this comparison is to compute the *unit price* of each pizza by dividing the total price of each pizza by a measure of its quantity. A good measure of quantity would be the pizza weight, but pizzas are not sold by weight—they are sold by size (diameter) measured in inches. Consequently, the best you can do is to use some meaningful measure of quantity based on pizza diameter. One such measure is pizza area. Using pizza area, you can define the unit price of a pizza as its price divided by its area.

The following data requirements list a pizza's size and price as problem inputs. Although the problem statement does not ask you to display the pizza's area, we are listing it as a problem output because the pizza's area will give you some idea of how many friends you can invite to share your pizza. The radius (half the diameter) is listed as a program variable because you need it to compute the pizza's area, but it is not a problem input or output.

Data Requirements

Problem Constant

```
MyPi = 3.14159;
```

Problem Inputs

```
Diameter : Real     {diameter or size of a pizza}
Price : Real        {price of a pizza}
```

Problem Outputs

```
UnitPrice : Real       {unit cost of a pizza}
Area : Real            {area of a pizza}
```

Program Variables

```
Radius : Real          {radius of a pizza}
```

Relevant Formulas

area of a circle = π × *radius*²
radius of a circle = *diameter* / 2
unit price = *total price* / *area*

DESIGN ▼

The initial algorithm here is similar to that of the previous case study. The step that computes the circle's circumference (step 3) has been replaced with one that computes the pizza's unit price.

Initial Algorithm

1. Read in the pizza's diameter and price.
2. Compute the pizza's area.
3. Compute the pizza's unit price.
4. Display the unit price and area.

The algorithm refinements follow. Step 2 requires refinement because you must compute the pizza's radius before you can compute its area.

Step 2 Refinement

2.1 Assign `Diameter / 2` to `Radius`.
2.2 Assign `MyPi * Radius * Radius` to `Area`.

Step 3 Refinement

3.1 Assign `Price / Area` to `UnitPrice`.

IMPLEMENTATION ▼

To write this program, edit the data requirements to develop the program declaration part and use the initial algorithm with refinements as a starting point for the program body. Figure 3.5 shows the Pascal program.

TESTING ▼

To test this program, run it with a few pizza sizes. You can verify that the program is working correctly by multiplying the unit price by the area. The product should equal the price of the pizza.

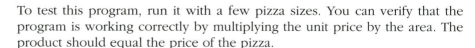

Figure 3.5
Pizza Program

Edit Window

```
program Pizza;
{Computes the unit price of a pizza}

  const
    MyPi = 3.14159;

  var
    Diameter,          {input - diameter or size of a pizza}
    Price,             {input - price of a pizza}
    UnitPrice,         {output - unit cost of pizza}
    Area,              {output - area of a pizza}
    Radius : Real;     {radius of a pizza}

begin
  {Read in the pizza diameter and price.}
  Write ('Diameter of pizza in inches >');
  ReadLn (Diameter);
  Write ('Price of pizza $');
  ReadLn (Price);

  {Compute the pizza area.}
  Radius := Diameter / 2;
  Area := MyPi * Radius * Radius;

  {Compute the pizza unit price.}
  UnitPrice := Price / Area;

  {Display the area and unit price.}
  WriteLn;
  Write ('The pizza unit price is $', UnitPrice :4:2);
  WriteLn (' per square inch.');
  WriteLn ('The area is ', Area :3:1, ' square inches.')
end.
```

Output Window

```
Diameter of pizza in inches >9.0
Price of pizza $7.45

The pizza unit price is $0.12 per square inch.
The area is 63.6 square inches.
```

Exercises for Section 3.1   **Self-Check**

1. Describe the problem inputs and outputs and write the algorithm for a program that computes an employee's gross salary given the hours worked and the hourly rate.
2. Write a preliminary version of the program from your solution to Exercise 1. Show the declaration part of the program and the program comments corresponding to the algorithm and its refinements.

3. What changes should you make to extend the payroll algorithm in Exercise 1 to include overtime hours to be paid at 1.5 times an employee's normal hourly rate when computing his or her gross salary? Assume that overtime hours are entered separately.

Programming

1. Add refinements to the program outline that follows and write the final Pascal program:

```
program SumAndAverage;
{Finds and prints the sum and average of two numbers}

   var
      One, Two,          {input - numbers to process}
      Sum,               {output - sum of One and Two}
      Average : Real;    {output - average of One and Two}

begin
   {1. Read two numbers.}
   {2. Compute sum of numbers.}
   {3. Compute average of numbers.}
   {4. Print sum and average.}
end.
```

2. Write a complete Pascal program for Self-Check Exercise 1.
3. Write a complete Pascal program for the revised payroll algorithm developed in Self-Check Exercise 3.

3.2 Functions

Functions and Reusability

A primary goal of structured programming is to write error-free code. One way to do so, called *reusability,* is to reuse whenever possible code that has already been written and tested. Stated more simply, "Why reinvent the wheel?" Pascal promotes reusability by providing many predefined functions for performing mathematical computations. A **function** is a separate module of code that computes a single result.

function
a separate module of code that computes a single result

Consider, for example, the Pascal function named Sqrt, which performs the square root computation. The expression part of the assignment statement,

function argument
a value passed into a function

function designator
the part of an expression that activates a function and passes arguments to the function

activates the code for function Sqrt, passing the **argument** X to the function. A function is activated by a **function designator** (Sqrt(X)) that is part of an expression. After the function executes, the function result is substituted for the function designator in the expression. If X is 16.0, the assignment statement is evaluated as follows:

1.   X is 16.0, so function Sqrt computes the square root of 16.0, or 4.0.
2.   The function result, 4.0, is assigned to Y.

A function can be thought of as a "black box" that is passed one or more input values and automatically returns a single output value. Figure 3.6 illustrates this process for the call to function Sqrt. The value of X (16.0) is the function input, and the function result, or output, is the square root of 16.0 (result is 4.0).

As another example, if W is 9.0, the assignment statement

```
Z := 5.7 + Sqrt(W)
```

is evaluated as follows:

1.   W is 9.0, so function Sqrt computes the square root of 9.0, or 3.0.
2.   The values 5.7 and 3.0 are added together.
3.   The sum, 8.7, is stored in Z.

EXAMPLE 3.1 ▼

The program in Fig. 3.7 displays the square root of two numbers provided as input data (First and Second) and the square root of their sum. To do so, it must call the Pascal function Sqrt three times:

```
Answer := Sqrt(First);
Answer := Sqrt(Second);
Answer := Sqrt(First + Second);
```

For the first two calls, the function arguments are variables (First and Second). The third call shows that a function argument can also be an expression (First + Second). For all three calls, the result returned by function Sqrt is assigned to variable Answer.

If you look closely at the program in Fig. 3.7, you will see that each statement contains a call to a Pascal procedure (Write, WriteLn, ReadLn) or a Pascal function (Sqrt)—we have used Pascal's predefined procedures and functions as building blocks to construct a new program.   ▲

Figure 3.6
Function Sqrt as a
"Black Box"

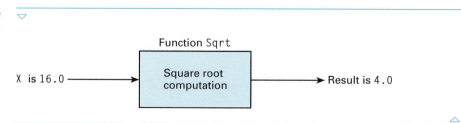

Figure 3.7
Program SquareRoots

Edit Window

```
program SquareRoots;
{Performs three square root computations}

   var
     First, Second,          {input - two data values}
     Answer : Real;          {output - a square root value}

begin
  {Get first number and display its square root.}
  Write ('Enter the first number >');
  ReadLn (First);
  Answer := Sqrt(First);
  WriteLn ('The square root of the first number is ',
           Answer :4:2);

  {Get second number and display its square root.}
  Write ('Enter the second number >');
  ReadLn (Second);
  Answer := Sqrt(Second);
  WriteLn ('The square root of the second number is ',
           Answer :4:2);

  {Display the square root of the sum of both numbers.}
  Answer := Sqrt(First + Second);
  WriteLn ('The square root of the sum of both numbers is ',
           Answer :4:2)
end.
```

Output Window

```
Enter the first number >9.0
The square root of the first number is 3.00
Enter the second number >16.0
The square root of the second number is 4.00
The square root of the sum of both numbers is 5.00
```

Program Style

Use of Color to Highlight New Constructs

In Fig. 3.7, program lines that illustrate new constructs are in color so that you can find them easily. We will continue to use color for this purpose in figures that contain programs.

Standard Pascal Functions

Table 3.1 lists the names and descriptions of some of Pascal's predefined functions. Except for Abs, Round, Sqr, and Trunc, each function in Table 3.1

returns a `Real` value regardless of its argument type (`Real` or `Integer`). The type of the result returned by `Abs` or `Sqr` is the same as the type of its argument.

Table 3.1
Standard Functions

Function	Purpose	Argument	Result
`Abs(X)`	Returns the absolute value of X	`Real` or `Integer`	Same as argument
`ArcTan(X)`	Returns the angle y in radians satisfying $X = \tan(y)$, where $-\pi/2 < y < \pi/2$	`Real` or `Integer`	`Real` (radians)
`Cos(X)`	Returns the cosine of angle X	`Real` or `Integer` (radians)	`Real`
`Exp(X)`	Returns e^X, where $e = 2.71828 \ldots$	`Real` or `Integer`	`Real`
`Ln(X)`	Returns the natural logarithm of X for $X > 0.0$	`Real` or `Integer`	`Real`
`Round(X)`	Returns the closest integer value to X	`Real`	`Integer`
`Sin(X)`	Returns the sine of angle X	`Real` or `Integer` (radians)	`Real`
`Sqr(X)`	Returns the square of X	`Real` or `Integer`	Same as argument
`Sqrt(X)`	Returns the positive square root of X for $X > 0.0$	`Real` or `Integer`	`Real`
`Trunc(X)`	Returns the integral part of X	`Real`	`Integer`

The functions `Round` and `Trunc` require type `Real` arguments and return type `Integer` values. These functions determine the integral part of a real-valued expression. Consequently, the expressions

```
Trunc(1.5 * Gross);
Round(Cents / 100)
```

have `Integer` values and may be assigned to `Integer` variables. `Trunc` simply *truncates,* or removes, the fractional part of its argument; `Round` *rounds* its argument to the nearest whole number. For example, `Trunc(17.5)` is 17, while `Round(17.5)` is 18; `Trunc(-3.8)` is -3, while `Round(-3.8)` is -4.

Most of the functions in Table 3.1 perform common mathematical computations. The arguments for `Ln` and `Sqrt` must be positive. The arguments for `Sin` and `Cos` must be expressed in radians, not degrees. `ArcTan` expresses its results in radians.

EXAMPLE 3.2 ▼

We can use the Pascal functions `Sqr` and `Sqrt` to compute the roots of a quadratic equation in *X* of the form

$$AX^2 + BX + C = 0$$

The two roots are defined as

$$Root_1 = \frac{-B + \sqrt{B^2 - 4AC}}{2A} \qquad Root_2 = \frac{-B - \sqrt{B^2 - 4AC}}{2A}$$

when the *discriminant* ($B^2 - 4AC$) is greater than zero. If we assume that this is the case, we can use the following assignment statements to assign values to `Root1` and `Root2`:

```
{Compute two roots, Root1 and Root2, for Disc > 0.0.}
Disc := Sqr(B) - 4 * A * C ;
Root1 := (-B + Sqrt(Disc)) / (2 * A);
Root2 := (-B - Sqrt(Disc)) / (2 * A)  ▲
```

EXAMPLE 3.3 ▼

If we know the length of two sides (*B* and *C*) of a triangle and the angle between them in degrees (*Alpha*) (see Fig. 3.8), we can compute the length of the third side (*A*) by using the formula

$$A^2 = B^2 + C^2 - 2BC \cos Alpha$$

To use Pascal's cosine function (`Cos`), we must express its argument angle in radians instead of degrees. To convert an angle from degrees to radians, we multiply the angle by $\pi/180$. If we assume that function `Pi` (see Table 3.2)

Figure 3.8
Triangle with Unknown
Side *A*

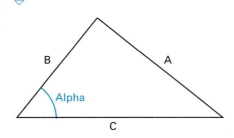

returns the constant π, the following Pascal assignment statement computes the unknown side length:

```
A := Sqrt(Sqr(B) + Sqr(C) - 2 * B * C * Cos(Alpha * Pi/180.0))
```

▲

EXAMPLE 3.4 ▼

Since Pascal has no exponentiation operator, it is not possible to write u^v directly when u and v are type `Real`. However, the theory of logarithms tells us that

$$\ln(u^v) = v \times \ln(u)$$

and

$$z = e^{\ln(z)}$$

where e is 2.71828 . . . . So if we substitute u^v for z in the preceding equation, we get

$$u^v = e^{\ln(u^v)} = e^{(v \times \ln(u))}$$

This formula can be implemented in Pascal as

```
UToPowerV := Exp(v * Ln(u))
```
▲

Additional Turbo Pascal Functions

Table 3.2 lists additional mathematical functions that are available in Turbo Pascal (but not standard Pascal). Functions `Frac` and `Int` can be used to extract the fractional part and the whole number part, respectively, of a real number. If X has the value `5.16123`, `Frac(X)` returns the `Real` value `0.16123` and `Int(X)` returns the `Real` value `5.0`.

Table 3.2
Turbo Pascal Functions

Function	Purpose	Argument	Result
`Frac(`*num*`)`	Returns the fractional part of its argument	`Real`	`Real`
`Int(`*num*`)`	Returns the whole number part of its argument	`Real`	`Real`
`Pi`	Returns an approximation to π	None	`Real`
`Random`	Returns a real random number ≥ 0.0 and < 1.0	None	`Real`
`Random (`*num*`)`	Returns a random integer ≥ 0 and $<$ *num*	`Integer`	`Integer`

The function Pi is unusual because it has no arguments. It always returns an approximation to the value of π (3.1415926536), so we could use it instead of the constant MyPi in Figs. 3.4 and 3.5.

The function Random generates a random number. A *random number* is a number that is selected at random from a specified range of numbers, each with an equally likely chance for selection. Random may be called with or without an argument. If it has an argument, Random returns a random integer from 0 up to, but not including, its argument. The Turbo Pascal procedure Randomize should be called prior to the first call to function Random. Random numbers can be used to simulate the toss of a coin (two possible values) or the throw of a die (six possible values).

EXAMPLE 3.5 ▼

Program MultQuest in Fig. 3.9 provides drill and practice in multiplication. It calls function Random twice, each time selecting an integer from 0 through 9. These random values are the operands (Factor1, Factor2) in a multiplication question. If 7 and 8 are the values returned by Random, for example, the question

```
What is the value of 7 * 8?
```

is displayed. The user's answer is read into Response, and the computer then displays the product of 7 and 8, so the user is able to check his or her answer.

In a more complete drill and practice program, the computer would compare the actual product computed from Factor1 and Factor2 to the value entered for Response. An appropriate message would be displayed indicating whether the value contained in Response is correct.   ▲

A Look at Where We Are Heading

Pascal also allows us to write our own functions. Let's assume that we have already written functions FindArea and FindCircum:

► Function FindArea(R) returns the area of a circle with radius R.
► Function FindCircum(R) returns the circumference of a circle with radius R.

We can reuse these functions in two programs shown earlier in this chapter (see Figs. 3.4 and 3.5). The program in Fig. 3.4 displays the area and the circumference of a circle whose radius is provided as input data; Fig. 3.10 shows a revised program that uses the two functions FindArea and FindCircum. In Fig. 3.10, the expression part for each of the two assignment statements

```
Area := FindArea(Radius);
Circum := FindCircum(Radius);
```

Figure 3.9
Program MultQuest

Edit Window

```
program MultQuest;
{
  Asks a random multiplication question and displays
  the correct product after the student responds
}
  const
    Limit = 10;                    {operand is < Limit}

  var
    Factor1, Factor2,              {two operands}
    Answer,                        {correct answer}
    Response          :  Integer;  {student response}
begin {MultQuest}
  Randomize;          {Initialize the random number generator}
  Factor1 := Random(Limit);   {Get first operand.}
  Factor2 := Random(Limit);   {Get second operand.}

  Write ('What is the value of ',
         Factor1 :1, ' * ', Factor2 :1, '? ');
  ReadLn (Response);

  Answer := Factor1 * Factor2;
  WriteLn ('My answer is ', Answer :1)
end. {MultQuest}
```

Output Window

```
What is the value of 7 * 8? 82
My answer is 56
```

is a function designator with argument Radius (the circle radius). The result returned by each function execution is stored in an output variable for the program (Area or Circum). To run this program, we need to complete the functions and insert them right after the comment

```
{Insert functions FindArea and FindCircum here.}
```

Section 6.5 shows you how to write your own functions.

Besides the advantage of reusing "tried and true" code, using these two functions frees us from the details of computing a circle's area or circumference when we write the main program. This is one way we can manage and reduce the complexity of writing programs.

Figure 3.10
Finding Area and
Circumference with
Functions

```
program CircleFunction;
{Finds area and circumference of a circle using functions}

   var
     Radius,        {input - radius of a circle}
     Area,          {output - area of a circle}
     Circum : Real; {output - circumference of a circle}

   {Insert functions FindArea and FindCircum here.}

begin
  {Read the circle radius.}
  Write ('Enter radius >');
  ReadLn (Radius);

  {Find the area.}
  Area := FindArea(Radius);

  {Find the circumference.}
  Circum := FindCircum(Radius);

  {Print the area and circumference.}
  WriteLn ('The area is ', Area :4:2);
  WriteLn ('The circumference is ', Circum :4:2)
end.
```

Exercises for Section 3.2   **Self-Check**

1. Rewrite the following mathematical expressions using Pascal functions:
   a. $\sqrt{U + V \times W^2}$ c. $\sqrt{(X - Y)^3}$
   b. $\log_n (X^Y)$ d. $|XY - W/Z|$

2. Evaluate the following function designators and indicate the type of the result:
   a. `Trunc(-15.8)`   e. `Sqrt(Abs(Round(-15.8)))`
   b. `Round(-15.8)`   f. `Round(3.5)`
   c. `Round(6.8) * Sqr (3)`   g. `Sqr(3.0)`
   d. `Int(-15.8) * Sqr(3)`   h. `Trunc(22.1) * Sqr(3)`

Programming

1. Write statements that read values into X and Y and compute and display the absolute difference (e.g., if X is 9 and Y is 7, the absolute difference is 2).
2. Using the `Round` function, write a Pascal statement to round any real value X to the nearest two decimal places. *Hint:* You will have to multiply the value by 100 before rounding, round the result, and then divide by 100.

3. Write a complete Pascal program that prompts the user for the Cartesian coordinates of two points, (*X1, Y1*) and (*X2, Y2*), and displays the distance between them computed by using the following formula:

$$distance = \sqrt{(X1 - X2)^2 + (Y1 - Y2)^2}$$

3.3   Top-Down Design and Structure Charts

top-down design

a problem-solving method in which you first break a problem up into its major subproblems and then solve the subproblems to derive the solution to the original problem

structure chart

a documentation tool that shows the relationships among the subproblems of a problem

Often the algorithm needed to solve a problem is more complex than those we have seen so far and the programmer has to break up the problem into subproblems to develop the program solution. In attempting to solve a subproblem at one level, we introduce new subproblems at lower levels. This process, called **top-down design**, proceeds from the original problem at the top level to the subproblems at each lower level. The splitting of a problem into its related subproblems is analogous to the process of refining an algorithm. The following case study introduces a documentation tool—the **structure chart**—that will help you to keep track of the relationships among subproblems.

CASE STUDY   ### Drawing Simple Diagrams

PROBLEM ▼

You want to draw some simple diagrams on your printer or screen. Two examples are the house and the female stick figure in Fig. 3.11.

ANALYSIS ▼

The house is formed by displaying a triangle without its base on top of a rectangle. The stick figure consists of a circular shape, a triangle, and a triangle without its base. We can draw both figures with these four basic components:

▶ A circle
▶ A baseline
▶ Parallel lines
▶ Intersecting lines

DESIGN ▼

To create the stick figure, you can divide the problem into three subproblems.

Initial Algorithm

1. Draw a circle.

Figure 3.11
House and Stick Figure

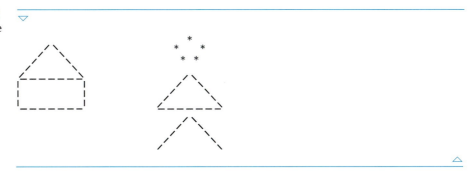

2. Draw a triangle.
3. Draw intersecting lines.

Algorithm Refinements

Because a triangle is not a basic component, you must refine step 2, generating the following subproblems:

Step 2 Refinement

2.1 Draw intersecting lines.
2.2 Draw a base.

You can use a structure chart to show the relationship between the original problem and its subproblems, as in Fig. 3.12, where the original problem (level 0) is in the darker color and its three subordinate subproblems are shown at level 1. The subproblem *Draw a Triangle* is also in color because it has its own subproblems (shown at level 2).

Figure 3.12
Structure Chart for
Drawing a Stick Figure

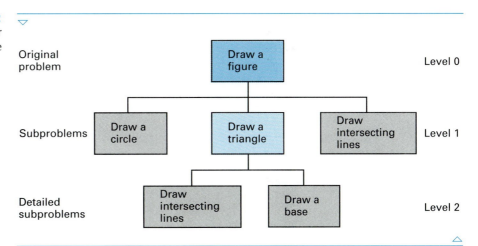

The subproblems appear in both the algorithm and the structure chart. The algorithm, not the structure chart, shows the order in which you carry out each step to solve the problem. The structure chart simply illustrates the subordination of subproblems to each other and to the original subproblem.

Exercises for Section 3.3   **Self-Check**

1. In which phase of the software development method do you apply top-down design to break the problem into suitable subproblems?
2. Draw the structure chart for the problem of drawing the house shown in Fig. 3.11.

3.4 Procedures

procedure
a separate program module solving a particular subproblem

Programmers often use procedures to implement top-down design in their programs. A **procedure,** like a function, is a separate program unit or module containing a group of program statements that solves a particular subproblem. Often a programmer will write one procedure for each subproblem in the structure chart. Procedures are more general than functions because they can return any number of results.

Chapter 2 introduced three procedures supplied by the Pascal compiler: `ReadLn`, `Write`, and `WriteLn`. Recall that you activated each of these procedures with a **procedure call statement.** In this section, you will learn to write and call your own procedures.

procedure call statement
an instruction that calls or activates a procedure

As an example of top-down design with procedures, you could use the program body in Fig. 3.13 to draw a stick figure. The three algorithm steps are coded as calls to three Pascal procedures. For example, the statement

```
DrawTriangle;          {Draw a triangle.}
```

calls a procedure (`DrawTriangle`) to implement the algorithm step *Draw a Triangle.*

➡A procedure is an independent program unit whose form is very similar to that of a program. A procedure begins with a *procedure heading,* which consists of the word `procedure` followed by the procedure name (an identifier)

Figure 3.13
Program Body to Draw a
Stick Figure

```
begin {StickFigure}
    DrawCircle;         {Draw a circle.}
    DrawTriangle;       {Draw a triangle.}
    DrawIntersect       {Draw intersecting lines.}
end. {StickFigure}
```

and a semicolon. The *declaration part* is optional and is needed only when the procedure has its own constants and variables. Each procedure has a *procedure body,* which starts with begin and ends with end;.

A procedure name is a user-defined identifier, so its usage must be declared in the declaration part of the program unit that calls it. You use a *procedure declaration* to declare a procedure.

SYNTAX DISPLAY

Procedure Declaration

Form:
```
procedure pname;
   declaration part
begin
   procedure body
end;
```

Example:
```
procedure Skip3Lines;
   {Skips three lines}

begin {Skip3Lines}
   WriteLn;
   WriteLn;
   WriteLn
end; {Skip3Lines}
```

Interpretation: The user-defined identifier *pname* is declared to be the name of a procedure. Any identifiers declared in the *declaration part* are defined only during the execution of the procedure, and can be referenced only within the procedure. The *procedure body* describes the data manipulation performed when the procedure is activated through a procedure call statement.

SYNTAX DISPLAY

Procedure Call Statement

Form: *pname*

Example: DrawCircle

Interpretation: The procedure call statement initiates the execution of procedure *pname*. After *pname* has finished executing, the program statement that follows the procedure call will be executed.

EXAMPLE 3.6 ▼

Figure 3.14 shows the declaration for procedure DrawCircle. The procedure body contains the three WriteLn statements that cause the computer to draw a circular shape. The procedure call statement

```
DrawCircle;
```

causes these WriteLn statements to execute.   ▲

Figure 3.14
Procedure DrawCircle

activates = Calls

```
procedure DrawCircle;  — Declaration part
{Draws a circle}

begin  {DrawCircle}
   WriteLn ('   *   ');
   WriteLn ('  *   *');  — Body part
   WriteLn ('   * *  ')
end;  {DrawCircle}
```

Activated by procedure call statement (DrawCircle)

The structure chart in Fig. 3.12 shows that the subproblem *Draw a Triangle* (level 1) depends on the solutions to its subordinate subproblems *Draw Intersecting Lines* and *Draw a Base* (both level 2). Figure 3.15 shows how to use top-down design to code procedure DrawTriangle. Instead of using WriteLn statements to display a triangular pattern, the body of procedure DrawTriangle calls procedures DrawIntersect and DrawBase to draw a triangle.

Placement of Procedure Declarations in a Program

Figure 3.13 showed the program body for the stick figure program. In the declaration part, you must declare the three procedures that are called in the program. The procedure declarations should follow the variable declarations in a Turbo Pascal program (required in standard Pascal).

The relative order of the procedure declarations does not affect their order of execution; that is determined by the order of execution of the procedure call statements. However, each procedure must be declared before you can write a procedure call statement that activates it. For this reason, you must declare the two procedures that are called by DrawTriangle (DrawIntersect and DrawBase) before DrawTriangle. That is the only restriction.

Figure 3.16 shows the completed stick figure program. To help you identify each procedure, its first and last lines are in color. In a program that uses procedures, we refer to the program body as the **main program**.

main program
the program body in a program with procedures

Figure 3.15
Procedure DrawTriangle

```
procedure DrawTriangle;  ←——— Procedure heading
{Draws a triangle}

begin {DrawTriangle}
   DrawIntersect;
   DrawBase              ←——— Procedure body
end; {DrawTriangle}
```

Program Style

Use of Comments in a Program with Procedures

Figure 3.16 includes several comments. Each procedure begins with a comment that describes its purpose. The begin and end that bracket each procedure body and the main program body are followed by a comment identifying that procedure or program.

Figure 3.16
Stick Figure Program

```
program StickFigure;
{Displays a stick figure}

  procedure DrawCircle;
  {Draws a circle}

  begin  {DrawCircle}
    WriteLn ('   *   ');
    WriteLn (' *   *');
    WriteLn ('  * *  ')
  end; {DrawCircle}

  procedure DrawIntersect;
  {Draws intersecting lines}

  begin  {DrawIntersect}
    WriteLn ('  / \  ');
    WriteLn (' /   \ ');
    WriteLn ('/     \')
  end; {DrawIntersect}

  procedure DrawBase;
  {Draws a base}

  begin  {DrawBase}
    WriteLn ('-------')
  end; {DrawBase}

  procedure DrawTriangle;
  {Draws a triangle}

  begin  {DrawTriangle}
    DrawIntersect;
    DrawBase
  end; {DrawTriangle}

begin {StickFigure}
  DrawCircle;          {Draw a circle.}
  DrawTriangle;        {Draw a triangle.}
  DrawIntersect        {Draw intersecting lines.}
end. {StickFigure}
```

Order of Execution of Procedures and Main Program

Because procedures appear in the declaration part of the program, which precedes the main program, the compiler translates the procedure declarations before it translates the main program. During translation, the compiler inserts a statement at the end of the procedure that causes a *return* from the procedure back to the statement that called it.

Figure 3.17 shows the main program and procedure DrawCircle of the stick figure program in separate areas of memory. Although the Pascal statements are shown in Fig. 3.17, it is actually the object code corresponding to each statement that is stored in memory.

When we run the program, the first statement in the main program is the first statement executed (the call to DrawCircle in Fig. 3.17). When the computer executes a procedure call statement, it transfers control to the referenced procedure (indicated by the colored line in Fig. 3.17). The computer allocates any memory that may be needed for constants and variables declared in the procedure and then performs the statements in the procedure body. After the last statement in procedure DrawCircle is executed, control returns to the main program (indicated by the black line in Fig. 3.17) and the computer releases any memory that was allocated to the procedure. After the return to the program, the next statement is executed (the call to DrawTriangle).

Advantages of Using Procedures

There are many advantages to using procedures. Their availability changes how an individual programmer organizes the solution to a programming problem. For a team of programmers working together on a large program, procedures simplify the apportioning of programming tasks; each programmer will be responsible for a particular set of procedures. Finally, they simplify programming tasks, as existing procedures can be used as the building blocks for new programs.

Figure 3.17
Flow of Control Between the Main Program and a Procedure

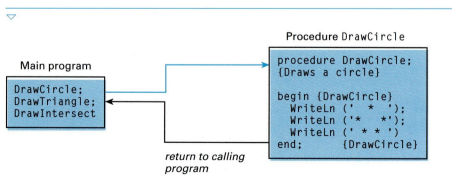

Main program

```
DrawCircle;
DrawTriangle;
DrawIntersect
```

Procedure DrawCircle

```
procedure DrawCircle;
{Draws a circle}

begin {DrawCircle}
  WriteLn ('  *  ');
  WriteLn ('*   *');
  WriteLn (' * * ')
end;      {DrawCircle}
```

return to calling program

step by step process

Procedural Abstraction

Procedures allow us to remove from the main program the code that provides the detailed solution to a subproblem. Because these details are provided in the procedures and not in the main program, we can write the main program as a sequence of procedure call statements as soon as we have specified the initial algorithm and before we refine any of the steps. We should delay writing the procedure for an algorithm step until we have finished refining that step. With this approach to program design, called **procedural abstraction,** we defer implementation details until we are ready to write an individual procedure module. Focusing on one procedure at a time is much easier than trying to write the complete program all at once.

no difference really, from divide and conquer.

Reuse of Procedures

procedural abstraction

a programming technique in which a main program consists of a sequence of procedure calls and each procedure is implemented as a separate program module

Another advantage of using procedures is that they can be executed more than once in a program. For example, procedure DrawIntersect is called twice in Fig. 3.16 (once by DrawTriangle and once by the main program). Each time DrawIntersect is called, the list of output statements shown in Fig. 3.16 is executed and a pair of intersecting lines is drawn. Without procedures, the WriteLn statements that draw the lines would have to be listed twice in the main program, thereby increasing the main program's length and the chance of error.

Finally, once you have written and tested a procedure, you can use it in other programs or procedures. For example, the procedures in program StickFigure could easily be used in programs that draw other diagrams.

reusage of procedure is a bonus - cutting down on length

Exercises for Section 3.4   ***Self-Check***

1. Assume that you have procedures PrintM and PrintO, each of which draws a large block letter (for example, PrintO draws a block letter O). Why would the following program body be more efficient using these procedures than if it did not use procedures at all?

```
begin {main}
  PrintM;
  PrintO;
  PrintM
end. {main}
```

2. Draw a structure chart for a program with three procedures that displays HI HO in block letters.

Programming

1. Write procedure DrawParallel that draws parallel lines and a procedure DrawRectangle that uses DrawParallel and DrawBase to draw a rectangle.
2. Write the main program and procedures for the problem described in Self-Check Exercise 2.

3. You have written a very good program called `GreatProgram` and you want all users to know you wrote it. Write a procedure called `Credits` that is executed upon program start and that tells the program name and its creator.

3.5   Procedures as Program Building Blocks

Programmers use procedures like building blocks to construct large programs. Procedures are more like Lego® blocks (Fig. 3.18) than the smooth-sided wooden blocks you might have used as a young child to demonstrate your potential as a budding architect. Your first blocks were big and did not link together, so buildings over a certain size would topple over. Legos, in contrast, have one surface with little protrusions and one surface with little cups. By placing the protrusions into the cups, you can build rather elaborate structures.

What does this have to do with programming? Procedures `DrawCircle` and `DrawParallel` are like simple wooden blocks. You can write some cute little programs with these procedures, but they are not particularly useful. To construct more interesting programs, we must provide procedures with protrusions and cups so they can be easily interconnected.

procedure parameters
information passed between a procedure and the program unit that calls it

procedure inputs
values passed into a procedure by the calling program unit

procedure outputs
results returned to the calling program unit by a procedure

The parameters of a procedure provide the linkage between a procedure and the main program or between two or more procedures. The **parameters** of a procedure receive values (**procedure inputs**) passed into the procedure from the calling module or they return results (**procedure outputs**) computed by the procedure back to the calling module. Figure 3.19 is a diagram of a procedure with inputs and outputs.

You have already encountered parameters in working with the `WriteLn` and `ReadLn` procedures. The procedure call statement

Figure 3.18
Lego® Blocks

Figure 3.19
Procedure with Inputs
and Outputs

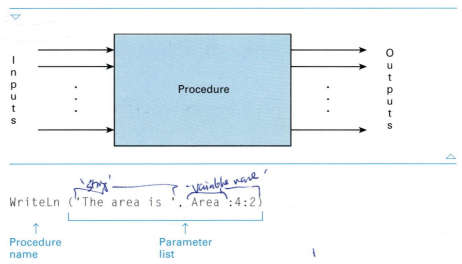

WriteLn ('The area is ', Area :4:2)

↑
Procedure
name

↑
Parameter
list

consists of two parts: the name of the Pascal procedure being called, WriteLn, and a parameter list enclosed in parentheses (containing two parameters, a string and a variable name, separated by a comma). Because it has a parameter list, procedure WriteLn is more versatile and hence more useful than procedure DrawCircle. Procedure DrawCircle can display only a circle shape, whereas procedure WriteLn can display whatever we want it to.

Chapter 6 discusses parameters in more detail. For the time being, we will restrict our use to procedures without parameters, to display lengthy messages or instructions to program users. We also will continue to use the Pascal ReadLn, Write, and WriteLn procedures for data entry and display. To learn more about procedure parameters, skip ahead to Section 6.1.

EXAMPLE 3.7: Displaying User Instructions ▼

Let's write a procedure that displays instructions to a user of the program that computes the area and the circumference of a circle (see Fig. 3.4). This simple procedure demonstrates one of the benefits of separating the statements that display user instructions from the main program body: Editing these instructions is simplified when they are separate from the code that performs the calculations.

If you place procedure Instruct (see Fig. 3.20) in the declaration part of the original program, you can begin the revised main program with the procedure call statement

```
Instruct;
```

The rest of the main program consists of the executable statements shown earlier. Figure 3.21 shows the output displayed by calling procedure Instruct. ▲

Figure 3.20
Procedure Instruct

```
procedure Instruct;
{Displays instructions to a user of program Circle}

begin {Instruct}
  WriteLn ('This program computes the area');
  WriteLn ('and circumference of a circle.');
  WriteLn;
  WriteLn ('To use this program, enter the radius of');
  WriteLn ('the circle after the prompt: Enter radius >');
  WriteLn;
  WriteLn ('The circumference will be computed in the');
  WriteLn ('same units of measurement as the radius.');
  WriteLn ('The area will be computed in the same ',
           'units squared');
  WriteLn
end; {Instruct}
```

Exercises for Section 3.5

Self-Check

1. How does the use of procedure parameters make it possible to write larger, more useful programs?
2. Why are the parameters for WriteLn, an output procedure, considered procedure inputs and the parameters for ReadLn, an input procedure, considered procedure outputs?

Programming

1. Show the revised program Circle with a call to Instruct.
2. Write a procedure like Instruct for the pizza program in Fig. 3.5, and show where to call it.

Figure 3.21
Output Displayed by
Procedure Instruct

```
This program computes the area
and circumference of a circle.

To use this program, enter the radius of
the circle after the prompt: Enter radius >

The circumference will be computed in the
same units of measurement as the radius.
The area will be computed in the same units squared
```

3.6 Introduction to Computer Graphics (Optional)

In normal computer output (called text mode), you use `Write` and `WriteLn` to display lines of characters. In Section 3.3 we showed how to write Pascal procedures for drawing simple stick figures using `WriteLn` statements. Turbo Pascal provides another mode of output (called graphics mode) that enables you to draw pictures or graphical patterns on your computer screen (**computer graphics**). In graphics programming, you cannot use procedure `Write` or `WriteLn` but must use Turbo Pascal's graphics procedures and functions instead. These functions allow you to draw lines and various geometric shapes (e.g., rectangles, circles, ellipses) anywhere on your screen and color and shade them in different ways.

computer graphics

drawing pictures or graphical patterns on a computer screen

Starting Graphics Programming

The following line should be the first line after the `program` statement in a graphics program:

```
uses Graph; {Enables access to graphics modules and constants}
```

The `uses` statement enables your program to access Turbo Pascal's predefined graphics modules and constants, found in a special file called a *unit* (i.e., in unit `Graph`). We discuss units in Chapter 9.

The object code generated in graphics mode is system dependent, so Turbo Pascal must know what kind of graphics hardware you are using. The declarations

```
var
   Driver, Mode : Integer; {Indicators of kind of graphics
                                    hardware}
```

allocate storage for two `Integer` variables (`Driver` and `Mode`) whose values indicate the kind of graphics hardware in your system. Use the procedure call statement

```
InitGraph (Driver, Mode, 'C:\BP\BGI'); {Initialize graphics
                                              mode}
```

to initialize graphics mode. Procedure `InitGraph` checks your graphics system to determine which values to store in `Driver` and `Mode`.

The string parameter `'C:\BP\BGI'` specifies which directory contains the software that controls the graphics system and is system dependent. The string with no characters (`''`) indicates that the current directory contains this software. To make our graphics programs portable, we will store the directory name in a string constant (`Directory`).

The Screen as a Graphics Palette

In text mode, you don't pay much attention to the position of each line of characters displayed on the screen. In graphics programming, in contrast, you control the location of each line or shape you draw on the screen. Consequently, you must know how your screen is laid out and how to reference the individual picture elements (called **pixels**) on the screen.

pixel

a picture element on a computer screen

palette

an X-Y grid of pixels

You can visualize your screen as an *X-Y* grid of pixels (called a **palette**). Most screens are wider than they are tall, so there are more pixels in the *X*-direction (horizontal) than in the *Y*-direction (vertical). Typical palette dimensions are 320 × 200, 640 × 350, and 640 × 480, where the first number in each pair gives the number of pixels in the *X*-direction.

The Turbo Pascal functions GetMaxX and GetMaxY return the position of the last pixel in the *X*- and *Y*-directions, respectively. Therefore, regardless of its actual dimensions, each screen has the layout shown in Fig. 3.22, with the coordinates for the four pixels at the screen corners. The pixel at the top-left corner has *X-Y* coordinates (0, 0), and the pixel at the top-right corner has *X-Y* coordinates (GetMaxX, 0). Functions GetMaxX and GetMaxY have no arguments.

Notice that Turbo Pascal numbers the pixels in the *Y*-direction differently from how we are accustomed. The pixel (0, 0) is at the top-left corner of the screen, and the *Y*-coordinate values increase as we move down the

Figure 3.22
Screen as a Palette

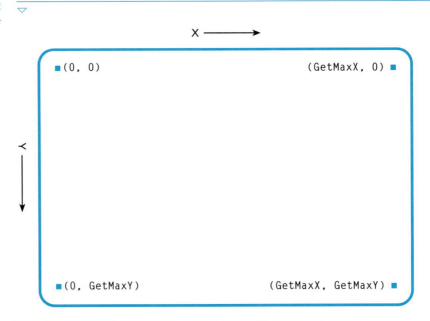

screen. In a normal *X-Y* coordinate system, the point (0, 0) is at the bottom-left corner.

EXAMPLE 3.8 ▼

The program in Fig. 3.23 displays the dimensions of your graphics palette. The statements

```
BigX := GetMaxX;          {Store largest X-coordinate.}
BigY := GetMaxY;          {Store largest Y-coordinate.}
```

store the largest *X*- and *Y*-coordinates in BigX and BigY, respectively. The statement

```
CloseGraph;               {Switch back to text mode.}
```

Figure 3.23
Displaying Palette
Dimensions

▽

Edit Window

```
program ShowDimensions;
{Displays palette dimensions}

  uses Graph; {Enable access to graphic modules and constants.}

  const
    Directory = 'C:\BP\BGI';        {Name of graphics directory}

  var
    Driver, Mode : Integer; {Indicators of kind of graphics hardware}
    BigX, BigY   : Integer;
begin {ShowDimensions}
  InitGraph (Driver, Mode, Directory); {Initialize graphics mode.}

  BigX := GetMaxX;      {Store largest X-coordinate.}
  BigY := GetMaxY;      {Store largest Y-coordinate.}

  CloseGraph;           {Switch back to text mode.}
  WriteLn ('Pixel at bottom-right corner is (',
          BigX :1, ', ', BigY : 1, ')' )
end. {ShowDimensions}
```

Output Window

```
Pixel at bottom-right corner is (639, 479)
```

△

switches the program back to text mode so that the values of BigX and BigY can be displayed in the normal way. Because pixel (0, 0) is at the top-left corner, the palette dimensions are 640 × 480. ▲

Background Color and Foreground Color

background color
the default color (black) used to display a pixel

foreground color
the color used to display a pixel when it is part of a line drawn on the screen

When in graphics mode, the computer displays all pixels continuously in one of 16 colors (or shades of gray if you don't have a color monitor). The default color used to display a pixel is called the **background color**. Consequently, your initial screen is blank because all its pixels are displayed in the background color. When you draw a line or a shape, the pixels it contains stand out because they are displayed in the **foreground color**.

Black and white are the default values for the background and foreground colors, respectively. The statements

```
SetBkColor (Green);        {Green is the background color.}
SetColor (Red)             {Red is the foreground color.}
```

reset the background color to Green and the foreground color to Red where Green and Red are predefined color constants (part of unit Graph). You select a color constant from the list shown in Table 3.3, using either the constant name or its numeric value as a parameter (e.g., Red or 4). Once you change the foreground or background color, it retains its new value until you change it again.

Table 3.3
Color Constants

Constant	Value	Constant	Value
Black	0	DarkGray	8
Blue	1	LightBlue	9
Green	2	LightGreen	10
Cyan	3	LightCyan	11
Red	4	LightRed	12
Magenta	5	LightMagenta	13
Brown	6	Yellow	14
LightGray	7	White	15

Drawing Lines

You can use procedure Line to draw a line on the screen. The procedure call statement

Figure 3.24
Line Through Points (*X1*, *Y1*) and (*X2*, *Y2*)

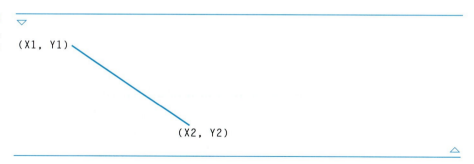

```
Line (X1, Y1, X2, Y2)
```

draws a line from point (X1, Y1) to point (X2, Y2) (Fig. 3.24).

EXAMPLE 3.9 ▼

The program in Fig. 3.25 draws a pair of diagonal lines intersecting at the center of the screen. The white line goes from (0, 0) to (GetMaxX, GetMaxY). The gray line goes from (GetMaxX, 0) to (0, GetMaxY). ▲

Figure 3.25
Drawing Intersecting Lines

Edit Window

```
program Intersect;
{Draws intersecting lines}

  uses Graph;                              {Enable access to graphic modules and constants.}

  const
    Directory = 'C:\BP\BGI';               {Name of graphics directory}

  var
    Driver, Mode : Integer;                {Indicators of kind of graphics hardware}
begin {Intersect}
  InitGraph (Driver, Mode, Directory);     {Initialize graphics mode.}

  Line (0, 0, GetMaxX, GetMaxY);           {Draw white line from top left (0,0)
                                            to bottom right (GetMaxX, GetMaxY).}

  SetColor (LightGray);
  Line (GetMaxX, 0, 0, GetMaxY)            {Draw gray line from top right to
                                            bottom left of screen.}
end. {Intersect}
```

▷ ▷ ▷ ▷ ▷ ▷

Output Window

Drawing Rectangles

We use procedure `Rectangle` to draw a rectangle on the screen. The procedure call statement

`Rectangle (X1, Y1, X2, Y2)`

draws a rectangle that has a diagonal with end points (X1, Y1) and (X2, Y2) (Fig. 3.26).

EXAMPLE 3.10 ▼

The program in Fig. 3.27 draws a house. The program begins by defining the corner points of the house, where the roof is a pair of lines intersecting at point (X2, Y2). The first call to `Rectangle` draws the rest of the house, and the second call to `Rectangle` draws the door.

We laid out the house for a palette size of 640 × 480. If your palette dimensions are smaller, you will need to redefine the coordinates of the corner points. We added labels (e.g., (X1, Y1)) in Fig. 3.27 to identify the corner points; the program does not display them.   ▲

Drawing Circles and Arcs

We use procedure `Circle` to draw a circle. The procedure call statement

`Circle (X, Y, Radius)`

Figure 3.26
Rectangle with Diagonal
Through (*X1, Y1*) and
(*X2, Y2*)

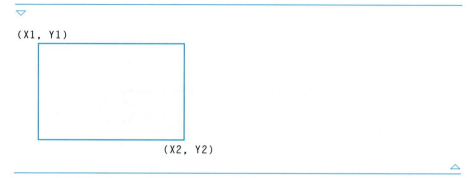

Figure 3.27
Drawing a House

Edit Window

```
program House;
{Draws a house}

  uses Graph;                        {Enable access to graphic modules and constants.}

  const
    Directory = 'C:\BP\BGI';          {Name of graphics directory}

  var
    Driver, Mode,                     {Indicators of kind of graphics hardware}
    X1, Y1, X2, Y2, X3, Y3,           {coordinates of 6 corner points}
    X4, Y4, X5, Y5, X6, Y6 : Integer;

begin {House}
  InitGraph (Driver, Mode, Directory);  {Initialize graphics mode.}

  {Define corners of house}
  X1 := 100; Y1 := 200;             {top-left corner}
  X2 := 300; Y2 := 100;             {roof peak}
  X3 := 500; Y3 := 200;             {top-right corner}
  X4 := 500; Y4 := 400;             {bottom-right corner}
  X5 := 325; Y5 := 400;             {bottom-right corner of door}
  X6 := 275; Y6 := 325;             {top-left corner of door}

  {Draw roof.}
  Line (X1, Y1, X2, Y2);
  Line (X2, Y2, X3, Y3);

  {Draw rest of house.}
  Rectangle (X1, Y1, X4, Y4);
```

▷ ▷ ▷ ▷ ▷ ▷

```
{Draw door.}
Rectangle (X5, Y5, X6, Y6)
end. {House}
```

Output Window

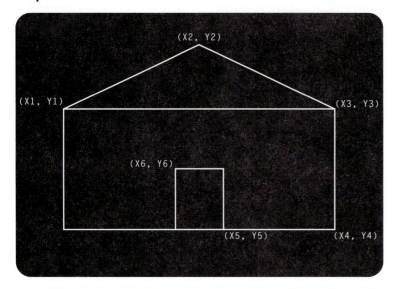

draws a circle whose center is at (X, Y). The third parameter is the circle radius.

Procedure Arc draws an arc, or part of a circle. To draw an arc, you must specify its starting angle and ending angle in degrees. The statement

```
Arc (X, Y, 0, 180, Radius)
```

draws the top half a circle with center at (X, Y) (Fig. 3.28). If you imagine a clock on the screen, 0 degrees is at 3 o'clock (horizontal direction), 30 degrees is at 2 o'clock, 60 degrees is at 1 o'clock, 90 degrees is at 12 o'clock (vertical direction), and so on.

Figure 3.28
Arc Drawn by Arc (X, Y, 0, 180, Radius)

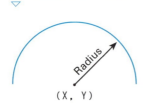

EXAMPLE 3.11 ▼

The program in Fig. 3.29 draws a happy face. It begins by completing an outer circle (radius HeadRadius), then it draws three smaller circles (radius EyeNoseRadius) representing the eyes and nose. Finally, it draws the smile as an arc from 210 degrees (8 o'clock) to 330 degrees (4 o'clock). The arc has the same center as the outer circle, but its radius is 75% as large.   ▲

Figure 3.29
Drawing a Happy Face

▽

Edit Window

```
program HappyFace;
{Draws a happy face}

  uses Graph;                        {Enable access to graphic modules and constants.}

  const
    Directory = 'C:\BP\BGI';         {Name of graphics directory}

  var
    Driver, Mode,                    {Indicators of kind of graphics hardware}
    MidX, MidY,                      {coordinates of center point}
    LeftEyeX, RightEyeX, EyeY,       {eye center points}
    NoseX, NoseY,                    {nose center point}
    HeadRadius,                      {head radius}
    EyeNoseRadius,                   {eye/nose radius}
    SmileRadius,                     {smile radius}
    StepX, StepY : Integer;          {X and Y increments}

begin {HappyFace}
  InitGraph (Driver, Mode, Directory);   {Initialize graphics mode.}

  {Draw head.}
  MidX := GetMaxX div 2;            {Center head in X-direction.}
  MidY := GetMaxY div 2;            {Center head in Y-direction.}
  HeadRadius := GetMaxY div 4;
  Circle (MidX, MidY, HeadRadius);      {Draw head.}

  {Draw eyes.}
  StepX := HeadRadius div 4;        {X-offset for eyes}
  StepY := StepX;                   {Y-offset for eyes and nose}
  LeftEyeX := MidX - StepX;         {X-coordinate for left eye}
  RightEyeX := MidX + StepX;        {X-coordinate for right eye}
  EyeY := MidY - StepY;             {Y-coordinate for both eyes}
  EyeNoseRadius := HeadRadius div 10;
```

▷ ▷ ▷ ▷ ▷

```
Circle (LeftEyeX,  EyeY, EyeNoseRadius);        {Draw left eye.}
Circle (RightEyeX, EyeY, EyeNoseRadius);        {Draw right eye.}

{Draw nose.}
NoseX := MidX;                                  {Nose is centered in X direction.}
NoseY := MidY + StepY;
Circle (NoseX, NoseY, EyeNoseRadius);

{Draw smile.}
SmileRadius := Round(0.75 * HeadRadius);        {3/4 of head radius}
Arc (MidX, MidY, 210, 330, SmileRadius)
end. {HappyFace}
```

Output Window

Program Style

Writing General Graphics Programs

The program in Fig. 3.29 is general and draws a similar image on any graphics screen, whereas the size and position of the house drawn by the program in Fig. 3.27 is system dependent. As you can see, it is generally easier to write programs that are system dependent; however, with a little practice you should be able to write general graphics programs. To generalize the program in Fig. 3.27, you could base the coordinates of the house corners on the screen dimensions as follows (see Self-Check Exercise 4).

```
X1 := GetMaxX div 4; Y1 := GetMaxY div 2;   {top-left corner}
X2 := GetMaxX div 2; Y2 := GetMaxY div 4;   {roof peak}
```

Drawing Filled Figures

So far all our graphics figures have been line drawings. To fill in sections of the screen using different colors and patterns, you would use procedure `SetFillStyle` to specify the pattern and color. The procedure call statement

```
SetFillStyle (SlashFill, Red)
```

sets the fill pattern to red slashes until you change it through another call to `SetFillStyle`. Table 3.4 shows the options for the first parameter in a call to `SetFillStyle`. Use either the constant name or its value (e.g., `Slash-Fill` or 4) and any color constant in Table 3.3 as the second parameter.

Table 3.4
Fill Pattern Constants

Constant	Value	Fill Pattern	Constant	Value	Fill Pattern
`EmptyFill`	0	Background color	`LtBkSlash-Fill`	6	\ \ \ (light)
`SolidFill`	1	Solid color	`HatchFill`	7	Hatch (light)
`LineFill`	2	- - -	`XHatchFill`	8	Crosshatch
`LtSlashFill`	3	/ / / (light)	`Interleave-Fill`	9	Interleaving line
`SlashFill`	4	/// (heavy)	`WideDot-Fill`	10	Dots (light)
`BkSlashFill`	5	\\\ (heavy)	`CloseDot-Fill`	11	Dots (heavy)

Use procedure `FloodFill` to actually fill in a portion of a diagram. The procedure call statement

```
FloodFill (X, Y, White)
```

fills with the current fill pattern an area on the screen that contains the point X, Y and is bounded by `White` lines. If the point X, Y is outside an area bounded by `White` lines, the exterior of the bounded figure is filled. Be careful when using `FloodFill`, as you may get unexpected results.

EXAMPLE 3.12 ▼

We can insert the following program fragment at the end of the program in Fig. 3.27 to paint the house (Fig. 3.30). The roof is painted in a gray hatch pattern, the house itself is painted in a white lined pattern, and the doorway is painted a solid blue.

Figure 3.30
Painted House

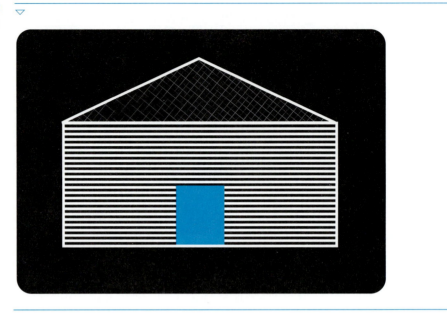

```
SetFillStyle (HatchFill, LightGray);
FloodFill (X2, Y2 + 10, White);        {Paint the roof.}

SetFillStyle (LineFill, White);
FloodFill (X2, Y1 + 10, White);        {Paint the house.}

SetFillStyle (SolidFill, Blue);
FloodFill (X2, Y6 + 10, White)         {Paint the door.}
```

We use X2, the midpoint in the *X*-direction, as the first parameter in each call to FloodFill. The second parameter (the *Y*-coordinate) determines which section (roof, house, or door) to fill in. All boundary lines for the house are white (the default foreground color), so the third parameter is White. ▲

Bars and Pie Slices

Turbo Pascal provides procedures to draw bars and pie slices. A *bar* is a filled rectangle, and a *pie slice* is a filled segment of a circle. The procedure call statement

```
SetFillStyle (XHatchFill, White);
Bar (X1, Y1, X2, Y2)
```

draws a filled rectangle that has a diagonal with end points (X1, Y1) and (X2, Y2).

Insert the statements

```
SetFillStyle (XHatchFill, White);
PieSlice (MidX, MidY, 10, 60, SmileRadius)
```

at the end of Fig. 3.29 to draw a white patch over the right eye of the happy face (Fig. 3.31). The patch is a pie slice with radius `SmileRadius` centered at point (`MidX, MidY`). The pie slice goes from 10 degrees to 60 degrees.

You can use the `PieSlice` and `Bar` procedures to draw pie charts and bar graphs (see Programming Project 9 at the end of the chapter). We describe how to display the message shown under the happy face next.

Adding Text to Drawings

In graphics mode, you cannot use `Write` or `WriteLn` to display characters or text, but you must instead draw characters just as you draw other shapes. Fortunately, Turbo Pascal provides a procedure that does this. The procedure call statement

```
OutTextXY (MidX - HeadRadius, GetMaxY - 20,
          'Pirate with an Eye Patch')
```

draws each character in a string (its third parameter) starting at the pixel whose *X-Y* coordinates are specified by its first two parameters. The string starts at the pixel whose *X*-coordinate is `MidX - HeadRadius` and whose *Y*-coordinate is 20 pixels above the bottom of the screen (Fig. 3.31).

Figure 3.31
Pirate with Eye Patch

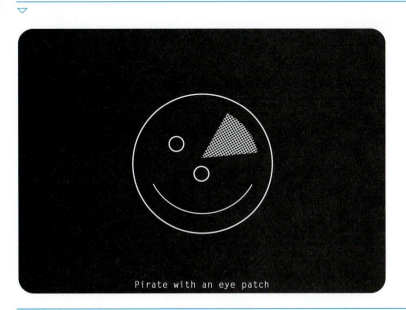

Pirate with an eye patch

Procedure or Function Call	Effect
InitGraph (Driver, Mode, 'C:\BP\BGI')	Initializes graphics mode and sets Driver and Mode when the graphics software is in directory C:\BP\BGI
CloseGraph	Switches from graphics to text mode
GetMaxX	Returns the position of the last pixel in the *X*-direction
GetMaxY	Returns the position of the last pixel in the *Y*-direction
SetColor (ForeColor)	Sets the foreground color to Fore-Color
SetBkColor (BackColor)	Sets the background color to Back-Color
Line (X1, Y1, X2, Y2)	Draws a line with end points (X1, Y1) and (X2, Y2)
Rectangle (X1, Y1, X2, Y2)	Draws a rectangle with a diagonal through points (X1, Y1) and (X2, Y2)
Circle (X, Y, R)	Draws a circle with center at (X, Y) and radius R
Arc (X, Y, Angle1, Angle2, R)	Draws an arc from angle Angle1 to Angle2 with center at (X, Y) and radius R
SetFillStyle (FilPat, FilCol)	Sets the fill pattern to FilPat and the fill color to FilCol
FloodFill (X, Y, Border)	Fills with the current fill pattern the figure containing the point (X, Y) and bounded by lines with color Border
Bar (X1, Y1, X2, Y2)	Draws a filled rectangle with a diagonal through points (X1, Y1) and (X2, Y2)
PieSlice (X, Y, Angle1, Angle2, R)	Draws a filled pie slice from angle Angle1 to Angle2 with center at (X, Y) and radius R
OutTextXY (X, Y, TextString)	Draws the characters for TextString starting at point (X, Y)

Exercises for Section 3.6   *Self-Check*

1. In Fig. 3.29, what is the reason for basing the head radius on `GetMaxY` and not `GetMaxX`?
2. Describe or show the drawing produced by the following fragment. Assume a 640 × 480 palette.

```
Circle (200, 50, 25);
Line (200, 75, 100, 100);
Line (200, 75, 300, 100);
PieSlice (200, 75, 245, 295, 100);
Line (200, 150, 100, 250);
Line (200, 150, 300, 250);
Bar (50, 250, 350, 300)
```

3. Write statements to add two windows to the second floor of the house in Fig. 3.27.
4. Modify the program in Fig. 3.27 so that it draws the house in the center of the screen and with the same relative size regardless of the actual palette dimensions.

Programming

1. Write the statements to draw a tennis racket in the appropriate place in the figure for Self-Check Exercise 2. At the end of a thin bar, draw a circle and fill it with a white crosshatch pattern.
2. Write a graphics program that draws a rocket ship consisting of a triangle (the cone) on top of a rectangle (the body). Draw a pair of intersecting lines under the rectangle. Fill the cone with a blue hatch pattern and the body with a red solid pattern.
3. Write a program that draws a pair of nested rectangles at the center of the screen, filling the inner rectangle in red and the outer rectangle in white. The outer rectangle should have a width 1/4 of the *X*-dimension and a height 1/4 of the *Y*-dimension of the screen. The height and width of the inner rectangle should be half that of the outer rectangle.
4. Write a program that draws a male and a female stick figure side-by-side.

3.7 Common Programming Errors

Remember to declare each procedure used in a program. Procedure declarations *must* precede procedure calls and are usually found in the declaration part of a program just after the variable declarations. If procedure A calls procedure B, you must declare procedure B first.

Syntax or run-time errors can occur when you use Pascal's predefined functions, so make sure that each function argument is the correct type. For example, the arguments for functions `Round` and `Trunc` should be type `Real`. If the argument for function `Sqrt` or `Ln` is negative, a run-time error will occur.

When you call procedure `InitGraph`, you must specify the correct directory for the software that controls your graphics system. If Turbo Pascal cannot find this software, it displays the message `BGI error: Graphics not initialized (use InitGraph)`.

CHAPTER REVIEW

1. Develop your program solutions from existing information. Use the system documentation derived from applying the software development method as the initial framework for the program. Edit the data requirements to obtain the declaration part, then use the refined algorithm as the starting point for the program body.
2. If a new problem is an extension of a previous one, modify the previous program rather than start from scratch.
3. Pascal's predefined functions can simplify mathematical computations. Write a function designator (consisting of the function name and argument list) in an expression to activate a function.
4. Use a structure chart to show subordinate relationships between subproblems.
5. Utilize modular programming by writing separate procedures to implement the different subproblems in a structure chart. Your main program will contain procedure call statements that activate the procedures listed in the declaration part.

Summary of New Pascal Constructs

Construct	Effect
Procedure Declaration	

`procedure Display;`
`{Prints 3 lines}`
`  const`
`    Star = '*';`
 	
`begin {Display}`
`  WriteLn (Star);`
`  WriteLn (Star);`
`  WriteLn (Star)`
`end; {Display}`
	Procedure `Display` is declared and can be called to print three lines of asterisks. The constant `Star` is defined only when `Display` is executing.

Procedure Call Statement	
`Display`	Procedure `Display` is called and begins execution.
Function Designator	
`Z := Sqrt(X + Y)`	Function `Sqrt` computes the square root of the expression `X + Y`, which is assigned to `Z`.

Quick-Check Exercises

1. Developing a program from its documentation means that every statement in the program has a comment. True or false?
2. The principle of reusability states that every procedure in your program must be used more than once. True or false?
3. Write this equation as a Pascal statement using functions Exp, Ln, and Sqr:

   $y = (e^n \ln b)^2$

4. Top-down design means writing the Pascal declaration section first, then the program body. True or false?
5. Each procedure is executed in the order in which it is declared in the main program. True or false?
6. What syntax is required in a Pascal program to invoke a procedure?
7. List the order of the declarations in a standard Pascal program.
8. What is a procedure parameter?
9. Explain how a structure chart differs from an algorithm.
10. A procedure can have inputs, outputs, or both. True or false?
11. What does the following procedure do?

```
procedure Nonsense;
begin {Nonsense}
   WriteLn ('*****');
   WriteLn ('*   *');
   WriteLn ('*****')
end; {Nonsense}
```

12. What does the following program body do?

```
begin
   Nonsense;
   Nonsense;
   Nonsense
end.
```

Answers to Quick-Check Exercises

1. False
2. False
3. `Y := Sqr(Exp(N * Ln(B)));`
4. False
5. False
6. A procedure call statement
7. Constants, variables, procedures
8. Parameters are used to receive information from the calling program unit or to pass results back to the calling program unit.
9. A structure chart shows the subordinate relationships between subproblems; an algorithm lists the sequence in which subproblems are performed.
10. True
11. It displays a rectangle.
12. It displays three rectangles on top of each other.

Review Questions

1. Define top-down design and structure charts.
2. In which section of a Pascal program should a procedure be declared? Where in the program can the procedure by called?
3. What are three advantages of using procedures?
4. When is a procedure executed, and where must it appear in the main program?
5. Is the use of procedures a more efficient use of the programmer's time or of the computer's time? Why?
6. How do functions differ from procedures?
7. Write a program that prompts the user for the two legs of a right triangle and makes use of the Sqr and Sqrt functions and the Pythagorean theorem to compute the length of the hypotenuse.
8. Write a program that draws a rectangle made up of asterisks. Use two procedures: `DrawSides` and `DrawLine`.

Programming Projects

1. Write two procedures, one that displays a triangle and one that displays a rectangle using text mode. Use these procedures to write a complete Pascal program from the following outline:

```
program StackHouses;
begin
   {1. Draw triangle.}
   {2. Draw rectangle.}
   {3. Print 2 blank lines.}
   {4. Draw triangle.}
   {5. Draw rectangle.}
end;
```

2. Add the procedures from Fig. 3.16 to the ones for Programming Project 1. Use these procedures in a program that draws a rocket ship (triangle over rectangles over intersecting lines), a male stick figure (circle over rectangle over intersecting lines), and a female stick figure standing on the head of a male stick figure. Write procedure `Skip5Lines` and call it to place five blank lines between each drawing.

3. Write a computer program that computes the duration of a projectile's flight and its height above the ground when it reaches the target. As part of your solution, write and call a procedure that displays instructions to the program user.

Problem constant
```
G = 32.17              {gravitational constant}
```

Problem input
```
Theta : Real           {input - angle (radians) of elevation}
Distance : Real        {input - distance (ft) to target}
Velocity : Real        {input - projectile velocity (ft/sec)}
```

Problem output
```
Time    : Real         {output - time (sec) of flight}
Height  : Real         {output - height at impact}
```

Relevant formulas
> $time = distance/(velocity \times cos\ Theta)$
> $height = velocity \times sin\ Theta \times time - (g \times time^2)/2$

4. Four track stars have completed the mile race at the Penn Relays. Write a program that will read in each of their race times (listed here) in minutes (`Minutes`) and seconds (`Seconds`) and compute and print the speed in feet per second (`FPS`) and in meters per second (`MPS`). (*Hint:* There are 5280 feet in one mile, and one kilometer equals 3282 feet.) Write and call a procedure that displays instructions to the program user.

Minutes	Seconds
3	52.83
3	59.83
4	00.03
4	16.22

5. In a new computer-assisted board game, moves are determined by selecting a random number, but players can influence their moves by taking risks. After a player enters a number n from 1 to 10, the computer generates a random integer r from 1 to 10. The player's move is then $(r - n + 1) * n$. A cautious player enters 1 and always moves forward, whereas an ambitious player enters higher numbers and may take larger forward moves or may move backward. Write a program to determine one move in the game and output the computer's integer selection and the move. (*Hint:* Be sure to call `Randomize` and use `Random (10) + 1` to get a random number x such that $1 \le x \le 10$.)

6. In shopping for a new house, you must consider several factors. In this problem, the initial cost of the house, the estimated annual fuel costs, and the annual tax rate are available. Write a program that will determine the total cost of a house after a five-year period for each of the following sets of data. You should be able to inspect your program output to determine the best buy.

Initial House Cost	Annual Fuel Cost	Tax Rate
$67,000	$2300	0.025
$62,000	$2500	0.025
$75,000	$1850	0.020

To calculate the house cost, add the initial house cost to the fuel cost for five years, then add the taxes for five years. Taxes for one year are computed by multiplying the tax rate by the initial cost. Write and call a procedure that displays instructions to the program user.

7. The first two verses of the song "99 bottles of beer on the wall" are:

99 bottles of beer on the wall.
99 bottles of beer.
Take one down and pass it around.
98 bottles of beer on the wall.

98 bottles of beer on the wall.
98 bottles of beer.
Take one down and pass it around.
97 bottles of beer on the wall.

Write a program that will print the first five verses of this song. Use procedures to minimize duplication of `WriteLn` statements.

8. Repeat Programming Project 2, this time using graphics mode.

9. Read in five values that represent the monthly amount spent on budget categories: food, clothing, transportation, entertainment, and rent. Write a program that displays a bar graph and a pie chart showing these values. In a bar graph, the length of each bar is proportional to the value it represents. Use a different color for each bar. (*Hint:* Multiply each value by the scale factor `GetMaxX div MaxExpense`, where `MaxExpense` is the largest possible expense.) For the pie chart, the arc length of each section should be proportional to the amount it represents. Use a different fill pattern and color for each section.

▼ **How would you define "human–computer interaction"? Why is it important?**

▲ I would define it by analogy to person-to-person communication. People communicate back and forth using a combination of words, gestures, and facial expressions to represent information that they want to convey to each other. Human–computer interaction addresses the ways in which humans and computers communicate. We have to tell the computer what we want and the computer has to tell us what information it has. Human–computer interaction looks at the language that encompasses this two-way communication: from the person to the computer and from the computer to the person.

The challenge is to design a language that makes it easy for the person to communicate to the computer and that enables the computer to respond in a form most understandable to people. Graphics plays an important part because graphical representations are often more understandable—that is, you can get information out of a chart of data, for example, more quickly than from a column of data.

Computer–human interaction is important in both an economic sense and a broader sense. In an economic sense, it is really the last frontier in the growth of the computer industry. The only thing keeping the computer industry growing is being able to do more and more things with computers. To get computers in the hands of more and more people, we need to find new forms of human–computer communication that will enable and facilitate new types of work.

In a broader sense, human–computer interaction strives to expand people's capabilities and intellectual leverage, so people can do their jobs more quickly, concentrate on the intellectually fulfilling parts of a job, and have access to more information more quickly.

▼ **What has influenced you the most in your own work?**

▲ I started out in graphics and came to realize that graphics was only an enabler—an important enabler, and one where research issues are plentiful—but the experience of building interactive computer graphics systems and seeing the power they brought to people got me interested in human–computer interaction, as well as continuing my interest in computer graphics.

▼ **It seems the most dramatic achievements in computer science have occurred in the area of graphics. Can the gains made in the 1980s be matched in the 1990s, or has this field matured to the point where achievements will be more evolutionary than revolutionary?**

▲ Yes, the achievements will be more evolutionary than revolutionary. As you go from year to year now, the gains in realism are smaller than they used to be because we've done all the easy things. Making pictures more and more realistic is essentially becoming a matter of dealing with mathematical formulations of physics, of how light interacts with surfaces, and of modeling of objects. We know how to model things that are geometrically shaped and to some extent those that are probabilistically or randomly shaped, like the branching patterns of trees, and we're making progress on doing things that don't have nice mathematical formulations.

INTERVIEW
▼
James D. Foley

James Foley is a professor of computer science and director of the new Graphics, Visualization, and Usability Center in the College of Computing at Georgia Institute of Technology. His interests include user interfaces and interactive computer graphics; his research focuses on building UIDE, the User Interface Design Environment.

A question that I and others keep asking is, How realistic is realistic enough? We sometimes get preoccupied with making pictures more and more realistic, but we may not always need the picture to be completely realistic. In fact, some studies have shown that realistic detail can sometimes get in the way of the message to be conveyed. I think the biggest growth for graphics is not in making pictures more and more realistic but in finding creative new ways in which graphics can be used to leverage productivity.

▼ **For someone electing to concentrate in the area of graphics, how important is it to understand the underlying hardware principles?**

▲ It depends on what you want to do. It's analogous to whether you want to be a race car driver or an automobile designer. If you're the race car driver, that would correspond to trying to get the most you can out of the current technology. You need to understand some of the underlying hardware in order to make it work as well as possible—which operations are fast and which are slow, how to organize the data so that access speeds are maximized, and so on. If you want to be an automobile designer, you need to understand the hardware very well. I think most people who study graphics are in the race car driver category.

▼ **What exciting things are being done today in the area of user interfaces?**

▲ Exciting things are going on in the area of virtual realities, creating 3D environments that appear to be real, that behave realistically, and with which you interact realistically. Speech recognition is another exciting area, as are the gesture-based interfaces, or what's now called "pen computing." Pen computing allow users to use a stylus on a liquid crystal display as they would write on a piece of paper. All three developments are making the way we interact with computers more like the way we interact with the real world, so we need to learn less about the system to transfer the skills and knowledge we use in the real world into working with the computer.

▼ **What advice do you have for students who want to work in human–computer interaction?**

▲ If you want to study human–computer interaction, there are two computing systems that you have to understand: the one on the desk and the one in your head. You need to understand the input/output channels for the human processor, as it is sometimes called—the eyes, ears, hands, and fingers—and you need to understand these capabilities as well as the capabilities of the computer. That means studying psychology, particularly cognitive psychology and perceptual psychology, and human factors. I like to compare people who get involved in human–computer interaction to the "Renaissance man," because to do a good job of designing computer interfaces you have to have a breadth of understanding beyond computer science, understanding both the human processor and the application area for which you are designing, and be open to learning about a new discipline.

CHAPTER FOUR

Selection Structures: if and case Statements

This chapter begins your study of statements that control the flow of program execution. You will learn to use Pascal if and case statements to select one statement to execute from many alternatives. First, the chapter discusses Boolean expressions because the if statement relies on them.

The case studies in this chapter extend your problem-solving abilities by introducing the techniques of solution by analogy and hand-tracing the execution of an algorithm. The chapter also introduces visual techniques to identify the data flow in structure charts and to represent Pascal constructs (language elements) in syntax diagrams.

4.1 Control Structures

control structures

combinations of individual instructions into a single logical unit with one entry point and one exit point

Structured programming utilizes **control structures** to control the flow of execution in a program or procedure. The Pascal control structures enable us to combine individual instructions into a single logical unit with one entry point and one exit point. We can then write a program as a sequence of control structures rather than as a sequence of individual instructions (Fig. 4.1).

Instructions are organized into three kinds of control structures to control execution flow: sequence, selection, and repetition. Until now we have been using only sequential flow. A **compound statement,** written as a group of statements bracketed by begin and end, is used to specify sequential flow:

compound statement

a group of statements bracketed by begin and end that are executed sequentially

```
begin
    statement₁ ;
    statement₂ ;
        .

        .

        .
    statementₙ
end
```

Control flows from *statement₁* to *statement₂*, and so on. You have been using compound statements all along—a program or procedure body consists of a single compound statement.

Figure 4.1

A Program as a Sequence of Three Control Structures

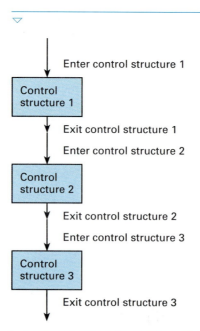

This chapter describes the Pascal control structures for selection. Some problem solutions require that choices be made between alternative steps, for which Pascal statements may or may not be executed, depending on the input data. A **selection control structure** chooses which alternative to execute.

selection control structure
a control structure that chooses among alternative program statements

4.2 Boolean Expressions

A program chooses among alternative steps by testing the value of key variables. For example, since different tax rates apply to various salary levels, an income tax program must select the rate appropriate for each worker's salary by comparing the salary value to the maximum salary for a particular income tax bracket. In Pascal, Boolean expresssons, or *conditions,* perform such comparisons. Each Boolean expression has two possible values, `True` or `False`, where `True` indicates a successful test and `False` indicates an unsuccessful test.

Boolean Variables and Constants

The simplest Boolean expression is a Boolean variable or constant. The statement

```
const
  LeapYear = True;
```

specifies that the Boolean constant `LeapYear` has the value `True`; the statement

```
var
  Switch, Flag : Boolean;
```

declares `Switch` and `Flag` to be Boolean variables—variables that may be assigned only the values `True` and `False`. Given these declarations, all these assignment statements are valid:

```
Switch := True;         {Switch gets True}
Flag := False;          {Flag gets False}
Switch := Flag          {Switch gets value of Flag}
```

After these statements execute, both `Flag` and `Switch` have the value `False`.

Boolean Expressions with Relational Operators

Boolean expressions that perform comparisons have one of these forms:

variable   relational-operator   variable
variable   relational-operator   constant

Relational operators are the following symbols:

< (less than)   > (greater than)
<= (less than or equal)   >= (greater than or equal)
= (equal)   <> (not equal)

The items being compared, or operands, are often two variables or a variable and a constant. If I is type `Integer`, the condition `I < 3` is true when I is negative or 0, 1, or 2.

The two operands of a relational operator must be the same data type (both type `Integer`, `Real`, `Char`, or `Boolean`), or one may be type `Real` and the other type `Integer`. If I is type `Integer`, the condition `I < '3'` causes a `type mismatch` syntax error because `'3'` is a type `Char` literal.

EXAMPLE 4.1 ▼

An individual's tax rate depends on his or her salary. Single persons who earn less than $18,550 are taxed at a rate of 15%, and those who earn between $18,550 and $44,900 pay 15% of the first $18,550 earned and 28% of the rest. If taxable income is stored in the type `Real` variable `Income`, the Boolean expression corresponding to the question "Is annual income less than $18,550?" is

```
Income < 18550.00
```

This expression evaluates to `True` when the answer is yes, and to `False` when the answer is no.   ▲

EXAMPLE 4.2 ▼

Table 4.1 lists the relational operators and some sample conditions. Each condition is evaluated assuming the variables have the following values:

X   Power   MaxPow   Y   Item   MinItem   MomOrDad   Num   Sentinel
-5   1024   1024   7   1.5   -999.0   M   999   999   ▲

<table>
<tr><td colspan="4">**Table 4.1**
Pascal Relational
Operators and
Sample Conditions</td></tr>
</table>

Operator	Condition	Meaning	Boolean Value
<=	X <= 0	X less than or equal to 0	True
<	Power < MaxPow	Power less than MaxPow	False
>=	X >= Y	X greater than or equal to Y	False
>	Item > MinItem	Item greater than MinItem	True
=	MomOrDad = 'M'	MomOrDad equal to 'M'	True
<>	Num <> Sentinel	Num not equal to Sentinel	False

Boolean Operators

We can form more complicated Boolean expressions by using the three Boolean operators—and, or, not—which require type Boolean operands. Two examples of Boolean expressions formed with these operators are

```
(Salary < MinimumSalary) or (Dependents > 5)
(Temperature > 90.0) and (Humidity > 0.90)
```

The first Boolean expression determines whether an employee is eligible for special scholarship funds. It evaluates to True if *either* condition in parentheses is true. The second Boolean expression describes an unbearable summer day, with temperature and humidity both in the nineties. The expression evaluates to True only when *both* conditions are true.

Boolean variables are Boolean expressions, so they also can be operands of Boolean operators. The Boolean expression

```
WinningRecord and (not Probation)
```

manipulates two Boolean variables (WinningRecord, Probation). A college team for which this expression is true has a winning record and is not on probation so it may be eligible for the postseason tournament. Note that although the expression

```
(WinningRecord = True) and (Probation = False)
```

is logically equivalent to the prior one, the prior one is preferred because it is more concise and more readable.

Table 4.2 shows that the and operator yields a true result only when both its operands are true. Table 4.3 shows that the or operator yields a false result only when both its operands are false. The not operator has a single

Table 4.2
The and Operator

operand1	operand 2	operand1 and operand 2
true	true	true
true	false	false
false	true	false
false	false	false

Table 4.3
The or Operator

operand1	operand2	operand1 or operand2
true	true	true
true	false	true
false	true	true
false	false	false

logical complement (negation)
the logical complement of True is False and vice versa.

operand; Table 4.4 shows that the not operator yields the logical **complement,** or **negation,** of its operand (that is, if Switch is True, not Switch is False and vice versa).

Table 4.4
The not Operator

operand1	not **operand1**
true	false
false	true

An operator's precedence determines its order of evaluation. Table 4.5 shows the precedence of all Pascal operators, including the relational operators. The not operator has the highest precedence, followed by the multiplicative operators (including and), the additive operators (including or), and last, the relational operators.

Table 4.5
Operator Precedence

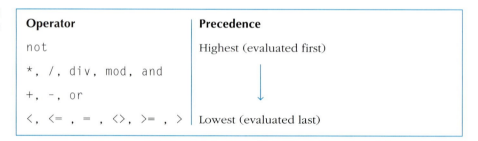

Operator	Precedence
not	Highest (evaluated first)
*, /, div, mod, and	
+, -, or	
<, <= , = , <>, >= , >	Lowest (evaluated last)

Because relational operators have the lowest precedence, you may need to place parentheses in expressions using them to prevent syntax errors. To illustrate, the Pascal compiler interprets the expression

X < Min + Max

correctly as

X < (Min + Max)

because + has higher precedence than <. However, the expression

Min <= X and X <= Max   {incorrect Boolean expression}

causes the syntax error type mismatch because the Pascal compiler interprets it as

Min <= (X and X) <= Max   {incorrect Boolean expression}

since and has higher precedence than <=. This is an error because the type Real variable X cannot be an operand of the Boolean operator and. Adding parentheses avoids a syntax error:

(Min <= X) and (X <= Max)

EXAMPLE 4.3 ▼

Expressions 1 to 4 contain different operands and operators. Each expression's value in the comment assumes X, Y, and Z are type Real, Flag is type Boolean, and the variables have the values:

X	Y	Z	Flag
3.0	4.0	2.0	False

```
1.  not Flag                            {not False is True}
2.  (X + Y / Z) <= 3.5                  {5.0 <= 3.5 is False}
3.  (not Flag) or ((Y + Z) >= (X - Z))  {True or True is True}
4.  not (Flag or ((Y + Z) >= (X - Z)))  {not (False or True) is
                                         False}
```

Figure 4.2 shows the evaluation tree for expression 3.   ▲

Writing English Conditions in Pascal

To solve programming problems, we must convert conditions expressed in English to Pascal. Many algorithm steps test whether a variable's value is within a specified range of values. For example, if Min represents the lower bound of a range of values and Max represents the upper bound (Min is less than Max), the expression

```
(Min <= X) and (X <= Max)
```

Figure 4.2
Evaluation Tree
for (not Flag)
or ((Y + Z) >= (X – Z))

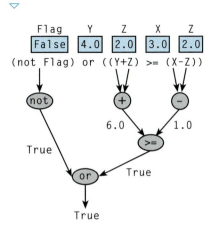

Figure 4.3
Range of True Values for
(Min <= X) and (X <= Max)

tests whether X lies within the range Min through Max, inclusive. In Fig. 4.3 this range is shaded. The expression is true if X lies within this range and false if X is outside the range.

EXAMPLE 4.4 ▼

Pascal expressions 1 to 5 implement an English condition shown in the comment on the right. The comments also show the evaluation of each expression assuming X is 3.0, Y is 4.0, and Z is 2.0.

```
1.  (Z > X) or (Z > Y)          {Z is greater than X or Y -
                                 False or False is False}
2.  (X = 1.0) or (X = 3.0)      {X equals 1.0 or 3.0 -
                                 False or True is True}
3.  (X > Z) and (Y > Z)         {X and Y are greater than Z -
                                 True and True is True}
4.  (Z <= X) and (X <= Y)       {X is in the range from Z to
                                 Y - True and True is True}
5.  (X < Z) or (X > Y)          {X is outside the range Z to
                                 Y - False or False is False}
```

Expression 1 is the Pascal code for the English condition "Z greater than X or Y". You may be tempted to write this condition as

```
Z > X or Y
```

but this expression is invalid because the type Real variables X and Y cannot be operands of the Boolean operator or.

Expression 4 is the Pascal code for the relationship Z <= X <= Y. The boundary values, 2.0 and 4.0, are included in the range of X values that yield a result of True.

Expression 5 is true if X lies outside the range bounded by Z and Y. In Fig. 4.4 the shaded areas represent the values of X that yield a True result. Both Y and Z are excluded from the set of values that yield a True result.   ▲

Boolean Assignment

You can write statements to assign a Boolean value to a Boolean variable. If Same is type Boolean, the statement

Figure 4.4
Range of True Values for
(X < Z) or (X > Y)

```
Same := True
```

assigns the value `True` to `Same`. Since assignment statements have the general form

variable := *expression*

you can use the statement

```
Same := (X = Y)
```

to assign the value of the Boolean expression (X = Y) to `Same`. The value of `Same` is `True` when X and Y are equal; otherwise, `Same` is `False`.

EXAMPLE 4.5 ▼

The following assignment statements assign values to two Boolean variables, `InRange` and `IsLetter`. `InRange` gets `True` if the value of N is in the range -10 through 10; `IsLetter` gets `True` if Ch is an uppercase or a lowercase letter.

```
InRange := (N > -10) and (N < 10);
IsLetter := (('A' <= Ch) and (Ch <= 'Z')) or
            (('a' <= Ch) and (Ch <= 'z'))
```

The expression in the first assignment statement is `True` if N satisfies both the conditions listed (N is greater than -10 and N is less than 10); otherwise, the expression is `False`. The expression in the second assignment statement uses the Boolean operators `and`, `or`. The subexpression on the first line is `True` if Ch is an uppercase letter; the subexpression on the second line is `True` if Ch is a lowercase letter. Consequently, `IsLetter` gets `True` if Ch is a letter; otherwise, `IsLetter` gets `False`. ▲

EXAMPLE 4.6 ▼

The next statement assigns the value `True` to `IsEven` (type `Boolean`) if 2 is a divisor of N (type `Integer`):

```
IsEven := (N mod 2 = 0)
```

Because all even numbers are divisible by 2, the value assigned to `IsEven` indicates whether N is even (`IsEven` is `True`) or odd (`IsEven` is `False`). ▲

Writing Boolean Values

Most Boolean expressions appear in control structures, where they determine the sequence in which Pascal statements execute. Because programs do not process Boolean data in the same way that they process numerical data, your programs will rarely read Boolean values as input data or display Boolean values as program results. If necessary, you can display the value of a Boolean variable with procedure Write or WriteLn, but you cannot use procedure ReadLn to read in a Boolean variable. If Switch is False, the statement

```
WriteLn ('Value of Switch is ', Switch)
```

displays the line

```
Value of Switch is FALSE
```

Exercises for Section 4.2 *Self-Check*

1. Which of the following Boolean expressions is incorrect and why? Assume X and Y are Real and P, Q, and R are Boolean.
   a. X < 5.1 and Y > 22.3   b. P and Q or Q and R
2. Draw evaluation trees for the following expressions:
   a. A = (B + A - B)
   b. (C = (A + B)) or not Flag
   c. (A <> 7) and (C >= 6) or Flag
   d. not (B <= 12) and (A mod 2 = 0)
   e. not ((A > 5) or (C < (A + B)))
3. Evaluate each expression in Exercise 2 if A is 5, B is 10, C is 15, and Flag is True.

Programming

1. Write a Boolean expression for each of the following relationships.
   a. Age is from 18 to 21 inclusive.
   b. Water is less than 1.5 and is greater than 0.1.
   c. Year is divisible by 4. (*Hint:* Use mod.)
   d. Speed is not greater than 55.
2. Write Boolean assignment statements for the following.
   a. Assign a value of True to Between if N is in the range -K to +K, inclusive; otherwise, assign a value of False.
   b. Assign a value of True to Uppercase if Ch is an uppercase letter; otherwise, assign a value of False.
   c. Assign a value of True to Divisor if M is a divisor of N; otherwise, assign a value of False.

4.3 The if Statement

In Pascal, the primary selection control structure consists of an if statement, which always contains a Boolean expression. The if statements determine which of several alternative code fragments executes in a particular situation. The if statements in this section select among one or two alternatives.

if Statement with Two Alternatives

The if statement

```
if Gross > 100.00 then
  Net := Gross - Tax
else
  Net := Gross
```

selects one of the two assignment statements. It either selects the statement following then if the Boolean expression is true (i.e., Gross is greater than 100.00), or it selects the statement following else if the Boolean expression is false (i.e., Gross is not greater than 100.00).

flowchart
a diagram that shows the step-by-step execution of a control structure or a program fragment

Figure 4.5(a) is a flowchart of the preceding if statement. In a **flowchart,** boxes and arrows diagram the step-by-step execution of a control structure or program fragment. A diamond-shaped box in a flowchart represents a decision, for which there is always one path in and two paths out (labeled True and False). A rectangular box represents an assignment statement or a process.

Figure 4.5(a) shows that the condition (Gross > 100.00) is evaluated first. If the condition is true, program control follows the arrow labeled True and the assignment statement in the right rectangle is executed. If the condition is false, program control follows the arrow labeled False and the assignment statement in the left rectangle is executed.

Figure 4.5
Flowcharts of if Statements with (a) Two Alternatives and (b) One Alternative

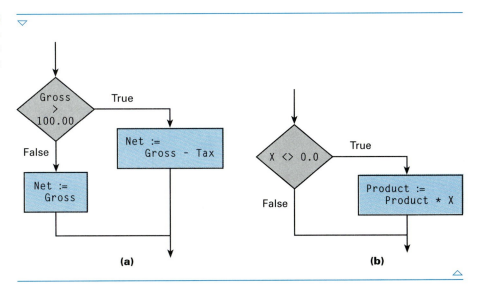

if Statement with One Alternative

The if statement in the last section has two alternatives but executes only one for a given value of Gross. You also can write if statements with a single alternative that executes only when the condition is true.

The if statement diagrammed in Fig. 4.5(b),

```
{Multiply Product by a non zero X only}
if X <> 0.0 then
  Product := Product * X
```

has one alternative, which is executed only when X is not equal to 0. It causes Product to be multiplied by X and the new value to be saved in Product, replacing the old value. If X is equal to 0, the multiplication is not performed.

A Comparison of One- and Two-Alternative if Statements

To differentiate between one- and two-alternative if statements, programmers often refer to an if statement with two alternatives as an if-then-else and an if statement with one alternative as an if-then.

EXAMPLE 4.7 ▼

The if statement

```
if MomOrDad = 'M' then
  WriteLn ('Hi Mom')
else
  WriteLn ('Hi Dad')
```

has two alternatives. It displays either 'Hi Mom' or 'Hi Dad', depending on the character stored in the variable MomOrDad (type Char).   ▲

EXAMPLE 4.8 ▼

The following if statement has one alternative: It displays the message 'Hi Mom' only when MomOrDad has the value 'M'. Whether 'Hi Mom' is displayed or not, the message 'Hi Dad' is always displayed. The semicolon terminates the if statement and is needed to separate the if statement from the second WriteLn.

```
if MomOrDad = 'M' then
  WriteLn ('Hi Mom');
WriteLn ('Hi Dad')
```

The next if statement is incorrect because there is a semicolon before the word else. The compiler will detect a syntax error when it reaches the else, because the semicolon terminates the if statement and a new statement cannot begin with else.

```
if MomOrDad = 'M' then
  WriteLn ('Hi Mom');
else                    {error - new statement begins with else}
  WriteLn ('Hi Dad')  ▲
```

SYNTAX DISPLAY

if Statement (One Alternative)

Form: if *condition* then
             statement$_T$

Example: if X > 0.0 then
             PosProd := PosProd * X

Interpretation: If *condition* evaluates to True, then *statement*$_T$ (the true task) is executed; otherwise, *statement*$_T$ is skipped.

SYNTAX DISPLAY

if Statement (Two Alternatives)

Form: if *condition* then
             statement$_T$
             else
             statement$_F$

Example: if X >= 0.0 then
             Write ('Positive')
             else
             Write ('Negative')

Interpretation: If *condition* evaluates to True, then *statement*$_T$ (the true task) is executed and *statement*$_F$ is skipped; otherwise, *statement*$_T$ is skipped and *statement*$_F$ (the false task) is executed.

Program Style

Format of the if Statement

All if statement examples in this text indent *statement*$_T$ and *statement*$_F$. The word else is typed on a separate line, aligned with the word if. The format of the if statement makes its meaning apparent and is used solely to improve program readability; the format makes no difference to the compiler.

Exercises for Section 4.3   **Self-Check**

1. What do these statements display?
   a. if 12 < 12 then
          WriteLn ('Less')
      else
          WriteLn ('Not less')
   b. Var1 := 25.12;
      Var2 := 15.00;
      if Var1 <= Var2 then
          WriteLn ('Less or equal')
      else
          WriteLn ('Greater than')

2. What value is assigned to X when Y is 15.0?
   a. ```
      X := 25.0;
      if Y <> (X - 10.0) then
         X := X - 10.0
      else
         X := X / 2.0
      ```
   b. ```
      if (Y < 15.0) and (Y >= 0.0) then
         X := 5 * Y
      else
         X := 2 * Y
      ```

Programming

1. Write Pascal statements to carry out the following steps.
   a. If Item is nonzero, then multiply Product by Item and save the result in Product; otherwise, skip the multiplication. In either case, print the value of Product.
   b. Store the absolute difference of X and Y in Y, where the absolute difference is (X - Y) or (Y - X), whichever is positive. Do not use the Abs function in your solution.
   c. If X is 0, add 1 to ZeroCount. If X is negative, add X to MinusSum. If X is greater than 0, add X to PlusSum.

4.4 Syntax Diagrams

syntax diagram

a graphical representation of the syntax of a Pascal construct

In addition to syntax displays, we can use **syntax diagrams** to describe Pascal constructs. Syntax diagrams are sometimes called railroad diagrams because they resemble track layout diagrams for a model railroad.

To learn how to read syntax diagrams, study the syntax diagram for *program* (Fig. 4.6). The diagram consists of a group of syntactic elements connected by arrows, with the category of each syntactic element indicated by its shape:

▶ Reserved words appear in gray ovals.
▶ Special symbols (punctuation marks and operators) appear in gray circles.
▶ Syntactic elements with their own syntax diagrams appear in colored rectangles.

Figure 4.6
Syntax Diagram for
program

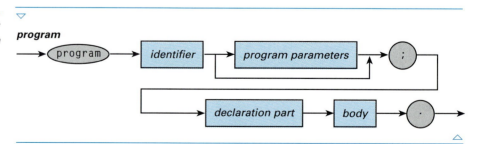

Trace through the syntax diagram in Fig. 4.6 following the arrows, starting at the leftmost arrow (into `program`) and exiting at the rightmost arrow (out of the symbol .). From the top row, notice that a Pascal program begins with the reserved word `program` followed by an *identifier*. The arrow from *identifier* splits in two: One path goes through *program parameters* to the symbol ; and one path bypasses *program parameters*, meaning that the syntactic element *program parameters* is optional. The program header

```
program First;
```

satisfies this part of the syntax diagram because `First` is an *identifier*. The rest of the syntax diagram for *program* indicates that the symbol ; should be followed by the syntactic elements *declaration part, body,* and the . symbol.

The syntax diagram for *identifier* (Fig. 4.7) shows that an identifier may be a single letter (A–Z, a–z). We determine this by tracing the horizontal arrow at the top of the diagram from left to right. By tracing through the loops in the diagram, we see that the initial letter may be followed by one or more letters, digits (0–9), or underscore symbols (for example, `R2D2`, `First`). This corresponds to our earlier definition of *identifier* (see Section 2.3).

The syntax diagrams for the syntactic elements *declaration part* and *body* complete the description of the syntactic element *program*. The diagram for *declaration part* is in Appendix C, along with the other syntactic elements of Pascal. The syntax diagram for *body* (Fig. 4.8) shows that a program *body* is a *compound statement,* or a sequence of one or more *statement* elements separated by semicolons and bracketed by `begin` and `end`.

Figure 4.9 shows the syntax diagram for an `if` statement. The arrow out of the *statement* element on the top row splits in two, with the arrow pointing to the right defining an `if` statement with one alternative (`if-then`). The arrow pointing down and to the left passes through the reserved word `else`, defining an `if` statement with two alternatives (`if-then-else`). The statement following the word `then` or `else` may be a single executable statement or a compound statement. Examples of such statements include assignment statements, procedure call statements, and other `if` statements.

Figure 4.7
Syntax Diagram for
identifier

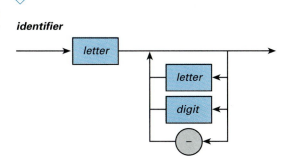

Figure 4.8
Syntax Diagrams for *body*
and *compound statement*

body

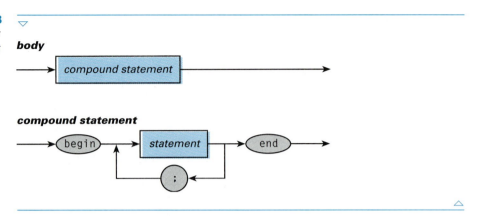

By comparing a program statement to its corresponding syntax diagram, you can verify that the statement is correct. If a syntax error occurs during debugging, you can refer to the appropriate syntax diagram to determine the correct form of the element that caused the problem. Appendix C contains all Pascal syntax diagrams.

Exercises for Section 4.4   **Self-Check**

1. Which of these identifiers satisfy the syntax diagram that follows?

    Ace   R2D2   R245   A23B   A1c   B34d5c   A23cd

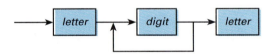

2. Draw a syntax diagram to describe `Real`-like numeric literals that begin with a digit, end with a digit, and contain a single decimal point somewhere in between.

Figure 4.9
Syntax Diagram for an if
Statement

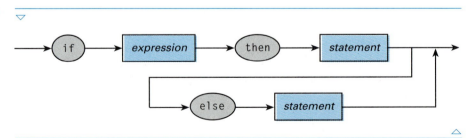

3. Modify the syntax diagram for *identifier* to show that an identifier may start with the underscore symbol or a letter.

4.5   if Statements with Compound Statements

Some if statements have compound statements following then or else. When the reserved word begin follows then or else, the Pascal compiler translates the statements between the begin and the end as a compound statement.

EXAMPLE 4.9 ▼

In many programming problems, you must order a pair of data values in memory so that the smaller value is stored in one variable (say, X) and the larger value in another (say, Y). The if statement in Fig. 4.10 rearranges any two values stored in X and Y so that the smaller number is in X and the larger number is in Y. If the two numbers are already in the proper order, the compound statement is not executed. Variables X, Y, and Temp should all be the same data type. Although the values of X and Y are being switched, an additional variable, Temp, is needed to store a copy of one of these values.

Table 4.6 simulates the execution of this if statement when X is 12.5 and Y is 5.0. The table shows that Temp is initially undefined (indicated by ?). Each line shows the part of the if statement that is being executed, followed by its effect. If any variable gets a new value, its new value is shown on that line. If no new value is shown, the variable retains its previous value. The last value stored in X is 5.0, and the last value stored in Y is 12.5.   ▲

Table 4.6
Step-by-Step Simulation of
if Statement

Statement Part	X	Y	Temp	Effect
	12.5	5.0	?	
if X > Y then				12.5 > 5.0 is true
Temp := X;			12.5	Stores old X in Temp
X := Y;	5.0			Stores old Y in X
Y := Temp		12.5		Stores old X in Y

Figure 4.10
if Statement to Order
X and Y

```
if X > Y then
   begin {switch X and Y}
      Temp := X;              {Stores old X in Temp}
      X := Y;                 {Stores old Y in X}
      Y := Temp              {Stores old X in Y}
   end {if}
```

EXAMPLE 4.10 ▼

As manager of a clothing boutique, you keep records of your checking transactions. When `TransType` is `'C'` in the next `if` statement, the compound statement following `then` processes a transaction (`TransAmount`) that represents a check you wrote to pay for goods received; otherwise, the compound statement following `else` processes a deposit made into your checking account. Both compound statements display an appropriate message and update the account balance (`Balance`).

```
if TransType = 'C' then
  begin {check}
    Write ('Check for $', TransAmount :4:2);
    Balance := Balance - TransAmount        {Deduct check.}
  end {check}
else
  begin  {deposit}
    Write ('Deposit of $', TransAmount :4:2);
    Balance := Balance + TransAmount        {Add deposit.}
  end {deposit and if}
```

The semicolons in the `if` statement separate the individual statements in each alternative. A common error would be to insert a semicolon after the first `end` (`end; {check}`), causing the `if` to separate into two statements. Because the second statement can't begin with `else`, the compiler would display an `unexpected symbol` error message. ▲

Program Style

Writing if Statements with Compound True or False Statements

Each `if` statement in this section contains at least one compound statement bracketed by `begin` and `end`. To improve our ability to read and understand the `if` statement, each compound statement is indented; indentation is ignored by the Pascal compiler.

The comment after each `end` helps to associate the `end` with its corresponding `begin`. The comments are not required but are included to improve program readability.

Semicolons are required between the individual statements within a compound statement, but they should not appear before or after the reserved words `then`, `else`, or `begin`. A semicolon may appear after an `end` that terminates the entire `if` statement.

Exercises for Section 4.5   ***Self-Check***

1. Insert semicolons where needed to avoid syntax errors and indent to improve readability:

```
{incorrect if statement}
if X > Y then
begin
X := X + 10.0
WriteLn ('X Bigger')
end
else
WriteLn ('X Smaller')
WriteLn ('Y is ', Y)
```

2. Explain why the program will not compile if you remove the bracketing `begin` and `end`.
3. What is the effect of placing a bracketing `begin` and `end` around the last two lines in Exercise 1?
4. Find the syntax error and logic error in the `if` statement:

```
if Num1 < 0 then
   begin
      Product := Num1 * Num2 * Num3;
      WriteLn ('Product is ', Product :1)
   end;
else
   Sum := Num1 + Num2 + Num3;
   WriteLn ('Sum is ', Sum :1)
```

5. What syntax diagrams would you use to validate the following `if` statement? Provide the label of every syntax diagram that describes an element of this statement.

```
if X > 0 then
   begin
      X := 25.0;
      WriteLn ('Positive')
   end
```

Programming

1. Write an `if` statement that, given two real values X and Y, will negate the two values if both are negative or both are positive.
2. Write an interactive program that computes the area of a rectangle (*area = base × height*) or a triangle (*area = 1/2 × base × height*) after prompting the user to type the first character of the figure name (R or T).

4.6 Decision Steps in Algorithms

decision step

an algorithm step that selects one of several actions

Algorithm steps that select from a choice of actions are called **decision steps.** The algorithm in the following payroll problem contains decision steps that are coded as Pascal `if` statements to compute an employee's gross pay and net pay.

CASE STUDY   **Payroll Problem**

PROBLEM ▼

Your company pays its employees time and a half for all hours worked over 40 hours a week. Employees who earn more than $100.00 a week pay union dues of $25 per week. Write a program to compute an employee's gross pay and net pay.

ANALYSIS ▼

You first must read the hours worked and the hourly rate for an employee (the problem inputs). After reading these data, compute gross pay. Employees who work 40 hours or less are to be paid the same rate for all hours worked. Those who work more than 40 hours are to be paid one rate for the first 40 hours and 1.5 times that rate for the overtime hours. Compute net pay by subtracting any union dues from gross pay.

Data Requirements

Problem Constants

```
MaxNoOvertime = 40.0        {maximum hours without overtime pay}
BonusRate = 1.5             {time and a half for overtime}
MaxNoDues = 100.00          {maximum salary without union dues}
Dues = 25.00               {union dues}
```

Problem Inputs

```
Hours : Real               {hours worked}
Rate : Real                {hourly rate}
```

Problem Outputs

```
Gross : Real               {gross pay}
Net : Real                 {net pay}
```

Relevant Formulas

gross pay = hours worked × hourly rate
gross pay = 40 × hourly rate + 1.5 × overtime hours × hourly rate
net pay = gross pay − union dues

Two formulas are listed for gross pay: the first for the employee who receives no overtime pay, the second for the employee eligible for overtime pay.

DESIGN ▼

The structure chart (Fig. 4.11) for this problem contains data flow information showing the inputs and outputs of each algorithm step. The structure chart shows that step 2, *Enter data,* provides values for Hours and Rate as

Figure 4.11
Structure Chart
for Payroll Problem

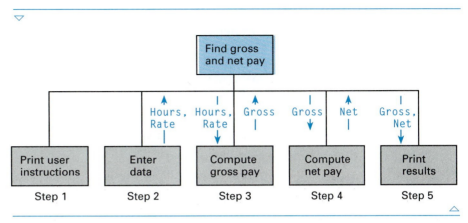

Figure 4.11
Structure Chart
for Payroll Problem

its outputs (data flow arrow points up). Similarly, the step *Compute gross pay* uses `Hours` and `Rate` as its inputs (data flow arrow points down) and provides `Gross` as its output.

Initial Algorithm

1. Display user instructions.
2. Enter hours worked and hourly rate.
3. Compute gross pay.
4. Compute net pay.
5. Display gross and net pay.

Algorithm Refinements

Refine algorithm steps 3 and 4 as decision steps.

Step 3 Refinement

3.1 `if` no overtime `then`
      3.2 Compute gross pay without overtime pay.
  `else`
      3.3 Compute gross pay with overtime pay.

Step 4 Refinement

4.1 `if` no union dues `then`
      4.2 `Net` gets `Gross`
  `else`
      4.3 `Net` gets `Gross` `-` `Dues`

pseudocode
a combination of English
phrases and Pascal constructs
to describe algorithm steps

These decision steps are expressed in **pseudocode,** which is a mixture of English and Pascal used to describe algorithm steps. The pseudocode uses indentation and the reserved words `if`, `then`, and `else` to show the logical structure of each step. Each decision step has a condition (following if) that can be written in English or Pascal, as can the sequentially numbered True and False tasks.

IMPLEMENTATION ▼

The program (Fig. 4.12) begins by calling procedure InstructPay to display the user instructions (the first ten lines of program output). After the input data are read, the if statement

```
{Compute gross pay.}
if Hours <= MaxNoOvertime then
  Gross := Hours * Rate                        {no overtime pay}
else
  Gross := MaxNoOvertime * Rate +
           BonusRate * (Hours - MaxNoOvertime) * Rate;
                                                    {overtime}
```

implements step 3. The first comment on the right is embedded in the if statement. The semicolon in the next-to-last line separates the if statement from the next if statement.

TESTING ▼

To test this program, run it with several data sets that yield all possible combinations of values for the two if statement conditions (True/True, True/False, False/True, False/False). As an example, to get the condition values True/True, hours worked should be less than 40 and gross pay should be less than $100.00. Also test the program with a data set for which hours worked is exactly 40 and one for which gross pay is exactly $100.00.

Figure 4.12
Program for
Payroll Problem

▽

Edit Window

```
program Payroll;
{
 Computes and prints gross pay and net pay given an hourly
 rate and number of hours worked. Overtime pay is included in
 the gross pay computation. The employee's net pay includes
 a possible deduction for union dues.
}
```

▷ ▷ ▷ ▷ ▷ ▷

```
const
   MaxNoOvertime = 40;      {maximum hours without overtime pay}
   BonusRate = 1.5;         {time and a half for overtime}
   MaxNoDues = 100.00;      {maximum salary without union dues}
   Dues = 25.00;            {union dues}

var
   Hours, Rate,             {inputs - hours worked, hourly rate}
   Gross, Net : Real;       {outputs - gross pay, net pay}

procedure InstructPay;
{Displays user instructions}

begin {InstructPay}
   WriteLn ('This program computes gross and net pay.');
   WriteLn ('Employees who work more than ', MaxNoOvertime :1);
   WriteLn ('hours receive overtime pay for the excess hours.');
   WriteLn ('Union dues of $', Dues :4:2, ' are deducted');
   WriteLn ('for an employee who earns more than $', MaxNoDues :4:2);
   WriteLn;
   WriteLn ('Enter hours worked and hourly rate');
   WriteLn ('on separate lines after the prompts.');
   WriteLn ('Press Enter after typing each number.');
   WriteLn
end; {InstructPay}

begin {Payroll}
   InstructPay;             {Display user instructions.}

   {Enter Hours and Rate.}
   Write ('Hours worked> ');
   ReadLn (Hours);
   Write ('Hourly rate> ');
   ReadLn (Rate);

   {Compute gross pay.}
   if Hours <= MaxNoOvertime then
      Gross := Hours * Rate                                          {no overtime pay}
   else
      Gross := MaxNoOvertime * Rate +
            BonusRate * (Hours - MaxNoOvertime) * Rate;             {overtime}

   {Compute net pay.}
   if Gross <= MaxNoDues then
      Net := Gross           {Deduct no dues.}
   else
      Net := Gross - Dues;   {Deduct union dues.}

   {Print Gross and Net.}
   WriteLn ('Gross pay is $', Gross :4:2);
   WriteLn ('Net pay is $', Net :4:2)
end.    {Payroll}
```

Output   Window

```
This program computes gross and net pay.
```

▷ ▷ ▷ ▷ ▷ ▷

```
Employees who work more than 40
hours receive overtime pay for the excess hours.
Union dues of $25.00 are deducted
for an employee who earns more than $100.00

Enter hours worked and hourly rate
on separate lines after the prompts.
Press Enter after typing each number.

Hours worked> 40.0
Hourly rate> 5.0
Gross pay is $200.00
Net pay is $175.00
```

Program Style

Using Constants to Enhance Readability and Maintenance

The constants MaxNoOvertime and BonusRate appear in the if statement in Fig. 4.12. We could just as easily have placed the literals 40 and 1.5 directly in the if statement:

```
{Compute gross pay.}
if Hours <= 40 then
  Gross := Hours * Rate                {no overtime pay}
else
  Gross := 40 * Rate +
          1.5 * (Hours - 40) * Rate;   {overtime pay}
```

However, using constants rather than literals has two advantages. First, the original if statement is easier to understand because it includes the descriptive names MaxNoOvertime and BonusRate rather than numbers, which have no intrinsic meaning. Second, a program written with constants is much easier to maintain than one written with literals. For example, to change the bonus for overtime to double pay instead of time and a half, you need to change only the constant declaration for BonusRate to 2.0. However, if you had inserted the literal 1.5 directly in the if statement, you would have to change the if statement and any other statements that manipulate that literal.

Note that the constants also appear in WriteLn statements in procedure InstructPay. It is perfectly permissible to reference program constants in a procedure body.

Using Data Flow Information in Structure Charts

In Fig. 4.11, the data flow information in the structure chart showed the inputs and outputs of each individual algorithm step. Data flow information is an important part of system documentation because it shows which program variables are processed by each step and the manner in which those variables are processed. If a step gives a new value to a variable, then that variable is considered an *output of the step*. If a step displays a variable's value or uses a variable in a computation without changing its value, the variable is considered an *input to the step.* For example, the step *Compute net pay* processes variables Gross and Net, using the value of Gross (its *input*) to compute Net (its *output*).

Figure 4.11 shows that a variable may have different roles for different subproblems in the algorithm. For example, in the context of the original problem statement, Hours and Rate are problem *inputs* (data supplied by the program user). In the context of the subproblem *Enter data,* however, where the task is to deliver values for Hours and Rate to the main program, they are considered *outputs.* In the context of the subproblem *Compute gross pay,* where the subproblem's task is to use Hours and Rate to compute Gross, they are *inputs* to this step. In the same way, the role of the variables Gross and Net changes as we go from step to step in the problem.

Solution by Analogy

solution by analogy

solving a new problem by adapting the solution to a similar problem

Sometimes a new problem is simply an old one presented in a new guise. Each time you face a problem, determine whether you have solved a similar one in the past and, if so, adapt the earlier solution. This problem-solving strategy—**solution by analogy**—requires a careful reading of the problem statement to recognize requirements that may be similar to those of earlier problems.

CASE STUDY

Computing Insurance Dividends

PROBLEM ▼

An insurance company sends annual dividend checks to its policyholders. The basic dividend rate is a fixed percentage (4.5%—0.045 in Pascal) of the policyholder's paid premium. If the policyholder has made no claims, the dividend rate for that policy is increased by a bonus rate (0.5%—0.005 in Pascal). Write a program to compute dividends.

ANALYSIS ▼

This problem is similar to the payroll problem. Just as there was a bonus pay rate for workers with overtime hours, there is a bonus dividend for policyholders with no claims. Begin by reading in the input data (the number of claims and the premium), then use a decision step to select either the basic dividend computation or the computation with a bonus dividend.

Data Requirements

Problem Constants

```
BasicRate = 0.045          {the basic dividend rate of 4.5%}
BonusRate = 0.005          {the bonus dividend rate of 0.5%}
```

Problem Inputs

```
Premium : Real              {premium amount}
NumClaims : Integer         {number of claims}
```

Problem Output

```
Dividend : Real             {dividend amount}
```

DESIGN ▼

The initial algorithm follows.

Initial Algorithm

1. Display user instructions.
2. Enter premium amount and number of claims.
3. Compute dividend including any bonus dividend.
4. Display dividend.

Algorithm Refinements

The refinement of step 3 is similar to the refinement of step 3 in the payroll problem.

Step 3 Refinement

3.1 if no claims then
    3.2 Compute dividend including a bonus dividend.
  else
    3.3 Compute dividend as the basic dividend.

IMPLEMENTATION AND TESTING ▼

We leave the program coding as a programming exercise. The if statement

```
{Compute dividend including any bonus dividend.}
if NumClaims = 0 then
  Dividend := Premium * BasicRate +      {basic dividend}
              Premium * BonusRate;       {bonus dividend}
else
  Dividend := Premium * BasicRate        {basic dividend}
```

implements algorithm step 3.

....

Exercises for Section 4.6

Self-Check

1. Change the refinement of step 4 of the payroll problem so that it uses a decision step with one alternative. *Hint:* Assign Gross to Net before the decision step, and use the decision step to change Net when necessary.
2. Predict the payroll program output when

a. Hours is 30.0, Rate is 5.00.
b. Hours is 20.0, Rate is 4.00.
c. Hours is 50.0, Rate is 2.00.
d. Hours is 50.0, Rate is 6.00.

3. Revise the pizza problem from Section 3.1 so that the user can compute the unit price of either a circular or a square pizza. Give the algorithm with refinements. Draw a structure chart with data flow information for the new pizza problem showing the relationship between the main program and its subproblems. Discuss how the role of the variable that represents pizza area (a problem output) changes for each subproblem.

Programming

1. Modify the program for the payroll problem to deduct union dues of 10% for gross salary over $100.00 and 5% otherwise. Also, deduct a 3% city wage tax for all employees.
2. Provide the structure chart and complete program for computing insurance company dividends.

4.7 Hand-Tracing an Algorithm

A critical step in algorithm design is to verify the algorithm's accuracy before you spend extensive time coding it. These few extra minutes often save hours of coding and testing time.

hand trace (desk check)
step-by-step simulation of an algorithm's execution

A **hand trace,** or **desk check,** is a careful, step-by-step simulation on paper of how a computer would execute an algorithm. The results should show the effect of each step's execution using data that are relatively easy to process by hand. In Section 4.5, we simulated the execution of an if statement that switches the values of two variables. Now we will trace the execution of the refined algorithm for the payroll problem solved in Section 4.6.

Refined Algorithm

1. Display user instructions.
2. Enter hours worked and hourly rate.
3. Compute gross pay.
    3.1 if no overtime then
        3.2 Compute gross pay without overtime pay.
     else
        3.3 Compute gross pay with overtime pay.
4. Compute net pay.
    4.1 if no union dues then
        4.2 Net gets Gross
     else
        4.3 Net gets Gross - Dues
5. Display gross and net pay.

Table 4.7 is a hand trace of steps 2 through 5 of the algorithm. Each step is listed at the left in the order of its execution, and the effect of each step is given in the last column. If a step changes the value of a variable, then the table shows the new value. If no new value is shown, the variable retains its previous value. For example, the table shows that the step

2. Enter hours worked and hourly rate.

stores the data values 30.0 and 10.00 in the variables Hours and Rate, respectively; Gross and Net are still undefined (indicated by ? in the first table row).

Table 4.7
Trace of Algorithm for Payroll Problem

Algorithm Step	Hours	Rate	Gross	Net	Effect
	?	?	?	?	
2. Enter hours and rate	30.0	10.00			Reads the data
3.1 if no overtime then					Hours <= 40 is true
3.2 Gross gets Hours * Rate			300.0		Compute gross with no overtime
4.1 if no union dues then					Gross <= 100.00 is false
4.3 Net gets Gross - Dues				275.0	Deduct union dues
5. Display Gross and Net					Displays 300.00 and 275.00

The trace in Table 4.7 shows that 300.0 and 275.0 are stored in Gross and Net, respectively, and displayed. To verify that the algorithm is correct, you must select other data that cause the two conditions to evaluate to different combinations of their values. Since there are two conditions and each has two possible values (True or False), there are two times two, or four, different combinations that should be tried. (What are they?) An exhaustive hand trace of the algorithm would show that it works for all combinations.

Besides the four cases already discussed, you should verify that the algorithm works correctly for unusual data. For example, what would happen if Hours were 40.0 (value of MaxNoOvertime) or if Gross were 100.0 (value of MaxNoDues)? Would the algorithm still provide the correct result? To complete the hand trace, you should show that the algorithm handles these special situations properly.

Take care when tracing each case, making sure to execute the algorithm exactly as the computer would. Often programmers assume how a particular step will be executed and don't explicitly test each condition and trace each step. A trace performed in this way is of little value.

Exercises for Section 4.7

Self-Check

1. Provide sample data that cause the first condition in the payroll problem to be false and the second to be true, and trace the execution for these data.
2. If Hours = MaxHours and Gross = MaxNoDues, which assignment steps in the algorithm would be performed? Provide a trace.

4.8 Nested if Statements and Multiple-Alternative Decisions

nested if statement

an if statement with another if statement as its true task or its false task

Until now we have used if statements to code decisions with one or two alternatives. In this section, we will use **nested if statements** (one if statement inside another) to code decisions with multiple alternatives.

EXAMPLE 4.11 ▼

The following nested if statement has three alternatives. It increases one of three variables (NumPos, NumNeg, or NumZero) by 1, depending on whether X is greater than zero, less than zero, or equal to zero, respectively. The boxes show the logical structure of the nested if statement: The second if statement is the false task (following else) of the first if statement.

{increment NumPos, NumNeg, or NumZero depending on X}

```
if X > 0 then
  NumPos := NumPos + 1
else
  if X < 0 then
    NumNeg := NumNeg + 1
  else {X = 0}
    NumZero := NumZero + 1
```

The execution of the nested if statement proceeds as follows: The first condition (X > 0) is tested; if it is true, NumPos is incremented and the rest of the if statement is skipped. If the first condition is false, the second condition (X < 0) is tested; if it is true, NumNeg is incremented; otherwise, NumZero is incremented. It is important to realize that the second condition is tested *only* when the first condition is false.

Table 4.8 traces the execution of this statement when X is -7. Because X > 0 is false, the second condition (X < 0) is tested. ▲

Table 4.8

Trace of if Statement in Example 4.11 for X = –7

Statement Part	Effect
if X > 0 then	-7 > 0 is false.
if X < 0 then	-7 < 0 is true;
NumNeg := NumNeg + 1	add 1 to NumNeg.

Comparison of Nested if and Sequence of ifs

Beginning programmers sometimes prefer to use a sequence of if statements rather than a single nested if statement. The nested if statement for Example 4.11 is logically equivalent to this sequence of if statements:

```
if X > 0 then
   NumPos := NumPos + 1;
if X < 0 then
   NumNeg := NumNeg + 1;
if X = 0 then
   NumZero := NumZero + 1
```

The nested if statement is more readable and more efficient, however, because the sequence doesn't clearly show that one and only one of the three assignment statements is executed for a particular X as the nested if does. With respect to efficiency, the nested if statement executes more quickly when X is positive because the first condition (X > 0) is true, so the part of the if statement following the first else is skipped. In contrast, all three conditions are always tested in the sequence of if statements. When X is negative, two conditions are tested in the nested if versus three in the sequence of if statements.

Pascal Rule for Matching else with if

The use of indentation conveys the logical structure of a nested if statement. The indentation in Example 4.11 clearly shows an if-then-else statement with a second if-then-else statement as its false task. The Pascal compiler disregards this indentation, however, and uses its own rule for matching each else with its corresponding if: Pascal matches each else with the closest preceding if that is not matched with a closer else. This rule is analogous to the rule for matching left and right parentheses in an expression, in that an if is like a left parenthesis and an else is like a right parenthesis.

EXAMPLE 4.12 ▼

In the nested if statement

```
{if-then-else as true task of an if-then}
```

```
if X > 0 then
    if Y > X then
        WriteLn ('Y > X > 0')
    else
        WriteLn ('(X > 0) and (Y <= X)')
```

Pascal matches the else with the second if. Therefore Pascal translates this statement as an if-then statement whose true task (following then) is an if-then-else statement.

If you want the else to go with the first if, not the second, then you must place a begin-end bracket around the inner if-then statement:

```
{if-then as true task of if-then-else}
```

```
if X > 0 then
    begin
        if Y > X then
            WriteLn ('Y > X > 0')
    end
else
    WriteLn ('X <= 0')
```

Pascal translates this statement as an if-then-else statement whose true task is an if-then statement.   ▲

Multiple-Alternative Decision Form of Nested if

Nested if statements can become quite complex. If there are more than three alternatives and indentation is not consistent, it may be difficult to determine the logical structure of the if statement. In situations like Example 4.11 in which each false task (except possibly the last) is followed by an if-then-else statement, you can code the nested if as the **multiple-alternative decision** described in the next display.

multiple-alternative decision
a nested if statement in which each false task (except possibly the last) is an if-then-else statement

SYNTAX DISPLAY

Multiple-Alternative Decision

Form: if *condition₁* then
              statement₁
          else if *condition₂* then
              statement₂
          else if *condition₃* then
              statement₃

```
        .
        .
        .
    else if condition_n then
        statement_n
    else
        statement_e
```

Example: {increment NumPos, NumNeg, NumZero depending on X}
```
    if X > 0 then
        NumPos := NumPos + 1
    else if X < 0 then
        NumNeg := NumNeg + 1
    else {X = 0}
        NumZero := NumZero + 1
```

Interpretation: The *conditions* in a multiple-alternative decision are evaluated in sequence until a true *condition* is reached. If a *condition* is true, the *statement* following it is executed and the rest of the multiple-alternative decision is skipped. If a *condition* is false, the *statement* following it is skipped and the next *condition* is tested. If all *conditions* are false, the *statement_e* following the last else is executed.

Note: It is not necessary to have an else *statement_e*. In this case, nothing happens if all *conditions* are false.

EXAMPLE 4.13 ▼

Suppose you want to assign letter grades based on exam scores.

Exam Score	Grade Assigned
90 and above	A
80 – 89	B
70 – 79	C
60 – 69	D
below 60	F

The following multiple-alternative decision displays the letter grade assigned according to this table. For an exam score of 85, the first true condition is Score >= 80, so B would be displayed and program control would pass to the WriteLn statement after the multiple-alternative decision.

```
if Score >= 90 then
    Write ('A')
else if Score >= 80 then
    Write ('B')
else if Score >= 70 then
    Write ('C')
```

```
else if Score >= 60 then
  Write ('D')
else
  Write ('F');
WriteLn (' is the exam grade - score is ', Score)  ▲
```

Program Style

Writing a Multiple-Alternative Decision

In the multiple-alternative decision, the reserved words `else if` and the next condition appear on the same line. All the words `else` align, and each task is indented under the condition that controls its execution.

Order of Conditions in a Multiple-Alternative Decision

When more than one condition in a multiple-alternative decision is true, only the task following the first true condition executes. Therefore the order of the conditions can affect the outcome.

The following multiple-alternative decision assigns grades incorrectly. All passing exam scores (60 or above) would be categorized as a grade of D because the first condition would be true and the rest would be skipped. The most restrictive condition (`Score >= 90`) should come first.

```
{incorrect grade assignment}
if Score >= 60 then
  Write ('D')
else if Score >= 70 then
  Write ('C')
else if Score >= 80 then
  Write ('B')
else if Score >= 90 then
  Write ('A')
else
  Write ('F')
```

EXAMPLE 4.14 ▼

You could use a multiple-alternative decision to implement a *decision table* that describes several ranges of values for a particular variable and the outcome for each range. For instance, let's say you are an accountant setting up a payroll system based on Table 4.9, which shows five different ranges for salaries up to $15,000.00. Each table line shows the base tax amount (column 2) and tax percentage (column 3) for a particular salary range (column 1). Given a person's salary, you can calculate the tax due by adding the base tax to the product of the percentage times the excess salary over the minimum salary for that range. For example, the second line of the table specifies that the tax due on a salary of $2000.00 is $225.00 plus 16% of the excess

Table 4.9
Decision Table for
Example 4.14

Salary Range	Base Tax	Percentage of Excess
0.00 – 1499.99	0.00	15%
1500.00 – 2999.99	225.00	16%
3000.00 – 4999.99	465.00	18%
5000.00 – 7999.99	825.00	20%
8000.00 – 15,000.00	1425.00	25%

salary over $1500.00 (i.e., 16% of $500.00, or $80.00). Therefore the total tax due is $225.00 plus $80.00, or $305.00.

The if statement in Fig. 4.13 implements the tax table. If the value of Salary is within the table range (0.00 to 15000.00), exactly one of the statements assigning a value to Tax will execute. Table 4.10 shows a hand trace of the if statement when Salary is 2000.00. Verify for yourself that the value assigned to Tax, 305.00, is correct. ▲

Table 4.10
Trace of if Statement in Fig.
4.13 for Salary = $2000.00

Statement Part	Salary	Tax	Effect
	2000.00	?	
if Salary < 0.0			2000.0 < 0.0 is false.
else if Salary < 1500.00			2000.0 < 1500.0 is false.
else if Salary < 3000.00			2000.0 < 3000.0 is true.
Tax := (Salary - 1500.00)			Evaluates to 500.00.
* 0.16			Evaluates to 80.00.
+ 225.00		305.00	Evaluates to 305.00.

Figure 4.13
if Statement for Table 4.9

▽

```
if Salary < 0.00 then
   WriteLn ('Error! Negative salary $', Salary :10:2)
else if Salary < 1500.00 then                    {first range}
   Tax := 0.15 * Salary
else if Salary < 3000.00 then                    {second range}
   Tax := (Salary - 1500.00) * 0.16 + 225.0
else if Salary < 5000.00 then                    {third range}
   Tax := (Salary - 3000.00) * 0.18 + 465.00
```

```
else if Salary < 8000.00 then                    {fourth range}
  Tax := (Salary - 5000.00) * 0.20 + 825.00
else if Salary <= 15000.00 then                  {fifth range}
  Tax := (Salary - 8000.00) * 0.25 + 1425.00
else
  WriteLn ('Error! Too large salary $', Salary :10:2)
```

Program Style

Validating the Value of Variables

If you validate the value of a variable before using it in a computation, you can avoid processing invalid or meaningless data. Instead of computing an incorrect tax amount, the if statement in Fig. 4.13 prints an error message if the value of Salary is outside the range covered by the table (0.0 to 15000.00). The first condition detects negative salaries; an error message is displayed if Salary is less than zero. All conditions evaluate to False if Salary is greater than 15000.00, so the task following else displays an error message.

Nested if Statements with More Than One Variable

In most of our examples, the use of nested if statements to test the value of a single variable has enabled us to write each nested if statement as a multiple-alternative decision. When several variables are involved, we cannot always use a multiple-alternative decision. Example 4.15 contains a situation in which we can use a nested if statement as a "filter" to select data that satisfy several different criteria.

EXAMPLE 4.15 ▼

The Department of Defense would like a program that identifies single males between the ages of 18 and 26, inclusive. One approach uses a nest of if-then statements whose conditions test the next criterion only if all previous criteria tested were satisfied. In the following nest of if-then statements, assume that all variables have initial values and that the Boolean variable Single has been set previously to indicate whether the individual is single (Single is True). Recall that the condition Single is preferable to Single = True. The WriteLn statement executes only when all conditions are true.

```
{Display message if all criteria are met.}
if Single then
  if Gender = 'M' then
    if (Age >= 18) and (Age <= 26) then
      WriteLn ('Current person satisfies the criteria.')
```

Another approach to solving this problem is to write a Boolean expression that combines all the individual conditions that must be true using the and operator. This expression appears on the right side of the following

Boolean assignment. The `if` statement following the Boolean assignment displays an appropriate message based on the value assigned to `AllMet`.

```
{Set AllMet to True if all criteria are met.}
AllMet := Single and (Gender = 'M') and
          (Age >= 18) and (Age <= 26);

{Display the result of the filtering operation.}
if AllMet then
  WriteLn ('Current person satisfies the criteria.')
else
  WriteLn ('All criteria are not satisfied.')   ▲
```

EXAMPLE 4.16 ▼

In a discussion about your options for college, your parents tell you that you may apply to your first-choice school if your SAT scores are above 1300 and you earn more than $2000 over the summer. If your SAT scores are not over 1300 but you still earn over $2000, then your parents suggest you apply to their alma mater and live at the dorm. If you cannot earn the necessary $2000, your parents want you to commute to a local college. The following nested `if` statement summarizes this decision process:

```
if Earnings > 2000.00 then
  if SAT > 1300 then
    WriteLn ('Apply to first-choice college')
  else
    WriteLn ('Apply to parents alma mater')
else
  WriteLn ('Apply to local college')
```

The first `WriteLn` executes when both conditions are `True`; the second `WriteLn` executes when the first condition is `True` and the second is `False`; the third `WriteLn` executes when the first condition is `False`.

We could also use the following multiple-alternative decision to implement this decision:

```
if (Earnings > 2000.00) and (SAT > 1300) then
  WriteLn ('Apply to first-choice college')
else if Earnings > 2000.00 then
  WriteLn ('Apply to parents alma mater')
else
  WriteLn ('Apply to local college')
```

The first `WriteLn` executes when both summer earnings and SAT scores are sufficient. Because the condition following `else if` is tested only when the first condition fails, it can be `True` only when earnings are sufficient but SAT scores are not. Note that it is not necessary to test the value of SAT in that condition. The third `WriteLn` executes when summer earnings are insufficient. ▲

Figure 4.14
Evaluation Tree for Flag or
((Y + Z) >= (X – Z))

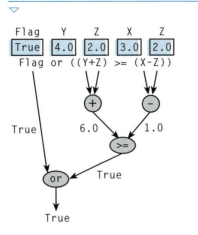

Short-Circuit Evaluation of Boolean Expressions

short-circuit evaluation

evaluating only as much of a Boolean expression as is necessary to determine its value

When evaluating Boolean expressions, some compilers employ a technique called **short-circuit evaluation.** A compiler using this technique stops evaluating a Boolean expression as soon as its value can be determined. For example, if the value of Flag is True, the expression in Fig. 4.14 must evaluate to True regardless of the value of the parenthesized expression following or (that is, True or (. . .) must always be True). Consequently, there is no need to evaluate the parenthesized expression following or when Flag is True. Similarly, we can show that False and (. . .) must always be False, so there is no need to evaluate the parenthesized expression following the and operator. By default, Turbo Pascal uses short-circuit evaluation of Boolean expressions; standard Pascal does not.

EXAMPLE 4.17 ▼

If X is zero, the if condition

```
if (X <> 0.0) and (Y / X > 5.0) then
```

is False because (X <> 0.0) is False, so False and (. . .) must be False. Consequently, there is no need to evaluate (Y / X > 5.0) when X is zero. If this expression is evaluated, however, a division by zero run-time error occurs because the divisor X is zero.

To prevent this run-time error for programs compiled by Pascal compilers that do not use short-circuit Boolean evaluation, the if condition should be split:

```
if (X <> 0.0) then
  if (Y / X > 5.0) then
```

The first condition guards the second and prevents the latter from being evaluated when X is zero. The result of evaluating these conditions is the same for short-circuit or complete evaluation.   ▲

Be wary of short-circuit evaluation and avoid writing Boolean expressions that rely on it. If you insert the special comment {$B+} in a program, the Turbo Pascal compiler generates code that causes complete evaluation of all Boolean expressions. Comments beginning with the symbols {$ are called **compiler directives** because they provide instructions to the compiler. The {$B+} compiler directive should precede the first Boolean expression for which complete evaluation is desired. Once enabled, complete Boolean evaluation remains in effect until the comment {$B-} is encountered.

compiler directive
a comment beginning with the symbols { $ that provides instructions to the compiler

SYNTAX DISPLAY

Boolean Evaluation Compiler Directive

Form: {$B-} or {$B+}
Default: {$B-}
Interpretation: In the default state, Turbo Pascal uses short-circuit Boolean evaluation. The compiler directive {$B+} causes the compiler to generate code for complete evaluation of every operand of a Boolean expression.
Note: Writing a Boolean expression that may fail when complete evaluation is used instead of short-circuit evaluation is not good programming practice.

Exercises for Section 4.8

Self-Check

1. Trace the execution of the nested if statement in Example 4.14 when Salary is 13500.00.
2. In Example 4.16, how many comparisons are required to execute the first if statement? What about the second? Which if statement is more efficient?
3. Evaluate the following expressions, with and without short-circuit evaluation, if X is 6 and Y is 7.

   a. (X > 5) and (Y div X <= 10)
   b. (X <= 10) or (X / (Y - 7) > 3)

Programming

1. Rewrite the if statement for Example 4.13 using only the relational operator < in all conditions. Test for a failing grade first.
2. Implement the following decision table using a nested if statement. Assume that the grade point average is within the range 0.0 through 4.0.

Grade Point Average	Transcript Message
0.0 – 0.99	Failed semester—registration suspended
1.0 – 1.99	On probation for next semester
2.0 – 2.99	(No message)
3.0 – 3.49	Dean's list for semester
3.5 – 4.0	Highest honors for semester

3. Write a Pascal program to roll a pair of dice. Use a random number generator to generate the six possible values of each die and print You Win! if a 7 or 11 is rolled, Snake Eyes! if a 2 is rolled, Try Again. otherwise. (*Hint:* Use Random(6) + 1 to determine a die roll.)

4.9 The case Statement

In addition to the if statement, the case statement can be used in Pascal to select one of several alternatives. The case statement is especially useful when selection is based on the value of a single variable or a simple expression (called the *case selector*). The case selector must be an **ordinal data type,** or a data type whose values may all be listed. Data types Integer, Boolean, and Char are ordinal types, but data types Real and string are not. (If you tried to list the real numbers between 3.1 and 3.2 as 3.11, 3.12, 3.13, . . . , you would be leaving out 3.111, 3.112, 3.113, ...)

ordinal data type
a data type having a finite set of values that can always be listed in order from the first to the last

EXAMPLE 4.18 ▼

The case statement

```
case MomOrDad of
  'M', 'm' : WriteLn ('Hello Mom - Happy Mother''s Day');
  'D', 'd' : WriteLn ('Hello Dad - Happy Father''s Day')
end; {case}
```

behaves the same way as the following if statement when the character stored in MomOrDad is one of the four letters listed (M, m, D, or d):

```
if (MomOrDad = 'M') or (MomOrDad = 'm') then
  WriteLn ('Hello Mom - Happy Mother''s Day')
else if (MomOrDad = 'D') or (MomOrDad = 'd') then
  WriteLn ('Hello Dad - Happy Father''s Day')
```

The message displayed by the case statement depends on the value of the case selector MomOrDad (type Char). If the case selector value is 'M' or 'm', the first message is displayed. If the case selector value is 'D' or 'd', the second message is displayed. The lists 'M', 'm' and 'D', 'd' are called *case labels*. ▲

EXAMPLE 4.19 ▼

The following case statement computes the gross pay a worker earns on a particular day, where the value of DayNumber indicates whether the day is a Saturday (DayNumber is 7), a Sunday (DayNumber is 1), or a weekday (DayNumber is 2 through 6). The worker is paid time and a half for weekend work. Of course, the values of DayNumber, DailyRate, and Hours must be defined before the case statement executes.

```
{Compute gross pay for a particular day}
case DayNumber of
   1, 7          : Gross := Hours * 1.5 * DailyRate;
   2, 3, 4, 5, 6 : Gross := Hours * DailyRate
end; {case}  ▲
```

One common error is using a string such as 'Saturday' or 'Sunday' as a case label. This causes the syntax error ordinal expression expected. Remember that only ordinal values (i.e., single characters, integers, or Boolean values) may appear in case labels.

We describe the case statement next and diagram it in Fig. 4.15.

Figure 4.15

Syntax Diagrams for case Statement and case Label

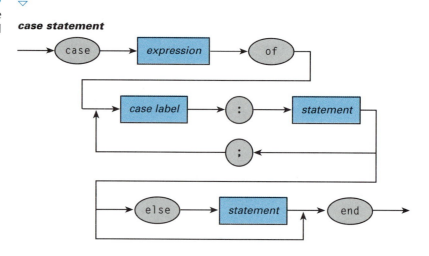

case statement

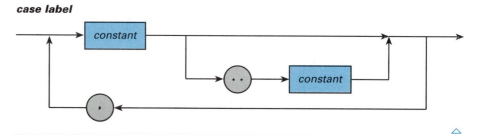

case label

SYNTAX DISPLAY

case Statement

Form: `case` *selector* `of`
           label₁ `:` *statement₁*;
           label₂ `:` *statement₂*;
                     .
                     .
                     .
           labelₙ `:` *statementₙ*
           `else`
           statementₑ
           `end` `{case}`

Example: `case N of`
           `1, 2 : begin`
                   `Write ('1, 2, ');`
                   `WriteLn ('Buckle my shoe')`
                   `end; {1, 2}`
           `3, 4 : WriteLn ('3, 4, Shut the door');`
           `5, 6 : WriteLn ('5, 6, Pick up sticks')`
           `else`
              `WriteLn (N :1, ' is out of range')`
           `end; {case}`

Interpretation: The *selector* expression is evaluated and compared to each *label*, which is a list of one or more possible values for the *selector*. Only one *statement* is executed; if the *selector* value is listed in *labelᵢ*, then *statementᵢ* is executed. Control is then passed to the first statement after `end` `{case}`. Each *statement* may be a single or a compound Pascal statement.
Note 1: If the value of the *selector* is not listed in any *label*, no *statement* is executed unless an `else` clause is provided. If present, the `else` clause (*statementₑ*) is executed. In standard Pascal, an `else` clause is not permitted, and a run-time error occurs when the *selector* value fails to match any *label*.
Note 2: A particular *selector* value may appear in, at most, one *label*.
Note 3: The type of each *selector* value must correspond to the type of the *selector* expression.
Note 4: Any ordinal data type is permitted as the *selector* type.

If no action is to be performed for a particular case *label*, the semicolon is placed right after the colon. Each *statement*, except the last, should be followed by a semicolon; the last *statement* is followed by the word `end`. There is no corresponding `begin` for a `case` statement.

else Clause

What happens if the program user enters a value that is not listed in a case label? In standard Pascal, a run-time error occurs. However, in Turbo Pascal nothing happens, and the next statement following the end {case} is executed. Turbo Pascal also allows the use of an else clause, which can display an error message or take some corrective action if the case selector has an unexpected data value. In the next case statement, the else clause displays the error message invalid day number if an unexpected value is stored in DayNumber. The else clause cannot be used in standard Pascal.

```
{Compute gross pay for a particular day}
case DayNumber of
  1, 7            : Gross := Hours * 1.5 * DailyRate;
  2, 3, 4, 5, 6 : Gross := Hours * DailyRate
else
  WriteLn ('invalid day number.')
end {case}
```

Subrange Notation in case Labels

subrange notation
using *min .. max* to indicate the ordinal range from *min* through *max*.

In Turbo Pascal, unlike standard Pascal, we can list a range of values in a case label using **subrange notation.** The next case statement shows that we needn't list each consecutive value from 2 to 6 individually in the second label. We simply list the starting and ending values separated by two periods. (We discuss subrange data types in Chapter 7.)

```
{Compute gross pay for a particular day.}
case DayNumber of
  1, 7 : Gross := Hours * 1.5 * DailyRate;
  2..6 : Gross := Hours * DailyRate
end {case}
```

Guarding a case Statement

In standard Pascal, programmers often guard a case statement with an if statement to prevent the occurrence of a case expression out of range error. In the next program fragment, the if statement guards the case statement nested inside it. The case statement executes only when the value of DayNumber is in the range 1 through 7, as required; an error message is printed when DayNumber is invalid. Note that no semicolon follows the end {case}. (Why?)

```
{Compute gross pay for a particular day.}
if (DayNumber >= 1) and (DayNumber <= 7) then
  case DayNumber of
    1, 7            : Gross := Hours * 1.5 * DailyRate;
    2, 3, 4, 5, 6 : Gross := Hours * DailyRate
  end {case}
else
  WriteLn ('invalid day number.')
```

Comparison of Nested if and case

Nested if statements, which are more general than a case statement, can be used to implement any multiple-alternative decision. A case statement, however, is more readable and should be used whenever practical. Remember not to use type Real values or strings as case labels.

Use the case statement when each case label contains a reasonably sized list of values (10 or fewer). When the number of values in a case selector is large or there are large gaps in those values, however, use a nested if statement.

Program Style

Type Boolean case Selectors

Although case statements may contain type Boolean case selectors, this rarely happens. The following case and if statements are equivalent, but the if statement is preferable:

```
case X = Y of                        if X = Y then
   True : WriteLn ('Equal');            WriteLn ('Equal')
   False : WriteLn ('Unequal')       else
end {case}                              WriteLn ('Unequal')
```

Exercises for Section 4.9   *Self-Check*

1. Write an if statement that corresponds to the following case:

   ```
   case X of
      2 : WriteLn ('Snake Eyes!');
      7, 11 : WriteLn ('Win!')
   else
      WriteLn ('Try again.')
   end {case}
   ```

2. Write a case statement that corresponds to the following if:

   ```
   if (Grade >= 'A') and (Grade <= 'C') then
      WriteLn ('Passing')
   else if (Grade = 'D') or (Grade = 'F') then
      WriteLn ('No credit')
   else
      WriteLn ('Invalid grade')
   ```

3. Can the nested if statements in Section 4.8 be rewritten using case statements? If not, why not?

Programming

1. Write a case statement that prints a message indicating whether NextCh (type Char) is an operator symbol (+, -, *, =, <, >, /), a punctuation mark (comma, semicolon, parenthesis, brace, bracket), or a digit. Your statement should print the category selected.
2. Write a nested if statement that is equivalent to the case statement described in Programming Exercise 1.
3. Guard the case statement described in Programming Exercise 1.

4.10 Common Programming Errors

The Boolean operators, and, or, and not, can be used only with Boolean expressions. In the expression

```
Flag and (X = Y)
```

the variable Flag must be type Boolean. The expression would be invalid without the parentheses unless X and Y were also type Boolean. In this case, Flag and X would be evaluated first because and has higher precedence than =.

Be careful when using semicolons inside an if statement. Use them only to separate the statements of a compound statement within an if statement, and place a semicolon after the if statement when more statements follow. Never use semicolons before or after the reserved words then or else in an if statement. If you use a semicolon just before else, the compiler will terminate the if statement and incorrectly assume that the else begins a new statement.

Don't forget to bracket a compound statement used as a true task or a false task with begin and end. If the begin-end bracket is missing, only the first statement will be considered part of the task, which can lead to a syntax error. In the following example, the missing begin-end bracket around the true task causes the compiler to assume that the semicolon after the assignment statement terminates the if statement. As a result, you get a ; expected syntax error when else is reached. If you then insert a semicolon at the end of the first WriteLn statement, you will get an error in statement syntax error because a statement cannot begin with else.

```
{if with missing begin - end}
if X > 0 then
   Sum := Sum + X;
   WriteLn ('X is positive')
else
   WriteLn ('X is not positive')
```

When writing a nested if statement, try to select the conditions in such a way that you can use the multiple-alternative format shown in Section 4.8. If more than one condition may be true at the same time, place the most restrictive condition first.

Remember that the Pascal compiler matches each `else` with the closest unmatched `if`. If careless, you may get an unexpected pairing that, while perhaps not causing a syntax error, will affect the outcome.

In `case` statements, make sure the case selector and labels are of the same ordinal type (`Integer`, `Char`, or `Boolean`, but not `Real` or `string`). Remember that lists of ordinal values or subranges (only in Turbo Pascal) may be used as case labels and that no value may appear in more than one case label. Use an `else` clause to print a warning message if the selector evaluates to a value not listed in any of the case labels. In standard Pascal, it is often wise to guard the `case` with an `if` statement. Don't forget to terminate a `case` statement with an `end {case}`; there is no matching `begin`.

CHAPTER REVIEW

1. Use control structures to control the flow of execution through a program. The compound statement is a control structure for sequential execution.
2. Boolean expressions appear in `if` statements and can be written
   ▶ using Boolean variables or constants
   ▶ using the relational operators ($<$, $<=$, $>$, $>=$, $=$, $<>$), to compare variables and constants of the same data type
   ▶ using the logical operators (`and`, `or`, `not`) with Boolean operands
3. Use selection control structures to represent decisions in an algorithm, and write them in algorithms using pseudocode. We use the `if` statement to code decision steps in Pascal.
4. Syntax diagrams describe the syntax of Pascal. To avoid syntax errors when you are unsure of the form of a statement, refer to the appropriate syntax diagrams (see Appendix C). If the compiler detects a syntax error that you don't understand, press the Help key (F1) or refer to the syntax diagram to determine the cause of the error.
5. Data flow information in a structure chart indicates whether a variable processed by a subproblem is used as an input or an output, or as both. An input provides data that are manipulated by the subproblem, and an output returns a value read or computed by the subproblem. The same variable can be an input to one subproblem and an output from another.
6. Solution by analogy is a problem-solving technique in which you solve a new problem by applying logic similar to that used in an earlier solution.
7. A hand trace of an algorithm verifies whether it is correct. You can discover errors in logic by carefully hand-tracing an algorithm. Hand-tracing an algorithm before coding it as a program will save you time in the long run.
8. Nested `if` statements are commonly used in Pascal to represent decisions with multiple alternatives. Programmers use indentation and the multiple-alternative decision form to enhance readability of nested `if` statements.
9. A second selection structure, the `case` statement, implements decisions with several alternatives, depending on the value of a variable or expression (the *case selector*). The *case selector* can be type `Integer`, `Char`, or `Boolean`, but not type `Real` or `string`.

Summary of New Pascal Constructs

Construct	Effect

Compound Statement

```
begin {group}
Write ('Enter X >');
  ReadLn (X);
  Positive := Abs(X);
  Root := Sqrt(Positive)
end {group}
```

The statements in the compound statement are executed in sequence.

if **Statement**

One Alternative

```
if X <> 0.0 then
  Product := Product * X
```

Multiplies Product by X only if X is nonzero.

Two Alternatives

```
if X >= 0.0 then
  WriteLn (X, ' positive')
else
  WriteLn (X, ' negative')
```

If X is greater than or equal to 0.0, displays X followed by positive; otherwise, displays X followed by negative.

Several Alternatives

```
if X < 0.0 then
  begin
    WriteLn ('negative');
    Sign := '-'
      end
else if X = 0.0 then
  begin
    WriteLn ('zero');
    Sign := '0'
  end
else
  begin
    WriteLn ('positive');
    Sign := '+'
  end
```

One of three messages is printed, depending on whether X is negative, positive, or zero. Sign (type Char) stores the sign of X.

case **Statement**

```
case NextCh of
  'A', 'a' : WriteLn ('Excellent');
  'B', 'b' : WriteLn ('Good');
  'C', 'c' : WriteLn ('O.K.');
  'D', 'd', 'F', 'f' :
    begin
```

Displays one of five messages based on the value of NextCh (type Char). If NextCh is 'D', 'd' or 'F', 'f', the student is put on probation. If NextCh is not listed in the case labels,

Construct	Effect

<pre>   Write ('Poor, student');
      WriteLn (' on probation')
    end
  else
    WriteLn ('Bad value')
  end {case}</pre>
	displays the message Bad value.

Quick-Check Exercises

1. An if statement is a control statement for _____.
2. What is a compound statement?
3. A case statement is often used instead of _____.
4. Why would the following statement fail in some Pascal implementations but not fail in others? Assume I and J are integer variables.

```
if (I > 0) and (J div I = 0) then
   WriteLn ('I is a factor of J')
```

5. The relational operator <> means _____.
6. What operator has the highest precedence? Name four that have the lowest precedence.
7. What is the purpose of a syntax diagram?
8. Correct the syntax errors in the following statement:

```
if X > 25.0 then
  begin
    Y := X - 25.0;
  else
    Y := X
  end {if}
```

9. What value is assigned to Fee by each of the following if statements when Speed is 75? Is the one on the left or the one on the right correct?

```
if Speed > 35 then          if Speed > 75 then
   Fee := 20.0                 Fee := 60.0
else if Speed > 50 then     else if Speed > 50 then
   Fee := 40.00               Fee := 40.00
else if Speed > 75 then     else if Speed > 35 then
   Fee := 60.00               Fee := 20.00
```

10. What output line(s) are displayed by the following statements when Grade is 'I'? When Grade is 'B'? When Grade is 'b'?

```
case Grade of
   'A' : Points := 4;
   'B' : Points := 3;
   'C' : Points := 2;
   'D' : Points := 1;
   'E', 'I' ,'W' : Points := 0
```

```
else
   Write ('Bad grade-')
end; {case}

if ('A' <= Grade) and (Grade <= 'D') then
   WriteLn ('Passed, points earned = ', Points)
else
   WriteLn ('No points earned')
```

11. Explain the difference between the statements on the left and the statements on the right. For each, what is the final value of X if the initial value of X is 1?

```
if X >= 1 then          if X >= 1 then
   X := X + 1              X := X + 1;
else if X >= 0 then     if X >= 0 then
   X := X + 2              X := X + 2
```

Answers to Quick-Check Exercises

1. selection or decision making
2. One or more statements bracketed by begin and end
3. a nested if statement or a multiple-alternative decision
4. This statement would fail when I is 0 if short-circuit evaluation is not used.
5. not equal
6. not; <, <=, >, >=, =, <>
7. To check the syntax of a Pascal construct
8. Remove begin and end and the semicolon.
9. 20.00 (first condition is true), 40.00; 40.00 is correct
10. When Grade is 'I': No points earned. When Grade is 'B': Passed, points earned = 3. When Grade is 'b': Bad grade-No points earned.
11. A nested if statement is on the left; a sequence of if statements is on the right. X becomes 2 on the left; X becomes 4 on the right.

Review Questions

1. Why are the relational operators placed in parentheses when the and or or operators are used?
2. How does a relational operator differ from a Boolean operator?
3. What is short-circuit Boolean evaluation? Why should its use be discouraged?
4. Trace the following program fragment and indicate which procedure will be called if a data value of 27.34 is entered:

```
WriteLn ('Enter a temperature>');
ReadLn (Temp);
if Temp > 32.0 then
   NotFreezing
else
   IceForming
```

5. Write a nested `if` statement to display a message that indicates the educational level of a student based on his or her number of years of schooling: `0—None, 1 through 5—Elementary School, 6 through 8—Middle School, 9 through 12—High School, > 12—College`. Print a message to indicate bad data as well.

6. Redo Review Question 5 using a `case` statement.

7. Given the following syntax diagram, which of the following words are valid?

   `pear    bread    drear    deaden    dad    drab`

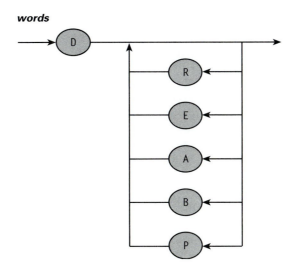

words

8. Write a guarded `case` statement to select an operation based on the value of `Inventory`. Increment `TotalPaper` by `PaperOrder` if `Inventory` is `'B'` or `'C'`; increment `TotalRibbon` by 1 if `Inventory` is `'E'`, `'F'`, or `'D'`; increment `TotalLabel` by `LabelOrder` if `Inventory` is `'A'` or `'X'`. Do nothing if `Inventory` is `'M'`.

9. Write the six pairs of words that satisfy the syntax diagram for *thing*.

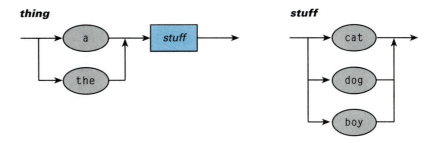

thing   **stuff**

10. What is solution by analogy?

Programming Projects

1. Write procedures to draw a circle, square, and triangle. Then write a program that reads a letter C, S, or T and, depending on the letter chosen, draws either a circle, square, or triangle.

2. Write a program that reads in four words and displays them in increasing alphabetical sequence and also in decreasing alphabetical sequence.

3. While spending the summer as a surveyor's assistant, you decide to write a program that transforms compass headings in degrees (0 to 360) to compass bearings. A compass bearing consists of three items: the direction you face (north or south), an angle between 0 and 90 degrees, and the direction you turn before walking (east or west). For example, to get the bearing for a compass heading of 110.0 degrees, you would first face due south (180 degrees) and then turn 70.0 degrees east (180.0 −70.0 is 110.0). Therefore, the bearing is south 70.0 degrees east. Be sure to check the input for invalid compass headings.

4. Write a program that reads in a room number, its capacity, and the size of the class enrolled so far and prints an output line showing the classroom number, capacity, number of seats filled, number of seats available, and a message indicating whether the class is filled. Call a procedure to display the following heading before the output line:

```
Room    Capacity    Enrollment    Empty seats    Filled/
                                                  Not filled
```

Display each part of the output line under the appropriate heading. Test your program with the following classroom data:

Room	Capacity	Enrollment
426	25	25
327	18	14
420	20	15
317	100	90

5. Write a program that determines the additional state tax owed by an employee. The state charges a 4% tax on net income. Determine net income by subtracting a $500 allowance for each dependent from gross income. Your program will read gross income, number of dependents, and tax amount already deducted. It will then compute the actual tax owed and print the difference between tax owed and tax deducted followed by the message 'SEND CHECK' or 'RE-FUND', depending on whether the difference is positive or negative.

6. Write a program to control a bread machine. Allow the user to input the type of bread as W for white and S for sweet. Ask the user whether the loaf size is double and whether the baking is manual. The program should fail if the user inputs are invalid. The following table details the time chart for the machine for each bread type. Print a statement for each step. If the loaf size is double, increase the baking time by 50%. If baking is manual, stop after the loaf shaping cycle and instruct the user to remove the dough for manual baking. Use a procedure to print program instructions.

Bread Time Chart

Operation	White Bread	Sweet Bread
Primary kneading	15 min	20 min
Primary rising	60 min	60 min
Secondary kneading	18 min	33 min
Secondary rising	20 min	30 min
Loaf shaping	2 sec	2 sec
Final rising	75 min	75 min
Baking	45 min	35 min
Cooling	30 min	30 min

7. Write a program that determines the day number (1 to 366) in a year for a date that is provided as input data. As an example, January 1, 1994, is day 1; December 31, 1993, is day 365; December 31, 1996, is day 366 since 1996 is a leap year. A year is a leap year if it is divisible by 4, except that any year divisible by 100 is a leap year only if it is divisible by 400. Your program should accept the month, day, and year as integers.

INTERVIEW
▼

Ellen Isaacs

Ellen Isaacs received her Ph.D. in 1989 from Stanford University. She has since authored a number of papers which address the development of video applications and presented "What Video Can and Can't Do for Collaboration" at ACM's 1993 Multimedia Conference. As a human-interface engineer in the Collaborative Computing group at SunSoft, Ellen Isaacs applies her knowledge of human communication skills to the design and development of video software for desktop computers.

▼ **You studied psychology and semiotics as an undergraduate and earned your Ph.D. in cognitive psychology. What attracted you to the computer science industry?**

▲ While in graduate school at Stanford, I studied ordinary conversation—how people work together to make sure they are understanding each other throughout a conversation. Some of my research involved observing how people communicate through various media. I became interested in how people interact with computers and signed on to a project that attempted to add a speech interface to a medical expert system. Using this prototype, a doctor could speak to the computer and report the results of a patient's visit. The goal of the project was to gain insight into how doctors adapted their speech to match the computer's capabilities. This was my first exposure to a more applied setting and I found it very gratifying to work on a tangible tool that would be used by real people.

My work continues to revolve around how computers can enhance human communication. I work in the Collaborative Computing (COCO) group at SunSoft, which designs, develops, and studies the use of video-based tools that enable people to communicate face-to-face from different locations. I bring to the group an understanding of how people cooperate in a conversation as well as experience studying groups to learn how they approach tasks we want to support on the computer.

▼ **What applications is the group currently developing? How will these tools be used and by whom?**

▲ The COCO group builds proof-of-concept prototypes that use video to enable people to collaborate across distance. We have two projects in development. *Forum* allows users to give interactive presentations or classes over the network. Using Forum, the audience sits at their desktops and receives live video and audio of the presenter as well as slides. The presenter can draw or write on these slides, and the marks are seen by the audience. The audience can interact with the presenter by speaking, sending in written comments, or by responding anonymously to yes/no and multiple-choice questions. (For example, a speaker might ask, "How many of you think the term *multimedia* has become a meaningless buzzword?" and she would see a bar chart indicating how many people were voting yes or no.) Audience members can also interact with each other via short text messages that can be sent back and forth throughout the presentation.

The other project we are working on, *Montage*, expands on basic video-conferencing tools by building in support for the "pre-interaction coordination" that goes on among people who are colocated. For example, when you want to speak to someone nearby, you might walk down the hall to check if they are in. If they're not you might leave a note indicating that you are looking for them. If they're on the phone, you might signal that you would like to talk to them when they are done. Montage seeks to provide these capabilities for people who are distributed across distance. It allows you to quickly and unobtrusively "glance" into someone's office. If they are not there, you can leave an electronic "stickup" message, check their calendar, or send e-mail. If they are there, you can see whether it is a good time to interact, and if so, enter into a full video conference.

▼ Do you foresee any technical or cultural obstacles in implementing video conferencing on a large scale?

▲ There are several obstacles to be overcome before such video-based tools are widely used, some technical and some social. I'm not an expert on the technical issues, but at the very least, the cost of video processing hardware needs to come down and high bandwidth networks need to become more widely available; both of these are starting to happen. Perhaps the biggest technical obstacle to software developers is the lack of interoperability. This term refers to the ability to run software (in this case, video-conferencing software) on numerous hardware platforms. Even within a single company, you cannot expect everyone to work on the same type of computer. Most large companies have some combination of PCs, Macs, UNIX boxes, and mainframes, all from different manufacturers. When you start talking about cross-company communication or communication into the home, it becomes essential to handle video connectivity across different platforms.

From a user point of view, the biggest obstacle to ubiquitous video conferencing is the privacy issue. I think we as researchers have already learned quite a bit about handling many of the practical issues surrounding privacy, but it will take a while until people feel that they have control over their privacy. For example, Montage permits only reciprocal audio and video. This means no one can watch or listen to you without your being able to see and hear them. Montage also provides varying levels of access. It permits the equivalent of closing your door but still allowing knocking, as well as completely locking visual access. These functions let people use their existing social mechanisms to keep from invading others' privacy. Montage was field-tested on a group of marketers and engineers. Some of the participants were extremely apprehensive about signing on. But once they started using Montage, they quickly became more comfortable with it. Soon enough, most ended up using the access modes to give *more* information about their whereabouts when they weren't in their offices.

▼ What guidelines do you apply in designing and developing user interfaces for these video tools?

▲ The best user interface feels invisible to the user. I think video, as well as audio and animation, provides an opportunity to reduce the amount of work required by the rest of the user interface. If you can build upon people's sophisticated skills in dealing with sounds and both static and moving images, you can reduce the amount of buttons, menus, and other artificial devices to manipulate an application. In addition, video conferencing (or any tool for that matter) needs to do a better job of integrating itself with other desktop tools. Users need the ability to quickly call up an image, share a text editor, or check e-mail messages whenever the need should arise during a video conference. If it takes too long or is too tedious to access another application, people are less likely to use the tools when they need them. On the whole, I think the key to designing good multimedia applications is to use the media as tools to enhance users' tasks rather than just showcasing multimedia technology for its own sake.

C H A P T E R   F I V E

Repetition: while, for, and repeat Statements

loop
the repetition of steps in a program

In the programs studied so far, the statements in the program body execute only once. In most commercial software, however, a process can be repeated many times. For example, in the Turbo Pascal editor, the user can move the cursor to a program line and perform an edit operation as often as necessary.

Repetition, you'll recall, is the third type of program control structure (*sequence, selection, repetition*), and the repetition of steps in a program is called a **loop.** In this chapter, we describe the three Pascal loop-control statements—while, for, and repeat—and the advantages of each and we explain when to use each one. Like if statements, loops can be nested, and this chapter demonstrates how to write and use nested loops in your programs.

5.1   The while Statement

Our study of loops begins with the most versatile loop-control statement, the while statement. The program fragment in Fig. 5.1 computes and displays the weekly pay for each of seven employees, assuming no overtime pay. The instructions that are repeated, called the **loop body,** follow the word do. The loop body is the compound statement bracketed by begin and end; {while} consisting of instructions that read an employee's payroll data and compute and display that employee's gross pay. After seven weekly pay amounts are displayed, the statement following the loop body executes and displays the message All employees processed.

loop body

the instructions that are repeated in the loop

The three lines in color in Fig. 5.1 control the looping process. The first statement,

```
CountEmp := 0;          {no employees processed yet}
```

stores an initial value of 0 in the variable CountEmp, which represents the count of employees processed so far. The next line evaluates the Boolean expression CountEmp < 7. If it is true, the loop body is executed, causing the program to read a new pair of data values and to compute and display a new pay amount. The last instruction in the loop body,

```
CountEmp := CountEmp + 1      {increment CountEmp}
```

adds 1 to the value of CountEmp. After the last instruction in the loop body has been executed, control returns to the line beginning with while, and the Boolean expression CountEmp < 7 is reevaluated for the next value of CountEmp.

The loop body is executed once for each value of CountEmp from 0 to 6. Eventually, CountEmp becomes 7, at which time the Boolean expression

Figure 5.1
Loop to Process Seven
Employees

```
CountEmp := 0;                        {no employees processed yet}
while CountEmp < 7 do                 {test value of CountEmp}
  begin
    Write ('Hours >');
    ReadLn (Hours);
    Write ('Rate >$');
    ReadLn (Rate);
    Pay := Hours * Rate;
    WriteLn ('Weekly pay is $', Pay :4:2);
    CountEmp := CountEmp + 1      {increment CountEmp}
  end; {while}

WriteLn ('All employees processed');
```

Loop
body

evaluates to `False`. At this point, the loop is exited and control transfers to the `WriteLn` statement following the loop body.

The Boolean expression after the reserved word `while`, called the **loop-repetition condition,** is evaluated before each repetition of the loop body. The loop body is repeated when this condition is true, and exited when this condition is false. The flowchart of the `while` loop in Fig. 5.2 illustrates this execution. The condition in the diamond-shaped box is evaluated first. If it is true, the loop body is executed and the process is repeated until the condition becomes false. At that point, the `while` loop is exited.

Make sure you understand the difference between the `while` statement in Fig. 5.1 and the `if` statement

```
if CountEmp < 7 then
   begin
      . . .
   end; {if}
```

The compound statement after the reserved word `then` executes at most one time. In a `while` statement, the compound statement after the reserved word `do` may execute more than once.

The variable `CountEmp` in Fig. 5.1 is called the **loop-control variable** because its value determines whether the loop body is repeated. The loop-control variable `CountEmp` must be *initialized, tested,* and *updated* for the loop to execute properly:

▶ *Initialization.* `CountEmp` is set to an initial value of 0 (*initialized to* 0) before the `while` statement is reached.
▶ *Testing.* `CountEmp` is tested before the start of each loop repetition (called an *iteration* or a *pass*).
▶ *Updating.* `CountEmp` is updated (its value increased by 1) during each iteration.

Similar steps must be performed for every `while` loop. Without the initialization, the initial test of `CountEmp` would be meaningless. The updating step ensures that the program progresses toward the final goal (`CountEmp >= 7`)

loop-repetition condition

the condition following `while` that controls loop repetition

loop-control variable

the variable whose value controls loop repetition

Figure 5.2
Flowchart of a while Loop

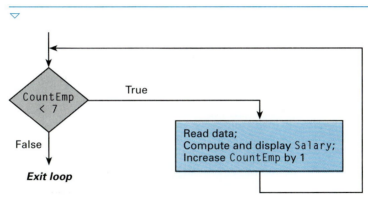

infinite loop
a loop that executes forever
counting loop
a loop whose required number of iterations can be determined before loop execution begins
counter
the loop-control variable for a counting loop

during each repetition of the loop. If the loop control variable were not updated, the loop would execute "forever." Such a loop is called an **infinite loop.**

The while loop in Fig. 5.1 is called a **counting loop** (or **counter-controlled loop**) because its repetition is controlled by a **counter** variable, whose value represents the number of loop iterations performed so far. We use a counting loop when we can determine prior to loop execution exactly how many loop repetitions are needed to solve our problem. The while condition should compare the counter to the number of loop repetitions needed. We describe the while statement syntax next and diagram it in Fig. 5.3.

SYNTAX DISPLAY

The while Statement

Form: while *expression* do
                statement
Example: {Display N asterisks.}
             CountStar := 0;
             while CountStar < N do
                begin
                   Write ('*');
                   CountStar := CountStar + 1
                end {while}

Interpretation: The *expression* (loop repetition condition) is tested; if it is true, *statement* (the loop body) is executed and *expression* is retested. *statement* is repeated as long as *expression* is true. When *expression* is tested and found to be false, the loop is exited, and the next program statement after the while statement is executed.

Note: If *expression* evaluates to false the first time it is tested, *statement* is not executed.

Position semicolons in a while statement carefully. Do not put a semicolon after the word do, or the Pascal compiler will execute what it assumes is an *empty statement* as your loop body. Such a "statement" will do nothing forever or until your patience or time expires.

Program Style

Formatting the while Statement

For clarity, indent the body of a while loop. If the loop body is a compound statement, bracket it with begin - end {while}.

Figure 5.3
Syntax Diagram for while
Statement

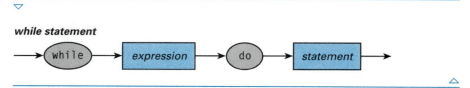

while statement

Exercises for Section 5.1   ***Self-Check***

1. How many times is the following loop body repeated? What is printed during each repetition of the loop body and after exit?

```
X := 3;
Count := 0;
while Count < 3 do
  begin
    X := X * X;
    WriteLn (X);
    Count := Count + 1
  end; {while}

WriteLn {Count}
```

2. Answer Exercise 1, assuming the last statement in the loop body is

```
Count := Count + 2
```

3. Answer Exercise 1, this time omitting the last statement in the loop body.

Programming

1. Write a `while` loop that displays each integer from 1 to 5 on a separate line together with its square.
2. Write a `while` loop that displays each integer from 4 down to -6 on a separate line. Display the values in the sequence 4, 2, 0, and so on.

5.2 Using Loops to Accumulate a Sum

Loops often accumulate a sum by repeating an addition operation, as demonstrated in Example 5.1.

EXAMPLE 5.1 ▼

The program in Fig. 5.4 has a `while` loop similar to the loop in Fig. 5.1. Besides displaying each employee's weekly pay, it computes and displays the company's total payroll (`TotalPay`). Prior to loop execution, the statements

```
TotalPay := 0.0;
CountEmp := 0;              {Start with first employee.}
```

initialize both `TotalPay` and `CountEmp` to 0, where `CountEmp` is the counter variable and `TotalPay` is an **accumulator** variable (it accumulates the total payroll value). Initializing `TotalPay` to 0 is critical; omitting this step will cause the final total to be off by whatever value happens to be stored in `TotalPay` when the program begins execution.

accumulator
a variable used to store a value being computed in increments during the execution of a loop

In the loop body, the assignment statement

```
TotalPay := TotalPay + Pay;              {Add next pay.}
```

Figure 5.4

Program to Compute
Payroll

Edit Window

```pascal
program Payroll;
{Computes the payroll for a company}

  var
    NumberEmp,                  {number of employees}
    CountEmp : Integer;         {current employee}
    Hours,                      {hours worked}
    Rate,                       {hourly rate}
    Pay,                        {weekly pay}
    TotalPay : Real;            {company payroll}

begin {Payroll}
  {Enter number of employees.}
  Write ('Enter number of employees >');
  ReadLn (NumberEmp);

  {Compute each employee's pay and add it to the payroll.}
  TotalPay := 0.0;
  CountEmp := 0;                {Start with first employee.}
  while CountEmp < NumberEmp do
    begin
      Write ('Hours >');
      ReadLn (Hours);
      Write ('Rate >$');
      ReadLn (Rate);
      Pay := Hours * Rate;
      WriteLn ('Pay is $', Pay :4:2);
      WriteLn;
      TotalPay := TotalPay + Pay;          {Add next pay.}
      CountEmp := CountEmp + 1
    end; {while}

  WriteLn ('All employees processed');
  WriteLn ('Total payroll is $', TotalPay :4:2)
end. {Payroll}
```

Output Window

```
Enter number of employees >3
Hours >5
Rate >$4.00
Pay is $20.00

Hours >6
Rate >$5.00
Pay is $30.00

Hours'>1.5
Rate >$10.00
Pay is $15.00

All employees processed
Total payroll is $65.00
```

Figure 5.5
Accumulating a Sum

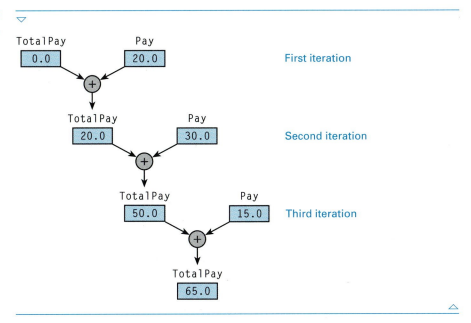

adds the current value of `Pay` to the sum being accumulated in `TotalPay`, thereby increasing the value of `TotalPay` with each loop iteration. Figure 5.5 traces the effect of repeating this statement for the three values of `Pay` shown in the sample run. Recall that iteration means a pass through the loop. ▲

Program Style

Writing General Loops

Because the loop in Fig. 5.1 uses the loop repetition condition `CountEmp < 7`, it processes exactly 7 employees. The more general loop in Fig. 5.4 uses the loop repetition condition `CountEmp < NumberEmp`, so it can process any number of employees. The number of employees to be processed in the latter loop must be read into variable `NumberEmp` before the `while` statement executes.

Exercises for Section 5.2   **Self-Check**

1. What output values are displayed by the following `while` loop for a data value of 5?

```
WriteLn ('Enter an integer> ');
ReadLn (X);
Product := 1;
Count := 0;
```

```
while Count < 4 do
   begin
      WriteLn (Product);
      Product := Product * X;
      Count := Count + 1
   end; {while}
```

2. What values are displayed if the call to `WriteLn` comes at the end of the loop instead of at the beginning?

3. What mathematical operation does the following segment compute?

```
Write ('Enter X> ');
ReadLn (X);
Write ('Enter Y> ');
ReadLn (Y);
Product := 1;
while Y > 0 do
   begin
      Product := Product * X;
      Y := Y - 1
   end; {while}
WriteLn ('Result = ', Product)
```

4. How would you modify the program in Fig. 5.4 to display the average employee salary, in addition to the total payroll amount?

Programming

1. When Robin's new baby was born, she opened a savings account with $1000.00. On each birthday, starting with the first, the bank added an additional 4.5% of the balance and Robin added another $500.00 to the account. Write a loop that will determine how much money was in the account on the child's 18th birthday.

5.3 Event-Controlled Loops

event-controlled loop

a loop whose repetition stops when a particular event occurs

Programmers use two kinds of loops: counter-controlled loops and event-controlled loops (or conditional loops). In the former, the loop body repeats a specified number of times. In an **event-controlled loop,** loop repetition stops when a particular event occurs.

For example, if faced with a pile of bills when sitting down to write monthly checks, you might not know how many checks to write. However, if you wanted to pay as many bills as possible, you could pay them in order by amount (smallest bill first) and stop writing checks when the event "account is overdrawn" occurs. In other words, you would continue writing checks as long as your account was not overdrawn, as indicated by the following pseudocode description:

```
while account is not overdrawn do
  begin
     Read the next bill
     Pay the bill if there are sufficient funds
     Update the balance
  end
```

The actual number of loop repetitions performed would depend on the amount of your initial checking account balance and the amount owed on each bill.

EXAMPLE 5.2 ▼

The program in Fig. 5.6 uses the preceding algorithm to pay bills, assuming that the total amount owed exceeds the initial checking account balance. The while loop reads each bill and processes it, and the if statement nested inside the loop determines whether to pay the bill by comparing the current account balance to the bill amount. If Balance >= Bill is true, the bill is paid; otherwise it is not paid and the last positive value of balance is displayed instead.

Figure 5.6
Paying Monthly Bills

▽

Edit Window

```
program PayBills;
{
  Authorizes payment of each bill as long as there are
  sufficient funds in the checking account. Assumes bills
  are entered in order starting with the smallest and the total
  amount owed exceeds the initial account balance.
}
  var
     Creditor : string;    {input - name of creditor}
     Bill,                 {input - amount of bill}
     InitBal,              {input - starting balance}
     Balance : Real;       {current account balance}

begin {PayBills}
  Write ('Enter initial account balance >$');
  ReadLn (InitBal);

  {
   Pay each bill as long as the account is not overdrawn.
   Decrease the balance by the bill amount after each bill is
   processed.
  }
  Balance := InitBal;
  while Balance >= 0.0 do
     begin
        WriteLn;                          {Skip a line.}
```

▷ ▷ ▷ ▷ ▷ ▷

```
     Write ('Enter next creditor >');
     ReadLn (Creditor);
     Write ('Enter amount owed >$');
     ReadLn (Bill);
     if Balance >= Bill then
       WriteLn ('Issue check for $', Bill :3:2,
                ' to ', Creditor)
     else
       WriteLn ('No check issued -- ',
                'Account balance is only $', Balance :3:2);
     Balance := Balance - Bill          {Update balance.}
   end; {while}

  WriteLn ('Insufficient funds to pay any more bills!')
end. {PayBills}
```

Output Window

```
Enter initial account balance >$120.00

Enter next creditor >Sam Jones
Enter amount owed >$65.00
Issue check for $65.00 to Sam Jones

Enter next creditor >Shirley Valentine
Enter amount owed >$70.00
No check issued -- Account balance is only $55.00
Insufficient funds to pay any more bills!
```

Table 5.1 traces the execution of the program for the data shown in the sample run. For brevity, we do not trace the string variable Creditor. During the first loop iteration, the if statement displays instructions for writing a check. During the second iteration, the if statement displays the last positive account balance. The next execution of the statement

```
Balance := Balance - Bill          {Update balance.}
```

assigns a negative value to Balance, so the loop would be exited when its repetition condition is retested.   ▲

Table 5.1
Trace of Program
in Fig. 5.6

Statement	InitBal	Balance	Bill	Effect
ReadLn (InitBal)	120.00	?	?	Enter start balance
Balance := InitBal;		120.00		Initialize Balance
while Balance >= 0.0 do				120.00 >= 0.0 is true

	Statement	InitBal	Balance	Bill	Effect
Table 5.1 Trace of Program in Fig. 5.6 (*continued*)	ReadLn (Bill);			65.00	Enter first bill
	if Balance >= Bill then				120.00 >= 65.00 is true
	WriteLn ('Issue check ...				Pay the bill
	Balance := Balance - Bill		55.00		Reduce Balance
	while Balance >= 0.0 do				55.00 >= 0.0 is true
	ReadLn (Bill)			70.00	Enter second bill
	if Balance >= Bill then				55.00 >= 70.00 is false
	WriteLn ('No check ...				Display Balance
	Balance := Balance - Bill		-15.00		Reduce Balance
	while Balance >= 0.0 do				-15.00 >= 0.0 is false, exit loop
	WriteLn ('Insufficient...				Display final message

Just like the counter in a counting loop, the loop-control variable Balance for an event-controlled loop must be *initialized, tested,* and *updated* for the loop to execute properly.

▶ *Initialization.* Balance is initialized to InitBal before the loop is reached.
▶ *Testing.* Balance is tested before each execution of the loop body.
▶ *Updating.* Balance is updated (reduced by the value of Bill) during each literation.

Remember to include similar steps in *every* loop that you write.

Checking Zero-Iteration Loops

zero-iteration loop
a loop whose body is not executed

Although we expect a loop body to be repeated, in some cases it will never execute (called a **zero-iteration loop**). The loop body will not execute if the loop-repetition condition evaluates to false when first tested. Because the loop initialization step is always performed, even for zero-iteration loops, it should always be written to ensure that a program with a zero-iteration loop generates meaningful results.

The bill-paying program of Fig. 5.6 has a zero-iteration loop when the initial account balance is negative. If InitBal is -120.00, the loop initialization step would assign -120.00 to Balance, the loop would be skipped, and the statements following the loop would execute. The program output would be:

```
Enter initial account balance >$-120.00
Insufficient funds to pay any more bills!
```

Exercises for Section 5.3

Self-Check

1. What is the least number of times that the body of a while loop can be executed?

2. When would the output of the following segment be erroneous? How could it be fixed?

```
Total := 0;
Write ('Enter number of items> ');
ReadLn (Num);
Count := 0;
while Count < Num do
  begin
    Write ('Enter a value> ');
    ReadLn (Value);
    Last := Value
  end; {while}
WriteLn ('The last value entered was ', Last)
```

3. Trace the program in Fig. 5.6 for the following data: 150.00, 75.00, 50.00, 25.00, 30.00.

4. a. How would you modify the loop in Fig. 5.6 so that it also determines the number of bills paid (CountBills)?

   b. How would you modify the loop in Fig. 5.6 if it is possible for all bills to be paid before the account becomes overdrawn? Assume that the number of bills to pay (NumberBills) as well as the initial account balance are provided as data. *Hint:* Use the loop repetition condition (Balance >= 0.0) and (CountBills < Number-Bills).

Programming

1. There are 9870 people in a town whose population increases by 10% each year. Write a loop that determines how many years (CountYears) it would take for the population to exceed 30,000.

5.4 Loop Design

It is one thing to analyze the operation of a loop and another to design your own loops. Loop design can be approached in two ways. One method analyzes the requirements for a new loop to determine the needed initialization, testing, and updating of the loop-control variable. The second method develops templates for frequently recurring loop forms and uses a template as the basis for a new loop.

Analyzing Loop Requirements

To gain some insight into the design of the loop needed for the bill paying program, let's study the comment in Fig. 5.6 that summarizes the goals of the loop:

```
{
  Pay each bill as long as the account is not overdrawn. Decrease
  the balance by the bill amount after each bill is processed.
}
```

To accomplish these goals, we must focus on loop control and loop processing. Focusing on loop control means making sure that the loop exit occurs when it should; focusing on loop processing means making sure that the loop body performs the required operations.

To formulate the necessary loop-control and loop-processing steps, we start by listing what we know about the loop. In this example, if `Balance` is the loop-control variable, we can make four observations:

1. `Balance` must be equal to `InitBal` just before the loop begins.
2. We pay the current bill if the account has sufficient funds.
3. `Balance` during the next pass must be less than `Balance` during the current pass by the amount of the current bill.
4. We stop paying bills when `Balance` becomes negative.

Requirement 1 tells us which initialization must be performed. Requirement 2 tells us when to pay the current bill (if `Balance >= Bill` is true). Requirement 3 tells us how to update `Balance` within the loop body (`Balance := Balance - Bill`). Requirement 4 tells us that the loop should be exited when the first bill to make `Balance` negative is processed. These requirements form the basis for the following algorithm design. The loop-repetition condition, `Balance >= 0.0`, is the opposite of the loop-exit condition, `Balance < 0.0`.

1. Initialize `Balance` to `InitBal`.
2. `while Balance >= 0.0 do`
    `begin`

3. Read the data for the current bill.
4. Display the check-writing information if the bill can be paid.
5. `Balance := Balance - Bill`
   `end {while}`

One common way to generate output from a loop is to arrange it in a table. In the next example, we analyze loop requirements to produce a table of values.

EXAMPLE 5.3: Designing a Loop to Display a Table of Values ▼

Your physics professor wants you to write a program that displays the effect of gravity on a free-falling object. Your results are to be listed in a table that shows the height of an object dropped from a tower for every second it is falling.

Assuming *t* is the time of free fall, we can make the following observations about the height of an object dropped from a tower:

1. At $t = 0.0$, the object height is the same as the tower height.
2. While the object is falling, its height is the tower height minus the distance it has traveled.
3. Free fall ends when the object height is less than or equal to 0.0.

These requirements determine the design of the `while` loop shown in Fig. 5.7. The object height, `Height`, is initialized to the tower height, `Tower` (from requirement 1). The `while` condition

`Height > 0.0`

ensures that loop exit occurs when the object hits the ground (from requirement 3). Within the loop body, the assignment statement

`Height := Tower - 0.5 * G * Sqr(T)`

Figure 5.7

Dropping an Object
from a Tower

Edit Window

```
program FreeFall;
{
  Displays the height of an object dropped
  from a tower until it hits the ground
}
  const
    G = 9.80665;      {gravitational constant for metric units}

  var
    Height,           {height of object}
    Tower,            {height of tower}
    T,                {elapsed time}
    DeltaT : Real;    {time interval}
```

▷ ▷ ▷ ▷ ▷ ▷

```
begin {FreeFall}
  {Enter tower height and time interval.}
  Write ('Tower height in meters> ');
  ReadLn (Tower);
  Write ('Time in seconds between table lines> ');
  ReadLn (DeltaT);

  {Display object height until it hits the ground.}
  WriteLn;
  WriteLn ('Time' :10, 'Height' :10);
  T := 0.0;
  Height := Tower;
  while Height > 0.0 do
    begin
      WriteLn (T :10:2, Height :10:2);
      T := T + DeltaT;
      Height := Tower - 0.5 * G * Sqr(T)
    end; {while}

  {Object hits the ground.}
  WriteLn;
  WriteLn ('SPLATT!!!')
end. {FreeFall}
```

Output Window

```
Tower height in meters> 100.0
Time in seconds between table lines> 1.0

        Time      Height
        0.00      100.00
        1.00       95.10
        2.00       80.39
        3.00       55.87
        4.00       21.55

SPLATT!!!
```

---

computes the object height (from requirement 2), where distance traveled is represented by the formula

distance $= \frac{1}{2}gt^2$

and *g* is the gravitational constant.

The number of loop iterations depends on the time interval between iterations (DeltaT) and the tower height (Tower), both of which are data values. During each iteration, the current elapsed time, T, and the current object height, Height, are displayed on a new table line, and new values are assigned to these variables. The message following the table is displayed when the object hits the ground. ▲

Program Style

Displaying a Table

The program in Fig. 5.7 displays a table of output values. Before the loop is reached, the statement

```
WriteLn ('Time' :10, 'Height' :10);
```

displays the two strings that appear in the table headings. Since a string is printed right-justified in its field (see Table 2.13), the rightmost character of the first string appears in column 10 and that of the second string in column 20 (10 + 10).

Within the loop body, the statement

```
WriteLn (T :10:2, Height :10:2);
```

displays a pair of output values each time it is executed. The rightmost digit of the first number appears in column 10 and that of the second number in column 20. Therefore a table consisting of two columns of numbers is displayed, each right-aligned with its respective heading. Make sure that the field width (10, in this case) is big enough to accommodate the largest value to be printed.

Another technique for using loop requirements to design a loop is to work backward from the results to determine which initial values will produce those results. In the next example, we use this technique to determine the initialization steps for a loop.

EXAMPLE 5.4: Working Backward to Determine Loop Initialization ▼

Your 10-year-old cousin is learning the binary number system and has asked you to write a program that displays all powers of 2 that are less than a certain value (say, 10,000). Assuming that each power of 2 is stored in the variable Power, we can make two observations about the loop:

1. Power during the next iteration is 2 times Power during the current iteration.
2. Power must be ≥ 10,000 just after loop exit.

Requirement 1 derives from the fact that the powers of 2 are all multiples of 2, and requirement 2 from the fact that only powers less than 10,000 are to be displayed. From requirement 1, we know that Power must be multiplied by 2 in the loop body. From requirement 2, we know that loop exit should occur if Power >= 10000 is true, so the loop repetition condition is Power < 10000.

These considerations lead us to the following outline:

1. Initialize `Power` to _____
2. `while Power < 10000 do`
    `begin`
        3. Display `Power`
        4. Multiply `Power` by 2
    `end`

One way to complete step 1 is to ask what value should be displayed during the first loop iteration. Since the value of any number raised to the power 0 is 1, initializing `Power` to 1,

1. Initialize `Power` to 1

will cause step 3 to display the correct value for `Power` during the first iteration. The second iteration will display 1×2 or 2 (2^1); the third iteration will display 2×2 or 4 (2^2); the fourth iteration will display 4×2 or 8 (2^3); and so on.   ▲

Using Templates to Design Loops

Because many loops have similar structures, we can create general frameworks, or templates, to use in designing these common loops.

Counter-Controlled Loops

We used counters to control the loops in Figs. 5.1 and 5.4. Although they can serve many different purposes, we can standardize the steps of a counter-controlled loop in the following template:

Template for Counter-Controlled Loop

1. Set *counter variable* to 0
2. `while` *counter variable* < *final value* `do`
    `begin`
      . . .
        3. Increase *counter variable* by 1
    `end`

Two more common loops are sentinel loops and loops controlled by Boolean flags. These loops, too, can be standardized into templates to help with their design.

Sentinel-Controlled Loops

Many programs with loops read one or more additional data items each time they repeat the loop body. Often we don't know how many data items the loop should process when it begins execution, and so we must find a way to signal the program to stop reading and processing new data.

One approach is to instruct the user to enter a unique data value, called a **sentinel value,** after the last data item. The loop-repetition condition tests each data item and causes loop exit when the sentinel value is read. Choose the sentinel value carefully; it must be a value that could not normally occur as data.

A program that calculates the sum of a collection of exam scores is a candidate for using a sentinel value. if the class is large, the instructor may not know the exact number of students who took the exam being graded. The program should work regardless of class size. The following loop uses Sum as an accumulator variable and Score as an input variable:

sentinel value

an end marker that follows the last data item

1. Initialize Sum to 0
2. Read the first score into Score
3. while Score is not the sentinel do
       begin
          4. Add Score to Sum
          5. Read the next score into Score
       end

Step 2 reads the first data value into Score before the loop is reached. In the loop body, step 4 adds each score to Sum (initial value is 0) and step 5 reads each data value in turn, including the sentinel value. The loop repeats as long as the previous data value read is not the sentinel, each iteration causing the previous data value to be added to Sum and the next data value to be read into Score. Because the loop exit occurs right after the sentinel value is read, the sentinel is not added to Sum.

Two of these steps read data into Score, steps 2 and 5. The initial read before the loop (step 2) reads only the first score and is called the *priming read*. This step is analogous to priming a pump, which is done by pouring a cup of water into the pump chamber before the pump can draw water out of a well.

Figure 5.8 shows a Pascal program that codes this loop. The sentinel value is -1 because all exam scores should be nonnegative. The constant declaration

```
const
   Sentinel = -1;              {sentinel value}
```

associates the constant Sentinel with the sentinel value.

Although it may seem strange at first to see the statement

```
ReadLn (Score);
```

at two different points in the program, this is a perfectly good programming practice and causes no problems. The sample run in Fig. 5.8 processes the scores 55, 33, and 77. The sentinel value (-1) is the last data value read, but it is not included in the sum.

Figure 5.8
Using a Sentinel-
Controlled Loop

Edit Window

```
program SumScores;
{Accumulates the sum of exam scores}

  const
    Sentinel = -1;              {sentinel value}

  var
    Score,                      {input - each exam score}
    Sum : Integer;              {output - sum of scores}
begin {SumScores}
  {Accumulate the sum.}
  Sum := 0;
  WriteLn ('When done, enter -1 to stop.');
  Write ('Enter the first score> ');
  ReadLn (Score);
  while Score <> Sentinel do
    begin
      Sum := Sum + Score;
      Write ('Enter the next  score> ');
      ReadLn (Score)
    end; {while}

  {Display the sum.}
  WriteLn;
  WriteLn ('Sum of exam scores is ', Sum :1)
end. {SumScores}
```

Output Window

```
When done, enter -1 to stop.
Enter the first score> 55
Enter the next  score> 33
Enter the next  score> 77
Enter the next  score> -1

Sum of exam scores is 165
```

We should verify that the program is correct when no data items remain to be processed. In that case, enter the sentinel value as the "first score." The loop exit would occur right after the first (and only) test of the loop-repetition condition, so the loop body would not execute (zero-iteration loop). Sum would retain its initial value of 0, which would be correct.

Template for a Sentinel-Controlled Loop

1. Read the first value of *input variable*
2. while *input variable* is not equal to the sentinel do
    begin

      . . .

      3. Read the next value of *input variable*
    end

The sentinel value must be a value that would not be entered as a normal data item and must not be processed in the loop body. To enhance program readability, we usually store the sentinel value in a constant.

Loops Controlled by Boolean Flags

Another common event-controlled loop is one whose execution is controlled by a Boolean variable. A **program flag,** or **flag,** is a Boolean variable whose value (True or False) signals whether a particular event occurs. The flag value should be set to False initially and reset to True when the event occurs. A flag-controlled loop executes until the event being monitored occurs.

For example, assume a program reads various data characters typed at the keyboard, but we are only interested in digit characters (0, 1, . . .). Consequently, our program should ignore any blanks, letters, symbols, and so on, and store the first digit character that it reads. A Boolean variable, say, DigitRead, could be used as a flag to monitor whether a digit character has been read:

Program variable
```
DigitRead : Boolean    {program flag - value is False until
                        a digit character is read; after a
                        digit character is read, value is True}
```

Because no characters have been read before the data entry loop executes, we should initialize DigitRead to False. The while loop must continue to execute as long as DigitRead is False, because this means that the event "digit character read as data" has not yet occurred. Therefore the loop repetition condition should be not DigitRead, because this condition is True when DigitRead is False. Within the loop body, we will read each data character and set the value of DigitRead to True if that data character is a digit. The while loop follows:

flag
a Boolean variable whose value is changed from False to True when a particular event occurs

```
DigitRead := False;        {Assume no digit character was read.}
while not DigitRead do
  begin
    Write ('Enter another data character >');
    ReadLn (NextChar);
    DigitRead := ('0' <= NextChar) and (NextChar <= '9')
  end {while}
```

Inside the loop body, the assignment statement

```
DigitRead := ('0' <= NextChar) and (NextChar <= '9')
```

assigns a value of True to DigitRead if NextChar is a digit character (within the range '0' through '9'); otherwise, DigitRead remains False. If DigitRead becomes True, loop exit occurs; if DigitRead remains False, the loop continues to execute until a digit character is finally read.

Template for a Flag-Controlled Loop

1. Initialize *flag* to False
2. while not *flag* do
    begin
        . . .
        3. Reset *flag* to True if the event being monitored occurs
    end

The last step in the loop body updates the flag value, setting it to True after the first occurrence of the event being monitored.

Exercises for Section 5.4

Self-Check

1. When generating a table in a loop, why is it necessary to add format specifiers to every output list item including integers (which cannot have decimal places)?
2. Why would it be incorrect to move the assignment statement in the sentinel-controlled loop of Fig. 5.8 to the end of the loop body?
3. Rewrite the sentinel-controlled loop in Fig. 5.8 as a flag-controlled loop. In this case the event being monitored would be "sentinel value was read."
4. When would a flag-controlled loop be a better choice than a sentinel-controlled loop?

Programming

1. Write a program to maintain a checkbook. It should first ask for a balance, then for transactions, and enter deposits as positive values and checks as negative values. After each check or deposit, the new balance should be printed. Use 0 as a sentinel value.

2. Write a program segment that allows the user to enter values and prints out the number of positive values entered and the number of negative values entered. Use 0 as the sentinel value.
3. Write a `while` loop that displays all powers of an integer, *n*, less than a specified value, `MaxPower`. On each line of a table, show the power (0, 1, 2, . . .) and the value of the integer *n* raised to that power.
4. Write a loop that prints a table of angle measures along with their sine and cosine values. Assume that the initial and final angle measures (in degrees) are available in `InitDeg` and `FinalDeg` (type `Real`), respectively, and that the change in angle measure between table entries is given by `StepDeg`. *Hint:* Don't forget to change degrees to radians.
5. Write a flag-controlled loop that continues to read pairs of integers until it reads a pair with the property that the first integer in the pair is evenly divisible by the second.

5.5   The for Statement

In addition to the `while` statement, Pascal provides another statement for writing counter-controlled loops. The `for` statement condenses the code for a counter-controlled loop, as you can see by comparing this pseudocode:

Pseudocode for `for` **Loop**	**Pseudocode for** `while` **Loop**

`for` *counter* := *initial* `to` *final* `do`
  `begin`
    . . .
  `end` {for}
	counter := *initial*;
	`while` *counter* <= *final* `do`
	    `begin`
	      . . .
	      counter := *counter* + 1
	    `end` {while}

The `for` loop header (the first line) specifies all manipulation of the counter variable (the color lines in the `while` loop). These three operations are as follows:

▶ Initialize *counter* to *initial*.
▶ Test if *counter* <= *final*
▶ Increment *counter* to its next value before each test.

EXAMPLE 5.5 ▼

The following two loops produce the same results:

for **loop**

```
{Print N blank lines.}
for Line := 1 to N do
   WriteLn
```

while **loop**

```
{Print N blank lines.}
Line := 1;
while Line <= N do
    begin
       WriteLn;
       Line := Line + 1
    end {while}
```

If Line is declared as an integer variable, the for statement causes the WriteLn operation to be performed N times. The for loop implementation is shorter because it does not require the assignment statements

```
Line := 1;
Line := Line + 1
```

which initialize and update the counter Line.   ▲

We describe the for statement syntax next and diagram it in Fig. 5.9.

SYNTAX DISPLAY

The for Statement

Form: for *counter* := *initial* to *final* do
                    statement

              for *counter* := *initial* downto *final* do
                    statement

Example: for I := 1 to 5 do
                    begin
                       ReadLn (InData, NextNum);
                       Sum := Sum + NextNum
                    end; {for}

              for CountDown := 10 downto 0 do
                    WriteLn (Countdown :2)

Interpretation: The *statement* that comprises the loop body is executed once for each value of *counter* between *initial* and *final*, inclusive. *initial* and *final* may be constants, variables, or expressions of the same ordinal type as *counter*. Use downto instead of to if *initial* is greater than *final*. In this case, *initial* is decremented by 1 after each loop repetition.

Note 1: The value of *counter* must not be modified in *statement*.

Note 2: The value of *final* is computed once, just before loop entry. Changing the value of *final* in the loop body will have no effect on the number of iterations performed.

Note 3: After the loop exit, the *counter* variable retains its value during the last iteration in Turbo Pascal, but not in standard Pascal.

Note 4: *statement* is not executed if *initial* is greater than *final*. (In the downto form, *statement* is not executed if *initial* is less than *final*.)

Figure 5.9
Syntax Diagram of the for Statement

for statement

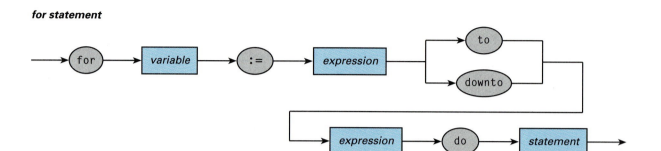

EXAMPLE 5.6 ▼

The for statement in Fig. 5.10 reads payroll data for seven employees and computes and displays each employee's weekly pay. Compare it with the while statement shown in Fig. 5.1.

Read the first line of Fig. 5.10 as "for each value of EmpNumber from 1 to 7 do." You needn't provide additional Pascal statements to set EmpNumber to an initial value or to update the value of EmpNumber; these two operations are automatically performed in a for loop.   ▲

Like a while statement, the counter variable in a for statement can be used in a computation; unlike a while statement, however, its value cannot be changed in the loop body. In the next example, you'll see a for statement that uses its counter variable as a function argument.

Figure 5.10
for Loop to Process Seven
Employees

```
for EmpNumber := 1 to 7 do
   begin
     Write ('Hours >');
     ReadLn (Hours);
     Write ('Rate >$');
     ReadLn (Rate);
     Pay := Hours * Rate;
     WriteLn ('Weekly pay is $', Pay :4:2)
   end; {for}

WriteLn ('All employees processed')
```

EXAMPLE 5.7 ▼

The `for` loop in Fig. 5.11 prints a list of integer values and their squares and square roots. During each repetition of the loop body, the statements

```
Square := Sqr(I);
Root := Sqrt(I);
```

compute the square and square root of the counter variable I; then the values of I, Square, and Root, are displayed. Table 5.2 traces the execution of the `for` loop.

Table 5.2
Trace of Program in
Figure 5.11

Statement	I	Square	Root	Effect
	?	?	?	
`for I := 1 to MaxI`	1			Initialize I to 1.
`  Square := Sqr(I);`		1		Assign 1 to Square.
`  Root := Sqrt(I);`			1.0	Assign 1.0 to Root.
`  WriteLn ...`				Print 1, 1, 1.0.
Increment and test I	2			2 <= 4 is true.
`  Square := Sqr(I);`		4		Assign 4 to Square.
`  Root := Sqrt(I);`			1.4	Assign 1.4 to Root.
`  WriteLn ...`				Print 2, 4, 1.4.
Increment and test I	3			3 <= 4 is true.
`  Square := Sqr(I);`		9		Assign 9 to Square.
`  Root := Sqrt(I);`			1.7	Assign 1.7 to Root.
`  WriteLn ...`				Print 3, 9, 1.7.
Increment and test I	4			4 <= 4 is true.
`  Square := Sqr(I);`		16		Assign 16 to Square.
`  Root := Sqrt(I);`			2.0	Assign 2.0 to Root.
`  WriteLn ...`				Print 4, 16, 2.0.
Increment and test I	5 4			5 <= 4 is false. Exit loop. Reset I to last value.

Figure 5.11
Table of Integers, Squares,
and Square Roots

Edit Window

```
program Squares;
{Displays a table of integers and their squares and square roots}

  const
    MaxI = 4;              {largest integer in table}

  var
    I,                     {counter variable}
    Square : Integer;      {output - square of I}
    Root : Real;           {output - square root of I}

begin {Squares}
  {Prints a list of integers, their squares, and their square roots}
  WriteLn ('I' :10, 'I * I' :10, 'Square root' :15);
  for I := 1 to MaxI do
    begin
      Square := Sqr(I);
      Root := Sqrt(I);
      WriteLn (I :10, Square :10, Root :15:1)
    end {for}
end. {Squares}
```

Output Window

```
         I     I * I    Square root
         1        1            1.0
         2        4            1.4
         3        9            1.7
         4       16            2.0
```

The trace in Table 5.2 shows that the counter variable I is initialized to 1 when the for loop is reached. After each loop repetition, I is incremented by 1 and tested to see whether its value is still less than or equal to MaxI (4). If the test result is true, the loop body is executed again, and the next values of I, Square, and Root are printed. If the test result is false, the loop is exited.

I is equal to MaxI during the last loop repetition. In Turbo Pascal, I retains its last value when the loop is exited. In standard Pascal, the value of I becomes undefined when the loop is exited. You should not reference the variable I again in standard Pascal until it is given a new value.   ▲

Type Char Counter Variables

The `for` loop can be used with other ordinal types besides `Integer`. The next example uses a counter variable of type `Char`.

EXAMPLE 5.8 ▼

The next `for` loop displays the uppercase letters on a line. The counter variable, `NextCh`, must be type `Char`.

```
for NextCh := 'A' to 'Z' do
  Write (NextCh);
WriteLn   ▲
```

Counting Down

The examples given so far have used the reserved word `to` and increased the value of the counter variable after each loop repetition. If the reserved word `downto` is used instead, the value of the counter variable decreases after each loop repetition.

EXAMPLE 5.9 ▼

A student wants a table equating Celsius temperatures from 5 degrees to −10 degrees with Fahrenheit temperatures. She could use the following `for` loop:

```
for Celsius := 5 downto -10 do
  begin
    Fahrenheit := 1.8 * Celsius + 32;
    WriteLn (Celsius :10, Fahrenheit :15:1)
  end {for}   ▲
```

Loops in Graphics Programs (Optional)

You can form many interesting geometric patterns on your screen by using a loop in a graphics program to repeatedly draw similar shapes. Each shape can have a different size, color, fill pattern, and position.

EXAMPLE 5.10 ▼

The program in Fig. 5.12 draws a nest of bars (filled rectangles), each a different color and fill pattern. Before entering graphics mode, the program prompts the user for the number of bars to draw. The first bar drawn is the outermost bar and fills the screen. Each subsequent bar is drawn inside the previous bar, so only a border from the previous bar remains on the screen. The statements

```
StepX := GetMaxX div (2 * NumBars);      {X increment}
StepY := GetMaxY div (2 * NumBars);      {Y increment}
```

define the change in *X*- and *Y*-values for the corners of each bar and are computed so that there will be room to display all the bars.

In the `for` loop, the statements

```
ForeColor := I mod 16;               {Pick foreground color.}
SetColor (ForeColor);
```

Figure 5.12
Drawing a Nest of
Rectangles

▽

Edit Window

```
program Quilt;
{Draws a nest of bars with different colors and fill patterns.}

  uses Graph;        {Enables access to graphic modules and constants.}

  const
    Directory = 'C:\BP\BGI';

  var
    Driver, Mode,          {Indicators of kind of graphics hardware}
    NumBars,                    {number of bars}
    X1, Y1,  X2, Y2,            {coordinates of corner points}
    StepX, StepY,               {change in coordinate values}
    I,                          {counter variable}
    Forecolor : Integer;        {foreground color (0 - 15)}
begin {Quilt}
  Write ('Enter number of bars> ');
  ReadLn (NumBars);
  InitGraph (Driver, Mode, Directory);   {Initialize graphics.}

  {Set corner points of outermost bar and X, Y increments.}
  X1 := 0;           Y1 := 0;              {top left corner}
  X2 := GetMaxX;     Y2 := GetMaxY;        {bottom right corner}
  StepX := GetMaxX div (2 * NumBars);   {X increment}
  StepY := GetMaxY div (2 * NumBars);   {Y increment}
  for I := 1 to NumBars do
    begin {for}
      ForeColor := I mod 16;      {Pick foreground color.}
      SetColor (ForeColor);
      SetFillStyle (I mod 12, ForeColor);              {Set fill style.}
      Bar (X1, Y1, X2, Y2);                            {Draw a bar.}
      X1 := X1 + StepX;  Y1 := Y1 + StepY;             {Change top left.}
      X2 := X2 - StepX;  Y2 := Y2 - StepY;             {Change bottom right.}
    end {for}
end. {Quilt}
```

▷ ▷ ▷ ▷ ▷ ▷

Output Window in Text Mode

```
Enter number of bars> 8
```

Output Window in Graphics Mode

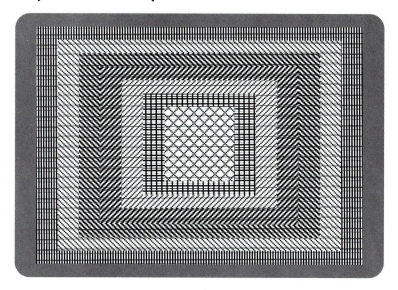

set the foreground color to one of 16 colors, based on the value of counter variable I. Similarly, procedure SetFillStyle sets the fill pattern to one of 12 possible patterns. After procedure Bar draws a bar, the statements

```
X1 := X1 + StepX;   Y1 := Y1 + StepY;   {Change top left.}
X2 := X2 - StepX;   Y2 := Y2 - StepY;   {Change bottom right.}
```

change the top-left corner (point X1, Y1) and the bottom-right corner (point X2, Y2) for the next bar, moving them closer together. For interesting effects, try running this program with different values assigned to StepX and StepY.   ▲

Exercises for Section 5.5   **Self-Check**

1. Trace the following program fragments:

```
J := 10;
for I := 1 to 5 do
  begin
    WriteLn (I, J);
    J := J - 2
  end; {for}
```

2. What is the minimum number of times the statement that comprises the `for` loop body can be executed? Give an example program fragment that will execute that minimum number of times.
3. Write `for` loop headers that process all values of `Celsius` (type `Integer`) in the following ranges:
   a. -10 through +10   c.   15 through 50
   b. 100 through 1   d.   50 through -75
4. Variables of which data types can be declared as `for` loop counter variables?
5. What would be drawn by the following fragment?

```
Radius := 20;
X := Radius;          Y := GetMaxY div 2;
for I := 1 to 10 do
  begin
    ForeColor := I mod 16;
    SetColor (ForeColor);
    Circle (X, Y, Radius);
    FloodFill (X, Y, ForeColor);
    X := X + Radius
  end; {for}
```

Programming

1. Write a `for` statement that computes the sum of the odd integers in the range 0 to 100, inclusive.
2. Write a program fragment with a `for` statement that accumulates the total number of days for the years 1950 to the year 2000. Remember, any year divisible by 4 is a leap year and has 366 days.

5.6   The repeat Statement

The `repeat` statement specifies a conditional loop that is repeated `until` its condition becomes true. Such a loop is called a *repeat-until* loop. To illustrate, compare two program segments that print the powers of 2 between 1 and 1000:

`repeat` **statement**	`while` **statement**
| ```
Power := 1;
repeat
  Write (Power :5);
  Power := Power * 2
until Power >= 1000
``` | ```
Power := 1;
while Power < 1000 do
  begin
    Write (Power :5);
    Power := Power * 2
  end {while}
``` |

logical complements
Boolean expressions with opposite values

The test in the `repeat-until` loop (`Power >= 1000`) is the **logical complement,** or opposite, of the test in the `while` loop. In the former, the loop body is repeated until the value of `Power` is greater than or equal to 1000. Since loop repetition *stops* when the condition is true, the test is called a **loop-termination test** rather than a loop-repetition test.

loop-termination test
the condition following `until` that causes loop exit when it becomes `True`

We describe the `repeat` statement syntax and diagram it in Fig. 5.13. Note that there is no need for a `begin-end` bracket around the loop body because the reserved words `repeat` and `until` perform this function.

SYNTAX DISPLAY

The repeat Statement (repeat-until Loop)

Form: `repeat`
                    loop-body
              `until` *termination-condition*
Example: `repeat`
                `Write ('Enter a digit> ');`
                `Read (Ch)`
              `until ('0' <= Ch) and (Ch <= '9')`

Interpretation: After each execution of *loop body, termination-condition* is evaluated. If *termination-condition* is true, loop exit occurs and the next program statement is executed. If *termination-condition* is false, *loop-body* is repeated. The *loop body* always executes at least once.

EXAMPLE 5.11 ▼

The program in Fig. 5.14 uses a `repeat-until` loop to find the largest value in a sequence of data items. The variable `Item` holds each data item, and the variable `LargestSoFar` saves the largest data value encountered. Within the loop, the `if` statement

```
if Item > LargestSoFar then
   LargestSoFar := Item        {Save the new largest number.}
```

redefines the value of `LargestSoFar` if the current data item is larger than all previous data values.

Figure 5.13
Syntax Diagram of the repeat Statement

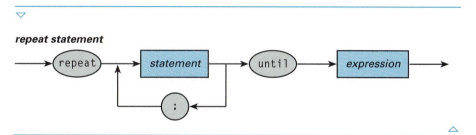

Figure 5.14
Finding the Largest Value

Edit Window

```
program Largest;
{Finds the largest number in a sequence of integer values}
  const
    MinValue = -MaxInt;      {a very small integer}

  var
    Item,                    {each data value}
    LargestSoFar : Integer;  {largest value so far}

begin  {Largest}
  {Initialize LargestSoFar to a very small integer.}
  LargestSoFar := MinValue;

  {Save the largest number encountered so far.}
  WriteLn ('Finding the largest value in a sequence:');
  repeat
    Write ('Enter an integer or ', MinValue :1, ' to stop> ');
    ReadLn (Item);
    if Item > LargestSoFar then
      LargestSoFar := Item        {Save the new largest number.}
  until Item = MinValue;

  WriteLn ('The largest value entered was ', LargestSoFar :1)
end. {Largest}
```

Output Window

```
Finding the largest value in a sequence:
Enter an integer or -32767 to stop> -999
Enter an integer or -32767 to stop> 500
Enter an integer or -32767 to stop> 100
Enter an integer or -32767 to stop> -32767
The largest value entered was 500
```

The constant `MinValue`, which represents a very small integer value, serves two purposes. Initializing `LargestSoFar` to `MinValue` before loop entry makes the condition `Item > LargestSoFar` true during the first iteration, so the first data item is saved as the largest value so far. `MinValue` is also a sentinel value because it is unlikely to be entered as a data item for a program that is finding the largest number in a sequence. ▲

menu-driven program
a program containing a loop that displays a menu of operations. The user selects the next operation from the menu.

EXAMPLE 5.12 ▼

When you use Turbo Pascal, a menu bar appears at the top of the screen displaying possible actions: run, compile, and so on. A program that uses a menu to determine its next operation is called a **menu-driven program.** For example, a statistics program might list its possible operations in the following menu form and the program user would enter an integer between 1 and 6 to select the next program operation.

```
1. Compute an average.
2. Compute a standard deviation.
3. Find the median.
4. Find the smallest and largest values.
5. Plot the data.
6. Exit the program.
```

A `repeat` statement can serve as the main control statement for a menu-driven program, as shown in this pseudocode:

repeat
    Display the menu
    Read the user's choice
    Perform the user's choice
until user's choice is exit program

The program fragment in Fig. 5.15 implements this loop. For each iteration, procedure `DisplayMenu` displays the menu and then the user's choice is read into `Choice` and passed on to procedure `DoChoice`. The loop repeats until the user's choice is `ExitChoice` (value is 6). ▲

Complementing a Boolean Expression

To replace a `while` statement with a `repeat` statement, you need to know the complement of the `while` loop repetition condition. To complement a simple comparison, change its operator as shown in the table (e.g., `Power >= 1000` and `Power < 1000` are complements):

Operator	Operator in Complement
<	>=
<=	>
>	<=
>=	<
=	<>
<>	=

Figure 5.15
Main Control Loop for
Menu-Driven Program

▽

```
repeat
    DisplayMenu;                              {Display the menu choices.}
    WriteLn ('Enter a number between 1 and ', ExitChoice :1);
    ReadLn (Choice);
    DoChoice (Choice)                         {Perform the user's choice.}
until Choice = ExitChoice
```

△

You would form the complement of a Boolean expression by preceding the entire expression with `not`. For example, the Boolean expression

```
(Ch >= 'a') and (Ch <= 'z')
```

is true when `Ch` is a lowercase letter. The complement of this expression is

```
not ((Ch >= 'a') and (Ch <= 'z'))
```

Also, *DeMorgan's theorem*, which is

not (*expression₁* and *expression₂*) = (not *expression₁*) or
                                              (not *expression₂*)

not (*expression₁* or *expression₂*) = (not *expression₁*) and
                                              (not *expression₂*)

provides another way to complement a Boolean expression containing `and` and `or` operators: Write the complement of each individual Boolean expression and change each `and` to `or` and each `or` to `and`. Using DeMorgan's theorem, the complement of the original expression would be

```
(Ch < 'a') or (Ch > 'z')
```

which is true if `Ch` is not a lowercase letter.

Review of for, while, and repeat Statements

Pascal contains three kinds of loop-control statements: `for`, `while`, and `repeat`. Use the `for` statement to write counting loops, that is, loops for which you know the number of iterations at the beginning of loop execution. The loop-control variable of a `for` statement must belong to an ordinal type (not `Real` or `string`).

Use the `while` and `repeat` statements to write event-controlled or conditional loops, loops whose number of iterations depends on the value (`True` or `False`) of a condition. The loop body in a `while` statement is repeated as long as its loop-repetition condition is true; the loop body in a `repeat` statement is repeated until its loop-termination condition becomes true. It is relatively easy to rewrite a `repeat-until` loop as a `while` loop by complementing the condition. However, not all `while` loops can be written as `repeat-until` loops, because the loop body of a `repeat-until` loop will always execute at least once, whereas a `while` loop body may be skipped entirely. For this reason, a `while` loop is preferred over a `repeat-until` loop unless it is certain that at least one loop iteration must always be performed.

To illustrate the three loop forms, Fig. 5.16 presents three versions of a simple counting loop. (The ellipses represent the loop body.) The `for` statement is the best choice in this situation. The `repeat-until` loop must be nested in an `if` statement to prevent it from being executed when `StartValue` is greater than `StopValue`. For this reason, the `repeat-until` version of a counting loop is least desirable.

Figure 5.16
Comparison of the Three
Loop Forms

```
for Count := StartValue to StopValue do        {for loop}
  begin
    ...
  end {for}

Count := StartValue;                           {while loop}
while Count <= StopValue do
  begin
    ...
    Count := Count + 1
  end {while}

Count := StartValue;                           {repeat-until loop}
if StartValue <= StopValue then
  repeat
    ...
    Count := Count + 1
  until Count > StopValue
```

In Fig. 5.16, `Count`, `StartValue`, and `StopValue` must all be the same ordinal type. The assignment statement

```
Count :- Count + 1
```

is used in both the `while` and `repeat` loops to update the loop-control variable `Count`, but is not required in the `for` loop.

Exercises for Section 5.6

Self-Check

1. Use DeMorgan's theorem to complement the following conditions:

   a. `(X <= Y) and (X <> 15)`   d. `Flag or not (X <> 15.7)`
   b. `(X <= Y) or (Z = 7.5)`   e. `not Flag and (X <= 8)`
   c. `(X <> 15) or (Z = 7.5) and (X <= Y)`

2. What would the following `repeat` statement display? What is the difference between `repeat ... until False` and `while False do`?

   ```
   repeat
     WriteLn ('False conditional example.')
   until False
   ```

3. When would you use a `repeat-until` loop rather than a `while` loop?

Programming

1. Write a program fragment that continues to read data values as long as they are not decreasing. The fragment should stop reading whenever a number smaller than the preceding one is entered. Write two versions: one with `repeat` and one with `while`.

2. Write a program fragment for the main control loop in a menu-driven program that updates an account balance (W = withdrawal, D = deposit, Q = quit). Assume that procedures ProcessWithdrawal and ProcessDeposit already exist and are called with the actual parameter Balance. Prompt the user for a transaction code (W, D, or Q) and call the appropriate procedure.

5.7   Nested Loops

Loops can be nested just as if statements are. Nested loops consist of an outer loop with one or more inner loops. Each time the outer loop is repeated, the inner loops are reentered, their loop-control expressions are reevaluated, and all required iterations are performed.

EXAMPLE 5.13 ▼

Figure 5.17 shows a sample run of a program with two nested for loops. The outer loop is repeated three times (for I equals 1, 2, 3). Each time the outer loop is repeated, the statement

Figure 5.17
Program with Nested
for Loops

Edit Window

```
program NestLoop;
{Illustrates a pair of nested for loops}

  var
    I, J : Integer;                    {loop-control variables}
begin  {NestLoop}
  WriteLn ('I' :12, 'J' :5);      {Print heading.}
  for I := 1 to 3 do
    begin {outer loop}
      WriteLn ('Outer' :5, I :7);
      for J := 1 to I do
        WriteLn ('Inner' :7, I :5, J :5)
    end {outer loop}
end.   {NestLoop}
```

Output Window

```
             I    J
Outer        1
   Inner     1    1
Outer        2
   Inner     2    1
   Inner     2    2
Outer        3
   Inner     3    1
   Inner     3    2
   Inner     3    3
```

```
WriteLn ('Outer' :5, I :7);
```

displays the string `'Outer'` and the value of I (the outer loop-control variable). Next the inner loop is entered, and its loop-control variable, J, is reset to 1. The number of times the inner loop is repeated depends on the current value of I. Each time the inner loop is repeated, the statement

```
WriteLn ('Inner' :7, I :5, J :5)
```

displays the string `'Inner'` and the value of I and J.

  The outer loop-control variable, I, is also the expression whose value determines the number of repetitions of the inner loop. Although this is perfectly valid, you cannot use the same variable as the loop-control variable of both an outer and an inner `for` loop in the same nest.   ▲

EXAMPLE 5.14 ▼

Program `Triangle` (Fig. 5.18) uses an outer loop (loop-control variable Row) and two inner loops to draw an isosceles triangle. Each time the outer loop is repeated, the two inner loops are executed. The first inner loop prints the leading blank spaces; the second inner loop prints one or more asterisks.

  The outer loop is repeated five times; the value of Row determines the number of repetitions performed by the inner loops. Table 5.3 lists the inner loop-control parameters for each value of Row. Four blanks and one asterisk are printed when Row is 1, three blanks and three asterisks are printed when Row is 2, and so on. When Row is 5, the first inner loop is skipped, and nine (2 * 5 - 1) asterisks are printed.   ▲

Table 5.3
Inner Loop-Control
Parameters

Row	LeadBlanks	CountStars	**Effect**
1	4 downto 1	1 to 1	Displays 4 blanks and 1 star
2	3 downto 1	1 to 3	Displays 3 blanks and 3 stars
3	2 downto 1	1 to 5	Displays 2 blanks and 5 stars
4	1 downto 1	1 to 7	Displays 1 blank and 7 stars
5	0	1 to 9	Displays 9 stars

Figure 5.18
Isosceles Triangle Program

Edit Window

```
program Triangle;
{Draws an isosceles triangle}

  const
    NumLines = 5;             {number of rows in triangle}
    Blank = ' ';              {output characters}
    Star = '*';

  var
    Row,                                {loop control for outer loop}
    LeadBlanks,               {loop control for first inner loop}
    CountStars : Integer; {loop control for second inner loop}
begin  {Triangle}
  for Row := 1 to NumLines do
    begin                              {Draw each row.}
      for LeadBlanks := NumLines - Row downto 1 do
        Write (Blank);                {Print leading blanks.}

      for CountStars := 1 to 2 * Row - 1 do
        Write (Star);                          {Print asterisks.}
      WriteLn                                   {Terminate line.}
    end  {for Row}
end.  {Triangle}
```

Output Window

```
    *
   ***
  *****
 *******
*********
```

Exercises for Section 5.7   **Self-Check**

1. What is displayed by the following program fragments, assuming M is 3 and N is 5?

   a. ```
   for I := 1 to N do
     begin
       for J := 1 to I do
         Write ('*');
       WriteLn
     end {for I}
   ```

   b.  ```
   for I := N downto 1 do
     begin
       for J := M downto 1 do
         Write ('*');
       WriteLn
     end {for I}
   ```

2. Show the output printed by the following nested loops:

```
for I := 1 to 2 do
  begin
    WriteLn ('Outer' :5, I :5);
    for J := 1 to 3 do
      WriteLn ('Inner' :7, I :3, J :3)
    for K := 2 downto 1 do
      WriteLn ('Inner' :7, I :3, K :3)
  end {for I}
```

Programming

1. Write a program fragment that, given an input value *N*, displays *N* rows of the form 1 2 . . . *N*, 2 3 . . . *N* + 1, and so on—a barber pole pattern of numbers. As an example, for an input value of 5, display:

   ```
   1 2 3 4 5
   2 3 4 5 6
   3 4 5 6 7
   4 5 6 7 8
   5 6 7 8 9
   ```

2. Write a program that prints a nicely labeled multiplication table for the digits 0 through 9.

5.8 Debugging and Testing Programs

In Section 2.9, we described the three general categories of errors: syntax errors, run-time errors, and logic errors. Sometimes the cause of a run-time error or the source of a logic error is apparent and the error can be fixed easily. Often, however, the error is not obvious and may require considerable time to locate.

The first step in locating a hidden error is to examine the program output to determine which part of the program is generating incorrect results. Then you can focus on the statements in that section to determine which are at fault. To find problem areas during debugging, insert extra WriteLn statements to display intermediate results at different points in your program. For example, if the loop in Fig. 5.8 is not computing the correct sum, the following diagnostic WriteLn statement in color will display each value of Score and Sum. The asterisks highlight the diagnostic output in the debugging runs and the diagnostic WriteLn statements in the source program.

```
ReadLn (Score);
while Score <> Sentinel do
  begin
    Sum := Sum + Score;
    WriteLn ('***** score is ', Score, ' sum is ', Sum);
    Write ('Enter the next score> ');
    ReadLn (Score)
  end {while}
```

Be careful when inserting diagnostic `WriteLn` statements. Sometimes you must add a `begin-end` bracket if a single statement inside an `if` or a `while` statement becomes a compound statement when you add a diagnostic `WriteLn`. If you insert a `WriteLn` statement after the last statement in a loop body, don't forget to precede the `WriteLn` with a semicolon.

Once it appears that you have located the error, avoid the temptation to take out the diagnostic `WriteLn` statements. Instead, as a temporary measure, turn the diagnostic statements into comments by enclosing them in braces. In this way, if the same errors crop up again in later testing, removing the braces will be easier than retyping the diagnostic statements.

Off-by-One Loop Errors

A fairly common logic error is a loop that executes one more or one less time than it should. If a sentinel-controlled `while` loop performs an extra repetition, it may erroneously process the sentinel value along with the regular data.

If a `while` loop performs a counting operation, make sure that the initial and final values of the loop-control variable are correct. For example, the following loop body executes `N + 1` times instead of `N` times. If you want the loop body to execute exactly `N` times, change the `while` condition to `Count < N`.

```
Count := 0;
while Count <= N do
  begin
    Sum := Sum + Count;
    Count := Count + 1
  end {while}
```

Checking Loop Boundaries

You can determine whether a loop is correct by checking the *loop boundaries,* that is, the initial and final values of the loop-control variable. For a `for` loop, carefully evaluate the *initial expression* and the *final expression* to see that their values make sense. Then substitute these values everywhere the counter variable appears in the loop body and verify that you get the expected results at the boundaries. As an example, in the `for` loop

```
Sum := 0;
for I := K to N - K do
  Sum := Sum + Sqr(I)
```

check that the first value of the counter variable `I` is supposed to be `K` and that the last value is supposed to be `N - K`. Next check that the assignment statement

```
Sum := Sum + Sqr(I)
```

is correct at these boundaries: When I is K, Sum gets the value of K squared, and when I is N - K, the value of $(N - K)^2$ is added to the previous Sum. As a final check, pick some small values of N and K (say, 3 and 1) and trace the loop execution to see that it computes Sum correctly for this case.

Using the Debugger

A *debugger program* can help to locate logic errors. The Turbo Pascal integrated environment contains its own debugger program, which allows you to interactively execute your program one statement at a time while observing changes made to selected variables or expressions. You also can halt execution of your program at certain statements (*breakpoints*) to inspect or change values of selected variables before resuming execution.

To use the Turbo Pascal debugger, select the Trace into option (function key F7) from the Run menu. An *execution bar* will appear over the begin line of the main program, and then will advance to the first program statement if you press function key F7. Each time you press F7, the statement under the execution bar executes, and the execution bar advances to the next statement. By repeatedly pressing function key F7, you will cause the debugger to execute your program one statement at a time.

The Watch Window

The User screen and the Output window can show the value of a variable only when it is displayed by a WriteLn statement. You can use Turbo Pascal's *Watch window* to see how the execution of each program statement changes the value of selected program variables or expressions. The window with label Watches in Fig. 5.19 shows two variables and their values just before the while loop executes for the first time.

You can open the Watch window or add a variable or expression to it at any time during program execution. To add a new variable, move the Edit cursor to that variable in the program, select the Debug menu from the Main menu bar, and choose the Add Watch option (or press Ctrl-F7), as shown in Fig. 5.19. A dialog box that contains in its Watch Expression field the variable under the Edit cursor will appear (Fig. 5.20). Select OK to add the variable in the Watch Expression field, along with its value, to the Watch window.

To place an expression in the Watch window, move the Edit cursor to the start of the expression and select Add Watch as before. Then press the right arrow key repeatedly until the whole expression is in the Watch Expression field. You can also type any variable name or expression directly into the Watch Expression field.

Use the F6 key to switch back and forth between the Edit window and the Watch window. To display both windows on the screen at the same time, reduce the size of the Edit window by clicking on the bottom right corner and dragging it up the screen.

Figure 5.19

Selecting Add Watch from
the Debug Menu

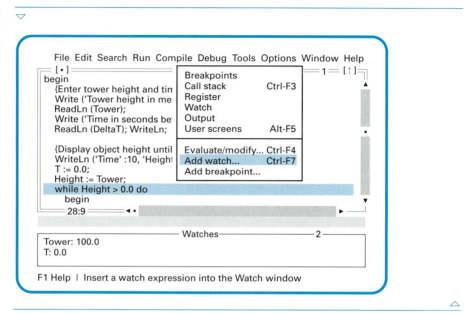

To delete a single expression from the Watch window, make it the active
window, use your mouse to highlight the expression to be deleted, and then
press the Delete key. To delete all watch expressions, close the Watch window.

Mixing Single-Statement and Normal Execution

If you suspect that a program bug lies in a certain section of your program,
you may want to execute all statements up to that section in the normal way.
Begin by moving the Edit cursor to the beginning of the section where you
believe the bug lies, then press F4. Turbo Pascal will execute all statements
up to the one selected and pause with the Execution bar over the selected
statement. At that point, you can add new variables to the Watch window
and begin single-statement execution.

Breakpoints

One approach to debugging is first to separate a program into segments and
then to execute all statements in a segment, pausing between segments to
examine Watch window values. In this way, you can determine which segments of a program are "buggy" and then rerun your program using single-
statement execution within buggy segments to find the bugs. You would
separate a program into segments by setting *breakpoints*, then pressing Ctrl-
F9 to execute all statements up to the next breakpoint or pressing F7 for
single-statement execution.

Figure 5.20
Add Watch Dialog Box

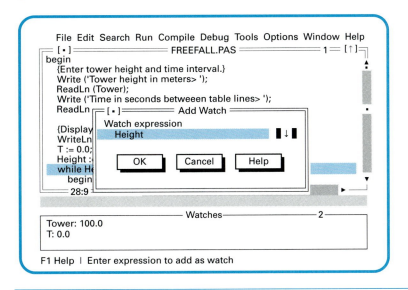

To set a breakpoint at some program statement, position the Edit cursor on that statement and press Ctrl-F8 (Toggle breakpoint). Or you could select the Debug menu and from it choose the Add breakpoint option, causing a dialog box to appear (Fig. 5.21). Select OK to set a breakpoint at the state-

Figure 5.21
Turbo Pascal Add
Breakpoint Dialog Box

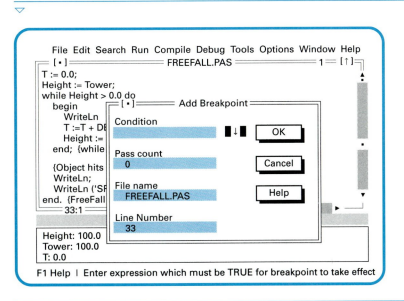

ment marked by the Edit cursor. Turbo Pascal sets a breakpoint and marks the statement with a highlight bar. Turbo Pascal allows you to set several breakpoints in your program and places a highlight bar over each breakpoint. If you have a color monitor, you will notice that Turbo Pascal uses different colors for breakpoints and the program execution bar.

To view a list of the breakpoints set in your program, select the Breakpoints option in the Debug menu. This brings up a dialog box similar to the one in Fig. 5.22. You can use your mouse to highlight any breakpoint displayed in the dialog box. By selecting the Delete button, you can remove the highlighted breakpoint from your program. The View button takes you to the program statement in the Edit window where the breakpoint is set, without executing your program.

The Edit button in Fig. 5.22 brings up a dialog box similar to the one in Fig. 5.21, which you can use to add a breakpoint or modify the condition under which execution should halt. You can use any valid Boolean expression in the Condition field; program execution will halt at that breakpoint only when that condition is true. The Pass count field is useful in monitoring the execution of loops, because you can specify the number of times a breakpoint is to be skipped before execution is halted. Select the New button to add a new breakpoint to your program. Select the Modify button to record any changes made to an existing breakpoint.

Figure 5.22
Turbo Pascal Edit
Breakpoint Dialog Box

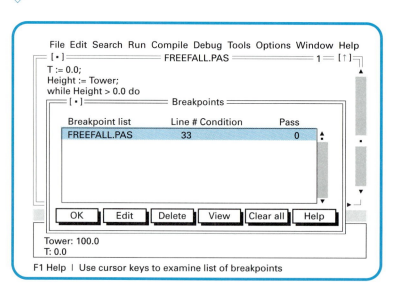

Restarting the Debugger

If you want to go back to the beginning of your program while in the middle of a debugging session, select Program Reset (Ctrl-F2) from the Run menu. This reinitializes the debugging system and positions the execution bar over the `begin` line of the main program.

Prior to loading a new program into the Turbo Pascal environment after a debugging session, select Program Reset to verify that the computer memory used by your old program is available for use by your new program. It is important to note that neither loading a new program into the Turbo Pascal system nor selecting Program Reset removes any of the expressions displayed in the Watch window or clears any of the program breakpoints. To remove Watch Expressions from the Watch window, close the Watch window. To clear all breakpoints, select the Clear all button shown in Fig. 5.22. You should do this prior to loading a new program into the Turbo Pascal environment.

Turbo Pascal will offer to restart the debugging session if you make any changes to a program's statements during debugging. For example, if you make a change to a program statement using an Edit command and then press one of the execution command keys (F7, F4, or Ctrl-F9), Turbo Pascal will display an Information dialog box with the message `Source has been modified. Rebuild?`. If you type `Y`, your program will be compiled again, the execution bar will be placed on the `begin` line of the main program, and the debugger will be reinitialized (as it would following a Program Reset). If you type `N`, the current debugging session will continue, and the changes made to your program will have no effect until it is recompiled.

Testing

After you have corrected all errors and the program appears to execute as expected, test it thoroughly to make sure it works. In Section 4.6, we discussed tracing an algorithm and suggested that you provide enough sets of test data to ensure that all possible paths are traced. The same is true for a completed program. Make enough test runs to verify that the program works properly for representative samples of all possible data combinations.

Exercises for Section 5.8   **Self-Check**

1. For the `while` loop in the subsection entitled "Off-by-One Loop Errors," add debugging statements to show the value of the loop-control variable at the start of each repetition. Add additional debugging statements to show the value of `Sum` at the end of each loop repetition.
2. Why does the following code fragment fail? What are the loop boundaries for this code fragment?

```
X := 10;
repeat
  X := X - 1;
  WriteLn (X, Sqrt(X))
until X < 0
```

5.9 Common Programming Errors

Beginners sometimes confuse if and while statements because both statements contain a condition. Always use an if statement to implement a decision step and a while statement to implement a conditional loop.

Be careful when you use tests for inequality to control the repetition of a while loop. For instance, the following loop is intended to process all transactions for a bank account while the balance is positive:

```
while Balance <> 0.0 do
  Update (Balance)
```

If the bank balance goes from a positive to a negative amount without being exactly 0.0, the loop will not terminate (an *infinite loop*). This loop would be safer:

```
while Balance > 0.0 do
  Update (Balance)
```

Be sure to verify that the repetition condition for a while loop will eventually become false. If you use a sentinel-controlled loop, remember to provide a prompt that tells the program user what value to enter as the sentinel. Make sure that the sentinel value cannot be confused with a normal data item.

If the loop body contains more than one statement, remember to bracket it with begin and end (unless it is a repeat-until loop). Otherwise, only the first statement will be repeated, and the remaining statements will be executed when and if the loop is exited. The following loop will not terminate, because the step that updates the loop-control variable is not considered part of the loop body. The program will continue to print the initial value of Power until you instruct the computer to terminate its execution. You can terminate a program by pressing Ctrl-C.

```
while Power <= 10000 do
  WriteLn ('Next power of N is ', Power :6);
  Power := Power * N
```

Be sure to initialize to 0 an accumulator variable used for accumulating a sum by repeated addition and to initialize to 1 a variable used for accumulating a product by repeated multiplication. Omitting this step leads to inaccurate results.

The value of the counter variable in a for statement either increases by 1 (to form) or decreases by 1 (downto form) after each repetition. If Larger is greater than `Smaller`, the following `WriteLn` statement will not execute because the initial value that would be assigned to `I` is larger than its final value:

```
for I := Larger to Smaller do
  WriteLn (I)
```

Similarly, the next `WriteLn` statement will not execute because the initial value that would be assigned to `I` is smaller than its final value:

```
for I := Smaller downto Larger do
  WriteLn (I)
```

A `repeat-until` loop always executes at least once. Use a `repeat` statement only when certain that there is no possibility of zero loop iterations; otherwise, use a `while` loop.

Be sure to trace each nest of loops carefully, checking the inner and outer loop-control variables. The loop-control variable of an outer `for` statement cannot be changed inside an inner `for` statement. Also, you cannot use the same loop-control variable in two `for` statements within the same nest.

CHAPTER REVIEW

1. To repeat steps in a program, use either of two kinds of loops: counter-controlled (or counting loops) and event-controlled (or conditional loops). For a counter-controlled loop, the number of iterations required can be determined before the loop is entered. For an event-controlled loop, repetition continues until a special event or condition occurs.
2. Pascal provides three statements for coding loops: `while`, `for`, and `repeat`. `while` and `repeat` can implement both kinds of loops; `for` can implement only counter-controlled loops.
3. In designing a loop, focus on both loop-control and loop-processing. For loop processing, make sure that the loop body contains steps that perform the operation that must be repeated. For loop control, you must provide steps that initialize, test, and update the loop control variable. Make sure that the initialization step leads to correct program results when the loop body is not executed (zero-iteration loop).
4. There are two common conditional loops: sentinel-controlled and flag-controlled. A sentinel-controlled loop stops repetition right after the sentinel value is read. Choose a value that cannot be a normal data item as the sentinel value. A flag-controlled loop tests a Boolean variable to determine whether a particular event has occurred.

Template for a Sentinel-Controlled Loop

Read the first value of *input variable*
`while` *input variable* is not equal to the sentinel `do`
  `begin`
    . . .

Read the next value of *input variable*
```
end
```

Template for a Flag-Controlled Loop

Initialize *flag* to False
```
while not flag do
   begin
      . . .
      Reset flag to True if the event being monitored occurs
   end
```

5. The `while` statement is the most general of the three Pascal loop statements. Unlike a `for` or `while`, the body of a `repeat-until` loop is always executed at least once. In a `for` statement, the counter variable may increase in value (`to` form) or decrease in value (`downto` form) after each loop iteration. Remember that the final value expression for the counter variable is evaluated when the loop is first reached and cannot be changed during loop execution.

6. Loops can be nested just like `if` statements. Each time an outer loop in a nest is repeated, every inner loop of the nest is reentered and executed to completion.

Summary of New Pascal Constructs

Construct	Effect
`while` *Statement*	
```Sum := 0;` `while Sum <= MaxSum do` ` begin` ` Write ('Next integer> ');` ` ReadLn (Next);` ` Sum := Sum + Next` ` end {while}```	A collection of input data items is read, and their sum is accumulated in Sum. This process stops when the accumulated sum exceeds MaxSum.
`for` *Statement*	
```for CurMonth := 3 to 9 do` ` begin` ` ReadLn (MonthSales);` ` YearSales := YearSales` ` + MonthSales` ` end {for}```	The loop body is repeated for each value of CurMonth from 3 to 9, inclusive. For each month, the value of MonthSales is read and added to YearSales.

Construct	Effect
repeat *Statement*	

`Sum := 0;`
`repeat`
  `ReadLn (NextInt);`
  `WriteLn (NextInt);`
  `Sum := Sum + NextInt`
`until NextInt = 0`
	Integer values are read, and their sum is accumulated in Sum. The process terminates after the first zero is read.

Quick-Check Exercises

1. If the loop condition is a Boolean variable, what type of loop is this?
2. It is an error if a `while` loop body never executes. True or false?
3. The priming step for a sentinel-controlled loop is what kind of statement? Where is this statement placed? What is the purpose of a similar statement in the loop body?
4. The sentinel value is always the last value added to a sum being accumulated in a sentinel-controlled loop. True or false?
5. Which loop form (`for`, `repeat`, or `while`)
   a. executes at least once?
   b. is the most general?
   c. condenses the code for a counting loop?
   d. should be used in a menu-driven program?
6. What does the following segment display?

```
Product := 1;
Counter := 2;
while Counter <= 5 do
   begin
      Product := Product * Counter;
      Counter := Counter + 1
   end; {while}
WriteLn (Product)
```

7. A loop that performs an incorrect computation during its last iteration has a problem at the _____.
8. During execution of the following program segment,

```
for I := 1 to 10 do
   begin
      for J := 1 to I do
         Write (I * J);
      WriteLn
   end
```

   a. how many times does the `Write` statement execute?
   b. how many times does the `WriteLn` statement execute?
   c. what is the last value displayed?

9.   What will be output by the following fragment?

```
N := 10;
for I := 1 to N do
   begin
      Write (I :3);
      N := N - I
   end; {for}
WriteLn (N :4)
```

Answers to Quick-Check Exercises

1.   Flag-controlled loop
2.   False
3.   An input operation; just before loop entry and as the last statement in the loop
      body. The input operation in the loop body reads all but the first data item,
      which is read by the input operation before loop entry.
4.   False—the sentinel should not be processed.
5.   a. repeat   b. while   c. for   d. repeat
6.   The value of 1 * 2 * 3 * 4 * 5, or 120.
7.   loop boundary
8.   a. 1 + 2 + 3 + ... + 9 + 10, or 55   b. 10   c. 100
9.   1 2 3 4 5 6 7 8 9 10 -45

Review Questions

1.   How does a sentinel value differ from a program flag as a means of loop con-
      trol?
2.   For correct use of a sentinel value when reading in data, where should the in-
      put statements appear?
3.   Write a program fragment that allows a user to input several pairs of values for
      X and Y and, for each pair, computes X raised to the Y power by repeated mul-
      tiplication. The program should keep obtaining values from the user until a sen-
      tinel value of 0 is entered for X.
4.   Hand trace the following program given these data:

```
4 2 8 4    1 4 2 1    9 3 3 1    -22 10 8 2    3 3 4 5

program Slopes;
   const
      StopValue = 0.0;
   var
      Slope, Y2, Y1, X2, X1 : Real;

begin {Slopes}
   WriteLn ('Enter four numbers separated by spaces');
   WriteLn ('The last two numbers cannot be the same, but');
   WriteLn ('The program terminates if the first two are.');
   WriteLn ('Enter four numbers> ');
   ReadLn (Y2, Y1, X2, X1);
```

```
Slope := (Y2 - Y1) / (X2 - X1);
while Slope <> StopValue do
   begin
      WriteLn ('Slope is ', Slope :5:2);
      WriteLn ('Enter four more numbers> ');
      ReadLn (Y2, Y1, X2, X1);
      Slope := (Y2 - Y1) / (X2 - X1)
   end {while}
end. {Slopes}
```

5. Can you always replace a `while` loop with a `for` or a `repeat` loop? Why or why not?

6. Consider the program segment

```
Count := 0;
for I := 1 to N do
   begin
      Read (X);
      if X = I then
         Count := Count + 1
   end {for}
```

   a. Write a `while` loop equivalent to the `for` loop.
   b. Write a `repeat-until` loop equivalent to the `for` loop.

Programming Projects

1. Write a program that will find the smallest, largest, and average values in a collection of N numbers. Read in the value of N before reading each value in the collection of N numbers.

2. Modify Programming Project 1 to compute and display both the range of values in the data collection and the standard deviation of the data collection. To compute the standard deviation, accumulate the sum of the data (Sum) and the sum of the squares of the data values (SumSquares) in the main loop. After loop exit, use the formula

$$\textit{Standard deviation} = \sqrt{\frac{\text{SumSquares} - \frac{\text{Sum}^2}{N}}{N}}$$

3. Bunyan Lumber Co. needs to create a table of the engineering properties of its lumber. The dimensions of the wood are given as the base and the height in inches. Engineers need to know the following information about lumber:

   cross-sectional area = base × height
   moment of inertia = (base × height³)/12
   section modulus = (base × height²)/6

   The height sizes are 2, 4, 6, 8, and 10 inches. Produce a table with appropriate headings to show these values and the computed engineering properties. Do not duplicate a 2-by-6 board with a 6-by-2 board.

4. Write a program to generate a yearly calendar. The program should accept the year and the day of the week for January 1 of that year (1 = Sunday, 7 = Saturday). Remember, February has 29 days if the year is divisible by 4. The calendar should be printed in the following form (for each month):

```
      January
                             1
   2   3   4   5   6   7   8
   9  10  11  12  13  14  15
  16  17  18  19  20  21  22
  23  24  25  26  27  28  29
  30  31
```

5. a. Write a program to read in a collection of exam scores ranging in value from 1 to 100. Your program should count and print the number of out standing scores (90–100), the number of satisfactory scores (60–89), and the number of unsatisfactory scores (1–59). It should also display the category of each score. Test your program on the following data:

    63 75 72 72 78 67 80 63 75
    90 89 43 59 99 82 12 100

    b. Modify your program to display the average exam score (a real number) at the end of the run.

6. Write a program to process weekly employee time cards for all employees of an organization. Each employee will have three data items: an identification number, the hourly wage rate, and the number of hours worked during a given week. Each employee is to be paid time and a half for all hours worked over 40. A tax amount of 3.625% of gross salary will be deducted. The program output should show the employee's number and net pay. Display the total payroll and the average amount paid at the end of the run.

7. Suppose you own a beer distributorship that sells Piels (ID number 1), Coors (ID number 2), Bud (ID number 3), and Iron City (ID number 4) by the case. Write a program to
    a. read in the case inventory for each brand for the start of the week.
    b. process all weekly sales and purchase records for each brand.
    c. print out the final inventory.
    Each transaction will consist of two data items: the brand identification number (an integer) followed by the amount purchased (a positive integer value) or the amount sold (a negative integer value). The weekly inventory for each brand (for the start of the week) will also consist of two items: the identification number and the initial inventory for that brand. For now, assume that you always have sufficient foresight to prevent depletion of your inventory for any brand. *Hint:* Your data entry should begin with eight values representing the case inventory, followed by the transaction values.

8. Revise Programming Project 7 to make it a menu-driven program. The menu operations supported by the revised program should be (E)nter Inventory, (P)urchase Beer, (S)ell Beer, (D)isplay Inventory, and (Q)uit Program. Negative quantities should no longer be used to represent goods sold.

9. Before high-resolution graphics displays became common, computer terminals were often used to display graphs of equations using only text characters. A typical technique created a vertical graph by spacing over on the screen, then drawing an *. Write a program that displays the graph of an increasing frequency sine wave this way. The program should ask the user for an initial step size in degrees and the number of lines of the graph to display. A sample output begins as:

```
                          *
                                *
                                    *
                                        *
                                            *
                                                *
                                                    *
                                                     *
                                                    *
                                                *
                                            *
                                    *
                                *
                          *
                    *
              *
        *
    *
  *
*
```

INTERVIEW

Marie desJardins

Marie desJardins graduated from Harvard University with an A.B. in computer science and later obtained a Ph.D. in artificial intelligence from the University of California at Berkeley. While at Berkeley Dr. desJardins was president of WICSE (Women in Computer Science and Engineering). Before entering the computer science industry Dr. desJardins worked as an instructor and lecturer, earning the Danforth Teaching Award for her work with undergraduate students. Since 1991, she has been a member of the Applied Artificial Intelligence Technology Program at SRI International.

▼ **What attracted you to the field of computer science?**

▲ I've always enjoyed mathematics and problem solving. Both of my parents work with computers, so I was exposed to them from a very early age. I can remember entering data on keypunch cards at my mother's office at NASA when I was eight or nine years old. In high school, I took a Fortran programming class and a problem-solving class at the local community college. I really enjoyed the logical thinking that was required, and the great feeling you get when you finally debug a complicated program—I even enjoyed pulling all-nighters to get class projects finished! By the time I finished the freshman series of programming courses in college, I was hooked.

▼ **You currently work on intelligent planning systems. When did your interest in artificial intelligence develop? How are intelligent planning systems "intelligent"?**

▲ My interests in artificial intelligence (AI) developed during my junior and senior years in college. I took several psychology classes and an AI class, and decided I really liked the combination of programming and cognitive psychology that AI represents, so I applied to graduate programs in AI, and eventually got my Ph.D. for research in machine learning.

Intelligent planning systems can be used autonomously or as "assistants" for human planners in many domains—such as space shuttle control, manufacturing, emergency response, and project management. These systems take knowledge about causality and problem solving within a specific domain and use general reasoning techniques to formulate plans based on that knowledge. Intelligent planning systems are capable of consolidating information into a plan and then analyzing the plan to determine where there might be bottlenecks, resource over-utilization, or conflicts between competing subgoals. Because they can continually synthesize incoming data, intelligent planning systems are a powerful tool with which a human planner can generate and maintain plans for very complex problems.

▼ **Are there problem-solving skills that are invaluable to you in tackling design problems?**

▲ In order to design a new piece of software, you need to be able to specify, very clearly and precisely, what problem it is you're trying to solve. This isn't always easy to do, even if you know what the problem is—and frequently in research, part of the design problem is to identify the problem being solved in the first place. Problem specification requires an ability to take intuitive, abstract, or vague concepts and break them down into manageable pieces; and to take these pieces and describe them "mathematically," in language that is clear enough that you can then start implementing a solution. Implementing a solution requires good programming skills. As I said before, you have to clearly specify, in a programming language, every step of the solution. Equally important are good debugging skills. Debugging requires patience, the application of careful testing methods, and the ability to "step back" from your expectations and observe what's *really* happening. When I helped students in the lab, I would frequently find that they were having trouble debugging their programs because they "knew," or rather thought they knew, what their program was doing, so they weren't testing the parts of the program that were causing the problem.

▼ **Through your years as a lecturer and teaching assistant, what topics did you find were most difficult for students learning introductory programming skills?**

▲ For beginning students, I think there are two particularly difficult concepts. The first is the idea that computers are actually very simplistic, deterministic devices that do *exactly* what they are told. This means that a computer program has to be correct in every detail: you can't skip any steps, make any assumptions, or have even a tiny error. Because we're so used to giving instructions to other human beings, who are very good at filling in gaps and at asking questions when there's something missing, it's hard at first to get used to the fact that in computer programming you have to specify every single step in order to solve a problem correctly.

The second difficult concept is that of recursion. The idea that a function can call itself with different arguments, and that the new call will eventually return to the spot in the same function where it was called—even if there were many more calls to the function within the recursive call—is not intuitive for most students. I found that different students respond to different explanations of this concept: some can grasp a particular metaphor, some need to "see" recursion happening in hands-on observation, some need to work it through on paper. My favorite part of teaching an introductory programming class is seeing the "Aha!" that many students experience when they finally get an intuitive understanding of recursion.

▼ **Looking back at your academic experience, what recommendations do you have for students pursuing computer science studies?**

▲ Computer science should be fun most of the time. Different students will enjoy different parts of the programming process—some people really like to design programs; some people like the programming itself; and some people enjoy testing and debugging. Sometimes it can be frustrating, especially when you feel like you've tried everything and just can't get a program to work. I really enjoy working with other people, so that when I get stuck, there's somebody else who knows what I'm working on that I can talk through the problem with. I think that developing the ability to work in a team is really important for computer science classes, and is invaluable in a work environment later on. The other recommendation I'd make is to pursue your other interests—music, history, literature, whatever. Not only will that make you a more well-rounded person (and help you to get away from the terminal every once in a while), but I frequently find that things I've learned in other classes actually come in handy in computer science classes. And you may find that you can combine computers with one or more of those interests, as I did with psychology and CS when I decided to study artificial intelligence.

Modular Programming

A carefully designed program constructed using procedures and functions shares some of the properties of a stereo system. Each stereo component is an independent device that performs a specific operation. You might know the purpose of each component, but you certainly have no need to know what electronic parts each contains or how it functions to play or record music.

Electronic audio signals move back and forth over wires linking the stereo components, via plugs on the back of the stereo receiver marked as inputs or outputs. Wires attached to the input plugs carry electronic signals into the receiver, where they are processed. These signals may come from the cassette deck, tuner, or CD player. The receiver sends new electronic signals through the output plugs to the speakers or back to the cassette deck for recording.

The introduction to procedures in Chapter 3 illustrated how to write the separate program components—the procedures—of a program. These procedures (or functions) correspond to the individual steps in a problem solution. In this chapter, you will learn how to connect the modules to create a program system—an arrangement of parts that makes your program function like a stereo system as it passes information from one module to another.

6.1   Introduction to Parameter Lists

Parameter lists provide the communication links between the main program and its modules. Parameters make procedures and functions more versatile because they enable a module to manipulate different data each time it is called. This section describes how programmers use parameters to pass information between a program and its modules, or between two modules.

Actual and Formal Parameters

Each procedure call statement has two parts: a *procedure name* and an **actual parameter list.** To illustrate, the graphics procedure Line draws a line from one point on the screen to another, and its procedure call statement

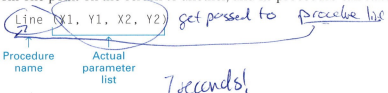

Procedure name   Actual parameter list

consists of the procedure name, Line, and the actual parameter list (X1, Y1, X2, Y2). The values of the four *actual parameters* are passed to procedure Line, which draws a line from point (X1, Y1) to point (X2, Y2). To continue drawing from point (X2, Y2) to (X3, Y3), we need the procedure call statement

Line (X2, Y2, X3, Y3)

In each procedure call, the programmer provides procedure Line with four variables or values that represent the X, Y coordinates of two points on the screen. Because the four coordinates can change each time Line is called, we must represent them somehow in the procedure declaration. To do this, we use dummy names called *formal parameters:*

procedure Line (XStart, YStart, XEnd, YEnd : Integer);

Procedure name   Formal parameter list

actual parameter list
parenthesized list of variables (or values) passed to the procedure; follows the procedure name in the procedure call

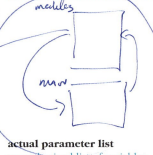

formal parameter list

parenthesized list of dummy names (with data types) used in the procedure to represent actual parameters; follows the procedure name in the procedure heading

The **formal parameters list** shows the four formal parameters used inside the procedure to represent the X, Y coordinates of the end points of the line to be drawn. The pair XStart, YStart represents one end point, and the pair XEnd, YEnd represents the other. The formal parameter list also indicates the data type, Integer, of these parameters.

Correspondence Between Actual and Formal Parameters

Procedure Line doesn't know what values it will receive until it is called. The calling program passes the information needed by Line via the actual parameter list, matching each actual parameter with its corresponding formal parameter.

Figure 6.1 shows part of a program containing procedure Line and one call to this procedure. The arrows show the information flow between the four actual and formal parameters. The parameter correspondence is summarized here:

Actual Parameter	corresponds to	Formal Parameter
X1		XStart
Y1		YStart
X2		XEnd
Y2		YEnd

Figure 6.1 shows that the value of main program variable X1 is passed to formal parameter XStart, and so on. Although not shown in the figure, the four actual parameters should have values assigned before the procedure call executes.

Notice that corresponding formal and actual parameters have different names in Fig. 6.1. This presents no problems, because the parameter correspondence is determined by *position* in each parameter list, not by name.

Figure 6.1
Main Program with Call to Procedure Line

```
program Main;

  var
    X1, X2, Y1, Y2, X3, Y3 : Integer;   Main program variables

                              Formal parameters
  procedure Line (XStart, YStart, XEnd, YEnd : Integer);
    . . .

  end; {Line}

begin {Main}

  Line (X1, Y1, X2, Y2);   Actual parameters
    . . .
end. {Main}
```

Information flow between corresponding parameters

EXAMPLE 6.1 ▼

Procedure ReportSumAve in Fig. 6.2 computes and displays the sum and the average of two type Real values that are passed into the procedure. The comment {input} identifies formal parameters Num1 and Num2 as procedure inputs.

local variables

variables declared in a procedure, not in the main program

Two **local variables**, Sum and Average, are declared in the procedure, the only place a procedure's local variables can be accessed. The statements

```
Sum := Num1 + Num2;
Average := Sum / 2.0;
```

assign values to these local variables as follows: The sum of the values passed into parameters Num1 and Num2 is stored in Sum, and their average is stored in Average.

For the procedure call statement

```
ReportSumAve (6.5, 3.5)
```

the value 6.5 is passed to formal parameter Num1 and the value 3.5 is passed to formal parameter Num2. The value assigned to Sum is 10.0, and the value assigned to Average is 5.0. The procedure displays these two values. The correspondence between the actual and the formal parameters follows:

Actual Parameter	**corresponds to**	*Formal Parameter*
6.5		Num1
3.5		Num2

For the procedure call statement

```
ReportSumAve (X, Y)
```

Figure 6.2
Procedure to Display a
Sum and an Average

```
procedure ReportSumAve (Num1, Num2 {input} : Real);
{
    Computes and displays the sum and average of Num1 and Num2.
    Pre : Num1 and Num2 are assigned values.
    Post: The sum and average value of Num1 and Num2 are
          computed and displayed.

    var
       Sum,                              {sum of Num1, Num2}
       Average : Real;                   {average of Num1, Num2}
begin {ReportSumAve}
    Sum := Num1 + Num2;
    Average := Sum / 2.0;
    WriteLn ('The sum is ', Sum :4:2);
    WriteLn ('The average is ', Average :4:2)
end; {ReportSumAve}
```

the value of X is passed to formal parameter Num1 and the value of Y is passed to formal parameter Num2:

Actual Parameter	corresponds to	Formal Parameter
X		Num1
Y		Num2

Figure 6.3 shows the main program data area and the data area for procedure ReportSumAve after this procedure call statement executes. The values 8.0 and 10.0 are passed into the formal parameters Num1 and Num2, respectively. The local variables, Sum and Average, are initially undefined; the execution of the procedure body changes the values of these variables to 18.0 and 9.0, respectively. ▲

The Procedure Data Area

Each time a procedure call statement is executed, an area of memory is allocated for storage of that procedure's data. The procedure data area includes storage cells for its formal parameters and any local variables or constants that may be declared in the procedure. Whenever the procedure terminates, the procedure data area is erased; it is re-created empty (all values undefined) when the procedure is called again.

Illegal Parameter Substitution Errors

The data type of each actual parameter must be assignment compatible (see Section 2.5) with the data type of its corresponding formal parameter, or a type mismatch syntax error will occur. How does the Pascal compiler de-

Figure 6.3
Data Areas After Call of
ReportSumAve

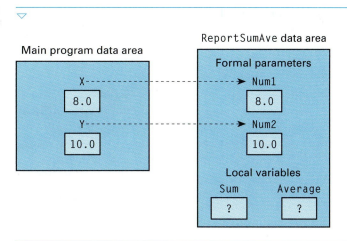

termine whether an actual parameter has a correct data type? The Pascal compiler knows the required data type for each actual parameter because a procedure's declaration must precede its first call. The formal parameter list (in the procedure declaration) specifies the data type of each procedure parameter.

Program Style

Choosing Formal Parameter Names

Although you can choose any valid identifiers as formal parameter names, you should continue to follow the convention of picking names that help to document the use of the formal parameter. Remember that the correspondence between an actual and a formal parameter is determined solely by position in the parameter lists, regardless of what names are used.

One purpose of procedures and functions is to facilitate the reuse of previously written and tested modules in future programs. Try to pick meaningful and generic formal parameter names rather than specific names tailored to a particular program application.

Preconditions and Postconditions

The multiple-line comment at the beginning of procedure `ReportSumAve` describes the procedure's operation. For comments that extend over multiple lines, use the commenting style

```
{
    ... comments ...
}
```

The comment line

```
Pre : Num1 and Num2 are assigned values.
```

precondition
condition assumed to be true before a procedure or function call

describes the condition that is true before the procedure is called; this condition is known as a **precondition.** The lines

```
Post: The sum and average value of Num1 and Num2 are
      computed and displayed.
```

describe the condition that is true after the procedure execution is completed; this condition is called a **postcondition**.

postcondition
condition assumed to be true after a procedure or function executes

Preconditions and postconditions document the procedure operation for other programmers who may use it. For example, preconditions tell a programmer what must be done before the procedure is called. In this case, two data values must be assigned or read into the actual parameters prior to calling `ReportSumAve`. Postconditions tell a programmer the effect of the procedure's execution on its parameters. In this case, their sum and average are computed and displayed.

Exercises for Section 6.1 ***Self-Check***

1. Consider procedure Down:

```
procedure Down (N : Integer);
begin {Down}
  while N > 0 do
    begin
      Write (N);
      N := N - 1
    end {while}
end; {Down}
```

  a. What is displayed when the procedure call statement Down (3) executes?

  b. If M is 5, what happens when the procedure call statement Down (M) executes?

  c. What is the value of the actual parameter M after the procedure executes?

  d. Where should M be declared, and what should its data type be?

2. Write preconditions and postconditions for procedure Down in Exercise 1.

Programming

1. Write a procedure that computes and displays the square root of a formal parameter X if X is greater than or equal to zero. Otherwise, the procedure should display an error message.

6.2 Returning Information from Procedures

In Section 6.1, we passed information from the main program to the procedure, where the information was processed. Procedures not only process information passed to them, but they also return information to the main program or another procedure for additional processing. This section describes how procedures return information to the calling module.

Variable and Value Parameters

value parameter
a type of formal parameter that receives information passed into a procedure

variable parameter
a type of formal parameter that returns a procedure result

Once again, the communication link between the procedure and the calling module is the parameter list. Formal parameters fall into two categories: value parameters and variable parameters. A **value parameter** receives information passed into a procedure, and a **variable parameter** returns a procedure result by changing its corresponding actual parameter value. So far we have used only value parameters.

Example 6.2 demonstrates the difference between value and variable parameters. As you follow the example, recall that when a procedure call executes, the computer allocates memory space in the procedure data area for each formal parameter. For input parameters, a copy of the value of each actual input parameter is stored in the memory cell allocated to its corresponding formal parameter. The procedure body can manipulate this value.

EXAMPLE 6.2 ▼

Procedure ComputeSumAve in Fig. 6.4 is similar to ReportSumAve (Fig. 6.2), the main difference being the former has four parameters: two for input (Num1 and Num2) and two for output (Sum and Average). Procedure ComputeSumAve computes the sum and the average of its inputs but does not display them. Instead these values are assigned to formal parameters Sum and Average and returned as procedure results to the calling module.

To see how this procedure works, assume that the main program declares X, Y, Total, and Mean as type Real variables. The procedure call statement

```
ComputeSumAve (X, Y, Total, Mean)
```

sets up the correspondence:

Actual Parameter	corresponds to	*Formal Parameter*
X		Num1
Y		Num2
Total		Sum
Mean		Average

The values of X and Y, associated with formal parameters Num1 and Num2, are passed into the procedure when it is first called. The statement

```
Sum := Num1 + Num2;
```

Figure 6.4
Procedure to Compute a
Sum and an Average

```
procedure ComputeSumAve (Num1, Num2 {input} : Real;
                         var Sum, Average {output} : Real);
{
   Computes the sum and average of Num1 and Num2.
   Pre : Num1 and Num2 are assigned values.
   Post: The sum and average of Num1 and Num2 are computed
         and returned.
}
begin {ComputeSumAve}
   Sum := Num1 + Num2;
   Average := Sum / 2.0
end; {ComputeSumAve}
```

stores the sum of the procedure inputs in the main program variable `Total` (the third actual parameter). The statement

`Average := Sum / 2.0`

divides the value stored in the main program variable `Total` by `2.0` and stores the quotient in the main program variable `Mean` (the fourth actual parameter). Figure 6.5 shows the main program data area and the procedure data area after the procedure call but before the procedure body begins execution; Fig. 6.6 shows these data areas just after the procedure body executes. The procedure execution sets the values of main program variables `Total` and `Mean` to `18.0` and `9.0`, respectively.   ▲

Figure 6.5 points out one important difference between formal parameters used as procedure inputs and those used as procedure outputs. Because formal parameters `Num1` and `Num2` are considered *value parameters,* each receives a copy of its corresponding actual parameter *value,* which the procedure uses in its computations. The *value* passed into formal parameter `Num1` is stored in the procedure data area at the time of the procedure call, and there is no further connection between formal parameter `Num1` and its corresponding actual parameter. The broken arrow in Fig. 6.5 indicates this condition, and its arrowhead shows that data flows in one direction only: from the calling module to the procedure.

Formal parameters `Sum` and `Average`, on the other hand, are *variable parameters*. The compiler stores in the procedure data area the memory *address* of the actual variable that corresponds to each variable parameter.

Figure 6.5
Data Areas After Procedure Call

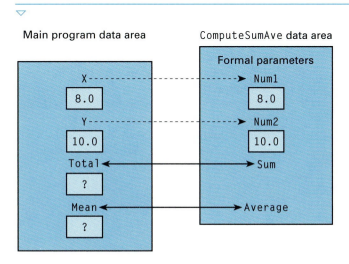

Figure 6.6
Data Areas After Procedure
Execution

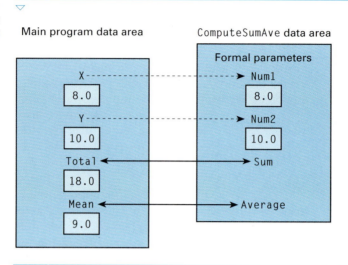

Main program data area   ComputeSumAve data area

Through this address, the procedure accesses the actual parameter in the calling module, so the procedure can change the actual parameter value or use it in a computation. In Fig. 6.5, this relationship is shown by a double-headed arrow connecting each variable parameter with its corresponding actual parameter. The double-headed arrow indicates that data can flow into the procedure and out of the procedure through a variable parameter.

Because the Pascal compiler must know whether a formal parameter is a value or variable parameter when it translates the procedure declaration, we identify variable parameters by preceding them with the reserved word `var` (see the second line in Fig. 6.4). Notice that `var` appears only in the formal parameter list, not in the actual parameter list.

Variable parameters are more versatile than value parameters because their values can be used in a computation as well as changed by the procedure's execution. Why not make all parameters, even input parameters, variable parameters? The reason is that value parameters offer some protection to data integrity: Because copies of value parameters are stored locally in the procedure data area, Pascal protects the actual parameter's value and prevents it from being erroneously changed by the procedure's execution. For example, if we add the statement

```
Num1 := -5.0
```

at the end of procedure `ComputeSumAve`, the value of formal parameter `Num1` will be changed to `-5.0`, but the value stored in `X` (the corresponding actual parameter) will still be `8.0`.

Should a programmer neglect to declare an output formal parameter as a variable parameter, then its value (not its address) will be stored in the procedure and any change to its value will not be returned to the calling program. This is a very common error in parameter usage.

Program Style

Writing Formal Parameter Lists

In Fig. 6.4 the formal parameter list

```
(Num1, Num2 {input} : Real;
 var Sum, Average {output} : Real);
```

is written on two lines to improve program readability. The value parameters are on the first line with the comment {input} to document their use as procedure inputs. The variable parameters are on the second line with the comment {output}.

Generally we follow the practice shown in Fig. 6.4 in writing formal parameter lists. Input parameters are listed first, and any output parameters are listed last.

When to Use a Variable Parameter or a Value Parameter

How do you decide whether to use a variable parameter or a value parameter? Here are some rules of thumb:

▶ If information is to be passed into a procedure but not returned or passed out of the procedure, then the formal parameter representing that information should be a value parameter (e.g., Num1 and Num2 in Figs. 6.2 and 6.4). A parameter used in this way is called an *input parameter*.

▶ If information is to be returned to the calling program from a procedure, then the formal parameter representing that information must be a variable parameter (e.g., Sum and Average in Fig. 6.4). A parameter used in this way is called an *output parameter*.

▶ If information is to be passed into a procedure, perhaps modified, and a new value returned, then the formal parameter representing that information must be a variable parameter. A parameter used in this way is called an *input/output parameter*.

Although we distinguish output parameters from input/output parameters, Pascal does not. Both kinds of parameters must be declared as variable parameters, so the address of the corresponding actual parameter is stored in the procedure data area when the procedure is called. For an input/output parameter, we assume there are some meaningful data in the actual parameter before the procedure executes; for an output parameter, we make no such assumption.

Passing Expressions to Value Parameters

Assignment-compatible expressions (or variables or constants) can serve as actual parameters corresponding to value parameters. For example, the procedure call statement

```
ComputeSumAve (X + Y, 10.5, MySum, MyAve);
```

calls `ComputeSumAve` to compute the sum (returned in `MySum`) and the average (returned in `MyAve`) of the expression `X + Y` and the real number `10.5`. However, only variables can correspond to variable parameters, so `MySum` and `MyAve` must be declared as type `Real` variables in the calling module. This restriction is imposed because an actual parameter corresponding to a variable parameter may be modified when the procedure executes; it is illogical to allow a procedure to change the value of either a constant or an expression.

Multiple Calls to a Procedure

Recall that parameters enable a procedure to execute one set of instructions on different sets of data each time the procedure is called. In Example 6.3, we demonstrate how a procedure may be called more than once in a given program and process different data in each call.

EXAMPLE 6.3: Sorting Three Numbers ▼

Program `Sort3Numbers` in Fig. 6.7 reads three data values into `Num1`, `Num2`, and `Num3` and rearranges the data so that they are in increasing sequence, with the smallest value in `Num1`. The three calls to procedure `Order` perform this **sorting** operation.

sort
a rearrangement of data such that the data are in increasing sequence

The body of procedure `Order` consists of the `if` statement from Fig. 4.10. The procedure heading contains the formal parameter list

```
(var X, Y {input/output} : Real)
```

which identifies X and Y as the formal parameters. X and Y are *input/output parameters* because the procedure uses the current actual parameter values as inputs and may return new values.

After `Order` executes, the smaller of its two parameter values is stored in its first actual parameter and the larger is stored in its second actual parameter. Therefore, the procedure call statement

```
Order (Num1, Num2); {Order the data in Num1 and Num2.}
```

stores the smaller of `Num1` and `Num2` in `Num1` and the larger in `Num2`. In the sample run shown, `Num1` is `8.0` and `Num2` is `10.0`, so these values are not changed by the procedure execution. However, the procedure call statement

```
Order (Num1, Num3); {Order the data in Num1 and Num3.}
```

Figure 6.7
Program to Order Three
Numbers

Edit Window

```
program Sort3Numbers;
{
  Reads three numbers and sorts them
  so that they are in increasing order
}
  var
    Num1, Num2, Num3 : Real;     {three variables being sorted}

  procedure Order (var X, Y {input/output} : Real);
  {
    Orders a pair of numbers represented by X and Y so that
    the smaller number is in X and the larger number is in Y.
    Pre : X and Y are assigned values.
    Post: X is the smaller of the pair and Y is the larger.
  }
    var
      Temp : Real;                {copy of number originally in X}

  begin {Order}
    if X > Y then
      begin {Switch the values of X and Y}
        Temp := X;               {Store old X in Temp.}
        X := Y;                  {Store old Y in X.}
        Y := Temp                {Store old X in Y.}
      end {if}
  end; {Order}

begin {Sort3Numbers}
  WriteLn ('Enter 3 numbers separated by spaces> ');
  ReadLn (Num1, Num2, Num3);

  {Sort the numbers}
  Order (Num1, Num2);    {Order the data in Num1 and Num2.}
  Order (Num1, Num3);    {Order the data in Num1 and Num3.}
  Order (Num2, Num3);    {Order the data in Num2 and Num3.}

  {Print the results.}
  WriteLn ('The three numbers in order are:');
  WriteLn (Num1 :8:2, Num2 :8:2, Num3 :8:2)
end. {Sort3Numbers}
```

Output Window

```
Enter 3 numbers separated by spaces>
8.0  10.0  6.0
The three numbers in order are:
    6.00    8.00   10.00
```

switches the values of Num1 (initial value is 8.0) and Num3 (initial value is 6.0). Table 6.1 traces the program execution.   ▲

Table 6.1
Trace of Program
Sort3Numbers

Statement	Num1	Num2	Num3	Effect
ReadLn (Num1, Num2, Num3);	8.0	10.0	6.0	Enters data
Order (Num1, Num2);				No change
Order (Num1, Num3);	6.0		8.0	Switches Num1 and Num3
Order (Num2, Num3);		8.0	10.0	Switches Num2 and Num3
WriteLn (Num1, Num2, Num3)				Displays 6.0, 8.0, 10.0

Exercises for Section 6.2   *Self-Check*

1. Assume X, Y, and Z are integer variables and X is 5, Y is 7, and Z is 2. Trace the execution of the call Shuffle (X, Y, Z):

```
procedure Shuffle (X, Y : Integer;
                        var Z : Integer);
  var
    Temp : Integer;

begin
  Temp := X;
  X := Y;
  Y := Z;
  Z := Temp
end; {Shuffle}
```

2. a. Show the output displayed by the following program in the form of a table of values for X, Y, Z, and W:

```
program Show;
  var
    W, X, Y, Z : Integer;

  procedure SumDiff (Num1, Num2 : Integer;
                        var Num3, Num4 : Integer);
  begin {SumDiff}
    Num3 := Num1 + Num2;
    Num4 := Num1 - Num2
  end; {SumDiff}

begin {Show}
  X := 5; Y := 3; Z := 7; W := 9;
```

```
        WriteLn ('  X   Y   Z   W');
        SumDiff (X, Y, Z, W);
        WriteLn (X :4, Y :4, Z :4, W :4);
        SumDiff (Y, X, Z, W);
        WriteLn (X :4, Y :4, Z :4, W :4);
        SumDiff (Z, W, Y, X);
        WriteLn (X :4, Y :4, Z :4, W :4);
        SumDiff (Z, Z, X, Y);
        WriteLn (X :4, Y :4, Z :4, W :4);
        SumDiff (Y, Y, Y, W);
        WriteLn (X :4, Y :4, Z :4, W :4)
     end. {Show}
```

    b.   Write the preconditions and postconditions for procedure
        `SumDiff`.

3.   A procedure has four formal parameters: W, X, Y, and Z (all type `Real`).
    During execution, the procedure stores the sum of W and X in Y and the
    product of W and X in Z. Which parameters are inputs and which are
    outputs?

Programming

1.   Write the procedure for Self-Check Exercise 3.
2.   Write a procedure that accepts as input the height *h* and radius *r* of a
    right circular cone and outputs the volume of the cone. The formula for
    the volume of a cone is: *volume* $= \pi r^2 h$.

6.3 Syntax Rules for Procedures with Parameter Lists

This section wraps up our discussion of parameters via syntax displays for
procedure declaration and call, a syntax diagram for formal parameter lists,
and rules for parameter list correspondence.

SYNTAX DISPLAY

Procedure Declaration (Procedure with Parameters)

Form: procedure *pname* (*formal parameters*);
           declaration section
           begin
             procedure body
           end;

Example: procedure Highlight (Ch {input} : Char;
                              var NumStars {output} : Integer);
         {
           Displays Ch between two asterisks and returns the
           numbers of asterisks printed.
           Pre : Ch is defined.
           Post: Returns 3 in NumStars if Ch = Border;
                otherwise, returns 2 in NumStars.
         }

```
        const
          Border = '*';

    begin {Highlight}
      Write (Border);   Write (Ch);   Write (Border);
      if Ch = Border then
        NumStars := 3
      else
        NumStars := 2
    end; {Highlight}
```

Interpretation: The procedure *pname* is declared, followed by the *formal parameters* enclosed in parentheses. The identifiers declared in the *declaration section* are local to the procedure and are defined only during the procedure execution. The *procedure body* describes the data manipulation to be performed by the procedure using the *formal parameters* as dummy names for the actual parameters. Value *formal parameters* receive data passed into the procedure, and variable *formal parameters* (preceded by word `var`) return procedure results to the calling module.

Procedure Call Statement (Procedure with Parameters)

Form: *pname* (*actual parameters*)
Example: `Highlight ('A', NumAsterisks)`
Interpretation: The *actual parameters* are enclosed in parentheses. When procedure *pname* is called into execution, the first *actual parameter* is associated with the first formal parameter, the second *actual parameter* with the second formal parameter, and so on. For a value parameter, the *actual parameter*'s value is stored in the procedure data area and the procedure processes the local value. For a variable parameter, the *actual parameter*'s address is stored in the procedure data area and the procedure processes the *actual parameter*.

Note: The *actual parameters* must satisfy the rules for parameter list correspondence discussed later in this section.

The following syntax diagram shows that a *formal parameter* list is always enclosed in parentheses and consists of one or more lists of identifiers. Each list may be preceded by `var` (optional), and must end with a colon followed by a data type name (e.g., `Real` or `Char`). Identifiers in a list are separated by commas, and lists of identifiers are separated by semicolons.

Formal Parameter List

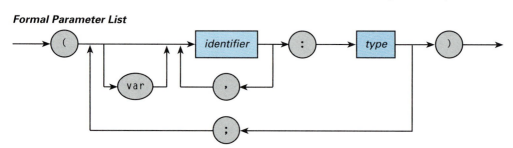

EXAMPLE 6.4 ▼

The following two formal parameter lists are printed on several lines to improve readability:

```
(Ch3 : Char;                (M, N, O : Integer;
  var X, Y, Z : Real)          var X, Y, Z : Real;
                                   A, B, C : Real)
```

In both lists, X, Y, Z are declared as type Real variable parameters. Ch3 is a type Char value parameter; A, B, and C are type Real value parameters; and M, N, and O are type Integer value parameters. ▲

This example points out a common error in formatting formal parameter lists: In the list on the right, the indentation of A, B, and C causes some students to think that the word var is implied and that A, B, and C are also variable parameters. Not so! The word var must always appear before *each* list of variable parameters.

The formal parameter list also determines the form of any actual parameter list in calls to the procedure. This form is determined during the translation of the program when the compiler processes the procedure declaration.

Later, when it reaches a procedure call statement, the compiler checks the actual parameter list for consistency with the formal parameter list. An actual parameter list may be a list of expressions, variables, or constants separated by commas. An actual parameter list and its corresponding formal parameter list must agree in **N**umber, **O**rder, and **T**ype (**NOT**), as described in the following rules.

Rules for Parameter List Correspondence

1. Correspondence between actual and formal parameters is determined by position in their respective parameter lists. These lists must be the same size, although the names of corresponding actual and formal parameters may differ.
2. For variable parameters, the types of corresponding actual and formal parameters must be identical. For value parameters, the actual parameter must be assignment compatible with its corresponding formal parameter (see Sections 2.5 and 7.6).
3. For variable parameters, an actual parameter must be a variable. For value parameters, an actual parameter may be a variable, a constant, or an expression.

EXAMPLE 6.5 ▼

A main program contains the declarations

```
var
  X, Y : Real;
  M : Integer;
  Next : Char;

procedure Test (A, B : Integer;
                var C, D : Real;
                var E : Char);
```

where only the heading for procedure Test is shown. Procedure Test has two value parameters (A and B) and three variable parameters (C, D, and E). Any of the following procedure call statements would be syntactically correct in the main program:

```
Test (M + 3, 10, X, Y, Next);
Test (M, MaxInt, Y, X, Next);
Test (35, M * 10, Y, X, Next)
```

The first actual parameter list shows that an expression (e.g., M + 3) or a constant (e.g., 10) may be associated with a value formal parameter. The correspondence specified by this parameter list is shown in Table 6.2.

Table 6.2

Parameter Correspondence for Test (M + 3, 10, X, Y, Next)

Actual Parameter	Formal Parameter	Parameter Kind
M + 3	A	Integer, value
10	B	Integer, value
X	C	Real, variable
Y	D	Real, variable
Next	E	Char, variable

All the procedure call statements in Table 6.3 contain syntax errors. The last procedure call statement points out an error often made in using procedures. The last three actual parameters (C, D, E) have the same names as their corresponding formal parameters. However, they are not declared as variables in the main program, so they cannot be used as actual parameters.

Procedure Call Statement	Error
Test (30, 10, M, X, Next)	Type of M is not Real.
Test (M, 19, X, Y)	Not enough actual parameters.
Test (M, 10, 35, Y, 'E')	Constants 35 and 'E' cannot correspond to variable parameters.
Test (M, 3.0, X, Y, Next)	Type of 3.0 is not Integer.
Test (30, 10, X, X + Y, Next)	Expression X + Y cannot correspond to a variable parameter.
Test (30, 10, C, D, E)	C, D, and E are not declared in the main program.

When writing relatively long parameter lists such as in this example, be careful not to transpose two actual parameters, or a syntax error may result. If no syntax is violated, the procedure execution will probably generate incorrect results. ▲

Exercises for Section 6.3 **Self-Check**

1. Arrange the other correct parameter lists shown in Example 6.5 in a format similar to Table 6.2.
2. Correct the syntax errors in these formal parameter lists:

```
(var A, B : Integer, C : Real)
(value M : Integer; var Next : Char)
(var Account, Real; X + Y , Real)
```

3. Assuming the declarations

```
var
   X, Y, Z : Real;
   M, N : Integer;

procedure Massage (var A, B : Real;
                        X : Integer);
```

which of the following are correct? Which are incorrect and why?

a.	Massage (X, Y, Z)	g.	Massage (A, B, X)
b.	Massage (X, Y, 8)	h.	Massage (Y, Z, M)
c.	Massage (Y, X, N)	i.	Massage (Y+Z, Y-Z, M)
d.	Massage (M, Y, N)	j.	Massage (Z, Y, X)
e.	Massage (25.0, 15, X)	k.	Massage (X, Y, M, 10)
f.	Massage (X, Y, M+N)	l.	Massage (Z, Y, MaxInt)

Programming

1. Write a procedure that displays a table showing all powers of its first argument from zero through the power indicated by its second argument (a positive integer). The procedure also should return the sum of all values displayed. For example, if the first argument is 10 and the second argument is 3, the procedure should display 1, 10, 100, and 1000 and return 1111 as its result.

6.4 Scope of Identifiers

identifier scope
the part of a program that can reference an identifier declared in the program

Every identifier in a Pascal program has a domain—the part of the program in which it is defined—called the **scope of the identifier.** An identifier can be referenced only by statements within its scope, which may be local or global as described next.

Scope Rule 1: Local and Global Scopes

global scope
the scope of an identifier declared in the main program
local scope
the scope of an identifier declared in a procedure or function

The scope of an identifier is the block (program or procedure) in which it is declared. Therefore, an identifier declared within the main program has **global scope** and can be referenced anywhere in the program. An identifier declared within a module has **local scope** and so can be referenced only within that module and any other modules that it declares.

The scope rules apply to all identifiers used in a program, including the names of constants, variables, procedures, and formal parameters. Thus, while a procedure declared in the main program declaration part has global scope, its formal parameter list is part of the procedure block and so has local scope.

Figure 6.8 illustrates scope rule 1 by boxing the program block and each procedure block. We placed each formal parameter list on a separate line to show that it is part of its procedure block. In color type next to each block, we show the identifiers whose scope is that block.

Variables Y and Z are global variables, which means that we can reference these variables anywhere (i.e., in the body of the main program or Proc1 or Proc2). (We will discuss why we cannot make the same statement for global variable X shortly.) Neither the main program nor procedure Proc2 can reference the local identifiers declared in Proc1 (formal parameters M, N, Me and local variables X, You).

Because Proc1 and Proc2 are global identifiers, we would expect that these procedures can be called anywhere. Table 6.4 shows that although procedure Proc2 can call Proc1, procedure Proc1 cannot call Proc2. The reason for this exception is that Proc2 is declared after Proc1, and the declaration of an identifier must precede its first use. If you have one procedure that calls another, be sure to declare the procedure being called before the caller.

Figure 6.8
Scope of Identifiers

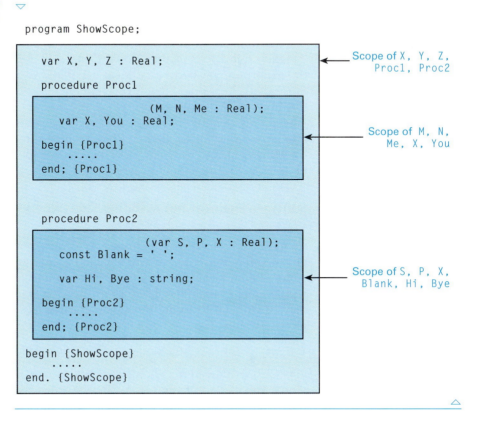

```
program ShowScope;

    var X, Y, Z : Real;                          ◄─── Scope of X, Y, Z,
                                                          Proc1, Proc2
    procedure Proc1

                        (M, N, Me : Real);
        var X, You : Real;
                                                 ◄─── Scope of M, N,
    begin {Proc1}                                        Me, X, You
      .....
    end; {Proc1}



    procedure Proc2

                        (var S, P, X : Real);
        const Blank = ' ';
                                                 ◄─── Scope of S, P, X,
        var Hi, Bye : string;                            Blank, Hi, Bye

    begin {Proc2}
      .....
    end; {Proc2}

begin {ShowScope}
  .....
end. {ShowScope}
```

Table 6.4
Valid Procedure Calls

Program or Procedure Body	Procedures That Can Be Called
ShowScope	Proc1, Proc2
Proc2	Proc1, Proc2
Proc1	Proc1

Table 6.4 shows that a procedure can call itself (a *recursive call*). We discuss recursive calls in Section 6.8.

Notice that identifier X in Fig. 6.8 has three separate declarations (global variable, local variable in Proc1, formal parameter in Proc2) and therefore three different scopes. We know that we cannot declare the same identifier twice in one block, but we can have multiple declarations for an identifier provided they are all in different blocks. Scope rule 2 tells us how Pascal handles multiple declarations of an identifier.

Scope Rule 2: Multiple Declarations of an Identifier

When an identifier has multiple declarations all in different blocks, then the most local declaration is used each time that identifier is referenced.

Scope rule 2 tells us that global identifier X is accessed when we use X in the main program body, that local variable X is accessed when we use X in the body of Proc1, and that formal parameter X is accessed when we use X in the body of Proc2. Because of scope rule 2, we needn't be concerned whether an identifier has been declared elsewhere when we declare and use it in a procedure. If an identifier has been declared elsewhere, Pascal ignores the other declarations when we reference that identifier within the procedure body. This feature simplifies writing procedures for reuse in other programs.

Software Engineering: Avoiding Side Effects

side effect

changing a nonlocal variable that does not correspond to a variable formal parameter through a procedure or function execution

Although global variables can be referenced anywhere in a program, you should avoid referencing them in a procedure body. Changing the value of a global variable in a procedure is called a **side effect** of the procedure execution. Often no documentation exists to indicate that a procedure manipulates a *global* variable; consequently, in a program with many procedures, it may be difficult to locate the statement that assigns an incorrect value to a global variable. If the statement

```
Y := Y + 3.5;      {Example of a side effect}
```

appeared in procedure Proc1, it would cause a side effect (adding 3.5 to global variable Y) whenever that procedure was called. However, a procedure can access a global variable without causing a side effect if the global variable is passed via the parameter list.

The formal parameter list and the local declarations for a procedure explicitly document the data to be manipulated. You should manipulate only local identifiers in a procedure, the only exceptions being global constants and type identifiers (discussed in later chapters). Because Pascal does not allow the value of a constant to be changed, you can reference a global constant in a procedure with no side effects.

Scope for Nested Procedures

Nested procedures occur when we declare one procedure inside another. Scope rule 1 tells us that the scope of an inner procedure is the block in which it is declared. Therefore, an inner procedure can be called by the procedure that declares it and by itself (a recursive call), but an inner procedure cannot be called by the main program or by any procedures outside the nest. This restriction limits the potential reuse of an inner procedure, so we recommend that you do not nest procedures.

Figure 6.9 illustrates the effect of procedure nesting on identifier scope, and Table 6.5 lists the identifiers that can be referenced in each block and

Figure 6.9
Scope for Nested
Procedures

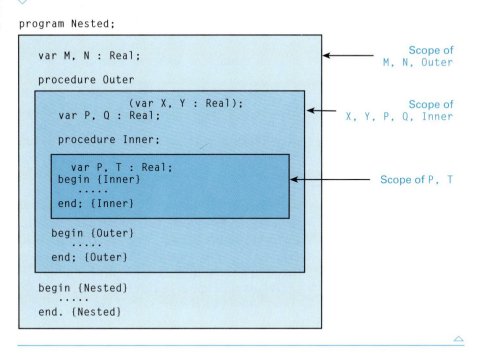

Table 6.5
Valid Identifier
References for
Fig. 6.9

Program or Procedure Body	Identifiers That Can Be Referenced
Nested	M, N (global variables)
	Outer (global procedure)
Outer	M, N (global variables)
	X, Y (parameters)
	P, Q (local variables)
	Outer (global procedure)
	Inner (local procedure)
Inner	M, N (global variables)
	X, Y (parameters for Outer)
	Q (variable declared in Outer)
	P, T (local variables)
	Outer (global procedure)
	Inner (procedure declared in Outer)

the procedures that can be called. The table shows that procedure Inner can reference its own local variables, all identifiers declared in the main program, and all identifiers declared in procedure Outer except for variable P. The reason for this exclusion is that Inner declares its own local variable P and that declaration takes precedence (scope rule 2).

Illustrating the Scope Rules

Example 6.6 illustrates bad programming practice, where identifier names are not meaningful and are unnecessarily redundant. However, studying this example should help you master the Pascal scope rules.

EXAMPLE 6.6 ▼

Figure 6.10 shows a procedure declared in a main program. W is declared as a variable in both the procedure and the main program; X is declared as a variable in the main program and as a parameter in the procedure; Y is declared as a variable in the main program only.

The main program begins by initializing global variables W, X, and Y to the values shown on the left side of Fig. 6.11. The procedure call statement

Change (W);

calls procedure Change with main program variable W corresponding to variable parameter X. Figure 6.11 shows the program and procedure data areas just after the procedure call.

In procedure Change, the assignment statement

X := 6.0;   {Change parameter X}

stores 6.0 in the main program variable W, and the assignment statement

Y := Y + 1.0;   {Side effect - change global Y.}

increments the main program variable Y to 4.0 (a side effect). The other two assignment statements in Change affect only its local variables W and Z (W becomes 35.0 and Z becomes 3.0)

The second WriteLn statement in Change displays the values of its local identifiers (W, X, and Z) and the global variable Y just before the procedure return. The WriteLn statement in the main program displays the values of the three main program variables after the return:

```
 W     X     Y
6.0   2.0   4.0
```

Figure 6.10
Program ScopeRules

Edit Window

```
program ScopeRules;
  var
    W, X, Y : Real;

  procedure Change (var X {input/output} : Real);
    var
      W, Z : Real;

  begin {Change}
    W := 35.0;      {Change local W.}
    X := 6.0;       {Change parameter X.}
    Y := Y + 1.0;   {Side effect - change global Y.}
    Z := 3.0;       {Change local Z.}
    WriteLn ('W' :5, 'X' :5, 'Y' :5, 'Z' :5);
    WriteLn (W :5:1, X :5:1, Y :5:1, Z: 5:1, ' in Change')
  end; {Change}

begin  {ScopeRules}
  W := 5.5;         {Initialize global W.}
  X := 2.0;         {Initialize global X.}
  Y := 3.0;         {Initialize global Y.}
  Change (W);       {Update global W.}
  WriteLn (W :5:1, X :5:1, Y :5:1, ' in ScopeRules' :19)
end. {ScopeRules}
```

Output Window

```
   W    X    Y    Z
 35.0  6.0  4.0  3.0  in Change
  6.0  2.0  4.0       in ScopeRules
```

Figure 6.11
Data Areas After Procedure
Call

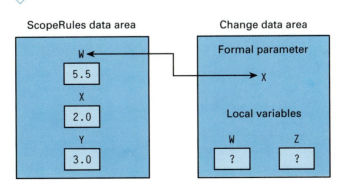

Notice that main program variable X is unchanged and that the value of W is 6.0 (not 35.0).

Consider what happens if X or Y is used as the actual parameter instead of W. That question is left as an exercise at the end of this section. ▲

Self-Check

1. In Fig. 6.8, why can't variable You declared in procedure Proc1 be referenced by the main program or procedure Proc2? Why can't procedure Proc2 be called from within the body of Proc1?
2. In Fig. 6.8, what would be the effect of executing the body of Proc1 as follows?

```
begin {Proc1}
   X := 5.5;
   Y := 6.6;
   M := 2;
   N := 3;
   You := M
end; {Proc1}
```

3. If the statement sequence in Exercise 2 appeared in a different block, some of the assignment statements would be syntactically incorrect. Identify the incorrect statements, and indicate the effect of executing the others if the statement sequence appeared as the body of
   a. Proc2
   b. ShowScope
4. Consider program ScopeRules in Fig. 6.10.
   a. What kind of error would occur if the assignment statement

   ```
   Z := 15.0;
   ```

   were inserted in the main program?
   b. Show the new values of W, X, and Y if X were the actual parameter in the call to procedure Change.
   c. What if Y were the actual parameter in the call to Change?
   d. What would be the effect of making formal parameter X a value parameter?
5. The outline of a program with nested procedures follows. Describe the scope of each identifier, including procedure names.

```
program NestScope;
   const Pi = 3.14159;

   procedure A (var X : Real);
      var B, C : Integer;

      procedure D (var S : Real);
         const Star = '*';
      begin
         . . . . .
```

```
      end; {D}
   begin {A}
    . . . . .
   end; {A}
   procedure F (var X, Y : Real);
     var D : Integer;
   begin
    . . . . .
   end; {F}
begin
 . . . . .
end. {NestScope}
```

6.5   Functions: Modules That Return a Single Result

Functions are independent modules like procedures, except that procedures can return any number of results whereas a function always returns a single result. In Section 3.2, we showed how to call a predefined function by writing a function designator in an expression. For example, the function designator Abs(X + Y) calls the predefined function Abs (absolute value), where the expression X + Y is the actual parameter passed to function Abs. In this section, we study how to write our own functions.

Writing User-Defined Functions

To define your own function, write a function declaration and place it in the declaration part of the calling program. Because a function does not return its result through its parameter list, a function declaration differs in the following ways from a procedure declaration:

▶ A function heading begins with the reserved word function instead of procedure.

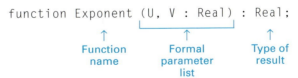

```
function Exponent (U, V : Real) : Real;
```

| Function
name | Formal
parameter
list | Type of
result |

▶ All function parameters should be value parameters.
▶ The data type of the function result is specified at the end of the function heading, following the formal parameter list.
▶ Within the function body, the function result is defined by assigning a value to the function name. The last value assigned to the function name is returned as the function result.

We illustrate these requirements for user-defined functions in Example 6.7.

EXAMPLE 6.7 ▼

Programmers typically use functions to simplify numeric computations. For instance, since Pascal has no exponentiation operator, a library function for raising a number to a power would be useful. Function Exponent (Fig. 6.12) raises its first argument, U, to the power indicated by its second argument, V (i.e., the function result is U^V). The function heading indicates that Exponent has two type Real value parameters; the type of the result, Real, is placed after the colon.

The if statement in the function body selects either an assignment statement or a WriteLn statement depending on the value passed into U. If the value of U is 0, the assignment statement

```
Exponent := 0.0
```

executes and defines the function result as 0. If the value of U is positive, the assignment statement

```
Exponent := Exp(V * Ln(U))
```

calls Pascal's built-in functions Exp and Ln to calculate the desired value using the formula derived in Example 3.4. Assigning this value to Exponent defines it as the function result.

If the value of U is negative, the WriteLn statement displays an error message but no value is assigned to Exponent, so the function result would be undefined. This is consistent with the function precondition, which states

Figure 6.12
Function Exponent

```
function Exponent (U, V : Real) : Real;
{
 Returns its first argument raised to the power specified
 by its second argument.
 Pre : U >= 0.0 and V is defined.
 Post: Returns U raised to the power V.
}
begin {Exponent}
  if U = 0.0 then
    Exponent := 0.0            {Result of 0.0 to any power is 0.0}
  else if U > 0.0 then
    Exponent := Exp(V * Ln(U)) {Result is U raised to power V}
  else
    WriteLn ('**** Error in first parameter of Exponent')
end; {Exponent}
```

that function `Exponent` should be called only when its first parameter is nonnegative.

Notice that the two assignment statements use the function name `Exponent` without parameters. If you use parameters after the function name, Pascal considers this a recursive call to the function.   ▲

Calling a User-Defined Function

If we have a main program with three type `Real` variables, `X`, `Y`, and `Z`, the main program statement

```
Z := Exponent(X, Y)
```

Function name — Actual parameter list

calls `Exponent`, passing it the values of actual parameters `X` and `Y`. The function body computes the value of X^Y. Upon return from the function, the function result is assigned to `Z`.

Figure 6.13 shows the main program data area and the function data area right after the function call. For the particular values of `X` and `Y` shown (`3.0` and `2.5`), the function execution defines the function result as `15.59`. Figure 6.14 shows the program data area and the function data area after the function body finishes execution but before the function return. Notice that there is no connection between main program variable `Z` and the memory cell in `Exponent`'s data area that represents the function result. The function result will be assigned to `Z` after the return to the main program.

Figure 6.13
Data Areas After Function Call

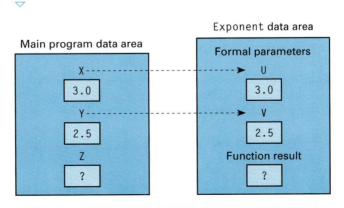

Figure 6.14
Data Areas After Function
Execution But Before
Return

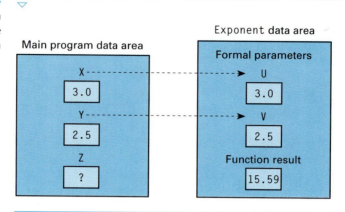

SYNTAX DISPLAY

Function Declaration

Form: function *fname* (*formal parameters*) : *ftype*;
    local declaration section
begin
   function body
end;

Example: function InverseSum (X, Y : Real) : Real;
    {Computes 1.0 divided by the sum of X, Y.}
      var
        SumXY : Real; {local storage for the sum of X, Y}

    begin {InverseSum}
      SumXY := X + Y;
      InverseSum := 1.0 / SumXY
    end; {InverseSum}

Interpretation: The function *fname* is declared, followed by the *formal parameters* enclosed in parentheses. The identifiers declared in the *local declaration section* are local to the function and are defined only during the execution of the function. A formal parameter cannot be declared as a local identifier.

The *function body* describes the data manipulation to be performed by the function using the formal parameters as dummy names in the description. When a formal parameter is referenced during function execution, the value of the corresponding actual parameter is manipulated.

The function returns a single result of type *ftype*. The function result is the value assigned to *fname* just prior to the return.

Note 1: The identifier *ftype* must be the name of a standard data type (Integer, Real, Boolean, or Char), a subrange type or enumerated type (described in Chapter 7), or a pointer type (described in Chapter 17). Turbo Pascal (but not standard Pascal) allows string and extended numeric types (described in Chapter 7) to be used as function return types.

Note 2: If there are no parameters, omit the *formal parameters* and the parentheses.

SYNTAX DISPLAY

Function Designator (Function Call)

Form: *fname* (*actual parameters*)

Example: InverseSum(3.0, Z)

Interpretation: The *actual parameters* are enclosed in parentheses. When function *fname* is called into execution, the first actual parameter corresponds to the first formal parameter, the second actual parameter corresponds to the second formal parameter, and so on. A function designator must always appear within an expression; after execution, the function result replaces the function designator in that expression.

Note: If there are no parameters, omit the *actual parameters* and the parentheses.

Software Engineering: Avoiding Function Side Effects

Because all function parameters in this book are input parameters, we omit the comment {input} from a function's formal parameter list. This restriction is imposed by programming style considerations, not by Pascal. You could return an additional result from a function by making one of its parameters a variable parameter, but any change to this parameter's value would be an undesirable *side effect* because it would not be expected and would contradict standard programming practice.

Testing Functions

In Example 6.8, we write a function that computes income tax owed and a small program whose sole purpose is to call and test that function. Such a program, used to test the operation of a function or a procedure, is called a **driver program.**

driver program
a small program written to test a procedure or function

EXAMPLE 6.8 ▼

Figure 4.13 contained an if statement that computed the income tax due for a particular salary based on the tax table shown in Table 4.10. Since this table appears in many different programs, your accountant has decided to place it in function FindTax (Fig. 6.15). The assignment statement

```
MyTax := FindTax(MySalary);
```

calls function FindTax, passing the value of MySalary into input parameter Salary. If the value passed into Salary is within the range of the table, the tax owed is computed and returned as the function result; otherwise, the function returns -1.0 to signal an input salary that is outside the table range.

Notice how the processing tasks are divided in Fig. 6.15. First, the ReadLn statement enters a salary value in the main program, not in function FindTax. The value read is passed into FindTax via its parameter list, as it should be. Never place statements to read a function's input data in the function body.

Figure 6.15

Driver Program with
Function FindTax

Edit Window

```
program Driver;
{Tests function FindTax}

  var
    MySalary,                          {input - salary}
    MyTax      : Real;                 {output - tax}

  function FindTax (Salary : Real) : Real;
  {
   Returns tax amount owed for a salary < $15000.
   Pre : Salary is assigned a value.
   Post: If Salary is within range, returns the tax owed;
         otherwise, returns -1.0.
  }
    const
      MaxSalary = 15000.00; {maximum salary for table}
      OutOfRange = -1.0;    {"tax" for an out-of-range salary}

  begin  {FindTax}
    if Salary < 0.0 then
      FindTax := OutOfRange              {salary too small}
    else if Salary < 1500.00 then        {first range}
      FindTax := 0.15 * Salary
    else if Salary < 3000.00 then        {second range}
      FindTax := (Salary - 1500.00) * 0.16 + 225.00
    else if Salary < 5000.00 then        {third range}
      FindTax := (Salary - 3000.00) * 0.18 + 465.00
    else if Salary < 8000.00 then        {fourth range}
      FindTax := (Salary - 5000.00) * 0.20 + 825.00
    else if Salary <= MaxSalary then     {fifth range}
      FindTax := (Salary - 8000.00) * 0.25 + 1425.00
    else
      FindTax := OutOfRange              {salary too large}
  end; {FindTax}

begin {Driver}
  Write ('Enter a salary less than or equal to $15000.00> $');
  ReadLn (MySalary);
  MyTax := FindTax(MySalary);
  if MyTax >= 0.0 then
    WriteLn ('The tax on $', MySalary :4:2,
             ' is $', MyTax :4:2)
  else
    WriteLn ('Salary $', Salary :4:2, ' is out of table range')
end. {Driver}
```

Output Window

```
Enter a salary less than or equal to $15000.00> $6000.00
The tax on $6000.00 is $1025.00
```

Second, the function result is computed in the function but is displayed by the WriteLn statement in the calling program. Generally, you should use WriteLn statements in functions only to display error messages.

Third, notice that the function body defines the function result by assigning a value to the function name, FindTax. After the function return, the assignment statement

```
MyTax := FindTax(MySalary);
```

in the main program assigns the function result to MyTax. Sometimes beginning programmers incorrectly assign a value to MyTax, instead of FindTax, in the function body. Because MyTax is a global variable, the function would compile without error, but the function result would be undefined so "garbage" would be assigned to MyTax after the function return. ▲

Program Style

Validating Input Parameters

The if statement in function FindTax tests for an invalid value of the input parameter Salary before performing the tax computation. All procedures and functions should validate their input parameters; there are no guarantees that the values passed to an input parameter will be meaningful.

Program Style

Cohesive Modules

Function FindTax only computes the payroll tax. It neither reads in a value for Salary nor displays the computed result, nor does it display an error message if the value passed to Salary is out of range. It simply returns a special value (-1.0), and the calling program displays the error message.

Modules that perform a single operation are called *cohesive modules*. Writing cohesive modules is good programming style, for they help to keep functions and procedures relatively compact and easy to read, write, and debug.

Program Style

Writing Driver Programs to Test Modules

The main program body in Fig. 6.15 consists of a statement for data entry, an assignment statement with a function designator in its expression part, and an if statement to display the function result. The sole purpose of the program is to test the function FindTax. Such a program is called a *driver program*.

Experienced programmers often use driver programs to pretest functions and procedures. Generally the small investment in time and effort required to write a short driver program pays off by reducing the total time spent debugging a large program system that contains several modules.

Exercises for Section 6.5 **Self-Check**

1. Since both procedures and functions can return a result and procedures are not limited to one output, why do we need functions?
2. In function `FindTax` in Fig. 6.15, why should you not replace each of the assignment statements

   ```
   FindTax := OutOfRange
   ```

   with the `WriteLn` statement

   ```
   WriteLn (Salary :4:2, ' is out of range')
   ```

3. a. What does the following function do?

   ```
   function Hypot (X, Y : Real) : Real;
   begin {Hypot}
     Hypot := Sqrt(Sqr(X) + Sqr(Y))
   end; {Hypot}
   ```

   b. Write a statement that calls this function with arguments `A` and `B` and stores the function result in `C`.
4. Which of the following tasks would be best implemented as a function and which as a procedure? Justify your answer.
   a. Computing the volume of a cone
   b. Displaying user instructions
   c. Testing whether a data value is in a specified range
   d. Computing the angle and muzzle velocity for a cannon based on the desired range

Programming

1. Write a driver program that tests function `FindTax` for all values of `Salary` from `-400.00` to `15100.00` in increments of `500.00`.
2. Write a function that raises a real number (X) to an integer power (N) by multiplying X by itself N times (use a `for` loop). Will your function work for negative values of X or N? *Hint:* To make your function work for negative values of N, use `Abs(N)` as the final expression in the `for` loop. Then use $X^N = 1 / X^{-N}$ to compute the correct result when N is negative.

6.6   Stepwise Design with Functions and Procedures

Using parameter lists to pass information to and from procedures and functions will improve your problem-solving skills. If the solution to a subproblem cannot be written easily using just a few Pascal statements, code it as a procedure or a function. The following case study demonstrates stepwise design of programs using procedures and functions.

CASE STUDY ## General Sum-and-Average Problem

PROBLEM ▼

Accumulate a sum and average a list of data values using procedure and functions modules. Because these tasks surface in many problems, design a general set of modules you can reuse in other programs.

ANALYSIS ▼

The loop in Fig. 5.4 computed a company's total payroll. We can use a similar loop to compute the sum of a collection of data values. To compute an average, you would divide a sum by the total number of items, being careful not to perform this division if the number of items is 0.

Data Requirements

Problem Inputs

```
NumItems : Integer      {number of data items to be summed}
Item : Real             {each data item}
```

Problem Outputs

```
Sum : Real              {sum of data items}
Average : Real          {average of data}
```

Relevant Formula

average = sum of data / number of data items

DESIGN ▼

Initial Algorithm

1. Read the number of items.
2. Read the data and compute the sum of the data.
3. Compute the average of the data.
4. Print the sum and the average.

The structure chart in Fig. 6.16 documents the data flow between the main problem and its subproblems. We will implement as a separate module each step that has a nontrivial solution; the label under a step denotes the name of the module that implements that step. Each step except the first is implemented in a separate module.

Figure 6.16 clarifies the data flow between the main program and each module. All variables whose values are set by a module are *module outputs*

Figure 6.16
Structure Chart with Data Flow Information

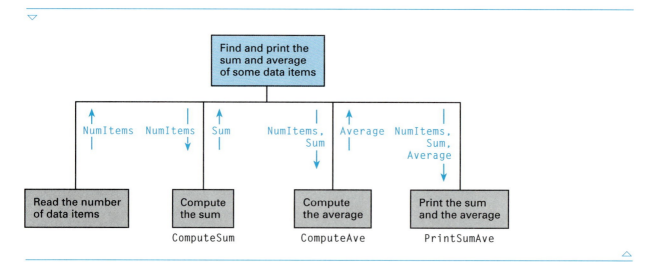

(indicated by an arrow pointing out of the module). All variables whose values are used in a computation but are not changed by the module are *module inputs* (indicated by an arrow pointing into the module). The role of each program variable depends on its usage in a module and changes from step to step in the structure chart.

Because the step *Read the number of data items* defines the value of NumItems this variable is an output of this step. Module ComputeSum needs the value of NumItems to know how many data items to read and sum; consequently, NumItems is an input to module ComputeSum. The variable Sum is an output of module ComputeSum but is an input to modules ComputeAve and PrintSumAve. The variable Average is an output of module ComputeAve but is an input to module PrintSumAve.

IMPLEMENTATION ▼

Using the data flow information in the structure chart, you can write the main program before refining the algorithm. Follow the approach described in Section 3.1 to write the main program. Begin by copying the data requirements into the program declaration part. Declare all the variables that appear in the structure chart in the main program, because they store data passed to a module or results returned from a module. Omit the declaration for variable Item, since it does not appear in the structure chart, but be sure to declare it in the module that uses it (ComputeSum). Next move the initial algorithm into the program body, writing each algorithm step as a comment (Fig. 6.17).

Figure 6.17
Main Program for General
Sum-and-Average Problem

```
program SumItems;
{Finds and prints the sum and average of a list of data items}

   var
     NumItems : Integer; {input - number of items to be added}
     Sum,                {output - sum being accumulated}
     Average : Real;     {output - average of the data}
     {
     Insert declarations for procedures ComputeSum and PrintSumAve
     and function ComputeAve here.
     }

begin {SumItems}
   Read the number of items.}
   Write ('How many numbers will be added> ');
   ReadLn (NumItems);

   {Read the data items and compute their sum.}
   ComputeSum (NumItems, Sum);

   {Compute the average of the data.}
   Average := ComputeAve(NumItems, Sum);

   {Print the sum and average.}
   PrintSumAve (NumItems, Sum, Average)
end. {SumItems}
```

To complete the main program, code each algorithm step *in-line* (as part of the main program code) or as a procedure or function call. Code the data entry step in-line, since it consists of a simple Write (for a prompt) and a ReadLn. Modules ComputeSum and ComputeAve return a single result, so you could write them as functions. However, code ComputeSum as a procedure because it reads the data items that are included in the sum. The data entry operations would be a side effect if ComputeSum were a function.

The data flow information in Fig. 6.16 tells you the actual parameters to use in each procedure or function call. In the case of a function, it also tells you the name of the main program variable that will hold the function result. For example, use the assignment statement

```
Average := ComputeAve(NumItems, Sum);
```

to call ComputeAve and set the value of Average. In this call, NumItems and Sum are passed as input parameters to function ComputeAve.

Call ComputeSum using the procedure call statement

```
ComputeSum (NumItems, Sum);
```

where NumItems is an input parameter and Sum is an output parameter.

Call `PrintSumAve` using the procedure call statement

```
PrintSumAve (NumItems, Sum, Average)
```

where all three parameters are procedure inputs.

Procedure ComputeSum

With the main program complete, you can concentrate on its individual modules, starting with procedure `ComputeSum`. Begin the data requirements for `ComputeSum` with the procedure inputs and outputs. `ComputeSum` also needs two local variables: one for storing each data item (`Item`) and one for loop control (`Count`).

Data Requirements for ComputeSum

Procedure Input

```
NumItems : Integer          {number of data items to be summed}
```

Procedure Output

```
Sum : Real                  {the sum of the data items}
```

Local Variables

```
Item : Real                 {each data item}
Count : Integer             {count of data items summed}
```

Before accumulating a sum in a loop, initialize the sum to zero prior to loop entry (see Section 5.2). The loop-control steps must ensure that the correct number of data items are read and included in the sum being accumulated. Since you know the number of items to sum beforehand (`NumItems`), use a counting loop. Use these steps to write the algorithm for `ComputeSum`; Fig. 6.18 shows the code for `ComputeSum`.

Algorithm for ComputeSum

1. Initialize `Sum` to 0
2. `for` each value of `Count` from 1 to `NumItems` do
   `begin`
   3. Read in the next item.
   4. Add it to `Sum`
   `end`

Figure 6.19 shows the parameter correspondence specified by the procedure call statement

```
ComputeSum (NumItems, Sum);
```

assuming the value 10 is read into `NumItems` just before the procedure call. The local variables, `Count` and `Item`, are undefined when the procedure is

Figure 6.18
Procedure ComputeSum

```
procedure ComputeSum (NumItems {input} : Integer;
                       var Sum {output} : Real);
{
  Computes the sum of a list of NumItems data items.
  Pre : NumItems is assigned a value.
  Post: NumItems data items are read; their sum is stored in
        Sum.
}

  var
    Count : Integer;        {count of items added so far}
    Item : Real;            {the next data item to be added}

begin  {ComputeSum}
  {Read each data item and add it to Sum.}
  Sum := 0.0;
  for Count := 1 to NumItems do
    begin
      Write ('Next number to be added> ');
      ReadLn (Item);
      Sum := Sum + Item
    end {for}
end; {ComputeSum}
```

Figure 6.19
Parameter Correspondence
for ComputeSum
(NumItems, Sum)

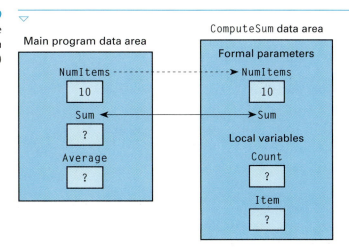

called. The procedure begins by initializing to 0 the main program variable Sum, which corresponds to variable parameter Sum. The for loop reads each data item into local variable Item and adds it to the main program variable Sum. The loop exit and procedure return occur after 10 items have been added.

Function ComputeAve and Procedure PrintSumAve

Both ComputeAve and PrintSumAve are relatively straightforward, as can be seen from their data requirements and algorithms, listed next. Both algorithms test NumItems, because it makes no sense to compute or display the average of the data items if NumItems is not positive. Figure 6.20 shows function ComputeAve, and Fig. 6.21 shows procedure PrintSumAve.

Data Requirements for ComputeAve

Function Inputs

```
NumItems : Integer          {the number of data items}
Sum : Real                  {the sum of all data}
```

Function Output

```
ComputeAve : Real           {the average of the data}
```

Algorithm for ComputeAve

1. if NumItems is positive then
    2. Set ComputeAve to Sum / NumItems
  else
    3. Set ComputeAve to 0

Figure 6.20
Function ComputeAve

```
function ComputeAve (NumItems : Integer; Sum : Real) : Real;
{
  Returns the average of NumItems data items with sum of Sum.
  Pre : NumItems and Sum are defined.
  Post: If NumItems is positive, returns Sum / NumItems;
        otherwise, returns zero
}
begin {ComputeAve}
  {Compute the average of the data.}
  if NumItems > 0 then
    ComputeAve := Sum / NumItems
  else
    ComputeAve := 0.0
end; {ComputeAve}
```

Figure 6.21
Procedure PrintSumAve

```
Procedure PrintSumAve  (NumItems {input} : Integer;
                        Sum, Average {input} : Real);
{
  Displays the sum and average of NumItems data items.
  Pre : NumItems, Sum, and Average are defined.
  Post: Displays Sum and also Average if NumItems > 0.
}
begin {PrintSumAve}
  if NumItems > 0 then
    begin
      WriteLn ('The sum is ', Sum :4:2);
      WriteLn ('The average is ', Average :4:2)
    end
  else
    WriteLn ('Sum and average are not defined')
end; {PrintSumAve}
```

Data Requirements for PrintSumAve

Procedure Inputs

```
NumItems : Integer          {the number of data items}
Sum : Real                  {the sum of all data}
Average : Real              {the average of the data}
```

Algorithm for PrintSumAve

1. if NumItems is positive then
   2. Display the sum and the average of the data

TESTING ▼

You must insert the function and procedure declarations in the declaration part of program SumItems (after the variable declarations) before you can run the program. In testing SumItems, make sure that the program displays the sum and the average correctly when NumItems is positive and displays an error message when NumItems is zero or negative. Figure 6.22 shows a sample run.

Figure 6.22
Sample Run of SumItems

```
How many numbers will be added> 3
Next number to be added> 5.0
Next number to be added> 6.0
Next number to be added> -7.0
The sum is 4.00
The average is 1.33
```

When to Use a Function or Procedure

In the four steps of the general sum-and-average program (see Fig. 6.16), all but the first step are performed by separate modules. It was obvious that step 1 could be implemented using a `Write` and a `ReadLn`, so that step was written directly in the main program. We used a procedure (`ComputeSum`) for step 2 because its algorithm was relatively complicated. Even though steps 3 and 4 were relatively easy to implement, we used a function (`ComputeAve`) for step 3 and a procedure (`PrintSumAve`) for step 4 because their implementations were rather lengthy. Follow this line of reasoning in determining whether to implement a step as a separate module. From this point on, your main program bodies should consist primarily of a sequence of procedure and function calls.

Multiple Declarations of Identifiers in a Program

The identifiers `Sum` and `NumItems` are declared as global variables in the main program and as formal parameters in the three modules called by the main program. From the discussion of scope of identifiers, you know that each of these declarations has its own scope and that the scope for each formal parameter is the module that declares it. The parameter lists associate global variable `Sum` with each of the other identifiers named `Sum`. The value of global variable `Sum` is initially defined when procedure `ComputeSum` executes because global variable `Sum` corresponds to `ComputeSum`'s output parameter `Sum`. This value is passed into function `ComputeAve` because global variable `Sum` corresponds to `ComputeAve`'s input parameter `Sum`, and so on.

To avoid the confusion of seeing the identifier `Sum` in multiple modules, we could have introduced different names in each module (e.g., `Total`, `My-Sum`). However, the program is easier to read if the name `Sum` is used throughout to refer to the sum of the data values. Make sure that you remember to link these separate uses of identifier `Sum` through parameter lists.

Exercises for Section 6.6   ***Self-Check***

1. Procedure `ComputeSum` returns a single value. Why do you think it was not implemented as a function?
2. Draw the main program data area and the function data area for the call to `ComputeAve`, assuming that `Sum` is `100.0` and `NumItems` is `10`.
3. Draw the main program data area and the procedure data area for the call to `PrintSumAve`.

6.7 Debugging and Testing Programs with Modules

As the number of statements in a program or module grows, the possibility of error increases. Keeping each module to a manageable size lowers the likelihood of error and enhances readability and testing of each module.

Just as you can simplify the overall programming process by writing a large program as a set of independent modules, you can simplify testing and debugging a program with multiple modules if you test in stages as the program evolves. Two kinds of testing are used: top-down testing and bottom-up testing. You should use a combination of these methods to test a program and its modules.

Top-Down Testing and Stubs

program system
a main program together with its modules

Whether a single programmer or a programming team is developing a **program system** (a main program and its modules), not all modules will be ready at the same time. It is possible, however, to test the overall flow of control between the main program and its level-1 modules and to test and debug the level-1 modules that are complete. The process of testing the flow of control between a main program and its subordinate modules is called **top-down testing.**

top-down testing
the process of testing flow of control between a main program and its subordinate modules

stub
a module with a heading and minimal body used in testing flow of control

Because the main program calls all level-1 modules, we need a substitute, called a stub, for all modules that are not yet coded. A **stub** consists of a procedure or function heading followed by a minimal body, which should display a message identifying the module being executed and should assign simple values to any outputs. Figure 6.23 shows a stub for procedure ComputeSum that could be used in a test of the main program in Fig. 6.17. The stub arbitrarily assigns a value of 100.0 to output parameter Sum, which is reasonable data for the remaining modules to process. Examining the program output tells us whether the main program calls its level-1 modules in the required sequence and whether data flows correctly between the main program and its level-1 modules.

Bottom-Up Testing and Drivers

A completed module can be substituted for its stub, of course, but always perform a preliminary test of a new module first. Locating and correcting er-

Figure 6.23
Stub for Procedure
ComputeSum

```
procedure ComputeSum (NumItems {input} : Integer;
                          var Sum {output} : Real);
{
   Computes the sum of a list of NumItems data items.
   Pre : NumItems is assigned a value.
   Post: NumItems data items are read; their sum is stored in
         Sum.
}
begin {ComputeSum stub}
   WriteLn ('Procedure ComputeSum entered');
   Sum := 100.0
end; {ComputeSum stub}
```

rors in a single module is easier than in a complete program system. You can test a new module by writing a short driver program similar to the one in Fig. 6.15.

Don't spend a lot of time creating an elegant driver program, because you will discard it as soon as the new module is tested. A driver program should contain only the declarations and executable statements necessary to test a single module. Moreover, it should begin by reading or assigning values to all input parameters and to input/output parameters, then call the module being tested. After calling the module, the driver program should display the module results.

bottom-up testing

the process of separately test-ing individual modules for a program system

Once you are confident that a module works properly, substitute it for its stub in the program system. The process of separately testing individual modules before inserting them into a program system is called **bottom-up testing**.

Through a combination of top-down and bottom-up testing, you can be-come fairly confident that the complete program system will be relatively free of errors when it is finally assembled. Consequently, the final debugging sessions should proceed quickly and smoothly.

Debugging Tips for Modular Programs

Here are some suggestions for debugging a program system:

1. As you write the code, carefully place comments to document each module parameter and local identifier. Also use comments to describe the module operation.
2. Leave a trace of execution by placing a WriteLn statement that displays the module name at the beginning of the module body.
3. Insert statements that display the values of all input and input/output parameters upon entry to a module. Check that these values make sense.
4. Insert statements that display the values of all module outputs after re-turning from a module. Hand-compute these values to verify that they are correct. For procedures, make sure that all input/output and output parameters are declared as variable parameters.
5. Make sure that a module stub assigns a value to each of its outputs.

It is a good idea to plan for debugging as you write each module rather than adding debugging steps afterwards. Include the output statements sug-gested for tips 2 to 4 in the Pascal code for the module. When satisfied that the module works as desired, remove the debugging statements. The sim-plest way is to change them to comments by enclosing them in braces; if you have a problem later, you can remove the braces, thereby changing the com-ments back to executable statements.

Another approach to turning debugging statements on and off is to use a global Boolean constant (say, Debug), which is declared in the main pro-gram. Use the declaration

```
const
  Debug = True;      {Turn debugging on.}
```

during debugging runs, and the declaration

```
const
  Debug = False;      {Turn debugging off.}
```

during normal runs. Within the main program body and its procedures, embed each diagnostic WriteLn statement in an if statement with Debug as its condition. If procedure ComputeSum begins with the following if statement, the WriteLn statements will execute only during debugging runs (Debug is True), as desired:

```
if Debug then
  begin
    WriteLn ('Procedure ComputeSum entered');
    WriteLn ('Input parameter NumItems has value ', NumItems :1)
  end; {if}
```

Using the Debugger to Trace a Procedure

As an alternative to displaying the initial values of a procedure's input and input/output parameters using special debugging statements, you can use the Turbo Pascal debugger and its trace feature (function key F7) to provide this information. If the next statement to be executed is a procedure call, pressing F7 will cause the procedure to be entered. The procedure body will appear in the Edit window with its begin line highlighted. Then you would designate the procedure parameters as Watch variables using the steps described in Section 5.8, and the initial parameter values will appear in the Watch window. As you execute each statement in the procedure (by pressing F7), any new values assigned to output parameters or input/output parameters will appear in the Watch window.

After the procedure return occurs, you can use the debugger to see what values were returned to the calling program. This time, designate as Watch variables any actual parameters that correspond to output parameters or to input/output parameters. The values returned by the procedure appear in the Watch window.

Using the Step Over Option

If you have thoroughly tested a procedure before using it in a new program, there is no need to execute each individual statement of that procedure when using the Turbo Pascal debugger. Whenever the next statement to be executed is a procedure call statement, you have the option of executing the complete procedure body at once, or of executing each statement in the procedure body individually. If you press F8 (Step over), the debugger executes the whole procedure body, stopping at the first statement after the procedure call. If you wish to trace the execution of each individual statement in the procedure body, press F7 (Trace into) to enter the procedure.

Identifier Scope and Watch Window Variables

The values displayed in the Watch window are determined by the normal scope rules for Pascal identifiers. Consequently, a procedure's local variables and formal parameters will be displayed with the value Unknown identifier until that procedure begins execution. Upon exit from the procedure, its local variables and formal parameters will again have Unknown identifier displayed as their value in the Watch window.

When identifiers having the same name are declared in different parts of a program, you can qualify a Watch variable by prefixing it with the name of the module in which it is declared so its value can be displayed throughout the execution of the program. For the watch variables shown in Fig. 6.24, ScopeRules.W refers to the global identifier W declared in the main program ScopeRules, and Change.W refers to the local identifier W declared in procedure Change. When procedure Change completes execution, the value displayed for Change.W is Cannot access this symbol, while the value of ScopeRules.W does not change.

Figure 6.24
Qualifying Watch
Variables

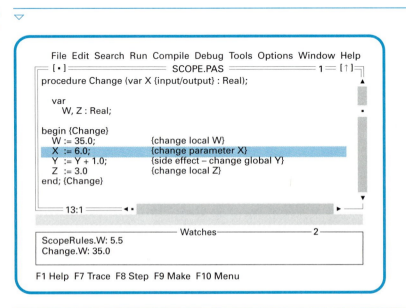

6.8   Recursive Functions (Optional)

recursive module

a procedure or function that
calls itself

factorial of N

the product of all positive integers ≤ N

Pascal allows a function or procedure to call itself. A module that calls itself
is a **recursive module.** We describe a recursive function in this section, one
that returns an integer value representing the factorial of its argument. The
factorial of N is the product of all positive integers less than or equal to N
and is written in mathematics as N!. For example, 4! is the product $4 \times 3 \times 2 \times 1$ or 24.

Figure 6.25 shows a nonrecursive factorial function that uses a loop to
accumulate partial products in local variable ProductSoFar. The for statement repeats the multiplication step when N is greater than 1. If N is 0 or 1,
the for statement does not execute, so ProductSoFar retains its initial value
of 1. After loop exit, the last value of ProductSoFar is assigned to Factorial, thereby defining the function result.

Figure 6.26 shows function Factorial rewritten as a recursive function,
in which the if statement implements the following formulas, which form
the recursive definition of N!:

$$N! = 1 \qquad\qquad \text{for } N = 0 \text{ or } 1$$
$$N! = N \times (N - 1)! \qquad \text{for } N > 1$$

When N is greater than 1, instead of executing a loop to repeat the multiplication, as in Fig. 6.25, the statement

```
Factorial := N * Factorial(N-1)
```

Figure 6.25
Function Factorial

```
function Factorial (N : Integer) : Integer;
{
   Computes N!
   Pre : N >= 0
   Post: Returns the product 1 * 2 * 3 * . . . * N for N > 1;
         returns 1 when N is 0 or 1.
}
   var
     I,                        {loop-control variable}
     ProductSoFar : Integer;   {accumulated product}

begin {Factorial}
   ProductSoFar := 1;        {Initialize accumulated product.}

   {Perform the repeated multiplication for N > 1.}
   for I := 2 to N do
     ProductSoFar := ProductSoFar * I;

   {Define function result.}
   Factorial := ProductSoFar
end; {Factorial}
```

Figure 6.26
Recursive Function
Factorial

```
function Factorial (N : Integer) : Integer;
{
 Computes N!
 Pre : N >= 0
 Post: Returns the product 1 * 2 * 3 * . . . * N for N > 1;
       returns 1 when N is 0 or 1.
}
begin {Factorial}
  if N <= 1 then
    Factorial := 1
  else
    Factorial := N * Factorial(N-1)
end; {Factorial}
```

executes, which is the Pascal form of the second formula. The expression part of this statement contains a function designator, Factorial(N-1), which calls function Factorial with an argument that is 1 less than the current argument. This function call is a *recursive call*. If the argument in the initial call to Factorial is 3, the following chain of recursive calls occurs:

Factorial(3) $\rightarrow$ 3 * Factorial(2) $\rightarrow$ 3 * (2 * Factorial(1))

In the last of these calls, N is equal to 1, so the statement

Factorial := 1

executes, stopping the chain of recursive calls.

When it finishes the last function call, Pascal must return a value from each recursive call, starting with the last one. The last call was Factorial(1) and it returns a value of 1. To find the value returned by each call for N greater than 1, multiply N by the value returned from Factorial(N-1). Therefore the value returned from Factorial(2) is 2 * the value returned from Factorial(1) or 2; the value returned from Factorial(3) is 3 * the value returned from Factorial(2) or 6 (see Fig. 6.27).

Exercises for Section 6.8   ***Self-Check***

1. Show the chain of recursive calls to function Mystery when M is 4 and N is 3. What do you think Mystery does?

```
function Mystery (M, N : Integer) : Integer;
begin {Mystery}
  if N = 1 then
    Mystery:= M
  else
    Mystery:= M * Mystery(M, N-1)
end; {Mystery}
```

Figure 6.27
Evaluating Factorial(3)

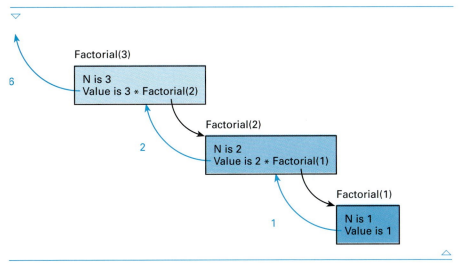

Programming

1. Write a recursive function that, given an input value of N, computes N + N-1 + . . . + 2 + 1.

2. Write a function C(N, R) that returns the number of different ways *R* items can be selected from a group of *N* items. The mathematical formula for C(N, R) follows. Test C(N, R) using both the recursive and the nonrecursive versions of function Factorial.

$$C(N, R) = \frac{N!}{R!(N-R)!}$$

6.9 Graphics Animation (Optional)

So far you have drawn figures at a single location on a screen. If a graphics procedure has parameters, you can vary the location of a figure or draw it at multiple locations on the screen. You can also animate a figure by drawing it at one point on the screen, erasing it, and then redrawing it at another point a few pixels away. By repeating these operations, the figure will appear to be moving across the screen.

EXAMPLE 6.9 ▼

Procedure DrawMan (see Fig. 6.28) draws a stick figure whose head is centered at point (X, Y), the procedure's first two parameters. The Boolean parameter Standing determines whether the stick figure's arms and legs are in the normal position (Standing is True) or raised in a jumping position (Standing is False).

Figure 6.28
Moving a Stick Figure

Edit Window

```
program JumpingJack;
{Moves a stick figure across the screen.}

  uses Graph, Crt;

  const
    Directory = 'C:\BP\BGI';                    {graphics directory}
    DelayTime = 250; {time between "frames" - 1/4 of a second}

  var
    XPosition, YPosition,      {position of stick figure}
    Driver, Mode,              {graphics system indicators}
    I : Integer;               {loop control variable}
    Standing : Boolean;        {flag - determines orientation}

  procedure DrawMan (X, Y {input} : Integer;
                          Standing {input} : Boolean);
    {
     Draws a standing or jumping stick figure.
     Pre : X, Y, Standing are defined.
     Post: Stick figure is drawn with head centered at pixel
           (X, Y) with arms and legs down if Standing is True
           and with arms and legs raised if Standing is False.
    }
    begin {DrawMan}
      Circle (X, Y, 20);                        {Draw head.}
      Line (X, Y + 20, X, Y + 60);           {Draw torso.}
      if Standing then
        begin {standing}
          Line (X, Y + 30, X - 20, Y + 60);   {Draw left arm.}
          Line (X, Y + 30, X + 20, Y + 60);   {Draw right arm.}
          Line (X, Y + 60, X - 20, Y + 100); {Draw left leg.}
          Line (X, Y + 60, X + 20, Y + 100)  {Draw right leg.}
        end   {standing}
      else
        begin {jumping}
          Line (X, Y + 30, X - 30, Y + 20);   {Draw left arm.}
          Line (X, Y + 30, X + 30, Y + 20);   {Draw right arm.}
          Line (X, Y + 60, X - 30, Y + 80);   {Draw left leg.}
          Line (X, Y + 60, X + 30, Y + 80)   {Draw right leg.}
        end {jumping}
    end; {DrawMan}

  begin {JumpingJack}
    InitGraph (Driver, Mode, Directory);  {Initialize graphics.}
    OutTextXY (10, 10, 'Press any key to stop the stick figure:');
    XPosition := 20;                      {Set initial X location.}
    YPosition := GetMaxY div 2;           {Set initial Y location.}
```

▷ ▷ ▷ ▷ ▷

```
{Draw the stick figure repeatedly.}
Standing := True;                {Start in standing position.}
repeat
   {Draw the stick figure.}
   SetColor (White);
   DrawMan (XPosition, YPosition, Standing);
   Delay (DelayTime);                            {Wait . . .}

   {Erase the stick figure.}
   SetColor (Black);
   DrawMan (XPosition, YPosition, Standing);

   {Move the stick figure and change its position.}
   XPosition := XPosition + 5;
   Standing := not Standing            {Switch position.}
   until KeyPressed          {continue until a key is pressed.}
end. {JumpingJack}
```

Output Window

In the main program loop, the statements

```
SetColor (White);
DrawMan (XPosition, YPosition, Standing);
Delay (DelayTime);                            {Wait . . .}
```

draw the stick figure in white and keep it displayed for a brief time period (250 milliseconds). Next, DrawMan is called again to erase the figure by drawing it in the same location in the background color (black). Then the statements

```
XPosition := XPosition + 5;
Standing := not Standing          {Switch position.}
```

change XPosition and Standing so a new stick figure will be drawn five pixels to the right of the previous one and in the opposite position.

The sample run shows the first two stick figures. The first figure, in gray, would be erased just before the second is drawn. As the draw and erase operations are repeated, the stick figure jumps across the screen. Procedure Delay (part of unit Crt) causes the program to pause or delay for the number of milliseconds indicated by its parameter; you can speed up or slow down the stick figure's motion by changing the value of DelayTime.

The repeat statement executes until its condition, KeyPressed, becomes true. Function KeyPressed (also in unit Crt) returns True if a key has been pressed; it returns False otherwise. Table 9.2 in Section 9.3 describes unit Crt's procedure and function modules.   ▲

Exercises for Section 6.9   *Programming*

1. Write a procedure MoveFigure that changes either the X or Y coordinate (input/output parameters) of the stick figure based on a direction character (input parameter) that can be U (up), D (down), R (right) or L (left).

6.10 Common Programming Errors

Proper use of parameters is difficult for beginning programmers to master, but it is an essential skill. Of the many opportunities for error when you use modules with parameter lists, the obvious pitfall occurs in not ensuring that the actual parameter list has the same number of parameters as the formal parameter list. The syntax errors "," expected and ")" expected indicate this problem.

Each actual parameter must be assignment compatible with its corresponding formal parameter (for a value parameter) or the same data type (for a variable parameter). An actual parameter that corresponds to a variable formal parameter must be a variable. A violation of the first rule results in a type mismatch syntax error; a violation of the second rule results in a variable identifier expected syntax error.

Return a procedure result to the calling module by assigning a value to a variable parameter. Any such value assigned to a value parameter is stored locally in the procedure and will not be returned. If your procedure seems to execute properly but does not return the expected results, it is possible that you forgot to declare an output or input/output parameter as a variable parameter.

Remember to return all function results by assigning a value to the function name. It is bad programming practice to return a second function result through a variable parameter (function side effect). It is also bad programming practice to directly manipulate a global variable in a procedure or function; all global variables should be passed to a module through its parameter list.

The Pascal scope rules determine where an identifier can be referenced. If an identifier is referenced outside its scope, an `identifier not declared` syntax error will result.

CHAPTER REVIEW

1. Parameters enable a programmer to pass data to functions and procedures and to return results from procedures. The parameter list provides a highly visible communication path between a module and its calling program. Using parameters enables a module to process different data each time it executes, thereby simplifying reuse of the module in other programs.
2. There are two types of parameters: value parameters and variable parameters. A value parameter is used only for passing data into a module, and a variable parameter is used to return results from a procedure. The actual parameter that corresponds to a value parameter can be an expression or a constant; the actual parameter that corresponds to a variable parameter must be a variable.
3. The scope of an identifier dictates where it can be referenced. An identifier can be referenced anywhere in the block that declares it. A global variable is one that is declared in the main program, and a local variable is one that is declared in a procedure or function module. A local variable is defined only during the execution of the module, and its value is lost when the module is exited. If there are multiple declarations of an identifier in different blocks, then the compiler uses the most local declaration when translating each block.
4. A function is a module that returns a single result. The function result is defined by assigning a value to the function name inside the function body. Function parameters should be value parameters.

Summary of New Pascal Constructs

Construct	Effect
Function Declaration	
```pascal function Sign (X : Real) : Char; begin {Sign} if X >= 0.0 then Sign := '+' else Sign := '-' end; {Sign} ```	Returns a character value that indicates the sign ('+' or '−') of its type Real argument X.

Construct	Effect
Procedure Declaration	
| ```pascal
procedure DoIt (X : Real;
                Op : Char;
                var Y: Char;
                var XSign : Char);
begin {DoIt}
  case Op of
    '+' : Y := X + X;
    '*' : Y := X * X
  end; {case}
  XSign := Sign(X)
end; {DoIt}
``` | If Op is '+', returns X + X through Y; if Op is '*', returns X * X through Y. Calls Sign to assign a character value that indicates the sign ('+' or '-') of X to XSign. |
| ***Procedure Call Statement*** | |
| ```pascal
DoIt (-5.0, '*', Y, MySign)
``` | Calls DoIt. Passes -5.0 into X, passes '*' into Op, returns 25.0 to Y, returns '-' to MySign. |

Quick-Check Exercises

1. The _____ parameters appear in the procedure call, and the _____ parameters appear in the procedure declaration.
2. Constants and expressions can correspond to formal parameters that are _____ parameters.
3. Formal parameters that are variable parameters must have actual parameters that are _____.
4. Formal parameters that are variable parameters must have actual parameters that are the _____ data type.
5. The data types of corresponding value parameters must be _____.
6. Which is used to test a new module, a driver or a stub?
7. Which is used to test main program flow, a driver or a stub?
8. A(n) _____ occurs when a function assigns a value to a variable parameter or when a procedure changes a global variable.
9. What are the values of main program variables X and Y after the following program executes?

```pascal
program Nonsense;
  var X, Y : Real;

  procedure Silly (X : Real);
    var Y : Real;
  begin
    Y := 25.0;
    X := Y
  end; {Silly}
```

```
begin {Nonsense}
   Silly (X)
end. {Nonsense}
```

10. Answer Exercise 9, this time assuming parameter X of Silly is a variable parameter.
11. The parameters of a function should be _____ parameters.
12. The part of a program where an identifier can be referenced is called the _____ of the identifier.
13. True or false: Within a procedure body, any other procedure declared in the program can be called.
14. How does a function return its value?

Answers to Quick-Check Exercises

1. actual, formal
2. value
3. variables
4. same or identical
5. assignment compatible
6. Driver
7. Stub
8. side effect
9. Both are undefined.
10. X is 25.0, Y is undefined.
11. value
12. scope
13. False, a procedure declared later in the main program cannot be called.
14. A function returns its single value by assigning a value to the function name.

Review Questions

1. Write the procedure heading for a procedure called Script that accepts three parameters passed to it. The first parameter is the number of spaces to print at the beginning of a line. The second parameter is the character to print after the spaces, and the third parameter is the number of times to print the second parameter on the same line.
2. Write a function called LetterGrade that has a parameter called Grade and that returns the appropriate letter grade using a straight scale (90–100 is an A, 80–89 is a B, and so on).
3. Why would you choose to make a formal parameter a value parameter rather than a variable parameter?
4. Write a procedure that accepts two real values as input and outputs the sum and difference of the two values.
5. Describe a circumstance where a procedure would give different results if a value parameter in the procedure was changed to a variable parameter.
6. Explain the use of a stub in testing a program.

7. In the chart that follows, write Yes for each procedure on the right that can be referenced (called) by the procedure on the left and No for each procedure that is inaccessible.

```
program ProcScope;

    procedure A;

        procedure B;

            procedure C;

            . . .

            end; {C}

            procedure D;

            . . .

            end; {D}

        . . .

        end; {B}

    . . .

    end; {A}

. . .

end. {ProcScope}
```

	Callable Procedures			
Calling Procedure	**A**	**B**	**C**	**D**
A				
B				
C				
D				

8. List two reasons for implementing a module as a procedure rather than as a function.

Programming Projects

1. The assessor in your town has estimated the market value of all properties and would like you to write a program that determines the tax owed on each property and the total tax to be collected. The tax rate is 12.5 cents per dollar of assessed value, and the assessed value of each property is 28% of its estimated market value. The market values are as follows:

$150,000 $148,000 $145,500 $167,000 $137,600 $147,100

$165,000 $153,350 $128,000 $158,000 $152,250 $148,000

$156,500 $143,700

You need to write procedures that correspond to the following procedure headers as part of your solution:

```
procedure PrintInstructions;
{Displays instructions to the user}

procedure ProcessProperties (var TotalTax {output} : Real);
{Reads market values and computes taxes on all properties}

function ComputeTax (Market : Real) : Real;
{Computes tax on a property with market value Market}

procedure PrintSummary (TotalTax {input} : Real);
{Displays value of TotalTax}
```

2. Revise Programming Project 1, assuming a 5% surcharge for all properties with market value over $150,000. Also grant a 10% discount for senior citizens. You will need to enter a second data item for each property to indicate whether its owner is a senior citizen. Write a separate procedure that reads and returns the current property market value and sets a Boolean parameter to True if the owner is a senior citizen.

3. The trustees of a small college are considering a 5.5% pay raise for its faculty members, but first they want to know how much this increase will cost. Write a program that prints the pay raise for each faculty member and the total amount of the raises, then prints the total faculty payroll before and after the raises. Test your program for the following salaries:

$32,500	$24,029.50	$36,000	$43,250
$35,500	$22,800	$30,000.50	$28,900
$43,780	$24,029.50	$44,120.25	$24,100

Refer to Programming Project 1 for a guide as to what procedures and functions will be needed.

4. Revise Programming Project 3, assuming that faculty earning less than $30,000 receive a 7% raise, faculty earning more than $40,000 receive a 4% raise, and all others receive a 5.5% raise. Write a new function that determines the raise percentage. Print the raise percentage as well as the amount for each faculty member.

5. A monthly magazine wants a program that prints out renewal and cancellation notices to its subscribers. Using procedures when advisable, write a program that first reads in the current month number (1 through 12) and year. For each subscription processed, read in four data items: the account number, the month and the year the subscription started, and the number of years paid for the subscription.

   Read in each set of subscription information and print a renewal notice if the current month is either the month prior to expiration or the month of expiration. A cancellation notice should be printed if the current month comes after the expiration month.

   Sample input might be as follows:

```
10 94                    for a current month of October 1994
1364  4  94  3           for account 1364, whose 3-year
                         subscription began in April 1994
```

6. Write a program that displays a running stopwatch. The user will enter the number of seconds that the stopwatch should run, starting at 0:00:00. Times should be displayed as *hours:minutes:seconds* with leading zeros on the minutes and seconds. For this program, you will need to use a procedure from the Turbo Pascal library: The procedure call `Delay (1000)` will delay for 1000 milliseconds (1 second). You will have to add `uses Crt;` to the beginning of your program to use this procedure. Write a procedure that displays a number as two digits with a leading zero. (Just test for less than 10 and output a zero and the number.) Write another procedure that accepts a time and displays it, using the last procedure to display the numbers. Finally, write a procedure that increments a time. Represent an elapsed time with three integer values.

7. The square root of a number N can be approximated by repeated calculation using the formula

    `NG = 0.5(LG + N / LG)`

    where NG stands for next guess and LG stands for last guess. Write a function that implements this process. The first parameter will be a positive real number, the second will be an initial guess of the square root, and the return value will be the computed result.

    The initial guess will be the starting value of LG. The function will compute a value for NG using the formula. The difference between NG and LG is checked to see whether these two guesses are almost identical. If so, the function is exited and NG is returned as the square root; otherwise, the new guess (NG) becomes the last guess (LG), and the process is repeated (i.e., another value is computed for NG, the difference is checked, etc.).

    For this program, the loop should be repeated until the magnitude of the difference is less than `0.005` (Delta). Use an initial guess of `1.0` and test the program for the numbers `4`, `120.5`, `88`, `36.01`, and `10000`.

8. The road stripe painters in your area have allied to form a monopoly. Each painter will paint up to two miles of stripes on the road. For roads longer than two miles, the painter will divide the area to be painted into three equal parts and subcontract each of those parts to three other painters, who will treat their sections the same way. Painters will charge $200.00 for each section they themselves paint and $100.00 to oversee the three they have hired. Write a program that allows a user to enter a road length and computes the cost to paint the entire road. *Hint:* Write a recursive function that returns 200 if the length is less than two miles or adds 100 to three recursive calls to the function with the length divided by 3. Try your program with 2, 54, 55, 100, and 1000 miles.

CHAPTER SEVEN

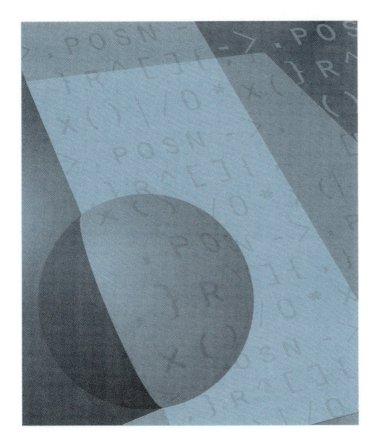

Simple Data Types

simple data type
a data type used to store a single value

We now take a closer look at Pascal's standard data types—Integer, Real, Char, and Boolean. We also describe some predefined functions for processing ordinal types.

No programming language can predefine all the data types a programmer may want to use, so Pascal allows a programmer to create new data types. In this chapter, you'll learn how to declare two new kinds of data types: subrange types and enumerated types. All these data types—standard types, subrange types, and enumerated types—are **simple,** or **scalar, data types** because only a single value can be stored in a variable of each type.

7.1   Numeric Data Types: Real and Integer

The data types `Integer` and `Real` represent numeric information. Although most numeric data are real, programmers typically use integers as loop counters and to represent whole-number data, such as exam scores.

Differences Between Numeric Types

We could represent an integer as a real number with a fractional part of 0, so why does Pascal need two numeric data types? On many computers, operations with integers are faster than those with real numbers and integers need less storage space than real numbers. Also, operations with integers are always precise, whereas there may be some loss of accuracy with real numbers.

These differences result from the way numbers are represented in the computer's memory. All data are represented in memory as *binary strings,* strings of 0s and 1s, but the binary string stored for, say, the integer 13 differs from that for the real number 13.0. The actual internal representation is computer dependent, and real numbers often require more bytes of computer memory.

Compare the sample integer and real formats shown in Fig. 7.1. The figure shows that integers are represented by binary numbers. For example, the integer 13 is represented as the binary number 0. . .01101. The leftmost bit represents the sign of the number; positive integers have a sign bit of 0 and negative integers have a sign bit of 1. Turbo Pascal uses 16 bits to store an integer.

Real format (also called *floating-point format*) is analogous to scientific notation. The storage area occupied by a real number is divided into two sections: the *mantissa* and the *exponent.* The *mantissa* is a binary fraction $\geq$ 0.0 and < 1.0, and the *exponent* is a power of 2. The mantissa and the exponent are chosen so that the following formula is correct:

real number = mantissa $\times$ $2^{exponent}$

Because memory cells have a finite size, not all real numbers in the range of reals can be represented precisely. Turbo Pascal uses 48 bits to store a real number.

Real numbers, unlike integers, can have a fractional part, and their range is considerably larger than that of integers. In Turbo Pascal, real numbers

Figure 7.1
Integer and Real Formats

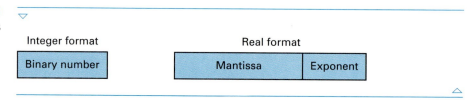

Integer format

| Binary number |

Real format

| Mantissa | Exponent |

range in value from 10^{-39} (a very small fraction) to 10^{+38}. The smallest positive integer is 1 and the largest integer, MaxInt, is 32767. The largest negative integer is -MaxInt - 1 or -32768.

Numerical Inaccuracies

One of the problems in processing real numbers is the chance of error in representing real data. Just as certain numbers cannot be represented exactly in the decimal number system (e.g., the fraction 1/3 is 0.333333 . . .), so some numbers cannot be represented exactly in real format. The size of this **representational error** depends on the number of binary digits (bits) used in the mantissa: The more bits, the smaller the error.

representational error
an error due to imprecise coding of a decimal number in binary form

For example, the decimal number 0.1 is a real number that cannot be represented exactly in the binary number system, resulting in a small error that would be magnified through repeated computations. Thus, because the result of adding 0.1 ten times is not exactly 1.0, the following loop may fail to terminate on some computers:

```
Trial := 0.0;
while Trial <> 1.0 do
  begin
    . . .

    Trial := Trial + 0.1
  end {while}
```

If the loop repetition test is changed to Trial < 1.0, the loop may execute 10 times on one computer and 11 times on another. To avoid this problem, use integer variables whenever possible in loop-repetition tests.

cancellation error
a computational error caused by processing a large number with a much small number

Other errors occur when manipulating very large and very small real numbers. Adding a large number and a very small number may cause the larger number to "cancel out" the smaller number, resulting in a **cancellation error.** If X is much larger than Y, then X + Y may have the same value as X (e.g., 100000.0 + 0.000001234 is equal to 100000.0 on some computers).

arithmetic underflow
an error caused by incorrectly representing a small computational result as zero

arithmetic overflow
an error caused by a computational result that is too large to be represented

The result of multiplying two very small numbers may be an amount so small it is represented as zero (**arithmetic underflow**). Similarly, if two very large numbers are multiplied, the result may be too large to be represented (**arithmetic overflow**).

Arithmetic overflow can occur even when processing relatively small integer values. For example, if Hours is 24, Min is 60, and Sec is 60, the statement

```
SecInDay := Hours * Min * Sec
```

assigns the number of seconds in a day (86400) to SecInDay. Because the result is too large for type Integer, an incorrect value (20864) is stored instead and no error is indicated. To avoid this error in standard Pascal, you would be forced to use type Real variables. Turbo Pascal has another solution as discussed next.

Additional Numeric Types in Turbo Pascal (Optional)

Turbo Pascal contains a data type, LongInt, having values between -2147483648 and 2147483647. A variable of type LongInt uses 32 bits of storage instead of the 16 bits allocated for variables of type Integer.

Table 7.1 lists the additional Integer data types available in Turbo Pascal, along with the range of values that can be stored in variables of each type. Two integer types, Byte and ShortInt, use only 8 bits per value. The data type Word stores only positive integers so its largest value is twice that of data type Integer. All Turbo Pascal operators that can be used with type Integer can also be used with the data types listed in Table 7.1.

Table 7.1
Integer Data Types

Type	Ranges
Byte	0..255
ShortInt	-128..127
Integer	-32768..32767
Word	0..65535
LongInt	-2147483648..2147483647

Turbo Pascal also provides several additional data types for real numbers. These data types are listed in Table 7.2, along with the range of values for each type and the number of significant digits for each type. All Turbo Pascal operators that can be used with type Real can also be used with the data types listed in Table 7.2.

Table 7.2
Real Data Types

Type	Ranges	Significant Digits
Single	1.5E-45..3.4E38	7–8
Real	2.9E-39..1.7E38	11–12
Double	5.0E-324..1.7E308	15–16
Extended	1.9E-4951..1.1E4932	19–20

While the additional Integer types are always available in Turbo Pascal, you may need special compiler directives to use the extended Real types. The compiler directives needed depend on whether your computer has a numeric coprocessor (a computer chip used for performing floating-point arithmetic operations). If the numeric coprocessor is installed, use the compiler directive pair {$N+, E-}, which instructs the compiler to perform floating-point numeric processing by calling procedures that utilize the coprocessor. If the coprocessor is not installed, use the compiler directive pair {$N+, E+}, which instructs the compiler to perform floating-point computations by calling procedures that *emulate* (simulate with software) the coprocessor.

SYNTAX DISPLAY

Numeric Support Compiler Directive

Form: {$N-} or {$N+}
Default: {$N-}
Interpretation: When passive (value −), the compiler generates code to perform floating-point calculations that do not require the numeric co-processor. When active (value +), the compiler generates code to perform floating-point calculations using the numeric coprocessor.
Note: The {$N+} state is required to make use of the Turbo Pascal extended Real data types: Single, Double, or Extended.

SYNTAX DISPLAY

Emulation Compiler Directive

Form: {$E-} or {$E+}
Default: {$E+}
Interpretation: When active (value +), the numeric coprocessor is emulated. When passive (value −), the numeric coprocessor is used directly.

Exercises for Section 7.1

Self-Check

1. Assuming a computer exhibits cancellation error such that 1000.0 + 0.0001234 is equal to 1000.0, what would be the result of the following assignment statement. Why?

   X := 1000.0001234;

Programming

1. Since the loop in the section on numerical inaccuracies may not operate correctly, write a loop that outputs the decimal fractions from 0.0 to 1.0 in steps of 0.1 using an integer as the loop counter.

7.2 The Boolean Data Type

Boolean variables have two values, True or False, which Pascal represents as the binary numbers 1 and 0, respectively. We can use the assignment operator with Boolean data and the Boolean operators and, or, not. Boolean expressions are used in if, while, and repeat statements.

Programmers write Boolean expressions that call Boolean functions to enhance program readability. Boolean functions return a value of True or False.

EXAMPLE 7.1: Boolean Functions ▼

We have written an algorithm that contains the following decision step. In this example, we have no interest in the details of the three procedures called in the `if` statement; we just want to make sure that the correct procedure is called.

```
if Ch is a letter then
   Call procedure ProcessLetter
else if Ch is a digit character then
   Call procedure ProcessDigit
else
   Call procedure ProcessSpecial
```

The `if` statement that follows implements this algorithm. The first Boolean expression calls function `IsLetter` (Fig. 7.2) to determine whether `Ch` is a letter; the second Boolean expression calls function `IsDigit` to determine whether `Ch` is a digit. The function designator `IsLetter(Ch)` returns a value of `True` if `Ch` is a letter and a value of `False` if `Ch` is not a letter. Similarly, the function designator `IsDigit(Ch)` returns a value of `True` if `Ch` is a digit character and a value of `False` otherwise.

```
if IsLetter(Ch) then
   ProcessLetter (Ch)
else if IsDigit(Ch) then
   ProcessDigit (Ch)
else
   ProcessSpecial (Ch)
```

Figure 7.2
Functions IsLetter
and IsDigit

```
function IsLetter (Ch : Char) : Boolean;
{
 Returns True when its argument is a letter; otherwise,
 returns False
}
begin {IsLetter}
   IsLetter := (('A' <= Ch) and (Ch <= 'Z')) or
               (('a' <= Ch) and (Ch <= 'z'))
end; {IsLetter}

function IsDigit (Ch : Char) : Boolean;
{
 Returns True when its argument is a digit character;
 otherwise, returns False
}
begin {IsDigit}
   IsDigit := ('0' <= Ch) and (Ch <= '9')
end; {IsDigit}
```

Functions `IsLetter` and `IsDigit` consist of a statement that assigns a Boolean value to the function name, thereby defining the function result. The value assigned (`True` or `False`) depends on the result of the character comparison specified by the Boolean expression. We discuss character comparisons in the next section. ▲

Exercises for Section 7.2

Self-Check

1. Evaluate each of the following when `Ch1` is `'a'` and `Ch2` is `'3'`:
   a. `IsLetter(Ch1) and IsDigit(Ch2)`
   b. `IsLetter(Ch1) or IsDigit(Ch2)`
   c. `IsLetter(Ch1) and IsDigit(Ch1)`
   d. `IsLetter(Ch1) or IsDigit(Ch1)`

Programming

1. Write a Boolean function that has two integer parameters, `M` and `N`, and returns `True` when the value of `M` is a divisor of `N` and `False` otherwise. Important: Zero is not considered a divisor of any number.

7.3 The Character Data Type

The character data type (`Char`) can store and manipulate individual characters such as those that make up a person's name, address, and other personal data. A type `Char` literal consists of a single character (a letter, a digit, a punctuation mark, or the like) in apostrophes. If `Next` is type `Char`, the assignment statement

```
Next := 'A'
```

stores the letter `A` in `Next`.

You can compare character data using relational operators. If `Next` and `First` are type `Char`, the Boolean expressions

```
Next = First
Next <> First
```

determine whether two character variables have the same or different values. The relational operators <, <=, >, and >= allow you to make order comparisons on character data.

To interpret the result of an order comparison, you must know something about the way characters are represented internally in your computer. Each character has its own unique numeric code whose binary form is stored in a memory cell that has a character value. These binary numbers are compared by the relational operators.

The character code used by Turbo Pascal is called ASCII (American Standard Code for Information Interchange). The ASCII code values are listed in

Appendix D. The digit characters, '0' through '9', are an increasing sequence of consecutive characters in ASCII and have code values of 48 through 57 (decimal). The following order relationship holds for the digit characters:

```
'0'<'1'<'2'<'3'<'4'<'5'<'6'<'7'<'8'<'9'
```

The uppercase letters and lowercase letters are also an increasing sequence of consecutive characters. In ASCII, the uppercase letters have the decimal code values 65 through 90 and the lowercase letters have the decimal code values 97 through 122. The following order relationships hold for uppercase and lowercase letters:

```
'A'<'B'<'C'< ... <'X'<'Y'<'Z'
'a'<'b'<'c'< ... <'x'<'y'<'z'
```

In ASCII the *printable characters* have codes from 32 (the code for a blank or a space) to 126 (the code for the symbol ~). The remaining codes represent normally nonprintable *control characters,* although Turbo Pascal does have printable symbols for these characters when they are displayed on the screen. Sending a control character to an output device causes the device to perform a special operation such as returning the cursor to column 1, advancing the cursor to the next line, or ringing a bell.

Exercises for Section 7.3

Self-Check

1. Evaluate the following:

```
'A' < 'a'     'A' <> 'a'     'Z' > 'A'      'Z' > 'a'
'0' <> 0      '0' <= '0'     '3' <= '9'    '9' <= 'A'
```

2. What does the following statement do?

```
for Ch := 'A' to 'Z' do
   Write (Ch)
```

7.4 Ordinal Functions and Character Functions

Ordinal Data Types

ordinal data type
a data type having a finite set of values that can be listed in order from the first to the last

The data types Integer, Boolean, and Char are classified as **ordinal data types.** The values of an ordinal data type can always be listed in order, with each value having a unique predecessor (except the first) and a unique successor (except the last). For example, the predecessor of 5 is 4 and the successor of 5 is 6.

The order or sequence of an ordinal data type is defined. For example, -MaxInt - 1 is the smallest integer, MaxInt is the largest integer, and the integers follow the sequence -MaxInt - 1, -MaxInt, ..., -1, 0, 1, ..., MaxInt - 1, MaxInt. The order of the Boolean values is False, True.

Ordinal Functions: Ord, Pred, and Succ

The Pascal function Ord determines the *ordinal number,* or relative position, of an ordinal value in its sequence of values. If the parameter of Ord is an integer, the ordinal number returned is the integer itself. For all other ordinal values, the ordinal number of the first value in the sequence is 0, the ordinal number of the second value is 1, and so on. For data type Boolean, Ord(False) is 0 and Ord(True) is 1. If variables A and B belong to the same ordinal type and A < B is true, then Ord(A) < Ord(B) also must be true.

The Pascal function Pred returns the predecessor of its parameter, and the Pascal function Succ returns the successor. These functions, like Ord, can be used only with parameters that are ordinal types.

EXAMPLE 7.2: Ordinal Functions with Integer and Boolean Data ▼

Table 7.3 shows the results of using the Ord, Succ, and Pred functions with an integer or Boolean parameter. The table shows that the last value in each ordinal type does not have a successor (MaxInt, True) and the first one does not have a predecessor (-MaxInt - 1, False). ▲

Table 7.3
Results of Some Ord, Succ, and Pred Functions

Parameter	Ord	Succ	Pred
15	15	16	14
0	0	1	-1
-30	-30	-29	-31
MaxInt	MaxInt	Undefined	MaxInt - 1
-MaxInt - 1	-MaxInt - 1	-MaxInt	Undefined
False	0	True	Undefined
True	1	Undefined	False

Although you can use the ordinal functions with any of the ordinal types, they are most often used with type Char and the enumerated types, which are discussed in Section 7.7. The ordinal number of a character is based on the character set code used (ASCII for Turbo Pascal).

EXAMPLE 7.3: Ordinal Functions with Character Data ▼

Table 7.4 shows some results of the `Ord`, `Succ`, and `Pred` functions for ASCII. The table shows that the digit `'0'` has the ordinal number 48 and the digit `'7'` has the ordinal number 55 in ASCII. Regardless of the character code used, the value of the expression

```
Ord('7') - Ord('0')
```

is 7 because the digit characters must be in consecutive sequence.

Table 7.4

Results of Some Ord, Succ, and Pred Functions for ASCII

Parameter	Ord	Succ	Pred
`'C'`	67	`'D'`	`'B'`
`'c'`	99	`'d'`	`'b'`
`'0'`	48	`'1'`	`'/'`
`'7'`	55	`'8'`	`'6'`
`'y'`	121	`'z'`	`'x'`
`' '`	32	`'!'`	Unprintable

Table 7.4 also shows that the character `'C'` has the ordinal number 67 in ASCII. Since the character `'D'` is the successor of the character `'C'`, it must have an ordinal number of 68. And since the letters are in consecutive sequence in ASCII, the value of the expression

```
Ord('C') - Ord('A')
```

is 2. In ASCII, the lowercase letters have larger code values than the uppercase letters, and the difference in code values for both cases of the same letter is 32 (e.g., `Ord('c') - Ord('C')` is 32). ▲

Character Functions

The function `Chr` returns a character as its result. The character returned is the one whose ordinal number is the function argument. For example, the result of the function reference `Chr(67)` is the character with ordinal number 67 (the letter C in the ASCII code).

If `Ch` is a type `Char` variable, the *nested function reference*

```
Chr(Ord(Ch))
```

has the same value as `Ch`. Therefore, the function `Chr` is the *inverse* of the `Ord` function for the characters.

EXAMPLE 7.4 ▼

Function LowerCase in Fig. 7.3 returns a type Char result—the lowercase form of an uppercase letter passed to its parameter Ch (e.g., if Ch is 'C', LowerCase returns 'c'). If Ch is 'C', the Boolean expression is true, and the first assignment statement is evaluated as

```
LowerCase := Chr(Ord('C') - Ord('A') + Ord('a'))
             Chr(67 - 65 + 97)
             Chr(99) = 'c'
```

If Ch does not contain an uppercase letter, function LowerCase returns Ch as its result.   ▲

EXAMPLE 7.5: Collating Sequence ▼

A *collating sequence* is a sequence of characters arranged by ordinal number. The program in Fig. 7.4 prints part of Turbo Pascal's collating sequence, the characters with ordinal numbers 32 through 90, inclusive. The first character printed is a blank (ordinal number 32).   ▲

Function UpCase

Another useful function provided in Turbo Pascal (but not standard Pascal) is UpCase. Function UpCase returns the uppercase equivalent of its Char argument. For example, UpCase('a') returns 'A'. UpCase returns its argument unchanged if it is not a lowercase letter. Table 7.5 summarizes the functions introduced in this section.

Figure 7.3
Function LowerCase

```
function LowerCase (Ch : Char) : Char;
{
  Returns the lowercase form of its argument.
  Pre : None.
  Post: Returns the lowercase equivalent of Ch if Ch is
        an uppercase letter; otherwise, returns Ch.
}
begin {LowerCase}
  if (Ch >= 'A') and (Ch <= 'Z') then
    LowerCase := Chr(Ord(Ch) - Ord('A') + Ord('a'))
  else
    LowerCase := Ch
end; {LowerCase}
```

Figure 7.4
Printing Part of a Collating
Sequence

Edit Window

```
program Collate;

{Prints part of the collating sequence}
  const
    Min = 32;                          {smallest ordinal number}
    Max = 90;                          {largest ordinal number}

  var
    NextOrd : Integer;                 {each ordinal number}

begin {Collate}
  {Print characters Chr(32) through Chr(90).}
  for NextOrd := Min to Max do
    Write (Chr(NextOrd));              {Print next character.}

  WriteLn
end. {Collate}
```

Output Window

```
!="#$%&'()*+,-./0123456789:;<=>@ABCDEFGHIJKLMNOPQRSTUVWXYZ
```

Table 7.5
Ordinal and
Character Functions

Function	Purpose	Argument	Result
Chr(N)	Returns the character whose ordinal number is N	Integer	Char
Ord(N)	Returns the ordinal number of its argument	Any ordinal type	Integer
Pred(N)	Returns the predecessor of its argument	Any ordinal type	Same as argument
Succ(N)	Returns the successor of its argument	Any ordinal type	Same as argument
UpCase(Ch)	Returns uppercase equivalent of argument	Char	Char

Exercises for Section 7.4   ***Self-Check***

1. Evaluate the following:
   a. `Ord(True)`   c. `Succ(False)`
   b. `Pred(True)`   d. `Ord(True) - Ord(False)`
2. Evaluate the following, assuming the letters are consecutive characters.
   a. `Ord('D') - Ord('A')`   f. `Ord('7') - Ord('6')`
   b. `Ord('d') - Ord('a')`   g. `Ord('7') - Ord('6')`
   c. `Succ(Pred('a'))`   h. `Succ(Succ(Succ('d')))`
   d. `Chr(Ord('C'))`   i. `Chr(Ord('A') + 5)`
   e. `Chr(Ord('Z') - Ord('A') + Ord('a'))`
3. Write a `while` loop equivalent to the following `for` loop:

   ```
   for Ch := 'A' to 'Z' do
     WriteLn (Ch, Ord(Ch));
   ```

Programming

1. Write a function `UpperCase` (your own version of `UpCase`) that returns as its value the uppercase equivalent of its character argument or, if there is none, returns the value of its argument.

7.5   Subrange Types

subrange type
an ordinal data type whose values are a subset of another ordinal type

host type (base type)
the data type whose range of values is restricted in a subrange type declaration

Pascal allows you to define your own data types. The first user-defined data type we consider is the **subrange type,** where a *subrange* defines a subset of the values associated with a particular ordinal type (the **host type** or **base type**). Subranges indicate the range of values allowed for an ordinal variable, so they enable Turbo Pascal to detect when a variable is given a value that is unreasonable in the problem environment.

EXAMPLE 7.6 ▼

To define a subrange, or any new data type, you write a type declaration that begins with the reserved word `type`. This example illustrates the declaration of two subrange types, as well as a variable of each new type:

```
type
  Letter = 'A'..'Z';
  DaysInMonth = 1..31;

var
  NextChar : Letter;      {NextChar is an uppercase letter.}
  InDay : DaysInMonth;    {InDay is an integer <= 31.}
```

The first subrange, `Letter`, has the host type `Char`, so any character value from `'A'` to `'Z'`, inclusive, can be stored in a variable of type `Letter`. The computer may display an error message and stop program execution if you attempt to read any other character into a variable of type Letter. The assignment statement

```
NextChar := 'a'
```

causes a compilation error in Turbo Pascal because the character value 'a' is not included in data type Letter.

DaysInMonth is a subrange with host type Integer. A variable of type DaysInMonth can store the day of the month, a number between 1 and 31 inclusive. The statement

```
ReadLn (InDay)
```

reads a data value into InDay (type DaysInMonth). ▲

The host type for a subrange is determined by the pair of values that defines the subrange; the ordinal number of the first value must be less than or equal to the ordinal number of the second value. Operations that are valid for the host type can be performed on any of its subrange types. Subrange type identifiers have the same scope rules as other Pascal identifiers.

SYNTAX DISPLAY

Subrange Type Declaration

Form: type *subrange-type* = *minvalue* .. *maxvalue*;
Example: type LowCase = 'a'..'z';
Interpretation: A new data type named *subrange-type* is defined. A variable of type *subrange-type* can be assigned a value from *minvalue* through *maxvalue*, inclusive. The values *minvalue* and *maxvalue* must belong to the same ordinal type (called the host type), and Ord(*minvalue*) must be less than or equal to Ord(*maxvalue*).
Note: *minvalue* and *maxvalue* may be constant identifiers of the same data type.

Range Checking

A range check error occurs when a program attempts to store a value that is too small or too large in a variable. Although subrange types provide the capability for detecting out-of-range values, Turbo Pascal (unlike standard Pascal) does not automatically perform this function. To implement range checking, place the compiler directive {$R+} in a program, and the Turbo Pascal compiler will generate range-checking code from that point on in the program. You can also turn range checking on through the Options menu, by selecting the Compiler submenu and placing an X in the check box for Range Checking.

SYNTAX DISPLAY

Range Checking Compiler Directive

Form: {$R-} or {$R+}
Default: {$R-}

Interpretation: In the {$R-} state, Turbo Pascal does not check for subrange errors during program execution. The compiler directive {$R+} causes the compiler to generate range-checking code and should be used during program debugging. When this option is active, a test for out-of-range values occurs before each assignment to a subrange variable.

Program Style

Motivation for Using Subranges and Range Checking

Most programmers want a program to stop executing as soon as it stores bad data in a variable, and not perform calculations that lead to meaningless results or a run-time error at some later point. Subrange types in combination with range checking provide this capability in Turbo Pascal. As soon as a program attempts to store an out-of-range value in a variable whose type is a subrange, the program will stop and indicate a Range check error. During compilation, Turbo Pascal displays a Constant out of range syntax error if an invalid constant is assigned to a variable whose type is a subrange type.

Subrange types also enhance program documentation. They clearly indicate to the program reader which variables have a restricted range of values.

The Order of Pascal Declarations

In standard Pascal, the type declarations for a subrange type or any other user-defined data type must come between the constant declarations and the variable declarations in a Pascal block. The form of the declaration part for a standard Pascal block is

constant declarations
type declarations
variable declarations
procedure and function declarations

Although Turbo Pascal does not require that this order be followed, you still must declare each identifier before its first use. This means that you must declare a user-defined data type before declaring a variable of that type.

Exercises for Section 7.5   **Self-Check**

1. Which of the following subranges are illegal and why?
   a. 1..MaxInt   f. 0..'9'
   b. 'A'..'Z'   g. 15..-15
   c. -15..15   h. 'ACE'..'HAT'
   d. 'A'..'z'   i. 'a'..'Z'
   e. -5.0..5.0   j. -MaxInt..-MaxInt + 5
2. The following type declaration and procedure is supposed to ensure the range of an input number is correct, but it generates range check errors anyway. Why?

```
{$R+}
type Year = 1990..2000;                    {valid years}

procedure SafeYear (var Y : Year);
begin {SafeYear}
  repeat
    Write ('Input year 1990-2000> ');
    ReadLn (Y)
  until (Y >= 1990) and (Y <= 2000)
end; {SafeYear}
```

Programming

1. Write a type declaration for a type `Month` appropriate to represent the month number and write a procedure `ReadMonth` that has an output parameter M (type `Month`). Your procedure should prompt the user to enter a month as a word and return a valid month number.

7.6 Type Compatibility and Assignment Compatibility

We discussed assignment compatibility in Section 2.5. Now that we can use more data types, we must reexamine our rules for data type compatibility.

Type Identical

type identical data types
data types that are equivalent

In Turbo Pascal, two data types are **type identical** (the same data type) when one of the following conditions holds:

▶ They are declared to be equivalent to each other.
▶ Each data type is declared to be equivalent to a third type identifier.

The type declarations

```
type
  Numbers = Integer;
  PosAndNeg = Numbers;
  IntType = PosAndNeg;
```

have the effect of making `Numbers`, `PosAndNeg`, `IntType`, and `Integer` identical types. However, `Percent` and `Hundred` as declared next are not identical types because each is declared to be identical to the same subrange (1..100), not the same type identifier:

```
type
  Percent = 1..100;
  Hundred = 1..100;
```

Type Compatibility

type compatible data types
data types that can be used
with the same operator

Two data types are **type compatible** in Turbo Pascal if any of the following conditions holds:

▶ They are type identical.
▶ Both data types are integer types (Byte, ShortInt, Integer, Word, LongInt), though not necessarily the same integer type.
▶ Both data types are real types (Single, Real, Double, Extended), though not necessarily the same real type.
▶ One type is a subrange of the other (for example, Letter and Char in Example 7.6).
▶ Both data types are subranges of the same host type.

Operands that are type compatible can be manipulated together. For example, the expression

```
NextChar <> '3'
```

is syntactically correct as long as NextChar is type Char or Letter. On the other hand, the expression

```
NextChar <> 3
```

causes a syntax error because the integer 3 is not type compatible with NextChar.

Assignment Compatibility

assignment compatible
an expression whose value is within the range allowed for the variable receiving it

An expression is **assignment compatible** with a variable in Turbo Pascal if any of the following conditions holds:

▶ Their types are type identical.
▶ They are compatible data types and the value of the expression falls within the range of possible values for the variable.
▶ The variable has one of the real types, the expression has one of the integer types, and the value of the expression falls within the range of possible values for the variable.

If a variable and an expression are assignment compatible, then the expression can be assigned to the variable without error.

Assuming the declarations

```
type
  Letter = 'A'..'Z';

var
  NextCh : Letter;      {NextCh is an uppercase letter.}
```

the assignment statement

```
NextCh := '3';
```

causes the syntax error Constant out of range because the literal '3' is not assignment compatible with the variable NextCh (type Letter). If Ch is of type Char and range checking is enabled using {$R+}, the assignment statement

```
NextCh := Ch;
```

will compile, but it may cause a `Range check error` at run time. This error occurs if the character stored in `Ch` is not an uppercase letter.

Parameter Correspondence and Type Compatibility

What are the requirements for types of corresponding parameters? For variable parameters, each actual parameter must be type identical with its corresponding formal parameter. For value parameters, each actual parameter must be assignment compatible with its corresponding formal parameter.

Exercises for Section 7.6

Self-Check

1. Assuming that `I` is type `0..10`, `J` is type `Integer`, and `K` is type `Real`, indicate whether each of the following expressions is assignment compatible with the variable on the left and what constraints are necessary to avoid an out-of-range error:

   a. `K := 3 * I + J`   e. `I := I / J`
   b. `I := 15`   f. `I := J mod 11`
   c. `J := Trunc(K) + 2 * I`   g. `J := 2 * K + 3`
   d. `I := I div J`

2. Explain why a compiler cannot determine whether a `Range check error` may occur at run time for a particular assignment statement.

7.7 Enumerated Types

The solution to many programming problems requires new data types. For example, in a budget program you might want to distinguish among the following categories of expenditures: entertainment, rent, utilities, food, clothing, automobile, insurance, miscellaneous. Although you could create an arbitrary code that associates entertainment with a character value of `'e'`, rent with a character value of `'r'`, and so on, Pascal allows you to create **enumerated types**, each with its own list of meaningful values.

enumerated type
a data type whose list of values is specified by the programmer in a type declaration

For example, the enumerated type `Expenses` has eight possible values enclosed in parentheses:

```
type
   Expenses = (Entertainment, Rent, Utilities, Food,
               Clothing, Automobile, Insurance, Miscellaneous);

var
   ExpenseKind : Expenses;
```

The variable `ExpenseKind` (type `Expenses`) can contain any of the eight values. The following `if` statement tests the value stored in `ExpenseKind`:

```
if ExpenseKind = Entertainment then
   WriteLn ('Postpone until after your payday.')
else if ExpenseKind = Rent then
```

```
     WriteLn ('Pay before the fifth of the month!')
. . .
```

EXAMPLE 7.7 ▼

The enumerated type Day has the values Sunday, Monday, and so on:

```
type
   Day =      (Sunday, Monday, Tuesday, Wednesday,
                Thursday, Friday, Saturday);    {days of the week}
```

The values associated with an enumerated type must be identifiers; they cannot be numeric, character, or string literals (e.g., 'Sunday' cannot be a value for an enumerated type). ▲

The scope rules for identifiers apply to enumerated types and their values. Each enumerated type value is treated as a constant identifier in the block containing the type declaration statement. The type declaration must precede any variable declaration that references it.

SYNTAX DISPLAY

Enumerated Type Declaration

Form: type *enumerated-type* = (*identifier-list*);
Example: type Class = (Freshman, Sophomore, Junior, Senior);
Interpretation: A new data type named *enumerated-type* is declared. The values associated with this type are specified in the *identifier-list*. Each value is defined as a constant identifier in the block containing the type declaration statement.
Note: A particular identifier can appear in only one *identifier-list* in a given block.

An identifier cannot appear in more than one enumerated type declaration. If type Day is already declared, the type declaration

```
type
   TDay = (Tuesday, Thursday);
```

is invalid because Tuesday and Thursday are associated with type Day.

Enumerated Type Operators

Like the standard types Integer, Boolean, and Char, each enumerated type is an ordinal type, so the order of its values is fixed when the enumerated type is declared. For type Day, the first value in its list (Sunday) has ordinal number 0, the next value (Monday) has ordinal number 1, and so on. The only operators that can be used with enumerated types are the relational and assignment operators. The following relations are all true:

```
Sunday < Monday
Wednesday = Wednesday
```

```
Wednesday >= Tuesday
Entertainment < Rent
```

An assignment statement can define the value of a variable whose type is an enumerated type. In the following example, assume that Day has been previously defined as an enumerated type. The variable declaration specifies that Today and Tomorrow are type Day.

```
var
  Today,                      {current day of the week}
  Tomorrow : Day;             {day after Today}
```

The variables can be assigned any of the values listed in the declaration for type Day. Consequently, the assignment statements

```
Today := Friday;
Tomorrow := Saturday;
```

assign the value Friday to variable Today and Saturday to variable Tomorrow. After the assignments, the following order relations are all true:

```
Today = Friday
Tomorrow = Saturday
Today < Tomorrow
Today <> Wednesday
Today >= Sunday
```

We can use the ordinal functions Succ, Pred, and Ord with enumerated types. In these examples, assume that Today is Friday and Tomorrow is Saturday:

```
Ord(Today) is 5
Ord(Tomorrow) is 6
Succ(Today) is Saturday
Pred(Today) is Thursday
Pred(Succ(Today)) is Friday
Succ(Tomorrow) is undefined
Pred(Tomorrow) is Friday
```

The next-to-last example is undefined because no value of type Day follows Saturday. Similarly, the value of Pred(Sunday) is undefined. Succ or Pred operations leading to undefined results may cause a Range check error during program execution.

EXAMPLE 7.8 ▼

The following if statement assigns the value of Tomorrow based on the value of Today (both type Day):

```
if Today = Saturday then
  Tomorrow := Sunday
else
  Tomorrow := Succ(Today)
```

Because the days of a week are cyclical, Tomorrow should be set to Sunday when Today is Saturday. The last value (Saturday) in the enumerated type Day is treated separately because Succ(Today) is undefined when Today is Saturday. ▲

Because enumerated types are ordinal types, we can use variables that belong to enumerated types as *counter* variables in for statements and as *case selectors* in case statements. The next two examples illustrate a for statement and a case statement.

EXAMPLE 7.9 ▼

The for loop in Fig. 7.5 reads the hours worked each weekday for an employee and accumulates the sum of the hours worked in WeekHours. If the counter variable Today is declared as the enumerated type Day, the loop executes for Today equal to Monday through Friday. During each iteration, the calls to Write and WriteDay display a prompt where WriteDay (see Programming Exercise 3 at the end of this section) displays the day name. When Today has the value Monday, the prompt is

```
Enter hours for Monday>
```

Next, each value read into DayHours is added to WeekHours. After loop exit, the final value of WeekHours is displayed. We explain why we need procedure WriteDay next. ▲

Reading and Writing Enumerated Type Values

Because different enumerated types and values can be used in each program, Pascal's input/output procedures were not designed to read or write enumerated type values. However, you can code your own procedures for this purpose.

Figure 7.5
Accumulating
Hours Worked

```
WeekHours := 0.0;
for Today := Monday to Friday do
  begin
    Write ('Enter hours for ');
    WriteDay (Today);
    Write ('>');
    ReadLn (DayHours);
    WeekHours := WeekHours + DayHours
  end; {for}

WriteLn ('Total weekly hours are ', WeekHours :4:2)
```

EXAMPLE 7.10 ▼

Given the declarations

```
type
  Color = (Red, Green, Blue, Yellow);

var
  Eyes : Color;
```

the statement

```
Write (Ord(Eyes) :1)
```

can be used for diagnostic printing during debugging. It does not print the value of Eyes, but it does display the ordinal number of the value that is an integer from 0 (for Red) to 3 (for Yellow).

Procedure WriteColor in Fig. 7.6 prints a string that represents a value of type Color. If the value of Eyes is defined, the statement

```
WriteColor (Eyes)
```

displays the value of Eyes as a string. Make sure you understand the difference between the string 'Blue' and the constant identifier Blue. ▲

Programmers often use case statements, such as the one in Fig. 7.6, whose case labels are values declared in an enumerated type. Be careful not to use a string such as 'Red' as a case label. This would cause a constant and case types do not match syntax error. Remember that only ordinal values or constants (including enumerated constants) can be case labels.

It is slightly more difficult to read the value of an enumerated type variable than it is to display it. The next example shows one method.

Figure 7.6
Procedure to Print a Value
of Type Color

```
procedure WriteColor (InColor {input} : Color);
{
  Displays the value of InColor.
  Pre : InColor is assigned a value.
  Post: The value of InColor is displayed as a string.
}
begin {WriteColor}
  case InColor of
    Red    : Write ('Red');
    Green  : Write ('Green');
    Blue   : Write ('Blue');
    Yellow : Write ('Yellow')
  end {case}
end; {WriteColor}
```

EXAMPLE 7.11 ▼

Procedure ReadLnColor in Fig. 7.7 returns a value of type Color through its output parameter ItemColor. The loop in Fig. 7.7 repeats until a valid color is assigned to ItemColor. The Boolean flag ValidColor controls loop repetition and is initialized to True. If a valid data character (R, G, B, or Y) is read, the if statement assigns its corresponding color value to ItemColor. If an invalid data character is read, ValidColor is set to False and the loop repeats.

If Black and Brown were added to the list of values for Color, it would be necessary to read additional characters when the first letter read was B. We leave this as an exercise (see Programming Exercise 2 at the end of this section). The procedure documentation indicates that ReadLnColor calls the Turbo Pascal function UpCase. ▲

Figure 7.7
Procedure ReadLnColor

```
procedure ReadLnColor (var ItemColor {output} : Color);
{
  Assigns a value to ItemColor based on an input character.
  Pre : None
  Post: ItemColor is defined as the color value whose first
        letter is the same as the data character.
  Calls: UpCase
}
  var
    ColorChar : Char;              {first letter of color name}
    ValidColor : Boolean;          {flag for valid color read}

begin {ReadLnColor}
  repeat
    ValidColor := True; {Assume a valid color will be read.}
    Write ('Enter first letter of color (R, G, B, or Y)> ');
    ReadLn (ColorChar);
    ColorChar := UpCase(ColorChar);  {Convert to uppercase.}

    {Assign the color value or reset ValidColor to False.}
    if ColorChar = 'R' then
      ItemColor := Red
    else if ColorChar = 'G' then
      ItemColor := Green
    else if ColorChar = 'B' then
      ItemColor := Blue
    else if ColorChar = 'Y' then
      ItemColor := Yellow
    else
      ValidColor := False {repeat - valid color was not read.}
  until ValidColor
end; {ReadLnColor}
```

Subranges of Enumerated Types

We can declare subranges of enumerated types. The following declarations specify that WeekDay (values Monday through Friday) is a subrange of type Day and that variable SchoolDay is type WeekDay:

```
type
  Day = (Sunday, Monday, Tuesday, Wednesday,
         Thursday, Friday, Saturday);       {days of the week}
  WeekDay = Monday..Friday;                 {weekdays only}

var
  SchoolDay : WeekDay;                       {a weekday}
```

The assignment statement

```
SchoolDay := Monday;
```

is valid, but the assignment statement

```
SchoolDay := Sunday;
```

causes a Constant out of range syntax error.

Why Use Enumerated Types?

At this point, you may be wondering whether enumerated types are worth using, considering the effort required to read and write their values. Also, if we need a code to enter the value of an enumerated type variable, why not use that code throughout the program? The reason is that enumerated types make the program considerably easier to read and understand.

EXAMPLE 7.12 ▼

The if statement

```
if DayNum = 1 then
  PayFactor := 2.0        {double pay for Sunday}
else if DayNum = 7 then
  PayFactor := 1.5        {time and a half for Saturday}
else
  PayFactor := 1.0        {regular pay}
```

might appear in a payroll program without enumerated types if Sunday and Saturday are "coded" as the integers 1 and 7, respectively. If we use the enumerated type Day and the variable Today (type Day), we can write this statement as

```
if Today = Sunday then
  PayFactor := 2.0
else if Today = Saturday then
  PayFactor := 1.5
else
  PayFactor := 1.0
```

The second example is obviously more readable because it substitutes values (Saturday and Sunday) that are meaningful to the problem. ▲

In a lengthy program, the extra overhead required to implement procedures for reading and writing the values associated with an enumerated type is insignificant. Placing these procedures in your own library of modules will simplify their reuse in future programs.

Another advantage of using enumerated types is the automatic creation of a range of values assignable to a variable. With an integer code, in contrast, any integer value can be assigned unless you take the trouble to declare a subrange type. In the preceding example, any integer value can be assigned to variable DayNum, but only one of the seven values listed in the declaration for enumerated type Day can be assigned to variable Today.

Exercises for Section 7.7 **Self-Check**

1. Evaluate each of the following expressions, assuming before each operation that Today (type Day) is Thursday:

    a. Ord(Monday)   f. Ord(Today) + 1
    b. Ord(Today)   g. Pred(Today)
    c. Today < Tuesday   h. Today >= Thursday
    d. Succ(Wednesday)   i. Pred(Sunday)
    e. Today + 1   j. Ord(Succ(Succ(Today)))

2. Indicate whether each of the following type declarations is valid or invalid. Explain what is wrong with each invalid type declaration.

    a. type Letters = ('A', 'B', 'C');
    b. type Letters = (A, B, C);
            TwoLetters = (A, C);
    c. type Letters = ('A'..'Z');
    d. type Statements = (begin, end, while, for);
    e. type
            Day = (Sun, Mon, Tue, Wed, Thu, Fri, Sat);
            WeekDay = Mon..Fri;
            WeekEnd = Sat..Sun;

Programming

1. Declare an enumerated type Month and rewrite the following if statement, assuming that CurMonth is type Month instead of type Integer. Also, write the equivalent case statement.

```
if CurMonth = 1 then
  WriteLn ('Happy New Year')
else if CurMonth = 6 then
  WriteLn ('Summer begins')
else if CurMonth = 9 then
  WriteLn ('Back to school')
else if CurMonth = 12 then
  WriteLn ('Happy Holidays');
```

2. Rewrite procedure `ReadLnColor` (see Fig. 7.7) assuming that `Black` and `Brown` are also values for enumerated type `Color`.
3. Write procedure `WriteDay` for enumerated type `Day`.

7.8 Iterative Approximations (Optional)

Numerical analysis is the branch of mathematics and computer science that develops algorithms for solving computational problems. Problems from numerical analysis include finding solutions to sets of equations, performing operations on matrices, finding roots of equations, and performing mathematical integration. The next case study illustrates methods for iteratively approximating a solution to a computational problem.

CASE STUDY   Approximating the Value of e

PROBLEM ▼

Many mathematical quantities can be represented by a series approximation, where a series is represented by a summation of an infinite number of terms. We can use this technique to compute *e* (value is 2.71828 . . .), the base of the natural logarithms.

ANALYSIS ▼

We can approximate the value of *e* by evaluating the series

$$1 + \frac{1}{1!} + \frac{1}{2!} + \frac{1}{3!} + \cdots + \frac{1}{N!}$$

where $N!$ is the factorial of N:

$$N! = N \times (N - 1)! \qquad \text{for } N > 1$$
$$N! = 1 \qquad \text{for } N = 0 \text{ or } 1$$

The previous series can be represented with summation notation as

$$\sum_{i=0}^{N} \frac{1}{i!}$$

where the first term is obtained by substituting 0 for i (1/0! is 1/1), the second term is obtained by substituting 1 for i (1/1!), and so on. The larger the value of N, the more terms will be included in the series, resulting in increased accuracy. The value of N is a problem input.

Data Requirements

Problem Input

```
N : Integer              {number of terms, N, in the sum}
```

Problem Output

```
E : Real                {approximate value of e}
```

Program Variables

```
IthTerm : Real          {ith term of the series}
I : Integer             {loop-control variable}
```

DESIGN ▼

Use a counting loop to implement the summation formula.

Initial Algorithm

1. Read in the value of N.
2. Initialize E to 1.0.
3. Initialize the *i*th term to 1.0.
4. `for` each I `from` 1 `to` N `do`
    `begin`
        5. Compute the *i*th term in the series.
        6. Add the *i*th term to E.
    `end`
7. Print the value of E.

IMPLEMENTATION ▼

The program is shown in Fig. 7.8. Inside the `for` loop, the statement

```
IthTerm := IthTerm / I;
```

computes the value of the *i*th term in the series by dividing the previous term by the loop-control variable I. The formula that follows shows that this division does indeed produce the next term in the series:

$$\frac{\dfrac{1}{(i-1)!}}{i} = \frac{1}{i x (i-1)!} = \frac{1}{i!}$$

Because 0! is 1, IthTerm must be initialized to 1.0. The statement

```
E := E + IthTerm;
```

adds the new value of IthTerm to the sum being accumulated in E. Trace the execution of this loop to satisfy yourself that IthTerm takes on the values 1/1!, 1/2!, 1/3!, and so on, during successive loop iterations.

TESTING ▼

To determine whether this algorithm works, run the program for a particular value of N and compare the result with *e*, which is 2.71828183. The sample

Figure 7.8
Series Approximation to *e*

Edit Window

```
program ESeries;
{Computes the value of e by a series approximation}

  var
    E,                    {output - value being approximated}
    IthTerm : Real;       {ith term in series}
    N,                    {input - number of terms in series}
    I : Integer;          {loop-control variable}

begin {ESeries}
  Write ('Enter the number of terms in the series> ');
  ReadLn (N);

  {Compute each term and add it to the accumulating sum.}
  E := 1.0;               {initial sum}
  IthTerm := 1.0;         {first term}
  I := 1;
  while I <= N do
    begin
      IthTerm := IthTerm / I;
      E := E + IthTerm;
      I := I + 1
    end; {while}

  {Print the result.}
  WriteLn ('The approximate value of e is ', E :20)
end. {ESeries}
```

Output Window

```
Enter the number of terms in the series> 15
The approximate value of e is      2.7182818285E+00
```

run shows that the value computed for N (15) is very close to the actual value. How does the value of N affect the accuracy of the final result? Programming Exercise 1 at the end of this section asks you to compute and display a table that demonstrates this.

Exercises for Section 7.8   **Programming**

1. Display a table that shows *e* and *N* for values of *N* from 3 to 15.
2. The value of e^x is represented by the series

   $$1 + x + x^2/2! + x^3/3! + \cdots + x^n/n! + \cdots$$

   Write a program to compute and print the value of this series for any *x* and *n*. Compare the result to Exp(X) and print a message '0.K.' or

'Not O.K.', depending on whether the difference between these results exceeds 0.0001.

7.9 Using the Debugger Evaluate and Modify Dialog Box

The Turbo Pascal debugger allows you to verify that a complicated expression in your program is correct. To activate this procedure, select the Evaluate option from the Debug menu after halting your program. Three fields will appear—Expression, Result, and New value—with the cursor in the Expression field.

Initially, the Expression field will contain a default expression consisting of the identifier under the Edit field cursor, or it will be blank if the Edit field cursor is not over an identifier. This expression can be edited or replaced by another expression. When editing is complete, press the Enter key to evaluate the contents of the Expression field. The value of this expression at the current location in your program will be displayed in the Result field.

Another way to enter an expression in the Expression field is to place the Edit cursor on the first operand of the expression you want to check just before bringing up the Evaluate and Modify dialog box (Fig. 7.9). This identifier will appear in the Expression field when the dialog box pops up. You can use the right arrow key to add additional operands and operators to the Expression field. Press the Enter key to evaluate the final expression.

Figure 7.9
Turbo Pascal Evaluate and Modify Dialog Box

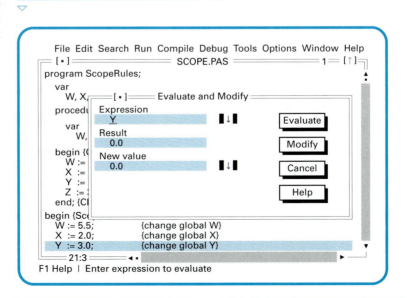

If the Expression field contains a single variable, you can modify its value. First move the cursor to the New value field using the Tab key or the mouse and type in a new value or expression for the variable. Pressing the Enter key causes the contents of the New value field to be evaluated and displayed in the Result field. The Turbo Pascal debugger retains the new value you entered if you select the Modify button before closing the dialog box.

7.10 Common Programming Errors

Be careful when working with complicated expressions, or you may inadvertently omit parentheses or operators. If you omit an operator or a single parenthesis, you will get a syntax error. But if you omit a pair of parentheses, the expression, although syntactically correct, may compute the wrong value.

A useful technique for working with complicated expressions is to break the expression into subexpressions. Assign the subexpressions to temporary variables and manipulate those temporary variables. For example, it is easier to write correctly the three assignment statements

```
Temp1 := Sqrt(X + Y);    {Assign 1st subexpression to Temp1.}
Temp2 := 1.0 + Temp1;    {Assign 2nd subexpression to Temp2.}
Z := Temp1 / Temp2       {Divide the subexpressions.}
```

than the single assignment statement

```
Z := Sqrt(X + Y) / (1.0 + Sqrt(X + Y))
```

which has the same effect. Using three assignment statements is also more efficient because Sqrt(X + Y) is evaluated only once; it is evaluated twice in the single assignment statement.

The only operators that you can use with type Char data are the relational operators. The Boolean expression

```
3 <> '3'              {incompatible operands}
```

is invalid because one operand is an integer and the other is a digit character.

Make sure you use parentheses properly in compound Boolean expressions. The Boolean operators and, or, and not have higher precedence than the relational operators, so parentheses are required in expressions such as

```
(-5.0 <= X) and (X <= 5.0)
```

Syntax or run-time errors can occur when you use built-in functions. The argument of the function Chr must be type Integer; the argument of the functions Ord, Succ, and Pred must be an ordinal type (not type Real). The results of the functions Succ, Pred, and Chr will be undefined for certain arguments.

Subranges can help you detect erroneous computations or data. If a value being assigned is outside the subrange and range checking is enabled, a Range check error occurs. The operations that can be performed on a variable with a subrange type are determined by the host type for that subrange. However, a variable whose type is a subrange type cannot correspond to a formal variable parameter whose type is the host type for that subrange.

When you declare enumerated types, remember that only identifiers can appear in the list of values for an enumerated type. Strings, characters, and numbers are not allowed. The same constant identifier cannot appear in more than one enumerated type declaration in a given block. It is permissible, however, for the same constant identifier to appear in more than one subrange type declaration. Remember that no standard procedures are available to read or write the values of an enumerated type.

CHAPTER REVIEW

1. Type Integer and Real data have different internal representations. Integer data are represented as binary numbers with the leftmost bit containing the sign of the number. Real data are represented by a binary exponent and mantissa.

2. Arithmetic with Real data may not be precise, because not all real numbers can be represented exactly. Other sources of numerical errors include cancellation errors (manipulating a very large number with a very small one) and arithmetic overflow and underflow.

3. The Boolean values, False and True, are represented as the binary numbers 0 and 1, respectively. Boolean functions can be used to make Boolean expressions more readable.

4. The functions Pred, Succ, and Ord manipulate ordinal data types. The function Chr, the inverse of Ord, finds the character corresponding to a given ordinal number.

5. Type Char data are represented by storing a binary code value for each symbol. Turbo Pascal uses the ASCII code.

6. You can declare your own data types in Pascal using the reserved word type. Subrange type declarations enhance readability by showing which ordinal variables have a restricted range of values. Run-time errors will occur if such variables are assigned out-of-range values when range checking has been enabled using the compiler directive {$R+}.

7. You declare an enumerated type by providing a list of identifiers (values of the data type) enclosed in parentheses. Using enumerated types makes programs more readable because an enumerated type's values are tailored to a particular programming application.

8. Numerical analysis is the branch of mathematics and computer science that develops algorithms for mathematical computation. We demonstrated how to use iterative approximations to evaluate a series that represents the value of *e*.

Summary of New Pascal Constructs

Construct	Effect
Subrange Declaration	
`type` `Digit = '0'..'9';`	A subrange of the characters is declared. This subrange (named `Digit`) consists of the character values `'0'` through `'9'`.
Enumerated Type Declaration	
`type` `BColor = (Blue, Black, Brown);`	An enumerated type `BColor` is declared with values `Blue`, `Black`, and `Brown`.

Quick-Check Exercises

1. What value is returned by the following function when its arguments are 5, 7? When its arguments are 7, 5? What does function `ThisDoesWhat` do?

```
function ThisDoesWhat (First, Second : Integer) : Boolean;
begin
   ThisDoesWhat := (First div Second) = 0
end; {ThisDoesWhat}
```

2. Which of the following can be an enumerated type value: an integer, a real number, an identifier, a Boolean value, a string value?
3. Explain how a subrange type can be used to detect an out-of-range integer value. How about an out-of-range real value?
4. What is the value of each of the following?
   a. `Chr(Ord('a'))`   c. `Ord('7') - Ord('0')`
   b. `Chr(Ord('a') + 3)`   d. `Ord('z') - Ord('a')`
5. Is a subrange type useful for preventing a user from entering an out-of-range value in a `ReadLn` statement? Why or why not?
6. a. Can a variable whose type is a subrange type correspond to a formal variable parameter whose type is the host type?
   b. What if the formal parameter is a value parameter?
7. If two variables are type compatible, can one always be assigned to the other?
8. If the value 1/3 is computed using `Real` variables, why will the result not be exactly 1/3.
9. What is wrong with the following enumerated type declaration?

   `type Prime = (2, 3, 5, 7, 9, 11, 13);`

10. Consider the enumerated type declaration

    `type Class = (Frosh, Soph, Jr, Sr);`

    What is the value of each of the following?

    a. `Ord(Succ(Pred(Soph)))`   b. `Pred(Pred(Jr))`

Answers to Quick-Check Exercises

1. True; false. The function tests $|First| < |Second|$.
2. Only an identifier
3. When range checking is activated through the {R+} compiler directive, Turbo Pascal generates code that will signal a run-time error when an out-of-range value is stored in a variable whose type is a subrange of the integers. Subranges cannot be defined over the real numbers.
4. a. 'a'   b. 'd'   c. 7   d. 25
5. The programmer must ensure that an invalid value is not entered. A subrange type can cause a Range check error if an invalid value is entered.
6. a. No   b. Yes
7. Yes, if they are the same type, or if the variable getting a new value is the host type and the other is a subrange of that host. If the variable getting a new value is a subrange type, the new value must be in range.
8. Because of representational error, the fraction 0.333333 . . . cannot be represented exactly in either decimal or binary.
9. Integers cannot appear as enumerated type values.
10. a. 1   b. Frosh

Review Questions

1. What are the advantages of the data type Integer over data type Real?
2. List and explain three computational errors that may occur in type Real expressions.
3. Write an enumerated type declaration for Fiscal as the months from July through June. Declare the subrange Winter as December through February.
4. Write procedures for reading and writing values for variables of enumerated type Season:

   ```
   type Season = (Winter, Spring, Summer, Fall);
   ```

5. Write a while loop equivalent to the following for loop. Assume variable Ch is type Char.

   ```
   for Ch := 'A' to 'Z' do
     Write(Ch)
   ```

6. a. Write a case statement that tests whether Today is a working day. Print either of the messages 'Workday' or 'Weekend'. Assume Today is type Day, an enumerated type that has the days of the week as its values.
   b. Is it necessary to guard this case statement?
7. Write a Boolean function that returns True or False based on the following conditions involving its arguments: either Flag is True or Color is Red, or both Money is Plenty and Time is Up. Show any type declarations that may be needed before the function is declared.
8. Write a Boolean function called OvertimeDue that returns a value of True only if a worker's weekly Hours are greater than 40.

9. Write an enumerated type declaration for days of the week and subrange types for weekdays and weekend days. How is the definition of the enumerated type constrained by the subrange requirements?

10. Write the Pascal statements necessary to enter an integer between 0 and 9, inclusive, and convert it to an equivalent character value (e.g., 0 to '0', 1 to '1') to be stored in a character variable Num.

11. Write a Pascal function with Integer argument N and Real argument X that returns as its value the first N terms of the series

$$X + 1/2X^2 + 1/3X^3 + 1/4X^4 + \cdots + 1/NX^N$$

Programming Projects

1. An integer N is divisible by 9 if the sum of its digits is divisible by 9. Develop a program to determine whether the following numbers are divisible by 9 using this technique. Declare N to be type LongInt.

   $N = 154368$
   $N = 621594$
   $N = 123456$

2. Redo Programming Project 1 by reading each digit of the number to be tested into the type Char variable Digit. Calculate the sum of the numeric values of the digits. *Hint:* The numeric value of Digit (type Char) is Ord(Digit) – Ord('0').

3. Since communications channels are often noisy, numerous ways have been devised to ensure reliable data transmission. One successful method uses a checksum. A checksum for a message can be computed by summing the ordinal values of the characters in the message and taking the modulo of 64. The ordinal value of a space character is added to this result to obtain the checksum. Since this value is within the range of the displayable characters, it is displayed as a character as well. Write a program that accepts single line messages ending with a period and displays the checksum for each message. Your program should continue displaying checksums until the user enters a line with only a period.

4. Write a program for printing a bar graph that summarizes the rainfall in Bedrock for one year. Include the average monthly rainfall and the maximum monthly rainfall during the year as part of the program output.

   Prompt the user for the amount of rainfall for a particular month and instruct the computer to send an appropriate output line to the printer. Assume that no one month will have more than 14 inches of rainfall. Your graph should resemble this one:

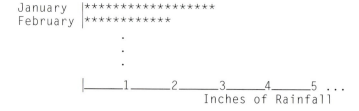

As part of your solution, write procedures that correspond to the procedure headers shown here:

```
procedure WriteMonth (Month {input} : Integer);
{Writes the string corresponding to the value of Month}

GetMonthlyTotal (Month {input} : Integer;
                var Inches {output},
                    MaxInches {input/output},
                    TotInches {input/output} : Real);

{
  User is prompted for Inches of rainfall during a Month.
  MaxInches and TotInches are updated so that they contain
  the maximum and total inches of rainfall input so far.
}

procedure DrawBar (Month {input} : Integer;
                   Inches {input} : Real);
{
  Draws a bar whose length is computed from Inches and whose
  label is determined by the value of Month
}

procedure DrawScaleLine;
{Draws scale and label at bottom of graph}
```

5. The interest paid on a savings account is compounded daily. This means that if you start with `StartBal` (in dollars) in the bank, at the end of the first day you will have a balance of

    StartBal $\times (1 + Rate/365)$

    where `Rate` is the annual interest rate (`0.10` if the annual rate is 10%). At the end of the second day, you will have

    StartBal $\times (1 + Rate/365) \times (1 + Rate/365)$

    and at the end of N days you will have

    StartBal $\times (1 + Rate/365)^N$

    dollars. Write a program that processes a set of data records, each of which contains values for `StartBal`, `Rate`, and `N`, and computes the final account balance.

6. The bisection method is one way of finding an approximate root for the equation $f(x) = 0$ on the interval `XLeft` to `XRight`, inclusive (assuming the function is continuous on this interval). The interval end points (`XLeft` and `XRight`) and the tolerance for the approximation (`Epsilon`) are entered by the user.

    The bisection method calls for the identification of an interval [`XLeft`, `XRight`] that is less than `Epsilon` in length over which $f(x)$ changes sign (from positive to negative or vice versa). The midpoint (`XMid = (XLeft +`

XRight)/2.0) of the interval will be an approximation to the root of the equation when $f($XMid$)$ is very close to 0. Of course, if you find a value of XMid so that $f($XMid$) = 0$, you have found a very good approximation of the root and the algorithm should stop.

One way to detect a sign change is to examine the value of the products $f($XLeft$) \times f($XMid$)$ and $f($XMid$) \times f($XRight$)$. If one of the products is negative, then a sign change has occurred over that interval (either [XLeft, XMid] or [XMid, XRight]). If neither product is negative, there is no root in the interval XLeft, XRight. If the sign change occurs in the interval [XLeft, XMid], let XRight = XMid and repeat the process. Similarly, if the sign change occurs in the interval [XMid, XRight], let XLeft = XMid and repeat the process. Figure 7.10 shows an example of a root in the interval [XLeft, XMid].

Write a program that uses the bisection method to determine an approximation to the equation

$$5x^3 - 2x^2 + 3 = 0$$

over the interval [-1, 1] using Epsilon = 0.0001.

7. We can approximate the area under the curve described by a function f by dividing the area into a number of rectangles and then accumulating the sum of all the rectangular areas. Figure 7.11 shows an example of the *midpoint method,* so named because the curve intersects each rectangle at its middle (as measured along the x-axis). The area of each rectangle is w (its width) times the function value at its midpoint. The area of the rectangle with left endpoint x_1 is $w \times f(x_1 + w/2)$. If the interval [a, b] is divided into n rectangles, the area under the curve is represented by the sum

$$Area = w \sum_{i=0}^{n-1} f(a + i \times w + w/2)$$

where w is $(b - a)/n$ and the first rectangle begins at $x = a$, the second at $x = a + w$, the third at $x = a + 2w$, and so on.

Figure 7.10
Root in Interval
[XLeft, XMid]

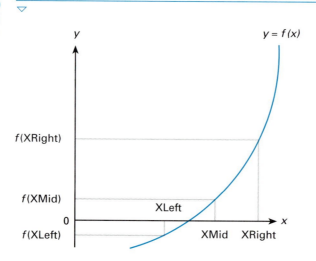

Figure 7.11
Midpoint Method

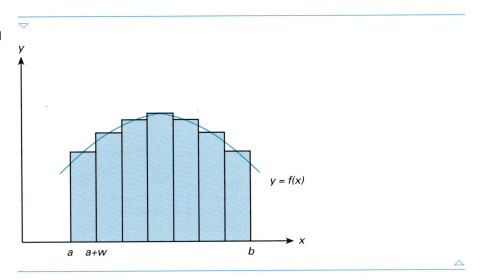

Figure 7.11
Midpoint Method

Write a program that uses the midpoint approximation to find the area under the curve (the value of the definite integral) for the function

$$f(x) = -3x^2 + 2x + 4$$

over the interval [-2, 3]. Test your program using several different values of n. The larger n is, the better the approximation should be.

8. A daisy wheel printer uses a print wheel with 95 characters representing the letters with ordinal values of 33 to 127. The printer works by rotating the print wheel left or right a number of steps until the correct letter is under the hammer, then striking. When the printer first starts, the wheel is positioned with the hammer over the letter A. Write a program that can drive a daisy wheel printer. Use the function ReadKey to read and return one keystroke at a time (include uses Crt in the beginning of your module). When the user presses a key, output the print wheel move that will most quickly move the correct letter under the hammer for striking and indicate the strike. Pressing return (ordinal value 13) should indicate a carriage advance, and pressing the Escape key (ordinal value 27) will end the program. Always display the shortest move, be it left or right. Remember, the space key does not print anything, repeating a letter does not move the wheel, and keys that don't print should be ignored. Create an enumerated type for the type of rotation (left or right) and a subrange type for the rotation distance.

9. We are used to counting in base 10, but that is not the only possible base. Create a subrange type that can express a base 9 digit using the integers 0 to 8. Write procedures to input, display, increment, and decrement three-digit base 9 numbers, where there is one procedure parameter per digit. Consider only positive numbers.

INTERVIEW

▼

Judith Schlesinger

Judith Schlesinger is a researcher at the Supercomputing Research Center in Bowie, Maryland, where she is currently involved in creating a system that "predicts" the performance capabilities of a parallel computer for any specified algorithm. Previously Dr. Schlesinger ran her own consulting business—JDS Consulting Services—and worked at the University of Denver, where she designed and implemented the master's program in computer science. Dr. Schlesinger earned her Ph.D. from Johns Hopkins University.

▼ **How did your interest in computer science develop?**

▲ During my junior year at Brooklyn College, I took an introductory programming class that I enjoyed immensely—much more than the math classes I was taking towards my major. Since that was the only course offered at my university, I elected to pursue computer science by going on for a master's degree.

Computer science programs were very new at that time—late '60s—and I didn't know much about them. I figured that there had to be more to it than "just" writing programs if master's and Ph.D. degrees were being granted. I also figured that if I hated it, I could always quit. I had a "nothing ventured, nothing gained" attitude.

It turns out that I loved it. For the first time in my life I was really excited about being in school. I've never regretted the decision.

▼ **What challenges face students beginning their computer science degrees?**

▲ As the field of computer science matures, it also expands. There are now a myriad of architectures, numerous programming languages and programming methodologies, and a host of other issues that did not previously exist. The challenge to educators is to evolve an effective course of study for computer science students. The challenge for students is to understand that there are many different methodologies and architectures and that the first they learned is not necessarily the "best" and only one they should know.

Students must be aware that they are part of a rapidly changing field. They must always be ready for something new and different and view these new concepts as exciting challenges and not as threats to their knowledge base. As exciting as I found the study of computers when I first began, the world to which I was exposed is dull in contrast to what is waiting for students today. Learning to write a program is of critical importance, but never forget that it is simply the means to harnessing the power of the computer and not an end in itself.

▼ **When and how did the first supercomputer come to be? How did you become involved in supercomputer research?**

▲ Depending on your definition of supercomputer, you might choose any of several different machines as being the first. The CDC 6600, in 1964, and the ILLIAC IV, in 1968, are the first machines that I can think of. One was a production machine and one was a major university research project. I guess it was an inevitable development step that components of a computer would be duplicated as happened with those machines.

I first became involved with supercomputers while on a consulting project. I was hired to develop a Fortran compiler for a new, parallel machine. The experience I gained led me to join the Supercomputing Research Center as a research staff member where I now continue research on using these computers.

▼ **What distinguishes a supercomputer from all others?**

▲ The term "supercomputer" has been used for some time and has had different meanings over the years. I define a supercomputer as any of a number of different computers that utilize parallelism to achieve greater speed of processing. Machines utilizing only pipelining or multiple function units are not generally considered to be supercomputers even though these are considered to be forms of parallelism. A supercomputer would use vector registers, multiple processors (numbering from just a few to thousands), or a combination of both to achieve massive speedups in processing.

These machines process data just as computers have always done: they store data in memory, apply computations to the data, and communicate results with the user or with other computers. However, depending on their configuration, these machines do introduce new programming issues related to how data is stored and accessed, what algorithms are most effective, and, what is the best way to program each machine to exploit all of its capabilities. Currently, a great deal of research is ongoing in these and related areas.

These machines can reduce the time it takes to run a program to completion. Jobs that required days of dedicated computer time can now be run in minutes; jobs that required weeks can now be run in days. These are gross estimates of the kinds of time improvements that have been achieved but I think they make the point. If a researcher in weather prediction, say, can now see results of data processed in minutes rather than days or weeks, we are that much closer to getting accurate weather forecasting. Certainly, everyone should be aware of the improved weather forecasts we now receive over those of just a few years ago.

▼ **In what ways do supercomputers currently affect our lives?**

▲ There are always applications that need more than whatever computer capability is available. These are the applications that are always being run on the biggest and fastest machines. Weather prediction, DNA and drug modeling, fluid dynamics, (financial) market modeling, demographic modeling, and oceanic and atmospheric modeling are just a few of many uses for supercomputers.

Very few of us are going to awaken any time in the near future and know that a supercomputer has directly affected our lives. However, as models of our environment, atmosphere, and oceans are improved, as medical breakthroughs are made, as new solutions to old problems (pollution, waste elimination, ecosystem destruction, etc.) are discovered due to the increased capabilities of supercomputers, we will assuredly be feeling the impact of these machines on our lives.

▼ **How does your research affect the computing industry as a whole?**

▲ The computing industry is very different from the days when everything was a mainframe. From individual desktop computers and more powerful workstations, to loosely coupled networks and workstation "farms," to very large vector and parallel machines, we now have an array of different architectures to meet different needs. Research and technology that are on the cutting edge today will be the production tools of tomorrow. The only current way to achieve significantly greater speeds from computers is to make them parallel. So, while supercomputer research focuses on specific uses, knowledge and skill being acquired will ultimately benefit everyone.

CHAPTER EIGHT

Text Files

interactive program
a program that reads all data from the keyboard and displays all output on the screen

All the example programs presented so far have been interactive. An **interactive program** reads all input data from the keyboard and displays all output on the screen. Interactive input and output is fine for programs that process small amounts of data, but this procedure is less effective for programs that must process large amounts of data. To improve efficiency, we can use data files for storing program input and output. Pascal can process two kinds of data files: text files and binary files. This chapter describes text files.

The input and output procedures we have used for interactive programs work with text files. In this chapter, we will describe one new procedure, Read, that is particularly useful for reading data from text files, in addition to describing several new procedures and functions for text files.

8.1 Text Files, Data Files, and Output Files

text file
a disk file that contains a collection of characters

data file (input file)
a file that contains the input data for a program

output file
a file that contains a program's results

A **text file** is a collection of individual characters stored under the same name on a disk. You can save all of the data to be processed by a program in a text file before you run that program. You can then instruct the program to read its data from the text file rather than reading it from the keyboard. A **data file** (or **input file**) is a file that contains the input data for a program. A data file may be a text file or a binary file (Chapter 16).

One advantage of a data file is that you can access it using an editor program (or word processor) and can correct any errors before the data file is processed by a program. Another advantage is that a data file can be read over and over again by a program. This property facilitates debugging because your program can read its data from the same data file each time it is run. In an interactive program, you would have to reenter each individual data item during every run of the program.

You can also instruct a program to write its results to a text file instead of to the screen, giving you a permanent version on disk of the program results. That disk file can be printed or even used as a data file for a second program that will process it further. An **output file** is a file that contains a program's results.

Organization of Information in a Text File

You can create and save a text file by using an editor. Each character that you type resides temporarily in main memory and is displayed on the screen. When you save the file, the information displayed on the screen is stored as a stream of characters on disk (see Fig. 8.1).

The text file in Fig. 8.1 contains a total of 45 characters or bytes, including digit characters, periods, blanks, letters, and two special characters, <eoln> and <eof>. <eoln>, the *end-of-line* character, is stored in a text file each time the Enter key on the keyboard is pressed. <eof>, the *end-of-file* character, is automatically inserted after the last character of a text file when the text file is saved. A text file can have many <eoln> characters but only one <eof> character.

Figure 8.1
Text File as a Stream of Characters

| 1 | 5 | 9 | 0 | 0 | . | 0 | 0 | | J | o | h | n | n | y | | J | o | n | e | s | <eoln> | 2 | 5 | 0 | 0 | 0 | . | 0 | 0 | | S | a | l | l | y | | S | m | y | t | h | e | <eoln> | <eof> |

Although the text file is *physically* stored on disk as one long stream of characters, it is *logically* organized as a sequence of characters separated into lines by `<eoln>` characters. If you use Turbo Pascal's editor to access the text file in Fig. 8.1, it will look like the information in Fig. 8.2, except that you will not see the `<eoln>` and `<eof>` characters.

You can view a text file using Turbo Pascal's editor or you can display a text file on the screen using the MS-DOS command

`>TYPE` *filename*

where *filename* is the name of the text file. Each file line will be displayed on a separate line of the screen. The MS-DOS command

`>PRINT` *filename*

prints file *filename*.

Reading Data from a Text File

You can use Pascal's `ReadLn` procedure to read data from a text file. Let's consider a program that contains the variable declarations

```
var
    Salary : Real;         {input - a salary}
    Name : string;         {input - a name}
    Separator : Char;      {input - blank between Salary and Name}
    MyData : Text;         {a text file used as a data file}
```

The last line declares `MyData` as a variable of type `Text`, which is the prede-fined data type for a text file. The statement

```
ReadLn (MyData, Salary, Separator, Name)
```

has four parameters: a `Text` file variable, a `Real` variable, a `Char` variable, and a `string` variable. It reads three data items from file `MyData`, storing the first in `Salary`, the second in `Separator`, and the third in `Name`. If `MyData` represented the text file in Fig. 8.2 and the first line were being read, this statement would store `15900.00` in `Salary`, the blank character in `Separa-tor`, and the string `'Johnny Jones'` in `Name`.

How does Pascal know to read the data from the text file instead of the keyboard? This is determined by the first parameter in the call to `ReadLn`. If the first parameter is a variable of type `Text`, Turbo Pascal reads data from the file indicated by that variable; otherwise, Turbo Pascal reads data from the keyboard.

Figure 8.2
Logical Organization of
Text File in Fig. 8.1

```
15900.00 Johnny Jones<eoln>
25000.00 Sally Smythe<eoln><eof>
```

ReadLn processes each line of a text file just like a data line entered at the keyboard. The first line of the file identified by variable MyData begins with a sequence of digit characters containing a decimal point. When ReadLn is reading data into a type Real variable, it skips any leading blanks and reads all digit characters up to the next blank or <eoln> character; consequently, it stores the real number 15900.00 in Salary. The next character to be read is the blank character between the digit 0 and the letter J; this blank is stored in Separator.

In Turbo Pascal (not standard), when ReadLn is reading data into a type string variable, it reads all characters through the next <eoln> character and stores all but the <eoln> character in the string variable. Therefore ReadLn stores the characters from J through s (i.e., the string 'Johnny Jones') in Name.

Some of the characters on a data line may be processed by ReadLn but not stored. The statement

```
ReadLn (MyData, Salary)
```

reads and stores in Salary the next number in a line of file MyData; it then skips the remaining characters on the data line (through the next <eoln>). This is not considered an error. The next ReadLn operation would begin reading data from the next data line of file MyData.

Procedure Read

A second input procedure, Read, also reads data from the keyboard or from a file. Unlike ReadLn, however, procedure Read processes only as many data characters as are needed to satisfy its input list.

EXAMPLE 8.1 ▼

The statements

```
Read (MyData, Salary);        {Read Salary from MyData.}
Read (MyData, Separator);     {Read the blank character.}
Read (MyData, Name);          {Read Name from MyData.}
ReadLn (MyData)      {Skip past <eoln> character in MyData.}
```

have the same effect as

```
ReadLn (MyData, Salary, Separator, Name)
```

The first Read statement reads into Salary the characters that comprise a real number, stopping at the blank character; the second Read statement reads the blank character into Separator; the third Read statement reads into Name all remaining characters up to the next <eoln> character; the ReadLn statement skips past the <eoln> character to the start of the next data line. Figure 8.3 shows the effect of executing these statements when

Figure 8.3
Effect of Read on First Line
of File MyData

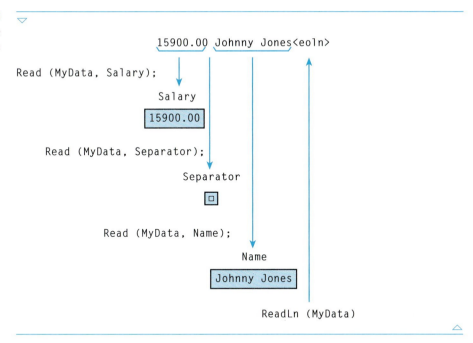

the first line of file `MyData` is being read. The blank character is shown as the symbol □ in `Separator`.   ▲

Review of Read and ReadLn

The number of characters read by `Read` or `ReadLn` depends on the type of variable receiving the data. When reading data into a type `Char` variable, a single character is read. When reading data into a numeric variable, the program skips over any leading blanks, control characters, or `<eoln>` characters until it encounters a character that is not a blank, a control character, or `<eoln>`. That first character must be a sign or a digit; if it is not, an execution error such as `Non-digit found while reading number` occurs, and the program stops. If the first character is a sign or a digit, the program continues reading digit characters (including a decimal point for type `Real`) until it encounters a blank, a control character, or an `<eoln>`. When reading data into a `string` variable, all characters up to, but not including, the next `<eoln>` character are read and stored. For `ReadLn` only, the `<eoln>` character is also read but not stored.

SYNTAX DISPLAY

Read, ReadLn Procedures

Form: Read (*infile, input list*)
             ReadLn (*infile, input list*)

Example: `Read (InData, X, Y, Z)`
`ReadLn (InData, Ch1, Ch2)`

Interpretation: A sequence of characters is read from the file identified by *infile* (type `Text`) into the variables specified in *input list*. The type of each variable in *input list* must be `Boolean`, `Char`, `Integer`, `Real`, `string`, or a subrange of `Char` or `Integer`. If the data type of a variable is `Char`, only a single character is read into that variable. If the data type of a variable is `Integer` or `Real`, any leading blanks or `<eoln>` characters are skipped and a sequence of numeric characters (including a decimal point for `Real`) is read and stored in that variable. If the data type is `string`, all characters up to the next `<eoln>` are read. After the *input list* for `Read` is satisfied, the next character to be read is the one that follows the last character that was read. If `ReadLn` is called, the next character to be read is the one that follows the next `<eoln>` character. If *infile* is omitted, the data items are read from the keyboard.

Table 8.1 lists several examples of `Read` and `ReadLn` statements and their effects. Assume that X is type `Real`, N is type `Integer`, C is type `Char`, S is type `string`, and the first character processed is the first character in the file shown on the right. The next character to be read after each `Read` or `ReadLn` operation is shown in color.

Table 8.1
Effects of Read and ReadLn

Statement and Effect	Next Character to Be Read
`Read (InData, X, N, C)` X is 1234.56, N is 789, C is ' '	1234.56□789□A345.67<eoln> W<eoln><eof>
`ReadLn (InData, X, N, C)` X is 1234.56, N is 789, C is ' '	1234.56□789□A345.67<eoln> W<eoln><eof>
`Read (InData, X, C, N)` X is 1234.56, C is ' ', N is 789	1234.56□789□A345.67<eoln> W<eoln><eof>
`ReadLn (InData, X, C, N)` X is 1234.56, C is ' ', N is 789	1234.56□789□A345.67<eoln> W<eoln><eof>
`Read (InData, C, X, N)` C is '1', X is 234.56, N is 789	1234.56□789□A345.67<eoln> W<eoln><eof>
`ReadLn (InData, C, X, N)` C is '1', X is 234.56, N is 789	1234.56□789□A345.67<eoln> W<eoln><eof>

`ReadLn (InData, X, N);`
`Read (InData, C)`
  X is 1234.56, N is 789, C is 'W'
	1234.56□789□A345.67<eoln>
	W<eoln><eof>

Statement and Effect	Next Character to Be Read
ReadLn (InData, X); ReadLn (InData, C) X is 1234.56, C is 'W'	1234.56□789□A345.67<eoln> W<eoln><eof>
ReadLn (InData, S); Read (InData, C) S is '1234.56 789 A345.67', C is 'W'	1234.56□789□A345.67<eoln> W<eoln><eof>

Table 8.1
Effects of Read and ReadLn
(continued)

Notice in Table 8.1 that C contains the blank character after the first four operations. In all these cases, C follows X or N in the input list. Therefore, a sequence of numeric characters up to (but not including) the blank character is read into X or N and the blank character is read into C.

Writing Results to a Text File

Use procedures Write and WriteLn to write results to a text file in the same way that you write to the screen. If the first parameter in a call to Write or WriteLn is a variable of type Text, the output characters are sent to the file identified by that variable rather than to the screen. Whenever WriteLn is used, an <eoln> character is placed in the file after the last output character.

A program writes a numeric value to a file as a sequence of digit characters. The minus character (⁻) precedes a negative number. The decimal point character (.) is inserted in a type Real value. You can use format specifications when writing to a text file (see Section 2.8).

SYNTAX DISPLAY

Write, WriteLn Procedures

Form: Write (*outfile, output list*)
        WriteLn (*outfile, output list*)
Example: Write (MyResult, Salary)
        WriteLn (MyResult, Hours :3:1, ' $', Salary :4:2)
Interpretation: The characters specified by *output list* are written to the end of file *outfile*. The type of each expression in *output list* must be Boolean, Char, Integer, Real, string, or a subrange of Char or Integer. If an expression is type Char, a single character is written to file *outfile;* otherwise, multiple characters may be written. Format specifications may be included in the *output list*. When WriteLn is called, an <eoln> character is written to *outfile* after the last character specified by the *output list*. If *outfile* is omitted, the output results are written to the screen.

The Keyboard and Screen as Text Files

In interactive programming, Pascal treats data entered at the keyboard as if they were read from the system file Input. These data are stored temporarily

input buffer

a temporary storage area for input data

in an **input buffer** (a storage area) until you press the Enter key. Up to that point, you can edit the data in the input buffer using the backarrow key to erase characters and retyping them. Pressing the Enter key inserts the <eoln> character in the input buffer and enables your program to begin processing the data line.

Similarly, displaying characters on the screen is equivalent to writing characters to system file Output. The WriteLn procedure places the <eoln> character in this file, thereby moving the cursor to the start of the next line of the screen. Both Input and Output are text files because their individual components are characters.

EXAMPLE 8.2 ▼

The statements

```
Write (Output, 'Enter a salary value> ');
ReadLn (Input, Salary)
```

display a prompting message on the screen (file Output) and read a value typed at the keyboard (file Input) into Salary. They are equivalent to the more familiar statements

```
Write ('Enter a salary value> ');
ReadLn (Salary)   ▲
```

Exercises for Section 8.1

Self-Check

1. a. For a computer program that handles the booking of airline reservations, would it be preferable to use a data file or to enter the data interactively? Explain your answer.
    b. What about a program for printing student transcripts at a university?
2. Explain when Read might be preferred to ReadLn as a means of obtaining numeric data from the user of an interactive program.
3. If text files are physically stored on disk as one long stream of characters, how can they appear as multiple lines on the screen of a text editor program?
4. Let X be type Real, N type Integer, C type Char, and S type string. Indicate the contents of each variable after each Read or ReadLn operation, assuming that the file consists of the following lines:

```
123 3.145 XYZ<eoln>
35 Z<eoln>
```

    a. ReadLn (InData, N, X); Read (InData, C)
    b. Read (InData, N, X, C)
    c. Read (InData, N, X, C, C)
    d. ReadLn (InData, N); Read (InData, C)
    e. ReadLn (InData, X); Read (InData, C, N)
    f. ReadLn (InData, C, C, C, X); Read (InData, N)

g. Read (InData, N, X, C, C, C, C, N)
h. Read (InData, N, X, C, C, C, C);
   ReadLn (InData, N, X); Read (InData, C)
i. Read (InData, N, S); Read (InData, C)
j. Read (InData, N, S); ReadLn (InData); Read (InData, C)

5. Repeat Exercise 4, substituting WriteLn for ReadLn, Write for Read, and OutData for InData. Show file OutData after each part. Assume that N is 512, X is 0.123, and C is '*'.

8.2 Procedures and Functions for Text Files

So far we have shown how to declare a text file, how to read from a text file used as a data file, and how to write output results to a text file used as an output file. In this section, we describe the additional Turbo Pascal procedures and functions needed to use a text file in a Pascal program.

To use a text file, you must carry out the following operations:

1. Declare variables used to identify text files as type Text.
2. Provide the directory name of the actual disk file that corresponds to each file variable.
3. For a text file that is being used as a data file, open the file and reset its file location marker to the first character in the file.
4. For a text file that is being used as an output file, open the file by creating an initially empty file on disk.
5. Use the file variable as the first parameter in all read or write operations involving the text file.
6. Close each text file before ending the program. This will write the <eof> character to the end of an output file.

We have already discussed operations 1 and 5; the remaining operations are described next.

External and Internal Names for Files

To enable Turbo Pascal to access a file saved on disk, you must provide its directory name, which is the name used to identify it in a disk's directory. A **disk directory** contains the directory names of all files stored on a disk together with other relevant information such as when a file was last modified, its size in bytes, and its disk address.

disk directory
a list of descriptive information about the files stored on a disk, including each file's directory name

To illustrate, the procedure call statement

Assign (MyData, 'A:INDATA.DAT');

associates file variable MyData with the file called INDATA.DAT in the directory for disk drive A. If the disk drive is not specified, Turbo Pascal uses the default drive.

You can also use a `string` variable as the second parameter for an `Assign` statement. In that case, the contents of the `string` variable are used as the file's directory name. This enables you to enter the directory name of the file as a data item during program execution.

The `Assign` statement is the only statement that references the directory name of the file. You use the file variable name in all other program statements. For this reason, programmers refer to `MyData` as the file's *internal name* and `A:INDATA.DAT` as its *external name.*

SYNTAX DISPLAY

Assign Procedure

Form: `Assign (`*filevar, dirname*`)`
Example: `Assign (MyData, 'A:INDATA.DAT')`
Interpretation: The file whose directory name is specified by the string *dirname* is associated with the file variable *filevar.*
Notes: Never use `Assign` on an open file. If *dirname* is the null string (`''`), *filevar* becomes associated with the standard `Input` or standard `Output` file, depending on whether *filevar* is later opened for input or output. Each file variable must have its own `Assign` statement. `Assign` is not part of standard Pascal.

Opening a Text File

opening a file
preparing a file for input or for output

Before a program can use a text file, the file must be prepared for input or output, or **opened.** A text file cannot be opened for both input and output at the same time. That is, if you are in the process of reading data from a text file, you cannot begin to write output results to the same file.

Reset Procedure

The procedure call statement

`Reset (InData)`

file location marker
a marker in each file that points to the next character to be processed in the file

prepares file `InData` for input to the program by moving its file location marker to the beginning of the file. The **file location marker** points to the next character to be processed in the file. After the `Reset` operation has been performed, the next character to be read is always the first character in the file. The `Reset` operation must be done before any characters are read from file `InData`, but, of course, the operation will fail if file `InData` was not previously saved on disk. To read and process a file a second time in the same program run, perform the `Reset` operation again.

Figure 8.4 shows file `MyData` after the `Reset` operation. The file location marker points to the first character.

SYNTAX DISPLAY

Reset Procedure

Form: `Reset (`*infile*`)`

Example: `Reset (MyData)`
Interpretation: File *infile* is prepared for input, and the file location marker for *infile* is moved to the first character in the file. The `Reset` operation is automatically performed on system file `Input`, so `Reset (Input)` is not required.

Rewrite Procedure

The procedure call statement

`Rewrite (OutData)`

prepares file `OutData` for receiving output. If the disk has no file corresponding to file `OutData`, a new, initially empty file is created. If a file corresponding to `OutData` is already saved on disk, its file location marker moves to the beginning of the file, effectively erasing the old file data.

Be sure to call procedure `Assign`, to associate the file variable with its directory name, before the initial call to `Reset` or `Rewrite`. Otherwise, a `File not assigned` run-time error will occur.

SYNTAX DISPLAY

Rewrite Procedure

Form: `Rewrite (`*outfile*`)`
Example: `Rewrite (MyData)`
Interpretation: File *outfile* is prepared for output, and *outfile* is initialized to an empty file. Any data previously stored in file *outfile* are lost. The `Rewrite` operation is automatically performed on system file `Output`, so `Rewrite (Output)` is not required.

Closing a File

After processing of an input file or an output file is complete, use Turbo Pascal's `Close` procedure (not part of standard Pascal) to disconnect the file from your program. Although you should close all files, take special care with output files. Because writing individual characters to an output file is very inefficient, Pascal temporarily stores output characters in an **output buffer** (storage area). When the output buffer is full, its contents are written as a block of characters to the corresponding output file. When you close an output file, any characters remaining in its output buffer are written to that file

output buffer

a temporary storage area for results to be written to an output file

Figure 8.4
File MyData After
Reset (MyData)

15900.00 Johnny Jones<eoln>25000.00 Sally Smythe<eoln><eof>

File location marker

along with the ⟨eof⟩ character. If you don't close an output file, the characters in its output buffer are not copied, so some program results may be lost.

Close Procedure

Form: Close (*filevar*)
Example: Close (InData)
Interpretation: The file denoted by *filevar* is closed. If *filevar* is an output file, any results remaining in memory are written to the file associated with *filevar* just before the ⟨eof⟩ character.
Note: If *filevar* is already closed when Close is called, a run-time error occurs. Close is not part of standard Pascal.

Testing for the End of a File: Function EOF

When reading a data file, you need to know when you have reached the end of the file. One way is to count the number of characters processed and compare this count to the number of characters in the file. Another way is to add a sentinel character at the end of each file. Both methods are unnecessary.

Each file automatically ends with an ⟨eof⟩ character, and Pascal's built-in function EOF (for End Of File) tests whether the next character to be read in a file is the ⟨eof⟩ character. The function designator

```
EOF(InFile)
```

returns True if all data characters in file InFile have been processed (i.e., the next character to be read is the ⟨eof⟩ character). It returns False if there are more characters remaining to be read.

EOF Function

Form: EOF(*filename*)
Example: EOF(InFile)
Interpretation: EOF returns True if the next character in file *filename* is ⟨eof⟩; otherwise, EOF returns False.
Note: If *filename* is omitted, the input file is assumed to be the system file Input (the keyboard). You can enter the ⟨eof⟩ character at the keyboard by pressing Ctrl-Z. If a read operation is attempted in standard Pascal when EOF(*filename*) is True, an Attempt to read past the end of the input file error occurs and the program stops.

Putting it All Together

Examples 8.3 and 8.4 use all the file operators discussed so far.

EXAMPLE 8.3: Writing a Table to an Output File ▼

The program in Fig. 8.5 reads a file containing a list of numbers (one per line) and writes each number followed by its square root and square to an output file. The program reads the directory name of the data file into `string` variable `InFileName`. After the loop exit, the files are closed and the directory name of the output file (`SQUARES.TXT`) is written to the screen, so the program user knows where to look for the file. Normally programmers use the extension `.TXT` (for TeXT) or `.DAT` (for DATa) with text files.

Figure 8.5
Program SquareAndRoot

Edit Window

```
program SquareAndRoot;
{Writes a table of squares and square roots to a file.}
  var
    InFile,                    {input file}
    OutFile : Text;            {output file}
    InFileName : string;       {directory name of input file}
    NextNum : Real;            {next number}

begin {SquareAndRoot}
  {Prepare files for input and output.}
  Write ('Input file name> ');
  ReadLn (InFileName);              {Get name of InFile.}
  Assign (InFile, InFileName);
  Reset (InFile);                  {Open InFile for input.}

  Assign (OutFile, 'SQUARES.TXT');
  Rewrite (OutFile);              {Open OutFile for output.}

  {Write table heading to output file.}
  WriteLn (OutFile, 'N' :10:2,
           'Square root' :15:2, 'Square' :12:2);

  {Read each number and write each line of the output file.}
  while not EOF(InFile) do
    begin
      ReadLn (InFile, NextNum);          {Read next number.}
      WriteLn (OutFile, NextNum :10:2,
               Sqrt(NextNum) :15:2, Sqr(NextNum) :12:2)
    end; {while}

  {Close the files.}
  Close (InFile);
  Close (OutFile);
  WriteLn ('Table of roots and squares is in file SQUARES.TXT')
end. {SquareAndRoot}
```

Output Window

```
Input file name> NUMBERS.TXT
Table of roots and squares is in file SQUARES.TXT
```

The sample run in Fig. 8.5 shows that two lines are displayed on the screen. The first output line contains a prompt followed by the external name of the input file. The program user types in the input file name (NUM-BERS.TXT), but the second Assign statement specifies the output file name (SQUARES.TXT).

After opening the files, the program writes the table heading to the output file. Inside the loop, the ReadLn statement reads each number from the input file, and the WriteLn statement writes three output results to the next line of the output file. Although the number of characters in a data line may vary, the program always writes 40 characters per output line, including the <eoln> character. The numbers that are read from the data file and written to the output file do not appear on the screen. Notice that there is no need for a prompt inside the loop because the data items are not entered interactively.

Notice also that no priming read is needed when using function EOF to control loop repetition. Instead, the ReadLn statement inside the loop reads all data lines including the first. If the data file is empty, the while loop does not execute and the files are closed. In this case, the output file would contain only the table heading, which was already written. We show a sample data file (left) and corresponding output file (right) next.

File NUMBERS.TXT | **File SQUARES.TXT**

	N	Square root	Square<eoln>
100<eoln>	100.00	10.00	10000.00<eoln>
4.00<eoln><eof>	4.00	2.00	16.00<eoln><eof>

▲

EXAMPLE 8.4: Copying a File ▼

The file copy program in Fig. 8.6 copies one line at a time from its input file (InFile) to its output file (OutFile). Before each repetition of the while loop, function EOF tests whether the end of file InFile has been reached. If the <eof> character is next, EOF(InFile) is True and not EOF(InFile) is False, so loop exit occurs. If the file does contain more data characters, EOF(InFile) is False and not EOF(InFile) is True, so the loop body continues executing. The ReadLn statement reads the next line of file InFile into string variable Line and the WriteLn statement writes it to the output file. ▲

Testing for the End of a Line: Function EOLN

Pascal also provides a function EOLN (for End Of LiNe) that enables a program to detect the <eoln> characters that separate a text file into lines. Function EOLN returns True when the next data character is <eoln>; otherwise, EOLN returns False.

Figure 8.6
Program CopyFile

Edit Window

```
program CopyFile;
{Copies a data file by writing each line to an output file.}
  var
    InFile,                     {input file}
    OutFile : Text;             {output file}
    InFileName,                 {directory name of input file}
    Line       : string;        {each file line}

begin {CopyFile}
  {Prepare files for input and output.}
  Write ('File to be copied> ');
  ReadLn (InFileName);              {Get name of InFile.}
  Assign (InFile, InFileName);
  Reset (InFile);                   {Open InFile for input.}

  Assign (OutFile, 'COPYFILE.TXT');
  Rewrite (OutFile);                {Open OutFile for output.}

  {Copy the data file line by line.}
  while not EOF(InFile) do
    begin
      ReadLn (InFile, Line);        {Read next line.}
      WriteLn (OutFile, Line)       {Write it to output file.}
    end; {while}

  {Close the files.}
  Close (InFile);
  Close (OutFile);
  WriteLn ('File ', InFileName, ' is copied to COPYFILE.TXT')
end. {CopyFile}
```

Output Window

```
File to be copied> A:MYDATA.TXT
File A:MYDATA.TXT is copied to COPYFILE.TXT
```

SYNTAX DISPLAY

EOLN Function

Form: EOLN(*filename*)

Example: EOLN(InFile)

Interpretation: The function result is True if the next character in file *filename* is <eoln>; otherwise, the function result is False.

Note: If *filename* is omitted, the input file is assumed to be the system file Input (the keyboard). In standard Pascal, it is an error to call the EOLN function if EOF(*filename*) is True.

EXAMPLE 8.5: Copying a Line of a File ▼

Procedure CopyLine in Fig. 8.7 copies one line of its first file parameter to its second file parameter. The while loop copies each character up to the ⟨eoln⟩ from file InFile to OutFile. After loop exit, the statements

```
ReadLn (InFile);                    {Skip the <eoln>.}
WriteLn (OutFile)                   {Write it to OutFile.}
```

skip over the ⟨eoln⟩ character in InFile and write the ⟨eoln⟩ character to OutFile. ▲

Because standard Pascal does not have a string data type, we cannot use ReadLn to read a data line into a string variable as we did in program CopyFile (Fig. 8.6). But we can use CopyLine to write a data line to an output file in standard Pascal. For example, we could call procedure CopyLine in program CopyFile to copy each line of the input file to the output file. In this case, the while loop would be rewritten as

```
{Copy each line from InFile to OutFile.}
while not EOF(InFile) do
  CopyLine (InFile, OutFile);
```

Figure 8.7
Procedure CopyLine

```
procedure CopyLine (var InFile {input file},
                        OutFile {output file} : Text);
{
 Copies one line of file InFile to file OutFile.
 Pre  : InFile is opened for input and OutFile for output.
 Post : Each character on the current line of file InFile is
        copied to OutFile. The <eoln> character is the last
        character written to OutFile and the file location
        marker for InFile is at the start of the next line.
}
  var
    Next : Char;         {each character}

begin {CopyLine}
  {Copy all characters up to the <eoln>.}
  while not EOLN(InFile) do
    begin
      Read (InFile, Next);
      Write (OutFile, Next)
    end; {while}

  {Process the <eoln> character.}
  ReadLn (InFile);                    {Skip the <eoln>.}
  WriteLn (OutFile)                   {Write it to OutFile.}
end; {CopyLine}
```

Although procedure CopyLine does not actually read the <eoln> character into Next, a Pascal program can read the <eoln> character. When this happens, Turbo Pascal stores the character corresponding to Ctrl-M in the variable receiving <eoln> as its data item; standard Pascal stores the blank character instead.

Program Style

Using ReadLn After a Loop

After the loop in Fig. 8.7 is exited, the statement

```
ReadLn (InFile);                    {Skip the <eoln>.}
```

executes, skipping over the <eoln> character. Placing ReadLn (InFile) right after a loop that uses not EOLN(InFile) as its loop-repetition test causes ReadLn to process the <eoln> character that caused loop repetition to terminate. If the <eoln> character were not processed, the next Read or ReadLn would read it instead of the first character in the next data line; possibly causing unexpected program results and a run-time error. In fact, if this statement were omitted from CopyLine, the loop

```
while not EOF(InFile) do
  CopyLine (InFile, OutFile);
```

would execute forever. The next character to process after a return from CopyLine would always be the <eoln> character. Consequently, in the next call to CopyLine, its while loop would be skipped and the statement

```
WriteLn (OutFile)                   {Write it to OutFile.}
```

would write another <eoln> character to OutFile instead of writing the next data line. This process would continue until the program user terminated the program.

File Parameters in User-Defined Procedures

File parameter InFile is listed as a variable parameter in the parameter list for procedure CopyLine. Because InFile represents an input file, it may seem strange to declare it as a variable parameter. However, Pascal requires all file parameters to be variable parameters because a local copy of a large file would require too much memory.

Using EOLN with Keyboard Data

You can use the EOLN function with parameter Input to test for the <eoln> character when reading data from the keyboard. Recall that the <eoln> character is placed in system file Input when the Enter key is pressed. The statement

```
CopyLine (Input, OutFile)
```

passes `Input` as the first file parameter to procedure `CopyLine` (see Fig. 8.7), so the next data line typed at the keyboard would be written to file `OutFile`.

It is easy to misuse `EOLN` or `EOF` to test for the `<eoln>` or `<eof>` character in the keyboard data. If you forget to specify the file parameter and write the function designator as just `EOLN` (as in `while not EOLN do`), Pascal will use system file `Input` as the default file parameter. Similarly, if you forget to use a file parameter with `Read` or `ReadLn`, Pascal will use `Input` by default, so your program will pause until you type in a data line.

Exercises for Section 8.2

Self-Check

1. Find the errors in the following fragment assuming `InFile` is type `Text` and `Next` is type `Char`. Which file is the input file, which file is the output file, and which file is tested by function `EOLN`?

```
Assign ('MYDATA.TXT', InFile);
Rewrite (InFile);
Reset (Input);
while not EOLN do
  begin
    Read (InFile, Next);
    Write (Next)
  end; {while}
```

2. Assume you are given an input file `NUMBERS.TXT` with integers, one per line, in it. Assuming variable `NumData` is type `Text`, what statements would be required to prepare for reading the file? What statement should be executed after you are through reading the file?

Programming

1. Write a procedure that reads a file that has integers, one per line, and computes the sum of the integers. The input to the procedure is a variable `FileName` of type `string` containing the name of the file to be read. The procedure output is the sum. If the file is empty, the sum should be zero.
2. Write a program that compresses a file by writing every other character in the file to an output file. The new file will contain approximately half as many characters as the original.
3. Write a procedure that returns a count of the number of occurrences of a particular character on the current line of a data file. The internal file name and the character being counted should be procedure inputs; the count of characters should be a procedure output.

8.3   Using Text Files

If one program writes its output to a disk file rather than to the screen, a second program may use that output file as its data file. In effect, the two programs communicate with each other through the disk file. The following case study develops a program whose output file is another program's data file.

CASE STUDY   **Preparing a Payroll File**

PROBLEM ▼

Your company's accountant has asked you to write two payroll programs. The first program will read a data file containing employee salary data, with data for each employee stored on two consecutive lines. The first line will house the employee's name. The second line will start with an indicator of employee status, with an H for an hourly employee or an S for a salaried employee. Either the employee's hourly rate (for an hourly employee) or the employee's annual salary (for a salaried employee) will follow. For hourly employees only the second line will end with an additional data value—the number of hours worked that week. A sample data file with one salaried and one hourly employee follows:

Data File

```
Peter Liacouras<eoln>
S 260000.00<eoln>
Caryn Koffman<eoln>
H 10.00 40.0<eoln><eof>
```

The first program should write each employee's name to an output file, followed by a line containing the employee's computed gross salary for the week. It should also compute and display the total payroll amount for the week. As shown in the following output file, the second line of the output file should list a salaried employee's annual salary (e.g., $260,000) divided by 52. The fourth line of the output file should list the product of an hourly employee's rate ($10.00) and hours (40.0).

Output File

```
Peter Liacouras<eoln>
5000.00<eoln>
Caryn Koffman<eoln>
400.00<eoln><eof>
```

The second program will read the output file and write payroll checks based on the contents of that file. For example, the first check issued should be for $5000.00 made out to Peter Liacouras.

ANALYSIS ▼

We will write the first program now and leave the second one as an exercise (see Programming Project 1 at the end of this chapter). The program must copy each employee's name to the output file. It must also compute each employee's weekly salary, write it to the output file, and add it to the payroll total.

Data Requirements

Problem Inputs (from Input File InEmp)

```
each employee's name
the category (hourly or salaried) of each employee
the pay rate for each employee
the hours worked for an hourly employee
```

Problem Outputs (to Output File OutEmp)

```
each employee's name
each employee's weekly salary
```

Problem Output (to screen)

```
Payroll : Real      {the payroll total}
```

DESIGN ▼

The main program prepares the files for input and output and calls procedure `ProcessEmp` to process all employees and accumulate the total payroll (step 2 in the following algorithm). After `ProcessEmp` is finished, the main program displays the final payroll total.

Algorithm for Main Program

1. Prepare files `InEmp` and `OutEmp`.
2. Process all employees and compute payroll total.
3. Display the payroll total.

Analysis and Design of ProcessEmp

`ProcessEmp` allocates storage for the variables that store an employee's salary data and final salary. The data requirements for `ProcessEmp` follow.

Data Requirements for ProcessEmp

Input Parameter

```
InEmp : Text            {file of employee data}
```

Output Parameter

```
OutEmp : Text          {payroll file}
```

Input/Output Parameter

```
Payroll : Real         {the payroll amount so far}
```

Local Variables

```
HourOrSal : Char   {input - hourly or salaried indicator}
Hours : Real       {input - hours worked}
Rate : Real        {input - hourly rate}
Salary : Real      {output - gross salary}
```

The algorithm for `ProcessEmp` follows. Step 3 of `ProcessEmp` is performed by procedure `CopyLine` (see Fig. 8.7). Step 4 is performed by procedure `ReadData` and step 5 is performed by function `ComputeSal`. Figure 8.8 shows the structure chart.

Figure 8.8
Structure Chart for Writing the Payroll File

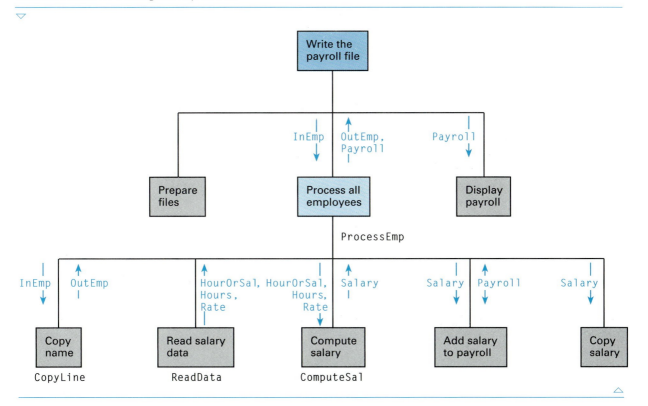

Algorithm for ProcessEmp

1. Initialize payroll total to 0.0.
2. `while` there are more employees `do`
      `begin`
      3. Read next employee's name from `InEmp` and write it to `OutEmp`.
      4. Read next employee's salary data.
      5. Compute next employee's weekly salary.
      6. Write next employee's salary to `OutEmp` and add it to payroll total.
      `end`

IMPLEMENTATION ▼

Coding the Main Program

Figure 8.9 shows the main program. Besides text files `InEmp` and `OutEmp`, the only variable declared in the main program is `Payroll`. We declare the variables needed to store and process an individual employee's data in `ProcessEmp`. This step is consistent with the policy of declaring a variable in the highest-level module that accesses it.

Figure 8.9
Writing a Payroll File

Edit Window

```
program WritePayroll;
{
  Writes each employee's name and weekly salary to an
  output file and computes total payroll amount.
}
  var
    InEmp,                 {data file}
    OutEmp : Text;         {output file}
    Payroll : Real;        {output - total payroll}

{Insert ReadData, ComputeSal, and ProcessEmp here.}

begin {WritePayroll}
  {Prepare InEmp and OutEmp.}
  Assign (InEmp, 'A:INEMP.DAT');
  Reset (InEmp);

  Assign (OutEmp, 'A:OUTEMP.DAT');
  Rewrite (OutEmp);

  {Process all employees and compute payroll total.}
  ProcessEmp (InEmp, OutEmp, Payroll);
```

▷ ▷ ▷ ▷ ▷ ▷

```
{Display result and close files.}
WriteLn ('Total payroll is $', Payroll :4:2);
Close (InEmp);
Close (OutEmp)
end. {WritePayroll}
```

Output Window

```
Total payroll is $5400.00
```

△

Coding the Modules

Figure 8.10 shows procedure ProcessEmp and its subordinate modules. Procedure ReadData reads the first data character and then reads either one or two numeric values, depending on whether the first character is S or H. Function ComputeSal computes the gross weekly salary for an employee, and that amount is assigned to Salary after the function return.

Figure 8.10
ReadData, ComputeSal, and ProcessEmp

▽

```
{Insert procedure CopyLine (see Fig. 8.7) here.}

procedure ReadData (var InEmp {input file} : Text;
                    var HourOrSal {output} : Char;
                    var Rate {output},
                        Hours {output} : Real);
{
 Reads the employee salary data.
 Pre  : File InEmp is opened for input.
 Post : HourOrSal contains the first data character on
        the data line.
        If HourOrSal is H, Rate contains the hourly rate
        and Hours contains the hours worked. If HourOrSal
        is S, Rate contains the annual salary and Rate is
        undefined. Otherwise, Hours and Rate are undefined.
}
begin {ReadData}
  Read (InEmp, HourOrSal);
  HourOrSal := UpCase(HourOrSal);
  if HourOrSal = 'H' then
    ReadLn (InEmp, Rate, Hours)    {Read hourly rate and hours.}
  else if HourOrSal = 'S' then
    ReadLn (InEmp, Rate)              {Read annual salary.}
  else
    begin
      ReadLn (InEmp);                      {Skip past <eoln>.}
      WriteLn ('Invalid character ', HourOrSal)
    end {if}
end; {ReadData}
```

▷ ▷ ▷ ▷ ▷

```
function ComputeSal (HourOrSal : Char;
                     Rate,
                     Hours : Real) : Real;
{
 Computes the weekly gross salary.
 Pre : HourOrSal and Rate are defined.
 Post: If HourOrSal is H, returns Rate * Hours;
       if HourOrSal is S, returns Rate / 52;
       otherwise, result is undefined.
}
begin
  if HourOrSal = 'H' then
    ComputeSal := Rate * Hours
  else if HourOrSal = 'S' then
    ComputeSal := Rate / 52.0
end; {ComputeSal}

procedure ProcessEmp (var InEmp {input file},
                          OutEmp {output file} : Text;
                      var Payroll {output} : Real);
{
 Processes all employees and computes payroll total.
 Pre : InEmp is prepared for input and OutEmp for output.
 Post: All employee names and weekly salaries are written
       to OutEmp and the sum of their salaries is returned
       through Payroll.
}
  var
    HourOrSal : Char;{input - hourly or salaried indicator}
    Hours,          {input - hours worked}
    Rate,           {input - hourly rate}
    Salary : Real;  {output - gross salary}

begin {ProcessEmp}
  Payroll := 0.0;
  while not EOF(InEmp) do
    begin
      CopyLine (InEmp, OutEmp);      {Copy employee name.}
      {Read salary data.}
      ReadData (InEmp, HourOrSal, Rate, Hours);
      Salary := ComputeSal(HourOrSal, Rate, Hours);
      if (HourOrSal = 'H') or (HourOrSal = 'S') then
        begin {good data}
          Payroll := Payroll + Salary;
          WriteLn (OutEmp, Salary :4:2)
        end {good data}
      else
        WriteLn (OutEmp, 'Salary is undefined')
    end {while}
end; {ProcessEmp}
```

The `while` loop in `ProcessEmp` tests whether the next character is `<eof>`. If it is not, `ProcessEmp` calls `CopyLine` to copy the next employee's name from the input file (`InEmp`) to the output file (`OutEmp`). `CopyLine` processes every other line of file `InEmp`, starting with the first line.

Next, the statement

```
ReadData (InEmp, HourOrSal, Rate, Hours);
```

in `ProcessEmp` calls `ReadData` to read an employee's salary data from `InEmp` and to advance the file location marker to the first letter of the next employee's name. If the character read into `HourOrSal` is not H or S, `ReadData` writes an error message to the screen and skips to the start of the next data line. The next statement in `ProcessEmp`

```
Salary := ComputeSal(HourOrSal, Rate, Hours);
```

calls `ComputeSal` to compute the weekly gross salary and to assign it to `Salary`. Finally, the statements

```
Payroll := Payroll + Salary;
WriteLn (OutEmp, Salary :4:2)
```

add the current employee's gross salary to `Payroll` and write it to file `OutEmp` provided `Salary` is defined.

TESTING ▼

Run the payroll program with sample payroll data to determine whether it computes weekly salaries and payroll correctly for both hourly and salaried employees. Also see what happens when the first character of an employee's salary data is not H or S. In this case, the program should display an error message and continue on to process the next employee's data. Check whether the program correctly processes later employees or whether errors propagate, causing an error in one employee's data to invalidate all other results.

The Importance of Advancing Past the <eoln> Character

It is easy to make an error when reading character data mixed with numeric data. Many problems are caused by not advancing past the `<eoln>` character. For example, consider what would happen if `ReadData` used the statement

```
Read (InEmp, Rate);
```

to read a salaried employee's data instead of calling procedure `ReadLn`. The difficulty is that the `Read` procedure advances the file location marker for file `InEmp` up to the `<eoln>` character but not past it:

S 260000.00<eoln>
        ↑
   File location marker

When CopyLine is called to copy the second employee's name, the while loop exit occurs immediately, without reading the name, because the next character is the <eoln> character. The <eoln> character is processed just before CopyLine returns to procedure ProcessEmp, and the next character is now the first letter of an employee's name. When ReadData is called again, the statement

```
Read (InEmp, HourOrSal);
```

reads the first letter, C, of the second employee's name, so an error message will be displayed on the screen.

Exercises for Section 8.3

Self-Check

1. a. What would be the effect, if any, of trailing blanks at the end of data lines in the data file for the program in Fig. 8.9?
   b. What would be the effect of blank lines?
2. Why does placing employee names and salary amounts on separate lines of file OutEmp simplify writing the program to print the payroll checks?

Programming

1. Write a program that reads file OutEmp produced by program WritePayroll (Fig. 8.9) and displays a count of the number of employees processed by WritePayroll and their average salary.

8.4 Debugging with Files

Preparing a data file that contains a representative set of test data for a new program makes it easier to debug a program. Each time it is run, the program can read the test data from this file, eliminating the need to retype the data items. After an interactive program has been debugged, replace the directory name in the Assign statement with the null string (''), so that Turbo Pascal will read data from the keyboard in subsequent runs.

You can use file identifiers as Watch variables. The value displayed in the Watch window for a file identifier is a parenthesized list that contains the directory name for the file as specified in the Assign statement. This list also contains a string entry indicating whether the file is open for input, open for output, or closed.

8.5   Common Programming Errors

Don't forget to use procedure `Assign` to associate each file identifier with its directory name before opening the file. The file name used in your program may differ from the directory name of the associated disk file. All file names must be declared as variables (type `Text`) except for system files `Input` and `Output`.

Always use the `Reset` or `Rewrite` procedure to prepare a file for input or output (except for system files `Input` and `Output`). If you rewrite an existing file, the data on that file may be lost. Make sure that you do not inadvertently place the `Reset` or `Rewrite` statement in a loop. If you do, a `Read` operation in the loop will repeatedly read the first file component; a `Write` operation in the loop will repeatedly write the first file component.

The `Read` or `ReadLn` procedure can be used only after a file has been prepared for input. Similarly, the `Write` or `WriteLn` procedure can be used only after a file has been prepared for output. When performing file input or output, be sure to specify the file name as the first procedure parameter; otherwise, the system file `Input` or `Output` will be assumed. The following loop will execute forever because data are read from system file `Input` (the default file) instead of file `MyData`, which is being tested for the <eoln> character:

```
while not EOLN(MyData) do
   begin
      Read (Next);          {incorrect read from keyboard}
      Write (Next)
   end; {while}
```

When you use function `EOLN` or `EOF` to control data entry, don't forget to include the data file name as the function argument. Remember to skip over the <eoln> character, using `ReadLn`, after you have reached the end of a data line. Be careful not to try to read data when the file location marker is at <eof>.

If you press the Enter key an extra time when you have finished creating a data file, you may place an extra empty line at the end of the data file. The following file contains one number per line and an empty line at the end:

```
500<eoln>
37<eoln>
<eoln><eof>
```

Although the empty line may seem harmless, if we use the `while` header

```
while not EOF(InData) do
```

to control a loop that reads and processes one number per line, the empty line will cause the loop to execute one extra time.

If an output file is missing or appears to be incomplete, it may be that you have forgotten to close the output file. Turbo Pascal saves data being written to a file in a temporary output buffer in memory; the `Close` statement copies any remaining data in the output buffer to the disk file.

CHAPTER REVIEW

1. You can read a program's data from a text file and write its results to a text file by specifying a file variable (type `Text`) as the first parameter in a `Read(Ln)` or `Write(Ln)`.
2. The `<eoln>` character separates a text file into lines. The `EOLN` function can test for an `<eoln>` character, and the `WriteLn` statement places an `<eoln>` character in a text file. An `<eoln>` character that is read into a type `Char` variable is stored as Ctrl-M in Turbo Pascal but as a blank in standard Pascal.
3. When text files are processed, sequences of characters are transferred between main memory and disk storage. The data type of a variable used in an input list or of an expression used in an output list must be `Boolean`, `Char`, `Integer`, `Real`, `string`, or a subrange of `Char` or `Integer`.
4. The `Assign` statement associates a file variable (the file's internal name) with the directory name of a file stored on disk (the file's external name). The `Reset` procedure moves the file location marker for an input file to the first character in the file. The `Rewrite` procedure creates an empty output file. The `EOF` function tests whether the end of the file has been reached and returns `True` if the next character is the `<eof>` character.

Summary of New Pascal Constructs

Construct	Effect
File Declaration	
```var MoreChars, MoreDigits : Text; I : Integer; NextCh : Char;```	`MoreChars` and `MoreDigits` are text files.
Assign Procedure	
```Assign (MoreDigits, 'A:DIGITS.DAT');```	File variable `MoreDigits` is associated with disk file `DIGITS.DAT`, located on drive A.

Construct	Effect
Reset and Rewrite Procedures	
`Reset (MoreDigits);` `Rewrite (MoreChars);`	`MoreDigits` is prepared for input, and `MoreChars` is prepared for output.
Read and Write Procedures	

`Read (MoreDigits, I);`
`WriteLn (MoreChars,`
`'number: ', I);`
	The next integer is read from file `MoreDigits` into variable `I` (type `Integer`). The string `'number: '` is written to `MoreChars` followed by the value of `I`.

EOF Function	

`Reset (MoreDigits);`
`Rewrite (MoreChars);`
`while not EOF(MoreDigits) do`
` begin`
`   ReadLn (MoreDigits, I);`
`   WriteLn (MoreChars, I)`
` end; {while}`
	File `MoreDigits` is prepared for input to the program and file `MoreChars` for output from the program. The first integer value on each line of file `MoreDigits` is written to a separate line of file `MoreChars`.

EOLN Function	

`Reset (MoreDigits);`
`while not EOLN(MoreDigits) do`
`  begin`
`    Read (MoreDigits, NextCh);`
`    Write (Output, NextCh)`
`  end;  {while}`
`ReadLn (MoreDigits)`
	File `MoreDigits` is prepared for input. Each character on the first line is read to `NextCh` and displayed on the screen. `ReadLn` advances the file location marker for `MoreDigits` to the first character of the second line.

Close Procedure	
`Close (MoreChars);`	File `MoreChars` is closed.

Quick-Check Exercises

1. The _____ operation associates a disk file with a file variable, but either _____ or _____ must be performed before the file can be read or written.
2. The _____ character separates a _____ file into lines, and the _____ character appears at the end of a file.
3. What data types can be read from or written to a text file?
4. Is it ever permissible to pass a file as a value parameter to a procedure?

5. True or false: The name of a variable of type Text must be the same as the name of the corresponding file.
6. Can a text file be used for both input and output by the same program?
7. Correct the following segment:

```
Reset (Number);
while not EOF do
    Read (InFile, Number);
```

Answers to Quick-Check Exercises

1. `Assign, Reset, Rewrite`
2. `<eoln>`, text, `<eof>`
3. A string or any of the standard data types (or a subrange thereof) except `Boolean` can be read; any of the standard types (or a subrange thereof) or a string literal can be written.
4. No.
5. False, the file's name is its directory name and it need not be the same as the file variable name.
6. Yes, but it may not be open for both input and output at the same time.
7.
```
Reset (InFile);
while not EOF(InFile) do
    Read (InFile, Number);
```

Review Questions

1. List three advantages to using files for input and output instead of interactive input and output.
2. a. Explain the difference between a file's internal and external names.
   b. What conventions are followed for choosing each name?
   c. Which name appears in the file variable declaration?
   d. Which name appears in an operating system command?
3. Explain how `Read` and `ReadLn` differ in reading data items from a text file.
4. Let X be type `Real`, N type `Integer`, and Ch type `Char`. Indicate the contents of each variable after each input operation is performed, assuming the file consists of the following lines and that the `Reset (InData)` operation occurs before each sequence of statements:

```
23 53.2 ABC<eoln>
145 Z<eoln><eof>
```

   a. `Read (InData, N, X);`
      `ReadLn (InData, Ch)`
   b. `ReadLn (InData, Ch, N)`
   c. `ReadLn (InData);`
      `Read (InData, X, Ch)`
5. Write a loop that reads up to 10 integer values from a data file and displays them on the screen. If there are not 10 integers in the file, the message `That's all folks` should be displayed after the last number.

6. Write a procedure that copies several data lines typed at the keyboard to a text file. The copy process should be terminated when the user enters an empty line.
7. Write a procedure that will open a file named MANY.TXT, read the first character from the file, and write that to a new file named FIRST.TXT. The procedure should not write the second file if the first file is empty.

Programming Projects

1. Write a procedure that reads the data for one employee from file OutEmp produced by program WritePayroll (see Section 8.3) and writes a payroll check to an output file. The format of the check should be similar to this one:

```
Temple University              Check No.      12372
Philadelphia, PA               Date:       03-17-94

Pay to the
Order of:   Peter Liacouras     $ 5000.00

                                Jane Smith
                                Bursar
```

2. Write a program that reads the initial check number and the data from the keyboard and then writes checks using the procedure from Programming Project 1 and a data file generated by running program WritePayroll. Write a separator line consisting of 80 underscore characters between checks.
3. Each year the state legislature rates the activity of the faculty of each state-supported college and university. The rating is based on reports submitted by the faculty members indicating the average number of hours worked per week during the school year. Each faculty member is rated, and the university receives an overall rating.

    The faculty activity ratings are computed as follows:
    a. "Highly productive" means over 55 hours per week reported.
    b. "Satisfactory" means reported hours per week are between 35 and 55.
    c. "Overpaid" means reported hours per week are less than 35.

    Read the following data from a file (assuming all names are padded with blanks in the data file to 10 characters):

Name	Hours
Herm	63
Flo	37
Jake	20
Maureen	55
Saul	72
Tony	40
Al	12

As part of your solution, your program should include procedures that correspond to the procedure headers shown next:

```
procedure PrintHeader;
{Displays table heading}
```

```
procedure DisplayProductivity (Hours {input} : Real);
{Displays productivity ranking based on value of Hours}

procedure ProcessName (var FacHours {input} : Text);
{Reads and displays one faculty name from file FacHours}

procedure ProcessData (var FacHours {input} : Text;
                       var Count {input/output} : Integer;
                       var Sum {input/output} : Real);
   {
    Reads all data lines from file FacHours and displays body
    of table and returns number of faculty (Count) and the sum
    of their hours worked (Sum). Calls: ProcessName and
    DisplayProductivity.
   }
```

4. Compute the monthly payment and the total payment for a bank loan, given the following:

   a. The amount of the loan
   b. The duration of the loan in months
   c. The interest rate for the loan

   Your program should read in one loan at a time, perform the required computation, and print the values of the monthly payment and the total payment.

   Test your program with at least the following data (and more if you want):

Loan	Months	Rate
16000	300	12.50
24000	360	13.50
30000	300	15.50
42000	360	14.50
22000	300	15.50
300000	240	15.25

   Hints:
   a. The formula for computing a monthly payment is

   $$monthpay = \frac{ratem \times expm^{months} \times loan}{expm^{months} - 1.0}$$

   where

   $ratem = rate/1200.00$

   $expm = (1.0 + ratem)$

   You will need a loop to multiply *expm* by itself *months* times.
   b. The formula for computing the total payment is

   $$total = monthpay \times months$$

5. Use the solution to Programming Project 4 as the basis for writing a program that will write a data file containing a table of the following form:

```
             Loan Amount: $1000
   Interest  Duration  Monthly  Total
   Rate      (years)   Payment  Payment
   6.00      20        _____   _____
   6.00      25        _____   _____
   6.00      30        _____   _____
   6.25      20        _____   _____
```

The output file produced by your program should contain payment information on a $1000 loan for interest rates from 6% to 10% with increments of 0.25%. The loan durations should be 20, 25, and 30 years.

6. Because text files can grow very large, some computer systems supply a handy utility program that displays the head and tail of a file, where the head is the first four lines and the tail is the last four lines. Write a program that asks the user for a file name, then displays the head of the file, a line of dots, and the tail of the file. If the file is eight or less lines long, just display the entire file.

7. Whatsamata U offers a service to its faculty in computing grades at the end of each semester. A program processes three weighted test scores and calculates a student's average and letter grade (based on an A as $90-100$, a B as $80-89$, etc.). Read the student data from a file and write each student's name, test score, average, and grade to an output file.

   Write a program to provide this valuable service. The data will consist of the three test weights followed by three test scores and a student ID number (four digits) for each student. Calculate the weighted average for each student and the corresponding letter grade. This information should be printed along with the initial three test scores. The weighted average for each student is equal to

   $$(weight_1 \times score_1) + (weight_2 \times score_2) + (weight_3 \times score_3)$$

   For summary statistics print the highest average, the lowest average, the average of the averages, and the total number of students processed.
   Sample data:

   ```
   0.35   0.25   0.4      test weights
   00   76      88   1014    test scores and ID
   ```

8. Write a program to manage a dictionary. Your dictionary is a text file named DICTION.TXT and consists of an alphabetized list of words, one per line. When a user inputs a word, scan the dictionary looking for the word. If the word is in the dictionary, say so. If not, display the word immediately preceding and immediately following the word in the dictionary, so that the user can see words close in spelling. Then, ask whether the user wants to add this new word to the dictionary. If the answer is yes, do so and go back to request the next word.

   To insert a word into a file in alphabetical order, simply copy the file to a new file named DICTION.TMP, and move words one at a time back to the original file, inserting the new word when you reach its correct position alphabetically.

9. Write a program that reads in a string of characters that represent a Roman numeral and then converts it to Arabic form (an integer). The character values for Roman numerals are as follows:

M	1000
D	500
C	100
L	50
X	10
V	5
I	1

Test your program with the following data: IX (9), LXXXVII (87), CCXIX (219), MCCCLIV (1354), MMDCLXXIII (2673), MCDLXXVI (1476).

What areas of computer science first attracted your interest? What was your first job in the industry?

▲ I chose to study electrical engineering and computer science because I was very interested in how computers are designed, built, and used. During college, my strongest technical interest became artificial intelligence. I enjoyed exploring how to develop computers that could adapt to the needs of the people using them as tools. My first job in the industry was at Lawrence Livermore Lab in California. I was a systems programmer, implementing magnetic fusion energy physics programs on LLL's new Cray computer. This was during the summer between my freshman and sophomore years in college. Later, I did summer internships at Bell Labs in Murray Hill, New Jersey, and at Xerox Palo Alto Research Center in California. When I got out of school I worked on expert system technology at Intellicorp for six years.

You have worked on a wide range of specialized projects—knowledge-based expert systems for 3M and other artificial intelligence software for Intellicorp, and Apple's Newton MessagePad. How difficult is it to adapt your management and engineering skills to the needs of these projects?

▲ From my point of view, everything I do uses everything I've ever learned. For example, skills I learned during childhood about valuing different perspectives of diverse people are the same skills that I used in blending a diverse engineering team for developing Newton software. I've been a relatively introverted "nerd" all my life, but my mother and sisters made sure that I developed strong verbal communication skills in addition to academic skills; now I use those communication skills every day in the workplace. My involvement in BESSA, the Black Engineering and Science Students' Association at UC Berkeley, was also very beneficial to me. Through BESSA, I met others with technology interests similar to my own; we worked on projects together to explore electrical engineering, computer science, and mechanical engineering ideas. As I took on leadership roles in BESSA, eventually serving as president, I began to develop my management and leadership skills. Technically, I draw daily from theory and practice in my engineering, science, and math background. Hands-on technical apprenticeships during college, as a complement to the theory I was learning, were invaluable in preparing me to use and re-use fundamental technical skills.

Your current position involves developing multimedia software for interactive television. How do you set expectations for the team? Do you foresee any constant obstacles to achieving the goals you establish?

▲ We're designing and implementing our broadband multimedia technology with maximum flexibility to support a variety of applications. Our customers will tell us what they're interested in when we begin field testing the early technology. The product goals develop as we receive feedback from the marketplace. We plan to listen to our customers and respond rapidly to their interests.

Major obstacles? Nothing out of the ordinary for developing new technology products. Network latencies are a foreseeable challenge. This is primarily because we are implementing the technology with

INTERVIEW

Donna Auguste

Donna Auguste is a technical director in the Multimedia Services Engineering and Development group at U S WEST Technologies. Previously, Ms. Auguste managed the Apple software engineering team that developed the industry's first Personal Digital Assistant, the Apple Newton. Her tireless commitment to projects and dynamic leadership skills have become her trademarks in the software development industry. Ms. Auguste began her studies at the University of California—Berkeley, where she earned a bachelor of science degree in electrical engineering and computer science. She then studied three years in the Carnegie-Mellon computer science Ph.D. program researching intelligent computer-aided instruction and user modeling.

computers and other network components that each require nanosecond and millisecond response times. Cumulatively, that adds up to a delay. Our customers expect response time close to an "instantaneous TV experience." We have to be creative with the technology in order to meet that expectation.

▼ **As a team manager, what are the key concepts you apply in directing your team?**

▲ LISTEN—All of us are experts at something related to our product development, so we ask each other a lot of questions and we listen to each other.
LEARN—Everyone on the team needs to constantly be in learning mode. For products based on (our!) brand-new technology, we have to realize that we're making this up as we go along.
HAVE FUN!

▼ **What next? Where do you see your career in the next few years?**

▲ There are lots of exciting options in this field. I have thoroughly enjoyed working in technology start-up environments—like my work at Intellicorp. I've also learned a tremendous amount and enjoyed working in larger corporate environments such as Apple and U S WEST. Outside of work, I devote a lot of time to learning and writing music—using a computer to help with composing and arranging—and enjoy this tremendously. My external interests, such as writing and music, may contribute to my choices in the future.

▼ **What recommendations do you have for students currently learning the introductory concepts of problem solving with computers?**

▲ I have one primary recommendation: Learn to give yourself honest feedback about progress toward your goals. Whether your goal is to master certain problem-solving techniques or to solve a very specific problem, you need to factor in input from others and give yourself your own feedback about whether or not your solution(s) will move you toward that goal. Re-examine solutions that do not move you toward your goals, and adjust them. The computer is one of many tools that you can apply to discover solutions. Understand what it can and cannot do as a problem-solving tool in your hands. Learn to trust your own intuition about how and when to use it.

CHAPTER NINE

Software Engineering and Units

software engineering
the study and use of tools and techniques for designing, coding, testing, and maintaining large software systems

The programs you've written and studied so far have been relatively short and designed to solve specific problems. Many problems, particularly those in industry, require larger, more complex programs. This type of large system programming, called *programming in the large*, is the focus of this chapter.

To implement large programs, professional programmers use a collection of tools and techniques for program design, coding, testing, and maintenance. The study and use of these tools and techniques is called **software engineering.** One technique to simplify the writing of large programs reuses code that accomplishes a particular task. In several earlier programs, you've extended problem solutions from one problem to another, but for the most part your programs were not general enough to solve more than one problem. To program a large system efficiently, the problem solution must be modularized so that many different programmers can write and test different sections of the program. Quite often a module used in one program can be part of another program. This chapter illustrates the benefits of files of modules, or *units,* in writing efficient, modular programs.

In addition to discussing how large programs are designed and written, this chapter also introduces testing techniques. Because this chapter describes concepts used by software professionals, it concludes with a discussion of professional behavior, ethics, and responsibilities.

9.1 Programming in the Large

To solve large-scale programming problems, programmers must have some way of attacking the problem systematically and managing its complexity. The techniques professional programmers use for this purpose are not very different from those you have been practicing so far. Programmers use the software development method to structure their solution, and they implement their solution by writing a collection of small, well-defined modules. Wherever possible, they reuse modules written to solve earlier problems. This section discusses how professional programmers use the software development method to develop a computer application or software system.

The System/Software Life Cycle

system/software life cycle
the steps in the development of a software system

Because the development of a software system proceeds in stages from its initial inception to its ultimate obsolescence, programmers refer to these different stages as the **system/software life cycle** (SLC). The system/software life cycle, like the software development method, consists of the following six steps:

1. Requirements specification
   a. Prepare a complete and unambiguous problem statement.
   b. Submit the requirements document to the users and analysts for review and obtain their written approval.
2. Analysis
   a. Understand the problem; determine problem outputs and required inputs.
   b. Evaluate alternative solutions.
   c. Choose the preferred solution.
3. Design
   a. Perform a top-down design of the system.
   b. For each module, identify key data elements and subordinate procedures using structure charts.

4. Implementation
   a. Write algorithms and pseudocode descriptions of individual procedures.
   b. Code the solution.
   c. Debug the code.
5. Testing and verification
   a. Test the code, verifying that it is correct.
   b. Include users and special testing teams in all system tests.
6. Operation, follow-up, and maintenance
   a. Run the completed system.
   b. Evaluate its performance.
   c. Remove new bugs as they are detected.
   d. Make required changes to keep the system up to date.
   e. Verify that changes are correct and do not adversely affect the system's operation.

Problem analysis should always precede problem solution (synthesis). Steps 1 and 2 of the SLC (requirements specification and analysis) are the analysis part, and steps 3 and 4 (design and implementation) are the synthesis part. System users take the lead in developing the initial requirements specification for a proposed software system. System analysts work closely with users to understand more thoroughly the problem requirements and to evaluate possible alternative solutions.

The SLC is iterative. During the design phase (step 3), problems may arise that necessitate modifying the requirements specification. Similarly, during implementation (step 4) it may become necessary to reconsider decisions made in the design phase. Systems analysts and system users must approve all changes.

Once implemented, the system must be thoroughly tested before entering its final stage (operation and maintenance). System changes identified in these stages may require repetition of earlier stages of the SLC to correct errors found during testing or to accommodate changes required by external sources (for example, a change in federal or state tax regulations).

Estimates vary as to the time necessary for each stage. For example, a typical system may require a year to proceed through the first four stages, three months of testing, then four or more years of operation and maintenance. Because the programmers who maintain the system may not have participated in its original design or implementation, software must be designed and documented so that it can be easily maintained.

Requirements Specification

Although we have illustrated most phases of the SLC (our software development method) in solving case studies, we have not studied in detail the requirements specification process. Programming problems used as examples for learning a programming language tend to be stated simply so that students can focus on the rudiments of the language and on programming techniques. For these reasons, each case study was preceded by a brief statement of the problem, and we began our solutions with the analysis phase.

To illustrate the requirements specification process, assume you have been given the following problem specification for a telephone directory program.

PROBLEM ▼

Write an interactive telephone directory program that contains a collection of names and telephone numbers. The directory user should be able to insert a new entry in the directory, retrieve an entry from the directory, change a directory entry, and delete a directory entry.

To plan the program, you need to know the format of the input data, the desired form of any output screens or printed forms, and the need for data validation. You might ask the user the following questions, among others:

▶ Is an initial list of names and numbers to be stored in the directory beforehand, or are all entries to be inserted at the same time? If there is an initial list, is it stored in a data file or will it be entered interactively?

▶ If the file is a text file, what are the formatting conventions (e.g., will the name start in position 1 and the phone number in position 20)? Are the name and number on the same data line or on separate lines?

▶ Is the final directory printed or stored as a file on disk?

▶ Can more than one number be associated with a particular name? If so, should the first number, the last number, or all numbers be retrieved?

▶ Is there a limit on the length of a name? How are the names stored (e.g., *lastname, firstname,* or *firstname lastname*)?

▶ Are phone numbers stored as numbers or as strings of characters? Do they contain area codes? Are there any special characters, such as hyphens and parentheses, in a phone number? Should you check for illegal characters in a number or for numbers that are too short or too long?

As you can see, the initial problem statement leaves plenty of questions unanswered. To complete the requirements specification, you should get answers to these questions and more.

Prototyping

prototyping
developing a system by
adding successive refinements
to an initial system model

An alternative to traditional system development is prototyping. In **prototyping**, systems analysts work closely with system users to develop a prototype, or model, of the actual system and refine that prototype in stages. Initially the prototype has few working features and just mimics the input/output interaction of the users with the system. At each stage, the users and the analysts decide what changes should be made and what new features should be added; these changes are then incorporated into the prototype. The process continues until a complete prototype is available that performs all the functions of the final system. The analysts and the users can then decide whether to use the prototype as the final system or as the basis of the design for a new system, which will perform the same operations as the prototype but which will be more efficient.

Programming Teams

One major difference between programming in college and in industry is that in industry it is rare for a large software project to be implemented by a single programmer. Most often, a large project is assigned to a team of programmers after the problem specification and analysis phases are complete. The team members then coordinate the overall organization of the project and meet regularly to exchange information and report progress.

Each team member is responsible for a set of modules, some of which may be accessed by other team members. After the initial organizational meeting, each team member should provide the other members with a specification for each procedure that he or she is implementing. Such a specification is similar to the documentation provided for each procedure in this text. It consists of a brief statement of the purpose of the procedure, its pre- and postconditions, and its formal parameter list. This information is all that a potential user of the procedure needs to know to call the procedure correctly.

Normally one team member acts as "librarian" by assuming responsibility for determining the status of each module in the system. Initially, the library of modules consists of a stub for each new module. As a module is completed and tested, its updated version replaces the version currently in the library. The librarian keeps track of the date that each version of a module is inserted into the library and makes sure that all programmers use the latest version of any module.

Section 9.2 discusses some techniques used to modularize a large program and to build libraries of modules in Turbo Pascal.

Exercises for Section 9.1   ***Self-Check***

1. Which phase or phases of the software life cycle are of most concern to the systems analyst? To the librarian?
2. List the six phases of the software life cycle. Which phase is usually the longest?

9.2 Introduction to Units

Whether programming as an individual or as a member of a team, we must be able to divide a program into a set of self-contained modules. In standard Pascal, these modules can be procedures or functions. Turbo Pascal offers an additional construct for building modular programs: units. The philosophy behind modular programming is one we've used in small programs: procedural abstraction.

Procedural Abstraction Revisited

Procedural abstraction is the philosophy that procedure development should separate the concern of *what* is to be achieved by a procedure from the details of *how* it is to be achieved. In other words, you can specify what you expect a procedure to do, then use that procedure in the design of a problem solution before you know how to implement the procedure.

To visualize the process, consider the implementation of two steps of an algorithm coded as procedure calls in the main program:

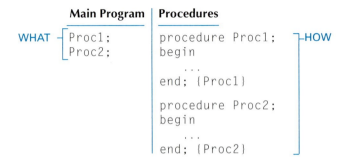

The main program calls two procedures, Proc1 and Proc2, to accomplish its first two tasks. The details of how these tasks are to be accomplished will be provided in the procedure declarations for Proc1 and Proc2 when they are written.

The practice of procedural abstraction in programming is analogous to following a recipe in cooking. An inexperienced cook working alone might follow without deviation each step in the recipe in the sequence in which it is listed. An experienced chef, on the other hand, would do much of the preparatory work (such as chopping ingredients, preparing the sauce) ahead of time or distribute these assignments to helpers. The chef would not care how, or in what sequence, these tasks were completed, as long as they were ready before needed in the final assembly and cooking. The experienced chef is using procedural abstraction, while the inexperienced cook is not.

Procedural Abstraction and Units

unit
a compilable Turbo Pascal file that can contain constant, variable, and type declarations and procedure and function modules

importing a unit
enabling access to a unit's constants, variables, data types, and modules in another unit or main program

You can realize the potential of procedural abstraction more fully with Turbo Pascal than with standard Pascal. Once you have designed and implemented a procedure that has some general use, Turbo Pascal (but not standard Pascal) allows you to encapsulate that procedure with others in your own library module or **unit**. You can then **import** that procedure into another program that needs the same operation performed and call it to carry out the operation. In that way, you can truly separate the *what* from the *how*. You can use a procedure as long as you know what it does and how to call it, even if you have no idea how the procedure is implemented.

You can save Turbo Pascal units as separate files on disk. A unit can contain related constants, data types, variables, procedures, and functions. When you write and save the unit, you should give it the extension .PAS. You can compile units separately from the programs that use them and correct any syntax errors in the units. If the source code for the unit is in file MYSTUFF.PAS, Turbo Pascal will save the object code in the file MYSTUFF.TPU (Turbo Pascal Unit).

Accessing Units with the uses Statement

Placing a uses statement at the start of a program makes a unit accessible to that program. For example, the statement

```
uses MyStuff, NewUtilities, Printer;
```

specifies the names of three units—MyStuff, NewUtilities, and Printer —whose object code will be linked to the program containing the uses statement. When the program is compiled, any identifiers referenced in the program but declared elsewhere will be imported from the unit in which they are declared. The object code for the complete program will include the object code for only those procedures and functions declared in a unit that are actually referenced by the program.

Figure 9.1 illustrates the process of separately compiling a unit and linking it to a program. The unit must be compiled before the main program.

Turbo Pascal assumes that the object code for a user-defined unit is stored in a disk file whose name consists of the unit name followed by the extension .TPU. If the unit name is longer than eight characters (e.g., unit NewUtilities), Turbo Pascal will look for a disk file whose name consists of the first eight characters of the unit name (NEWUTILI.TPU).

There are several advantages to using previously compiled units:

▶ The object code for procedures in units is accessible, thereby saving compilation time.

▶ The new programs that are written will be simpler and more concise because they need not contain declarations for constants, variables, data types, procedures, or functions defined in previously compiled units.

▶ It is easier to debug a program system that uses tried and tested procedures contained in a library unit instead of new, untested procedures.

▶ It is easier to apportion a large project to individual programming team members. If each team member's modules are saved as a unit in a separate file, other team members can import these modules as needed through a uses statement.

▶ The details of a unit's code can be changed without requiring recompilation of the programs that use it.

Figure 9.1
Compiling and Linking a Unit to a Program

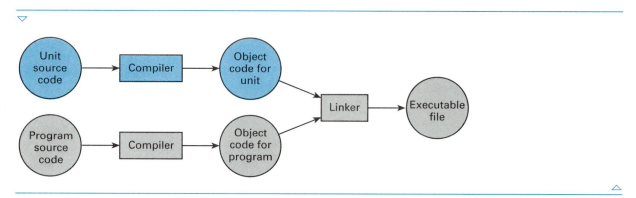

SYNTAX DISPLAY

Uses Statement

Form: uses *unitlist*;

Example: uses Printer, Crt, EnterData;

Interpretation: The Turbo Pascal compiler must import portions of the object code for units listed in *unitlist* when generating the object code for a program or another unit containing the uses statement.

Note 1: The units contained in the Turbo Pascal run-time library (Printer, Crt, Dos, etc.) are stored in the disk file TURBO.TPL. All other units are assumed to reside in the disk files whose names are derived from the first eight characters of the unit name with the extension .TPU.

Note 2: Turbo Pascal first looks in the current directory to find the object code file for a given unit. If the file is not found, Turbo Pascal looks in the directory for Unit directories (specified in the Directories submenu of the Options menu).

In the following sections, we will discuss two predefined units that are provided in Turbo Pascal and show how to write your own units.

Exercises for Section 9.2   *Self-Check*

1. What two pieces of information must you know about a library procedure before you can call it?
2. In what file would Turbo Pascal expect to find the object code for a unit named MyTools? How does Turbo Pascal determine the directory in which this file resides?

9.3   Predefined Units and User Interfaces

Turbo Pascal comes with several predefined and precompiled units, which are described in Appendix B. In the optional graphics sections, we showed how to use unit Graph to generate graphics output. In this section, we describe unit Printer, which you can use to send program results directly to the printer. We also describe unit Crt, which provides additional capability for keyboard input and screen output, enabling you to create your own dialog boxes or *user interfaces* for your programs.

Unit Printer

Unit Printer declares file variable Lst, associates it with the system printer, and opens the output file associated with the printer. The program in Fig. 9.2 prints the contents of a text file. Compare it to program CopyFile in Fig. 8.6, which copies a file. Because Lst is its first parameter, the WriteLn statement

Figure 9.2
Printing a File

Edit Window

```
program PrintFile;
{Prints a data file by writing every line to the printer.}

uses Printer;              {Associate file Lst with the printer.}

  var
    InFile : Text;         {input file}
    InFileName,            {directory name of input file}
    Line       : string;   {each file line}

begin {PrintFile}
  {Prepare data file for input.}
  Write ('File to be printed> ');
  ReadLn (InFileName);              {Get name of InFile.}
  Assign (InFile, InFileName);
  Reset (InFile);                   {Open InFile for input.}

  {Print the data file line by line.}
  while not EOF(InFile) do
    begin
      ReadLn (InFile, Line);        {Read next line.}
      WriteLn (Lst, Line)           {Send it to the printer.}
    end; {while}

  {Close the file.}
  Close (InFile);
  WriteLn ('File ', InFileName, ' is printed.')
end. {PrintFile}
```

Output Window

```
File to be printed> A:MYDATA.TXT
File A:MYDATA.TXT is printed.
```

```
WriteLn (Lst, Line)              {Send it to the printer.}
```

sends its output list (`string` variable `Line`) to the printer instead of to the screen.

Unit Crt

Unit `Crt` contains several procedures that provide you with more control over the keyboard and display screen. The screen (Fig. 9.3) consists of a grid of character positions with 80 columns (*X*-dimension) and 25 rows (*Y*-dimension). Instead of using the full screen for data entry and display, you can use a subarea of the screen, or a **window.** Procedure `Window` defines a rectangular text window on the screen and moves the cursor to the top-left corner of the window. Procedure `ClrScr` (Clear Screen) clears the current window, removing any characters that were displayed. Procedure `GoToXY` moves the cursor to a specified row and column of the current window.

Procedures `TextBackground` and `TextColor` specify the background color of the current window and the color of text, respectively. Each procedure has one parameter, a color constant, chosen from the list shown in Table 9.1. Use either the constant name or its numeric value as a parameter (e.g., `Red` or 4). Once you change the background color or text color, it retains its new value until you change it again. For background color, select a constant less than or equal to 7.

window

a rectangular subarea of the screen used for data entry and display

Figure 9.3
Screen as a Grid of
Character Positions

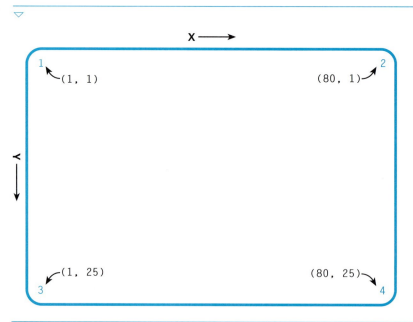

Table 9.1
Color Constants

Constant	Value	Constant	Value
Black	0	DarkGray	8
Blue	1	LightBlue	9
Green	2	LightGreen	10
Cyan	3	LightCyan	11
Red	4	LightRed	12
Magenta	5	LightMagenta	13
Brown	6	Yellow	14
LightGray	7	White	15

EXAMPLE 9.1: Procedures Restore and PopUpWindow ▼

Figure 9.4 shows two procedures to create dialog boxes for data entry. The first procedure, Restore, resets the screen to its normal mode. The statement

```
Window (1, 1, 80, 25);      {Full screen display}
```

defines a text window from point (1, 1), the top-left character position, to point (80, 25), the bottom-right character position. The next statements set the background color to black, set the text color to white, and clear the screen.

Procedure PopUpWindow displays a dialog box for data entry with a prompting message, Prompt, displayed inside it. The statement

```
Window (20, 10, 60, 15);          {Center the dialog box.}
```

defines a window with 41 columns and 6 rows in the center of the screen. The statements

```
TextBackground (WinColor);                    {Set box color.}
ClrScr;                                        {Clear the box.}
GoToXY (5, 3);                          {Go to third row of box.}
WriteLn (Prompt);
```

show the box in its background color, WinColor, and display the message Prompt in row 3 of the box. The statement

```
Window (24, 14, 24 + WinSize, 14);   {Define 1-line window.}
```

defines a one-line data entry window at row 14 of the full screen display (row 4 of the dialog box) with capacity for WinSize characters. The next statements show this window in gray and display the prompt symbol > in black.

Figure 9.4

Procedures Restore and
PopUpWindow

```
procedure Restore;
{
 Resets the display to a full screen and clears it.
 Pre : none
 Post: Display screen is cleared.
}
begin {Restore}
   Window (1, 1, 80, 25);     {Full screen display}
   TextBackground (Black);
   TextColor (White);
   ClrScr                     {Clear the screen.}
end; {Restore}

procedure PopUpWindow (Prompt {input} : string;
                       WinSize,
                       WinColor {input} : Integer);
{
 Displays a dialog box for entering one data item.
 Pre : none
 Post: Displays a box with color WinColor containing
       the message Prompt. Up to WinSize characters
       may be typed in a 1-line data entry window.
}
begin {PopUpWindow}
   Window (20, 10, 60, 15);           {Center the dialog box.}
   TextBackground (WinColor);              {Set box color.}
   ClrScr;                                 {Clear the box.}
   GoToXY (5, 3);                    {Go to third row of box.}
   WriteLn (Prompt);
   Window (24, 14, 24 + WinSize, 14); {Define 1-line window.}
   TextBackground (LightGray);
   TextColor (Black);
   ClrScr;                        {Clear the data entry window.}
   Write ('>')                {Display prompt symbol in window.}
end; {PopUpWindow}
```

You can use the statements

```
PopUpWindow ('Check amount', 10, Blue); {Display box.}
ReadLn (Check);
Restore
```

to create a dialog box for reading a value into variable Check (Fig. 9.5). After the data characters are typed in the data entry window, ReadLn reads
the data into variable Check and Restore resets the screen to its normal
mode. ▲

A summary of unit Crt procedures and functions is given in Table 9.2.

Figure 9.5
Dialog Box Created by
PopUpWindow

Table 9.2
Summary of Crt Procedures
and Functions

Procedure or Function Call	Effect
Window (X1, Y1, X2, Y2)	Defines a text window on the screen with top-left corner at (X1, Y1) and bottom-right corner at (X2, Y2), where X1, X2 range from 1 to 80 and Y1, Y2 range from 1 to 25. The cursor is placed at (X1, Y1).
ClrScr	Clears the current window, displaying it in the background color. Places the cursor at the window's top-left corner.
GoToXY (X, Y)	Places the cursor at point (X, Y) in the current window where (1, 1) denotes the top-left corner of the window.
TextBackground (Color)	Sets the background color of the current window to Color, a constant from 0 to 7.
TextColor (Color)	Sets the color of text in the current window to Color, a constant from 0 to 15.
Delay (DelayTime)	Pauses approximately DelayTime milliseconds.
KeyPressed	Returns true if a key has been pressed; otherwise, returns false.

Self-Check

1. Sketch the user interface created by the following fragment:

```
Restore;
Window (20, 10, 60, 20);
TextBackground (Blue); ClrScr;
GoToXY (1, 1);
Write ('Enter C for check, D for deposit >');
ReadLn (CheckOrDepositChar);
GoToXY (1, 6);
Write ('Enter Amount $');
ReadLn (Amount)
```

Programming

1. Write a program that allows you to use the printer as a typewriter so that every line of text entered by the user is printed on the printer. End the program by entering a blank line.
2. Write a procedure that colors the four quarters of the screen in blue, green, red, and magenta.

9.4 Writing New Units

You can use your own units in much the same way you use predefined units. You can compile each unit individually, and later Turbo Pascal can link the object code for a procedure in a compiled unit to a program that calls it. This section discusses how to create and use your own units.

Efficient programmers write library procedures to perform useful operations that are not included in Pascal. For example, because Pascal's ReadLn procedure cannot read a Boolean value, you might want to write your own input procedure that does this. Another useful input procedure is one that reads and returns an integer value within a specified range (e.g., an integer from −5 to +5). Next, we discuss a unit that contains these procedures.

Unit EnterData

The structure of a unit is similar to the structure of a Turbo Pascal program. The first line of a unit begins with the reserved word unit instead of program, and end. is the last line of a unit.

Unit EnterData (Fig. 9.6) contains the two input procedures just discussed, ReadLnBool and EnterInt, as well as procedures Restore and PopUpWindow from the previous section. It also declares a variable, CountBad, which counts the number of times EnterInt is called with an invalid range.

Figure 9.6
Unit EnterData

```
unit EnterData;
{
 Contains procedures Restore, PopUpWindow, ReadLnBool, and
 EnterInt. Variable CountBad counts the number of times
 EnterInt is called with an invalid range.
}
interface
  uses Crt;                {EnterData is a client of unit Crt.}

  var
    CountBad : Integer;    {Count of bad data ranges}

  procedure Restore;
  {
   Resets the display to a full screen and clears it.
   Pre : none
   Post: Display screen is cleared.
  }

  procedure PopUpWindow (Prompt {input} : string;
                             WinSize,
                             WinColor {input} : Integer);
  {
   Displays a dialog box for entering one data item.
   Pre : none
   Post: Displays a box with color WinColor containing
         the message Prompt. Up to WinSize characters
         may be typed in a 1-line data entry window.
  }

  procedure ReadLnBool (var BoolVal {output} : Boolean);
  {
   Reads a Boolean value (represented by a T or F) into
   BoolVal.
   Pre : none
   Post: BoolVal is set to True if T or t is read;
         otherwise, BoolVal is set to False.
  }

  procedure EnterInt (MinN, MaxN {input} : Integer;
                       var N {output} : Integer);
  {
   Reads an integer between MinN and MaxN into N. Increases
   CountBad by 1 if range is invalid.
   Pre : MinN and MaxN are assigned values.
   Post: Returns in N the first data value between MinN and
         MaxN if MinN <= MaxN is true; otherwise, N is not
         defined and CountBad is increased by 1.
  }
```

▷ ▷ ▷ ▷ ▷ ▷

```
implementation
  {Insert procedures Restore and PopUpWindow from Fig. 9.4.}

  procedure ReadLnBool (var BoolVal {output} : Boolean);
    var
      NextChar : Char;             {data character}

  begin {ReadLnBool}
    repeat
      Write ('Type T or F> ');
      ReadLn (NextChar);
      NextChar := Upcase(NextChar);
      BoolVal := (NextChar = 'T')        {Is NextChar 'T'?}
    until (NextChar = 'T') or (NextChar = 'F')
  end; {ReadLnBool}


  procedure EnterInt (MinN, MaxN {input} : Integer;
                          var N {output} : Integer);
    var
      InRange : Boolean;  {program flag - loop control}

  begin {EnterInt}
    if MinN <= MaxN then
      InRange := False       {no valid value in N as yet}
    else
      begin
        WriteLn ('Error - empty range for EnterInt');
        CountBad := CountBad + 1;
        InRange := True     {Skip data entry loop.}
      end; {if}

    {Keep reading until valid number is read.}
    while not InRange do
      begin
        Write ('Enter an integer from ');
        Write (MinN :1, ' to ', MaxN :1, '> ');
        ReadLn (N);
        InRange := (MinN <= N) and (N <= MaxN)  {Is N valid?}
      end {while}
  end; {EnterInt}

begin {EnterData}
  CountBad := 0                    {no bad entries read yet}
end. {EnterData}
```

interface section (public part)

the part of a unit that contains information needed by a programmer to use the unit and by Turbo Pascal to compile it

A unit consists of two required sections, interface and implementation, and one optional section, initialization. The **interface section** of a unit begins with the reserved word interface and is called the **public part** of a unit because it contains all the information that a programmer needs to know to use the unit. It also contains all declarations required by the Turbo

client
the user (a program or another unit) of a unit

Pascal compiler to check that a unit is being used correctly by a program or another unit (called a **client**). The procedure headings in the interface section describe the function performed by each procedure.

The scope of identifiers declared in the interface section includes all clients of the unit, so these identifiers are considered *visible* to a client. Any constant, type, and variable declarations are written using the usual Pascal syntax. However, only procedure headings and documentation appear in the interface section; procedure bodies appear in the implementation section.

implementation section (private part)
the part of a unit that contains procedure and function declarations and other declarations (constants, variables, and data types) that are used internally by the unit

The **implementation section** contains complete declarations for procedures and functions whose headings appear in the interface section. There also may be some new identifiers declared in the implementation section. Because the new identifiers cannot be accessed outside the unit, the implementation section is called the **private part** of the unit, and the new identifiers and procedure bodies are said to be *hidden* from a user.

When writing the implementation section, you needn't repeat the parameter lists for procedures first listed in the interface section. If parameter lists are included for those procedures, however, they must be identical to those appearing in the interface section. We recommend that you include the parameter lists in both interface and implementation sections so Turbo Pascal can check that they match. Because of space limitations, we have omitted the procedure documentation, which already appears in the unit interface section.

The end of a unit is indicated by the line

```
end.
```

initialization section
the part of a unit that contains initialization code for variables declared in the unit

There is no need to have a corresponding begin unless the unit has an initialization section. The **initialization section** assigns initial values to any unit variables, and it executes before any client of the unit. In Fig. 9.6, the initialization section sets CountBad to 0, and procedure EnterInt increases the value of CountBad by 1 each time it is called with an invalid range.

SYNTAX DISPLAY

Unit Definition

Form: unit *unitname*;

interface
    public declarations

implementation
    private declarations
    public procedure and function declarations
    initialization section
end.

Example: `unit TwoItems;`

```
interface
  procedure SwapTwo (var X, Y {input/output} :
                            Real);
  {
   Swaps two real values.
   Pre : X, Y are defined.
   Post: X is old Y and Y is old X.
  }

implementation
  procedure SwapTwo (var X, Y {input/output} :
                            Real);
    var Temp : Real;
  begin {SwapTwo}
    Temp := X;
    X := Y;
    Y := Temp
  end; {SwapTwo}

end. {TwoItems}
```

Interpretation: Unit *unitname* is a separate program module that can be compiled to disk and then used by other units or programs. The interface part contains *public declarations*. The public identifiers can be referenced by any program or unit that lists *unitname* in its `uses` statement. For public procedures and functions, only their headings appear in the interface part; their complete declarations appear in the implementation part.

The implementation part contains *private declarations* as well as declarations for public procedures and functions. Any private identifiers declared in the implementation part cannot be referenced outside unit *unitname*.

If present, the *initialization* section starts with the reserved word `begin` and is used to initialize any variables declared in the unit. It executes before the client program.

Notes: Unit *unitname* may be a client of other units. If so, the other units must be listed in a `uses` statement that follows the `interface` line or the `implementation` line in unit *unitname*. If a unit is listed after the `interface` line, its public identifiers may be referenced anywhere in unit *unitname* and in its clients. If a unit is listed after the `implementation` line, its public identifiers may be referenced only in the implementation part of unit *unitname*.

Program Style

Validating a Library Procedure's Parameters

Procedure `EnterInt` begins by checking whether its user correctly entered its input parameters, `MinN` and `MaxN`. If the parameters define an empty range, an error message is displayed and the `while` loop is skipped. Make sure that you carefully validate input parameters for procedures that are candidates for inclusion in a library. Since library procedures can be reused many times and by many different programmers, this extra effort can pay valuable dividends.

Units Using Other Units

A unit can be the client of another unit. You would indicate this fact by placing the `uses` statement right after the reserved word `interface` or `implementation` in the client unit. The position of the `uses` statement determines the scope of identifiers imported into the client unit. The statement sequence

```
interface
    uses Crt;                  {EnterData is a client of unit Crt.}
```

in Fig. 9.6 enables you to reference identifiers declared in unit `Crt` anywhere in unit `EnterData`.

If you use the statement sequence

```
implementation
    uses Crt;                  {EnterData is a client of unit Crt.}
```

instead, you can reference identifiers declared in unit `Crt` only in unit `EnterData`'s implementation section. This would not cause an error because all references to unit `Crt`'s procedures appear in the implementation section of `EnterData` (inside procedures `Restore` and `PopUpWindow`).

Compiling and Using Your Own Units

Before you can use unit `EnterData`—or any unit that is not predefined—you should compile it to disk. To compile a program or a unit to disk, first load the source file into the Edit window and then select the Compile menu. When the Compile menu is displayed, press the D key to change the storage destination for the object code from Memory to Disk. (To change the destination back to Memory, simply press the D key again.) After changing the destination to Disk, you can compile your unit. Compiling a unit to disk creates an object code file with the extension `.TPU`; compiling a program to disk creates an object code file with the extension `.EXE` (i.e., an EXEcutable file).

The Turbo Pascal compiler expects to find the object code for a unit used by a client program in a file that has a name derived from the first eight characters of the unit name followed by the extension `.TPU`. If the statement

```
uses EnterData;
```

appears in a client program, Turbo Pascal will link file `ENTERDAT.TPU` with the object code for the program being compiled. If file `ENTERDAT.TPU` does not exist, or Turbo Pascal cannot find it, you will get a `File not found` error.

Once unit `EnterData` has been compiled to disk, you can use it just as you would the predefined unit `Printer`. However, since a client program may be on a different disk or directory than the .TPU files it imports, you may need to use the Options menu to tell the Turbo Pascal compiler where your .TPU files reside before you compile a client program or unit. To do so, select the Options menu, then highlight and select the Directories option, as shown in Fig. 9.7. This will cause the Directories dialog box to appear on screen (see Fig. 9.8).

Figure 9.7
Turbo Pascal Options
Menu

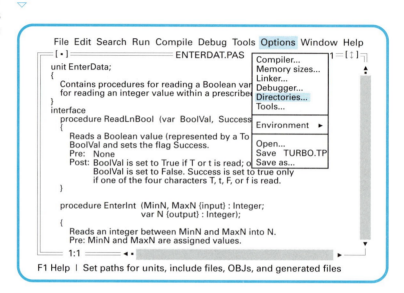

Figure 9.8
Turbo Pascal Directories
Dialog Box

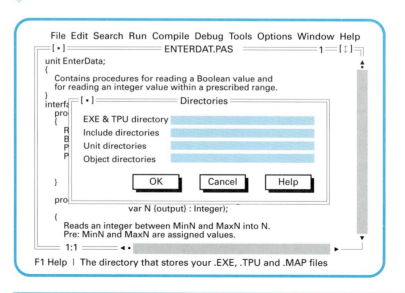

The EXE & TPU directory field will be selected by default. You should type an MS-DOS path specification telling Turbo Pascal where your .TPU files are located. A path specification can consist of a disk drive name (e.g., A:), a disk drive name followed by a subdirectory name (e.g., C:\PASCAL), or a subdirectory name by itself (e.g., \TP\TOOLS). If your .TPU files reside in several disk locations, you can give a list of path specifications with the items separated by semicolons (e.g., A:;C:\PASCAL;\TP\TOOLS). Pressing the Enter key after typing a path specification closes the dialog box.

EXAMPLE 9.2 ▼

A driver program that tests procedures ReadLnBool and EnterInt is shown in Fig. 9.9. This program can be compiled and run in the normal way. ReadLnBool returns True to variable NextBool, and EnterInt returns 0 to variable Num. The driver program displays these values and the final value of variable CountBad, declared in unit EnterData.   ▲

Figure 9.9
Program TestEnterData

Edit Window

```pascal
program TestEnterData;
{Tests procedures in unit EnterData.}

  uses EnterData;

  var
    NextBool : Boolean;      {input - Boolean data value}
    Num : Integer;           {input - an in-range integer}

begin {TestEnterData}
  ReadLnBool (NextBool);       {Read a Boolean into NextBool.}
  WriteLn ('Boolean value read was ', NextBool); WriteLn;

  EnterInt (5, -5, Num);       {Read an integer from 5 to -5.}
  EnterInt (-5, 5, Num);       {Read an integer from -5 to 5.}
  WriteLn ('Integer read was ', Num :1);
  WriteLn (CountBad :1, ' invalid data range for EnterInt.')
end. {TestEnterData}
```

Output Window

```
Type T or F> b
Type T or F> t
Boolean value read was TRUE

Error - empty range for EnterInt
Enter an integer from -5 to 5> 0
Integer read was 0
1 invalid data range for EnterInt.
```

Exercises for Section 9.4   ***Self-Check***

1. Why is it important that, when library procedures change, the procedure parameters remain the same?

Programming

1. Write procedure `EnterChar` that returns a data character that lies within a specified range of characters. Your procedure should display an error message if the specified range is invalid.
2. Write a program that tests the procedure written in Programming Exercise 1. Describe how you can effectively test the procedure using this test program, and list all input you will use for testing.

9.5   Units and Abstract Data Types

In many programming problems, you need to process information relating to the day of the week. To facilitate this processing, you can declare an enumerated type `Day` that has as its values the days of the week. You would have to write your own procedures for reading and writing the days of the week, because Pascal cannot read and write enumerated type values directly. In Turbo Pascal, you can place the data type and procedure declarations in the same unit. This combination of a data type and procedures for processing that type is called an **abstract data type (ADT)**. We will discuss abstract data types further in Chapter 13.

abstract data type (ADT)
a combination of a data type and procedures and functions for manipulating the data type

Figure 9.10 shows a unit, `DayADT`, that implements the abstract data type just described. It begins with the type declaration for `Day`. Clients of the ADT must be able to reference data type `Day`, so its declaration appears in the interface section of the unit. Next come the headings for procedures `ReadLnDay` and `WriteDay`, along with comments documenting each procedure. As before, the procedure bodies appear in the unit's implementation section.

Figure 9.10
Unit DayADT

```
unit DayADT;
{
 Abstract data type Day: contains declarations for enumerated
 type Day and procedures for reading and displaying values of
 type Day.
}

interface                          {type specification}
   type
      Day = (Sunday, Monday, Tuesday, Wednesday,
             Thursday, Friday, Saturday);
```

▷ ▷ ▷ ▷ ▷ ▷

```
procedure ReadLnDay (var OneDay {output} : Day);
{
  Reads a value into OneDay.
  Pre : None.
  Post: OneDay is assigned a value when the two characters
        read are SU, MO, TU, WE, TH, FR, or SA;
        Value of OneDay corresponds to data characters.
}

procedure WriteDay (OneDay {input} : Day);
{
  Displays the value of OneDay.
  Pre : OneDay is defined.
  Post: Displays OneDay as a string.
}

implementation                {procedure definitions}

procedure ReadLnDay (var OneDay {output} : Day);
  var
    DayCh1,               {input - first letter in day}
    DayCh2  : Char;       {input - second letter in day}
    ValidDay : Boolean;   {flag - indicates if data are valid}

begin {ReadLnDay}
  repeat
    Write ('Enter the first two letters of the day name> ');
    ReadLn (DayCh1, DayCh2);
    DayCh1 := Upcase(DayCh1);
    DayCh2 := Upcase(DayCh2);

    {Convert to day of week}
    ValidDay := True;                     {Assume valid day.}
    if (DayCh1 = 'S') and (DayCh2 = 'U') then
      OneDay := Sunday
    else if (DayCh1 = 'M') and (DayCh2 = 'O') then
      OneDay := Monday
    else if (DayCh1 = 'T') and (DayCh2 = 'U') then
      OneDay := Tuesday
    else if (DayCh1 = 'W') and (DayCh2 = 'E') then
      OneDay := Wednesday
    else if (DayCh1 = 'T') and (DayCh2 = 'H') then
      OneDay := Thursday
    else if (DayCh1 = 'F') and (DayCh2 = 'R') then
      OneDay := Friday
    else if (DayCh1 = 'S') and (DayCh2 = 'A') then
      OneDay := Saturday
    else
      ValidDay := False     {Day is invalid - repeat loop}
  until ValidDay
end; {ReadLnDay}
```

▷ ▷ ▷ ▷ ▷ ▷

```
procedure WriteDay (OneDay {input} : Day);

begin {WriteDay}
  case OneDay of
    Sunday    : Write ('Sunday');
    Monday    : Write ('Monday');
    Tuesday   : Write ('Tuesday');
    Wednesday : Write ('Wednesday');
    Thursday  : Write ('Thursday');
    Friday    : Write ('Friday');
    Saturday  : Write ('Saturday')
  end {case}
end; {WriteDay}

end. {DayADT}
```

EXAMPLE 9.3 ▼

The program shown in Fig. 9.11 is a driver program that tests unit DayADT. It reads and displays the "day of the week" stored in variable Today (type Day). Notice that WriteDay does not advance the cursor to the next line, so we used the statement pair

```
WriteDay (Today);
WriteLn;
```

to display the value of Today and to advance the cursor.   ▲

Figure 9.11
Testing Unit DayADT

Edit Window

```
program TestDay;
{
  Test abstract data type DayADT.
  Imports: Day, ReadLnDay, WriteDay from DayADT (Fig. 9.10)
}
  uses DayADT;

  var
    Today : Day;              {input - day being read}

begin {TestDay}
  WriteLn ('What day is Today?');
  ReadLnDay (Today);
  Write ('Today is ');
  WriteDay (Today);
  WriteLn;
  if Today = Sunday then
    WriteLn ('Today is the first day of the week')
end. {TestDay}
```

Output Window

```
What day is today?
Enter the first two letters of the day name> SU
Today is Sunday
Today is the first day of the week
```

Self-Check

1. Draw a structure chart for program `TestDay` that shows the data flow between program procedures.

Programming

1. Write an ADT `MonthADT` that contains the declaration for an enumerated type `Month`, procedures `ReadMonth` and `WriteMonth`, and function `MonthEquivalent`. Function `MonthEquivalent` has an integer argument of 1 through 12 and returns a value of type `Month`.
2. Write a client program that tests your `MonthADT`.

9.6 Debugging with Units

Earlier we stated that you should debug and test all procedures in a unit before making them a permanent part of your programming library. Since it is not possible to execute a unit's source file directly, you will need to write a driver program to test its procedures. Once you have thoroughly tested a unit's procedures, you can assume that their execution in future programs will be error free.

Turbo Pascal's integrated debugger lets you use the F8 key (Run/Step Over) when the next statement is a call to a library procedure in a unit. The F7 key (Run/Trace Into) can be used to step through each statement in a procedure defined in a unit. Unit names, followed by a period, can be used to qualify Watch variable expressions if variables with the same name have been declared in different units (e.g., `MyTools.Ch` references variable `Ch` declared in unit `MyTools`).

When debugging a large program that uses several program units, it often is difficult to keep track of where you are in the program. In this case, you can use the Search menu Find procedure to help locate the source code for a particular procedure. Begin by selecting the Search menu and then the Find procedure option, as shown in Fig. 9.12.

Figure 9.12
Turbo Pascal Search Menu

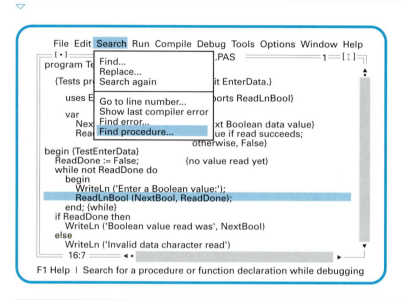

Figure 9.13
Turbo Pascal Find
Procedure Dialog Box

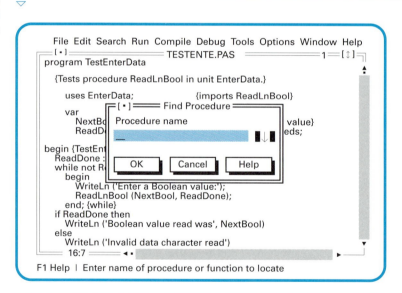

The Find Procedure dialog box will then appear on the screen (Fig. 9.13). If you type the name of a procedure in the Procedure name field, the debugger will search the various source files used by your program. If the search is successful, the debugger will load the appropriate source file into a new Edit window. You can use a unit name to qualify the procedure name if the same procedure name has been declared in more than one unit.

It is important to note that the Find procedure command does not change the current debugging state. This means that the next line to be executed in your program will be the same before and after the use of Find procedure. To have your program execute up to the first line of the procedure located by Find procedure, press function key F4 (Go to Cursor).

So far we have discussed how Turbo Pascal units can help you write large programs by making it easier to reuse code that has been previously written and tested. In the next two sections, we will discuss techniques for testing and verifying large programs.

Exercise for Section 9.6   **Self-Check**

1. When would it be appropriate to trace the source code for a procedure when debugging with units? When would it be appropriate to step over?

9.7 Testing Large Programs

It doesn't matter how carefully designed and efficient a program is if it doesn't do what it is supposed to do. One way to show that a program is correct is by testing it. But how much testing should be done? Often errors appear in a software product after it is delivered, some of the more notable errors having caused power brownouts, telephone network saturation, and space flight delays.

Preparing a Test Plan Early

A test plan specifies how the software will be tested, when the tests will take place, and who will do the testing. Normally, testing is done by the programmer, by other members of the programming team who did not code the module being tested, and by users of the software product. Some companies have special testing groups that are expert at finding bugs in other programmers' code.

Even though testing and verification appear at the end of the system life cycle, software development will proceed more smoothly if you consider the tests that each module will go through as it is being designed. If the test plan is developed early in the design stage, testing can take place concurrently with design and coding. The earlier an error is detected, the easier and less expensive it is to correct.

By thinking about testing early, you can write each module so that it will be able to handle correctly many situations that would otherwise cause problems or execution errors. A good programmer will practice **defensive programming** and include code that detects unexpected or invalid data values. For example, if a procedure has the precondition

```
{Pre : N greater than zero}
```

it would be a good idea to place the `if` statement

```
if N <= 0 then
  WriteLn ('Invalid value for parameter N - ', N :1);
```

at the beginning of the procedure. This `if` statement will provide a diagnostic message in the event that the parameter passed to the procedure is invalid.

Similarly, if a data value read from the keyboard is supposed to be between 0 and 40, a defensive programmer would use procedure `EnterInt` from unit `EnterData` (see Fig. 9.6), as shown next:

```
WriteLn ('Enter number of hours worked:');
EnterInt (Hours, 0, 40)
```

The second and third parameters of `EnterInt` define the range of acceptable values for its first parameter.

Structured Walkthroughs

In one important testing technique, called a **structured walkthrough,** the programmer describes, or "walks through," the logic of a new module as part of a presentation to other members of the programming team. During the walkthrough, team members attempt to identify design errors or bugs that the programmer may have overlooked before they become part of the code.

Black Box Versus White Box Testing

There are two ways to test a module or a complete system: black box, or specification-based, testing and white box testing. **Black box testing** assumes that the program tester has no idea of the code inside the module or system. The tester's job is to verify that the module does what its specification says it will. For a procedure, this means ensuring that its postconditions are satisfied whenever its preconditions have been met. For a system, this means ensuring that it does indeed satisfy its original requirements specification. Because the tester cannot look inside the module or system, he or she must prepare sufficient sets of test data to determine that the system outputs are correct for all valid system inputs. The tester especially should check the **system boundaries**, that is, particular values for the program variables where the system performance changes. A boundary for a payroll program would be the value of hours worked that triggers overtime pay. Moreover, the

defensive programming
guarding against program failure due to invalid data entry

structured walkthrough
a detailed, step-by-step presentation of the algorithm to other members of the programming team whose purpose is to find design errors overlooked by the programmer

black box testing
a testing process that assumes that the tester has no knowledge of the code; tester must compare a system's performance with its specification

system boundaries
values that cause a change in system performance

white box testing
a testing process that assumes the tester knows how the system is coded and requires checking all possible execution paths

module or system should not crash when presented with invalid inputs. Black box testing most often is done by a special testing team or by program users.

In **white box testing,** the tester has full knowledge of the code for the module or system and must verify that each and every section of code has been thoroughly tested. For a selection statement (`if` or `case`), this means checking all possible paths through the selection statement. The tester must determine that the correct path is chosen for all possible values of the selection variable, taking special care at the boundary values where the path changes.

For a loop, the tester must check that it always performs the correct number of iterations and that the number of iterations is not off by 1. The tester must also verify that the computations inside the loop are correct at the boundaries, that is, for the initial and final values of the loop-control variable. Finally, the tester must make sure that the module or system still meets its specification when a loop executes zero times and that there are no circumstances under which the loop could execute forever.

Integration Testing

Section 6.7 discussed the differences between top-down and bottom-up testing. Another type of testing is called *integration testing.* In integration testing, the program tester must determine whether the individual components of a system that have been tested separately (using top-down or bottom-up testing or some combination) can be integrated with other like components. Each phase of integration testing deals with larger units, progressing from individual modules, through subsystems, and ending with the entire system. For example, after two subsystems have been completed, integration testing must determine whether the two subsystems can work together. Once the entire system has been completed, integration testing must determine whether that system is compatible with other systems in the computing environment in which it will be used.

Exercises for Section 9.7   ***Self-Check***

1. Explain why a procedure interface error would not be discovered through white box testing.
2. Devise a set of data to test procedure `EnterInt` (Fig. 9.6) using each of the following:
   a. White box testing
   b. Black box testing

9.8   Formal Methods of Program Verification

In Section 9.7, we asked, How much testing is enough? Although we described testing procedures and recommended that testing go hand-in-hand with program design and implementation, we really did not answer the question directly. How would a systems analyst know for sure that the testing team has tried enough different sets of test data or that all possible paths through the program have been executed?

To address this issue, computer scientists have developed an alternative method of demonstrating the correctness of a program called **formal verification.** In this method, the verifier uses formal rules to prove that a program meets its specification in the same way that a mathematician proves a theorem using definitions, axioms, and previously proved theorems.

A thorough discussion of formal verification is beyond the scope of this book. However, we introduce two key concepts, assertions and loop invariants, and use them to help document and clarify some modules.

formal verification

using formal techniques to prove that a program is correct

Assertions

assertion

a logical statement that is always true

Part of formal verification concerns documenting a program through **assertions**—logical statements about the program that are "asserted" to be true. An assertion is written as a comment and describes what is supposed to be true about the program variables at that point.

EXAMPLE 9.4 ▼

The following program fragment contains a sequence of assignment statements, each followed by an assertion written as a comment:

```
A := 5;              {assert: A is 5}
X := A;              {assert: X is 5}
Y := X + A;          {assert: Y is 10}
```

The truth of the first assertion, {A is 5}, follows from executing the first statement with the knowledge that 5 is a constant. The truth of the second assertion, {X is 5}, follows from executing X := A with the knowledge that A is 5. The truth of the third assertion, {Y is 10}, follows from executing Y := X + A with the knowledge that X is 5 and A is 5. The assertions document the change in a program variable after each assignment statement executes. ▲

The goal of formal verification is to prove that a program fragment meets its specification. For the preceding fragment, this means proving that the final assertion, or *postcondition* (in this case, {Y is 10}), follows from the initial presumption, or *precondition* (in this case, {5 is a constant}), after the program fragment executes. The assignment rule (described next) is critical to this process. If we know that {A is 5} is true, the assignment rule allows us to make the assertion {X is 5} after executing the statement X := A.

The Assignment Rule

{P(A)}

```
X := A;
{P(X)}
```

Explanation: If P(A) is a logical statement (assertion) about A, the same statement will be true of X after the assignment statement X := A executes.

For our purposes, we use assertions as a documentation tool to improve our understanding of programs rather than as a method of formally proving them correct. Our assertions will be written in informal English, not in a formal language for logical statements. We have already used assertions to document the effect of executing a procedure.

Preconditions and Postconditions

A procedure's precondition is a logical statement about its input parameters. A procedure's postcondition may be a logical statement about its output parameters, or it may be a logical statement describing the change in program state caused by the procedure's execution. Any of the following activities changes the program state: changing the value of a variable, writing additional program output, reading new input data.

EXAMPLE 9.5 ▼

The precondition and the postcondition for procedure EnterInt (see Fig. 9.6) are repeated next:

```
procedure EnterInt (MinN, MaxN {input} : Integer;
                        var N {output} : Integer);
{
 Reads an integer between MinN and MaxN into N. Increases
 CountBad by 1 if range is invalid.
 Pre : MinN and MaxN are assigned values.
 Post: Returns in N the first data value between MinN and
       MaxN if MinN <= MaxN is True; otherwise, N is not
       defined and CountBad is increased by 1.
}
```

The precondition tells us that input parameters MinN and MaxN are defined before the procedure begins execution. The postcondition tells us that the procedure's execution assigns the first data value between MinN and MaxN to the output parameter N whenever MinN <= MaxN is true. ▲

Loop Invariants

loop invariant

a logical statement about variables processed in the loop that is true just before the first loop repetition and remains true after each loop repetition

Errors frequently occur in loops because it is difficult to determine that a loop body executes exactly the right number of times or that loop execution causes the desired change in program variables. A special type of assertion, a loop invariant, helps prove that a loop meets its specification. A **loop invariant** is a logical statement about variables processed by a loop that is true before the loop is entered and after each execution of the loop body. It must therefore be true just after the loop is exited. An invariant is so-called because it is a relationship that remains true as loop execution progresses.

As an example of a loop invariant, let's examine the following loop, which accumulates the sum of the integers 1, 2, . . . , N, where N is a positive integer, and Sum, I, and N are type Integer:

```
{
Accumulate the sum of integers 1 through N in Sum.
 assert: N >= 1
}
Sum := 0;
I := 1;
while I <= N do
   begin
      Sum := Sum + I;
      I := I + 1
   end; {while}
```

{assert: Sum is 1 + 2 + 3 + . . . + N-1 + N}

The first assertion, {N >= 1}, is the precondition for the loop, and the last assertion is its postcondition.

We stated previously that the loop invariant must be true before the loop begins execution and after each loop repetition. Since it traces the loop's progress, the loop invariant should be a logical statement about the loop-control variable I and the accumulating sum.

Figure 9.14 sketches the loop's progress for the first three iterations of the loop. At the end of the third iteration, I is 4 and Sum is 6—the sum of all integers less than 4 (1 + 2 + 3). When loop repetition finishes, I will be N+1 and Sum will contain the desired result (1 + 2 + 3 + . . . + N). Therefore we propose the invariant

{invariant: I <= N+1 and Sum is 1 + 2 + . . . + I-1}

Figure 9.14
Sketch of Summation Loop

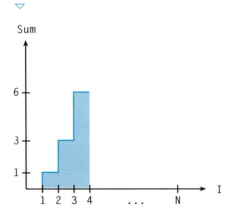

In English, this means that, after each loop repetition, I must be less than or equal to N+1 and Sum is equal to the sum of all positive integers less than I.

You may be wondering why the first part of the invariant is I <= N+1 instead of I <= N. The reason is that the loop invariant must be true after the last iteration of the loop. Since the last step taken in the loop body is to increment I, the last value assigned to I just prior to loop exit is N+1.

The loop invariant also must be true before loop execution begins. At that point, I is 1 and 1 <= N+1 is true for N >= 1 (the precondition). Also, the invariant requires that the value of Sum be equal to the summation of all positive integers less than 1. Because Sum is initialized to 0, this is also the case.

In program verification, the loop invariant proves that the loop meets its specification. For our purposes, we will use the loop invariant to document what we know about the loop's behavior, and we will place it just before the loop body, as shown next.

```
{
 Accumulate the sum of integers 1 through N in Sum.
 assert: N >= 1
}
Sum := 0;
I := 1;
while I <= N do
   {invariant: I <= N+1 and Sum is 1 + 2 + . . . + I-1}
   begin
     Sum := Sum + I;
     I := I + 1
   end; {while}

{assert: Sum is 1 + 2 + 3 + . . . + N-1 + N}
```

Loop Invariants as a Design Tool

Some computer scientists recommend writing the loop invariant as a preliminary step before coding the loop. The invariant serves as a specification for the loop and as a guide to determining the loop initialization, the loop repetition condition, and the loop body. For example, the following loop invariant describes a summation loop that adds N data items:

```
{invariant:
   Count <= N and
   Sum is the sum of all data read so far
}
```

From the loop invariant we can infer the following:

▶   The loop initialization is

```
    Sum := 0.0;
    Count := 0;
```

▶ The loop repetition test is

```
Count < N
```

▶ The loop body is

```
Read (Next);
Sum := Sum + Next;
Count := Count + 1
```

Given all this information, it becomes a simple task to write the summation loop (see Programming Exercise 2 at the end of this section).

Invariants and the for Statement

Since the loop invariant states what we know to be true about a loop after each iteration, we should be able to write an invariant for a `for` statement as well as a `while` statement. So that the loop invariant will remain true, we will assume that the loop-control variable in a `for` statement is incremented just before loop exit and retains its final value. This assumption allows us to use a loop invariant to document the following `for` loop:

```
{assert: N >= 1}

Sum := 0;
for I := 1 to N do
   {invariant: I <= N+1 and Sum is 1 + 2 + . . . + I-1}
   Sum := Sum + I;

{assert: Sum is 1 + 2 + 3 + . . . + N-1 + N}
```

More Loop Invariants

This subsection provides another example of the use of a loop invariant and assertions to document a loop.

EXAMPLE 9.6 ▼

Figure 9.15 shows a sentinel-controlled `while` loop that computes the product of a collection of data values. Loop exit occurs after the sentinel value (value of `Sentinel`) is read. The loop invariant indicates that `Product` is the product of all values read before the current one and that none of these values was the sentinel. The preconditions and postconditions for the loop are written as assertions.   ▲

Exercises for Section 9.8   *Self-Check*

1. a. Write the loop invariant and the assertion following the loop for the `while` loop in procedure `EnterInt` (Fig. 9.6).
   b. What other assertions should be added to procedure `EnterInt` to facilitate its verification?

2. If the sentinel-controlled loop in Fig. 9.15 were rewritten as a flag-controlled loop, what would the new loop invariant look like? The flag NoZero should remain true until a zero value is read.

3. In Programming Exercise 1, why is Number >= 0 used instead of Number > 0?

Programming

1. Write a function that returns the count (Count) of the number of nonzero digits in an arbitrary integer (Number). Your solution should include a while loop for which the following loop invariant is valid:

```
{invariant:
    Count >= 0 and Number >= 0 and the original
    Number has been divided by 10 Count times.
}
```

and this assertion would be valid following the loop:

```
{assert: Number is 0 and Count is the number of digits in N.}
```

2. Write a program fragment that implements the loop whose invariant is described in the subsection "Loop Invariants as a Design Tool."

Figure 9.15
Sentinel-Controlled Loop
with Invariant

```
{
 Compute the product of a sequence of data values.
 assert: Sentinel is a constant.
}
Product := 1;
WriteLn ('When done, enter ', Sentinel :1, ' to stop.');
WriteLn ('Enter the first number> ');
ReadLn (Num);
while Num <> Sentinel do
   {invariant:
      Product is the product of all prior values read into Num
      and no prior value of Num was the sentinel
   }
   begin
     Product := Product * Num;
     WriteLn ('Enter the next number> ');
     ReadLn (Num)
   end; {while}

{assert:
   Product is the product of all numbers
   read into Num before the sentinel.
}
```

9.9   Ethics and Responsibilities

Software engineers and computer programmers should act like the professionals they are. As part of their jobs, computer programmers may access large data banks that contain sensitive personnel information, information that is classified "secret" or "top secret," or financial transaction data. Programmers should behave in a socially responsible manner and not retrieve information they are not entitled to see. They should not use any information that they access for their own personal gain or do anything that would be considered illegal, unethical, or harmful to others.

The media often report stories of "computer hackers" who have broken into secure data banks. Some hackers sell classified information to intelligence agencies of other countries. Others retrieve similar information for their own amusement, as a prank, or just to demonstrate that they can. Regardless of the intent, such activity is illegal and subject to government prosecution.

Another illegal activity sometimes practiced by hackers is the insertion of special code, called a *virus,* into a computer's disk memory. A virus may cause sporadic activities to occur that disrupt the operation of the host computer. For example, unusual messages may appear on the screen at certain times. Viruses can also cause the host computer to erase portions of its own disk memory, thereby destroying valuable information and programs. Viruses are spread from one computer to another when data are copied from the infected disk and processed by a different computer. Certainly, these kinds of activities should not be considered harmless pranks; they are illegal and often cause irreparable damage.

A programmer who changes information in a database containing financial records is guilty of *computer theft* or *computer fraud.* Such acts are a felony and can lead to fines and imprisonment.

Another example of unprofessional behavior is using someone else's program or code without permission. While it is certainly permissible to use procedures in libraries that have been developed for reuse by your own company's programmers, you should not use another programmer's personal code or code from another company without permission. Failure to obtain such permission could lead to an expensive lawsuit against you or your company.

Many commercial software packages are protected by copyright laws and cannot be copied or duplicated. It is illegal to make additional copies of copyrighted software that you may be using at work for use on your home computer. In addition to being illegal, using software copied from another computer increases the possibility that your computer will receive a virus. You should act ethically and honor any copyright agreements that pertain to a particular software package.

Exercises for Section 9.9   **Self-Check**

1. Why might it be easier for a computer programmer to commit computer theft than for other users of a computer system?
2. What might be some ethical responsibilities of the program tester?

9.10 Common Programming Errors

To use a library procedure, you must know the name of the unit in which the procedure is found and have a description of the procedure interface. Specifically, you must know the number, order, and type of the procedure's parameters. Make sure that all variable formal parameters correspond to actual parameters that are variables of the same or identical type. Also make sure that all preconditions for a procedure's parameters (as listed in the procedure interface) are satisfied before each call to the procedure. Finally, the unit containing the procedure you are using must be linked to your program before you attempt to run it.

When writing user-defined units, insert only the procedure headings in the unit's interface section; the complete procedure declarations must appear in the unit's implementation section. Any constant, type, variable, or procedure that is intended for use by client modules must be declared in the unit's interface section. You should compile a unit to disk before attempting to compile a client of that unit.

Any time a change is made to the interface section of a unit, the client units using that unit must be recompiled. If you forget to recompile any of the client units, a `Unit version mismatch` error results when you attempt to compile a program or unit that uses one of those client units. If only the unit's implementation or initialization section is changed, client units do not need to be recompiled. However, client programs must always be recompiled whenever a change is made to a unit in order to access the most recent version of the unit.

CHAPTER REVIEW

1. A large program or system has a life cycle consisting of the following phases:

   ▶ Requirements specification
   ▶ Analysis
   ▶ Design
   ▶ Implementation
   ▶ Testing and verification
   ▶ Operation, follow-up, and maintenance

2. During the requirements specification phase, programmers and analysts in the programming team work together with users to ensure that everyone understands the planned capabilities of the new program system.

3. Use of a library of procedures and functions facilitates the implementation phase. Program development proceeds more quickly and smoothly if you reuse previously tested modules in a new program instead of writing new modules.

4. You can combine related procedures and functions in a Turbo Pascal unit. Each unit may contain public identifiers declared in the interface section and private identifiers declared in the implementation section. The public identifiers may be data types or variables that are imported by a client of the unit. You list procedure and function headings in the unit interface section and provide the complete declarations in the unit implementation section.

5. Using units simplifies apportioning pieces of a large project to members of a programming team. Once a unit has been completed, it can be compiled and its procedures can be imported and reused by other units.

6. You can create an abstract data type by placing a data type declaration together with procedures and functions that operate on data of that type in a separate unit.

7. The test plan for a large program should be developed during the design phase. The test plan discusses the kind of testing to be done, the amount of testing, and who will do the testing. Programmers should keep the test plan in mind as they implement the program's modules.

8. Different techniques for testing include structured walkthroughs, black box testing, white box testing, and integration testing. A programming team should use all of these techniques.

9. Formal verification is an alternative to testing. Assertions and loop invariants are logical statements. An assertion is always true. A loop invariant is a logical statement that is true before the first loop repetition and after each repetition of the loop.

Summary of New Pascal Constructs

Construct	Effect
Unit Definition	
| ```
unit Letter;

interface

  const
    Num = 3;

  procedure DisplayNum
      (Ch {input} : Char);

implementation

  procedure DisplayNum
      (Ch {input} : Char);
    var
      I : Integer;
``` | Declares unit Letter and makes procedure DisplayNum and constant Num available for export to a client unit or program |
```

Construct	Effect

```
begin {DisplayNum}
   for I := 1 to Num do
      Write (Ch);
   WriteLn
end; {DisplayNum}
end. {Letter}
```

uses Statement

```
uses Printer, Letter;
```

Enables Turbo Pascal to use constant, type, variable, and procedure declarations from units `Printer` and `Letter` when compiling a client program or unit

Quick-Check Exercises

1. Place the following six phases of the software life cycle (SLC) in their correct order:

   testing and verification   design   requirements specification
   operation and maintenance   implementation   analysis

2. In which phases are users of a software product likely to participate?
3. In which phases of the SLC are programmers and analysts likely to participate?
4. In Turbo Pascal, what is the name for a library module?
5. Name the two sections of a unit that implements an abstract data type. Where is the data type declaration found? Where are the procedure declarations found?
6. _____ testing requires the use of test data that exercise each statement in a module.
7. _____ testing focuses on testing the functional characteristics of a module.
8. Why is a loop invariant not equivalent to placing an assertion at the beginning of the loop body?
9. The use of loop invariants is useful for which of the following: loop control, loop design, loop verification?
10. Write a loop invariant for the following code segment:

    ```
    Product := 1;
    Counter := 2;
    while Counter <= 5 do
      begin
        Product := Product * Counter;
        Counter := Counter + 1
      end;
    ```

Answers to Quick-Check Exercises

1. Requirements specification, analysis, design, implementation, testing and verification, operation and maintenance
2. Requirements specification, testing and verification, operation and maintenance
3. All phases
4. Unit
5. Interface and implementation sections; interface; implementation but headings appear in interface too
6. White box
7. Black box
8. The assertion must be true before each iteration of the loop; the loop invariant must be true before and after each iteration.
9. Loop design, loop verification
10. ```
    {invariant:
        Counter <= 6 and
        Product contains product of all integers < Counter
    }
    ```

Review Questions

1. Define the terms *procedural abstraction* and *loop invariant*.
2. Which of the following are likely to occur in a programmer's library of procedures? Explain your answers.
    a. A procedure that raises a number to a specified power
    b. A procedure that writes the user instructions for a particular program
    c. A procedure that displays the name of an application program in block letters
    d. A procedure that displays the block letter M
3. Define an abstract data type for the positions on a baseball team (pitcher, catcher, infield, outfield) with procedures to read and write those positions and code the ADT as a unit.
4. Write the interface section for an abstract data type Money that allows you to do basic arithmetic operations (addition, subtraction, multiplication, and division) on real numbers having exactly two digits to the right of the decimal point.
5. Which of the following statements is incorrect?
    a. Loop invariants are used in loop verification.
    b. Loop invariants are used in loop design.
    c. A loop invariant is always an assertion.
    d. An assertion is always a loop invariant.
6. Briefly describe a test plan for the telephone directory program described in Section 9.1. Assume that integration testing is used.
7. Write a procedure that computes the average number of characters found on the lines of a text file. Include loop invariants and any other assertions necessary to verify that the procedure is correct.
    ```

Programming Projects

1. Write an abstract data type that consists of data type `ColorType` and operators for reading and writing the colors (red, yellow, green, blue, black, brown, orange, purple, and white).

2. Create a Turbo Pascal unit containing a set of library procedures (or functions) that can be used to determine the following information for an integer input parameter:

   a. Is it a multiple of 7, 11, or 13?
   b. Is the sum of the digits odd or even?
   c. What is the square root value?
   d. Is it a prime number?

   Write a client program that tests your library procedures using the following input values: 104, 3773, 13, 121, 77, and 3075.

3. Each month a bank customer deposits $50 into a savings account. Assume that the interest rate is fixed and is a problem input. The interest is calculated on a quarterly basis. For example, if the account earns 6.5% annually, it earns one-fourth of 6.5% every three months. Write a program to compute the total investment, the total amount in the account, and the interest accrued for each of the 120 months of a 10-year period. Assume that the rate is applied to all funds in the account at the end of a quarter, regardless of when the deposits were made.

   Print all values accurate to two decimal places. The table printed by your program when the annual interest rate is 6.5% should begin as follows:

MONTH	INVESTMENT	NEW AMOUNT	INTEREST	TOTAL SAVINGS
1	50.00	50.00	0.00	50.00
2	100.00	100.00	0.00	100.00
3	150.00	150.00	2.44	152.44
4	200.00	202.44	0.00	202.44
5	250.00	252.44	0.00	252.44
6	300.00	302.44	4.91	307.35
7	350.00	357.35	0.00	357.35

4. Redo Programming Project 3, adding columns to allow comparison of interest compounded monthly (one-twelfth of annual rate every month) with continuously compounded interest. The formula for continuously compounded interest is

   $$amount = principal \times e^{\, rate \times time}$$

   where *rate* is the annual interest rate and *time* is expressed in years.

5. Many computer program user interfaces place windows on the screen that consist of a user area bordered by a different color. In the top edge of the border, the title of the window is displayed centered. Write a library module to create such windows on the screen. Your module should include a procedure that accepts the window's coordinates and background and foreground colors, the

color of the window edge, and the color of the title and a title string. Supply a program that adequately tests the library module. *Hint:* You can draw an edge by simply displaying spaces using the edge color as the background color.

6. A very popular effect in the user interface of many programs is the so-called "genie out of the bottle" effect. In this effect, instead of simply appearing on the screen, a Window starts as a small rectangle and then expands until full size. Add a procedure to the library module developed in Programming Project 5 to provide this effect. Again, adequately test the library module. *Hint:* On very fast computers, it may be necessary to use the Delay procedure to slow down the effect.

7. You have been assigned the task of writing a library module to compute factorials and Fibonacci numbers for the Turbo Pascal data type LongInt. Since this library module will be a component of the flight software of a satellite, it is of utmost importance that it be absolutely correct. Therefore you are to supply loop invariants for all loops and sufficient assertions to show program correctness. You must also supply a test program and a written test procedure that will support your claims of correctness.

Factorials are described in detail in Section 6.8. For a given number N, the Nth Fibonacci number is computed as follows: If N is 0 or 1, the Fibonacci number is 1. Otherwise, the Fibonacci number is the sum of the last two Fibonacci numbers. As an example, the first eight Fibonacci numbers are 1, 1, 2, 3, 5, 8, 13, 21. Each number is the sum of the previous two. Do not use a recursive solution for either of these problems.

▼ **What was the major influence on your choosing computer science as a profession?**

▲ I like to program. I think that's a primary reason why most people are in the profession. In ancient times (the early 1960s), quite a bit of effort was required to get near a computer, and you would be crazy to even try to do it if you didn't like it. Getting a hundred-line program to work was something that might require a week's work, since one-day turnaround was common. You turned in your card deck one day and got your printout the next day. Under those circumstances, you were strongly motivated to outsmart the system, and it was quite satisfying to be able to actually do so.

▼ **Why are algorithms and data structures fundamental to computer science?**

▲ Algorithms and data structures represent an abstraction of the notion of a particular program running on a particular machine. This abstraction has served us well, because algorithms and data structures have been remarkably robust across generations of machines. The best available sorting method today is the same as the best available sorting method 30 years ago, and the same goes for data structures and algorithms for searching and many other problems. Thus, though one might think that new technology would make old methods obsolete, it has turned out that algorithms and data structures can be thought of as representative of the knowledge built up over the years in all the programs that have been written. When you develop a program for sorting or searching or some other classical problem, then either you are inventing something that has eluded others over the years, or you are reinventing some classical algorithm. The former happens sufficiently often to make the field still exciting, even for newcomers, and the latter happens sufficiently often that it is worthwhile to study the best classical methods and take advantage of others' experience.

▼ **Is there a connection between famous classical problems like Towers of Hanoi, dining philosophers, or traveling salesman and the study of areas like software engineering or computer graphics?**

▲ Most of the "classical problems" in computer science are not too old and not too far removed from practical problems. Anyone involved in a serious endeavor solving a practical problem with a computer is very likely to encounter recursion (as typified by Towers of Hanoi), synchronization (as typified by dining philosophers), and NP-completeness (as typified by the traveling salesman problem). An educated computer scientist will have a better chance to cope, having studied the classical problems.

▼ **Universal models of computation, Turing machines and the like, seem like games theoreticians play that aren't that important for computing professionals making a living in the real world. What is the link between computational models and applications?**

▲ Sometimes there are direct links. Often the very best way to solve a problem is to invent an abstract machine (computational model) suited to the problem, then write a simple simulator for the machine. Other times the links are indirect but also very important. For example, inten-

INTERVIEW
▼
Robert Sedgewick

Robert Sedgewick is a professor of computer science at Princeton University. He has held visiting research positions at Xerox PARC, Institute for Defense Analyses, and INRIA. Sedgewick is a widely published author whose research interests include mathematical analysis of algorithms, structures and algorithms, and program visualization.

sive study of computational models related to problems like the traveling salesman problem has led to the development of the theory of "NP-completeness," which tells the practicing programmer not to expect to easily find a tricky way to solve the traveling salesman problem efficiently, and that there are a vast number of similar "NP-complete" problems. By studying the theory, one can perhaps learn to more easily recognize (and perhaps avoid) the onset of NP-completeness in practice. This is a very significant advance over the situation faced by practicing programmers even in 1975.

▼ **What major events do you foresee in research in algorithms and data structures in the 1990s?**

▲ Serendipity is one of the most attractive aspects of working in research. No one can know where the real breakthroughs will come, so I'll pass on this question.

▼ **Among the goals of studying algorithms is the design of more efficient programs. Efficiency of a similar kind is also a goal for those who build computers—the architects. In what ways do hardware and software designers share information to achieve common goals?**

▲ Given a specific program, a good hardware designer can build a machine that will do an outstanding job executing that program, but a great hardware designer will come up with a machine that is fast for a large class of similar programs. Conversely, given a specific machine, a good software designer can write a program that will run fast on a large class of similar machines. The best way to generalize in both cases is through abstraction: Settle on a specific set of operations that the hardware should be built to perform and that should be used to build the software. Common goals are best served when both sides agree on the same set of operations. Actually, this is frequently the case in successful machine designs. Note that this goes back to your earlier question on the value of models of computation.

CHAPTER TEN

Arrays

data structure

a composite of related data items stored under the same name

Simple data types, whether built-in (Integer, Real, Boolean, Char) or user-defined (e.g., enumerated type Day), use a single memory cell to store a variable. To solve many programming problems, it is more efficient to store related data items together than to store each data item in a different variable. A program that processes exam scores for a class, for example, would be easier to write if all the scores were stored together and could be accessed as a group. Pascal allows a programmer to group such related data items together into a single composite **data structure.** In this chapter, we look at one such data structure: the array.

10.1 The Array Data Structure

array
a collection of data items of the same type

The **array** is a data structure in which we store a collection of data items of the same type (e.g., all the exam scores for a class). By using an array, we can associate a single variable name (e.g., Scores) with the entire collection of data (see Fig. 10.1). We can also reference individual items in the array. The naming process is like the one used to describe families and their members. The Koffman household refers to all five members of my immediate family, and individual names—Deborah Koffman, for example—designate individuals in my family.

Pascal stores an array in consecutive storage locations in main memory, one item per memory cell. We can perform some operations, such as passing the array as a parameter to a procedure, on the whole array. We also can access individual items stored in the array (called **array elements**) and process them like other simple variables. In this section, we describe how to declare arrays in Pascal programs and how to reference individual array elements.

array element
a data item that is part of an array

Declaring Arrays

Normally, we first describe the structure of an array in an *array type declaration*. Then we can allocate storage for one or more arrays of that type.

```
                            8 elements  Element type
type
   RealArray = array [1..8] of Real;    {array type declaration}
var
   X : RealArray;                       {Allocate storage for array X.}
```

In this example, the array type, RealArray, is declared in the type declaration. The symbols [1..8] tell Pascal to allocate 8 memory cells for any variable with type RealArray. Because variable X is declared with type RealArray, X is an array of 8 elements, and each element contains a single Real value.

Keep in mind that an array type declaration does not cause the Pascal compiler to allocate storage space in memory. The array type merely describes the structure of an array. Only variables actually store information

Figure 10.1
Array Scores with Five
Array Elements

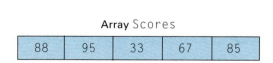

Array Scores

and require storage. Pascal does not allocate storage space until a variable of this type is declared.

SYNTAX DISPLAY

Array Type Declaration

Form: type
                array type = array [*subscript type*] of *element type*;
Example: type
                SmallArray = array [1..5] of Char;

Interpretation: The identifier *array type* describes a collection of array elements; each element can store an item of type *element type*. The *subscript type* can be either of the standard ordinal types Boolean or Char, an enumerated type, or a subrange type. There is one array element for each value in the *subscript type*.

The *element type* describes the type of each element in the array. All elements of an array are the same type.

Note 1: The standard types Real and Integer cannot be used as a *subscript type*; however, a subrange of the integers can be a *subscript type*.

Note 2: The *element type* can be any standard or user-defined type.

Note 1 in the syntax display states that the standard types Integer and Real cannot be used as subscript types. Type Integer is not allowed because an array with subscript type Integer would have one element for each integer in the range -MaxInt - 1 to MaxInt (a very large array!). Type Real is not allowed because it is not an ordinal type.

Array Subscripts

To process the data stored in an array, we must be able to access its individual elements. We use the array name (a variable) followed by the array subscript (sometimes called an **index**) to do so. The **array subscript,** enclosed in brackets, selects a particular array element for processing and must be assignment compatible with the subscript type specified in the array type declaration.

array subscript (index)
a value or expression enclosed in brackets after the array name, specifying which array element to access

If X is a variable of type RealArray,

```
type
  RealArray = array [1..8] of Real;  {array type declaration}

var
  X : RealArray;                      {Allocate storage for array X.}
```

the subscript type is the Integer subrange 1..8, so the allowable subscripts are integers in this subrange. We therefore use X[1] (read as "X sub 1") to reference the first element of array X, X[2] for the second element, and X[8] for the eighth element (see Fig. 10.2). We cannot use X[0] or X[9] to reference elements in array X. (Why not?)

subscripted variable
a variable followed by a subscript in brackets

We call a variable followed by a subscript in brackets (e.g., X[1]) a **subscripted variable**. A subscripted variable has the same data type as the ar-

Figure 10.2
The Eight Elements of
Array X

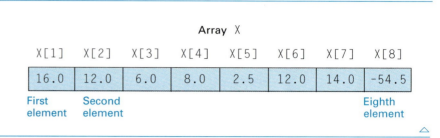

ray element it references. Because the elements of array X are type Real, we can manipulate X[1] like any other Real variable. Specifically, we can use X[1] with the arithmetic operators, the relational operators, and the assignment operator. We also can pass X[1] as a parameter to procedures Read(Ln) and Write(Ln) and to any of Pascal's built-in functions that accept type Real parameters.

To store a value in an array element, we write an assignment statement of the form

subscripted variable := expression

To retrieve or access a value stored in an array element, just write the corresponding subscripted variable in an expression.

EXAMPLE 10.1: Storing and Retrieving Values in an Array ▼

Let X be the array first shown in Fig. 10.2. Some statements that manipulate elements of this array are shown in Table 10.1. The contents of array X after execution of these statements are shown in Fig. 10.3. Notice that only array elements X[3] and X[4] have changed, because they are the only ones that are assigned new values.

Table 10.1
Storing and Retrieving
Values in Array X

Statement	Explanation
WriteLn (X[1])	Displays the value of X[1], or 16.0.
X[4] := 25.0	Stores the value 25.0 in X[4].
Sum := X[1] + X[2]	Stores the sum of X[1] and X[2], or 28.0, in the variable Sum.
Sum := Sum + X[3]	Adds X[3] to Sum. The new Sum is 34.0.
X[4] := X[4] + 1.0	Adds 1.0 to X[4]. The new X[4] is 26.0.
X[3] := X[1] + X[2]	Stores the sum of X[1] and X[2] in X[3]. The new X[3] is 28.0

Figure 10.3
Array X After Execution of
Statements in Table 10.1

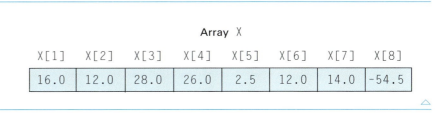

Array X

X[1]	X[2]	X[3]	X[4]	X[5]	X[6]	X[7]	X[8]
16.0	12.0	28.0	26.0	2.5	12.0	14.0	-54.5

Each subscript in Table 10.1 is a literal enclosed in square brackets (e.g., [4]). In Example 10.2, we show that an array subscript may be an expression that is assignment compatible with the subscript type. ▲

EXAMPLE 10.2: Manipulating Array Elements ▼

The statements in Table 10.2 manipulate elements in array X (Fig. 10.3). I is a type Integer variable with value 6. When I is 6, the subscripted variable X[I + I] references element X[12], which is not in the array. Standard Pascal would display an Index expression out of bounds run-time error. Turbo Pascal, in contrast, does not check for invalid array subscripts unless range checking is enabled with the {$R+} compiler directive. If range checking is enabled, Turbo Pascal would display a Range check error message. Always enable range checking when writing and testing a program with arrays.

Table 10.2
Using Subscript
Expressions with Array X

Statement	Effect
Write (8, X[8])	Displays 8 and -54.5 (value of X[8])
Write (I, X[I])	Displays 6 and 12.0 (value of X[6])
Write (X[I] + 1)	Displays 13.0 (value of X[6] + 1)
Write (X[I] + I)	Displays 18.0 (value of X[6] + 6)
Write (X[I + 1])	Displays 14.0 (value of X[7])
Write (X[I + I])	Illegal attempt to display X[12]
Write (X[2 * I - 4])	Displays -54.5 (value of X[8])
Write (X[Trunc(X[5])])	Displays 12.0 (value of X[2])
X[I] := X[I + 1]	Assigns 14.0 (value of X[7]) to X[6]
X[I - 1] := X[I]	Assigns 14.0 (new value of X[6]) to X[5]
X[I] - 1 := X[I - 1]	Illegal assignment statement

The last Write statement in Table 10.2 uses X[5] as an argument for function Trunc and Trunc(X[5]) as a subscript expression. X[5] has the value 2.5 and Trunc(X[5]) is 2, so the value of X[2] (not X[5]) is printed. An error would occur if the value of Trunc(X[5]) were outside the allowable range (1 through 8).

Two different subscripts are used in the last three assignment statements in the table. The first assignment statement copies the value of X[7] to X[6] (subscripts I + 1 and I); the second assignment statement copies the value of X[6] to X[5] (subscripts I and I - 1). The last assignment statement causes a syntax error because X[I] - 1 is an expression, not a variable. ▲

SYNTAX DISPLAY

Array Element Reference

Form: *array name* [*subscript*]
Example: X[3 * I - 2]
Interpretation: The *subscript* must be an expression that is assignment compatible with the subscript type specified in the declaration for *array name*. If the expression is the wrong data type, the syntax error Index type is not compatible with declaration is detected. If the expression value is not in range and range checking is enabled using {$R+}, a Range check error occurs during run time.

More Array and Subscript Types

The arrays declared so far had subscript types that were subranges of the integers and were used to store numeric values. This, of course, is not required in Pascal, because subscript types can be any ordinal type (except Integer) and array elements can be any standard or previously declared type. A number of different array types are described in Table 10.3.

As the table shows, the array Name has 10 elements and can store the letters of a person's name. The array Fahrenheit, with 21 elements, stores the Fahrenheit temperature equivalent to each Celsius temperature in the range -10 through +10 degrees Celsius. For example, Fahrenheit[0] would be the Fahrenheit temperature, 32.0, corresponding to 0 degrees Celsius. Arrays LetterCount and LetterFound have the same subscript type (i.e., the uppercase letters) but different element types. The array Answers has only two elements, with subscript values True and False.

EXAMPLE 10.3 ▼

The declaration section for a plant operations program is shown next. The type declaration declares two simple data types, EmpRange and Day, and two array types, EmpArray and DayArray. Two arrays, Vacation and Plant-Hours, are declared in the variable declarations.

```
const
  NumEmp = 8;                          {number of employees}

type
  EmpRange = 1..NumEmp;               {subscript range}
  EmpArray = array [EmpRange] of Boolean;
  Day = (Sunday, Monday, Tuesday, Wednesday,
         Thursday, Friday, Saturday);
  DayArray = array [Day] of Real;
```

Table 10.3
Some Array Types and
Applications

Array Type	Subscript Type	Application
type NameArray = array [1..10] of Char; var Name : NameArray;	integer subrange	Name[1] := 'A'; stores a person's name using 10 characters.
type Temps = array [-10..10] of Real; var Fahrenheit : Temps;	integer subrange	Fahrenheit[0] := 32.0; stores Fahrenheit temperatures equivalent to −10 through 10 degrees Celsius.
type Counters = array ['A'..'Z'] of Integer; var LetterCount : Counters;	character subrange	LetterCount['A'] := 0; stores the number of times each uppercase letter occurs.
type Flags = array ['A'..'Z'] of Boolean; var LetterFound : Flags;	character subrange	LetterFound['X'] := False; stores a set of Boolean values indicating which letters occur and which do not.
type BoolCounts = array [Boolean] of Integer; var Answers : BoolCounts;	Boolean	Answers[True] := 15; stores the number of true answers and false answers to a quiz.

```
var
  Vacation : EmpArray;
  PlantHours : DayArray;
```

Consider the declaration for array type EmpArray first. The subscript type is EmpRange (the subrange 1..NumEmp), so the subscript type for an array of type EmpArray (e.g., Vacation) is 1..8. Each element of array Vacation can store a Boolean value (see Fig. 10.4). The contents of this array could indicate which employees are on vacation (Vacation[1] is True if employee 1 is on vacation). If employees 1, 3, 5, and 7 are on vacation and the rest are not, array Vacation would have the values shown in Fig. 10.4.

Next consider the declaration for array type DayArray. Because the subscript type is the enumerated type Day, the subscripts for an array of type DayArray are the enumerated type values Sunday, Monday, and so on. Because PlantHours is type DayArray, each element of array PlantHours can store a type Real value. The array element PlantHours[Sunday] could indicate how many hours the plant was operating on Sunday of the past week.

Figure 10.4
Arrays Vacation and
PlantHours

The array in Fig. 10.4 indicates that the plant was closed on the weekend and operated a single shift on Monday and Thursday (open 8.0 hours), double shifts on Tuesday and Friday, and triple shifts on Wednesday.

We could eliminate the declarations for the constant NumEmp and data type EmpRange and just declare the array type EmpArray:

```
type
  EmpArray = array [1..8] of Boolean;
```

There are three advantages to the original declarations, however. First, it is easy to change the declared size of array Vacation: By simply redefining the constant NumEmp, we change the array size. Second, the constant NumEmp can be referenced in the program body. Finally, the data type EmpRange can be used as a type identifier elsewhere in the program. ▲

Anonymous Array Types

Although we will not do so in this text, it is possible to declare an array without first declaring its type. The variable declaration

```
var
  X : array [1..20] of Integer;  {anonymous type array}
```

anonymous type

an unnamed type used in a variable declaration

allocates storage for an array X of 20 integers. Because there is no array type declaration, the type of array X is an **anonymous type**. It is bad programming practice to declare arrays with anonymous types.

Exercises for Section 10.1 ***Self-Check***

1. Given the statements Y := X3 and Y := X[3], supply type and variable declaration such that these statements are valid. Assume Y is of type Real.
2. If an array is declared to have 10 elements, can you always reference the array elements using subscripts 1 through 10?
3. For the following declarations, how many memory cells are reserved for data and what type of data can be stored there? Is the memory allocated after the type declaration or after the variable declaration?

    ```
    type
       IndexRange = 1..5;
       AnArray = array [IndexRange] of Char;

    var
       Grades : AnArray;
    ```

4. Describe the following array types and indicate how many elements can be stored in arrays of each type:
    a. array [1..20] of Char
    b. array ['0'..'9'] of Boolean
    c. array [-5..5] of Real
    d. array [Boolean] of Char

5. Write the variable and type declarations for only the valid array descriptions:
    a. subscript type Boolean, element type Real
    b. subscript type 'A'..'F', element type Integer
    c. subscript type Char, element type Boolean
    d. subscript type Integer, element type Real
    e. subscript type Char, element type Real
    f. subscript type Real, element type Char
    g. subscript type Day (enumerated type), element type Real
6. Provide array type declarations for representing the following:
    a. A group of rooms (living room, dining room, kitchen, etc.) that have a given area
    b. Elementary school grade levels (1 through 6) with a given number of students per grade
    c. A group of colors with letter values assigned according to the first letter of their name (e.g., 'B' for blue)

10.2 Sequential Access to Array Elements

Many programs require that all the elements of an array be processed in sequence, starting with the first element. To enter data into an array, print its contents, or perform other sequential processing tasks, we would use a `for` loop whose loop-control variable (`I`) is also the array subscript (`X[I]`). Increasing the value of the loop-control variable by 1 would cause the next array element to be processed.

EXAMPLE 10.4: Storing Data in an Array ▼

The array `Cube`, declared as follows, stores the cubes of the first 10 integers (for example, `Cube[1]` is 1, `Cube[10]` is 1000):

```
type
  IndexRange = 1..10;
  IntArray = array [IndexRange] of Integer;

var
  Cube : IntArray;        {array of cubes}
  I : Integer;            {loop-control variable}
```

The `for` statement

```
for I := 1 to 10 do
  Cube[I] := I * I * I
```

stores values into this array as follows:

Array Cube

[1]	[2]	[3]	[4]	[5]	[6]	[7]	[8]	[9]	[10]
1	8	27	64	125	216	343	512	729	1000

▲

EXAMPLE 10.5: Reading and Displaying an Array ▼

Data must always be read into an array one element at a time, and displayed one array element at a time. In Fig. 10.5, the declarations

```
const
  MaxItems = 8;                          {number of data items}

type
  IndexRange = 1..MaxItems;
  RealArray = array [IndexRange] of Real;

var
  X : RealArray;                         {array of data}
  I : IndexRange;                        {loop-control variable}
```

allocate storage for an array `X` of `Real` elements with subscripts in the range `1..8`. Three `for` loops process the array `X`, and the loop-control variable `I` ($1 \le I \le 8$) is the array subscript in each loop. The first `for` loop

```
for I := 1 to MaxItems do
  Read (X[I]);
```

reads one data value into each array element (the first item is stored in X[1], the second item in X[2], etc.). The Read statement is repeated for each value of I from 1 to 8; each repetition causes a new data value to be read and stored in X[I]. The subscript I determines which array element will receive the next data value.

Figure 10.5
Table of Differences

Edit Window

```
{$R+}
program ShowDiff;
{
  Computes the average value of an array of data and
  prints the difference between each value and the average
}
  const
    MaxItems = 8;                        {number of data items}

  type
    IndexRange = 1..MaxItems;
    RealArray = array [IndexRange] of Real;

  var
    X : RealArray;                       {array of data}
    I : IndexRange;                      {loop-control variable}
    Average,                             {average value of data}
    Sum    : Real;                       {sum of the data}

begin {ShowDiff}
  {Enter the data.}
  Write ('Enter ', MaxItems :1, ' numbers> ');
  for I := 1 to MaxItems do
    Read (X[I]);

  {Compute the average value.}
  Sum := 0.0;                            {Initialize Sum.}
  for I := 1 to MaxItems do
    Sum := Sum + X[I];                   {Add each element to Sum.}
  Average := Sum / MaxItems;             {Get average value.}
  WriteLn ('The average value is ', Average :3:1); WriteLn;

  {Display the difference between each item and the average.}
  WriteLn ('Table of differences between X[I] and average');
  WriteLn ('I' :4, 'X[I]' :8, 'Difference' : 14);
  for I := 1 to MaxItems do
    WriteLn (I :4, X[I] :8:1, X[I] - Average :14:1)
end. {ShowDiff}
```

▷ ▷ ▷ ▷ ▷ ▷

Output Window

```
Enter 8 numbers> 16.0  12.0  6.0  8.0  2.5  12.0  14.0  -54.5
The average value is 2.0

Table of differences between X[I] and average
    I     X[I]     Difference
    1     16.0        14.0
    2     12.0        10.0
    3      6.0         4.0
    4      8.0         6.0
    5      2.5         0.5
    6     12.0        10.0
    7     14.0        12.0
    8    -54.5       -56.5
```

The last `for` loop,

```
for I := 1 to MaxItems do
   WriteLn (I :4, X[I] :8:2, X[I] - Average :14:2)
```

displays a table that shows each array element, `X[I]`, and the difference between that element and the average value, `X[I] - Average`.

The second `for` loop,

```
Sum := 0.0;                          {Initialize Sum to zero.}
for I := 1 to MaxItems do
   Sum := Sum + X[I];                {Add each element to Sum.}
```

accumulates the sum of all eight elements of array `X` in the variable `Sum`. Each time the `for` loop is repeated, `I` increases by 1, so the statement

```
Sum := Sum + X[I];                   {Add each element to Sum.}
```

adds the next element of array `X` to `Sum`. The execution of this program fragment is traced in Table 10.4 for the first three repetitions of the loop. ▲

Table 10.4
Partial Trace of for Loop

Statement Part	I	X[I]	Sum	Effect
`Sum := 0.0;`			0.0	Initializes Sum.
`for I := 1 to MaxItems do` `   Sum := Sum + X[I]`	1	16.0	 16.0	Initializes I to 1; adds X[1] to Sum.
`increment and test I` `   Sum := Sum + X[I]`	2	12.0	 28.0	2 <= 8 is True; adds X[2] to Sum.
`increment and test I` `   Sum := Sum + X[I]`	3	6.0	 34.0	3 <= 8 is True; adds X[3] to Sum.

Exercises for Section 10.2 *Self-Check*

1. The following sequence of statements changes the contents of array X displayed in Fig. 10.5. Describe what each statement does to the array, and show the final contents of array X after all statements execute.

```
I := 3;
X[I] := X[I] + 10.0;
X[I - 1] := X[2 * I - 1];
X[I + 1] := X[2 * I] + X[2 * I + 1];
for I := 5 to 7 do
   X[I] := X[I + 1];
for I := 3 downto 1 do
   X[I + 1] := X[I]
```

2. Write program statements that do the following to array X shown in Fig. 10.5:
    a. Replace the third element with 7.0
    b. Copy the element in the fifth location into the first one
    c. Subtract the first element from the fourth and store the result in the fifth element
    d. Increase the sixth element by 2
    e. Find the sum of the first five elements
    f. Multiply each of the first six elements by 2 and place each product in an element of the array AnswerArray
    g. Display all even-numbered elements on one line

Programming

1. Write a loop to compute the product of all elements of an array of real numbers. Write a suitable type for this array.

10.3 Arrays as Parameters and Operands

In this section, we show how to pass individual array elements and entire arrays as parameters. We also discuss another operation that can be performed on whole arrays: copying an array.

Array Elements as Parameters

In Fig. 10.5 the subscripted variable X[I] is an actual parameter for the Pascal Read and WriteLn procedures. We can pass individual array elements as actual parameters to procedures or functions that we write. In this case, the formal parameters must have the same data type as the array elements.

EXAMPLE 10.6 ▼

Procedure Switch in Fig. 10.6 exchanges the values of its two type Real prameters. The procedure call statement

Figure 10.6
Procedure Switch

```
procedure Switch (var P, Q {input/output} : Real);
{
  Exchanges the values of P and Q.
  Pre : P and Q are assigned values.
  Post: P has the value passed into Q and vice versa.
}
  var
    Temp : Real;          {temporary variable for the exchange}

begin {Switch}
  Temp := P;
  P := Q;
  Q := Temp
end; {Switch}
```

```
Switch (X[2], X[1])
```

uses this procedure to exchange the contents of the first two elements (type
Real) of array X from Fig. 10.5. The actual parameter X[2] corresponds to
formal parameter P, and the actual parameter X[1] to formal parameter Q.
This correspondence is shown in Fig. 10.7.

Although we can pass array elements as actual parameters, we cannot use
them as formal parameters. The procedure declaration

```
procedure Switch (var X[I], X[J] {input/output} : Real);
```

would cause a syntax error because the formal parameter names must be
Pascal identifiers. ▲

Copying an Array

In all array operations so far, we processed one array element at a time. Pascal allows us, however, to copy an entire array of values by using the assignment operator. To illustrate, given the declarations

Figure 10.7
Parameter Correspondence
for Switch (X[2], X[1])

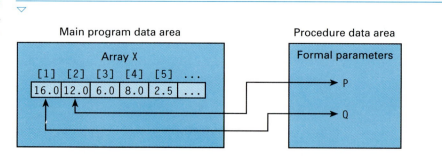

```
const
  MaxSize = 100;

type
  IndexRange = 1..MaxSize;
  TestArray = array [IndexRange] of Real;

var
  X, Y : TestArray;
```

the assignment statement

```
X := Y                          {copy array Y to array X}
```

copies each value in array Y to the corresponding element of array X (i.e., Y[1] is copied to X[1], Y[2] to X[2], and so forth). Array copies can be performed only when the arrays involved are the same array type.

Array Parameters

We can write modules that have array parameters. The module can manipulate some or all of the elements corresponding to its actual array parameter.

EXAMPLE 10.7: Initializing an Array ▼

Figure 10.8 shows a procedure that sets the initial values of all elements of an array of type TestArray to InValue. We can use the procedure call statements

```
FillArray (X, 0.0);
FillArray (Y, 1.0)
```

to fill arrays X and Y declared earlier. After these statements execute, array X will contain all zeros and array Y will contain all ones.

In procedure FillArray, the formal array parameter is declared as a variable parameter of type TestArray. The following procedure heading

Figure 10.8
Procedure FillArray

```
procedure FillArray (var W {output} : TestArray;
                        InValue {input} : Integer);
{
  Sets all elements of its array parameter to InValue.
  Pre : InValue is defined.
  Post: W[I] = InValue, for 1 <= I <= MaxSize.
}
  var
    I : IndexRange;          {array subscript and loop control}

begin {FillArray}
  for I := 1 to MaxSize do
    W[I] := InValue
end; {FillArray}
```

```
procedure FillArray (var W : array [IndexRange] of Real;
                     InValue {input} : Integer);
```

is invalid because each parameter type must be an identifier.   ▲

Variable and Value Array Parameters

When an array is passed as a variable parameter, Pascal passes the address of the first actual array element into the procedure data area. Because the array elements are stored in adjacent memory cells, the entire array of data can be accessed. The procedure directly manipulates the actual array.

When an array is passed as a value parameter, a local copy of the array is made when the procedure is called. The local array is initialized so that it contains the same values as the corresponding actual array. The procedure manipulates the local array, and any changes made to the local array do not alter the contents of the actual array.

Example 10.8 illustrates these differences, assuming the following declarations:

```
const
  MaxSize = 5;

type
  IndexRange = 1..MaxSize;
  TestArray = array [IndexRange] of Real;

var
  X, Y, Z : TestArray;
```

EXAMPLE 10.8 ▼

Although it is possible to use a single assignment statement to copy one array to another, the assignment statement

```
Z := X + Y     {illegal addition of arrays}
```

is invalid because the operator + cannot have an array as an operand. You might use procedure AddArray (Fig. 10.9) to add two arrays of type Test-Array.

The parameter correspondence for arrays established by the procedure call statement

```
AddArray (X, Y, Z)
```

is shown in Fig. 10.10. Arrays A and B in the procedure data area are local copies of arrays X and Y. As indicated by the solid arrow, the address of the first element of array Z is stored in parameter C. The procedure results are stored directly in array Z. After execution of the procedure, Z[1] will contain the sum of X[1] and Y[1], or 3.5; Z[2] will contain 6.7; and so on. Arrays X and Y will be unchanged.   ▲

Figure 10.9
Procedure AddArray

```
procedure AddArray (A, B {input} : TestArray;
                    var C {output} : TestArray);
{
  Stores the sum of A[I] and B[I] in C[I]. Array elements
  with subscripts 1..MaxSize are summed, element by element.
  Pre : A[I] and B[I] (1 <= I <= MaxSize) are defined.
  Post: C[I] := A[I] + B[I] (1 <= I <= MaxSize).
}
  var
    I : IndexRange;          {loop control and array subscript}

begin {AddArray}
  {Add corresponding elements of each array.}
  for I := 1 to MaxSize do
    C[I] := A[I] + B[I]
end; {AddArray}
```

Program Style

Efficiency of Variable Parameters Versus Protection of Value Parameters

Parameters A and B in Fig. 10.9 are declared as value parameters because they only store data passed into procedure AddArray and their values should not be changed by AddArray. Pascal must create a local copy of

▶▶▶▶▶▶

Figure 10.10
Parameter Correspondence for AddArray (X, Y, Z)

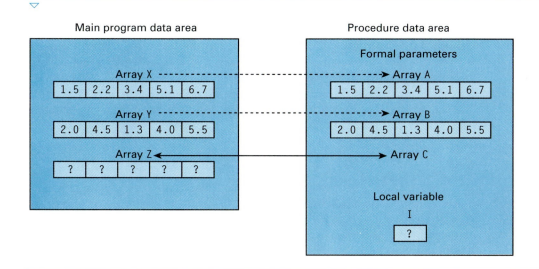

these two arrays each time procedure `AddArray` is called. This copying uses valuable computer time and memory space. If the arrays being copied are very large, the program may terminate with an error because all its memory space has been used.

To conserve time and memory space, experienced programmers sometimes declare arrays that are used only for module inputs as variable parameters rather than as value parameters. This means, however, that the corresponding actual array is directly manipulated by the module and is no longer protected from accidental modification by the module. Any changes made to the actual array are an undesirable side effect of the module's execution. If an array corresponds to a value parameter, the changes are made to a local copy, and the actual array is unaffected. To avoid side effects, declare array parameters used only for module inputs as value parameters unless the arrays are quite large (say, more than 500 elements).

EXAMPLE 10.9: Comparing Two Arrays ▼

Function `SameArray` in Fig. 10.11 determines whether two arrays (of type `TestArray`) are identical. We consider two arrays to be identical if the first element of one is the same as the first element of the other, the second element of one is the same as the second element of the other, and so forth.

We can determine that the arrays are not identical by finding a single pair of unequal elements. Consequently, the `while` loop may be executed anywhere from one time (first elements unequal) to `MaxSize` - 1 times. Loop exit occurs when a pair of unequal elements is found or just before the last pair is tested.

After loop exit, the Boolean assignment statement

```
SameArray := (A[I] = B[I])                {Define result.}
```

defines the function result. If loop exit occurs because the pair of elements with subscript I are not equal, the function result is `False`. If loop exit occurs because the last pair of elements is reached (I = MaxSize), the function result is `True` if the elements at I are equal and `False` if they are not.

As an example of how you might use function `SameArray`, the `if` statement

```
if SameArray(X, Y) then
  Z := X
else
  AddArray (X, Y, Z)
```

either copies array X to array Z (when X and Y are identical) or stores the sum of arrays X and Y in array Z (when X and Y are not identical).

Because the arrays have `MaxSize` elements, a common error is to use the condition

```
(I <= MaxSize) and (A[I] = B[I])
```

Figure 10.11
Function SameArray

```
function SameArray (A, B : TestArray) : Boolean;
{
  Returns a value of True if the arrays A, B are identical;
  otherwise, returns a value of False.
  Pre : A[I] and B[I] (1 <= I <= MaxSize) are defined.
  Post: Returns True if A[I] = B[I] for all I in range
        1..MaxSize; otherwise, returns False.
}
  var
    I : Integer;                       {array subscript}

begin
  I := 1;                             {Start with first pair.}
  {Test corresponding elements of arrays A and B.}
  while (I < MaxSize) and (A[I] = B[I]) do
    {invariant:
        1 <= I <= MaxSize and
        A[I] = B[I] for all prior values of I
    }
    I := I + 1;                       {Advance to next pair.}

  {assert:
    An unequal pair was found or all but the
    last pair were compared.
  }
  SameArray := (A[I] = B[I])          {Define result.}
end;  {SameArray}
```

as the `while` condition in Fig. 10.11, causing all element pairs to be tested by the `while` condition if the arrays are equal. When `I` is `MaxSize + 1`, the first part of this condition evaluates to `False` but the second part still must be evaluated unless short-circuit evaluation is used. This can lead to a `Range check error` because array element `A[MaxSize + 1]` does not exist. ▲

The next case study demonstrates two different methods for array access: sequential access and random access. We discuss their differences after the case study.

CASE STUDY　　**Home Budget Problem**

PROBLEM ▼

Write a program that keeps track of monthly expenses by category. The program should read each expense amount, add it to the appropriate category total, and print the total expenditure by category. The input data consist of the category and the amount of each purchase made during the past month.

ANALYSIS ▼

The budget categories are entertainment, food, clothing, rent, tuition, insurance, and miscellaneous. The program must accumulate seven separate totals, each of which can be associated with a different element of a seven-element array. The program must read each expenditure, determine to which category it belongs, and then add that expenditure to the appropriate array element. After processing all expenditures, the program should print a table that shows each category and its accumulated total. As in all programs that accumulate a sum, each total must be initialized to zero.

You could simply use an array with subscripts 1 through 7 to store your budget entries, but the program would be more readable if you declared a data type `BudgetCat` and used this data type as the array subscript type. To enhance modularity and ease of development, you can treat the `BudgetCat` data type as an abstract data type and declare it, together with its operators `ReadBudgetCat` and `WriteBudgetCat`, in unit `BudgetCatADT` (see Programming Exercise 4 at the end of this section). Data type `BudgetCat`, shown next, has an extra "category," `Done`, which is used to indicate that all expenditures have been processed.

Data Requirements

Data Type

```
BudgetCat = (Entertainment, Food, Clothing, Rent,
             Tuition, Insurance, Miscellaneous, Done);
```

Problem Inputs

Each expenditure and its category

Problem Output

The array of expenditure totals (`Budget`)

DESIGN ▼

Initial Algorithm

1. Initialize all category totals to zero.
2. Display the possible budget categories.
3. Read each expenditure and add it to the appropriate total.
4. Print the accumulated total for each category.

Structure Chart and Refinements

The structure chart in Fig. 10.12 shows the relationships among steps 1, 3, and 4, which manipulate the array `Budget`. Procedures `Initialize` and

Figure 10.12
Structure Chart for Home
Budget Problem

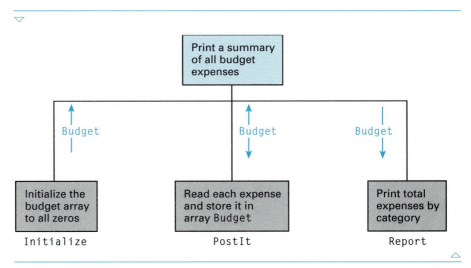

PostIt store information in this array, and procedure Report displays this
information. Step 2 is implemented by procedure DisplayMenu (not shown),
which simply lists the budget categories for the benefit of the program user.

IMPLEMENTATION ▼

Coding the Main Program

Figure 10.13 shows the program. The main program contains declarations for
the data type BudgetArray and the array Budget (type BudgetArray). Array Budget appears in each parameter list and is passed between each procedure and the main program.

The loop-control variable NextCat (type BudgetCat) is declared as a local variable in each procedure. In procedure Initialize, the assignment
statement

```
Budget[NextCat] := 0.0
```

is repeated once for each value of NextCat and sets each element of Budget
to 0. In procedure Report the statements

```
WriteBudgetCat (NextCat);  {Display budget category.}
WriteLn (Budget[NextCat] :15:2)
```

call procedure WriteBudgetCat (from unit BudgetCatADT) to display a
budget category name and WriteLn to display the category total.

Procedure PostIt must read each expenditure and add it to the appropriate array element. The total of all entertainment expenditures is accumulated

Figure 10.13
Home Budget Program

```
{$R+}
program HomeBudget;
{Prints a summary of all expenses by budget category}

uses
   BudgetCatADT;          {Import type BudgetCat and
                             ReadBudgetCat and WriteBudgetCat.}

   type
     BudgetArray = array [BudgetCat] of Real;    {array type}

   var
     Budget : BudgetArray;          {output - array of totals}

   procedure Initialize (var Budget {output} : BudgetArray);
   {
     Initializes array Budget to all zeros.
     Pre : None.
     Post: Each element of Budget is 0.0.
   }
     var
       NextCat : BudgetCat;          {loop-control variable}
                                     {      array subscript}
   begin {Initialize}
     for NextCat := Entertainment to Miscellaneous do
       Budget[NextCat] := 0.0
   end; {Initialize}

   procedure DisplayMenu;
   {Displays the budget categories}
     var
       NextCat : BudgetCat;

   begin
     WriteLn ('LIST OF BUDGET CATEGORIES:');
     for NextCat := Entertainment to Done do
       begin
         WriteBudgetCat (NextCat);
         WriteLn
       end {for}
   end; {DisplayMenu}

   procedure PostIt (var Budget {input/output} : BudgetArray);
   {
     Reads each expenditure amount and adds it to the
     appropriate element of array Budget.
     Pre : Each array element Budget[NextCat] is 0.0.
     Post: Each array element Budget[NextCat] is the sum of
           expense amounts for category NextCat.
   }
```

▷ ▷ ▷ ▷ ▷

```
begin {PostIt stub}
  WriteLn ('Procedure PostIt entered')
end; {PostIt stub}

procedure Report (Budget {input} : BudgetArray);
{
  Prints the expenditures in each budget category.
  Pre  : Array Budget is defined.
  Post : Displays each budget category name and amount.
  Calls: WriteBudgetCat
}
  var
    NextCat : BudgetCat;         {loop-control variable,}
                                 {array subscript}
begin {Report}
  WriteLn;                                {Display table heading.}
  WriteLn ('  Category      ' :15, 'Expenses' :15);
  {Print each category name and the total.}
  for NextCat := Entertainment to Miscellaneous do
    begin
      WriteBudgetCat (NextCat);   {Display category.}
      WriteLn (Budget[NextCat] :15:2)
    end {for}
end; {Report}

begin  {HomeBudget}
  {Initialize array Budget to all zeros.}
  Initialize (Budget);

  {Display list of budget categories.}
  DisplayMenu;

  {Read and process each expenditure.}
  PostIt (Budget);

  {Print the expenditures in each category.}
  Report (Budget)
end. {HomeBudget}
```

in Budget[Entertainment], all food expenditures are accumulated in Budget[Food], and so forth.

Coding Procedure PostIt

Procedure PostIt, shown in Fig. 10.14, uses procedure ReadBudgetCat (from unit BudgetCatADT) to read the budget category. Procedure PostIt calls ReadBudgetCat to read the next category into NextCat. The while loop body is executed for each value of NextCat that is not Done (the sentinel). The assignment statement

Figure 10.14
Procedure PostIt

```
procedure PostIt (var Budget {input/output} : BudgetArray);
{
  Reads each expenditure amount and adds it to the
  appropriate element of array Budget.
  Pre  : Each array element Budget[NextCat] is 0.0.
  Post : Each array element Budget[NextCat] is the sum of
         expense amounts for category NextCat.
  Calls: ReadBudgetCat
}
  var
    NextCat : BudgetCat;    {next budget category}
    Expense : Real;         {expenditure amount}

begin   {PostIt}
  {Read each budget category and expense and add to Budget.}
  ReadBudgetCat (NextCat);
  while NextCat <> Done do
    {invariant:
        no prior value of NextCat is Done
        and Budget[NextCat] is the sum of all budget entries
        so far for each category NextCat.
    }
    begin
      Write ('Enter the expenditure amount $');
      ReadLn (Expense);
      Budget[NextCat] := Budget[NextCat] + Expense;
      WriteLn;
      ReadBudgetCat (NextCat)
    end {while}
end; {PostIt}
```

```
Budget[NextCat] := Budget[NextCat] + Expense;
```

adds the expense amount to whatever element of array Budget is selected by NextCat.

TESTING ▼

Before running the program, you must save and compile to disk file BUD-GETCA.PAS, which contains unit BudgetCatADT (see Programming Exercise 4 at the end of this section). A sample run of the home budget program in Fig. 10.15 indicates that the input data do not have to be in order by category. You should verify that all budget categories without expenses remain zero and that invalid category values do not cause the program to terminate

Figure 10.15

Sample Run of Home
Budget Program

```
LIST OF BUDGET CATEGORIES:
Entertainment
Food
Clothing
Rent
Tuition
Insurance
Miscellaneous
Done

Enter the first letter of the category> C
Enter the expenditure amount $25.00

Enter the first letter of the category> M
Enter the expenditure amount $25.00

Enter the first letter of the category> C
Enter the expenditure amount $15.00

Enter the first letter of the category> E
Enter the expenditure amount $675.00

Enter the first letter of the category> D

    Category        Expenses
    Entertainment    675.00
    Food               0.00
    Clothing          40.00
    Rent               0.00
    Tuition            0.00
    Insurance          0.00
    Miscellaneous     25.00
```

prematurely. Notice that it is sufficient to enter only the first letter of each budget category because all are unique.

Sequential Versus Random Access to Arrays

The home budget program illustrates two common ways of selecting array elements for processing. Often we need to manipulate all elements of an array in some uniform manner (for instance, we might want to initialize them all to zero). In such situations, it makes sense to process the array elements in sequence (*sequential access*), starting with the first and ending with the last. In procedures `Initialize` and `Report`, we accomplish sequential access by using a `for` loop whose loop-control variable is also the array subscript.

In procedure PostIt, the order in which the array elements are accessed depends completely on the order of the data. The value read into NextCat determines the element to be incremented. This approach is called *random access* because the order is not predictable.

Exercises for Section 10.3   **Self-Check**

1. When is it better to pass an entire array of data, rather than individual elements, to a procedure?
2. When is a copy of an entire array made for an array that is a procedure parameter? What happens to the copy after the procedure executes?
3. In function SameArray (Fig. 10.11), what will be the value of I when the statement

   ```
   SameArray := (A[I] = B[I])
   ```

   executes if array A is equal to array B? If the third elements do not match? If only the last elements do not match?

Programming

1. Write a procedure that assigns a value of True to element I of the output array if element I of one input array has the same value as element I of the other input array; otherwise, assign a value of False. If the input arrays have subscript type IndexType, the output array should have the following type:

   ```
   type
      BoolArray = array [IndexType] of Boolean;
   ```

2. Write a procedure that copies each value stored in one array to the corresponding element of another array. For example, if the arrays are InArray and OutArray, copy InArray[1] to OutArray[1], then copy InArray[2] to OutArray[2], and so on.
3. Write an array equivalent of the Switch procedure of Fig. 10.6 that does not allocate a local, temporary array. Hence SwitchArray, given input arrays Aarray and Barray, would switch Aarray[1] with Barray[1], Aarray[2] with Barray[2], and so on.
4. Write unit BudgetCatADT. *Hint:* See unit DayADT in Fig. 9.10.

10.4   Subarray Processing

Usually, it isn't known prior to program execution exactly how many elements will be stored in an array. As an example, a professor processing exam scores might have 150 students in one class, 200 in the next, and so on. Because you must declare the array size before program execution begins (at *compile time*), you must allocate enough storage space so that the program can process the largest expected array without error.

When you read the array data into memory, you should begin filling the array starting with the first element and be sure to keep track of how many data items are actually stored in the array. The part of the array that contains data is called the **filled subarray.** The **length** of the filled subarray is the number of data items that are actually stored in the array.

filled subarray
the portion of an array that contains actual data
length of a subarray
the number of elements in a subarray

EXAMPLE 10.10 ▼

The array Scores, declared as follows, can accommodate a class size of up to 250 students. Each array element can contain an integer value.

```
const
   ClassSize = 250;              {maximum class size}

type
   ClassIndex = 1..ClassSize;   {subscript type for ScoreArray}
   ScoreArray = array [ClassIndex] of Integer;

var
   Scores : ScoreArray;         {array of exam scores}
   ClassLength : Integer;       {length of filled subarray}
```

Procedure ReadScores in Fig. 10.16 reads up to 250 exam scores and prints a warning message when the array is filled. The output parameter ClassLength represents the length of the filled subarray and is initialized to zero. Within the while loop, the statements

Figure 10.16
Reading Part of an Array

```
procedure ReadScores (var Scores {output} : ScoreArray;
                      var ClassLength {output} : Integer);
{
   Reads an array of exam scores (Scores)
   for a class of up to ClassSize students.
   Pre : None.
   Post: The filled subarray is Scores[1..ClassLength]
         and ClassLength is the number of values read
         (0 <= ClassLength <= ClassSize).
}
   const
     Sentinel = -1;              {sentinel score}

   var
     TempScore : Integer;     {temporary storage for a score}

begin
   Write ('Enter next score after the prompt or enter ');
   WriteLn (Sentinel :1, ' to stop:');

   {Read each array element until done.}
   ClassLength := 0;                {initial class length}
   Write ('Score> ');
```

▷ ▷ ▷ ▷ ▷ ▷

```
    ReadLn (TempScore);
    while (TempScore <> Sentinel) and (ClassLength < ClassSize) do
      {invariant:
         No prior value of TempScore is Sentinel,
         ClassLength <= ClassSize,
         and Scores[1..ClassLength] is the filled subarray
      }
      begin
        ClassLength := ClassLength + 1; {Increment ClassLength.}
        Scores[ClassLength] := TempScore;      {Save the score.}
        Write ('Score> ');
        ReadLn (TempScore)
      end; {while}

    {assert: Sentinel was read or array is filled.}
    if TempScore <> Sentinel then
      WriteLn ('Cannot store ', TempScore, '- array is full.')
end;  {ReadScores}
```

```
ClassLength := ClassLength + 1; {Increment ClassLength.}
Scores[ClassLength] := TempScore;      {Save the score.}
```

increment ClassLength and store the score just read (value of TempScore) in the next array element. After loop exit, the value of ClassLength is the length of the filled subarray.

In any subsequent processing of array Scores, use the variable ClassLength to limit the number of array elements processed. Because only the subarray with subscripts 1 through ClassLength (i.e., Scores[1..ClassLength]) contains meaningful data, array elements with subscripts larger than ClassLength should not be manipulated. ClassLength should be passed as a parameter to any procedure that processes the filled subarray.   ▲

Exercises for Section 10.4   *Self-Check*

1. In procedure ReadScores, what prevents the user from entering more than ClassSize scores?
2. Given the ability to do subarray processing, what are the consequences of always declaring a larger array bounds than is needed?
3. Why do we read the next data value into TempScore instead of reading it directly into the next array element?

Programming

1. Rewrite the while loop in ReadScores as a repeat-until loop. Why is the while loop better? Why can't we use a for loop?

10.5 Searching and Sorting an Array

This section discusses two common problems in processing arrays: *searching* an array to determine the location of a particular value and *sorting* an array to rearrange the array elements in numerical order. As an example of an array search, we might want to search the array to determine which student, if any, got a particular score. An example of an array sort would be rearranging the array elements so that they are in increasing order by score. Such a sort would be helpful if we wanted to display the list in order by score or if we needed to locate several different scores in the array.

Finding the Smallest Value in an Array

We begin by solving a simpler search problem: finding the smallest value in an array.

Algorithm for Finding the Smallest Value in an Array

1. Assume that the first element is the smallest so far and save its subscript as the subscript of the smallest so far.
2. for each array element do
    3. if the current element < the smallest so far then
        4. Save the subscript of the current element as the subscript of the smallest so far.

Function `FindMin` in Fig. 10.17 implements this algorithm for an array of type `ScoreArray` (see Example 10.10). During each iteration of the loop, `MinIndex` is the subscript of the smallest element so far and `W[MinIndex]` is its value. The function returns the last value assigned to `MinIndex`, which is the subscript of the smallest value in the array. Parameters `StartIndex` and `EndIndex` define the boundaries of the subarray `W[StartIndex..EndIndex]` whose smallest value is being found. Passing these subscripts as arguments results in a more general function.

Note that function `FindMin` returns the subscript (or index) of the smallest value, not the smallest value itself. Assuming `Next` is type `Integer`, and `ClassLength` is the number of array elements containing data, the following statements display the smallest value in array `Scores` (type `ScoreArray`):

```
IndexOfMin := FindMin(Scores, 1, ClassLength);
WriteLn ('The smallest exam score is ', Scores[IndexOfMin] :1)
```

Although not as easy to read, the single statement that follows is equivalent; it uses the function designator as the subscript expression.

```
WriteLn ('The smallest exam score is ',
        Scores[FindMin(Scores, 1, ClassLength)] :1)
```

Figure 10.17
Function FindMin

```
function FindMin (W {input} : ScoreArray;
                  StartIndex, EndIndex {input} : ClassIndex) :
                                                        Integer;
{
  Returns the subscript of the smallest element in the
  subarray W[StartIndex..EndIndex].
  Pre : StartIndex and EndIndex are defined and
        W[StartIndex..EndIndex] is part of the filled subarray.
  Post: Returns K if W[K] <= W[I] for all I in subrange
        StartIndex..EndIndex. If the smallest value appears in
        two or more elements, K is the subscript of the first.
}
  var
    MinIndex,               {index of smallest so far}
    NextIndex : Integer;    {index of current element}
begin {FindMin}
  MinIndex := StartIndex;   {Assume first entry is smallest.}
  for NextIndex := StartIndex + 1 to EndIndex do
    if W[NextIndex] < W[MinIndex] then
      MinIndex := NextIndex; {Value at NextIndex is smallest.}

  {assert:
    All elements are examined and
    MinIndex is the index of the smallest element.
  }
  FindMin := MinIndex                  {Define result.}
end; {FindMin}
```

Searching an Array

We can search an array for a particular score by comparing each array element, starting with the first, to the *target score,* the value we are seeking. If a match occurs, we have found the target score in the array and can return its subscript as the search result. Otherwise, we continue searching until we either get a match or test all array elements without success.

Data Requirements for Search Function

Input Parameters

```
Scores: ScoreArray        {array to be searched}
ClassLength : ClassIndex  {number of elements in Scores}
Target : Integer          {score being searched for}
```

Function Output

The subscript of the first element containing `Target` or zero if `Target` was not found

Program Variables

```
Next : Integer      {subscript of next score to test}
NoTarget: Boolean   {program flag - true if target
                     has not been found in elements
                     tested so far}
```

Algorithm for Search Function

1. Start with the first array element.
2. Set `NoTarget` to `True`.
3. `while` the target is not found and there are more elements `do`
    4. `if` the current element contains the target score `then`
        Set `NoTarget` to `False`.
        `else`
        Try the next element.
5. `if` the target was not found `then`
    Return 0.
    `else`
    Return the target's subscript.

The `while` loop in step 3 executes until it finds an array element that contains the target score or it has tested all array elements without success. Step 4 compares the current array element (selected by subscript `Next`) to the target score and sets `NoTarget` to `False` if they match. If they do not match, the subscript `Next` is increased by 1. After loop exit, the `if` statement (step 5) defines the function result as 0 (target was not found) or as the value of `Next` when the match occurred. Figure 10.18 shows function `Search`.

The program flag `NoTarget` controls loop repetition and communicates the results of the search loop to the `if` statement that follows the loop. `NoTarget` is set to `True` before entering the search loop and reset to `False` as soon as a tested element matches the target. The only way `NoTarget` can remain true throughout the entire array search is if no array element matches the target. The `if` statement returns 0 when `NoTarget` remains true; otherwise, it returns the value of subscript `Next` that caused `NoTarget` to be changed to `False`.

The loop invariant is

```
{invariant:
   Target was not found in subarray Scores[1..Next - 1]
   and Next is <= ClassLength + 1.
}
```

Figure 10.18
Function Search

```
function Search (Scores : ScoreArray;
                 ClassLength : ClassIndex;
                 Target : Integer)      : Integer;
{
  Searches for Target in array Scores.
  Pre : 1 <= ClassLength <= ClassSize and
        Scores[1..ClassLength] is the filled subarray.
  Post: Returns the subscript of Target if found;
        otherwise, returns zero.
}
  var
    Next : Integer;              {index of the current score}
    NoTarget : Boolean;          {program flag - true if target
                                  has not been found in elements
                                  tested so far}

begin  {Search}
  {Compare each element of Scores to Target until done.}
  Next := 1;                     {Start with the first score.]
  NoTarget := True;              {Target is not found.}
  while NoTarget and (Next <= ClassLength) do
    {invariant:
       Target was not found in subarray Scores[1..Next - 1]
       and Next is <= ClassLength + 1.
    }
    if Scores[Next] = Target then
      NoTarget := False          {Target is found.}
    else
      Next := Next + 1;          {Advance to next score.}

  {assert:
    Target was found or all elements tested without success.
  }
  if NoTarget then
    Search := 0                  {Target was not found.}
  else
    Search := Next               {Target found at Scores[Next].}
end; {Search}
```

This means that for each value of Next (starting with 1), the target was not found in an array element with a smaller subscript than Next. Because Next <= ClassLength + 1 must also be true after loop exit, Scores[ClassLength] is the last array element that can be compared to the target.

In the following sketch of array Scores,

Array Scores

[1] [2]   . . .   [Next-1] [Next] . . . [ClassLength]

| Elements tested without success | Elements not yet tested |

the elements in the color part of the array are the ones that have already been tested, and the element with subscript `Next` will be tested in the current loop iteration. If `Scores[Next]` does not match the target, the portion of the array in color will grow by one element, and the value of `Next` will increase by 1.

The invariant is true before the first iteration (`Next` is 1) because there are no array elements that precede the element with subscript 1. If the current element matches the target, loop exit will occur without changing `Next`, so the invariant will still be true. If `Next` becomes `ClassLength + 1`, all array elements will have been tested without success (the entire array will be in color), and loop exit will occur.

Sorting an Array

Many programs execute more efficiently if the data they process are sorted before processing begins. For example, a check processing program executes more quickly if all checks are in order by checking account number. Other programs produce more understandable output if the information is sorted before it is displayed. For example, your university might want your instructor's grade report sorted by student ID number. In this section, we describe one simple sorting algorithm from among the many that have been studied by computer scientists.

The *selection sort* is a fairly intuitive sorting algorithm. To perform a selection sort of an array with N elements (subscripts `1..N`), we locate the smallest element in the array and then switch the smallest element with the element at subscript 1, thereby placing the smallest element at position 1. Then we locate the smallest element remaining in the subarray with subscripts `2..N` and switch it with the element at subscript 2, thereby placing the second smallest element at position 2. Then we locate the smallest element remaining in the subarray with subscripts `3..N` and switch it with the element at subscript 3, and so on.

Figure 10.19 traces the operation of the selection sort algorithm on a subarray of length 4. The first array shown is the original array. Then we show each step as the next smallest element is moved to its correct position. The subarray in color represents the portion of each array that is sorted. Note that, at most, `N-1` exchanges will be required to sort an array with N elements.

Algorithm for Selection Sort

1. `for Fill := 1 to N-1 do`
   2. Find the position of the smallest element
      in subarray `Scores[Fill..N]`.
   3. `if Fill` is not the position of the smallest element `then`
      4. Exchange the smallest element with the one at position
         `Fill`.

Figure 10.19
Trace of Selection Sort

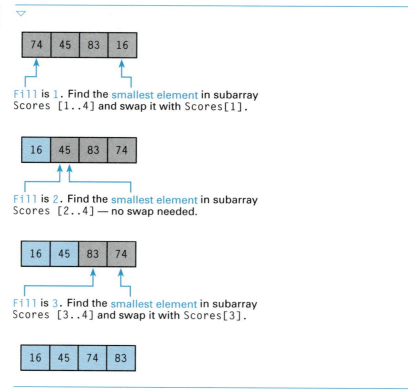

Fill is 1. Find the smallest element in subarray Scores [1..4] and swap it with Scores[1].

Fill is 2. Find the smallest element in subarray Scores [2..4] — no swap needed.

Fill is 3. Find the smallest element in subarray Scores [3..4] and swap it with Scores[3].

We can use function FindMin (see Fig. 10.17) to perform step 2. Procedure SelectSort in Fig. 10.20 implements the selection sort algorithm for the array Scores with ClassLength elements. Local variable IndexOfMin holds the index of the smallest exam score found so far in the current subarray. At the end of each pass, we call procedure Switch (see Fig. 10.6) to exchange the elements with subscripts IndexOfMin and Fill when IndexOfMin and Fill differ. After execution of procedure SelectSort, the exam scores will be in increasing order by exam score. We must modify procedure Switch to accept type Integer parameters.

The loop invariant for the outer loop

```
{invariant:
    The elements in Scores[1..Fill-1] are in
    their proper place and Fill <= ClassLength.
}
```

summarizes the progress of the selection sort. The subarray whose elements are in their proper place is shown in the color part of array Scores in the

Figure 10.20

Selection Sort Procedure

```
procedure SelectSort (var Scores {input/output} : ScoreArray;
                          ClassLength {input} : Integer);
{
 Sorts the data in array Scores.
 Pre : 1 <= ClassLength <= ClassSize and the
       filled subarray is Scores[1..ClassLength].
 Post: The values in Scores[1..ClassLength] are in
       increasing order.
 Calls:Procedures Switch and FindMin
}
  var
    Fill, {index of element to contain next smallest score}
    IndexOfMin : Integer;      {index of next smallest element}

begin {SelectSort}
   for Fill := 1 to ClassLength - 1 do
     begin
       {invariant:
          The elements in Scores[1..Fill-1] are in
          their proper place and Fill <= ClassLength.
       }
       {Find smallest score in Scores[Fill..ClassLength].}
       IndexOfMin := FindMin(Scores, Fill, ClassLength);

       {Exchange elements at Fill and IndexOfMin.}
       if IndexOfMin <> Fill then
          Switch (Scores[IndexOfMin], Scores[Fill])
     end {for Fill}
end; {SelectSort}
```

following sketch. The remaining elements are not yet in place and are all larger than `Scores[Fill-1]`.

Array `Scores`

[1] [2] . . . [Fill-1]	[Fill] . . . [ClassLength]
Elements in their proper place	**Elements larger than** `Scores[Fill-1]`

During each pass, the portion of the array in color grows by one element and `Fill` is incremented to reflect this. When `Fill` is equal to `ClassLength`, the first `ClassLength-1` elements will be in their proper place, so `Scores[ClassLength]` must also be in its proper place.

Program Style

Creating and Using General Purpose Modules

Function FindMin is a general purpose module that finds the smallest element in any subarray of its array parameter. Writing FindMin in this way enables us to use it in procedure SelectSort, simplifying the coding of SelectSort.

Exercises for Section 10.5 **Self-Check**

1. For the Search function in Fig. 10.18, what happens if
   a. the last student score matches the target?
   b. several scores match the target?
2. Trace the execution of the selection sort on the following two lists:

   10 55 34 56 76 5   5 15 25 35 45 45

   Show the arrays after each exchange occurs. How many exchanges are required to sort each list? How many comparisons?
3. How could you modify the selection sort algorithm to get the scores in descending order (largest score first)?

Programming

1. Write a procedure to find the next to the smallest element of an array. Assume that there are no duplicate entries in the array. Return StartIndex if the array only has one item.
2. Another method of performing the selection sort is to place the largest value in position N, the next largest in position N-1, and so on. Write this version.
3. A technique for implementing an array search without introducing a program flag is to use a while loop that increments Next as long as both of the following statements are true: The target does not match the current element, and Next is less than ClassLength. After loop exit, the element at position Next can be retested to determine the function result. If the element matches the target, the result is Next; otherwise, the result is 0. Write the function body.

10.6 Analysis of Algorithms: Big-O Notation (Optional)

Many algorithms for searching and sorting arrays are available. Because arrays can have many elements, executing these algorithms can be very time consuming. Therefore, it is important to have some idea of the relative efficiency of different algorithms. Given the difficulty of measuring precisely the performance of an algorithm or program, programmers normally try to approximate the effect on an algorithm of a change in the number of items, N, that the algorithm processes. Programmers can compare two algorithms by seeing how each algorithm's execution time increases with N.

For example, if

$2N^2 + N - 5$

expresses the relationship between processing time and N, the algorithm is an $O(N^2)$ algorithm, where O is an abbreviation for order of magnitude. This notation is known as *Big-O notation*. The reason that this is an $O(N^2)$ algorithm instead of an $O(2N^2)$ algorithm or an $O(2N^2 + N - 5)$ algorithm is that the fastest-growing term (the one with the largest exponent) is dominant for large N and we ignore constants.

To search an array of N elements for a target using function `Search`, we have to examine all N elements if the target is not present in the array. If the target is in the array, then we have to search only until we find it. However, the target could be anywhere in the array—it is equally likely to be at the beginning of the array as at the end. So on average we have to examine $N/2$ array elements to locate a target value in an array. This means that an array search is an $O(N)$ process, so the growth rate is linear.

To determine the efficiency of a sorting algorithm, we focus on the number of array element comparisons and exchanges that it requires. Performing a selection sort on an array with N elements requires $N - 1$ comparisons during the first pass through the array, $N - 2$ comparisons during the second pass, and so on. Therefore the total number of comparisons is represented by the series

$1 + 2 + 3 + \cdots + (N - 2) + (N - 1)$

The value of this series is expressed in the closed form

$N \times (N - 1)/2 = N^2/2 - N/2$

so the number of comparisons performed in sorting an array of N elements is $O(N^2)$.

The number of array element exchanges varies, depending on the initial ordering of the array elements. If an element is already in its correct position, it is not exchanged. If the array happens to be sorted before procedure `SelectSort` is called, all its elements will be in their proper place, so there will be zero exchanges (*best-case situation*). If no elements are in their correct positions, there will be one exchange at the end of each pass through the array, or a total of $N - 1$ exchanges (*worst-case situation*). Therefore, the number of array element exchanges for an arbitrary initial ordering is between zero and $N - 1$, which is $O(N)$.

Because the number of comparisons is $O(N^2)$, selection sort is a *quadratic sort* (i.e., its growth rate is proportional to the square of the number of elements). What difference does it make whether an algorithm is an $O(N)$ process or an $O(N^2)$ process? Table 10.5 evaluates N and N^2 for different values of N. A doubling of N causes N^2 to increase by a factor of 4. Since N^2 increases much more quickly than *N*, the performance of an $O(N)$ algorithm is not as adversely affected by an increase in array size as is an $O(N^2)$ algorithm. For large values of *N* (say, 100 or more), the differences in performance for an $O(N)$ and an $O(N^2)$ algorithm are significant (see the last three lines of Table 10.5).

Table 10.5
Table of Values of *N*
and N^2

N	N^2
2	4
4	16
8	64
16	256
32	1024
64	4096
128	16384
256	65536
512	262144

Other factors besides the number of comparisons and exchanges affect an algorithm's performance. For example, one algorithm may take more time preparing for each exchange or comparison than another. Or one algorithm might exchange subscripts, whereas another might exchange the array elements themselves, which can be more time-consuming. Another measure of efficiency is the amount of memory required by an algorithm.

Exercises for Section 10.6 **Self-Check**

1. Determine how many times the WriteLn statement is displayed in each of the following fragments. Indicate whether the program fragment is $O(N)$ or $O(N^2)$.

   a. ```
   for I := 1 to N do
       for J := 1 to N do
           WriteLn (I, J)
   ```
   b. ```
   for I := 1 to N do
       for J := 1 to 2 do
           WriteLn (I, J)
   ```
   c. ```
   for I := 1 to N do
       for J := N downto I do
           WriteLn (I, J)
   ```
   ```

Programming

1. Write a program fragment that displays the values of *Y1* and *Y2*, defined as follows, for values of *N* from 10 to 100 in increments of 10. Does the result surprise you?

   $Y1 = 100N + 10$

   $Y2 = 5N^2 + 2$

10.7 Arrays with Type Char Elements and Subscripts

Many arrays contain numerical values, such as exam scores or hours worked. The arrays we introduce in this section store character data. In addition to storing character data in arrays, we can use characters as array subscripts.

Arrays of Characters Versus String Variables

Turbo Pascal allows us to use either an array of characters or a string variable to store a collection of characters in memory. The following declarations allocate storage for array `FirstName` and string variable `LastName`, each of which provides storage for 20 characters:

```
const
  StringSize = 20;

type
  IndexRange = 1..StringSize;
  CharArray = array [IndexRange] of Char;
  String20 = string[StringSize];

var
  FirstName : CharArray;    {array of 20 characters}
  LastName : String20;      {string of up to 20 characters}
```

We would process array `FirstName` just like any other array in Pascal. A loop is necessary to read data into array `FirstName` or to display its contents.

The type declaration for `String20` indicates that a variable of this type (e.g., `LastName`) can store up to 20 characters instead of the default maximum for a string variable, which is 255 characters. You can work more easily with string variable `LastName` than array `FirstName` for several reasons:

▶ You can use the Pascal Read(Ln) and Write(Ln) procedures to read a data value into `LastName` or to display the value in `LastName`.
▶ You can compare `LastName` to a string value or another string variable using the relational operators. For example, `LastName = 'ZZZZZ'` is true if `LastName` contains five Z characters; `LastName < 'ZZZZZ'` is true if `LastName` is less than the string of five Z characters.
▶ You can use an assignment statement such as

```
LastName := 'Washington'
```

to store a string value in LastName.

The length of string variable LastName is *dynamic* (changeable) and is defined as the number of characters actually stored (10 for the preceding assignment). The function designator Length(LastName) returns the length of LastName.

We can reference individual characters in both FirstName and LastName. For example, FirstName[1] and LastName[1] access the first character of the array and string. The subscripted variable LastName[Length(LastName)] accesses the last character stored in string LastName. Chapter 15 describes string processing in more detail.

SYNTAX DISPLAY

Length Function (for String Variables)

Form: Length(*string*)
Example: Length(Name)
Interpretation: The function Length returns an integer indicating the number of characters currently stored in *string*.

Arrays with Type Char Subscripts

Often you can use an array with subscript type Char (or a subrange of Char) to simplify a program that processes characters. Example 10.11 and the case study that follows use arrays whose subscripts are the uppercase letters.

EXAMPLE 10.11 ▼

The program in Fig. 10.21 displays the number of occurrences of each letter in a line of text. It uses array LetterCount (subscript type 'A'..'Z') to store the number of occurrences of each letter (e.g., LetterCount['A'] is the number of occurrences of the letter A). Procedure CountLetters reads each data character into Ch and increments the element of array LetterCount selected by data character Ch. Function UpCase (see Section 7.4) converts the case of each letter read to uppercase so that both t and T cause the count for

Figure 10.21
Counting Letters in a Line

▽

Edit Window

```
{$R+}
program Concordance;
{
  Finds and prints the number of occurrences of each letter.
  The case of each letter is immaterial. Letters with counts
  of zero are not displayed.
}
```

```
type
   Letter = 'A'..'Z';
   CountArray = array [Letter] of Integer;

var
   LetterCount : CountArray; {output - array of counts}

{Insert procedure FillCountArray here.}

procedure CountLetters (var LetterCount {output} : CountArray);
{
 Counts the number of occurrences of each letter.
 Pre  : LetterCount is initialized to all zeros.
 Post : Reads next data line and LetterCount[Ch] is the
        number of occurrences of letter Ch in the line.
}
   var
      Ch : Char;                          {each data character}

begin {CountLetters}
   WriteLn ('Type in a data line:');
   while not EOLN do
      begin
         Read (Ch);                       {Get next character.}
         Ch := UpCase(Ch);               {Convert to uppercase.}
         if (Ch >= 'A') and (Ch <= 'Z') then
            LetterCount[Ch] := LetterCount[Ch] + 1
      end; {while}
   ReadLn                                 {Skip the <eoln>.}
end; {CountLetters}

procedure PrintCount (LetterCount {input} : CountArray);
{
 Prints counts of letters.
 Pre  : LetterCount is initialized.
 Post : Displays each letter and its count if non-zero.
}
   var
      NextChar : Letter;             {loop control and subscript}

begin {PrintCount}
   WriteLn;
   WriteLn ('Letter', 'Occurrences' :16);
   for NextChar := 'A' to 'Z' do
      if LetterCount[NextChar] > 0 then
         WriteLn (NextChar :6, LetterCount[NextChar] :16)
end; {PrintCount}

begin  {Concordance}
   {Initialize LetterCount.}
   FillCountArray (LetterCount, 0);

   {Count the letters in a line.}
   CountLetters (LetterCount);
```

▷ ▷ ▷ ▷ ▷ ▷

```
{Print counts of letters that are in the line.}
PrintCount (LetterCount)
end. {Concordance}
```

Output Window

```
Type in a data line:
This is it!

Letter  Occurrences
   H              1
   I              3
   S              2
   T              2
```

letter T to be incremented. Procedure FillCountArray is similar to FillAr-ray (see Fig. 10.8). Procedure PrintCount displays a table showing each letter and the number of occurrences of each letter.   ▲

CASE STUDY   ## Cryptogram Generator Problem

A cryptogram is a coded message formed by substituting a code character for each letter of the original message. Computers can be programmed to generate these coded messages.

PROBLEM ▼

Create a cryptogram program in which the substitution is performed uniformly throughout the original message—for instance, every A is replaced by an S, every B is replaced by a P, and so forth. All punctuation (including spaces between words) remains unchanged.

ANALYSIS ▼

The program must examine each character in the message and replace each character that is a letter by its code symbol. We can store the code symbols in an array Code with subscript type 'A'..'Z' and element type Char. The character stored in Code['A'] will be the code symbol for the letter 'A'. This will enable us to look up the code symbol for a letter simply by using that letter as an index to the array Code. In the sample array Code shown next, every letter is replaced by the next letter in the alphabet and letter Z is replaced by A.

Array Code

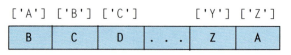

Data Requirements

Problem Inputs

```
Code : array [Letter] of Char    {array of code symbols}
```

Each message character

Problem Outputs

Each character of the cryptogram

DESIGN ▼

Initial Algorithm

1. Read in the code symbol for each letter.
2. Read each message character and display the cryptogram.

Algorithm Refinements and Structure Chart

As shown in the structure chart (Fig. 10.22), procedure `ReadCode` performs step 1 and procedure `Encrypt` performs step 2. The data requirements and algorithms for these procedures follow.

Local Variable for ReadCode

```
NextLetter : 'A'..'Z'    {Loop-control variable and
                          array subscript}
```

Algorithm for ReadCode

1. Display the alphabet.
2. for each letter do
   3. Read in the code symbol and store it in array `Code`.

Figure 10.22
Structure Chart for
Cryptogram Generator

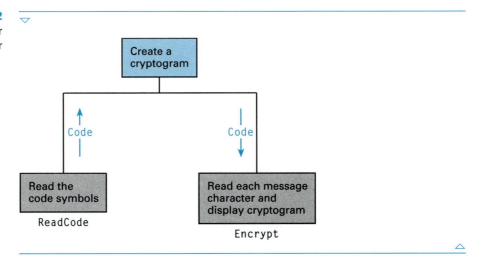

Local Variable for Encrypt

```
Ch : Char    {each message character}
```

Algorithm for Encrypt

1. while there are more message characters do
    begin
        2. Read the next message character.
        3. Display the message character or its code symbol.
    end

IMPLEMENTATION ▼

The program in Fig. 10.23 assumes that the uppercase letters are consecutive characters, as they are in the ASCII character set.

Figure 10.23
Cryptogram Generator

Edit Window

```
{$R+}
program Cryptogram;

{Generates cryptograms corresponding to input messages}

   type
      Letter = 'A'..'Z';
      CodeArray = array [Letter] of Char;

   var
      Code : CodeArray;        {input - array of code symbols}

   procedure ReadCode (var Code {output} : CodeArray);
   {
     Reads in the code symbol for each letter.
     Pre : None.
     Post: 26 data values are read into array Code.
   }
      var
         NextLetter : Letter;              {each letter}

   begin {ReadCode}
      WriteLn ('First specify the code.');
      WriteLn ('Enter a code symbol under each letter.');
      WriteLn ('ABCDEFGHIJKLMNOPQRSTUVWXYZ');
      {Read each code symbol into array Code.}
      for NextLetter := 'A' to 'Z' do
        Read (Code[NextLetter]);
      ReadLn;                              {Skip the <eoln>.}
      WriteLn                              {Skip a line.}
   end;   {ReadCode}
```

```
procedure Encrypt (Code {input} : CodeArray);
{
  Reads each character and prints it or its code symbol.
  Pre : Array Code is defined.
  Post: Reads a data line. A code symbol was printed for
        each letter; each nonletter was printed
}
  var
    Ch : Char;        {input - each message character}

begin  {Encrypt}
  WriteLn ('Enter each character of your message:');
  while not EOLN do
    begin
      Read (Ch);
      Ch := UpCase(Ch);              {Convert to uppercase.}
      if (Ch >= 'A') and (Ch <= 'Z') then
        Write (Code[Ch])             {Print code symbol.}
      else
        Write (Ch)                   {Print nonletter.}
    end; {while}
  ReadLn                             {Skip the <eoln>.}
end; {Encrypt}

begin  {Cryptogram}
  {Read in the code symbol for each letter.}
  ReadCode (Code);

  {Read each character and print it or its code symbol.}
  Encrypt (Code)
end. {Cryptogram}
```

Output Window

```
First specify the code.
Enter a code symbol under each letter.
ABCDEFGHIJKLMNOPQRSTUVWXYZ
BCDEFGHIJKLMNOPQRSTUVWXYZA

Enter each character of your message:
A tiny one!#
B UJOZ POF!#
```

TESTING ▼

In the preceding sample run, the code symbol for each letter is entered directly beneath that letter and read by procedure ReadCode. The sample run ends with two lines of output: the first contains the message; the second contains its cryptogram. For a simple test, try using each letter as its own code symbol. In that case, both lines should be the same. Make sure the program encodes lowercase as well as uppercase letters. The program should not change characters that are not letters.

....

Self-Check

1. What changes would have to be made to the cryptogram generator so that, given the same code, it would decode rather than encrypt?

Programming

1. Make changes to the cryptogram program to encode the blank character and the punctuation symbols , ; : ? ! . . *Hint:* Use subscript type Char.
2. The cryptogram generator program does not work correctly if the user inputs the same code symbol more than once. Modify ReadCode so that such an error forces the user to reenter an unambiguous code.

10.8 Debugging Programs with Arrays

When debugging programs (or modules) that process arrays, it is best to test them on arrays having a small number of elements. If constants are used in array size declarations, then these constants should be small values. After your program is error free, you can change the constants to their normal values. Remember to enable range checking by using the {$R+} compiler directive.

If you use a variable or an expression as an array subscript, use the Watch window to observe the subscript value as the program executes. You can place an array element (a subscripted variable) or an entire array in a Watch window. The array element value in a Watch window is determined by the current subscript value. If X is the array displayed in Fig. 10.5 and X[I] is placed in the Watch window, the value displayed for X[I] is 16.0 when the value of I is 1. When the value of I becomes 2, the value displayed for X[I] is 12.0. The {$R+} compiler directive should be used to ensure that X[I] is a valid array reference.

If you place the array name in the Watch window, the entire array is displayed with the array element values separated by commas and enclosed in parentheses. If X is the array displayed in Fig. 10.5 and the identifier X is placed in the Watch window, the Watch window will look like Fig. 10.24. Strange looking values may be displayed for array elements that have not been assigned values.

If the array is too large to fit in the Watch window, use the F6 key to move to the Watch window. Then use the left and right arrow keys (or your mouse and the Watch window's horizontal scroll bar) to scan through the array.

Figure 10.24
Watch Window for Array
in Fig. 10.5

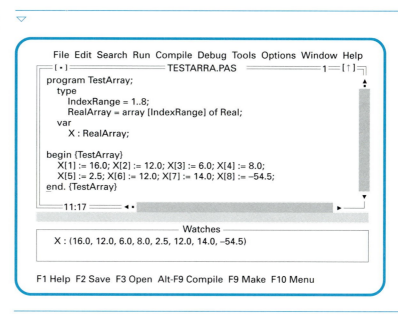

Alternatively you can display a portion of the array in the Watch window by entering a subscripted variable followed by a comma and a repeat count as a Watch expression. For example, the Watch expression

```
X[3],4
```

causes the following line to be displayed in the Watch window:

```
X[3],4: 6.0,8.0,2.5,12.0
```

This line represents the values of four array elements: `X[3]`, `X[4]`, `X[5]`, and `X[6]`. Similarly, a subscripted variable followed by a repeat count could be used to display a portion of a string.

For a loop that processes individual array elements, you might prefer to place breakpoints before and after the loop rather than trace each statement in the loop body as it executes. This procedure would be particularly beneficial for a loop that reads data into an array: It makes little sense to watch each value being stored, and the breakpoints would allow you to compare the array contents before and after loop execution.

10.9 Common Programming Errors

The most common error in the use of arrays is a subscript expression whose value goes outside the allowable range during program execution. If that happens when range checking is not being performed (the default in Turbo Pascal), storage locations outside the array or even program instructions could be modified without your knowledge. For this reason, it is very important that you enable range checking using the {$R+} compiler directive when testing and debugging programs. You should also keep range checking enabled during normal runs unless the execution speed of your program is of critical concern.

Subscript range errors most often are caused by an incorrect subscript expression. If the subscript is also the loop-control variable and is incremented before each loop iteration, subscript range errors can result from nonterminating loops or from loops that execute one more time than required.

Subscript range errors are most likely for subscript values at the loop boundaries. If these values are in range, it is likely that all other subscript references in the loop are in range as well.

As with all Pascal data types, make sure there are no type inconsistencies. The subscript type and element type used in all array references must correspond to those specified in the array type declaration.

Similarly, two arrays used in an array copy statement or as corresponding parameters must be type identical. Remember to use only identifiers without subscripts as formal array parameters and to specify the types of all array parameters using identifiers.

CHAPTER REVIEW

1. Arrays are data structures that store collections of data items of the same type. An array is characterized by its subscript type and element type. You declare an array type before you declare a variable (the array) with that type. Pascal allocates storage at compile time for each array listed in the variable declarations.

2. You can reference the entire collection of data using the array name; you can reference individual items using the array name followed by a subscript (a subscripted variable). The subscript must be a constant or expression that is compatible with the subscript type for that array. Array subscripts can be integers, characters, enumerated type values, and Boolean values.

3. You can use a for statement to reference the individual elements of an array in sequence. Some common array operations written using for loops are initializing arrays, reading arrays, and printing arrays. You can also reference array elements in arbitrary or random order (called *random access*).

4. You can write modules that have array parameters. When you call a procedure that has an array as a value parameter, a copy of the array is stored in the procedure data area and manipulated. The actual array is a module input and cannot be changed. When you call a procedure that has an array as a variable parameter, the address of the first actual array element is passed to the procedure and the actual array is manipulated. This enables you to change the contents of the actual array which is a module output.

5. You can write modules that search an array for a specific target value and sort the array so that its contents are ordered in an increasing, or decreasing, sequence. You can use Big-O notation to compare the efficiency of two searching or sorting algorithms.

Summary of New Pascal Constructs

Construct	Effect
Array Declaration	
```type IndexRange = 1..10; IntArray = array [IndexRange] of Integer; var Cube, Count : IntArray;```	The data type `IntArray` describes an array with 10 type `Integer` elements. `Cube` and `Count` are arrays with this structure.
Array References	
```for I := 1 to 10 do Cube[I] := I * I * I;```	Saves I cubed in the `Ith` element of array `Cube`.
```if Cube[5] > 100 then Write (Cube[1], Cube[2])```	Displays the first two cubes, if `Cube[5]` is greater than `100`.
Array Copy	
```Count := Cube```	Copies contents of array `Cube` to array `Count`.

Quick-Check Exercises

1. What is a data structure?
2. Which standard types cannot be array subscript types? Array element types?
3. Can values of different types be stored in an array?
4. If an array is declared to have 10 elements, must the program use all 10?
5. When can the assignment operator be used with array operands? Answer the same question for the equality operator.
6. The two methods of array access are _____ and _____.
7. The _____ loop allows us to access the elements of an array in _____ order.
8. What is a filled subarray? What is its length? What is the relationship between the last element in a filled subarray and its length?
9. Explain why variable parameters are a more efficient use of memory when passing arrays to a procedure.
10. Declare variables `Name` and `Age` that can be used to store a person's name (a string) and age (an integer) in separate arrays. Assume up to 50 names and ages need to be stored.

Answers to Quick-Check Exercises

1. A data structure is a grouping of related values in memory.
2. `Real` and `Integer`; all can be element types.
3. No.
4. No.
5. If the arrays are the same type; if the arrays are strings.
6. Random, sequential
7. `for`, sequential
8. A filled subarray is the portion of an array that has meaningful data. Its length is the number of elements in the filled subarray. The last element's subscript is the same as the length.
9. A local copy of each array used as a value parameter is made when a procedure is called.
10.
```
type
    IndexRange = 1..50;
    NameArray = array [IndexRange] of string;
    IntArray = array [IndexRange] of Integer;

var
    Age : IntArray;
    Name : NameArray;
```

Review Questions

1. Identify the error in the following code segment. When will the error be detected?

```
program Test;
  type
    AnArray = array [1..8] of Integer;

  var
    X : AnArray;
    I : Integer;

begin {Test}
  for I := 1 to 9 do
    X[I] := I
end. {Test}
```

2. Declare an array of reals called `Week` that can be referenced by using any day of the week as a subscript, where `Sunday` is the first subscript.
3. Indicate which of the assignment statements in the following code segment are incorrect. For each incorrect statement, describe what the error is and when it will be detected.

```
program Errors;
  type
    AnArray = array [1..8] of Real;

  var
    X, Y : AnArray;
    I : Integer;
```

```
begin
  I := 1;
  X[I] := 7.329;
  X[1..8] := 9.25;
  X(I) := -23.5;
  X := Y;
  X[1..5] := Y[1..5]
end;
```

4. What are two common ways of selecting array elements for processing?
5. How would the parameters differ for two procedures that manipulate arrays if one does subarray processing and the other does not?
6. The parameters for a procedure are two arrays (type RealArray) and an integer that represents the length of the arrays. The procedure copies the first array in the parameter list to the other array in reverse order. Write the procedure.
7. List three advantages to using strings.
8. What would be a valid reason for not passing an array that provides input to a procedure as a value parameter?
9. How many exchanges are required to sort the following list of integers using selection sort? How many comparisons?
   20   30   40   25   60   80
10. What is the efficiency of selection sort in Big-O notation? Why?

Programming Projects

1. Write a program for the following problem. You are given a file that contains a collection of scores (type Integer) for the last exam in your computer course. You are to compute the average of these scores and assign grades to each student according to the following rule:

   If a student's score is within 10 points (above or below) of the average, assign a grade of Satisfactory. If a student's score is more than 10 points higher than the average, assign a grade of Outstanding. If a student's score is more than 10 points below the average, assign a grade of Unsatisfactory.

   The output from your program should consist of a labeled two-column list that shows each score and its corresponding grade. As part of the solution, your program should include functions and procedures that correspond to the function and procedure headers that follow:

```
procedure ReadStuData (var RawScores {input} : Text;
                       var Score {output} : ArrayType;
                       var Count {output} : Integer;
                       var TooMany {output} : Boolean);
{
  Reads exam scores from file RawScores into array Scores.
  Count contains number of students read. TooMany is set
  to True if RawScores contains more than ClassSize scores.
}

procedure PrintGrade (OneScore {input} : Integer;
                      Average {input} : Real);
```

```
{Prints student grade after comparing OneScore to Average}

function Mean (Score : ArrayType; Count : Integer) : Real;
{Computes average of Count student scores}

procedure PrintTable (Score {input} : ArrayType;
                            Count {input} : Integer);
{
  Prints a table showing each student's score and grade
  on a separate line.
  Calls: PrintGrade.
}
```

2. Redo Programming Project 1, assuming that each line of file RawScores contains a student's ID number (an integer) and an exam score. Allocate three arrays for storing ID numbers, exam scores, and grades. Modify procedure ReadStuData to read the ID number and the score from the Ith data line into array elements ID[I] and Score[I], respectively. Write a new procedure AssignGrades that assigns values to the array Grades based on the exam scores. Modify procedure PrintTable to display a three-column table with the following headings:

   ID   Score   Grade

3. Write a program to read N data items into two arrays, X and Y, of size 20. Store the product of corresponding elements of X and Y in a third array, Z, also of size 20. Print a three-column table displaying the arrays X, Y, and Z. Then compute and print the square root of the sum of the items in Z. Make up your own data, with N less than 20.

4. If an array is sorted, we can search for an item in the array much faster by dividing the array and searching decreasing halves. This is called a binary search. Given a beginning and an end in an array, the binary search determines a middle index and compares the middle value to the search value. If they are equal, the procedure can return a found condition. If the middle is less than the search value, we search to the right of the middle, repeating the same process. Write a binary search procedure for an array of integers and a test program that searches for each value in an ordered array of 1000 numbers (1 to 1000). Have the program count the total number of comparisons required. Compare this number to the 5,005,500 comparisons required by the simple search function.

5. The results of a true–false exam given to a computer science class have been coded for input to a program. The information available for each student consists of a student identification number and the student's answers to 10 true–false questions. The available data are as follows:

Student Identification	Answer String
0080	FTTFTFTTFT
0340	FTFTFTTTFF
0341	FTTFTTTTTT
0401	TTFFTFFTTT

0462	TTFTTTFFTF
0463	TTTTTTTTTT
0464	FTFFTFFTFT
0512	TFTFTFTFTF
0618	TTTFFTTFTF
0619	FFFFFFFFFF
0687	TFTTFTTFTF
0700	FTFFTTFFFT
0712	FTFTFTFTFT
0837	TFTFTTFTFT

Write a program that first reads in the answer string representing the 10 correct answers (use FTFFTFFTFT as data). Next read each student's data into two arrays. Then compute and store the number of correct answers for each student in the corresponding element of another array. Determine the best score, Best. Then print a three-column table that displays the ID number, the score, and the grade for each student. The grade should be determined as follows: If the score is equal to Best or Best-1, give an A; if it is Best-2 or Best-3, give a C. Otherwise, give an F.

6. An array can be used to represent a polynomial. If we consider a polynomial such as $a+bx+cx^2+dx^3$, we could put a, b, c, and d in array locations indexed by 1, 2, 3, and 4, respectively. The maximum index of the array would determine the maximum degree of the polynomial we could compute. Write a program that will input a polynomial of degree up to 10 and output a table of the computed values of the polynomial for x values from -1.0 to 1.0 in steps of 0.1.

7. The results of a survey of the households in your township are available for public scrutiny. Each record contains data for one household, including a four-digit integer identification number, the annual income for the household, and the number of household members. Write a program to read the survey results into three arrays and perform the following analyses:

   a. Count the number of households included in the survey and print a three-column table displaying the data. (Assume that no more than 25 households were surveyed.)

   b. Calculate the average household income and list the identification number and income of each household that exceeds the average.

   c. Determine the percentage of households that have incomes below the poverty level. Compute the poverty level income using the formula

   $$p = \$6500.00 + \$750.00 \times (m - 2)$$

   where m is the number of members of each household. This formula shows that the poverty level depends on the number of family members, m, and that the poverty level income increases as m gets larger.

Test your program on the following data.

Identification Number	Annual Income	Household Members
1041	12,180	4
1062	13,240	3
1327	19,800	2
1483	22,458	8
1900	17,000	2
2112	18,125	7
2345	15,623	2
3210	3,200	6
3600	6,500	5
3601	11,970	2
4725	8,900	3
6217	10,000	2
9280	6,200	1

8. Assume that your computer has the very limited capability of reading and writing only single-integer digits and adding together two integers consisting of one decimal digit each. Write a program that can read in two integers of up to 30 digits each, add these digits together, and display the result. Test your program using pairs of numbers of varying lengths.

    Hints: Store the two numbers in two integer arrays of size 30, one digit per array element. If the number is less than 30 digits in length, enter enough leading zeros (to the left of the number) to make the number 30 digits long.

    You will need a loop to add the digits in corresponding array elements starting with subscript 30. Don't forget to handle the carry digit if there is one! Use a Boolean variable to indicate whether the sum of the last pair of digits is greater than 9.

9. A prime number is any number divisible only by one and itself. Write a program to compute all the prime numbers less than 2000. One way to generate prime numbers is to create an array of Boolean values that are true for all prime numbers, false otherwise. Initially set all the array entries to true. Then, for every number from 2 to 1000, set the array locations indexed by multiples of the number (but not the number itself) to false. When done, output all numbers whose array location is true. These will be the prime numbers.

10. Write a program that generates the Morse code for a sentence that ends in a period and contains no other characters except letters and blanks. After reading the Morse code into an array of strings, your program should read each word of the sentence and display its Morse equivalent on a separate line. The Morse code is as follows:

```
A ·-    B -···   C -·-·   D -··   E ·   F ··-·   G --·   H ····   I ··
J ·---   K -·-   L ·-··   M --   N -·   O ---   P ·--·   Q --·-   R ·-·
S ···   T -   U ··-   V ···-   W ·--   X -··-   Y -·--   Z --··
```

Your program should include procedures corresponding to the procedure headers shown next.

```
procedure ReadCode (var CodeFile {input} : Text;
                    var Code {output} : CodeArray);
{Stores Morse codes read from CodeFile in array Code}

procedure SkipBlanks (Sentence {input} : StringType;
                      var I {input/output} : StringIndex);
{If Sentence[I] is blank, advances I to next nonblank
 in Sentence.}

procedure WriteCode (Code {input} : CodeArray;
                     Letter : Char);
{Writes Morse equivalent for a letter}
```

11. Write an interactive program that plays the game of Hangman. Read the word to be guessed into Word. The player must guess the letters belonging to Word. The program should terminate when either all letters have been guessed correctly (player wins) or a specified number of incorrect guesses have been made (computer wins).

    Hint: Use Solution to keep track of the solution so far. Initialize Solution to a string of symbols '*'. Each time a letter in Word is guessed, replace the corresponding '*' in Solution with that letter.

CHAPTER ELEVEN

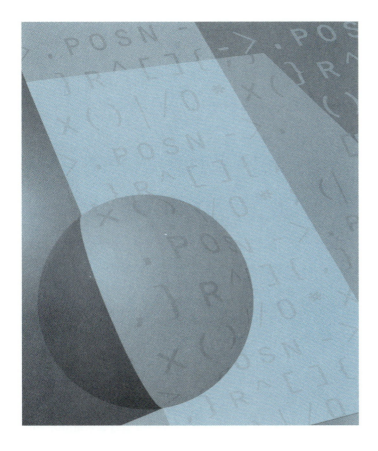

Multidimensional Arrays

multidimensional array
an array with two or more dimensions

The array data structure allows a programmer to organize information in arrangements that are more complex than the linear or one-dimensional arrays you've seen so far. We can declare and use arrays with several dimensions, each with a different subscript type. Although **multidimensional arrays** allow more flexibility in arranging data than one-dimensional arrays, the rules for element types are the same: The array elements may be simple or structured, but they must all be the same type.

11.1   Two-Dimensional Arrays: Arrays of Arrays

Two-dimensional arrays, the most common of the multidimensional arrays, store information normally represented in tabular form. An example would be a classroom seating plan that lists each student's name in the location (row and seat) of that student's desk (see Fig. 11.1).

Declaring Two-Dimensional Arrays

Examples 11.1 to 11.3 demonstrate how to declare two-dimensional arrays.

EXAMPLE 11.1 ▼

A familiar two-dimensional object is a tic-tac-toe board. The declarations

```
type
  MoveRange = 1..3;
  BoardArray = array [MoveRange, MoveRange] of Char;
```

```
var
  TicTacToe : BoardArray;
```

allocate storage for array `TicTacToe` (see Fig. 11.2), which is type `BoardArray`. An array of type `BoardArray` has two dimensions, each with subscript type `MoveRange`. Therefore `TicTacToe` is a two-dimensional array with three rows and three columns. This array has nine elements, each of which must be referenced by specifying a row subscript (1, 2, or 3) and a column subscript (1, 2, or 3).

To reference an element of a two-dimensional array, you must specify the array name and provide two subscript expressions. The first subscript is the row subscript, and the second subscript is the column subscript. The subscripted variables

```
TicTacToe[2, 3]              TicTacToe[2][3]
```

Array	Row	Column		Array	Row	Column
name	subscript	subscript		name	subscript	subscript

Figure 11.1
Classroom Seating Plan (11 Rows and 9 Seats per Row)

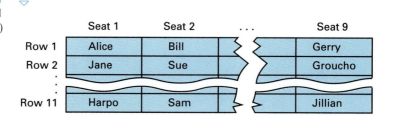

Figure 11.2
A Tic-Tac-Toe Board Stored
as Array TicTacToe

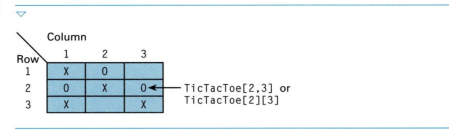

select the array element in row 2, column 3 of the array in Fig. 11.2; it contains the character 0. The form TicTacToe[2, 3] is more commonly used. ▲

EXAMPLE 11.2 ▼

Your instructor wants to store the seating plan (Fig. 11.1) for a class on a computer. The declarations

```
const
   RowMax = 11;              {number of rows in the room}
   SeatsPerRow = 9;          {number of seats in a row}
   StringSize = 10;          {characters in a string}

type
   RowRange = 1..RowMax;
   SeatRange = 1..SeatsPerRow;
   StringType = string[StringSize];
   SeatPlan = array [RowRange, SeatRange] of StringType;

var
   MyClass : SeatPlan;       {seating plan for MyClass}
```

allocate storage for a two-dimensional array of strings called MyClass. Array MyClass could be used to hold the first names of the students seated in a classroom with 11 rows and 9 seats in each row. Because each string can contain up to 10 characters, the array requires 990 bytes of storage (11 × 9 × 10). The statement

```
MyClass[6, 5] := 'Marilyn'
```

places a student named Marilyn in row 6, seat 5, the center of the classroom. ▲

EXAMPLE 11.3 ▼

The declarations

```
const
   NumberSalesPeople = 5;              {number of salespeople}
```

```
type
  People = 1..NumberSalesPeople;
  Quarter = (Fall, Winter, Spring, Summer);
  SalesArray = array [People, Quarter] of Real;

var
  Sales : SalesArray;
```

allocate storage space for a two-dimensional array of real numbers called Sales. The first dimension is type People and the second type Quarter. The array contains 20 (5 × 4) elements (see Fig. 11.3). Sales[1, Winter] stores the amount of sales (1250.00) for salesperson 1 during the Winter quarter.   ▲

Arrays of Arrays

Arrays can have elements that are structured types rather than simple types. An example of an array with elements that are structured types is an array of arrays. The declarations

```
type
  MoveRange = 1..3;
  BoardRow = array [MoveRange] of Char;
  BoardArray = array [MoveRange] of BoardRow;

var
  TicTacToe : BoardArray;
```

allocate storage for the array TicTacToe shown in Fig. 11.2. These statements declare BoardRow as an array type with three elements of type Char and BoardArray as an array type with three elements of array type BoardRow. Consequently, the variable TicTacToe (type BoardArray) is an array of arrays, or a two-dimensional array.

SYNTAX DISPLAY

Array Type Declaration (Multidimensional)

Form: type
$$multidim = \text{array } [subscript_1, \ subscript_2, \ldots, \ subscript_n]$$
$$\text{of } element \ type;$$

Figure 11.3
Array Sales

	[Fall]	[Winter]	[Spring]	[Summer]
[1]	1200.00	1250.00	1700.00	1200.00
[2]	3500.00	2400.00	1500.00	1000.00
[3]	4500.00	3000.00	2500.00	1500.00
[4]	2500.00	2000.00	3000.00	1200.00
[5]	1250.00	2500.95	2700.00	1500.00

or

```
type
    multidim = array [subscript₁] of array [subscript₂]
                . . .
                    of array [subscriptₙ] of element type;
```
Example: `type`
```
        Month = (Jan, Feb, Mar, Apr, May, Jun,
                 Jul, Aug, Sep, Oct, Nov, Dec);
        Candidate = 'A'..'E';
        Precinct = 1..10;
        YearRange = 1900..1999;
        YearByMonth = array [YearRange, Month] of Real;
        Election = array [Candidate] of array
                     [Precinct] of Integer;
```
Interpretation: *subscript*$_i$ represents the subscript type of dimension *i* of array type *multidim*. Each subscript type can be either of the standard ordinal types `Boolean` or `Char`, an enumerated type, or a subrange type. The *element type* can be any standard data type or a previously defined simple or structured data type.

Storage of Two-Dimensional Arrays

Pascal compilers store two-dimensional arrays in adjacent memory cells to simplify accessing the individual elements. The elements of a two-dimensional array normally are stored in order by row (i.e., first row 1, then row 2, etc.), a process called *row-major order*. To access a particular array element, the compiler computes the *offset* of that element from the first element stored. To perform this computation, the compiler must know the size of each element in bytes and the number of elements per row. Both values are available from the array type declaration.

For example, the array `TicTacToe` would be stored as shown in Fig. 11.4. In this array, each row has three elements, each occupying one byte of storage. The offset for element `TicTacToe[`*row,col*`]` is computed from the formula

$$offset = rowsize \times (row - 1) + (col - 1)$$

Because *rowsize* is 3 (i.e., 3 columns per row), this formula gives a value of 0 as the offset for element `TicTacToe[1,1]` and a value of 5 as the offset for element `TicTacToe[2,3]`.

Exercise for Section 11.1   **Self-Check**

1. Assuming the following declarations,

Figure 11.4
Array TicTacToe
in Memory

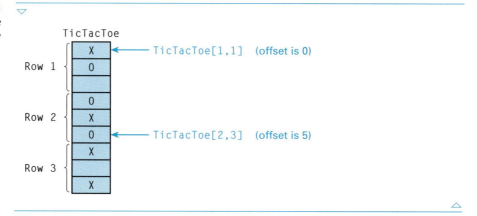

```
type
   RowRange = 1..5;
   ColRange = 1..4;
   MatrixType = array [RowRange, ColRange] of Real;

var
   Matrix : MatrixType;
```

answer these questions:

a. How many elements are in array `Matrix`?
b. Write a statement to display the element in row 3, column 4.
c. What is the offset for this element?
d. What formula computes the offset for `Matrix[I,J]`?

11.2 Processing Two-Dimensional Arrays

We have two methods for accessing elements of a one-dimensional array: random access and sequential access. For a two-dimensional array or table, we have three methods of access:

1. *Random access.* The order is arbitrary, depending on data entered by the program user.
2. *Row-by-row access.* All elements in the first row are processed, then all elements in the second row, and so on.
3. *Column-by-column access.* All elements in the first column are processed, then all elements in the second column, and so on.

Nested loops are used to access a two-dimensional array, either row-by-row or column-by-column. In row-by-row access, the outer loop-control variable is the row subscript and the inner loop-control variable is the column subscript. These roles are reversed in column-by-column access, as shown in the following templates summarizing the loop forms.

Template for Row-by-Row Access of Array Table

```
for row-subscript ... do          {Specify the row.}
   for column-subscript ... do     {Access each column of row.}
      Process Table[row-subscript, column-subscript]
```

Template for Column-by-Column Access of Array Table

```
for column-subscript ... do        {Specify the column}
   for row-subscript ... do         {Access each row of column.}
      Process Table[row-subscript, column-subscript]
```

Here are some of the more common operations that we perform on two-dimensional arrays and their recommended method of access:

▶ Initialize all array elements to a specified value—either row-by-row or column-by-column access.
▶ Find the sum of all the elements in a table—either row-by-row or column-by-column access.
▶ Display the elements in a table—row-by-row access.
▶ Find the sum for each row—row-by-row access.
▶ Find the sum for each column—column-by-column access.
▶ Update array elements as determined by input data—random access.

We show how to perform some of these operations next.

Initializing an Array

Procedure `Initialize` (Fig. 11.5) initializes each element of its array parameter `Sales` (Fig. 11.3) to `InValue`. The procedure accesses the array elements row-by-row. The outer `for` loop cycles through the rows and the inner `for` loop cycles through the columns. During the first iteration of the outer loop `NextPerson` is 1, so the inner loop sets the four array elements in row 1 to `InValue`. Next, it sets the four array elements in row 2 to `InValue`, and so on.

Computing Row Sums

For the array shown in Fig. 11.3, computing the sum for one row will give the annual sales total for one person (e.g., 1200.00 + 1250.00 + 1700.00 + 1200.00 is the annual sales total for the first salesperson). The program fragment

```
Sum := 0.0;
for NextQuarter := Fall to Summer do
   Sum := Sum + Sales[1, NextQuarter];
WriteLn ('Sales for person 1 are $', Sum :3:2)
```

Figure 11.5

Initializing a Two-
Dimensional Array

```
procedure Initialize (var Sales {output} : SalesArray;
                          InValue {input} : Real);
{
  Initializes all elements of its array parameter to InValue.
  Pre  : InValue is defined.
  Post : Sets each element of its array parameter to InValue.
}
  var
    NextPerson : People;         {Row subscript}
    NextQuarter : Quarter;       {Column subscript}

begin {Initialize}
  for NextPerson := 1 to NumberSalesPeople do
    for NextQuarter := Fall to Summer do
      Sales[NextPerson, NextQuarter] := InValue
end; {Initialize}
```

computes this sum by adding the four array elements in row 1 to Sum. Notice that only the column subscript changes with each loop iteration. The fragment initializes Sum to 0 before the loop and displays its final value after loop exit.

You must use nested loops to find the sum for every row. Procedure Sum-Rows (Fig. 11.6) performs this operation. Instead of displaying each sum, the procedure returns the sum for row I in array element RowSum[I](type RowArray). We declare type RowArray before the procedure.

Procedure SumRows accesses the array elements row-by-row. Its outer for loop cycles through the rows and its inner for loop cycles through the columns. The outer loop initializes Sum to 0 before each pass through the columns and assigns its final value after each pass to the element of array RowSum selected by the row subscript.

Computing Column Sums

Computing the sum for each column would give us the annual sales for each quarter (e.g., 1200.00 + 3500.00 + 4500.00 + 2500.00 + 1250.00 gives us the total sales during the Fall quarter). To compute the sum for a given column, we must add the five elements in each row of that column. Procedure SumColumns (Fig. 11.7) accesses the array elements column-by-column and returns the four column sums through array ColSum. Fig. 11.8 shows the relationship among arrays Sales, RowSum, and ColSum.

Figure 11.6
Procedure SumRows and
Type RowArray

```
type
  RowArray = array [People] of Real;

procedure SumRows (Sales {input} : SalesArray;
                          var RowSum {output} : RowArray);
{
 Sums the rows of array Sales, returning the sums in RowSum.
 Pre  : Array Sales is defined.
 Post : RowSum[I] is the sum of elements in row I.
}
  var
    NextPerson : People;         {Row subscript}
    NextQuarter : Quarter;       {Column subscript}
    Sum : Real;                  {Each row sum}

begin {SumRows}
  for NextPerson := 1 to NumberSalesPeople do
    begin
      Sum := 0.0;
      for NextQuarter := Fall to Summer do
        Sum := Sum + Sales[NextPerson, NextQuarter];
      RowSum[NextPerson] := Sum      {Return next row sum}
    end {outer for}
end; {SumRows}
```

Figure 11.7
Procedure SumColumns
and Type ColArray

```
type
  ColArray = array [Quarter] of Real;

procedure SumColumns (Sales {input} : SalesArray;
                          var ColSum {output} : ColArray);
{
 Sums the columns of array Sales, returning the sums in ColSum
 Pre  : Array Sales is defined.
 Post : ColSum[I] is the sum of elements in column I.
}
  var
    NextPerson : People;         {Row subscript}
    NextQuarter : Quarter;       {Column subscript}
    Sum : Real;                  {Each column sum}

begin {SumColumns}
  for NextQuarter := Fall to Summer do
    begin
      Sum := 0.0;
      for NextPerson := 1 to NumberSalesPeople do
        Sum := Sum + Sales[NextPerson, NextQuarter];
      ColSum[NextQuarter] := Sum      {Return next column sum}
    end {outer for}
end; {SumColumns}
```

Figure 11.8
Array Sales, RowSum, and ColSum

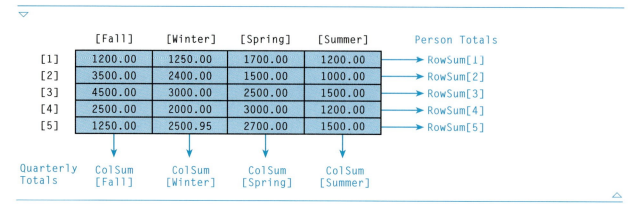

CASE STUDY   **Analysis of Sales Data**

PROBLEM ▼

The sales manager of your company needs a sales analysis program to track sales performance by salesperson and by quarter. The program will read all sales transactions from a text file. The data for each transaction will be the salesperson's number, the quarter in which the sale took place, and the sales amount. The sales transactions should be in no particular order. After reading all sales transactions, the program should display a table in the form shown in Fig. 11.8, which includes the totals by person and by quarter.

ANALYSIS ▼

You will need separate arrays to hold the sales table, the row sums, and the column sums.

Data Requirements

Problem Inputs

Sales transactions file

```
Sales : SalesArray;    {array of sales amounts}
```

Problem Outputs

```
RowSum : RowArray;     {array of row sums}
ColSum : ColArray;     {array of column sums}
```

DESIGN ▼

Initial Algorithm

1. Initialize all elements of the sales array to zero.
2. Read in the sales data.
3. Compute the row sums.
4. Compute the column sums.
5. Display the sales table showing the row and column sums.

IMPLEMENTATION ▼

Coding the Main Program

We have already written procedures for steps 1, 3, and 4 (Figs. 11.5–11.7). We will write the main program next (Fig. 11.9) and then write the procedures for steps 2 and 5.

Figure 11.9
Sales Analysis
Main Program

```
{$R+}
program SalesAnalysis;
{Reads in sales figures for one year and stores them in a table
 organized by salesperson and quarter. Displays the table and
 the annual totals for each person and the sales totals for
 each quarter.
}
  const
    NumberSalesPeople = 5;        {number of salespeople}

  type
    People = 1..NumberSalesPeople;
    Quarter = (Fall, Winter, Spring, Summer);
    SalesArray = array [People, Quarter] of Real;
    RowArray = array [People] of Real;
    ColArray = array [Quarter] of Real;

  var
    Sales : SalesArray;           {2-D sales table}
    RowSum : RowArray;            {row totals}
    ColSum : ColArray;            {column totals}

{Insert procedures Initialize, SumRows, and SumColumns.}
{Insert procedures ReadQuarter, ReadTable and DisplayTable.}

begin {SalesAnalysis}
  Initialize (Sales, 0.0);
  ReadTable (Sales);
  SumRows (Sales, RowSum);
  SumColumns (Sales, ColSum);
  DisplayTable (Sales, RowSum, ColSum)
end. {SalesAnalysis}
```

Coding Procedure ReadTable

Procedure ReadTable (Fig. 11.10) reads in the sales table data from the sales transaction file after preparing the data file for input. Each transaction specifies the salesperson, the quarter in which the sale took place, and the sales amount. Procedure ReadQuarter (see Programming Exercise 1 at the end of this section) returns the sales quarter value read through its second parame-

Figure 11.10
Procedure ReadTable

```pascal
procedure ReadTable (var Sales {output} : SalesArray);
{
 Reads the sales table data from a data file and saves the
 sales results in a sales table.
 Pre  : Sales is initialized to all zeros.
 Post : Each entry of Sales represents the sum of sales
        for a particular salesperson and quarter.
 Calls: ReadQuarter to read the sales quarter.
}
  var
    TranAmount : Real;              {transaction amount}
    TranPerson : Integer;          {salesperson number}
    TranQuarter : Quarter;         {sales quarter}
    SalesFile : Text;              {sales file variable}
    FileName : string;             {external file name}
    ValidQuarter : Boolean;        {flag indicating whether
                                    a valid quarter was read}

begin {ReadTable}
  {Prepare data file for input.}
  Write ('Enter name of sales data file> ');
  ReadLn (FileName);
  Assign (SalesFile, FileName);
  Reset (SalesFile);

  {Read and store all valid sales data.}
  while not EOF(SalesFile) do
    begin
      Read (SalesFile, TranPerson);
      ReadQuarter (SalesFile, TranQuarter, ValidQuarter);
      ReadLn (SalesFile, TranAmount);
      if ValidQuarter and (TranPerson >= 1) and
                          (TranPerson <= 5) then
        Sales[TranPerson, TranQuarter] :=
              Sales[TranPerson, TranQuarter] + TranAmount
      else
        WriteLn ('Invalid person or quarter - ',
                 'person is ', TranPerson :1,
                 '; amount is ', TranAmount :3:2)
    end {while}
end; {ReadTable}
```

ter and a `Boolean` value through its third parameter, indicating whether a valid quarter was read.

The `if` statement tests whether the salesperson and quarter are valid. If so, the statement

```
Sales[TranPerson, TranQuarter] :=
    Sales[TranPerson, TranQuarter] + TranAmount
```

adds the current sales amount to the total being accumulated for the salesperson selected by `TranPerson` (row subscript) and `TranQuarter` (column subscript). Because the data are in no particular order, the array elements are randomly accessed.

Coding Procedure DisplayTable

You should display the information in a two-dimensional array in the same way that humans visualize it: as a table whose rows correspond to the array's first dimension and whose columns correspond to the array's second dimension. To accomplish this, access and display the array elements row-by-row.

Procedure `DisplayTable` (Fig. 11.11) displays the data in the sales table array in the form shown in Fig. 11.8. Besides the array data (first parameter), the procedure also displays the row sums (second parameter) and column sums (third parameter). To enhance readability, `DisplayTable` also displays the row and column labels shown in Fig. 11.8.

Figure 11.11
Procedure DisplayTable

```
procedure DisplayTable (Sales {input} : SalesArray;
                        RowSum {input} : RowArray;
                        ColSum {input} : ColArray);
{
 Displays the sales table data in table form and the row
 and column sums.
 Pre  : Sales, RowSum, and ColSum are defined.
 Post : The values stored in the three arrays are displayed.
}
  var
    NextPerson : People;            {Each salesperson}
    NextQuarter : Quarter;          {Each quarter}

begin
  {Display the heading.}
  WriteLn;
  WriteLn ('SALES TABLE' :40);
  WriteLn ('[Fall]' :20, '[Winter]' :10, '[Spring]' :10,
                          '[Summer]' :10, ' Person Totals');
```

▷ ▷ ▷ ▷ ▷

```
{Display one table row for each salesperson.}
for NextPerson := 1 to NumberSalesPeople do
  begin
    Write ('[' :8, NextPerson :1, ']');
    for NextQuarter := Fall to Summer do
      Write (Sales[NextPerson, NextQuarter] :10:2);
    WriteLn (RowSum[NextPerson] : 14:2)
  end; {for NextPerson}

{Display the column totals.}
WriteLn;
Write ('Quarterly' :10);
for NextQuarter := Fall to Summer do
  Write (ColSum[NextQuarter] :10:2);
WriteLn;
WriteLn ('Totals')
end; {DisplayTable}
```

TESTING ▼

To test the sales analysis program, create a sample data file. Verify that incorrect data for salesperson or quarter do not cause a `Range check error` during run time. Figure 11.12 shows a sample run. The person totals column and quarterly totals row should both sum to the same amount (`4200.00` for the sample run).

Figure 11.12
Sample Run of Sales
Analysis Program

```
Enter name of sales data file> SALEDATA.TXT
Invalid person or quarter - person is 6; amount is 1200.00
Invalid person or quarter - person is 3; amount is 850.00

                        SALES TABLE
            [Fall]   [Winter]   [Spring]   [Summer] Person Totals
     [1]   1000.00       0.00       0.00    1500.00       2500.00
     [2]      0.00       0.00     100.00     500.00        600.00
     [3]    100.00       0.00    1000.00       0.00       1100.00
     [4]      0.00       0.00       0.00       0.00          0.00
     [5]      0.00       0.00       0.00       0.00          0.00

Quarterly   1100.00       0.00    1100.00    2000.00
Totals
```

Exercises for Section 11.2 **Self-Check**

1. For each fragment, which array locations are displayed and in which order?
   a. `for NextQuarter := Fall to Summer do`
      `    Write (Sales[1, NextQuarter])`
   b. `for NextPerson := 1 to 5 do`
      `    Write (Sales[NextPerson, Spring]);`
   c. `for NextQuarter := Fall to Summer do`
      `    begin`
      `      for NextPerson := 1 to 5 do`
      `        Write (Sales[NextPerson, NextQuarter]);`
      `      WriteLn`
      `    end; {for}`

Programming

1. Procedure `ReadQuarter` reads two characters representing the quarter (`FA, WI, SP, SU`) from a data file and returns the corresponding quarter value (`Fall, Winter, Spring, Summer`) if the data characters are correct. Write procedure `ReadQuarter`.
2. Write an array type declaration for 10×10 square matrices that contain real numbers.
3. For the array type declared in Programming Exercise 2, do the following:
   a. Write a loop that computes the sum of the elements in row 5.
   b. Write a loop that computes the sum of the elements in column 6.
   c. Write nested loops that compute the sum of all the array elements.
4. Write a function that determines who has won a game of tic-tac-toe. The function should first check all rows to see whether one player occupies all the cells in that row, next check all columns, and then check the two diagonals. The function should return a value from the enumerated type (`NoWinner, XWins, OWins`).

11.3 Three-Dimensional Arrays

Pascal does not limit the number of dimensions an array may have, though arrays with only two and three dimensions are most common. Be aware that large amounts of memory space can be allocated for storage of a multidimensional array. For that reason, avoid passing multidimensional arrays as value parameters. In this section, we study some examples of three-dimensional arrays.

EXAMPLE 11.4 ▼

The array RoomHeat (Fig. 11.13) declared as

```
type
   Length = 1..12;        {12 feet long}
   Width = 1..10;         {10 feet wide}
   Height = 1..8;         {8 feet high}
   TempArray = array [Length, Width, Height] of Real;

var
   RoomHeat : TempArray;
```

has three dimensions and requires three subscripts. The first subscript can have values from 1 to 12; the second, from 1 to 10; and the third, from 1 to 8. A total of 12 × 10 × 8, or 960, real numbers can be stored in the array RoomHeat. We can use this array to store the room temperature measured at discrete points in a 12-by-10-foot room with an 8-foot ceiling. ▲

EXAMPLE 11.5 ▼

Your job is to computerize a small office. The first step is to store the information in your boss's two file cabinets, labeled "Business" and "Personal" (Fig. 11.14). Each file cabinet contains two drawers, and each drawer has 26 folders labeled A through Z. Each folder contains a memo of up to 255 characters. The following declarations allocate storage for an array Office that will hold all the information in the two filing cabinets:

Figure 11.13
Array RoomHeat

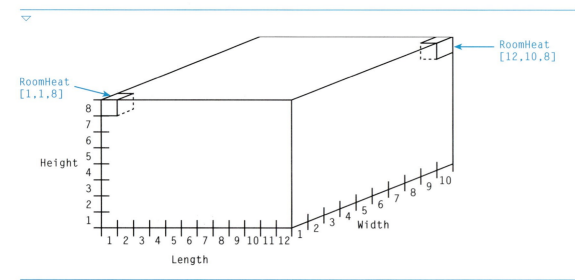

Figure 11.14
Office Files to Be
Computerized

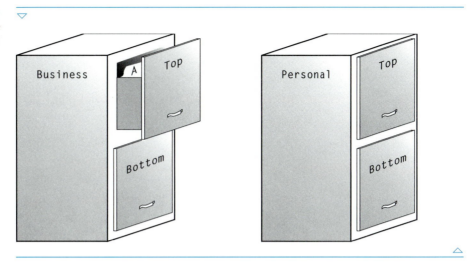

```
const
   MemoLength = 255;

type
   CabinetType = (Business, Personal);
   DrawerType = (Top, Bottom);
   FolderType = 'A'..'Z';
   Memo = string[MemoLength];
   FileCabinet = array [CabinetType, DrawerType, FolderType]
                                                of Memo;

var
   Office : FileCabinet;
```

You need three subscripts to access an element of this array. The subscripted variable `Office[Business, Top, 'A']` accesses the folder with label A in the open drawer shown in Fig. 11.14. The statement

```
Write (MemoFile, Office[Business, Top, 'A'])
```

copies the memo in this folder to output file `MemoFile` (type `Text`).

The array `Office` occupies a large amount of storage space. Using 1K bytes to mean 1024 bytes, the array would require 26K bytes of storage ($2 \times 2 \times 26 \times 256$). ▲

EXAMPLE 11.6 ▼

A university offers 50 courses at each of five campuses. The registrar's office wants to break down enrollment information according to student rank. To do this, they need to store the enrollment information in a three-dimensional array with 1000 elements (50 × 5 × 4). This array is declared next and is shown in Fig. 11.15.

```
const
    MaxCourse = 50;                     {maximum number of courses}

type
    Campus = (Main, Ambler, Center, Delaware, Montco);
    Rank = (Freshman, Sophomore, Junior, Senior);
    CourseRange = 1..MaxCourse;
    ClassArray = array [CourseRange, Campus, Rank] of Integer;

var
    ClassEnroll : ClassArray;           {class enrollment}
    CurCampus : Campus;                 {current campus}
    ClassRank : Rank;                   {current rank}
    Total : Integer;                    {student totals}
```

The subscripted variable ClassEnroll[1, Center, Senior] represents the number of seniors taking course 1 at Center campus.

The program fragment

```
Total := 0;
for ClassRank := Freshman to Senior do
    Total := Total + ClassEnroll[1, Center, ClassRank]
```

Figure 11.15
Three-Dimensional Array ClassEnroll

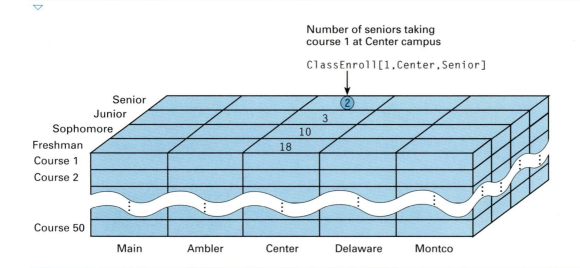

computes the total number of students of all ranks in course 1 at Center campus.

The program fragment

```
Total := 0;
for CurCampus := Main to Montco do
    for ClassRank := Freshman to Senior do
        Total := Total + ClassEnroll[1, CurCampus, ClassRank]
```

computes the total number of students in course 1 (regardless of rank or campus).   ▲

Exercises for Section 11.3   *Self-Check*

1. Declare a three-dimensional array type in which the first subscript consists of letters from 'A' to 'F', the second subscript consists of integers from 1 to 10, and the third consists of the user-defined type Day (days of the week). Real numbers will be stored in the array. How many elements can be stored in an array of this type?

2. Declare a three-dimensional array that can keep track of the number of students in the math classes (Math1, Algebra, Geometry, Algebra2, Trigonometry, Calculus) at your old high school according to the grade level and the gender of the students. How many elements are in this array?

3. Extend row-major order to three dimensions and show how the array ClassEnroll might be stored. What would be the offset for the array element ClassEnroll[1, Center, Senior] and the general formula for ClassEnroll[*i, j, k*]?

Programming

1. Redefine MaxCourse (Example 11.6) as 5, and write code fragments that perform the following operations:
   a. Enter the enrollment data.
   b. Find the number of juniors in all classes at all campuses. Count students once for each course in which they are enrolled.
   c. Find the number of sophomores on all campuses who are enrolled in course 2.
   d. Compute and print the number of students at Main campus enrolled in each course and the total number of students at Main campus in all courses. Count students once for each course in which they are enrolled.
   e. Compute and print the number of upper-class students in all courses at each campus, as well as the total number of upper-class students enrolled. (Upper-class students are juniors and seniors.) Again, count students once for each course in which they are enrolled.

11.4 Debugging Multidimensional Arrays

You can use the Watch window to display single elements of multidimensional arrays, several adjacent array elements, or entire multidimensional arrays. Multidimensional arrays are displayed in the Watch window as nested, parenthesized lists. To display all values in the two-dimensional array shown in Fig. 11.2, use the Watch expression

```
TicTacToe
```

The Watch window displays the contents of the array `TicTacToe` as

```
TicTacToe: (('X','O',' '),('O','X','O'),('X',' ','X'))
```

The elements of `TicTacToe` appear in row-major order, with row 1 followed by rows 2 and 3. If you use the Watch expression

```
TicTacToe[2]
```

elements of the second row of array `TicTacToe` appear in the Watch window as

```
TicTacToe[2]: ('O','X','O')
```

Repeat counts in Watch expressions display several adjacent elements of array `TicTacToe` or several adjacent rows of array `TicTacToe`. The Watch expression

```
TicTacToe[2,1],2
```

displays the first and second elements of row 2 in array `TicTacToe` as

```
TicTacToe[2,1],2: 'O','X'
```

Use some caution with repeat counts because adjacent array elements are not necessarily in the same row. The Watch expression

```
TicTacToe[2,3],2
```

displays array elements `TicTacToe[2,3]` and `TicTacToe[3,1]` in the Watch window. The Watch expression

```
TicTacToe[1],2
```

displays the first and second rows of array `TicTacToe` as

```
TicTacToe[1],2: ('X','O',' '),('O','X','O')
```

11.5 Common Programming Errors

When you use multidimensional arrays, make sure the subscript for each dimension is consistent with its declared type. If any subscript value is out of range, you may get a `Range check error` during runtime.

If you use nested `for` loops to process the array elements, make sure that loop-control variables used as array subscripts are in the correct order. The order of these variables determines the sequence in which the array elements are processed.

CHAPTER REVIEW

1. Use two-dimensional arrays, or arrays of arrays, to represent tables of information and game boards. You can use arrays of higher dimension to represent more complicated organizations of information.
2. Access the elements of a multidimensional array in a systematic way using nested loops. The correspondence between the loop-control variables and the array subscripts determines the order in which the array elements are processed. To access a two-dimensional array row-by-row, use the row subscript as the outer loop-control variable and the column subscript as the inner loop-control variable. Reverse this order to access the elements column-by-column.

Summary of New Pascal Constructs

Construct	Effect
Declaring Multidimensional Arrays	

`type`
`  Day = (Sunday,Monday,Tuesday,Wednesday,`
`         Thursday,Friday,Saturday);`
`  Matrix = array [1..52, Day] of Real;`
 	
`var`
`  Sales : Matrix;`
	Matrix describes a two-dimensional array with 52 rows and 7 columns (days of the week). Sales is an array of this type and can store 364 real numbers.

Multidimensional Array References	
`Write (Sales[3, Monday])`	Displays the element of Sales for day Monday of week 3.

`for Week := 1 to 52 do`
`  for Today := Sunday to Saturday do`
`    Sales[Week, Today] := 0.0`
	Initializes each element of Sales to 0.

`ReadLn (Sales[1, Sunday])`	Reads the value for the first Sunday into Sales.

Quick-Check Exercises

1. What are the three modes of access for a two-dimensional array?
2. What is the difference between row-major and column-major order? Which does Pascal use?
3. Write the type declaration for an array that stores the current worm population in a stack of worm boxes. The boxes are arranged in a rectangular pallet of 10 boxes × 7 boxes and there are 5 pallets in a stack.
4. Write a program segment to display the sum of the values (type Real) in each column of a two-dimensional array Table with data type array [1..5, 1..3] of Real. How many column sums will be displayed? How many elements are included in each sum?
5. Write the type declaration for an array that stores the batting averages by position (Catcher, Pitcher, FirstBase, etc.) for each of 10 baseball teams in two leagues (American and National).

Answers to Quick-Check Exercises

1. Random access, row-by-row access, column-by-column access
2. In row-major order, the first row of the array is placed at the beginning of the memory area allocated to the array. It is followed by the second row, and so on. In column-major order, the first column is placed at the beginning of the array memory area. Pascal uses row-major order.
3.
```
type
    LengthRange = 1..10;
    WidthRange = 1..7;
    StackRange = 1..5;
    WormStack = array [LengthRange, WidthRange, StackRange]
                    of Integer;
```
4.
```
for Column := 1 to 3 do
    begin
        ColumnSum := 0.0;
        for Row := 1 to 5 do
            ColumnSum := ColumnSum + Table[Row, Column];
        WriteLn ('Sum for column ', Column :1, ' is ',
                ColumnSum :3:2)
    end {for Column}
```
Three column sums; five elements added per column
5.
```
type
    League = (American, National);
    Team = 1..10;
    Position = (Pitcher, Catcher, FirstBase,
                SecondBase, ThirdBase, ShortStop,
                LeftField, CenterField, RightField);
    BAArray = array [League, Team, Position] of Real;
```

Review Questions

1. Declare an array that can be used to store each title of the Top40 hits for each week of the year given that the TitleLength will be 20 characters.

2. Write the declaration of the array `YearlyHours` to store the hours each of five employees works each day of the week, each week of the year.

3. Write a procedure to compute and display the total number of hours worked by each employee on a specified day (an input parameter).

4. Write a procedure to compute and display the total number of hours worked by a given employee (an input parameter).

5. Write the declarations for the array `CPUArray` that will hold 20 elements of type `CPU` where `CPU` is an array type that contains storage for five real items.

Programming Projects

1. Write a set of procedures to manipulate a pair of matrices. Provide procedures for addition, subtraction, and multiplication. Each procedure should validate its input parameters (i.e., check all matrix dimensions) before performing the required data manipulation.

2. Write a program that uses a two-dimensional array to store election results. The program should call the following procedures. Parameter `Tally` stores the election results.

   Procedure `Initialize (var Tally)`: Reads in the number of precincts (up to 10) and the letter (up to J) corresponding to the last candidate; initializes all vote totals to zero.

   Procedure `ReadTally (var Tally)`: Reads in the votes by precinct for each candidate.

   Procedure `WriteTable (Tally)`: Displays the election results in the form shown.

   Procedure `CountBallot (var Tally)`: Determines the count of votes received by each candidate and the corresponding percentage of the total votes cast.

   Procedure `FindWinner (Tally, var Cand1, var Cand2, var Over50)`: Determines the letters of the highest-scoring candidate (`Cand1`) and the second-highest-scoring candidate (`Cand2`) and sets `Over50` to `True` if the highest scoring candidate receives more than 50% of the vote.

   Procedure `DisplayWinner (Cand1, Cand2, Over50)`: Displays the name of `Cand1` and the message `Won the election` if `Over50` is true; otherwise, displays the message `Runoff election between 2 highest-scoring candidates` and `Cand1` and `Cand2`.

   Write a main program that calls these procedures, and run the program for the data in the following table and also when candidate C receives only 108 votes in precinct 4.

Precinct	Candidate A	Candidate B	Candidate C	Candidate D
1	192	48	206	37
2	147	90	312	21
3	186	12	121	38
4	114	21	408	39
5	267	13	382	29

3. Modify Programming Project 2 to make it an interactive menu-driven program. Menu options should include initializing the vote table (prompt the user for the number of candidates, their names, and the number of precincts), displaying the vote table with row and column totals, displaying the precinct totals, displaying the candidates' names and votes received (raw count and percentage of votes cast), displaying winner's name (or names in the event of a tie), and exiting the program.

4. For the sales analysis problem (see Section 11.2) provide these procedures:

    `EditData (var Sales)`: Prompts the user to determine the person, quarter, and new amount for a sales entry to be changed and then changes that entry.

    `SaveTable (Sales)`: Stores the table values in an output file. Writes each table entry in the same format as sales transactions in the data file.

    Add these options to the program and test them. Change the main program so that it is a menu-driven program.

5. The Queen in the game of chess can move horizontally, vertically, or diagonally on an 8 × 8 board. Write a program that displays a chess board as characters. The squares of the chess board are displayed as one of the following letters: E for an empty and available square, Q if the square now contains a queen and X if the location is protected by a queen already on the board. The board starts with all locations empty. The user can place Queens by supplying a row and column location that contains an E. The program ends when there are no E squares left. Try to see how many Queens you can place on the board. It is possible to place 8.

▼ **People often seem confused about what artificial intelligence is and is not. In your text, *Artificial Intelligence*, you define the goals of AI as "[attempting] to make computers more useful [and] to understand the principles that make intelligence possible." Has your thinking about the goals of AI changed since that was written nine years or so ago?**

▲ I would say my sense of the goals of AI is more precise perhaps, but not fundamentally changed. Now I tend to say that the engineering goal of artificial intelligence is to solve real-world problems using artificial intelligence as an armamentarium of ideas about representing knowledge, using knowledge, and assembling systems. The scientific goal, on the other hand, is to determine which ideas about representing knowledge, using knowledge, and assembling systems account for various sorts of intelligence.

▼ **Of all the choices you could have made, why did you choose AI? What influenced you most in that decision?**

▲ Well, I have always wanted to understand what thinking is all about. When I was a graduate student, I looked for answers, as many do, by taking subjects offered in psychology and neuroanatomy. But even though I learned a lot, I felt that something was missing. Luckily, that was about the time I heard that the students of Marvin Minsky and Seymour Papert were not only trying to understand intelligence, they were trying to *produce* it. I resolved instantly to be one of those students. And when I did, I learned that what was missing was the idea that you can study the computations that make intelligence possible without concerning yourself too much with the particular computer that happens to be performing those computations, be it natural or made of silicon.

▼ **What comes to mind when you think of the major achievements in AI over the past decade? Who do you think has benefited the most from the accomplishments of AI?**

▲ Lots. Especially in the last half of the decade, which has been especially exciting because so much conventional wisdom has been overturned. For example, we now know that the memory required to do visual recognition need not involve any explicit three-dimensional models—an idea that used to seem ridiculous 10 years ago. But this is just one example; similar stories can be told for just about every subfield of AI. I've taken to telling my students that the exams stay the same from year to year, but all the answers change.

▼ **One sometimes hears of the MIT or Carnegie-Mellon or some other institutional view of artificial intelligence, suggesting that several views of AI are extant. Do you think such diversity of viewpoints exists in the field, and if so do you think it's healthy?**

▲ Certainly there are lots of approaches, and many are championed by advocates with almost religious zeal. And on the whole, this is a good thing because AI, like most fields, benefits from diverse ideas and excited people. And besides, any adequate account of intelligence, from a computational point of view, is unlikely to rest on just a few elegant laws like electromagnetism rests on Maxwell's equations. There is room

INTERVIEW
▼

Patrick H. Winston

Patrick H. Winston is a professor of computer science at the Massachusetts Institute of Technology and director of the interdepartmental Artificial Intelligence Laboratory there. He is also author of Artificial Intelligence *and co-author of* Lisp, *two of the most widely used texts on these subjects. He is currently involved in the study of learning, precedent-based reasoning, common-sense problem solving, problem solving via abstraction, and applications of artificial intelligence (AI) to database mining, scheduling, and dynamic resource allocation.*

for lots of approaches to be right with respect to some part of the total picture.

▼ **What significant achievements can we look forward to in AI in the 1990s?**

▲ Making predictions in AI is always dangerous because there are critics who take failure to meet some claimed objective at a predicted time to mean *never* instead of *not yet*. Also, we still need breakthroughs in AI, and it is hard to predict when someone will have a breakthrough idea. But if you force me, nevertheless, to hazard something, I would claim that the results of the past few years suggest that the next decade will be the decade of learning. Ten years from now, we will know a great deal about how to learn using a combination of already known facts and a little observation, and conversely, we will know a great deal about how to dig regularities out of lots of data with no background knowledge. Some of this is bound to change the world, at least in a minor way, and maybe in a major way, especially if the technolgy can be harnessed, for example, to individually tailored product marketing or to, say, pharmaceutical development.

CHAPTER TWELVE

Records

We introduce a new structured data type in this chapter: records. Like arrays, records are composed of related data items, but, unlike arrays, record components can contain data of different types. We could use a record to store various items of information about a person: name, address, year of birth, and gender, for example. We could not save this information in an array because name and address would be strings, year of birth would be an integer, and gender would be a character.

Finally, we can use arrays whose elements are records and records whose components are other records to represent more complex organizations of information.

12.1 The Record Data Type

record
an aggregate of related data items of different types

Although arrays are useful as data structures that can collect related data, they are limited because all the data they store must be of the same type. Many programming problems can be easily solved if we are able to organize related data having different data types. With the **record** data structure, we can store related data of different types in a single data structure. In this section, we show how to declare and process records.

Declaring Record Types

To keep organized, accessible information about her staff members, the manager of a software firm wants to save the information like the following about each employee:

```
ID: 1234
Name: Caryn Jackson
Gender: F
Number of Dependents: 2
Hourly Rate: 6.00
Total Wages: 240.00
```

record data type
a template that describes the format of a record including the name and type of each data element
record field
a data element in a record

We can store this information in a record with six data elements. The **record data type** is a template that describes the format of each record including the name and type of each data element, or record **field.** To store the preceding information, we can use the record type `Employee` shown next with two integer fields, a string field, a character field (for gender), and two real fields:

```
const
  StringLength = 20;

type
  IDRange = 1111..9999;
  StringType = string[StringLength];

  Employee = record
              ID : IDRange;
              Name : StringType;
              Gender : Char;
              NumDepend : Integer;
              Rate, TotWages : Real
            end; {Employee}
```

The type declaration for record `Employee` is bracketed by the words `record` and `end`. Each field description consists of the field name (a Pascal identifier) followed by the field data type. A colon separates the field name from the data type. The field data type can be a standard data type (`Char`, `Integer`, `Real`), a user-defined simple type (`IDRange`), or a structured data type (`StringType`).

A variable declaration is required to allocate storage space for a record. The record variable Clerk (see Fig. 12.1) is declared:

```
var
  Clerk : Employee;
```

The record variable Clerk has the structure specified in the declaration for record type Employee. Thus the memory allocated consists of storage space for six distinct values.

As with other identifiers in Pascal programs, field names should describe the information to be stored and the data type should be appropriate for that kind of information. For example, record type Employee uses a string field for storage of an employee's name.

SYNTAX DISPLAY

Record Type Declaration

Form: type
        rec type = record
                    id list$_1$: *type*$_1$;
                    id list$_2$: *type*$_2$;
                        . . .
                    id list$_n$: *type*$_n$
              end;

Example: type
            Complex = record
                  RealPart, ImaginaryPart : Real
              end;

Interpretation: The identifier *rec type* is the name of the record structure being described. Each *id list*$_i$ is a list of one or more field names separated by commas; the data type of each field in *id list*$_i$ is specified by *type*$_i$.

Notes: Field names must be unique within a record type. Each *type*$_i$ can be any standard or user-defined data type, including a structured type. If *type*$_i$ is a user-defined data type, it can be defined either before the record or as part of the record description.

Figure 12.1
Record Variable Clerk

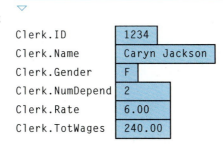

Clerk.ID	1234
Clerk.Name	Caryn Jackson
Clerk.Gender	F
Clerk.NumDepend	2
Clerk.Rate	6.00
Clerk.TotWages	240.00

Accessing Record Fields

We can access a field in a record by using a *field selector,* which consists of the record variable name followed by the field name. A period separates the record name from the field name:

record-variable.field-name

EXAMPLE 12.1 ▼

The following statements store data in the record variable `Clerk`. Figure 12.1 shows the contents of `Clerk` after these statements execute.

```
Clerk.ID := 1234;                {Store 1234 in ID field.}
Clerk.Name := 'Caryn Jackson';   {Store string in Name field.}
Clerk.Gender := 'F';             {Store F in Gender field.}
Clerk.NumDepend := 2;            {Store 2 in NumDepend field.}
Clerk.Rate := 6.00;              {Store 6.00 in Rate field.}
Clerk.TotWages := 0.0;           {Initialize TotWages field.}
Clerk.TotWages := Clerk.TotWages + 40.0 * Clerk.Rate
```

Once data are stored in a record, they can be manipulated in the same way as other data in memory. For example, the last assignment in our example computes the clerk's new total wages by adding this week's wages to her previous total wages (`0.0` in this case). The computed result is saved in the record field `Clerk.TotWages`.

The statements

```
Write ('The clerk is ');
case Clerk.Gender of
  'F', 'f' : Write ('Ms. ');
  'M', 'm' : Write ('Mr. ')
end; {case}
Write (Clerk.Name)
```

display the clerk's name after an appropriate title (`'Ms. '` or `'Mr. '`); the output line follows:

```
The clerk is Ms. Caryn Jackson
```
▲

Arrays as Record Fields

The `Name` field of record `Clerk` is a string, which is really an array of characters:

`Clerk.Name` `C a r y n   J a c k s o n`

We can reference individual characters in a string field (or array field) by writing the field selector followed by a subscript enclosed in brackets:

Record
variable   Field
   ↓   ⌒⌒⌒⌒
`Clerk.Name[I]`
     ↗   ↑
   String   Subscript
   variable

The function designator `Length(Clerk.Name)` returns the number of characters stored in field `Clerk.Name`. The `for` loop that follows accesses each character, from the first (C) to the last (n):

```
Write ('The clerk''s initials are: ');
for I := 1 to Length(Clerk.Name) do
  if (Clerk.Name[I] >= 'A') and (Clerk.Name[I] <= 'Z') then
    Write (Clerk.Name[I]);
WriteLn
```

The `if` statement condition is true if `Clerk.Name[I]` is an uppercase letter, so the program fragment displays the output line

```
The clerk's initials are: CJ
```

Exercises for Section 12.1 Self-Check

1. Each part in an inventory is represented by its part number, a descriptive name, the quantity on hand, and the price. Define a record type `Part`.
2. A computer graphics program computes the intensity of pixels on the screen. Define a record type `Pixel` for this program that will represent a pixel, where each pixel has an integer *X* and *Y* location, and real valued intensities for colors red, green, and blue.

12.2 Records as Operands and Parameters

In addition to accessing individual record fields to perform arithmetic operations, logical operations, or input or output operations, programmers often need to write procedures that process entire records. Usually it is more convenient to pass the record itself as a procedure parameter rather than to pass the individual fields. Programmers also need to copy the contents of one record variable to another. This section describes operations on entire records.

Record Copy or Assignment

We can copy all the fields of one record variable to another record variable of the same type with a record copy (assignment) statement. To illustrate, if `Clerk` and `Janitor` are both record variables of type `Employee`, the statement

```
Clerk := Janitor      {copy Janitor to Clerk}
```

copies each field of Janitor into the corresponding field of Clerk.

Records as Parameters

A record can be passed as a parameter to a function or a procedure, provided the actual parameter is the same type as its corresponding formal parameter. The use of records as parameters can shorten parameter lists considerably, because one parameter (the record variable) can be passed instead of several related parameters.

You can't use Pascal's input procedures to read data from the keyboard or a text file into an entire record. Similarly, you can't use Pascal's output procedures to write the contents of an entire record to the screen or a text file. You will need to code your own procedures to perform these common operations, as we show in Examples 12.2 and 12.3. Each procedure has a single parameter: the record to be read or written.

EXAMPLE 12.2: Reading a Record ▼

Procedure ReadEmployee in Fig. 12.2 reads data into all fields of a record variable of type Employee. The procedure call statement

```
ReadEmployee (Clerk)
```

causes the data read to be stored in record variable Clerk. ▲

Figure 12.2
Procedure ReadEmployee

```
procedure ReadEmployee (var AnEmp {output} : Employee);
{
  Reads one employee record into AnEmp.
  Pre : None.
  Post: Data are read into record AnEmp.
}
begin {ReadEmployee}
  Write ('ID> ');
  ReadLn (AnEmp.ID);
  Write ('Name> ');
  ReadLn (AnEmp.Name);
  Write ('Gender (F or M)> ');
  ReadLn (AnEmp.Gender);
  Write ('Number of dependents> ');
  ReadLn (AnEmp.NumDepend);
  Write ('Hourly rate> ');
  ReadLn (AnEmp.Rate);
  Write ('Total wages to date> ');
  ReadLn (AnEmp.TotWages)
end; {ReadEmployee}
```

EXAMPLE 12.3: Writing a Record ▼

In a grading program, the summary statistics for an exam are the average score, the highest and lowest scores, and the standard deviation. Previously we would have stored these data in separate variables, but now we are able to group them together as a record:

```
type
   ScoreRange = 0..100;
   ExamStats = record
                  Low, High : ScoreRange;
                  Average, StandardDev : Real
               end; {ExamStats}
```

Procedure `PrintStat` (Fig. 12.3) displays the value stored in each field of its record parameter (type `ExamStats`).   ▲

Exercises for Section 12.2   *Self-Check*

1. What does the following fragment do? Provide the declarations for variables `Exam1` and `Exam2`.

```
PrintStat (Exam1);
Exam2 := Exam1;
Exam2.High := Exam2.High - 5.0;
PrintStat (Exam2)
```

2. Which of the following are incorrect and why for `Exam1` and `Exam2` from Exercise 1? Correct each invalid statement.
   a. `var Exam1, Exam 2 : Exam;`
   b. `Exam1 := Exam2`
   c. `ReadLn (Exam1.Average)`
   d. `Exam1.High := Exam2`

Figure 12.3
Procedure PrintStat

```
procedure PrintStat (Exam {input} : ExamStats);
{
   Prints the exam statistics.
   Pre : The fields of record parameter Exam are assigned
         values.
   Post: Each field of Exam is displayed.
}
begin {PrintStat}
   WriteLn ('High score: ', Exam.High :1);
   WriteLn ('Low score: ', Exam.Low :1);
   WriteLn ('Average: ', Exam.Average :3:1);
   WriteLn ('Standard deviation: ', Exam.StandardDev :3:1)
end; {PrintStat}
```

```
e.  Exam2.Low := Exam1.High
f.  Exam2.Low := Exam1.Average
g.  WriteLn (Exam1)
```

Programming

1. Write a procedure that reads in the data for a pixel and returns the data through its parameter. See Self-Check Exercise 2 for Section 12.1.

12.3 The with Statement

Writing the complete field selector each time you reference a field of a record is tedious business. Instead, you can use the with statement to shorten the field selector. This with statement processes the record variable Clerk shown in Fig. 12.1:

```
with Clerk do
  begin
    Write ('The clerk is ');
    case Gender of
      'F', 'f' : Write ('Ms. ');
      'M', 'm' : Write ('Mr. ')
    end; {case}
    WriteLn (Name);

    TotWages := TotWages + 40.0 * Rate;
    WriteLn ('The clerk''s total wages are $', TotWages :4:2)
  end; {with}
```

As you can see, you needn't specify both the record variable and the field names inside a with statement. Because the record variable Clerk is identified in the with statement header, only the field name is needed, not the complete field selector (e.g., Rate instead of Clerk.Rate). The with statement is particularly useful when you are manipulating several fields of the same record variable.

SYNTAX DISPLAY

with Statement

Form: with *record var* do
              statement
Example: with Clerk do
              if NumDepend > 3 then
                Rate := 1.5 * Rate

Interpretation: *statement* can be a single statement or a compound statement. *record var* is the name of a *record* variable. Anywhere within *statement,* you can reference a field of *record var* by specifying only its field name.

EXAMPLE 12.4 ▼

Many programs need to keep track of the time of day, and normally do so by updating the time of day after a certain period has elapsed. The record type Time is declared as follows, assuming a 24-hour clock:

```
type
  Time = record
           Hour : 0..23;
           Minute, Second : 0..59
         end; {Time}
```

Procedure ChangeTime in Fig. 12.4 updates the time of day, TimeOfDay (type Time), after a time interval, ElapsedTime, which is expressed in seconds. Each statement that uses the mod operator updates a particular field of the record represented by TimeOfDay. The mod operator ensures that each updated value is within the required range; the div operator converts multiples of 60 seconds to minutes and multiples of 60 minutes to hours.

Using the with statement simplifies writing procedure ChangeTime. Without it, the first assignment statement would be coded as

```
NewSec := TimeOfDay.Second + ElapsedTime;   {total seconds}   ▲
```

Figure 12.4
Procedure ChangeTime

```
procedure ChangeTime (ElapsedTime {input} : Integer;
                          var TimeOfDay {input/output} : Time);
{
 Updates the time of day, TimeOfDay, assuming a 24-hour clock
 and an elapsed time of ElapsedTime in seconds.
 Pre : ElapsedTime and record TimeOfDay are assigned
       values.
 Post: TimeOfDay is incremented by ElapsedTime.
}
  var
    NewHour, NewMin, NewSec : Integer; {temporary variables}

begin {ChangeTime}
  with TimeOfDay do
    begin
      NewSec := Second + ElapsedTime;      {total seconds}
      Second := NewSec mod 60;             {seconds over 60}
      NewMin := Minute + (NewSec div 60);  {total minutes}
      Minute := NewMin mod 60;             {minutes over 60}
      NewHour := Hour + (NewMin div 60);   {total hours}
      Hour := NewHour mod 24               {hours over 24}
    end {with}
end;   {ChangeTime}
```

Program Style

A Word of Caution About the with Statement

Although the `with` statement is helpful in reducing the length of program statements that manipulate record components, it also can reduce the clarity of those statements. For example, in the preceding assignment statement, the field selector `TimeOfDay.Second` shows clearly that `Second` is a field of record parameter `TimeOfDay`. This role is not documented as clearly in the statement

```
NewSec := Second + ElapsedTime;      {total seconds}
```

used in procedure `ChangeTime`.

Exercises for Section 12.3

Self-Check

1. If a procedure declared a local variable with name `Second`, how would the use of `with` be restricted if a variable of type `Time` were also declared?
2. If all fields of variable `Now` (type `Time`) are initially 0, how is `Now` changed by the execution of the following fragment?

```
ChangeTime (3600, Now);
ChangeTime (7125, Now)
```

Programming

1. Write a procedure that initializes all fields of a variable of type `Time` to 0.
2. Write a function that accepts a parameter of type `Time` and computes the equivalent time in seconds. Return the result as a `LongInt`. (Why?)

12.4 Arrays of Records

Arrays and records are two basic data structures in Pascal. Just as we use the basic program modules, procedures and functions, as building blocks of larger programs, we can use these basic data structures to model more complicated organizations of data.

Storing a Database as an Array of Records

database

a collection of facts or information about related items usually organized as a file or table of records

One common method of organizing data in real life is to build a **database**, a collection of facts or information about related items. A hospital, for example, might maintain a database of employees, a database of patients, and a database of prescription drugs. We could use a record to represent each item in a database, and we could use an array of records to store each database in memory. Often we read a database from a disk file before we access it and we write a database out to disk when we are finished updating it.

A simple example of a database is a collection of student records for a class. For each student, we might want to store the student's name, three exam scores, the average score, and the student's grade. We can store the information for each student in a record of type Student. The data structure declared next stores the class data in an array of student records. Array Class is shown in Fig. 12.5.

```
const
    MaxClass = 200;
    StringLength = 20;
    NumberExams = 3;

type
    ClassIndex = 1..MaxClass;
    StringType = string[StringLength];
    ScoreArray = array [1..NumberExams] of Integer;
    Student = record
                Name : StringType;
```

Figure 12.5
Array of Records

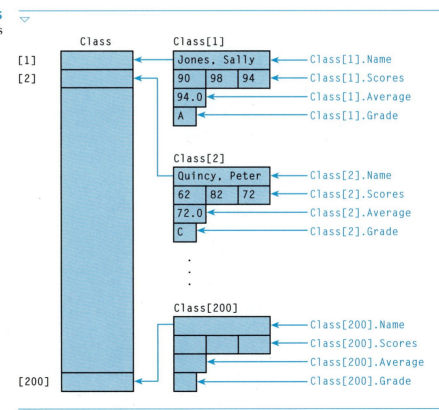

```
                    Scores : ScoreArray;
                    Average : Real;
                    Grade : Char
                end; {Student}

    StudentArray = array [ClassIndex] of Student;

var
    Class : StudentArray;
```

In Fig. 12.5, the data for the first student are stored in record Class[1]. The individual data items are Class[1].Name, Class[1].Scores[1], Class[1].Scores[2], Class[1].Scores[3], Class[1].Average and Class[1].Grade. Notice that two subscripts are needed to access an exam score. The first subscript selects an element of array Class; the second subscript selects an element of the Scores array. As shown, Class[1].Scores[1] is 90.

EXAMPLE 12.5 ▼

Procedure ReadClass (Fig. 12.6) reads data into the array of student records. The procedure returns two results: the array of student data and the number of student records stored. The for statement

```
for I := 1 to ClassSize do
  ReadStudent (Class[I])
```

```
procedure ReadClass (var Class {output} : StudentArray;
                     var ClassSize {output} : Integer);
{Returns the number of students in the class through
 ClassSize. Fills the subarray Class[1..ClassSize] with
 student data.
 Pre  : None
 Post : 1 <= ClassSize <= MaxClass and Class[I] contains
        the input data for the Ith student.
 Calls: EnterInt (Fig. 9.6) and ReadStudent
}
  var
    I : Integer;            {loop control and array subscript}

begin {ReadClass}
  WriteLn ('Enter number of students:');
  EnterInt (1, MaxClass, ClassSize);

  {Read the student data.}
  WriteLn ('Enter each student''s data:');
  for I := 1 to ClassSize do
    ReadStudent (Class[I])
end; {ReadClass}
```

fills the array `Class`. Each time `ReadStudent` (see Programming Exercise 1 at the end of this section) is called, the record returned (type `Student`) will be stored as the Ith element (1 ≤ I ≤ `ClassSize`) of array `Class`. The details of reading each record are left to procedure `ReadStudent`.   ▲

Using the with Statement with an Array of Records

Be careful when you use a `with` statement to process an array of records. For example, the `with` statement that begins

```
with Class[I] do
```

uses the subscripted variable `Class[I]` as its record variable. The particular array element referenced depends on the value of I. If I is undefined or is out of range, a run-time error will result.

If I is updated inside the `with` statement, the array element referenced will not change. For example, the following statements display the first student's name `MaxClass` times. Because I is 1 when the `with` statement is reached, `Class[1]` is the record referenced in the `with` statement body. Even though the `for` loop changes the value of I, `Class[1]` is still the record referenced, so `Class[1].Name` will be displayed repeatedly.

```
I := 1;
{incorrect attempt to display all student names}
with Class[I] do
  for I := 1 to ClassSize do
    WriteLn (Name)
```

The correct way to sequence these statements is

```
{Display all student names.}
for I := 1 to ClassSize do
  with Class[I] do
    WriteLn (Name)
```

Now all student names will be printed, because I is changed by the `for` statement external to the `with` statement. Each time the `with` statement is reached, it references a new record. Whenever a `for` statement accesses an array of records in sequential order, the `with` statement should be nested inside the `for` statement, not vice versa.

Effect of Data Structures on Program Design

The data structure chosen for a problem can have a significant effect on program design. When you code procedures that process the class data, take advantage of the fact that each student's data are stored in a separate record and use procedures associated with that record type. For example, procedure `ReadClass` calls procedure `ReadStudent` to read each student record. Often you will find that procedures like `ReadStudent` will already be coded. This choice of data structure simplifies coding `ReadClass`.

An alternative for storing the student data would be to use four separate arrays: one array with `MaxClass` elements could store all the student names, a two-dimensional array (`MaxClass` × 3) could store the exam scores, and two more arrays with `MaxClass` elements could store the average score and semester grade for each student. The Ith student's data would be stored in row I of all four arrays (see Fig. 12.7).

Although we will not go into detail on how to process these arrays, it should be clear that procedure `ReadClass` would be much more complicated. Instead of filling one array of records, it would need to read data into four separate arrays, one with two dimensions.

Another possibility for storing the class data would be to combine the student information with information about the class as a whole in a single record. Record type `GradeBook` declared next has three fields: `ClassID` for storing the class identification (a string), `ClassSize` for storing the class size, and `Class` for storing the student data. Figure 12.8 sketches record variable `MyClass` (type `GradeBook`).

```
type
   {Insert declarations for StringType and StudentArray.}
   GradeBook = record
                  ClassID : StringType;
                  ClassSize : Integer;
                  Class : StudentArray
               end; {GradeBook}

var
   MyClass : GradeBook;         {a grade book page}
```

You can store all the information for a class in one record variable (e.g., `MyClass`) of type `GradeBook`. Use `MyClass.ClassID` to access the class

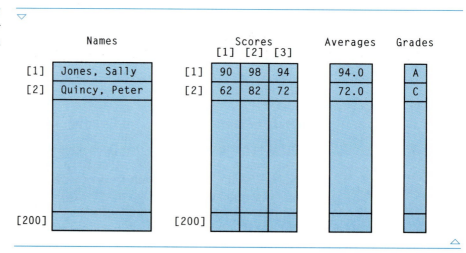

Figure 12.7
Four Arrays for
Student Data

Figure 12.8
Record Variable MyClass

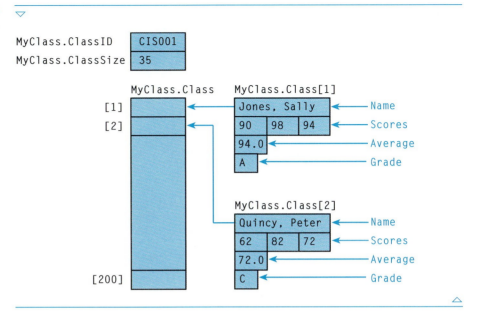

identification, MyClass.ClassSize to access the number of students, MyClass.Class[I] to access the Ith student record, MyClass.Class [I].Name to access that student's Name, and MyClass.Class[I].Score[1] to access that student's first exam score.

You can rewrite procedure ReadClass to read the class identification, class size, and student data into a record of this type (see Programming Exercise 2 at the end of this section). The new procedure would have just one parameter because all information about the class would be read into different fields of the same record. Example 12.6 shows how to sort the array field Class so its records are in alphabetical order by student name.

EXAMPLE 12.6 ▼

Procedure SortStudents (Fig. 12.9) sorts the class array so that all student data are in sequence by student name. Compare it to procedure SelectSort shown in Fig. 10.20.

Procedure SwitchStu exchanges the student records at positions Fill and IndexOfMin of array field Class. Notice that SwitchStu uses three record copy statements to exchange all student data, not just the student names.

Function FindMinName (see Programming Exercise 3 at the end of this section) returns the position of the student record with the alphabetically smallest name in the subarray Class[Fill..ClassSize]. The array field Class is the first function argument and it should correspond to a formal parameter of type StudentArray. ▲

Figure 12.9
Procedures SwitchStu and
SortStudents

```
procedure SwitchStu (var Stu1, Stu2 {input/output} : Student);
{Switches the values stored in Stu1 and Stu2.}
   var
      TempStu : Student;          {temporary student record}

begin {SwitchStu}
   TempStu := Stu1;      Stu1 := Stu2;      Stu2 := TempStu
end; {SwitchStu}


procedure SortStudents (var MyClass {input/output} :
                                             GradeBook);
{
 Sorts the data in array field Class of record MyClass.
 Pre : The record MyClass is defined and the filled
        subarray is MyClass.Class[1..MyClass.ClassSize].
 Post: The records in MyClass.Class[1..MyClass.ClassSize] are
        in alphabetical order by student name.
 Calls: Procedures SwitchStu and FindMinName.
}
   var
      Fill,                    {index of element to be filled next}
      IndexOfMin : Integer;    {index of next smallest element}

begin {SortStudents}
   with MyClass do
      for Fill := 1 to ClassSize - 1 do
         begin
            {invariant:
               The records in MyClass.Class[1..Fill-1] are in
               their proper place and Fill <= MyClass.ClassSize.
            }
            {Find position of student with smallest name.}
            IndexOfMin := FindMinName(Class, Fill, ClassSize);

            {Exchange students at positions Fill and IndexOfMin.}
            if IndexOfMin <> Fill then
               SwitchStu (Class[IndexOfMin], Class[Fill])
         end {for and with}
end; {SortStudents}
```

Exercises for Section 12.4   *Self-Check*

1. For the array of records Class (see Fig. 12.5), what value is displayed
   by each valid statement? Correct the invalid statements.
   a. WriteLn (Class[1].Name[4])
   b. WriteLn (Class[1].Score[4])
   c. WriteLn (Class.Grade[3])
   d. WriteLn (Class[1].Name)

```
  e.  WriteLn (Class[1].Name[4].Grade)
  f.  WriteLn (Class[1].Grade)
  g.  WriteLn (Class[1])
  h.  WriteLn (Class.Name[4])
```

Programming

1. Write procedure `ReadStudent`. Read each student's name and score; leave the grade field undefined.
2. Write a modified procedure `ReadClass` to read all class data into a record of type `GradeBook`. Assume that the number of records and class identification are data items and are returned as procedure results along with the student array.
3. Write function `FindMinName` (see Fig. 10.17).

12.5 Hierarchical Records

In addition to constructing arrays with record components, it is possible to declare a record type with fields that are other record types. A record with one or more fields that are record types is a **hierarchical record.**

hierarchical record

a record with one or more record fields

In this section, we modify record type `Employee` by adding new fields for storage of the employee's address, starting date, and date of birth. The record type `NewEmployee` is declared in Fig. 12.10, along with two additional record types, `Date` and `Address`. `Programmer` is a record variable of type `NewEmployee`. The hierarchical structure of this record variable is shown in Fig. 12.11. This diagram provides a graphic display of the record form.

Figure 12.10
Declaration of a
Hierarchical Record

```
const
   StringLength = 20; {length of all strings except zipcode}
   ZipStringSize = 5; {length of zipcode string}

type
   IDRange = 1111..9999;
   StringType = string[StringLength];
   ZipString = string[ZipStringSize];
   Month = (January, February, March, April, May, June, July
            August, September, October, November, December);

   Employee = record
                ID : IDRange;
                Name : StringType;
                Gender : Char;
                NumDepend : Integer;
                Rate, TotWages : Real
              end; {Employee}
```

▷ ▷ ▷ ▷ ▷

```
Address = record
             Street, City, State : StringType;
             ZipCode : ZipString
         end; {Address}

Date = record
          ThisMonth : Month;
          Day : 1..31;
          Year : 1900..1999
      end; {Date}

NewEmployee = record
                 PayData : Employee;
                 Home : Address;
                 StartDate, BirthDate : Date
             end; {NewEmployee}
var
   Programmer : NewEmployee;
```

Record `Programmer` has fields `PayData`, `Home`, `StartDate`, and `Birth-Date`. Each of these fields is itself a record (called a *subrecord* of `Programmer`). The fields of each subrecord are indicated under that subrecord.

To reference a field in this diagram, we must trace a complete path to it starting from the top of the diagram. For example, the field selector

`Programmer.StartDate`

references the subrecord `StartDate` (type `Date`) of the variable `Programmer`. The field selector

`Programmer.StartDate.Year`

references the `Year` field of the subrecord `Programmer.StartDate`. The field selector

`Programmer.Year`

is incomplete (which `Year` field?) and would cause a syntax error. The record copy statement

`Programmer.StartDate := DayOfYear`

is valid if `DayOfYear` is a record variable of type `Date`. This statement copies each field of `DayOfYear` into the corresponding field of the subrecord

`Programmer.StartDate`

In many situations we can use the `with` statement to shorten the field selector. The statement

```
with Programmer.StartDate do
   WriteLn ('Year started: ', Year:4, ', day started: ', Day:1)
```

Figure 12.11
Record Variable Programmer (Type NewEmployee)

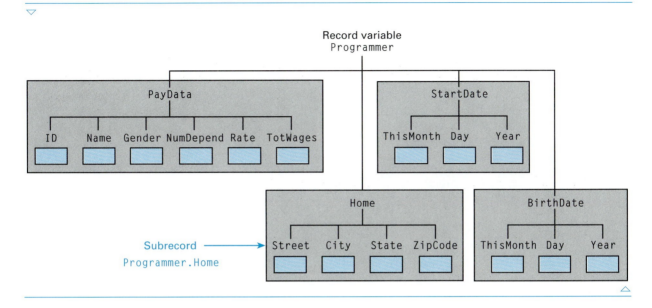

displays two fields of the subrecord `Programmer.StartDate`. The computation for updating total wages could be written as

```
with Programmer.PayData do
   TotWages := TotWages + Rate * 40.0
```

The `with` statement

```
with Programmer do
   WriteLn (PayData.Name, ' started work in ',StartDate.Year:4)
```

displays an output line of the form

```
Caryn Jackson started work in 1986
```

It is also possible to nest `with` statements. The following nested `with` statement also displays the preceding output line.

```
with Programmer do
   with PayData do
      with StartDate do
         WriteLn (Name, ' started work in ', Year :4)
```

The record variable name (`Programmer`) must precede the field names, as shown. The order of the field names `PayData` and `StartDate` is not important.

We can also use a list of record variable names and field names in a with statement. The statement

```
with Programmer, PayData, StartDate do
  WriteLn (Name, ' started work in ', Year :4)
```

is equivalent to the one just discussed.

Procedure ReadNewEmp in Fig. 12.12 could be used to read in a record of type NewEmployee. It calls procedures ReadEmployee (see Fig. 12.2), ReadAddress, and ReadDate (see the programming exercise at the end of this section).

Exercises for Section 12.5 *Self-Check*

1. What must be the type of NewAddress if the following statement is correct?

   ```
   Programmer.Home := NewAddress
   ```

2. Write Pascal statements to perform the following actions:
   a. Increase the programmer's salary by 10%.
   b. Display the city, state, and zip code of the programmer.
   c. Display the programmer's month of birth.
   d. Display the month the programmer started working.

Programming

1. Write procedures ReadAddress and ReadDate.

Figure 12.12
Procedure ReadNewEmp

```
procedure ReadNewEmp (var NewEmp {output} : NewEmployee);
{
    Reads a record into record variable NewEmp.
    Pre  : None.
    Post : Reads data into all fields of record NewEmp.
    Calls: Procedures ReadEmployee (see Fig. 12.2),
           ReadAddress, and ReadDate (see programming exer-
           cise)
}
begin {ReadNewEmp}
  with NewEmp do
    begin
      ReadEmployee (PayData);
      ReadAddress (Home);
      ReadDate (StartDate);
      ReadDate (BirthDate)
    end {with}
end; {ReadNewEmp}
```

12.6 Variant Records (Optional)

variant record
a record that has a fixed and
a varying component
fixed part
the part of a record that is
always the same
variant part
the part of a record that is
changeable

All record variables of type NewEmployee have the same form and structure. It is possible, however, to use **variant records** to store data collections in which some fields are always the same (the **fixed part**) and some fields may be different (the **variant part**).

For example, we might want to include additional information about an employee based on marital status. For all married employees, we might want to know the spouse's name and the number of children. For all divorced employees, we might want to know the date of the divorce. For all single employees, we might want to know whether the employee lives alone.

This new employee type, Executive, is declared in Fig. 12.13 and uses several data types declared earlier in Fig. 12.10.

Figure 12.13
Record Type Executive and
Record Variable Boss

```
const
    StringLength = 20;   {length of all strings except zipcode}
    ZipStringSize = 5;   {length of zipcode string}

type
    IDRange = 1111..9999;
    StringType = string[StringLength];
    ZipString = string[ZipStringSize];
    Month = (January, February, March, April, May, June, July,
             August, September, October, November, December);

    Employee = record
                   ID : IDRange;
                   Name : StringType;
                   Gender : Char;
                   NumDepend : Integer;
                   Rate, TotWages : Real
               end; {Employee}

    Address = record
                  Street, City, State : StringType;
                  ZipCode : ZipString
              end; {Address}

    Date = record
               ThisMonth : Month;
               Day : 1..31;
               Year : 1900..1999
           end; {Date}
```

▷ ▷ ▷ ▷ ▷ ▷

```
                MaritalStatus = (Married, Divorced, Single);
                Executive = record
                              PayData : Employee;
                              Home : Address;
                              StartDate, BirthDate : Date;
                            case MS : MaritalStatus of
                              Married  : (SpouseName : StringType;
                                              NumberKids : Integer);
                              Divorced : (DivorceDate : Date);
                              Single   : (LivesAlone : Boolean)
                            end; {Executive}

                var
                  Boss : Executive;
```

The fixed part of a record always precedes the variant part. The fixed part of record type `Executive` has the form of record type `NewEmployee`. The variant part follows the line

```
case MS : MaritalStatus of
```

which defines a special field `MS`, of type `MaritalStatus`. The value of the **tag field** `MS` (`Married`, `Divorced`, or `Single`) indicates the form of the remainder of the record. If the value of the tag field is `Married`, there are two additional fields, `SpouseName` (type `StringType`) and `NumberKids` (type `Integer`); otherwise, there is only one additional field, `DivorceDate` (type `Date`) or `LivesAlone` (type `Boolean`).

Figure 12.14 shows three variants of record variable `Boss`, starting with the tag field. The fixed parts of all these records (not shown) have the same form.

tag field

the record field whose value determines the form of that record's variant part

Figure 12.14
Three Variants of Record
Variable Boss

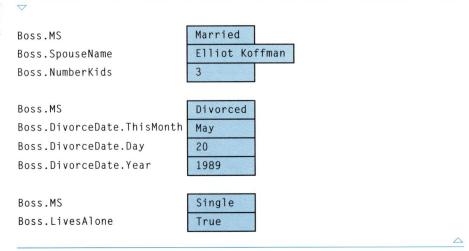

For each variable of type Executive, the compiler allocates sufficient storage space to accommodate the largest of the record variants. However, only one variant is defined at any given time, and that particular variant is determined by the tag field value.

The amount of storage required for each variant depends on how many bytes are used to store integer values and enumerated type values on a particular computer. The first variant in Fig. 12.14 requires more than 20 bytes of storage (one byte per character of the spouse's name) and should be the largest.

EXAMPLE 12.7 ▼

If the value of the tag field Boss.MS is Married, then only the variant fields SpouseName and NumberKids can be referenced correctly; all other variant fields are undefined. Assuming the first variant shown in Fig. 12.14 is stored in record Boss, the program fragment

```
with Boss do
  begin
    WriteLn ('The spouse''s name is ', SpouseName, '.');
    WriteLn ('They have ', NumberKids :1, ' children.')
  end {with}
```

displays the lines

```
The spouse's name is Elliot Koffman.
They have 3 children.
```

We must ensure that the variant fields that are referenced are consistent with the current tag field value. The compiler and the run-time system do not normally check this. If the value of Boss.MS is not Married when the preceding fragment is executed, the information displayed will be meaningless. For that reason, a case statement is often used to process the variant part of a record. Using the tag field as the case selector, we can ensure that only the currently defined variant is manipulated.   ▲

EXAMPLE 12.8 ▼

The fragment in Fig. 12.15 displays the data stored in the variant part of record Boss. The value of Boss.MS determines what information is displayed.   ▲

SYNTAX DISPLAY

Record Type with Variant Part

Form: type

$rec\ type$ = record

$id\ list_1$: $type_1$;
$id\ list_2$: $type_2$;
. . .
$id\ list_n$: $type_n$;

Fixed part

Figure 12.15
Displaying a Variant
Record

```
{Display the variant part.}
with Boss do
   case MS of
      Married :
            begin
               WriteLn ('The spouse''s name is ', SpouseName, '.');
               WriteLn ('They have ', NumberKids :1, ' children.')
            end; {Married}
      Divorced :
            with DivorceDate do
               WriteLn ('Divorced on ', Ord(ThisMonth) + 1 :2,
                              '/', Day :2, '/', Year :4);
      Single :
            if LivesAlone then
               WriteLn ('Lives alone')
            else
               WriteLn ('Does not live alone')
   end {case}
```

case *tag* : *tag type* of
   label₁ : (*field list₁*) ;
   label₂ : (*field list₂*) ; } **Variant part**
        . . .
   labelₖ : (*field listₖ*)
   end;

Example: type
```
         Face = record
                     Eyes : Color;
                  case Bald : Boolean of
                     True : (WearsWig : Boolean);
                     False : (HairColor : Color)
                  end;
```

Interpretation: The fixed part is declared before the word case. The variant part starts with the reserved word case. The identifier *tag* is the name of the *tag* field of the record; the tag field name is separated by a colon from its type (*tag type*), which must be type Boolean, an enumerated type, or a subrange of an ordinal type.

The case labels (*label₁*, *label₂*, . . . , *labelₖ*) are lists of values of the tag field as defined by *tag type*. *Field listᵢ* describes the record fields associated with *labelᵢ*. Each element of *field listᵢ* specifies a field name and its type; the elements in *field listᵢ* are separated by semicolons. *Field listᵢ* is enclosed in parentheses.

Note 1: All field names must be unique. The same field name may not appear in the fixed and variant parts or in two field lists of the variant part.
Note 2: An empty field list (no variant part for that case label) is indicated by an empty pair of parentheses, ( ).
Note 3: A field list may have a variant part, and that part must follow the fixed part of that field list.
Note 4: There is only one end for the record type declaration; there is no separate end for the case.

When you initially store data in a record with a variant part, the tag field value should be read first. Once the value of the tag field is defined, data can be read into the variant fields associated with that value.

Exercises for Section 12.6 **Self-Check**

1. How many bytes do you need to store each variant for a record of type Executive, assuming two bytes for an integer or an enumerated type value and one byte for a character or a Boolean value? Don't include the tag field in your calculations.

2. Write a statement that displays Boss.SpouseName if defined or the message Not married.

Programming

1. Write a procedure to display a record of type Face as declared in the syntax display in this section.

12.7 Debugging Records

To display the value of a record field in the Watch window, you must use the fully qualified field name as a Watch expression. To display the value of field ID of the record variable Clerk shown in Fig. 12.1, you would use Clerk.ID as a Watch expression. The with statement has no effect on field identifiers used in Watch expressions.

To display all fields of a record variable, the record identifier is used as a Watch expression. Like an array, the record's field values are displayed in the Watch window as a list enclosed in parentheses. If Clerk is the Watch expression having the field values shown in Fig. 12.1, Turbo Pascal displays the first line in the Watch window at the bottom of Fig. 12.16. Strange looking values may be displayed for record fields that have not been assigned values.

If all the values displayed do not fit in the Watch window, use your mouse or the F6 key to move to the Watch window. Then use either the left or the right arrow key (or your mouse and the Watch window horizontal scroll bar) to scan through the values.

Figure 12.16
Watch Window for
a Record

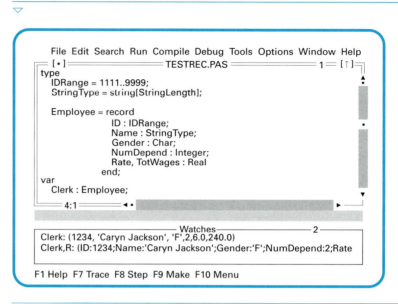

If you use the Watch expression

```
Clerk,R
```

Turbo Pascal displays each field name of `Clerk` followed by its value as shown in the second line of the Watch window of Fig. 12.16. The *Debug expression format character* R causes this result.

Debugging Records with Structured Components

Hierarchical records are displayed in the Watch window as nested, parenthesized lists of values. The same is true for records that contain arrays as fields. You can display subrecords and record fields that are arrays if you use their fully qualified names as Watch expressions. They will be displayed as a list of values enclosed in parentheses.

Debugging Arrays of Records

You can also use the Watch window to display all or portions of arrays whose elements are record types. Arrays of records are displayed as nested, parenthesized lists of values. If we type `Class` as a Watch expression assuming that `MaxClass` is 4, the Watch window displays the following array:

```
Class: (('Jones, Sally',(90,98,94),94.0,'A'),('Quincy,
Peter',(62,82,72),72.0,'C'),('Philips, Susan',
(60,65,70),65.0,'D'),('Austin, Tracy',(80,86,92),86.0,'B'))
```

Both repeat counts and Debug expression format characters can be used in Watch expressions for arrays of records. The Watch expression

```
Class[2]
```

displays the second record of array `Class` in the Watch window. The Watch expression

```
Class[2],2
```

displays the second and third records of `Class`, while the Watch expression

```
Class[2],R
```

displays the field names and values of the second record of array `Class`. As a final example, the Watch expression

```
Class[2],2R
```

displays the field names and values for the second and third records of the array `Class` in the Watch window.

12.8 Common Programming Errors

The most common error when using records is incorrectly specifying the record field to be manipulated. The full field selector (record variable and field name) must be used, unless the record reference is nested inside a `with` statement or the entire record is to be manipulated. So far we have discussed the latter option only for record copy statements and for records passed as parameters.

If a record variable name is listed in a `with` statement header, only the field name is required to reference fields of that record inside the `with` statement. You still must use the full field selector to reference fields of any other record variable.

Errors in Arrays of Records

When an array of records is processed, the array name and the subscript must be included as part of the field selector (e.g., `X[I].Key` references field `Key` of the Ith record). If you use a `for` statement to process all array elements in sequence, then you must nest any `with` statement that references the array records inside the `for` statement, as shown here:

```
for I := 1 to N do
  with X[I] do
```

As the loop-control variable `I` changes, the next array record is processed by the `with` statement. If the nesting order is reversed, as in

```
with X[I] do
  for I := 1 to N do
```

then the same array record is processed N times. The record that is processed is determined by the value of I when the with statement is first reached. Changing the value of I inside the with statement has no effect.

Errors in Variant Records

For variant records, remember that the value of the tag field determines the form of the variant part that is currently defined. Manipulating any other variant causes unpredictable results. You must ensure that the correct variant is being processed—the computer does not check this. So always reference a variant record in a case statement with the tag field as the case selector to ensure that the proper variant part is being manipulated.

CHAPTER REVIEW

1. Use records to store a collection of related data items of different types. Reference individual record fields using a field selector consisting of the record variable name and a period followed by the field name.

2. You can assign one record variable to another record variable of the same type (record copy statement) or pass a record as a parameter to a procedure or function.

3. You can shorten a field selector using a with statement. If you specify the record variable name in a with statement header, then you only need to write the field name inside the with statement.

4. Using arrays of records to organize data collections can simplify programming. A procedure that processes the entire array of records can call other procedures to process each individual record.

5. Represent more complicated data organizations using hierarchical records (records with record components). Use variant records to store data with both a fixed and varying component.

Summary of New Pascal Constructs

Construct	Effect
Record Declaration	
```type Part = record ID : 1111..9999; Quantity : Integer; Price : Real end; {Part} var Nuts, Bolts : Part;```	A record type Part is declared with fields that can store two integers and a real number. Nuts and Bolts are record variables of type Part.

Construct	Effect

Record Variant Declaration

```
type
   ChildKind = (Girl, Boy);
   Child = record
              First, Last : Char;
              Age : Integer;
           case Sex : ChildKind of
              Girl : (Sugar, Spice :
                                Real);
              Boy : (Snakes, Snails,
                        Tails : Integer)
           end; {Child}
var
   Kid : Child;
```

A record type with a variant part is declared. Each record variable can store two characters and an integer. One variant part can store two real numbers, and the other can store three integers. The record variable `Kid` is type `Child`.

Record Reference

```
TotalCost := Nuts.Quantity
                * Nuts.Price;
WriteLn (Bolts.ID :4)
```

Multiplies two fields of `Nuts`.
Prints `ID` field of `Bolts`.

Record Copy

```
Bolts := Nuts
```

Copies record `Nuts` to `Bolts`.

with Statement

```
with Bolts do
   Write (ID :4, Price :8:2)
```

Prints two fields of `Bolts`.

Declaring Arrays of Records

```
type
   AElement = record
                 Data : Real;
                 Key : Integer
              end; {AElement}
   DataArray = array [1..10] of
                 AElement;
var
   MyData : DataArray;
```

`DataArray` is an array type with 10 elements of type `AElement` (a record). Each element has fields named `Data` and `Key`.

`MyData` is a variable of type `DataArray`.

Referencing an Array of Records

```
MyData[1].Data := 3.14159;
MyData[10].Key := 9999;
```

The real value `3.14159` is stored in the first `Data` field of array `MyData`; the value `9999` is stored in the last `Key` field.

Construct	Effect
Referencing a Record Variant	

`with Kid do`
`  case Sex of`
`    Girl :`
`      begin`
`        Write (Pounds of sugar>');`
`        ReadLn (Sugar)`
`      end; {Girl}`
`    Boy :`
`      begin`
`        Write ('Count of snakes>');`
`        ReadLn (Snakes)`
`      end {Boy}`
	Uses a `case` statement to read data into the variant part of record variable `Kid`. If tag field `Sex` is `Girl`, reads a value into the field `Sugar`. If tag field `Sex` is `Boy`, reads a value into the field `Snakes`.

Quick-Check Exercises

1. What is the primary difference between a record and an array? Which would you use to store the catalog description of a course? To store the names of the students in the course?
2. Write a type declaration that describes a computer display that is 640 columns by 480 rows of pixels, where each pixel has a red, green, and blue intensity value (of integer type).
3. When can you use the assignment operator with record operands? When can you use the equality operator?
4. For `AStudent` declared as follows, provide a statement that displays the initials of `AStudent`:

```
type
   StringType = string[StringLength];
   Student = record
                First, Last : StringType;
                Age, Score : Integer;
                Grade : Char
             end; {Student}

var
   AStudent : Student;
```

5. If an integer uses two bytes of storage and a character one, and `StringLength` is 20, how many bytes of storage are occupied by `AStudent`?
6. Write a procedure that displays a variable of type `Student`.
7. Why do we use a `with` statement? What is a disadvantage of using the `with` statement?
8. Write the type declaration for a data structure that stores a player's name, salary, fielding position, batting average, fielding percentage, and number of hits, runs, runs batted in, and errors.
9. Write the type declaration for a data structure that stores the information in Quick-Check Exercise 8 for a team of 25 players.
10. When should you use a record variant?

Answers to Quick-Check Exercises

1. The values stored in an array must all be the same type, whereas the values stored in a record do not have to be the same type; record for catalog item; array for list of names.

2.
```
type
   Pixel = record
              Red, Blue, Green : Integer
            end; {Pixel}
   Screen = array [1..640, 1..480] of Pixel;
```

3. When the records are the same type; never

4. `WriteLn (AStudent.First[1], AStudent.Last[1])`

5. 45

6.
```
procedure WriteStudent (OneStu {input} : Student);
   begin
      WriteLn ('Student is ', OneStu.FirstName,
               ' ', OneStu.LastName);
      WriteLn ('Age is ', OneStu.Age :1);
      WriteLn ('Score is ', OneStu.Score :1);
      WriteLn ('Grade is ', OneStu.Grade)
   end;
```

7. A `with` statement allows us to shorten field selectors. It is helpful when we must reference several fields of the same record. Its disadvantage is that it makes the program less readable because it separates the record variable name from the field name. It is particularly confusing when there are multiple records of the same type or when a record has nested subrecords.

8.
```
type
   Position = (Pitcher, Catcher, FirstBase,
               SecondBase, ThirdBase, ShortStop,
               LeftField, CenterField, RightField);
   StringType = string[20];
   Player = record
              Name : StringType;
              Salary : Real;
              FieldPos : Position;
              BatAve, FieldPct : Real;
              Hits, Runs, RBIs, Errors : Integer
            end; {Player}
```

9.
```
type
   StringType = . . .
   Player = . . .
   TeamArray = array [1..25] of Player;
```

10. When an object has some fields that are always the same and some fields that may be different

Review Questions

1. Declare a record called `Subscriber` that contains the fields `Name`, `StreetAddress`, `MonthlyBill` (how much the subscriber owes), and which paper the subscriber receives (`Morning`, `Evening`, or `Both`).

2. Write a Pascal program to enter and then print out the data in record Compe-tition declared as follows:

```
const
  StringLength = 20;

type
  StringType = string[StringLength];
  OlympicEvent = record
                    Event,
                    Entrant,
                    Country : StringType;
                    Place : Integer
                 end; {OlympicEvent}
var
  Competition : OlympicEvent;
```

3. Identify and correct the errors in the following program.

```
program Report;
  type
    String15 = string[15];
    SummerHelp = record
                    Name : String15;
                    StartDate : String15;
                    HoursWorked : Real
                 end; {SummerHelp}

  var
    Operator : SummerHelp;

begin {Report}
  with SummerHelp do
    begin
      Name := 'Stoney Viceroy';
      StartDate := 'June 1, 1995';
      HoursWorked := 29.3
    end; {with}
  WriteLn (Operator)
end. {Report}
```

Use the following declarations for Review Questions 4 through 9.

```
const
  TotalEmployees = 20;

type
  EmpRange = 1..TotalEmployees;
  Employee = record
                ID : Integer;
                Rate, Hours : Real
             end; {Employee}
  EmpArray = array [EmpRange] of Employee;

var
  Employees : EmpArray;
```

4. Write the function `TotalGross` that will return the total gross pay given the data stored in array `Employees`.

5. Explain what is wrong with the following fragment and fix it:

```
I := 1;
with Employees[I] do
   while I <= TotalEmployees do
      begin
         WriteLn (Hours :12:2);
         I := I + 1
      end {while}
```

6. Explain what is wrong with the following fragment and fix it:

```
I := 1;
while (Employees[I].ID <> 999) and (I<=TotalEmployees) do
   I := I + 1;
```

7. Write a fragment that displays the ID number of each employee who works between 10 and 20 hours per week.

8. Write a fragment that displays the ID number of the employee who works the most hours.

9. Write a procedure that, given an employee ID, displays the wages of that employee.

10. Write the declarations for the record `Quotations` that contains an integer count of the number of quotations stored and an array of up to 100 records of type `Quote`. Each record of type `Quote` should have the following fields: `The-Quote` (80 characters in length), `Author` (30 characters), and `Year` (integer).

11. Write the variant declaration for `Supplies`, which consists of `Paper`, `Ribbon`, or `Labels`. For `Paper`, the information needed is the number of sheets per box and the size of the paper. For `Ribbon`, the size, color, and kind (`Carbon` or `Cloth`) are needed. For `Labels`, the size and number per box are needed. For each supply, the cost, the number on hand, and the reorder point also must be stored. Use whatever data types are appropriate for each field.

Programming Projects

1. Represent an article of clothing using a record that consists of the article's description (a string), color (enumerated type `ColorType`), and price. Write a new abstract data type `ClothingADT` with operators that read and display a single article of clothing. `ClothingADT` should use the ADT developed for Programming Project 1 in Chapter 9. Use `ClothingADT` in a client program that reads and displays the data for each clothing item from a text file in which each item's data takes up three lines: description, color, price. Read each item's data into the same program variable.

2. Modify Programming Project 1 to display a summary table that indicates the count of items read in each color. Also, display the total value of all items. You should use an array of integers with subscript type `ColorType` to keep track of the count of items in each color.

3. A number expressed in scientific notation is represented by its mantissa (a decimal fraction) and its exponent. Write a procedure that reads separately the mantissa and exponent of a number and stores them in a record with two `Real` fields. Write a procedure that prints the contents of each record as a real value.

Also write a procedure that computes the sum, the product, the difference, and the quotient of the two numbers. Test your procedures.

4. We all have demands on our time and must determine the best use of that time. Write a program that allows a user to enter up to 40 activities and then computes a maximum number of nonoverlapping activities that can be performed. Each activity has a description (40 character string), a start time (of type `Time`), and an end time (also of type `Time`).

There is an easy way to generate such a list. Sort the list of activities by increasing end time. Then select the first item in this list, which takes up time until its end time. Thereafter, select the next item in the sorted list with a start time after the previously selected item's end time (so that it is not overlapped by that item). Continue this process until the list is exhausted. The selected items are surely in order and do not overlap. This is the maximum number of activities that can be performed.

5. Write a student grading program that uses the data structure `GradeBook` declared in Section 12.4. Provide the following procedures. Assume that parameter `MyClass` is type `GradeBook`.

`ReadExamFile (var InFile, var MyClass)`: Reads in the student exam data from data file `InFile`. Reads each student's name and stores three exam scores per student.

`AddStudent (var MyClass)`: Reads a student record from the keyboard and adds it to the collection of student records.

`GetStudent (MyClass, StudentName, var StuData)`: Returns through `StuData` the record for the student specified by `StudentName`.

`PutStudent (var MyClass, StudentName, StuData)`: Stores new exam data (passed through `StuData`) in the record for the student specified by `StudentName`.

`AssignGrade (var MyClass)`: Computes the average exam score for each student. Assigns letter grades using a predetermined exam scale (e.g., 90–100, A; 80–89, B; and so on).

`EditStudent (var MyClass)`: Prompts the user for the name of a student whose grade may be changed; reads in the new grade and calls `PutStudent` to make the change.

`DisplayGrade (MyClass)`: Displays the information stored in array `MyClass` in a legible format.

Write a menu-driven program which tests these procedures.

6. Use a three-dimensional array to represent a building (floors 1 to 3, wings A and B, and rooms 1 to 5). Each entry in the array will be a record containing a person's name and phone number. Provide operators to create an initially empty building (all names are blank), read data into the building, display the entire building, display a particular floor of the building, retrieve the entry for a particular room, and store a new entry in a particular room. To designate a particular room, the program user must enter the floor number, wing letter, and room number as data. You will also need an abstract data type to represent, read, and display a single entry.

7. Write a program that simulates the movement of radioactive particles in a 20-by-20-foot two-dimensional shield around a reactor. Particles enter the shield at some random position in the shield coordinate space. Once a particle enters the shield, it moves 1 foot/second in one of four directions. The direction for the next second of travel is determined by a random number between 1 and 4 (forward, backward, left, right). A change in direction is interpreted as a collision with another particle, which results in a dissipation of energy. Each particle can have only a limited number of collisions before it dies. A particle exits the shield if its position places it outside the shield coordinate space before K collisions occur. Determine the percentage of particles that exit the shield, where K and the number of particles are input as data items. Also compute the average number of times a particle's path crosses itself during travel time within the shield. *Hint:* Mark each array position occupied by a particle before it dies or exits the shield.

8. Many supermarkets use computerized scanning equipment that allows the checkout clerk to drag an item across a sensor that reads the bar code on the product container. After the computer reads the bar code, the store inventory database is examined, the item's price and product description are located, counts are reduced, and a receipt is printed. Your task is to write a program that simulates this process.

   Your program will need to read the inventory information from the data file on disk into an array of records. The data in the inventory file is written one item per line, beginning with a 2-digit product code, followed by a 30-character product description, its price, and the quantity of that item in stock. Your program will need to copy the revised version of the inventory to a new data file after all purchases have been processed.

   Processing customers' orders involves reading a series of product codes representing each person's purchases from a second data file. A zero product code is used to mark the end of each customer order. As each product code is read, the inventory list is searched to find a matching product code. Once located, the product price and description are printed on the receipt, and the quantity on hand is reduced by 1. At the bottom of the receipt, you are to print the total for the goods purchased by the customer.

INTERVIEW
▼

Adele Goldberg

*Adele Goldberg is the chairman
and founder of ParcPlace Systems.
ParcPlace Systems provides a broad
range of products and services
based on object-oriented technologies, including development tools for
Smalltalk and for C ++, that serve
the applications development needs
of corporate programmers. Previously, Dr. Goldberg was a research
laboratory manager at Xerox PARC,
where she wrote several books on the
Smalltalk-80 system* (Smalltalk-80:
The Language, *with David Robson,
and* Smalltalk-80: The Interactive
Programming Environment) *and
led the effort to design, implement,
and distribute the Smalltalk-80
development system on standard
microprocessors.*

▼ **What influenced you to become a computer scientist?**

▲ I received a bachelor's degree in mathematics from the University of
Michigan, where my degree work had been mostly theoretical. However, I worked as a programmer at the Center for Research on Learning
and Teaching at the university and I also worked in an IBM business
office in Chicago. After seeing what kind of work was available and
seeing opportunities in the application of computing to education, I decided to obtain more advanced training. I attended graduate school in
information sciences at the University of Chicago and arranged to do
my doctoral research at Stanford University at the Institute for Mathematical Studies in the Social Sciences (IMSSS). My particular long-term
interests were, and still are, in the use of computers to augment both
formal and informal learning.

▼ **How did your interests in learning lead you to the Smalltalk development team?**

▲ My interests in the use of computer technology for learning naturally
led me to consider accessibility issues; that is, to be truly beneficial,
tools taught in the classroom should be accessible wherever and whenever the person thinks of using them. When I met Alan Kay, I immediately resonated with his ideas for the Dynabook, a personal computer
that would have the same portability and ease of use as a printed book.
The vision of the Dynabook incorporated the vision of a system structure in which people would find immediately usable applications but
would also be able to easily learn how to specify applications and uses
of their own invention. I joined Xerox Palo Alto Research Center in
1973, shortly after the start of the Smalltalk project. All the people involved in the Smalltalk project were, at one time or another, invited into
the Dynabook project by Alan, who was looking for people to tackle
the software and hardware issues associated with creating a truly per-
sonalizable and accessible system. Creating a language that would be
easy enough to be accessible by almost anyone, yet powerful enough to
allow the user to customize the system, was part of the challenge.

▼ **Smalltalk, the first uniformly object-oriented language, revolutionized
programming for the personal computer in the 1980s. How was the
language developed?**

▲ Smalltalk is based on ideas gleaned from the Simula language and from
early work on visual programming, such as Sutherland's Sketchpad. The
earliest versions of Smalltalk were highly influenced by the tales of success from MIT with the Logo Project. We started out with the notion of
a single language that would be learnable by children as well as adults,
although I found that this spectrum was better understood as a series
of tightly related languages. The Smalltalk system evolved gradually over
the years, with an interesting research cycle: We would design and implement the language along with the user interface and development
tools, reimplement any known applications, invent and implement new
applications, then determine what was hard and what was easy to implement and why. We would then modify the language system design and
repeat the cycle. The vision of the language remained the same, but its
embodiment changed because of new ideas about usage and how to
learn and also because of new technologies.

▼ **What is object-oriented programming, and to what do you attribute its popularity?**

▲ Software engineering technology encompasses all aspects of engineering, from programming languages to analysis and design methods to measures. By object-oriented technology, we mean technology that embodies the use of objects. An object is a software description of a set of behaviors that occur in the real world. Programming using object-oriented languages involves an analysis of the required system behaviors, and then the design of which parts of a system will take responsibility for providing these behaviors. These system parts are called objects. The behaviors are often referred to as the services provided by the objects. Objects are describable as compositions or refinements of other objects. An important aspect of object-oriented programming is designing the relationships among the objects.

My early work with the Smalltalk project focused on determining design factors that contributed to learnability. This included devising pedagogical techniques, setting up special resource centers, and teaching. I typically taught students ages 10–13 years old. I observed that they were able to learn to program when they extended and customized example programs. This is one of the basic concepts behind object programming. An object is the basic system component, or building block, and lends itself to customization or extension, making it unnecessary for a programmer to start from scratch with every application. An object consists of some private memory and a set of operations. It responds to a set of messages that specify which of its operations should be carried out. Messages may request an operation, but do not specify how it should be carried out. This not only minimizes interdependence between system components, but makes it possible for a user to employ an object without knowing the details of its internal implementation. This model of communicating objects applies to the most primitive objects as well as the high-level interaction between the computer and user in the Smalltalk system, and was important to us as we worked toward a powerful but very accessible system.

The modularity of object-oriented systems is a key reason for their popularity today. The value of modularity becomes apparent when designing and implementing large applications. As long as the message interface on which other objects depend is not destroyed, components may be redesigned, tested, and implemented without disrupting the rest of the program's operation. The other reason is the somewhat inaccurate belief that you cannot have a graphical, interactive application unless you use an object-oriented style of implementation.

▼ **What advice would you give a student majoring in computer science today?**

▲ I would like students to understand that studies in computer science cannot be treated in isolation from a vision of how technology can be put to work to improve some aspect of work, education, or recreational life. We study programming languages, we invent new technologies for hardware and software, we study mathematics and psychology, and we study the introduction of technology into large and small organizations. And all these studies are directed at applying our knowledge of the foundations of computing science to improve our ability to employ the computer as a tool.

CHAPTER THIRTEEN

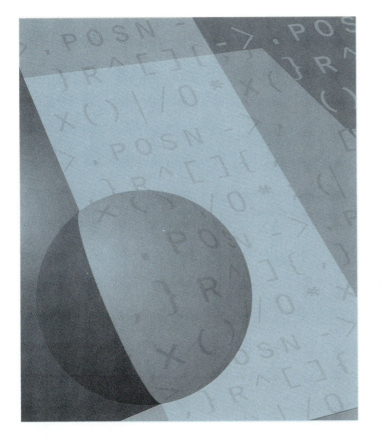

Data Abstraction and Object-Oriented Programming

data abstraction

program design technique that focuses on the data objects needed by a program and the operations on those objects

Procedural abstraction is the philosophy that procedure development should separate the concern of *what* is to be achieved by a procedure from the details of *how* it is to be achieved. Using procedural abstraction, you can specify what you expect a procedure to do, then use that procedure in the design of a problem solution before you know how to implement the procedure. Applying procedural abstraction in combination with top-down design results in modular programs that are easier to read and maintain than nonmodular programs.

In this chapter, we introduce another type of abstraction, data abstraction. The idea of **data abstraction** is to specify *what* data objects are needed for a problem and *what* operations must be performed on these objects without being overly concerned with *how* the data objects will be represented and stored in memory. This approach allows us to use the data objects in our programs before pinning down the details of their actual organization in memory and before implementing them. Applying data abstraction and procedural abstraction results in a set of reusable program units that serve as building blocks for future software development.

In this chapter, we introduce two different approaches to using data abstraction in programming. The first method uses familiar Turbo Pascal units and data types. The second method uses Turbo Pascal objects that facilitate a new style of programming called object-oriented programming.

13.1   Data Abstraction and Abstract Data Types

You have already practiced data abstraction—you have used the data type `Real` to represent real numbers, without knowing much about the internal representation of this data type on a computer. In fact, `Real` representations vary considerably from one computer to another. Some computers use a floating-point processor to perform real arithmetic; others use software to perform real arithmetic. The point is that you have been using real literals, variables, and operations with confidence, without knowing or even caring how they are represented.

Data abstraction enables you to make implementation decisions in stages. At the top levels of the design, you focus on how to use a data object and on what *operators* (procedures and functions) are needed; at the lower levels of design, you work out the implementation details.

To use a data object in a client program, you must declare a variable of that type. A variable with the same type as a data object is called an **instance** of the object.

instance of a data object
a variable with the same type as the data object

Information Hiding

When writing a client program that uses a data object, you are still at the top level and may not know the details of the data object's implementation. Therefore, when the client module accesses the data object, it can do so only through its operators. Concealing the details of a data object's implementation is called **information hiding.**

information hiding
concealing the details of a low-level module's implementation from a higher-level module

To see how information hiding works, let's consider how we might organize and process information to be stored in a personal telephone directory. At the very least, we would want to store each person's name and telephone number in the directory. If we assume that we have operator functions named `GetName` and `GetNumber`, we can write programs that manipulate the information in a particular entry without knowing how the person's name and number are actually stored. If `AnEntry` is an entry in our telephone directory, the function designator `GetName(AnEntry)` returns the name stored in `AnEntry` and the function designator `GetNumber(AnEntry)` returns the number stored in `AnEntry`. To the user of these functions, it makes no difference whether `AnEntry` is a record with two string fields or an array containing two string elements. The implementor, however, must know the internal organization of data type `AnEntry` before coding these functions. Both `GetName` and `GetNumber` are called **accessor** operators because they access a data object and return a value stored in that object.

accessor operator
a function or procedure that retrieves a value stored in a data object

From a software engineering viewpoint, not knowing the details of a data object's implementation is an advantage rather than a limitation. It allows the designer to modify the data object at a later date and possibly choose a more efficient method of internal representation or implementation. Because the client module accesses a data object only through its operators, the client will not have to be rewritten and may not even need to be recompiled after the data object is modified.

Encapsulation

A goal of software engineering is to write *reusable code,* which can be reused in many different applications, preferably without having to be recompiled. One method *encapsulates,* or combines, a data type together with its operators in a separate program module. In Section 9.5, we stated that the combination of a data type together with its operators is called an *abstract data type* (ADT).

Figure 13.1 illustrates an abstract data type. The data values stored in the ADT are hidden inside the oval wall. The purpose of this wall is to indicate that these data values can be accessed only by going through the ADT's operators.

In Turbo Pascal, you can implement each ADT as a separate unit. If you compile the unit to disk, then Turbo Pascal can link the executable code with other programs that use it. If you were careful to include a fairly complete set of operator procedures in the ADT, you will not need to modify or recompile the ADT before reusing it in a new application.

specification
description of the data type and operators of an ADT

Before coding an ADT, you should write its **specification,** which provides a complete description of the data type and its operators and therefore

Figure 13.1
Diagram of an ADT

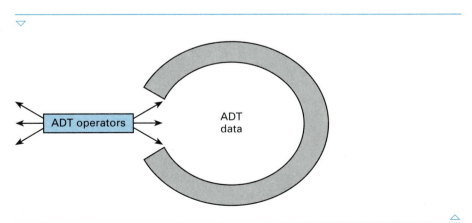

contains all the information needed by a programmer using the ADT. In Turbo Pascal, you would code the unit's interface section from the ADT specification. This section contains the information needed by Turbo Pascal to link the unit to a client program. We illustrate the specification and coding of an ADT next.

ADT for a Telephone Directory Entry

We mentioned earlier that a telephone directory entry should contain a person's name and telephone number. We will assume that both of these data items are character strings and that each entry has a unique name whose value we use to distinguish between entries. A data object component used in this way is called a **key.** Table 13.1 provides a specification for ADT `Entry`.

Before we write the specification (Table 13.1), we list the operators that might be required to process a directory entry.

key
a data object component that has a unique value for each instance of the data object

Operators for a Directory Entry

▶ Create and define an entry.
▶ Read and store data for an entry.
▶ Display an entry.
▶ Test whether two entries have the same key value.
▶ Retrieve the name of an entry.
▶ Retrieve the phone number of an entry.

Table 13.1
Specification for ADT Entry

Structure
A telephone directory entry contains two strings representing the person's name and telephone number.

Operators
The descriptions of the operators use the following parameters:

> `AnEntry, Entry2` are type `Entry`
> `AName` is a name string
> `ANumber` is a phone number string

`Init (var AnEntry, AName, ANumber)`   Stores `AName` and `ANumber` in an entry.

`ReadEntry (var AnEntry, var InFile, FileName)`   Reads a name and phone number from file `InFile` (external name `FileName`) into an entry.

`EqualTo(AnEntry, Entry2)`   (function) Tests whether `AnEntry` and `Entry2` have the same key value.

`GetName(AnEntry)`   (function) Retrieves the name associated with an entry.

`GetNumber(AnEntry)`   (function) Retrieves the number associated with an entry.

`DisplayEntry (AnEntry)`   Displays a name and phone number.

As shown in Table 13.1, operators `Init` and `ReadEntry` store data in a directory entry. Operator `DisplayEntry` displays an entry, and operators `GetName` and `GetNumber` retrieve the data values stored in an entry. Operator `EqualTo` determines whether two entries have the same key value.

Figure 13.2 shows `EntryADT` coded as a Turbo Pascal unit. Data type `Entry` is a record type with two fields: `Name` and `Number`. Procedure `ReadEntry` can read its data from either the keyboard or a data file. The string passed through parameter `FileName` is the external name of the data file. If `FileName` is the null string, `ReadEntry` reads data from the keyboard; otherwise, it reads data from the text file passed through parameter `InFile`.

Figure 13.2
Unit EntryADT

```pascal
unit EntryADT;
{Abstract data type for a telephone directory entry}

interface

  type
    KeyType = string[20];              {type of an entry's key}
    StringType = string[12];

    Entry = record
              Name : KeyType;          {Name is key field.}
              Number : StringType
            end; {Entry}

  procedure Init (var AnEntry {output} : Entry;
                  AName : KeyType;
                  ANumber : StringType);

  procedure ReadEntry (var AnEntry {output} : Entry;
                       var InFile {input} : Text;
                       FileName {input} : string);

  function GetNumber (AnEntry : Entry): StringType;

  function GetName (AnEntry : Entry): KeyType;

  function EqualTo (AnEntry, Entry2 : Entry) : Boolean;

  procedure DisplayEntry (AnEntry {input} : Entry);

implementation

  procedure Init (var AnEntry {output} : Entry;
                  AName : KeyType;
                  ANumber : StringType);
  {
   Creates a directory entry with contents AName and
   ANumber.
   pre : AName and ANumber are defined.
   post: AName and ANumber are stored in a directory entry.
  }
```

▷ ▷ ▷ ▷ ▷ ▷

```
begin {Init}
  AnEntry.Name := AName;
  AnEntry.Number := ANumber
end; {Init}

procedure ReadEntry (var AnEntry {output} : Entry;
                     var InFile {input} : Text;
                     FileName {input} : string);
{
 Reads a name and phone number into an entry.
 pre : InFile is opened and FileName is defined.
 post: Name and number are read into a directory entry.
}
begin {ReadEntry}
  if FileName = '' then
    begin {from keyboard}
      Write ('Name> ');
      ReadLn (AnEntry.Name);
      Write ('Number> ');
      ReadLn (AnEntry.Number)
    end {from keyboard}
  else
    begin {from InFile}
      ReadLn (InFile, AnEntry.Name);
      ReadLn (InFile, AnEntry. Number)
    end {from InFile}
end; {ReadEntry}

function GetNumber (AnEntry : Entry) : StringType;
{
 Returns the phone number stored in a directory entry.
 pre : AnEntry is defined.
 post: Returns phone number.
}
begin {GetNumber}
  GetNumber := AnEntry.Number
end; {GetNumber}

function GetName (AnEntry : Entry) : KeyType;
{
 Returns the name stored in a directory entry.
 pre : AnEntry is defined.
 post: Returns name.
}
begin {GetName}
  GetName := AnEntry.Name
end; {GetName}

function EqualTo (AnEntry, Entry2 : Entry) : Boolean;
{
 Determines whether AnEntry and Entry2 have the same key.
 pre : AnEntry and Entry2 are defined.
 post: Return True if keys are equal;
       otherwise, returns False.
}
```

▷ ▷ ▷ ▷ ▷

```
begin {EqualTo}
  EqualTo := (AnEntry.Name = Entry2.Name)
end; {EqualTo}

procedure DisplayEntry (AnEntry {input} : Entry);
{
 Displays the contents of a directory entry.
 pre : AnEntry is defined.
 post: Name and number are displayed.
}
begin {DisplayEntry}
  WriteLn (AnEntry.Name);
  WriteLn (AnEntry.Number)
end; {DisplayEntry}

end. {EntryADT}
```

Figure 13.3 diagrams EntryADT. As with any ADT, a client module should access the data fields only through the operators listed on the left.

Using EntryADT

Figure 13.4 shows a small driver program that tests EntryADT. First, the program creates an empty directory entry and then it reads and stores data into that entry. Next, it reads a name and displays the telephone number if that name was stored; otherwise, it displays a Not listed message. Finally, it displays the directory entry.

Program Style

Use of Init

We call procedure Init to create an empty directory entry before calling ReadEntry to read data into that entry. Although we needn't call Init first, we usually follow the convention of creating an instance of a data object before referencing that instance.

Figure 13.3
Sketch of EntryADT

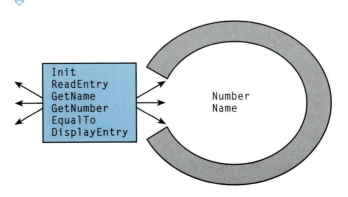

Figure 13.4
Driver Program for
EntryADT

Edit Window

```
program ClientEntry;
{Driver program to test EntryADT}

uses EntryADT;      {imports KeyType, Entry, and its operators.}

  var
    AnEntry, Entry2 : Entry;         {directory entries}
    AName : KeyType;                 {name being searched for}

begin {ClientEntry}
  Init (AnEntry, '', '');            {Create an empty entry.}
  WriteLn ('Enter a directory entry:');
  ReadEntry (AnEntry, Input, '');    {Read an entry.}

  {Check for match and display result.}
  WriteLn;  Write ('Enter a name to match> ');
  ReadLn (AName);
  Init (Entry2, AName, '');          {AName is key for Entry2.}
  if EqualTo(AnEntry, Entry2) then
    WriteLn ('Number is ', GetNumber(AnEntry))
  else
    WriteLn ('Not listed');

  WriteLn;  WriteLn ('The directory entry follows:');
  DisplayEntry (AnEntry)
end. {ClientEntry}
```

Output Window

```
Enter a directory entry:
Name> Judith Wilson
Number> 215-555-9876

Enter a name to match> Judith Wilson
Number is 215-555-9876

The directory entry follows:
Judith Wilson
215-555-9876
```

Problems with Record Types in ADT Units

To declare a record type for an ADT implemented as a unit, we must declare it in the interface section of the unit. Because the data type is declared in the interface section, its components are visible outside the unit and can be accessed directly by a client module without using an operator. Although direct access is undesirable, Turbo Pascal permits it. This means that we can write the if statement in Fig. 13.4 as

```
if AnEntry.Name = Entry2.Name then
  WriteLn ('Number is ', AnEntry.Number)
else
  WriteLn ('Not listed');
```

This `if` statement is less desirable, however, because it is dependent on the internal organization of data type `Entry` and would have to be rewritten if data type `Entry` were modified.

Another disadvantage of declaring record types inside an ADT is that we cannot easily modify the structure of a such an ADT, say by adding new fields. If we attempt to do so, we will probably have to add several new accessor functions and recode operator procedures that process all fields of the data object. Examples of the latter would be operators that initialize a data object, read information into a data object, or display information stored in a data object.

In the next section, we will discuss the Turbo Pascal object feature that provides solutions to both of these problems.

Exercises for Section 13.1 **Self-Check**

1. List the Pascal operators and standard functions that should be considered part of the complete specifications for the following built-in data types:
   a. `Real`　　b. `Char`　　c. `Boolean`
2. What is information hiding? Why is it important to a software designer?
3. What does the following program segment do? What does it display for the two records shown? What data types are required for `MyEmp`, `YourEmp`, `Name1`, and `Name2`?

```
Init (MyEmp, 'Jennie Moss', '215-555-1233');
Init (YourEmp, 'Jackie Moss', '215-555-1234');
if EqualTo(MyEmp, YourEmp) then
  WriteLn ('Duplicate entry for ', GetName(MyEmp) :1)
else
  begin
    Name1 := GetName(MyEmp);
    Name2 := GetName(YourEmp);
    WriteLn (Name1, '***** ', Name2)
  end; {if}
```

4. Suppose you were asked to provide an ADT that would allow up to 10 type `Entry` items to be placed in a phone book. What would be the structure for the phone book? Describe, but don't write, operators for adding a new phone book entry and finding an entry by name in the phone book.

Programming

1. Code the operators in Self-Check Exercise 4.

13.2 Objects and Object-Oriented Programming

Object-oriented programming (OOP) has become widely used in the past few years. Its popularity is due to its facility in writing reusable program modules and to the availability of objects in languages like Turbo Pascal and C++.

object
the encapsulation of data fields together with operators in a single entity

Turbo Pascal allows the programmer to encapsulate data fields along with operators in a single entity known as an **object.** Object types can be defined so that their data fields can be manipulated only by their operators. For this reason, objects are a natural means of implementing abstract data types. Objects may be defined in a hierarchical manner, with *descendant types inheriting* attributes from their *ancestor types*. This feature enables the programmer to create new objects from existing objects rather than starting from scratch.

OOP Versus Traditional Programming

In traditional procedure-oriented programming, we focus on the procedures needed to solve a problem. In OOP, we focus on data objects and the services they need. The object-oriented view is that the data objects are fixed and the client program sends a message to a given data object. The data object receives the message and generates a result by carrying out the indicated action:

message → (*object*) → *result*

For example, if `AnEntry` is an instance of a data object and `GetName` is one of the object's operators, the statement

```
AnEntry.GetName
      ↑         ↑
  Recipient  Message
```

message
a request to an object instance to invoke a particular operation
recipient
the object instance that receives and responds to a message

sends a **message** to `AnEntry`, the message **recipient.** The object's response is to invoke the `GetName` operator, returning the name stored in `AnEntry` as a result. The recipient name, `AnEntry`, qualifies the operator name, `GetName`, so there is no need to pass `AnEntry` as a parameter to `GetName`. The general form of a message is

recipient. *operator*

Declaring Objects

methods (method members)
an object's operators
data members
an object's data fields

Figure 13.5 shows the declaration for object type `Entry` (a telephone directory entry). Object type `Entry` begins with a list of headers for the object's operators, which in OOP are called **methods** or **method members.** The object's **data members** (`Name` and `Number`) are listed after the reserved word `private`.

The reserved word `private` separates the object's public part from its private part. The identifiers in the public part, the object's method members, are visible outside the unit declaring the object type and may be referenced by its clients. The identifiers in the private part, the data members, can be referenced only within the module declaring the object type. This means they are not visible outside the unit containing the declaration for object `Entry`. A client program can therefore access the `Name` and `Number` fields of an instance of object `Entry` only through its methods, which is a requirement of true information hiding. Notice that you must place a semicolon after the last method member and after the last data member.

The method headers in Fig. 13.5 do not correspond exactly with the operator headers in Fig. 13.2, because formal parameter `AnEntry` is deleted. For example, we use the method header

```
procedure ReadEntry (var InFile : Text;
                         FileName : string);
```

instead of

```
procedure ReadEntry (var AnEntry {output} : Entry;
                         var InFile : Text;
                         FileName : string);
```

Method `ReadEntry` does not need a parameter, because, whenever we send a message to an object, we write the message recipient before the method name. If `MyEntry` is declared as type `Entry` in a client program, we use

Figure 13.5
Declarations for Object
Type Entry

```
type
   KeyType = string[20];
   StringType = string[12];

Entry = object
        procedure Init (AName : KeyType;
                          ANumber : StringType);
        procedure ReadEntry (var InFile : Text;
                               FileName : string);
        function GetName : KeyType;
        function GetNumber : StringType;
        function EqualTo (Entry2 : Entry) : Boolean;
        procedure DisplayEntry;

     private
        Name : KeyType;
        Number : StringType;
     end; {Entry}
```

```
MyEntry.ReadEntry (Input, '')
```

to send the ReadEntry message to object instance MyEntry.

Object Type Declaration

Form: type *object type* = object
                     data member list;
                     method header list;

                  private
                     data member list;
                     method header list;
                  end;

Example: type Point = object
                     procedure Init (X1, Y1 : Real);
                     function DistanceOrigin : Real;
                     function GetX : Real;
                     function GetY : Real;

                  private
                    X, Y : Real;
                  end; {Point}

Interpretation: The identifier *object type* is an object with data members (described in the *data member list*) and method members (described in the *method header list*). The *data member list* is similar to the *field list* appearing in a record type declaration. The *method header list* consists of a list of procedure and function headers only.

    The reserved word private indicates that the method members and data members that follow are for internal use only and cannot be referenced outside the unit in which the object type is declared.

Note: When declared in a unit, the object type declaration appears in the interface section of the unit and the complete method declarations appear in the implementation section of the unit.

Declaring Objects in Units

Figure 13.6 shows Turbo Pascal unit EntryObjADT, which declares object type Entry. The unit's interface section contains the object type declaration from Fig. 13.5. Its implementation section contains complete declarations for the object's method members based on the operators shown in Fig. 13.2. In the header for each method, the object's name qualifies the method name (e.g., Entry.ReadEntry). Inside each method, the data member names (Name and Number) are not qualified. When a method is invoked, they will be qualified by the message recipient.

Figure 13.6
Unit EntryObjADT

```
unit EntryObjADT;
{
 Abstract data type for a telephone directory entry declared
 as an object.
}
interface

    {Insert declaration for object type Entry. See Fig. 13.5.}

implementation

    procedure Entry.Init (AName: KeyType;
                          ANumber : StringType);
    {
     Stores AName and ANumber in a new entry.
     pre : AName and ANumber are defined.
     post: AName and ANumber are stored in an entry.
    }
    begin {Init}
      Name := AName;
      Number := ANumber
    end; {Init}

    procedure Entry.ReadEntry (var InFile : Text;
                               FileName : string);
    {
     Reads a name and phone number into an entry.
     pre : InFile is opened and FileName is defined.
     post: Name and number are read into an entry.
    }
    begin {ReadEntry}
      if FileName = '' then
        begin {from keyboard}
          Write ('Name> ');
          ReadLn (Name);
          Write ('Number> ');
          ReadLn (Number)
        end {from keyboard}
      else
        begin {from InFile}
          ReadLn (InFile, AName);
          ReadLn (InFile, ANumber)
        end {from InFile}
    end; {ReadEntry}

    function Entry.GetNumber : StringType;
    {
     Returns the phone number stored in an entry.
     pre : The entry is defined.
     post: Returns its phone number.
    }
    begin {GetNumber}
      GetNumber := Number
    end; {GetNumber}
```

▷ ▷ ▷ ▷ ▷ ▷

```
function Entry.GetName : KeyType;
{
 Returns the name stored in an entry.
 pre : The entry is defined.
 post: Returns name.
}
begin {GetName}
  GetName := Name
end; {GetName}

function Entry.EqualTo (Entry2 : Entry) : Boolean;
{
 Determines whether the message recipient and its
 parameter have the same key.
 pre : The recipient and Entry2 are defined.
 post: Returns True if the recipient and Entry2 have the
       same key; otherwise, returns False.
}
begin {EqualTo}
  EqualTo := (Self.Name = Entry2.Name)
end; {EqualTo}

procedure Entry.DisplayEntry;
{
 Displays the contents of an entry.
 pre : The entry is defined.
 post: Name and number are displayed.
}
begin {DisplayEntry}
  WriteLn (Name);
  WriteLn (Number)
end; {DisplayEntry}

end. {EntryObjADT}
```

Program Style

Use of Self

The statement

```
EqualTo := (Self.Name = Entry2.Name)
```

uses the standard identifier `Self` to denote the recipient of the `EqualTo` message. Although we don't need to qualify field names of a message recipient, using `Self` clarifies which `Name` field is being compared to `Entry2.Name`. It would be just as correct, but less readable, to write this statement as

```
EqualTo := (Name = Entry2.Name)
```

Using EntryObjADT

Figure 13.7 shows a driver program that tests `EntryObjADT`. Notice that we qualify each method name with object instance `AnEntry` (data type `Entry`). The sample output (not shown) would be identical to that shown in Fig. 13.4.

Exercises for Section 13.2   ***Self-Check***

1. How does the implementation of a method member for an object type differ from the implementation of an operator with the same name and purpose for a record type that is an ADT?
2. What would happen if you replace the `if` statement in Fig. 13.7 with the following fragment? What does your result illustrate?

```
if AnEntry.Name = Entry2.Name then
  WriteLn ('Number is ', AnEntry.Number)
else
  WriteLn ('Not listed');
```

Figure 13.7
Driver Program for
EntryObjADT

```
program ClientEntryObj;
{Driver program to test EntryObjADT}

uses EntryObjADT; {imports KeyType, object Entry & its methods}

  var
    AnEntry, Entry2 : Entry;        {directory entries}
    AName : KeyType;                {name being searched for}

begin {ClientEntryObj}
  AnEntry.Init ('', '');           {Create an empty entry.}
  WriteLn ('Enter a directory entry:');
  AnEntry.ReadEntry (Input, '');            {Read an entry.}

  {Check for match and display result.}
  WriteLn;  Write ('Enter a name to match> ');
  ReadLn (AName);
  Entry2.Init (AName, '');          {AName is key for Entry2.}
  if AnEntry.EqualTo(Entry2) then
    WriteLn ('Number is ', AnEntry.GetNumber)
  else
    WriteLn ('Not listed');

  WriteLn;  WriteLn ('The directory entry follows:');
  AnEntry.DisplayEntry
end. {ClientEntryObj}
```

3. Why would we want data members to be private? When would we want a method header to be private?

Programming

1. Write a new method member LessThan for object type Entry that returns true if its recipient's key is smaller than its parameter's key.
2. Rewrite the code fragment for Self-Check Exercise 3 of Section 13.1, assuming Entry is an object type.
3. Declare an object type Student with data members Name, Age, Gender, and Grade and method members Init, ReadStu, and DisplayStu as well as accessor methods for each data member.

13.3   Object-Oriented Design

In this section, we solve a programming problem using OOP. We focus on the telephone directory and its operators with the goal of designing a reusable object to house the telephone directory.

A complete discussion of *object-oriented design* is beyond the scope of this text, but a summation of the steps involved in the object-oriented design methodology follows:

1. Identify the objects and define the services to be provided by each object.
2. Identify the interactions among objects in terms of services required and services provided.
3. Determine the specification for each object.
4. Implement each object.

Unlike traditional software design, there is no sharp division between the analysis phase and the design phase. In fact, in object-oriented design, programmers often follow the prototyping design practice of designing a little, implementing a little, and testing a little, rather than attempting to build a complete piece of software all at once.

CASE STUDY   Design of a Telephone Directory

PROBLEM ▼

Design a program to store and retrieve a growing collection of names and telephone numbers in a telephone directory. Create the directory by reading from a data file the names and numbers of people called frequently. The directory program should also be able to insert new names and numbers, change numbers, retrieve selected telephone numbers, and delete names and numbers.

ANALYSIS AND DESIGN ▼

In OOP, we focus on the data objects and the services (operators) they need. This problem presents two distinct data objects to consider: the directory as a whole and each individual entry. We have already identified the operators required for each individual entry, so we list the operators needed for the directory next.

Operators for a Directory Object

► Create an empty directory.
► Read a directory from a text file.
► Insert a new entry in the directory.
► Replace an entry in the directory.
► Delete an entry from the directory.
► Search for a particular entry in the directory.
► Retrieve a particular entry from the directory.
► Retrieve the count of entries in the directory.
► Sort the directory.
► Display the directory.

These operators are quite general and may be required by many other objects used to store collections of individual entries. We will therefore design a generic object of type `List` to house our directory. Table 13.2 provides the specification of a list ADT.

Operators `Replace`, `Delete`, `Search`, and `GetEntry` succeed only if there is an entry in the list with the same key as the operator's first parameter. They indicate success by returning `True` through their last parameter. Operator `Insert` succeeds if the list is not full.

IMPLEMENTATION ▼

Coding a Client Program

Figure 13.8 contains a client program that creates and reads in a directory (`MyDirectory`), inserts a new entry, replaces the phone number of an entry, retrieves the phone number in an entry, and finally displays the directory. Notice that both units `ListADT` and `EntryObjADT` must be listed in the `uses` statement.

Structure
A list is a collection of elements, each with a key field that uniquely identifies it.

Operators
The descriptions of the operators use the following parameters:

    AnEntry (type Entry)
    Success (type Boolean)
    PosEntry (type Integer)

Several operators use the Boolean parameter Success to indicate whether the operation succeeds (returns True) or fails (returns False).

List.Init   Creates a list that is initially empty.

List.ReadList   Reads the entries from a text file and stores them in the list.

List.Insert (AnEntry, var Success)   Inserts a new entry at the end of the list if the list is not full.

List.Replace (AnEntry, var Success)   Substitutes AnEntry for the list entry with the same key as AnEntry.

List.Delete (AnEntry, var Success)   Deletes the entry with the same key as AnEntry.

List.Search (AnEntry, var PosEntry, var Success)   Returns through PosEntry the relative position of AnEntry in the list if AnEntry is found.

List.GetEntry (var AnEntry, var Success)   Retrieves the entry with the same key as AnEntry.

List.GetCount   (function) Returns the count of entries in the list.

List.Sort   Sorts the list entries in increasing order by key.

List.DisplayList   Displays all list entries.

The program first calls Init to create an empty directory and ReadList to read data into it. Next, it calls ReadEntry (from EntryObjADT) to read an additional entry and method Insert to insert it at the end of the directory:

MyDirectory Before		MyDirectory After	
Bill	555-123-4567	Bill	555-123-4567
Sam	555-123-5678	Sam	555-123-5678
Carol	555-123-6789	Carol	555-123-6789
		Robin	**555-222-3333**

Figure 13.8
Client Program for ListADT

Edit Window

```
{$R+}
program ClientList;
{Tests ListADT and EntryObjADT}

  uses EntryObjADT, ListADT; {import type Entry, List}

  var
     MyDirectory : List;        {my phone directory}
     AName : StringType;        {one name}
     AnEntry : Entry;           {one entry}
     Success : Boolean;         {program flag}

begin {ClientList}
   {Read in a directory.}
   MyDirectory.Init;            {Create empty directory.}
   MyDirectory.ReadList;        {Read and store its data.}
   WriteLn (MyDirectory.GetCount :1, ' items in directory');
   WriteLn;

   {Insert a new element at end.}
   WriteLn ('Type in new entry:');
   AnEntry.ReadEntry (Input, '');           {Read a new entry.}
   MyDirectory.Insert (AnEntry, Success);   {Insert it.}
   WriteLn (MyDirectory.GetCount :1, ' items in directory');
   WriteLn;

   {Change Sam's phone number.}
   AnEntry.Init ('Sam', '555-111-2222');    {Sam's new entry}
   WriteLn ('Changing number for ', AnEntry.GetName);
   MyDirectory.Replace (AnEntry, Success);    {Replace entry.}
   if not Success then
     WriteLn ('Replacement not performed.');
   WriteLn;

   {Retrieve a person's number.}
   Write ('Find number for> ');
   ReadLn (AName);
   AnEntry.Init (AName, '');
   MyDirectory.GetEntry (AnEntry, Success);        {Get number.}
   if Success then
     AnEntry.DisplayEntry                       {Display entry.}
   else
     WriteLn ('Name not found in directory.');

   {Display the list.}
   WriteLn;
   MyDirectory.DisplayList
end.  {ClientList}
```

▷ ▷ ▷ ▷ ▷ ▷

Output Window

```
Enter the data file name> PHONE.TXT
3 items in directory

Type in new entry
Name> Robin
Number> 555-222-3333
4 items in directory

Changing number for Sam

Find number for> Bill
Bill
555-123-4567

List of entries:
Bill
555-123-4567
Sam
555-111-2222
Carol
555-123-6789
Robin
555-222-3333
```

To change the phone number associated with a particular entry (for example, to change Sam's number to 555-111-2222), method Init (from EntryObjADT) creates an entry with Sam's new phone number. If Sam is in the directory, method Replace (from ListADT) replaces Sam's entry with the new entry:

MyDirectory Before	**MyDirectory After**
Bill 555-123-4567	Bill 555-123-4567
Sam 555-123-5678	Sam 555-111-2222
Carol 555-123-6789	Carol 555-123-6789
Robin 555-222-3333	Robin 555-222-3333

Next, the program reads in a name, Bill, whose number is requested and method Init (from EntryObjADT) creates an entry with name Bill and with number unspecified (number is the null string). Method GetEntry retrieves Bill's actual data, and method DisplayEntry displays it. Finally, method DisplayList displays the entire directory.

Each method name in Fig. 13.8 is qualified by an object instance (AnEntry or MyDirectory). Notice there are two Init operators, one for object type Entry and one for object type List. The type of the recipient of each Init message tells Turbo Pascal which Init operator to invoke.

Coding Unit ListADT

The final step is to implement the List ADT (unit ListADT). The interface section (Fig. 13.9) follows from the specification given in Table 13.2.

The first line of the interface section,

```
uses EntryObjADT;        {imports type Entry}
```

indicates that unit ListADT is a client of unit EntryObjADT. Next we declare the constant MaxEntry (value is 100) and object type List. The object declaration shows ten method members and two data members. The first data member (array Entries) stores the individual list entries, and the second data member (Count) specifies the number of entries currently in the list.

Figure 13.9
Interface Section for
ListADT

```
unit ListADT;

interface
  uses EntryObjADT;                    {imports type Entry}

const
  MaxEntry = 100;                      {maximum entries}

type
  EntryRange = 1..MaxEntry;           {subscripts of entries}
  EntryArray = array [EntryRange] of Entry;

  List = object
          procedure Init;
          procedure ReadList;
          procedure Insert (AnEntry : Entry;
                              var Success : Boolean);
          procedure Replace (AnEntry : Entry;
                              var Success : Boolean);
          procedure Delete (AnEntry : Entry;
                              var Success : Boolean);
          procedure Search (AnEntry : Entry;
                              var PosEntry : Integer;
                              var Success : Boolean);
          procedure GetEntry (var AnEntry : Entry;
                               var Success : Boolean);
          function GetCount : Integer;
          procedure Sort;
          procedure DisplayList;

        private
          Entries : EntryArray;      {array of entries}
          Count : Integer;           {number of entries}
        end; {List}
```

Next we show the full declarations for the method members, beginning with Init and ReadList (Fig. 13.10). Init simply sets the count of entries to 0. The while loop in ReadList calls ReadEntry (from EntryObjADT) to read each entry into AnEntry, and the statement

```
Entries[Next] := AnEntry                {Store next entry.}
```

Figure 13.10
Methods Init and ReadList

```
implementation

  procedure List.Init;
  {
   Creates an initially empty list.
   pre : none
   post: List with 0 elements is defined.
  }
  begin {Init}
    Count := 0
  end; {Init}

  procedure List.ReadList;
  {
   Reads a data file into a list.
   pre : Data file is saved on disk.
   post: Entries in data file are stored in the list.
  }
    var
      Next : Integer;         {next subscript for a new entry}
      AnEntry : Entry;        {a new entry}
      InFile : Text;          {internal file variable}
      FileName : string;      {directory name of input file}

  begin {ReadList}
    Write ('Enter the data file name> ');
    ReadLn (FileName);
    Assign (InFile, FileName);
    Reset (InFile);              {Open the data file.}

    Next := 0;
    while not EOF(InFile) and (Next < MaxEntry) do
      begin
        AnEntry.ReadEntry (InFile, FileName);    {Read entry.}
        Next := Next + 1;
        Entries[Next] := AnEntry              {Store next entry.}
      end; {while}

    Count := Next;                       {Count is number of entries.}
    if not EOF(InFile) then
      WriteLn ('Warning - not all file data was read.');
    Close (InFile)
  end; {ReadList}
```

inserts the entry just read into the next element of array field `Entries`. After loop exit, the statement

```
Count := Next;                    {Count is number of entries.}
```

sets `Count` to the number of entries read from the data file. The `if` statement displays a warning message if the data file contains more than `MaxEntry` entries.

In method `Insert` (Fig. 13.11), the statements

```
Count := Count + 1;        {one more entry}
Entries[Count] := AnEntry;  {Entry is new last entry.}
```

increase the `Count` field by 1 and store the new entry (`AnEntry`) in array element `Entries[Count]`. Methods `Replace` and `Delete` call method `Search` to locate the element in array field `Entries` with the same key as parameter `AnEntry`. If the search is successful, the intended operation is performed.

Figure 13.11
Methods Insert, Search, Replace, and Delete

```
procedure List.Insert (AnEntry {input} : Entry;
                       var Success {output} : Boolean);
{
 Inserts entry AnEntry into a list.
 pre : AnEntry is defined.
 post: If the list was not full, AnEntry is last entry in
       list and Success is True; otherwise, Success is False.
}
begin {Insert}
  if Count < MaxEntry then
    begin {add entry}
      Count := Count + 1;         {one more entry}
      Entries[Count] := AnEntry; {AnEntry is new last entry.}
      Success := True
    end {add entry}
  else
    Success := False
end; {Insert}


procedure List.Search (AnEntry {input} : Entry;
                       var PosEntry {output} : Integer;
                       var Success {output} : Boolean);
{
 Searches for AnEntry in the list.
 pre : AnEntry is defined.
 post: If AnEntry is found, Success is True and PosEntry is
       its position; otherwise, Success is False.
}
  var
    Next : Integer;     {next element in list}
```

▷ ▷ ▷ ▷ ▷

```
begin {Search}
  {Compare each element of List to AnEntry until done.}
  Next := 1;                        {Start with the first entry.}
  Success := False;                 {AnEntry is not found.}
  while not Success and (Next <= Count) do
    {invariant:
        AnEntry was not found in subarray Entries[1..Next - 1]
        and Next is <= Count + 1.
    }
    if AnEntry.EqualTo(Entries[Next]) then
      Success := True               {AnEntry is found.}
    else
      Next := Next + 1;             {Advance to next entry.}

  {assert:
    AnEntry was found or all entries tested without success.
  }
  if Success then
    PosEntry := Next          {AnEntry matched Entries[Next].}
end; {Search}


procedure List.Replace (AnEntry {input} : Entry;
                        var Success {output} : Boolean);
{
 Replaces entry with same key as AnEntry with AnEntry.
 pre: AnEntry is defined.
 post: Entry with same key as AnEntry has same number too
       and Success is True; otherwise, Success is False.
}
  var
    PosEntry : Integer;  {position of AnEntry in list.}

begin {Replace}
  Search (AnEntry, PosEntry, Success);  {Find AnEntry.}
  if Success then
    Entries[PosEntry] := AnEntry              {Replace it.}
end; {Replace}


procedure List.Delete (AnEntry {input} : Entry;
                       var Success {output} : Boolean);
{
 Deletes the entry with the same key as AnEntry.
 pre : AnEntry is defined.
 post: If AnEntry is found, the last entry takes the place of
       AnEntry and Success is True;
       otherwise, Success is False.
}
  var
    PosEntry : Integer;       {position of AnEntry in list.}
```

▷ ▷ ▷ ▷ ▷

```
begin {Delete}
  Search (AnEntry, PosEntry, Success);  {Find AnEntry.}
  if Success then
    begin
      Entries[PosEntry] := Entries[Count]; {Copy last entry.}
      Count := Count - 1                   {Decrement Count.}
    end {if}
end; {Delete}
```

△

Method `Search` (Fig. 13.11) is based on function `Search` in Fig. 10.18. Unlike function `Search`, it returns the position of its target element through its parameter list (`PosEntry`) and the search result through a Boolean parameter (`Success`). The `if` condition

```
AnEntry.EqualTo(Entries[Next])
```

uses method `EqualTo` (from `EntryObjADT`) to compare the name stored in each array element to the name stored in `AnEntry`.

In `Delete`, the statement

```
Search (AnEntry, PosEntry, Success);  {Find AnEntry.}
```

calls `Search` to locate `AnEntry` in the object instance receiving the `Delete` message. If the search is successful, the statements

```
Entries[PosEntry] := Entries[Count];  {Copy last entry.}
Count := Count - 1                    {Decrement Count.}
```

copy the last entry in the list to the position of the one being deleted and then decrement `Count`. The net effect is to replace the original entry at `PosEntry` with the original last entry, and then remove the last entry. It doesn't matter that the order of the entries has changed.

Figure 13.12 shows the accessor methods `GetEntry` and `GetCount`. Method `GetEntry` first calls `Search` to locate the entry with the desired name. Method `GetCount` returns the value stored in field `Count`. In Method `DisplayList`, the statement

```
Entries[Next].DisplayEntry;    {Display next entry.}
```

sends the `DisplayEntry` message to the next element in the list.

Review and Summary of OOP

Unit `ListADT` is complete with the exception of method `Sort` (see Programming Exercise 1 at the end of this section). To use this unit in a client program, you must perform the following sequence of operations.

▶ Compile unit `EntryObjADT` (file `ENTRYOBJ.PAS`) to disk (file `ENTRY-OBJ.TPU`).

Figure 13.12

Methods GetEntry,
GetCount, and DisplayList

```
procedure List.GetEntry (var AnEntry {output} : Entry;
                         var Success {output} : Boolean);
{
 Retrieves the entry with the same key as AnEntry.
 pre : AnEntry is defined.
 post: AnEntry contains data in element of Entries with
       the same key and Success is True; otherwise,
       Success is False.
}
  var
    PosEntry : Integer;      {position of AnEntry in list}

begin {GetEntry}
  Search (AnEntry, PosEntry, Success);   {Find AnEntry.}
  if Success then
    AnEntry := Entries[PosEntry]     {Return the data.}
end; {GetEntry}


function List.GetCount : Integer;
{
 Returns the count of entries in the list.
 pre : none
 post: Returns the count of entries.
}
begin {GetCount}
  GetCount := Count
end; {GetCount}


procedure List.DisplayList;
{
 Displays the list.
 pre : none
 post: Each entry in the list is displayed.
}
  var
    AnEntry : Entry;        {next entry}
    Next : Integer;         {next subscript}

begin {DisplayList}
  WriteLn ('List of entries:');
  for Next := 1 to Count do
    begin
      Entries[Next].DisplayEntry;     {Display next entry.}
      WriteLn
    end {for}
end; {DisplayList}

end. {ListADT}
```

▶ Compile unit `ListADT` (file `LISTADT.PAS`) to disk (file `LISTADT.TPU`).
▶ Compile and run the client program.

We stated there are several advantages to OOP. We demonstrated two of them in this section: First, through OOP we can encapsulate a data object together with its methods in a unit; second, OOP enforces information hiding because a client program can access an object's data members only through its methods.

A third advantage is that objects are reusable. For example, you can use an object of type `List` to house any list of elements, not just a telephone directory. To accomplish this, first write and compile to disk a unit containing a new object type that provides the same methods as object type `Entry`. Next, change the `uses` statement in unit `ListADT` to import this unit instead of `EntryObjADT`.

Exercises for Section 13.3   **Self-Check**

1. Assume the following statements appear in Fig. 13.8. Correct each invalid statement, and explain what the valid and corrected statements do.
    a. `MyDirectory.ReadEntry`
    b. `MyDirectory.GetEntry (AnEntry, Success)`
    c. `AnEntry.Insert (MyDirectory, Success)`
    d. `MyDirectory.Init ('Silly Sam', '215-555-4578')`
    e. `AnEntry.Init ('Silly Sam', '');`
        `MyDirectory.Delete (AnEntry, Success)`
2. Assume the following statements appear in the method declarations for object `List` (Figs. 13.10–13.12). Correct each invalid statement. Explain what the valid and corrected statements do.
    a. `Directory.Entries[Count] := AnEntry`
    b. `Entries[Count].ReadEntry`
    c. `AnEntry.Init (Entries[Count])`
    d. `AnEntry := GetEntry ('Carol', '')`
    e. `Success := EqualTo(Entries[Count], AnEntry)`
3. Would it be valid to write the `for` statement header in `DisplayList` as

    `for Next := 1 to Self.GetCount do`

    What is the effect of deleting `Self` from this line? What is the advantage of the approach used in Fig. 13.12?
4. Write statements to delete the entry for Carol.

Programming

1. Write method member `Sort` for object type `List`, which performs a selection sort (Fig. 10.20). Method `Sort` should use method `LessThan` (Programming Exercise 1 in Section 13.2).

13.4   Inheritance

inheritance
using a previously declared
object to define new objects
ancestor
the original object that is the
basis for new or modified
objects
descendant (specialization)
a new object formed by modifying an existing object

Besides easy reuse of objects using OOP, programmers can extend or modify a previously declared object. **Inheritance** enables programmers to create new objects from existing ones. Each new object inherits the methods
and data members of its **ancestor** object and can also define its own methods and data members. Each new object created in this way is a **descendant** or **specialization** of the existing object. An ancestor object may have
several descendants, but each descendant object can have only a single ancestor.

We can use OOP and inheritance to define a collection of figure objects.
All the figures—rectangle, square, circle, and so on—have several properties
in common, such as a name, an area, a perimeter, and a location on the
screen. But each of these objects also has its own special properties; for example, a circle has a radius, whereas a rectangle has a length and a width.

Figure 13.13 is a sketch of a general figure object and its descendants.
Rather than represent a square as a direct descendant of Figure, we have
shown Square as a descendant of Rectangle (i.e., a square is a rectangle
whose length and width are the same).

Figure 13.14 is a more detailed description of this object hierarchy. It
shows each object along with its method and data members. As shown, the
general type Figure object has five data members: Name, PosX, PosY, Area,
and Perimeter. All descendant objects inherit these data members and may
add data members of their own (e.g., Length and Width for Rectangle).
The object Square does not have any data members of its own, since a
square is a rectangle whose length and width are equal. Each object, including the general Figure object, has its own Init and Display method members. Each object, except for the general Figure object and the Square

Figure 13.13
Ancestor Tree for
Geometric Figures

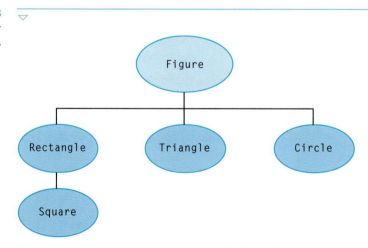

Figure 13.14
Object Hierarchy with Method and Data Members

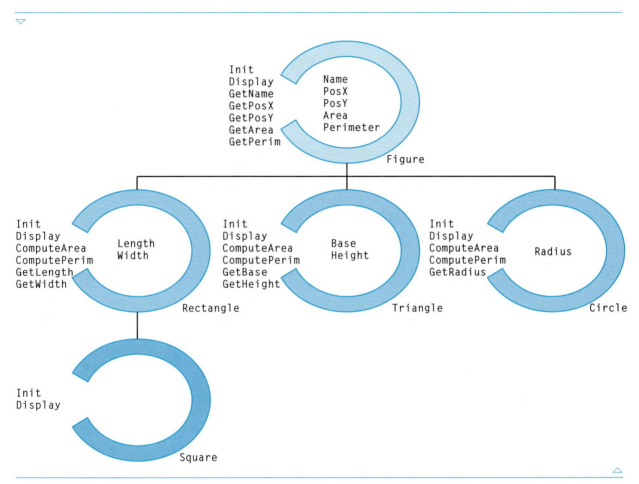

object, has its own method for computing area and perimeter. The Square object inherits these methods from Rectangle.

Figure 13.15 shows a more complete specification of object Rectangle. The data and method members that are inherited are shown in italics.

Figure 13.16 shows the interface section for unit FigFamilyADT. For brevity, we have shown just three object types: Figure, Rectangle, and Square. Notice that the header of the declaration for each descendant object shows its ancestor in parentheses (e.g., Rectangle = object(Figure)).

Two new reserved words appear in Fig. 13.16: constructor and virtual. The reserved word virtual, which follows method Display, first ap-

Figure 13.15
Object Rectangle with
Inherited Members in
Italics

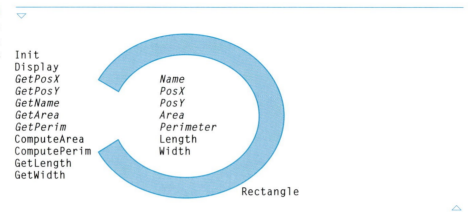

```
Init
Display
GetPosX          Name
GetPosY          PosX
GetName          PosY
GetArea          Area
GetPerim         Perimeter
ComputeArea      Length
ComputePerim     Width
GetLength
GetWidth
                                    Rectangle
```

pears in object Figure and is redefined in both Rectangle and Square. Each object type requires its own Display method because each object must display values stored in its own distinct fields as well as its inherited fields. Turbo Pascal recommends the use of the virtual directive after methods that are redefined. All method headers for a particular virtual method must have identical parameter lists, as in Fig. 13.16, where each Display method has an empty parameter list.

Using virtual after a method declaration enables Turbo Pascal to wait until run time to determine which Display method to call when it encounters a Display message. Although that is not an issue now, situations can arise in which this decision cannot be made during compilation.

If an object has one or more virtual methods, Turbo Pascal requires that an Init method classified as a constructor be used to create an instance of that object. A constructor method is declared and called just like a procedure. A constructor method cannot be declared as virtual because Turbo Pascal must know at compile time exactly how much storage to allocate for an instance of an object.

The implementation section (Fig. 13.17) shows the methods for all three objects, starting with Figure. Method Figure.Init creates a new Figure object with an empty Name field. Method Figure.Display displays the fields that are inherited by all descendants of Figure. To save space, we have omitted the accessor methods (GetName, GetPosX, and so on) and comments.

Method Rectangle.Init creates a rectangle object (Name field is 'Rectangle') and stores a length and width value in it. Method Square.Init assigns the same value (SideVal) to its data members Length and Width, both of which are inherited from object Rectangle.

Method Rectangle.Display and Square.Display begin with a call to Figure.Display to display the inherited data members. Next, Rectan-

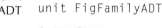

Figure 13.16
Interface Section for Unit
FigFamilyADT

```
unit FigFamilyADT;

interface

type
  Figure = object
            constructor Init;
            procedure Display; virtual;
            function GetName : string;
            function GetPosX : Real;
            function GetPosY : Real;
            function GetArea : Real;
            function GetPerim : Real;

        private
          Name : string;              {name as a string}
          PosX, PosY : Real;          {X, Y coordinates}
          Area, Perimeter : Real;
        end; {Figure}

  Rectangle = object(Figure)
            constructor Init (LengthVal, WidthVal, X, Y :
                                  Real);
            procedure Display; virtual;
            function GetLength : Real;
            function GetWidth : Real;
            procedure ComputeArea;
            procedure ComputePerim;

          private
            Length, Width : Real;
          end; {Rectangle}

  Square = object(Rectangle)
            constructor Init (SideVal, X, Y : Real);
            procedure Display; virtual;
          end; {Square}
```

gle.Display displays the Width and Length of a Rectangle object;
method Square.Display displays the value stored in Length.

Object Square does not have its own method to compute perimeter and
area, so it inherits methods ComputePerim and ComputeArea from object
Rectangle. Because Width and Length are set to the same value when
Square.Init executes, the values computed by these inherited methods
will be correct.

Accessor methods GetName, GetArea, GetPerim, GetPosX, GetPosY (see
Programming Exercise 1 at the end of this section) are defined in object Figure and are inherited by all its descendants. Object Rectangle defines two

Figure 13.17
Implementation Section for
Unit FigFamilyADT

```
implementation

  constructor Figure.Init;
  begin {Init}
    Name := ''
  end; {Init}

  procedure Figure.Display;
  begin {Display}
    if Name = '' then
      WriteLn ('Figure is not defined')
    else
      begin
        WriteLn ('Figure is ', Name);
        WriteLn ('Center at (', PosX :3:1,
                 ', ', PosY :3:1, ')');
        WriteLn ('Area is ', Area :3:1);
        WriteLn ('Perimeter is ', Perimeter :3:1)
      end {if}
  end; {Display}

{
 Insert accessor functions GetName, GetPosX, GetPosY,
 GetArea and GetPerim.

 Rectangle methods
}
  constructor Rectangle.Init (LengthVal, WidthVal, X, Y
                                                 : Real);
  begin {Init}
    Name := 'Rectangle';
    Length := LengthVal;      PosX := X;
    Width := WidthVal;        PosY := Y;
  end; {Init}

  procedure Rectangle.ComputeArea;
  begin {ComputeArea}
    Area := Length * Width
  end; {ComputeArea}

  procedure Rectangle.ComputePerim;
  begin {ComputePerim}
    Perimeter := 2 * (Length + Width)
  end; {ComputePerim}

  procedure Rectangle.Display;
  begin {Display}
    Figure.Display;
    WriteLn ('Width is ', Width :3:1);
    WriteLn ('Length is ', Length :3:1)
  end; {Display}
```

▷ ▷ ▷ ▷ ▷ ▷

```
{
 Insert GetWidth and GetLength here.

 Square methods
}

  constructor Square.Init (SideVal, X, Y : Real);
  begin {Init}
    Name := 'Square';
    Width := SideVal;         PosX := X
    Length := SideVal;        PosY := Y
  end; {Init}

  procedure Square.Display;
  begin {Display}
    Figure.Display;
    WriteLn ('Side is ', Width :3:1)
  end; {Display}

end. {FigFamilyADT}
```

△

additional accessor methods, GetLength and GetWidth, that retrieve values from fields that are not inherited from Figure.

Program Style

Advantages of Object Inheritance

There are several important advantages to using inheritance:

▶ Inheritance reduces the effort required to introduce a new geometric figure type, as each new figure can inherit data and method members from its ancestor. For example, we were able to add object type Square by providing just two new method members.

▶ A new figure (say, Triangle or Circle) can be added without modifying the objects and methods that have already been written.

▶ New objects can be placed in a separate unit and all ancestor objects and their methods imported by placing the statement

```
uses FigFamilyADT;
```

in the interface section of the new unit. The new unit can then be compiled without recompiling FigFamilyADT.

Using FigFamilyADT

Figure 13.18 shows a client program that initializes a general figure object, a rectangle, and square objects. After the objects are initialized, the areas and

Figure 13.18
Client Program for
FigFamilyADT

Edit Window

```
program ClientOfFigFamily;

uses FigFamilyADT;

  var
    MyFigure : Figure;
    MyRectangle : Rectangle;
    MySquare : Square;

begin {ClientOfFigFamily}
  MyFigure.Init;                        {Create a general figure.}
  MyFigure.Display;    {Display general figure object instance.}
   WriteLn;

  MyRectangle.Init (5.0, 10.0, 0.0, 0.0); {Create a rectangle.}
  MyRectangle.ComputePerim;
  MyRectangle.ComputeArea;
  MyRectangle.Display;       {Display Rectangle object instance.}
   WriteLn;

  MySquare.Init (7.0, 15.0, 20.0);              {Create a square.}
  MySquare.ComputePerim;
  MySquare.ComputeArea;
  MySquare.Display;              {Display Square object instance.}
   WriteLn;

  MyFigure := MyRectangle;    {Assign MyRectangle to MyFigure.}
  MyFigure.Display              {Display Figure object instance.}
end. {ClientOfFigFamily}
```

Output Window

```
Figure is not defined

Figure is Rectangle
Center at (0.0, 0.0)
Area is 50.0
Perimeter is 30.0
Width is 10.0
Length is 5.0

Figure is Square
Center at (15.0, 20.0)
Area is 49.0
Perimeter is 28.0
Side is 7.0

Figure is Rectangle
Center at (0.0, 0.0)
Area is 50.0
Perimeter is 30.0
```

perimeters of the rectangle and square are computed and their characteristics are displayed.

Object Type Compatibility

The program in Fig. 13.18 ends with

```
MyFigure := MyRectangle;   {Assign MyRectangle to MyFigure.}
MyFigure.Display           {Display Figure object instance.}
end. {ClientOfFigFamily}
```

The first statement assigns object instance `MyRectangle` (type `Rectangle`) to object instance `MyFigure` (type `Figure`). You can assign an instance of a descendant object (`MyRectangle`) to an instance of an ancestor object (`MyFigure`). The assignment copies over only those fields of `MyRectangle` that were inherited from ancestor object `Figure`. The values in data fields `Length` and `Width` are not copied to `MyFigure`. The message `MyFigure.Display` displays the values of the inherited fields in the last three lines of the sample run.

The assignment statement

```
MyRectangle := MyFigure      {invalid assignment}
```

is invalid because you cannot copy an instance of an ancestor object to an instance of a descendant object. The reason is that a descendant object may have its own data fields that are not inherited from its ancestor; these data fields would be undefined after the assignment.

Exercises for Section 13.4 Self-Check

1. Assume the following statements appear in Fig. 13.18. Correct each invalid statement. Explain what the valid and corrected statements do.
   a. `MySquare := MyRectangle;`
      `MySquare.Display`
   b. `MyRectangle := MySquare;`
      `MyRectangle.Display`
   c. `MySquare.Init (5.5, 5.5)`
   d. `Figure := Square;`
      `Figure.Display;`
      `Square.Display`
2. If `Figure` has a method called `Display` and `Rectangle` inherits the methods of `Figure`, why is it not an error that `Rectangle` declares `Display` as a member as well? Which one will be used?
3. Would it have made sense for the `List` object in Section 13.3 to be a descendent of the `Entry` object? Why or why not?

Programming

1. In Fig. 13.16, add a declaration for object type `Circle` with a new data member `Radius`. Write the method declarations for `Circle` as they would appear in Fig. 13.17.
2. Modify Figs. 13.16 and 13.17 to include a new method member named `ReadFig` for the family of figure objects. Method `ReadFig` reads the data for a figure from the keyboard.

13.5 Common Programming Errors

When programming with objects, always precede each method name in a message with its recipient, which must be an object instance of the appropriate type. The most common errors in using objects are omitting the object instance and using an object instance that is the wrong type.

In the object implementation section, remember to qualify each method declaration with its object type. Otherwise, an `Unknown identifier` syntax error will result each time you reference an object's data member or another method member. Also be sure that each method header is consistent with the one used for the object type declaration in the interface section.

Each client program must import the object types that it references through a `uses` statement. Remember to compile the unit containing the object type to disk before compiling the client program. Make sure that you declare each object instance processed by the client and qualify each method appearing in the client program with the required object instance. Do not attempt direct access of an object's method members in the client program, or a `Field identifier expected` syntax error will result.

When declaring objects with inherited fields, use the reserved word `virtual` after each method header that appears in an ancestor and descendant object declaration. Do not use `virtual` in the implementation section. You can assign a descendant object to an ancestor object; however, assigning an ancestor object to a descendant object causes a `Type mismatch` syntax error.

CHAPTER REVIEW

1. Through data abstraction, you can focus on data objects and their required operations. You can write clients that manipulate these objects without knowledge of their internal structure or organization. Information hiding enables you to process data objects and access the information they store through their operators. If a data object's implementation should change, you need not rewrite its client programs.
2. An abstract data type (ADT) is encapsulated with its operators in a separate unit. Although you can implement abstract data types using records with operators that are procedures and functions, Turbo Pascal does not prevent you from directly accessing a record's fields in an external program.
3. With Turbo Pascal objects, you can encapsulate an object type and its methods (operators) in an object type declaration. Turbo Pascal prevents clients from di-

rectly accessing an object's private data members; you must use a method member to access a private data member. To invoke a method member, you send a message to the object where a message has the form *object-instance. method*.

4. Using inheritance, you can create new objects (descendants) by modifying existing objects (ancestors). An ancestor can have several descendants, but each descendant object can have only one direct ancestor. A type declaration beginning with

descendant = object(*ancestor*)

indicates that the object type *descendant* has the object type in parentheses as its direct ancestor. Object type *descendant* inherits all data members and method members of object type *ancestor*.

Summary of New Pascal Constructs

Construct	Effect
Declaring Objects	
```pascal‎ type Person = object constructor Init (N :string; A : Integer; G : Char); procedure Display; virtual; function GetName : string; function GetAge : Integer; function GetGender : Char; private Name : string; Age : Integer; Gender : Char; end; {Person} ```	Declares object type Person with three data members and five methods.
```pascal‎ Student = object(Person) constructor Init (N : string; A : Integer; G : Gender; M : string; GP : Real); procedure Display; virtual; function GetMajor : string; function GetGPA : Real; private Major : string; GPA : Real; {grade point} end; {Student} ```	Declares object type Student as a descendant of type Person with two new data members and four new or redefined method members.

Quick-Check Exercises

1. _____ is hiding low-level details of implementation from a higher-level module.
2. How does an object type declaration differ from a record type declaration?
3. What advantages do object types have over record types for implementing ADTs?
4. If an object instance named `AnObject` of the object type `TheObject` has a method named `Init`, what would be the form of a message to that object?
5. Which method members and data members of an ancestor object are available for use by an instance of a descendant of that object?
6. When should the virtual directive be used in declaring an object type method?
7. When is a constructor used?
8. What does a descendant object inherit from its ancestor?
9. Object types can be declared as local identifiers in procedures. True or false?
10. What is the purpose of using the reserved word `private` in an object type declared in a unit?

Answers to Quick-Check Exercises

1. Information hiding
2. Object type declarations contain method headers and private parts.
3. If the object's data members are private, you cannot access the data members directly—you must use a method member. Also, objects support inheritance, facilitating the creation of new objects from existing ones.
4. `AnObject.Init`
5. All are available, though some may have to be fully identified using the ancestor's name if they have been redefined in the descendant.
6. When a method is likely to be redefined by a descendant object and the method heading will not need to be changed
7. Declare method `Init` as a constructor for each object type in an object hierarchy.
8. The ancestor's data members and method members
9. False
10. To prevent a client module from accessing the fields or methods that follow the reserved word `private` in an object type declaration

Review Questions

1. Define the terms procedural abstraction and data abstraction.
2. Explain why the principle of information hiding is important to the software designer.
3. What is an accessor function? Why should it be used?
4. Write an abstract data type interface section for describing a radio station using records. A station has a four-letter call sign, can be AM or FM, and has a real number frequency.
5. Write an abstract data type interface section for describing a radio station as in Review Question 4 using an object.

6. List the steps of the object-oriented design method.
7. Define an object `Player` for the positions on a baseball team (pitcher, catcher, infielder, outfielder) with methods for reading and writing `Player` objects.

Programming Projects

1. A polynomial can be expressed as $c_0 + c_1x + c_2x_2 + \cdots + c_dx_d$, where c_0, c_1, $\cdots$, c_d are called the coefficients of a polynomial of degree d. Write an abstract data type for polynomials of degree up to 10. Your ADT should provide the ability to read the polynomial degree and coefficients from the user and to evaluate the polynomial for a given value of x. Write a suitable test program for your ADT and demonstrate its proper operation. Use a record ADT.
2. Repeat Programming Project 1, using an object ADT.
3. Write a program to manage a checkbook. Create an ADT for checkbook transactions. There should be an object for a transaction consisting of a date, number, description, and amount. Negative amounts indicate checks and positive amounts indicate deposits. Create another ADT for the checkbook itself. A checkbook is simply a list of transactions. Your program should keep the contents of the checkbook in a file and provide a menu for adding checks and deposits and printing a statement. The current balance should always be displayed. *Hint:* Create an empty checkbook file using the Turbo Pascal editor before running your program.

4. Each month a bank customer deposits $50 into a savings account. Assume that the interest rate is fixed and is a problem input. The interest is calculated on a quarterly basis. For example, if the account earns 6.5% annually, it earns one-fourth of the 6.5% investment every three months. Write a program to compute the total amount in the account and the interest accrued for each of the 120 months of a 10-year period. Assume that the rate is applied to all funds in the account at the end of a quarter, regardless of when the deposits were made.

    Print all values accurate to two decimal places. The table printed by your program when the annual interest rate is 6.5% should begin as follows:

MONTH	INVESTMENT	NEW AMOUNT	INTEREST	TOTAL SAVINGS
1	50.00	50.00	0.00	50.00
2	100.00	100.00	0.00	100.00
3	150.00	150.00	2.44	152.44
4	200.00	202.44	0.00	202.44
5	250.00	252.44	0.00	252.44
6	300.00	302.44	4.91	307.35
7	350.00	357.35	0.00	357.35

    Your solution should make use of an `Account` object that contains account information for a single month and has methods for initializing, updating, and displaying its data fields.
5. Redo Programming Project 4, adding columns to allow comparison of interest compounded monthly (one-twelfth of annual rate every month) with continuously compounded interest. The formula for compounded interest is

amount = principal $\times$ rate $\times$ time

where *rate* is the annual interest rate and *time* is expressed in years.

6. An employee time card is represented as a single line in a text data file. Write a program that processes a data file containing several employee data lines to produce a payroll report, which is written to text file. Each data line has the following form:

```
Positions                         Data
1-4              Employee identification number
5                Blank
6-7              Number of regular hours (whole number)
8                Blank
9-14             Hourly rate (dollars and cents)
15               Blank
16-17            Number of dependents
18               Blank
19-20            Number of overtime hours (whole number)
```

Define an object type Employee that has the preceding data fields as well as fields GrossPay and NetPay as defined here:

$gross\ pay = (regular\ hours + overtime\ hours \times 1.5) \times rate$
$federal\ tax = 0.14 \times (gross - 13 \times dependents)$
$social\ security = 0.052 \times gross$
$net\ pay = gross - (federal\ tax + social\ security)$

7. Write a menu-driven program that contains options for creating the data file to be processed by the payroll program described in Programming Project 6 (the user should be prompted to enter several time cards from the keyboard), displaying the time cards in the file on the system printer, adding new time cards to the end of an existing data file, deleting a time card from the file by ID number, and quitting the program.

CHAPTER FOURTEEN

Recursion

recursive module
a procedure or function that
calls itself

A recursive procedure or function is one that calls itself. Each time it is called, the **recursive module** can operate on different parameters. Recursion can be an alternative to iteration (looping), although a recursive solution is usually less efficient, in terms of computer time, than an iterative one because of the overhead for the extra procedure calls. In many instances, however, recursion enables us to specify a natural, simple solution to a problem that otherwise would be difficult to solve. For this reason, recursion is an important and powerful tool in problem solving and programming.

14.1   Recursive Modules

In this section, we demonstrate recursion by using a simple function and we develop rules for writing recursive modules from this example. Consider the computer solution to the problem of multiplying 6 by 3, assuming you can add but not multiply. The problem of multiplying 6 by 3 can be split into two problems:

Problem 1: Multiply 6 by 2.

Problem 2: Add 6 to the result of problem 1.

Because your computer can add, it can solve problem 2 but not problem 1. Problem 1, however, is simpler than the original problem. We can split problem 1 into two problems, 1.1 and 1.2, leaving three problems to solve, two of which are additions.

Problem 1.1: Multiply 6 by 1.

Problem 1.2: Add 6 to the result of problem 1.1.

Problem 2: Add 6 to the result of problem 1.

Even though your computer cannot multiply, you can program it to recognize that the result of multiplying any number by 1 is that number. Therefore solving problem 1.1 (the answer is 6) and problem 1.2 gives the solution to problem 1 (the answer is 12). Solving problem 2 gives the final answer, 18.

Figure 14.1 implements this approach to multiplication as the recursive Pascal function `Multiply`, which returns the product, $M \times N$, of its two arguments. If N is greater than 1, the statement

```
Multiply := M + Multiply(M, N-1)     {recursive step}
```

executes, splitting the original problem into the two simpler problems:

Figure 14.1
Recursive Function
Multiply

```
function Multiply (M, N : Integer) : Integer;
{
   Performs multiplication using + operator.
   Pre : M and N are defined and N > 0.
   Post: Returns M * N.
}
begin {Multiply}
   if N = 1 then
     Multiply := M                       {stopping case}
   else
     Multiply := M + Multiply(M, N-1)   {recursive step}
end; {Multiply}
```

Problem 1: Multiply M by N-1.

Problem 2: Add M to the result.

recursive step
the step in a program or algorithm that contains a recursive call

The first of these problems is solved by calling `Multiply` again with N-1 as its second argument. If the new second argument is greater than 1, there will be additional calls to function `Multiply`. We call this case (N > 1) the **recursive step** because it contains a call to function `Multiply`.

Note the two different uses of the identifier `Multiply` in the recursive step in Fig. 14.1. The one without parameters defines the function result; the other calls the function recursively.

When the condition N = 1 is finally true, the statement

```
Multiply := M                          {stopping case}
```

stopping case
the statement that causes recursion to terminate

executes, so the answer is M. We call this case (N = 1) the **stopping case** because it is always the last case reached.

Tracing a Recursive Function

Hand-tracing an algorithm's execution demonstrates how that algorithm works. We can trace the execution of the function designator `Multiply(6, 3)` by drawing an activation frame that corresponds to each call of the function. An **activation frame** is a device that shows the parameter values for each call and summarizes its execution.

activation frame
a device showing the parameter values for each recursive call and its execution

Figure 14.2 shows the three activation frames generated to solve the problem of multiplying 6 by 3. The part of each activation frame that executes before the next recursive call is in color; the part that executes after the return from the next call is in gray. The darker the color of an activation frame, the greater the depth of recursion.

The value returned from each call appears alongside each black arrow. The return arrow from each function call points to the operator +, because the addition is performed just after the return.

Figure 14.2 shows that there are three calls to function `Multiply`. Parameter M has the value 6 for all three calls; parameter N has the values 3, 2, and finally 1. Because N is 1 in the third call, the value of M (6) is returned as the result of the third and last call. After the return to the second activation frame, the value of M is added to this result, and the sum (12) is returned as the result of the second call. After the return to the first activation frame, the value of M is added to this result, and the sum (18) is returned as the result of the original call to function `Multiply`.

Properties of Recursive Problems and Solutions

Problems that can be solved by recursion have the following characteristics:

▶ One or more stopping cases have a simple, nonrecursive solution.

Figure 14.2
Trace of Function Multiply

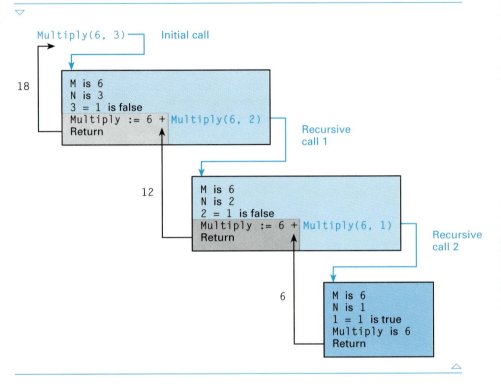

▶ The other cases of the problem can be reduced (using recursion) to problems that are closer to stopping cases.

▶ Eventually the problem can be reduced to stopping cases only, which are relatively easy to solve.

Follow these steps to solve a recursive problem:

1. Understand the problem.
2. Determine the stopping cases.
3. Determine the recursive steps.

The recursive algorithms that we write generally consist of an if statement with the form:

```
if the stopping case is reached then
    Solve it.
else
    Split the problem into simpler cases using recursion.
```

Figure 14.3 illustrates these steps. Assume that for a particular problem of size *N*, we can split the problem into one of size 1 that we can solve (a stopping case) and one of size *N* - 1. We can split the problem of size *N* - 1 into another problem of size 1 and a problem of size *N* - 2, which we can split further. If we split the problem *N* times, we end up with *N* problems of size 1, all of which we can solve.

A Recursive Procedure

In Fig. 14.4, Reverse is a recursive procedure that reads in a string of length N and prints it out backward. If the procedure call statement

Reverse (5)

is executed, the five characters entered are displayed in reverse order. If the characters abcde are entered when this procedure is called, the lines

abcde
edcba

appear on the screen. The color letters are entered as data and the black letters are printed. If the procedure call statement

Reverse (3)

is executed instead, only three characters are read, and the lines

abc
cba

appear on the screen.

terminating condition
a condition that is true when a recursive module reaches a stopping case

Like most recursive procedures, the body of procedure Reverse consists of an if statement that evaluates a **terminating condition**, N = 1. When

Figure 14.3
Splitting a Problem into Smaller Problems

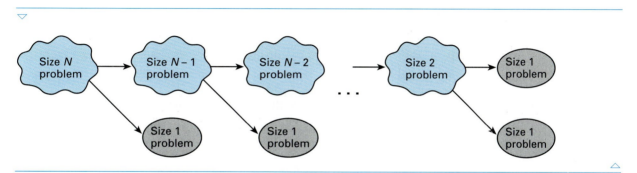

Figure 14.4

Procedure Reverse

```
procedure Reverse (N : Integer);
{
  Displays a string of length N in
  the reverse order from which it is entered.
  Pre : N is greater than or equal to one.
  Post: Displays N characters.
}
  var
    Next : Char; {next data character}

begin {Reverse}
  if N = 1 then
    begin {stopping case}
      Read (Next);
      Write (Next)
    end {stopping case}
  else
    begin {recursion}
      Read (Next);
      Reverse (N-1);
      Write (Next)
    end {recursion}
end; {Reverse}
```

the terminating condition is true, the problem has reached a stopping case—a data string of length 1—and the Read and Write statements are executed.

When the terminating condition is false (N > 1), the recursive step (following else) is executed and the Read statement enters the next data character. The procedure call statement

```
Reverse (N-1);
```

calls the procedure recursively, with the parameter value decreased by 1. The character just read is not displayed until later, because the Write statement follows the recursive procedure call. Consequently, the Write statement cannot be performed until after the procedure execution is completed and control is returned to the Write statement. For example, the character that is read when N is 3 is not displayed until after the procedure execution for N equal to 2 is done. Hence, this character is displayed after the characters that are read when N is 2 and N is 1.

To see why this is so, trace the execution of the procedure call statement

```
Reverse (3)
```

The trace shown in Fig. 14.5 assumes the letters abc were entered as data. The trace shows three activation frames for procedure Reverse, each beginning with a list of the initial values of N and Next for that frame. The value of

Figure 14.5

Trace of Reverse (3)

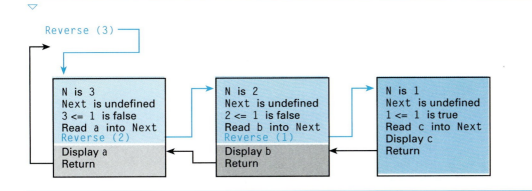

N is passed into the procedure when it is called, because N is a value parameter; the value of Next is initially undefined, because Next is a local variable.

The statements in color in Fig. 14.5 are recursive procedure calls and result in a new activation frame, as indicated by the colored arrows. A procedure return occurs when the procedure end is reached, as indicated by the word Return and a black arrow pointing to the statement in the calling frame to which the procedure returns. Tracing the colored arrows and then the black arrows in Fig. 14.5 gives us the list of statements in Fig. 14.6. To help you understand this list, all the statements for a particular activation frame are indented to the same column.

Figure 14.6

Sequence of Statements
for Reverse (3)

Call Reverse with N equal to 3.
    Read the first character (a) into Next.
    Call Reverse with N equal to 2.
        Read the second character (b) into Next.
        Call Reverse with N equal to 1.
            Read the third character (c) into Next.
            Display the third character (c).
            Return from third call.
        Display the second character (b).
        Return from second call.
    Display the first character (a).
    Return from original call.

Note the three calls to procedure `Reverse`, each with a different parameter value. The procedure returns always occur in the reverse order of the procedure calls; that is, we return from the last call first, then we return from the next to last call, and so on. After we return from a particular execution of the procedure, the procedure displays the character that was read into `Next` just prior to that procedure call. The expression **unwinding the recursion** describes the return from a series of recursive calls.

unwinding the recursion
the process of returning from
a series of recursive calls

Exercises for Section 14.1   *Self-Check*

1. Show how the problem generated by the function designator `Multiply(5, 4)` can be split into smaller problems as in Fig. 14.3.
2. Trace the execution of `Multiply(5, 4)`.
3. Given the following procedure and the call `WhatDo (4)`, what would be the output?

```
procedure WhatDo (I : Integer);
begin {WhatDo}
  if I > 1 then
    begin
      Write (I :2);
      WhatDo (I - 1);
      Write (I :2)
    end {if}
end; {WhatDo}
```

Programming

1. Write a recursive function `Divide(A, B)` to compute `A div B` using only integer subtraction and no multiplication or division.

14.2   Parameter and Local Variable Stacks

stack
a data structure in which the
last component stored is the
first one removed

Pascal uses a special data structure called a **stack** to keep track of the values of the parameters of a recursive module as they change from call to call. A stack is analogous to a stack of dishes or trays. In a buffet, clean dishes are always placed on top of the stack of dishes. When a dish is needed, the last one placed on the stack, the one on top, is removed. This causes the next to last dish placed on the stack to move to the top of the stack.

Whenever a new procedure call occurs, the parameter value associated with that call is placed on the top of the parameter stack. Also, a new memory cell whose value is initially undefined is placed on top of the stack that is maintained for each local variable. In procedure `Reverse`, whenever `N` or `Next` is referenced, the value at the top of the corresponding stack is always used. When a procedure return occurs, the value currently at the top of each stack is removed, and the value just below it moves to the top.

Stacks for Procedure Reverse

As an example, let's look at the two stacks right after the first call to Reverse. There is one cell on each stack, as follows:

After first call to Reverse

The letter a is read into Next just before the second call to Reverse.

After the second call to Reverse, the number 2 is placed on top of the stack for N, and the top of the stack for Next becomes undefined again. The value in color is at the top of each stack.

After second call to Reverse

The letter b is read into Next just before the third call to Reverse:

However, Next becomes undefined again right after the third call:

After third call to Reverse

During this execution of the procedure, the letter c is read into Next, and c is echo printed immediately because N is 1 (the stopping case):

The procedure return causes the values at the top of the stack to be removed:

After first return

Because control is returned to a `Write` statement, the value of `Next` (b) at the top of the stack is then displayed. Another return occurs, causing the values currently at the top of the stack to be removed:

After second return

N   Next

Again, control is returned to a `Write` statement, and the value of `Next` (a) at the top of the stack is displayed. The third and last return removes the last pair of values from the stack, and N and `Next` both become undefined:

After third return

N   Next

Chapter 18 shows you how to declare and manipulate stacks yourself. Because these steps are all done automatically by Pascal, we can write recursive procedures without worrying about the stacks.

Implementation of Parameter Stacks in Pascal

For illustrative purposes, we have used separate stacks for N and `Next` in our discussion; the compiler, however, actually maintains a single stack. Each time a call to a procedure or a function occurs, all its parameters and local variables are pushed onto the stack along with the memory address of the calling statement. The latter gives the computer the return point after execution of the procedure or function. Although multiple copies of a procedure's parameters may be saved on the stack, only one copy of the procedure body is in memory.

Exercises for Section 14.2 **Self-Check**

1. Why is N a value parameter in Fig. 14.4?
2. Assume the characters `*+-/` are entered for the procedure call statement

   `Reverse (4)`

   Show the contents of the stacks immediately after each procedure call and return.
3. For the function designator `Multiply(5, 4)`, show the stacks after each recursive call.

14.3 Recursive Mathematical Functions

Many mathematical functions are defined recursively. An example is the factorial of a number n (represented as $n!$):

▶ 0! is 1
▶ *n*! is *n* × (*n* − 1)!,   for *n* > 0   Definition of *n*!

Thus 4! = 4 × 3! = 4 × 3 × 2!, and so on. It is easy to implement this recursive mathematics definition as a recursive function in Pascal.

EXAMPLE 14.1 ▼

Function Factor in Fig. 14.7 computes the factorial of its argument N. The recursive step

```
Factor := N * Factor(N-1)
```

implements the second line of the factorial definition. This statement means that the result of the current call (argument N) is determined by multiplying the result of the next call (argument N-1) by N.
    A trace of

```
Fact := Factor(3)
```

is shown in Fig. 14.8. The value returned from the first call, Factor(3), is 6, and this value is assigned to Fact. Be careful when you use the factorial function; its value increases rapidly and could lead to an integer-overflow error (for example, 10! is 24320).   ▲

Although the recursive implementation of function Factor follows naturally from its definition, this function can be implemented easily using iteration. The iterative version (FactorIt) is shown in Fig. 14.9. Notice that FactorIt contains a loop as its major control structure, whereas the recursive version contains an if statement. Also, a local variable, Factorial, is needed in FactorIt to hold the accumulating product.

Figure 14.7
Recursive Function Factor

```
function Factor (N : Integer) : Integer;
{
  Computes the factorial of N (N!).
  Pre : N is defined and N >= 0.
  Post: Returns N!
}
begin {Factor}
  if N = 0 then
    Factor := 1
  else
    Factor := N * Factor(N-1)
end; {Factor}
```

Figure 14.8
Trace of Fact := Factor(3)

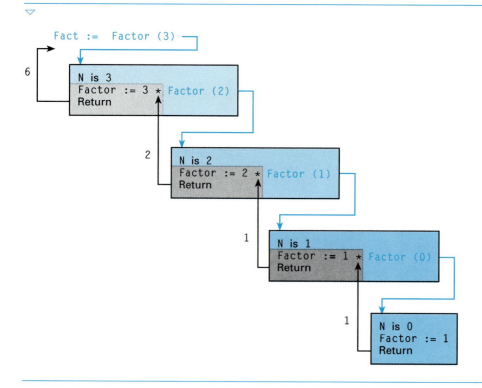

Figure 14.9
Iterative Function FactorIt

```
function FactorIt (N : Integer) : Integer;
{
  Computes the factorial of N (N!).
  Pre : N is defined and N >= 0.
  Post: Returns N!
}
  var
    I,                        {loop-control variable}
    Factorial : Integer;   {the accumulating product}

begin {FactorIt}
  Factorial := 1;
  for I := 2 to N do
    Factorial := Factorial * I;

  FactorIt := Factorial       {Define result.}
end; {FactorIt}
```

EXAMPLE 14.2 ▼

The Fibonacci series is a sequence of numbers that have varied uses. They were originally intended to model the growth of a rabbit colony. We will not describe that model here, but you can see that the Fibonacci sequence 1, 1, 2, 3, 5, 8, 13, 21, 34, . . . increases rapidly. The fifteenth number in the sequence is 610 (that's a lot of rabbits!). The Fibonacci sequence is defined as follows:

▶ Fib_1 is 1.
▶ Fib_2 is 1.
▶ Fib_n is $Fib_{n-2} + Fib_{n-1}$, for $n > 2$.

Verify for yourself that the sequence of numbers in the preceding paragraph is correct.

A recursive function that computes the Nth Fibonacci number is shown in Fig. 14.10. Although easy to write, the Fibonacci function is not very efficient, because each recursive step generates two calls to function Fibonacci. ▲

EXAMPLE 14.3 ▼

Euclid's algorithm for finding the greatest common divisor of two positive integers, M and N, is defined recursively as follows. The *greatest common divisor* (GCD) of two integers is the largest integer that divides them both.

▶ GCD(M, N) is N if N <= M and N divides M.
▶ GCD(M, N) is GCD(N, M) if M < N.
▶ GCD(M, N) is GCD (N, remainder of M divided by N).

Figure 14.10
Recursive Function
Fibonacci

```
function Fibonacci (N : Integer) : Integer;
{
  Computes the Nth Fibonacci number.
  Pre : N is defined and N > 0.
  Post: Returns the Nth Fibonacci number.
}
begin {Fibonacci}
  if N <= 2 then
    Fibonacci := 1
  else
    Fibonacci := Fibonacci(N-2) + Fibonacci(N-1)
end; {Fibonacci}
```

Figure 14.11
Function GCD

Edit Window

```
program FindGCD;

{Prints the greatest common divisor of two integers}
  var
    M, N : Integer;                {two input items}

  function GCD (M, N : Integer) : Integer;
  {
    Finds the greatest common divisor of M and N.
    Pre : M and N are defined and both are > 0.
    Post: Returns the greatest common divisor of M and N.
  }
  begin {GCD}
    if (N <= M) and (M mod N = 0) then
      GCD := N
    else if M < N then
      GCD := GCD(N, M)
    else
      GCD := GCD(N, M mod N)
  end; {GCD}

begin {FindGCD}
  Write ('Enter two positive integers> ');
  ReadLn (M, N);
  WriteLn ('Their greatest common divisor is ',
           GCD (M, N) :1)
end. {FindGCD}
```

Output Window

```
Enter two positive integers> 24 84
Their greatest common divisor is 12
```

This algorithm states that the GCD is N if N is the smaller number and if N divides M. If M is the smaller number, then the GCD determination should be performed with the arguments transposed. If N does not divide M, the answer is obtained by finding the GCD of N and the remainder of M divided by N. The declaration and use of function GCD are shown in Fig. 14.11. ▲

Exercises for Section 14.3 **Self-Check**

1. What is the output of the following program? What does function Puzzle compute?

    ```
    program TestPuzzle;

      function Puzzle (N : Integer) : Integer;
      begin  {Puzzle}
    ```

```
        if N = 1 then
          Puzzle := 0
        else
          Puzzle := 1 + Puzzle(N div 2)
     end; {Puzzle}

begin {TestPuzzle}
  WriteLn (Puzzle(8))
end. {TestPuzzle}
```

2. Complete the following recursive function, which calculates the value of a number (Base) raised to a power (Power). Assume that Power is positive.

```
function PowerRaiser (Base, Power : Integer) : Integer;
begin
  if Power = _____ then
    PowerRaiser := _____
  else
    PowerRaiser := _____
end;
```

3. What would happen if the terminating condition for function Fibonacci is N <= 1?

4. If a program had the statement F := Fibonacci(5), how many calls to Fibonacci would be performed?

Programming

1. Write a recursive function, FindSum, that calculates the sum of successive integers starting at 1 and ending at N (e.g., FindSum(N) = 1 + 2 + . . . + (N-1) + N).

2. Write an iterative version of the Fibonacci function.

3. Write an iterative function for the greatest common divisor.

14.4 Recursive Modules with Array Parameters

So far our recursive examples have used parameters that are simple types. Recursive modules also can process parameters that are structured types. This section shows recursive modules with array parameters.

CASE STUDY Summing the Values in an Array

PROBLEM ▼

Write a recursive function that finds the sum of the values in an array X with subscripts 1..N.

ANALYSIS

The stopping case occurs when N is 1, that is, the sum is X[1] for a single-element array. If N is not 1, then we must add X[N] to the sum we get when we add the values in the subarray with subscripts 1..N-1.

Data Requirements

Problem Inputs

```
X : IntArray       {array of integer values}
N : Integer        {number of elements in the array}
```

Problem Output

The sum of the array values

DESIGN

Initial Algorithm

1. if N is 1 then
   2. The sum is X[1].
   else
   3. Add X[N] to the sum of values in the subarray with subscripts 1..N-1.

IMPLEMENTATION ▼

Function FindSum in Fig. 14.12 implements this algorithm. The result of calling FindSum for a small array (N is 3) is also shown.

TESTING ▼

Figure 14.13 traces the function call FindSum(X, 3). As before, the colored part of each activation frame executes before the next recursive function call,

---

Figure 14.12
Using Recursive Function
FindSum

Edit Window

```
program TestFindSum;

{Tests function FindSum}

  type
     IndexRange = 1..20;
     IntArray = array [IndexRange] of Integer;

  var
     N : Integer;
     X : IntArray;
```

▷ ▷ ▷ ▷ ▷ ▷

```
function FindSum (var X : IntArray;
                       N : Integer) : Integer;

{
    Finds the sum of the values in elements 1..N of array X.
    Pre : Array X and N are defined and N > 0.
    Post: Returns sum of first N elements of X.
}
begin {FindSum}
  if N = 1 then
    FindSum := X[1]
  else
    FindSum := X[N] + FindSum(X, N-1)
end; {FindSum}

begin {TestFindSum}
  N := 3;
  X[1] := 5;  X[2] := 10;   X[3] := -7;
  WriteLn ('The array sum is ', FindSum(X, 3) :3)
end. {TestFindSum}
```

Output Window

```
The array sum is 8
```

Figure 14.13
Trace of FindSum(X, 3)

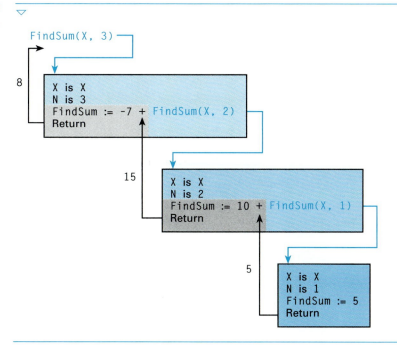

and each colored arrow points to a new activation frame. The gray part of each activation frame executes after the return from a recursive call, and each black arrow indicates the return point (the operator +) after a function execution. The value returned is indicated alongside the black arrow. The value returned for the original call, `FindSum(X, 3)`, is 8, which is printed.

Recursive Boolean Functions

Functions that return Boolean values (`True` or `False`) also can be written recursively. These functions do not perform a computation, yet their result is still determined by evaluating an expression (type `Boolean`) containing a recursive call. The function in Example 14.4 searches an array and the one in Example 14.5 compares two arrays.

EXAMPLE 14.4: Recursive Array Search ▼

The Boolean function `Member` in Fig. 14.14 returns the value `True` if the argument `Target` is in the subarray `X[1..N]`; otherwise, it returns the value `False`. For a single-element array (a stopping case), the result is determined by comparing `X[1]` and `Target`. For larger arrays, the result is `True` if the last element, `X[N]`, equals `Target` (another stopping case). Otherwise, the result depends on whether `Target` occurs in the subarray `X[1..N-1]`, as indicated by the recursive step:

```
Member := Member(X, Target, N-1) {Search rest of array.}
```

Figure 14.14
Recursive Function
Member

```
function Member (var X : IntArray;
                     Target,
                     N : Integer) : Boolean;
{
   Searches for Target in array X with subscripts 1..N.
   Pre : Target, N, and array X are defined and N > 0.
   Post: Returns True if Target is located in array X;
         otherwise, returns False.
}
begin {Member}
   if N = 1 then
      Member := (X[1] = Target)          {Check single element.}
   else if X[N] = Target then
      Member := True                     {Found - return True.}
   else
      Member := Member(X, Target, N-1) {Search rest of array.}
end; {Member}
```

Figure 14.15
Trace of Function Member

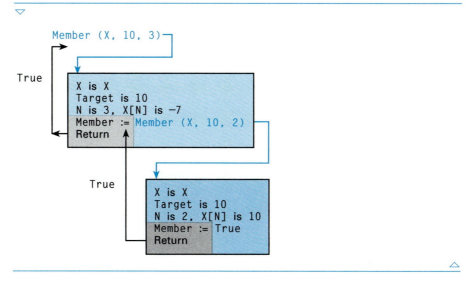

The function result is the value assigned to Member when a stopping case is reached.

The function designator Member(X, 10, 3) is traced in Fig. 14.15 for the array X defined in Fig. 14.12. The value returned is True, because the expression X[N] = Target is True when N is 2 (the second activation frame). ▲

EXAMPLE 14.5: Comparing Two Arrays ▼

The Boolean function Equal returns the value True if two arrays, say X and Y, of N elements are the same (e.g., X[1] = Y[1], X[2] = Y[2], . . ., X[N] = Y[N]). This function (see Fig. 14.16) looks similar to function Member. For single-element arrays, the function result depends on whether X[1] = Y[1]. For larger arrays, the result is False if X[N] <> Y[N]. Otherwise, the result depends on whether the subarrays with subscripts 1..N-1 are equal. ▲

Program Style

Variable Array Parameters in Recursive Modules

Earlier we stated that programmers often declare large arrays as variable parameters to conserve memory even if the arrays are input parameters. We recommend that you do this for recursive modules; otherwise, a separate copy of an array parameter would be made for each recursive call.

Figure 14.16
Recursive Function Equal

```
function Equal (var X, Y : IntArray;
                     N : Integer) : Boolean;
{
   Compares arrays X and Y with elements 1..N.
   Pre : Arrays X and Y are defined and N > 0.
   Post: Returns True if arrays X and Y are equal; otherwise,
         returns False.
}
begin {Equal}
   if N = 1 then
      Equal := (X[1] = Y[1])       {Compare 1-element arrays.}
   else if X[N] <> Y[N] then
      Equal := False                {Found an unequal pair.}
   else
      Equal := Equal(X, Y, N-1)     {Compare rest of arrays.}
end; {Equal}
```

Comparison of Iterative and Recursive Functions

In function MemberIt (Fig. 14.17), the iterative version of Member, a loop is needed to examine each array element. Without recursion it is not possible to use the function name in an expression, so a local variable, Found, is needed to represent the result so far. Before the return from the function, the final value of Found is assigned as the function result.

The iterative function would execute faster than the recursive version. However, many programmers would argue that the recursive version is esthetically more pleasing. It is certainly more compact (a single if statement) and requires no local variables. Once you are accustomed to thinking recursively, the recursive form is somewhat easier to read and understand than the iterative form.

Some programmers like to use recursion as a conceptual tool. Once they have written the recursive form of a function or procedure, they can always translate it into an iterative version if run-time efficiency is a constraint. In the next section, we will describe a much more efficient searching algorithm.

Exercises for Section 14.4   ***Self-Check***

1. Trace the execution of recursive function Equal for the three-element arrays X (element values 1, 15, 10) and Y (element values 1, 5, 7).
2. Answer Exercise 1 for the recursive function Member and array X when searching for 15 and for 3.
3. What does the following recursive function do? Trace its execution on array X in Exercise 1.

Figure 14.17
Iterative Function
MemberIt

```
function MemberIt (var X : IntArray;
                       Target,
                       N : Integer) : Boolean;
{
   Searches for Target in array X with subscripts 1..N.
   Pre : Target, N, and array X are defined and N > 0.
   Post: Returns True if Target is located in array X;
         otherwise, returns False.
}
   var
     Found : Boolean;                    {local flag}
     I : Integer;                        {loop-control variable}

begin {MemberIt}
   Found := False;                       {Assume Target not found.}
   {Search array X for Target.}
   I := 1;                               {Start at beginning.}
   while not Found and (I <= N) do
     if X[I] = Target then
       Found := True                     {Found Target.}
     else
       I := I + 1;                       {Try next element.}

   {assert: Target is found or all elements are tested.}
   MemberIt := Found                     {Define result.}
end; {MemberIt}
```

```
function Mystery (X : IntArray;
                    N : Integer) : Integer;

   var
     Temp : Integer;
begin {Mystery}
   if N = 1 then
     Mystery := X[1]
   else
     begin
       Temp := Mystery(X, N-1);
       if X[N] > Temp then
         Mystery := X[N]
       else
         Mystery := Temp
     end {if}
end; {Mystery}
```

Programming

1. Write a recursive procedure that returns the smallest value in an array
    and its location.

14.5 Binary Search

This section describes a recursive search algorithm called binary search. Binary search is an example of an $O(\log_2 N)$ algorithm—a significant improvement over the sequential search algorithm, $O(N)$ (see Section 10.6).

CASE STUDY — **Recursive Binary Search**

Section 10.5 demonstrated one technique for searching for a target key in an array. Function Search (Fig. 10.18) performs a sequential search of its array argument and returns the index of the target key or the value 0 if the target is not present. Because the function requires N comparisons to determine that a target key is not in an array of N elements, sequential search is not very efficient for large arrays ($N > 100$). If the elements of the array being searched have been sorted and are in sequence by key value, we can make use of a more efficient search algorithm known as binary search.

Function Search returns 0 for a failed search. However, if 0 is allowed as a valid subscript for the array being searched, then returning 0 as the function value is inconclusive. To eliminate this ambiguity, we can implement an array-search algorithm as a procedure that has two output parameters: the index of the target value if found and a program flag indicating whether the target was found.

PROBLEM

Write an improved search algorithm that takes advantage of the sorted array elements and allows the use of 0 as a subscript in the array being searched.

ANALYSIS

The *binary-search algorithm* uses the ordering of array elements to eliminate half the array elements with each probe into the array. Consequently, if the array has 1000 elements, it either locates the target value or eliminates 500 elements with its first probe, 250 elements with its second probe, 125 elements with its third probe, and so on. For this reason, a binary search of an ordered array is an $O(\log_2 N)$ process. This means that you could use the binary-search algorithm to find a name in a large metropolitan telephone directory using 30 or fewer probes.

Because the array is ordered, all we have to do is compare the target value with the middle element of the subarray we are searching. If their values are the same, we are done. If the middle element value is larger than the target value, we should search the left half of the subarray; otherwise, we should search the right half of the subarray.

The subarray being searched has subscripts First..Last. The variable Middle is the subscript of the middle element in this range. Figure 14.18 shows an example in which the target is 35, First is 1, Last is 9, and Middle is 5. The right half of the array (subscripts Middle..Last) is eliminated by the first probe.

Last must be reset to Middle - 1 to define the new subarray to be searched, and Middle should be redefined as shown in Fig. 14.19. The target value, 35, would be found on this probe.

The binary-search algorithm can be defined clearly using recursion. The stopping cases are as follows:

▶ The array bounds are improper (First > Last).
▶ The middle value is the target value.

In the first case, the procedure returns False as the value of the program flag and the index of the target value is not defined. In the second case, True is returned as the value of the program flag and Middle is returned as the index of the target value. The recursive step is to search the appropriate subarray.

Data Requirements

Problem Inputs

```
Table  : IntArray    {array of integers to be searched}
Target : Integer     {target being searched for}
First  : Integer     {first subscript in the subarray}
Last   : Integer     {last subscript in the subarray}
```

Problem Outputs

```
Index : Integer      {location of Target in Table}
Found : Boolean      {flag - set to True if Target found}
```

Figure 14.18
First Probe of Binary Search

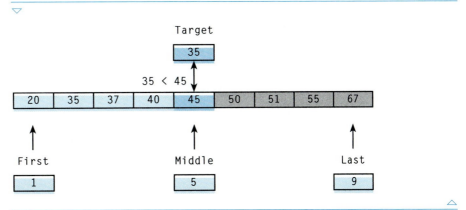

Figure 14.19
Second Probe of Binary
Search

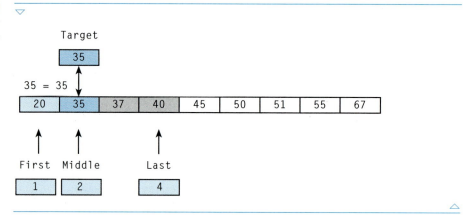

DESIGN ▼

Binary-Search Algorithm

1. Compute the subscript of the middle element.
2. if the array bounds are improper then
    3. Return with failure.
  else if the target is the middle value then
    begin
      4. Middle value is target location.
      5. Return with success.
    end
  else if the target is less than the middle value then
    6. Search subarray with subscripts First..Middle - 1.
  else
    7. Search subarray with subscripts Middle + 1..Last.

For each of the recursive steps (steps 6 and 7), the bounds of the new subarray must be listed as actual parameters in the recursive call. The actual parameters define the search limits for the next probe into the array.

IMPLEMENTATION ▼

In the initial call to the recursive procedure, First and Last should be defined as the first and last elements of the entire array, respectively. For example, you could use the procedure call

```
BinSearch (X, 35, 1, 9, Location, Success);
```

to search an array X with subscripts 1..9 for the target value 35 (assuming X has type IntArray). The position of the target element in array X will be returned as the value of the actual parameter Location if 35 is found. The actual parameter Success will be set to True if 35 is found and will be False otherwise. Procedure BinSearch is shown in Fig. 14.20.

The assignment statement

```
Middle := (First + Last) div 2;
```

computes the subscript of the middle element by finding the average of First and Last. The value has no meaning when First is greater than Last, but it does no harm to compute it.

TESTING ▼

Check for targets in the first and last elements of the array. Check for targets that are not present. Check the algorithm for even- and odd-length arrays and for arrays with lower subscripts that are negative. Also check arrays with

Figure 14.20
Recursive Binary Search
Procedure

```
procedure BinSearch (var Table {input} : IntArray;
                         Target {input} : Integer;
                         First, Last {input} : Integer;
                         var Index {output} : Integer;
                         var Found {output} : Boolean);
{
  Pre : The elements of Table are in increasing order and
        First and Last are defined.
  Post: If Target is in the array, return its position
        in Index and set Found to True; otherwise, set
        Found to False and leave Index undefined.
}
  var
    Middle : Integer;

begin {BinSearch}
  Middle := (First + Last) div 2;   {Compute middle
                                          subscript.}
  if First > Last then                 {Test array bounds.}
    Found := False
  else if Target = Table[Middle] then
    begin
      Found := True;                   {successful search}
      Index := Middle
    end
  else if Target < Table[Middle] then
    BinSearch (Table, Target, First, Middle - 1,
               Index, Found)
  else
    BinSearch (Table, Target, Middle + 1, Last,
               Index, Found)
end; {BinSearch}
```

multiple target values. See what happens when the array size gets very large, say, 1000.

Self-Check

1. Trace the execution of BinSearch for the array shown in Fig. 14.19 and a Target value of 40.
2. What would happen if BinSearch were called with the precondition of elements in increasing order violated? Would BinSearch still find the item?

Programming

1. Sorting algorithms need to know where in a sorted array a new item should be inserted. Write a recursive function InsertLocation that returns a location where Target could be inserted into an array and still maintain correct ordering.

14.6   Problem Solving with Recursion

To solve the Towers of Hanoi problem, you must move a specified number of disks that gradually increase in size from one tower (or one peg) to another. Legend has it that the world will come to an end when the problem is solved for 64 disks. You may be familiar with a children's game that is a 3-disk version of this puzzle.

The version of the problem shown in Fig. 14.21, has five disks (numbered 1 through 5) and three towers or pegs (lettered A, B, and C). The goal is to move the five disks from peg A to peg C subject to the following rules:

1. Only one disk may be moved at a time, and this disk must be the top disk on a peg.
2. A larger disk can never be placed on top of a smaller disk.

Figure 14.21
Towers of Hanoi

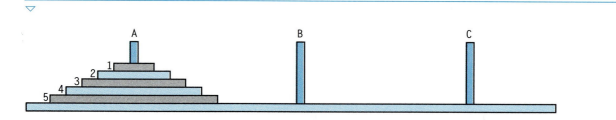

A stopping case of the problem is the movement of only one disk (e.g., "move disk 2 from peg A to peg C"). Simpler problems than the original would be to move four disks subject to conditions 1 and 2, to move three disks, and so on. We therefore want to split the original five-disk problem into one or more problems involving fewer disks. Let's consider splitting the original problem into three problems:

1.   Move four disks from peg A to peg B.
2.   Move disk 5 from peg A to peg C.
3.   Move four disks from peg B to peg C.

Step 1 moves all disks but the largest to tower B, an auxiliary tower. Step 2 moves the largest disk to the goal tower, tower C. Step 3 then moves the remaining disks from B to the goal tower, where they will be placed on top of the largest disk. Let's assume that we can perform step 1 and step 2 (a stopping case); Fig. 14.22 shows the status of the three towers after completion of these steps. At this point it should be clear that we can solve the original five-disk problem if we can complete step 3 (move four disks from peg B to peg C). In step 3, peg C is the goal tower and peg A becomes the auxiliary tower.

Unfortunately, we still don't know how to perform step 1 or step 3. Both steps, however, involve four disks instead of five, so they are easier than the original problem. We should be able to split them into even simpler problems. In step 3, we must move four disks from peg B to peg C, so we can split it into two 3-disk problems and a single 1-disk problem:

3.1 Move three disks from peg B to peg A.
3.2 Move disk 4 from peg B to peg C.
3.3 Move three disks from peg A to peg C.

Figure 14.23 shows the towers after completion of steps 3.1 and 3.2. The two largest disks are now on peg C. Once we complete step 3.3, all five disks will be on peg C. Although we still do not know how to solve steps 3.1

Figure 14.22
Towers of Hanoi After Steps 1 and 2

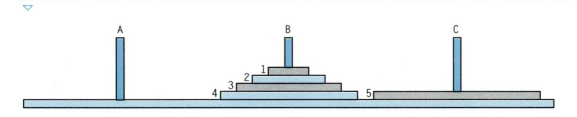

Figure 14.23
Towers of Hanoi After Steps 1, 2, 3.1, and 3.2

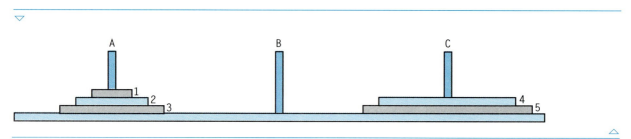

and 3.3, they are at least simpler problems than the four-disk problem from which they are derived.

By splitting each *N*-disk problem into two problems involving (*N* − 1) disks and a one-disk problem, we eventually reach the point where all the cases manipulate only one disk, cases that we know how to solve. Next, we use this process to write a Pascal program that solves the Towers of Hanoi problem.

CASE STUDY   **Towers of Hanoi Problem**

PROBLEM ▼

Solve the Towers of Hanoi problem for N disks, where N is a parameter.

ANALYSIS ▼

The solution to the Towers of Hanoi problem consists of a printed list of individual disk moves. We need a recursive procedure that moves any number of disks from one peg to another, using the third peg as an auxiliary. The role of each peg (source, destination, auxiliary) changes with each call.

Data Requirements

Problem Inputs

```
FromPeg : 'A'..'C'        {the from peg}
ToPeg : 'A'..'C'          {the to peg}
AuxPeg : 'A'..'C'         {the auxiliary peg}
N : Integer               {number of disks to be moved}
```

Problem Output

A list of individual disk moves

DESIGN ▼

Initial Algorithm

1. `if N is 1 then`
      2. Move disk 1 from the *from* peg to the *to* peg.
    `else`
      `begin`
          3. Move N-1 disks from the *from* peg to the *auxiliary* peg using the *to* peg as an intermediary.
          4. Move disk N from the *from* peg to the *to* peg.
          5. Move N-1 disks from the *auxiliary* peg to the *to* peg using the *from* peg as an intermediary.
    `end`

If N is 1, a stopping case is reached. If N is greater than 1, the recursive step (following `else`) splits the original problem into three smaller subproblems, one of which (step 4) is a stopping case. Each stopping case displays a move instruction. Verify that the recursive step generates the three original subproblems, repeated next, when N is 5, the *from* peg is A, and the *to* peg is C.

1. Move four disks from peg A to peg B.
2. Move disk 5 from peg A to peg C.
3. Move four disks from peg B to peg C.

IMPLEMENTATION ▼

The implementation of this algorithm is shown as procedure `Tower` in Fig. 14.24. Procedure `Tower` has four parameters. The procedure call statement

```
Tower ('A', 'C', 'B', 5)
```

solves the problem posed earlier of moving five disks from tower A to tower C using B as an auxiliary peg.

In Fig. 14.24, the stopping case (move disk 1) is implemented as a call to procedure `WriteLn`. Each recursive step consists of two recursive calls to `Tower`, with a call to `WriteLn` sandwiched between them. The first recursive call solves the problem of moving N-1 disks to the *auxiliary* peg. The call to `WriteLn` displays a message to move disk N to the *to* peg. The second recursive call solves the problem of moving the N-1 disks back from the *auxiliary* peg to the *to* peg.

TESTING ▼

The procedure call statement

```
Tower ('A', 'C', 'B', 3)
```

Figure 14.24
Recursive Procedure Tower

```
procedure Tower (FromPeg,
                 ToPeg,
                 AuxPeg {input} : Char;
                 N       {input} : Integer);
{
  Moves N disks from FromPeg to ToPeg
  using AuxPeg as an intermediary.
  Pre : FromPeg, ToPeg, AuxPeg, and N are defined.
  Post: Displays a list of move instructions that transfer
        the disks.
}
begin  {Tower}
  if N = 1 then
    WriteLn ('Move disk 1 from peg ', FromPeg,
             ' to peg ', ToPeg)
  else
    begin {recursive step}
      Tower (FromPeg, AuxPeg, ToPeg, N-1);
      WriteLn ('Move disk ', N :1, ' from peg ', FromPeg,
               ' to peg ', ToPeg);
      Tower (AuxPeg, ToPeg, FromPeg, N-1)
    end {recursive step}
end; {Tower}
```

solves a simpler three-disk problem: to move three disks from peg A to peg C. Its execution is traced in Fig. 14.25; the output generated is shown in Fig. 14.26. Verify for yourself that this list of steps does solve the three-disk problem.

Comparison of Iterative and Recursive Procedures

It is interesting to consider that procedure Tower in Fig. 14.24 will solve the Towers of Hanoi problem for any number of disks. The three-disk problem results in a total of 7 calls to procedure Tower and is solved by 7 disk moves. The five-disk problem would result in a total of 31 calls to procedure Tower and is solved in 31 moves. In general, the number of moves required to solve the N-disk problem is $2^N - 1$. Because each procedure call requires the allocation and initialization of a local data area in memory, computer time increases exponentially with problem size. For this reason, be careful about running the program with a value of N larger than 10.

The dramatic increase in processing time for larger towers is a function of the problem, not of recursion. In general, however, if there are recursive and iterative solutions to the same problem, the recursive solution requires more time and space because of the extra procedure calls.

Figure 14.25
Trace of Tower ('A', 'C', 'B', 3)

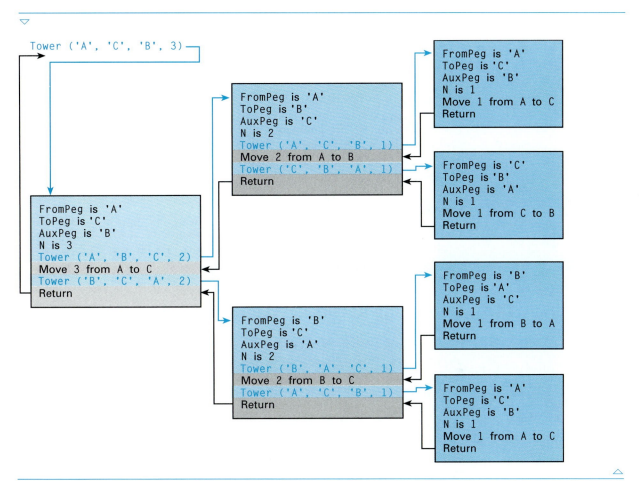

Figure 14.26
Output Generated by
Tower ('A', 'C', 'B', 3)

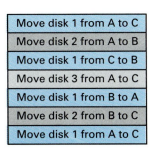

Although recursion was not really needed to solve the simpler problems in this chapter, it was extremely useful in formulating an algorithm for the Towers of Hanoi. For certain problems, recursion leads naturally to solutions that are much easier to read and understand than their iterative counterparts. In those cases, the benefits gained from increased clarity far outweigh the extra cost in time and memory of running a recursive program.

Exercises for Section 14.6   *Self-Check*

1. What problems are generated when you attempt to solve the problem "Move three disks from peg B to peg A"? When you attempt to solve the problem "Move three disks from peg A to peg C"?
2. How many moves are needed to solve the six-disk problem?

Programming

1. Write a main program that reads in a data value for N (the number of disks) and calls procedure Tower to move N disks from A to B.

14.7   Debugging Recursive Algorithms

Use the Turbo Pascal debugger as an aid in debugging a recursive function or procedure. If you place a value parameter in the Watch window, you can see how that parameter's value changes during successive calls to the recursive subprogram. If your subprogram's local variables are in a Watch window, you can observe their values as you single-step through the subprogram using the F7 function key.

The Call Stack window can help trace the execution of a recursive module. Each time a procedure or function is called, the Turbo Pascal debugger remembers the call by placing a record on the Call Stack. This record contains the subprogram name along with the values of the actual parameters used in the subprogram call. When the procedure or function is exited, its record is removed from the Call Stack. Whenever execution pauses during a debugging session, you can view the contents of the Call Stack by pressing Ctrl-F3. This opens a window similar to that shown in Fig. 14.27.

The Call Stack window contains a list of the calls to the currently active modules. If this list is too long to fit on the screen, use the mouse or the F6 key to move to the Call Stack window and then use the mouse or the arrow keys to scroll through the list of calls.

You also can determine the statement currently executing in any of the active calls. Normally, the most recent call is highlighted in the Call Stack window, and its currently executing statement is highlighted in the Edit window.

Figure 14.27
Call Stack Window

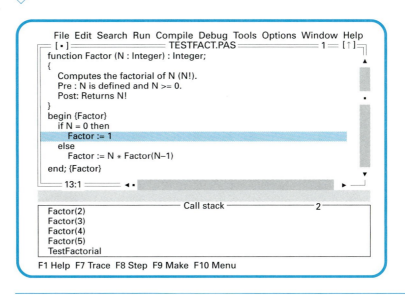

If you select another call in the Call Stack window (using the arrow keys or the mouse), the Call Stack window will disappear and the Edit window cursor will be positioned at the statement currently executing in that call. You can bring back the Call Stack window by pressing Ctrl-F3 again.

14.8 Common Programming Errors

The most common problem with a recursive function or procedure is that it may not terminate properly. For example, if the terminating condition is not correct or is incomplete, the procedure may call itself indefinitely or until all available memory is used up. Normally, a `stack overflow` run-time error indicates that a recursive procedure is not terminating. Make sure you identify all stopping cases and provide a terminating condition for each one. Also be sure that each recursive step leads to a situation that is closer to a stopping case and that repeated recursive calls eventually lead to stopping cases only.

Large arrays or other data structures used as value parameters can quickly consume all available memory. Unless absolutely essential for data protection, arrays should be passed as variable parameters. Any expression such as `N-1` must be passed as a value parameter.

CHAPTER REVIEW

1. A recursive module or function is one that calls itself. You can use recursion to solve problems by splitting them into smaller versions of themselves.
2. Each recursive module has one or more stopping cases and recursive steps. The stopping cases can be solved directly; the recursive steps lead to recursive calls of the module.
3. Recursive modules can be used with parameters that are simple types or structured types. Recursive functions can implement mathematical operations that are defined by recursive definitions.
4. Binary search is a recursive search procedure that can search a large array in $O(\log N)$ time.

Quick-Check Exercises

1. How are stacks used in recursion?
2. Can the stopping case also have a recursive call in it?
3. Which control statement is always in a recursive procedure or function?
4. What are the two uses of the function name in a recursive function?
5. What is the relation between a terminating condition and a stopping case?
6. Returning from a series of recursive calls is called _____ the recursion.
7. What is the problem with value array parameters in recursion?
8. In a recursive problem involving N items, why must N be a value parameter?
9. What causes a stack overflow error?
10. What can you say about a recursive algorithm that has the following form?

   if *condition* then
      Perform recursive step.

Answers to Quick-Check Exercises

1. The stack is used to hold all parameter and local variable values and the return point for each execution of a recursive module.
2. No, if it did, recursion would continue.
3. The if statement
4. To assign a value to the function and to call it recursively
5. A recursive module reaches a stopping case when a terminating condition is true.
6. Unwinding
7. A copy of the array must be pushed onto the stack each time a call occurs. All available stack memory could be exhausted.
8. If N was a variable parameter, it would not be possible to use the expression N-1 as an actual parameter in a recursive call.
9. Too many recursive calls—all stack memory is allocated.
10. Nothing is done when the stopping case is reached.

Review Questions

1. Differentiate between a recursive step and a stopping case in a recursive algorithm.
2. Discuss the time and space efficiency of recursive procedures versus iterative procedures.
3. What basic characteristics must a problem have for a recursive solution to be applicable?
4.` Write a recursive procedure that prints the accumulating sum of ordinal values corresponding to each character in a string. For example, if the string value is 'a boy', the first value printed would be the ordinal number of a, then the sum of ordinals for a and the space character, then the sum of ordinals for a, space, b, and so on.
5. Differentiate between the use of value and variable parameters in a recursive procedure. When would each be applicable?
6. Convert the following program from an iterative process to a recursive function that calculates an approximate value for *e*, the base of the natural logarithms, by summing the series

    $$1+1/1! + 1/2! + \ldots + 1/N!$$

    until additional terms do not affect the approximation:

```
program ELog;

  var
    ENL, Delta, Fact : Real;
    N : Integer;

begin {ELog}
  ENL := 1.0;
  N := 1;
  Fact := 1.0;
  Delta := 1.0;
  repeat
    ENL := ENL + Delta;
    N := N + 1;
    Fact := Fact * N;
    Delta := 1.0 / Fact
  until ENL = (ENL + Delta);
  Write ('The value of e is ', E :18:15)
end. {ELog}
```

Programming Projects

1. The expression for computing $c(n, r)$, the number of combinations of n items taken r at a time, is

    $$c(n, r) = n!/r!(n - r)!$$

    Write and test a function for computing $c(n, r)$, given that $n!$ is the factorial of n.

2. A palindrome is a word that is spelled exactly the same when the letters are reversed, for example, level, deed, and mom. Write a recursive function that returns the Boolean value True if a word passed as a parameter is a palindrome.

3. Write a recursive procedure that lists all subsets of pairs of letters for a given set of letters, for example,

    ['A','C','F','G'] →['A','C'], ['A','E'], ['A','G'],
                       ['C','E'], ['C','G'], ['E','G']

4. Write a procedure that accepts an 8 × 8 array of characters that represents a maze. Each position can contain either an 'X' or a blank. Starting at position [1,1], list any path through the maze to get to location [8,8]. Only horizontal and vertical moves are allowed (no diagonal moves). Make sure your algorithm avoids retracing previously tried paths. If no path exists, write a message indicating this condition.

    Moves can be made only to locations that contain a blank. If an 'X' is encountered, that path is blocked and another must be chosen. Use recursion.

5. Programming Project 6 in Chapter 7 described the bisection method, which finds an approximate root for the equation $f(X) = 0$ on the interval XLeft to XRight, inclusive (assuming the function is continuous on this interval). The interval end points (XLeft and XRight) and the tolerance for the approximation (Epsilon) are input by the user.

    One stopping criterion for the bisection method is the identification of an interval [XLeft,XRight] that is less than Epsilon in length over which $f(X)$ changes sign (from positive to negative or vice versa). The midpoint [XMid = (XLeft + XRight)/2.0)] of the interval will be an approximation to the root of the equation when $f(XMid)$ is very close to zero. Of course, if you find a value of XMid such that $f(XMid) = 0$, you have found a very good approximation of the root, and the algorithm should also stop.

    To perform the recursive step, replace either XLeft or XRight with XMid, depending on which one has the same sign as XMid. Write a program that uses the bisection method to determine an approximation to the equation

    $5x^3 - 2x^3 + 3 = 0$

    over the interval [-1,1] using Epsilon = 0.0001.

6. Write a program that finds the size of a blob in a rectangular grid where a blob is a connected group of filled cells. Represent the grid as an 8 × 8 array. Read the data for the array, designating each cell as filled or empty. Also enter the starting cell for the blob you are investigating. If the starting cell is not in the grid or the starting cell is empty, the blob has a size of 0. Otherwise, the size of a blob is determined by moving out from the start cell to its eight neighbors (assuming the cell is not on a grid boundary) and determining the size of the blob each neighbor is part of. Add 1 to this sum to account for the start cell. Make sure you reset a cell to empty when it is counted as part of a blob.

7. Write a program that, given a list of up to 10 integer numbers and a sum, will find a subset of the numbers whose total is that sum if one exists or indicate that none exists otherwise. For example, for the list 5, 13, 23, 9, 3, 3 and sum = 28, your program should find 13, 9, 3, 3.

8. MergeSort is an $O(N \times \log N)$ sorting technique with the following recursive algorithm:

    if the array to sort has more than 1-element then
      begin
        MergeSort the left-half of the array.
        MergeSort the right-half of the array.
        Merge the two sorted subarrays to form the sorted array.
      end

    For example: to MergeSort the array 10, 20, 15, 6, 5, 40, follow these steps:

    MergeSort the subarray 10, 20, 15 giving 10, 15, 20.

    MergeSort the subarray 6, 5, 40 giving 5, 6, 40.

    Merge the two sorted subarrays giving 5, 6, 10, 15, 20, 40.

    Each call to MergeSort above will generate two more recursive calls (one for a 1-element array and one for a 2-element array). MergeSort for a 1-element array is a stopping case. See Section 16.3 for a discussion of merging.

CHAPTER FIFTEEN

Sets and Strings

15.1 Set Data Type
15.2 Set Operators
15.3 Variable-Length Strings
15.4 String Processing Illustrated
      Case Study: Text Editor
15.5 Common Programming Errors
      Chapter Review

This chapter introduces a new user-defined, structured data type: sets. Sets are useful for determining whether a variable has a value that is included in a list of values. In this chapter, you will learn what sets are, which operators are used with sets, and how to use them in programs.

The string data type is the second topic covered in this chapter. Strings are used in programs that process textual data (e.g., word processors, text editors, and business data-processing applications). Turbo Pascal provides a dynamic string data type, along with several functions and procedures that allow us to work with string variables. In Section 10.7, we introduced the Turbo Pascal string data type and compared it to an array of characters. In this chapter, we will complete our discussion of the Turbo Pascal string data type and operators for string variables.

15.1 Set Data Type

set
an unordered list of elements that are values of the same ordinal type

Sets are structured variables that contain lists of integers, characters, or enumerated type values. A set is like an array in that it can house a collection of simple elements. Unlike an array, however, the elements of a set are not ordered.

You probably have studied sets in a mathematics course. In mathematics, a set is represented by a list of **set elements,** or **set members,** enclosed in curly braces. For example, the set {1, 3, 5, 7, 9} is the set of odd integers from 1 through 9. In Pascal, set elements are enclosed in square brackets so the preceding set is written as [1, 3, 5, 7, 9]. Because the elements of a set are not ordered, the set [9, 5, 7, 1, 3] is equivalent to [1, 3, 5, 7, 9].

set element (set member)
a value in a set

Declaring Sets

You declare a set or set variable just as you declare other structured types. First declare a set data type and then declare a variable of that type.

EXAMPLE 15.1 ▼

The declarations

```
type
   DigitSet = set of 0..9;  {set type of integer elements}

var
   Odds, Evens, Middle, Mixed : DigitSet;        {4 sets}
```

declare a set type DigitSet and four set variables: Odds, Evens, Middle, and Mixed. Each set variable of type DigitSet can contain between zero and 10 elements chosen from the integers in the subrange 0..9. Although memory space is allocated for four sets, their contents are undefined. To work with a set, you must define it using a set assignment, as shown shortly. ▲

SYNTAX DISPLAY

Set Type Declaration

Form: type
                 set type = set of *base type*;

Example: `type`
        `LetterSet = set of 'A'..'Z';`

Interpretation: The identifier *set type* is defined over the values specified in *base type*. A variable declared to be of type *set type* is a set whose elements are chosen from the values in *base type*. The *base type* must be an ordinal type.

Notes: Most implementations limit the number of values in the *base type* of a set. Turbo Pascal limits this number to the number of values in the data type `Char` (256), allowing you to declare `set of Char` as a set type. Given this limitation, you cannot use the data type `Integer` as a *base type,* but you can use a subrange of type `Integer` with up to 256 values.

Set Assignment and Set Literals

The set assignment statement places values in a set. The statements

```
Odds := [1, 3, 5, 7, 9];
Evens := [0, 2, 4, 6, 8]
```

set literal
a list of values enclosed in brackets

assign values to two of the set variables declared in Example 15.1. Each assignment statement assigns a set literal to a set variable, where a **set literal** is a list of values from the set base type enclosed in brackets. After these assignments, the set `Odds` contains the set of odd digits in the subrange 0 through 9, and the set `Evens` contains the set of even digits in the same range. We could use these two sets to determine whether a variable contained an odd or an even number.

The set literal `['0'..'9','+','-','E','.']` is the set of characters that can appear in a real number. This set contains 14 elements. It is more convenient to use the *subrange notation* `'0'..'9'` to denote the 10 digit characters rather than list each digit character separately.

SYNTAX DISPLAY

Set Literal

Form: [*list-of-elements*]
Example: `['+', '-', '*', '/', '<', '>', '=']`
Interpretation: A set is defined whose elements are the *list-of-elements* enclosed in brackets. The elements of a set must belong to the same ordinal type or to compatible ordinal types (defined in Section 7.6). Commas separate elements in the *list-of-elements*. A group of consecutive elements may be specified with subrange notation (i.e., *minvalue .. maxvalue,* where *minvalue* and *maxvalue* are type-compatible expressions and *minvalue* is considered less than or equal to *maxvalue*).
Note: In Turbo Pascal `Ord(`*minvalue*`)` must be ≥ 0 and `Ord(`*maxvalue*`)` must be ≤ 255.

SYNTAX DISPLAY

Set Assignment

Form: *set var* := *set expression*
Example: Uppercase := ['A'..'Z'] {set of uppercase letters}
Interpretation: The variable, *set var,* is defined as the set whose elements are determined by *set expression*. The *set expression* may be a set literal or another set variable. Alternatively, a *set expression* may specify the manipulation of two or more sets using the set operators. The base type of *set var* and *set expression* must be type compatible, and all the elements in *set expression* must be included in the base type of *set var.*

Empty Set and Universal Set

Two special set literals are associated with each set type: the empty set and the universal set. The **empty set** has zero elements and is denoted by a pair of brackets, []. To create an empty set, you must use an assignment such as

Middle := []

empty set
a set having zero elements denoted by []

An empty set can be distinguished from an **undefined set,** where the set is declared but its elements are unknown.

undefined set
a set variable that is declared but is not assigned any values
universal set
a set containing all possible values for a set

A **universal set** contains all the values in the base type for a particular set type. For a set of type Digits (Example 15.1), the base type is the subrange 0..9 so a universal set would be denoted as [0..9]. The assignment

Mixed := [0..9]

defines set variable Mixed as a universal set. We often initialize a set variable to the empty set or universal set before using it.

Sets with Enumerated Type Values

You also can define sets with values chosen from your own enumerated data type.

EXAMPLE 15.2 ▼

In the following declarations, we declare and use an enumerated type (Cars) as the base type for a set type (CarSet). Next, we declare three set variables of type CarSet:

```
type
   Cars = (Dodge, Ford, Lincoln, Cadillac, Fiesta, Pontiac,
           Corvette, Buick, Chevrolet, Mercury, Mustang);
   CarSet = set of Cars;

var
   Avis, Hertz, Merger : CarSet;
```

The assignments

```
Avis   := [Dodge, Lincoln, Fiesta];
Hertz  := [Dodge..Cadillac, Mercury];
Merger := [Dodge..Mustang]
```

define the set Avis consisting of the three elements listed, the set Hertz consists of five elements (what are they?), and the set Merger, which is the universal set for type CarSet.

You may place a set variable on the right of the assignment statement, provided both set variables have compatible base types. The next assignment changes the value of set Merger:

```
Merger := Hertz   ▲
```

Exercises for Section 15.1 ***Self-Check***

1. Which of the following sets are valid? Which are invalid? What are the elements of the valid sets?

   a. `[1, 3, 1..5]`   d. `['1', '3', 'A'..'C']`
   b. `['1', '3', '1'..'5']` e. `[1, 10, 500..501]`
   c. `[1, 3, '1'..'5']`

2. Write a set that consists of the special characters used in Pascal for punctuation or as operator symbols.

15.2 Set Operators

Several operations may be performed on sets. In this section, we describe one new operator, in, and show how to use other familiar operators with sets.

Testing for Set Membership

You use a search module (see Figs. 10.18 and 14.14) to determine whether a particular value is in an array and, if so, its location. Pascal provides a set membership operator, in, to determine whether a particular value is a set element. An expression with operator in returns a Boolean value.

You can use the in operator with a set instead of a compound condition. For example, you can write the condition

```
(Ch = '.') or (Ch = '?') or (Ch = ';') or (Ch = '!')
```

more succinctly as

```
Ch in ['.', '?', ';', '!']
```

Both conditions are true if Ch is one of the characters in the set.

EXAMPLE 15.3 ▼

Some programs require that we determine whether a character variable contains a vowel, a lowercase letter, or an uppercase letter. We can use the three sets defined next to help with this determination:

```
type
  CharSet = set of Char;        {set type of Char elements}
var
  Vowels, Uppercase, Lowercase : CharSet;        {3 sets}
  NextChar : Char;                      {a data character}
begin
  Vowels := ['A','a', 'E','e', 'I','i', 'O','o', 'U','u'];
  Uppercase := ['A'..'Z'];
  Lowercase := ['a'..'z']
```

The following loop repeats until NextChar contains a letter. The if statement displays a message about NextChar based on its contents.

```
repeat
  Write ('Enter a letter> ');
  ReadLn (NextChar);

  {Display message about NextChar.}
  if NextChar in Vowels then
    WriteLn (NextChar, ' is a vowel')
  else if NextChar in Uppercase then
    WriteLn (NextChar, ' is an uppercase consonant')
  else if NextChar in Lowercase then
    WriteLn (NextChar, ' is a lowercase consonant')
  else
    WriteLn (NextChar, ' is not a letter')
until NextChar in ['A'..'Z', 'a'..'z']
```

Be careful when complementing an expression containing the set membership operator. The complement of the until condition is

```
not (NextChar in ['A'..'Z', 'a'..'z'])      {not a letter}
```

A common error is to write this expression as

```
NextChar not in ['A'..'Z', 'a'..'z']  {invalid expression}
```    ▲

SYNTAX DISPLAY

Set Membership Operator in

Form: *element* in [*list-of-elements*]
Example: NextCh in ['+','-','*','/','<','>','=']
Interpretation: The set membership operator in describes a condition that evaluates to True when *element* is included in *list-of-elements*; otherwise, the condition evaluates to False. The data type of *element* must be compat-

ible with the set elements. Operator `in` has the same precedence as the relational operators.

Set Union, Intersection, and Difference

If you have studied sets in mathematics, you know that three operations are commonly performed on sets: union, intersection, and difference. These operations manipulate two sets to form a third set. In Pascal we specify these operations using the operators + (set union), * (set intersection), and - (set difference).

The *union* of two sets (set operator +) is the set of elements that are contained in either or both sets:

```
[1,3,4] + [1,2,4] is [1,2,3,4]
[1,3] + [2,4] is [1,2,3,4]
['A','C','F'] + ['B','C','D','F'] is ['A','B','C','D','F']
['A','C','F'] + ['A','C','D','F'] is ['A','C','D','F']
```

The *intersection* of two sets (set operator *) is the set of elements that are common to both sets:

```
[1,3,4] * [1,2,4] is [1,4]
[1,3] * [2,4] is []
['A','C','F'] * ['B','C','D','F'] is ['C','F']
['A','C','F'] * ['A','C','D','F'] is ['A','C','F']
```

The *difference* of set A and set B (set operator -) is the set of elements that are in set A but not in set B:

```
[1,3,4] - [1,2,4] is [3]
[1,3] - [2,4] is [1,3]
['A','C','F'] - ['B','C','D','F'] is ['A']
['A','C','F'] - ['A','C','D','F'] is []
['A','C','D','F'] - ['A','C','F'] is ['D']
```

commutative operator

an operator that produces the same result regardless of the order of its operands

The set operator - is not **commutative.** This means that A - B and B - A can have different values. The set operators + and *, however, are commutative.

In Pascal expressions, the operators +, *, and - specify arithmetic operations when their operands are type `Real` or `Integer`, and they specify set operations when their operands are sets. When an operator has more than one meaning, this condition is called **operator overloading.** The precedence rules for the operators +, *, and - are the same regardless of their use (see Table 4.5). When in doubt, use parentheses to specify the intended order of evaluation.

operator overloading

giving an operator more than one meaning

unit set

a set containing a single element enclosed in brackets

Often a new element must be inserted into an existing set. Such an insertion is achieved by forming the union of the existing set and a **unit set,** which contains only the new element. The set [2], which follows, is a unit set:

```
[1,3,4,5] + [2] is [1,2,3,4,5]
```

Avoid the common error of omitting the brackets around a unit set. For example, the expressions

```
[1,3,4,5] + 2        {2nd operand is not a set}
Avis + Cadillac      {2nd operand is not a set}
```

are invalid because one operand is a set and the other is a constant (see Example 15.2). Likewise, the expression

```
[Avis] + [Cadillac]  {1st operand is not a set}
```

is invalid; the brackets around Avis are not needed because Avis is a set.

Set Relational Operators

The relational operators =, <>, <=, and >= compare two sets. The two sets being compared must have the same base type. The result of a comparison is a Boolean value.

The operators = and <> test whether two sets contain the same elements:

```
[1,3] = [1,3] is True      [1,3] <> [1,3] is False
[1,3] = [2,4] is False     [1,3] <> [2,4] is True
[1,3] = [3,1] is True      [1,3] <> [3,1] is False
  [] = [1] is False           [] <> [1] is True
```

As indicated by the next-to-last line, the order in which the elements of a set are listed is not important ([1,3] and [3,1] denote the same set). However, we normally list the elements of a set in increasing ordinal sequence.

The relational operators <= and >= determine subset and superset relationships:

▶ Set A is a *subset* of set B (A <= B) if every element of A is also an element of B:

```
[1,3] <= [1,2,3,4] is True
[1,3] <= [1,3] is True
[1,2,3,4] <= [1,3] is False
[1,3] <= [] is False
[] <= [1,3] is True
```

The empty set, [], is a subset of every set.

▶ Set A is a *superset* of set B (A >= B) if every element of B is also an element of A:

```
[1,3] >= [1,2,3,4] is False
[1,3] >= [1,3] is True
[1,2,3,4] >= [1,3] is True
[1,3] >= [] is True
[] >= [1,3] is False
```

The set operators are summarized in Table 15.1.

Table 15.1
Set Operators

Operator	Meaning	Example
+	Set union	`['A'] + ['B'] is ['A', 'B']`
−	Set difference	`['A', 'B'] - ['A'] is ['B']`
*	Set intersection	`['A', 'B'] * ['A'] is ['A']`
=	Set equality	`['A', 'B'] = ['B', 'A'] is True`
<>	Set inequality	`['A', 'B'] <> ['A'] is True`
<=	Subset	`['A', 'B'] <= ['A'] is False`
>=	Superset	`['A', 'B'] >= ['B'] is True`

Reading and Writing Sets

Like most other data structures, a set cannot be a parameter of the standard Read or Write procedures. Data items to be stored in a set must be read individually and inserted in an initially empty set using the set union operator.

EXAMPLE 15.4: Reading Sets ▼

Procedure ReadSet in Fig. 15.1 reads a sentence terminated by . and inserts the uppercase form of each letter in the set represented by parameter Letters (set type CharSet). The statement

```
Letters := [];                    {Initialize Letters.}
```

initializes set Letters to the empty set, and the if statement

```
if NextChar in ['A'..'Z'] then
  Letters := Letters + [NextChar];  {Insert a letter.}
```

inserts each new uppercase letter in set Letters.   ▲

Figure 15.1
Procedure ReadSet

```
procedure ReadSet (var Letters {output} : CharSet);
{
  Reads a sentence terminated by a period and
  stores the uppercase form of each letter in Letters.
  Pre : None.
  Post: Returns through Letters all the letters read
        before the period.
}
  const
    Sentinel = '.';                    {sentinel character}
```

```
    var
      NextChar : Char;                        {next input character}

begin  {ReadSet}
  Letters := [];                             {Initialize Letters.}
  WriteLn ('Enter a sentence ending with symbol ', Sentinel);
  Read (NextChar);                           {Read first character.}
  while NextChar <> Sentinel do
    {invariant:
       No prior value of NextChar is the sentinel and
       Letters contains each uppercase letter read so far.
    }
    begin
      NextChar := UpCase(NextChar);   {Convert to uppercase.}
      if NextChar in ['A'..'Z'] then
        Letters := Letters + [NextChar];    {Insert a letter.}
      Read (NextChar)                        {Read next character.}
    end  {while}

  {assert: Last character read was the sentinel.}
end; {ReadSet}
```

EXAMPLE 15.5: Writing Sets ▼

To print a set, you must test whether every value in the base type is a set element. Only values that are set elements should be printed. Procedure PrintSet in Fig. 15.2 prints the uppercase letters in the set represented by its parameter Letters. If you call PrintSet with ['A', 'C', 'Z'] as its parameter, PrintSet displays {A, C, Z, }. ▲

```
procedure PrintSet (Letters {input} : CharSet);
{
  Prints the uppercase letters in set Letters.
  Pre : Letters is defined.
  Post: Each uppercase letter in Letters is displayed.
}
  var
    NextLetter : Char;              {loop-control variable}

begin {PrintSet}
  Write ('{');
  for NextLetter := 'A' to 'Z' do
    if NextLetter in Letters then
      Write (NextLetter, ', ');                {Print a set member.}
  WriteLn ('}')
end; {PrintSet}
```

1. Given that A is the set [1,3,5,7], B is the set [2,4,6], and C is the set [1,2,3], evaluate the following set expressions.
    a. A + (B - C)   g. C + (A - C)
    b. A + (B * C)   h. C - (A - B)
    c. A + B + C   i. (C - A) - B
    d. (C - A) <= B   j. A - C - [5,7] = []
    e. [] <= A * B * C   k. 2 in A
    f. A + B <> [1..7]   l. 2 in A + B
2. Given two sets A and B, write a Boolean expression to determine whether A is a proper subset of B. A is a proper subset of B if every element of A is in B and one element in B is not in A.

Programming

1. Modify PrintSet to print a set of type DigitSet.

15.3   Variable-Length Strings

The rest of this chapter describes the processing of character strings, used to store textual data for many applications. The text for this book, for example, was written on a word processor and its pages were composed using a desktop publishing system and set into type using a computerized typesetting machine. Programs that work with strings also generate "personalized" junk mail and create mailing labels, and language scholars use computers to analyze great works of literature.

   If you have ever used a word processor, you are familiar with the kinds of operations performed on string data. For example, we frequently want to insert one or more characters into an existing string, delete a portion of a string, overwrite or replace one substring of a string with another, search for a target substring, or join two strings together to form a longer string. In this section, we learn how to perform these operations using Turbo Pascal's built-in procedures and functions (not part of standard Pascal).

The Null String

The length of a string variable is dynamic and is determined by the data stored in it. This length cannot exceed the declared maximum for that variable. Sometimes we need to initialize a string variable to a string of zero characters, or a **null string.** If Name is a string variable, the statements

null string
a string with zero characters

```
Name := '';
WriteLn ('Length is ', Length(Name) :1)
```

assign the null string to `Name` and call function `Length` to display the message

`Length is 0`

Converting a String to a Number

Turbo Pascal has a built-in procedure, `Val`, that converts a string to a number. The string involved in the conversion must be a numeric string. A **numeric string** is one that satisfies the syntax requirements for a valid Pascal number (for example, `'1234'`, `'0.12E5'`).

numeric string

a string whose contents are a number

Assuming that `IntNum` and `Error` are type `Integer`, the procedure call statement

`Val ('1234', IntNum, Error);`

causes the integer value `1234` to be stored in `IntNum` and `0` in `Error`. Procedure `Val` returns an error indication through its third parameter (variable `Error`). `Val` returns a value of `0` when there is no error.

The procedure call statement

`Val ('12#34%', IntNum, Error);`

returns the value `3` to `Error`, indicating that the character in position 3 is not numeric. When an error occurs, the conversion cannot be performed, so the value of `IntNum` is undefined.

Table 15.2 lists the results of several calls to `Val`, assuming that `RealNum` is type `Real` and `IntNum` and `Error` are type `Integer`. The type of the second parameter determines whether an `Integer` or a `Real` value will be returned. As shown in the last two lines, blanks cannot appear in the numeric string being converted.

Table 15.2

Using the Val Procedure

Call to `Val`	**Values Returned**
`Val ('-3507', IntNum, Error)`	`IntNum` is `-3507`, `Error` is `0`.
`Val ('-3507', RealNum, Error)`	`RealNum` is `-3507.0`, `Error` is `0`.
`Val ('1.23E3', RealNum, Error)`	`RealNum` is `1230.0`, `Error` is `0`.
`Val ('1.23E3', IntNum, Error)`	`IntNum` is undefined, `Error` is `2`.
`Val ('1.23E 3', RealNum, Error)`	`RealNum` is undefined, `Error` is `6`.
`Val (' 1.2E3', RealNum, Error)`	`RealNum` is undefined, `Error` is `1`.

EXAMPLE 15.6 ▼

The program fragment

```
repeat
  Write ('Enter an integer value> ');
  ReadLn (NumStr);
  Val (NumStr, IntNum, Error)
until Error = 0;
```

stores an integer value in `IntNum`. If a valid numeric string is read into `Num-Str` (a string variable), procedure `Val` returns its numeric value in `IntNum` (type `Integer`). If an invalid numeric string is read, procedure `Val` returns a nonzero value in `Error` (type `Integer`), and the loop is repeated.

Such code validates numeric input to a program. If the program user entered an incorrect integer, this loop would prevent an `Invalid numeric format` error. If the loop weren't used, the program would abort. ▲

SYNTAX DISPLAY

Val Procedure

Form: `Val` (*numeric string, number, error*)

Example: `Val` ('-5', N, E)

Interpretation: A *numeric string* is converted to a numeric value, which is returned in *number*. The data type of the number passed into *numeric string* must match the data type (`Real` or `Integer`) of *number*. The value returned for *error* indicates the position of the first invalid character (0 if *numeric string* satisfies the syntax for a number). The parameter *error* must be type `Integer`.

Notes: If range checking is enabled using {$R+}, out-of-range values will generate a run-time error. If range checking is disabled (default), the value returned in *number* may contain an incorrect result even though the value returned in *error* is 0.

Converting a Number to a String

The `Str` procedure performs the inverse of the operation performed by `Val`: It converts a number to a numeric string. The procedure call statement

```
Str (345 :5, NumStr);
```

stores the string ' 345' in `NumStr` (a string variable), where the format specification :5 causes the result string to have a field width of 5. The procedure call statement

```
Str (345.126 :7:2, NumStr);
```

causes the string ' 345.12' to be stored in `NumStr`. The procedure call statement

```
Str (345.126 :3:1, NumStr)
```

causes the string '345.1' to be stored in `NumStr`.

SYNTAX DISPLAY

Str Procedure

Form: Str (*number* : *format*, *numeric string*)
Example: Str (N :1, S)
Interpretation: The value passed to *number* is converted to a *numeric string.* The *format* specification determines the form and the length of *numeric string,* as it would if used with the Write procedure.

Substrings and the Copy Function

substring
a segment of a string

Sometimes we need to extract segments, or **substrings,** of a larger character string. For example, we might want to examine the three components (month, day, year) of the string 'Jun 25, 1994'. Function Copy can be used to do this, as shown next.

EXAMPLE 15.7 ▼

Assume that a date string (stored in Date) always has the form 'MMM DD, YYYY' where the characters represented by MMM are the month name (positions 1–3), DD the day of the month (positions 5 and 6), and YYYY the year (positions 9–12). Assuming Date, Month, Day, and Year are variable-length strings, the statement

```
Month := Copy(Date, 1, 3);
```

assigns to Month the substring of Date starting at position 1 and consisting of the first three characters. The statement

```
Day := Copy(Date, 5, 2);
```

assigns to Day the two characters that represent the day of the month (positions 5 and 6). Finally, the statement

```
Year := Copy(Date, 9, 4);
```

assigns to Year the four characters that represent the year (positions 9–12). If the contents of Date are 'Jun 25, 1994', the contents of the variable length strings Month, Day, and Year become 'Jun', '25', and '1994', respectively. ▲

EXAMPLE 15.8 ▼

Procedure PrintWords in Fig. 15.3 displays each word found in its parameter Sentence on a separate line. It assumes that there is always a single blank character between words.

Figure 15.3
Procedure PrintWords

```
procedure PrintWords (Sentence {input} : string);
{
  Displays each word of a sentence on a separate line.
  Pre : Variable-length string Sentence is defined.
  Post: Each word in Sentence is displayed on a separate
        line.
}
  const
    WordSeparator = ' ';

  var
    Word : string;              {each word}
    SentLen,                    {length of Sentence}
    First,                      {first character in each word}
    Next : Integer;             {position of next character}

begin {PrintWords}
  {Display each word of Sentence on a separate line.}
  First := 1;                {First word starts at position 1.}
  SentLen := Length(Sentence);
  for Next := 1 to SentLen do
    begin
      if Sentence[Next] = WordSeparator then
        begin
          {Get word.}
          Word := Copy(Sentence, First, Next-First);
          WriteLn (Word);
          First := Next + 1
        end {if}
    end; {for}

  {Display last word.}
  Word := Copy(Sentence, First, SentLen-First+1);
  WriteLn (Word)
end; {PrintWords}
```

The variable First always points to the start of the current word and is initialized to 1. During each execution of the for loop, the Boolean expression

```
Sentence[Next] = WordSeparator
```

tests whether the next character is a blank. If so, the substring occupying positions First through Next-1 in Sentence is copied to Word by the statement

```
Word := Copy(Sentence, First, Next-First);
```

The values of `First` and `Next` are shown in the following display just before the fourth word of a string stored in `Sentence` is displayed. The value of `Next-First` is 5, so the substring `short` is shown.

```
This is a short example
          ↑     ↑
        First   Next
```

11		16

After each word is printed, `First` is reset to `Next + 1`, the position of the first character of the next word. After loop exit, the statement

```
Word := Copy(Sentence, First, SentLen-First+1);
```

stores the last word of `Sentence` in `Word`. For this sentence, the value of `First` is 17 and the value of the third parameter is 7 (`23 - 17 + 1`), so the last word displayed is `example`. ▲

SYNTAX DISPLAY

Copy Function

Form: Copy (*source, index, size*)

Example: Copy ('Mr. John Doe', 5, 4)

Interpretation: The function returns the substring of *source* at position *index* and consisting of *size* characters. The parameter *source* must be a string variable or value; *index* and *size* must be type `Integer`.

Notes: If *index* is larger than the length of *source,* an empty string is returned. If *size* specifies more characters than remain following position *index,* only the remainder of the string is returned.

Concatenating Strings

concatenating strings
joining strings together to form a new string

The `Concat` function **concatenates,** or joins, strings to form a new string.

EXAMPLE 15.9 ▼

The following statements concatenate their string arguments, and store the string result in `Name`. For the string contents (the symbol □ denotes a blank)

```
Title       First       Last
```

Ms.□		Bo□		Peep

the statement

```
Name := Concat(Title, Last);
```

stores the string `'Ms. Peep'` in `Name`. The statement

```
Name := Concat(Title, First, Last);
```

stores the string 'Ms. Bo Peep' in Name. The statement

```
Name := Concat(Last, ',', First, Title);
```

stores the string 'Peep, Bo Ms. ' in Name.

The operator + also can be used to concatenate strings. The preceding assignment statement can also be written as

```
Name := Last + ',' + First + Title;
```

When the operands are strings, Turbo Pascal interprets the operator + as "concatenate" instead of "add" or "union." ▲

EXAMPLE 15.10: String Concatenation in Graphics Mode ▼

String concatenation is used when writing text in graphics mode. The graphics output procedure OutTextXY draws the characters in its string argument on the screen. The statements

```
Str (Check, NumStr :4:2);      {Convert Check to a string.}
OutTextXY (X, Y, 'The check amount is $' + NumStr)
```

display at pixel (X, Y) the string formed by concatenating the string literal 'The check amount is $' with NumStr, the string equivalent of the value of Check. ▲

EXAMPLE 15.11 ▼

Function Reverse in Fig. 15.4 uses the Concat function to reverse the string passed to its argument string InString. After being initialized to the null string, TempString stores the string being formed. Characters are taken one at a time from InString, starting with the last character, and joined to the end of TempString. The first character of InString is the last character joined to TempString. Table 15.3 traces the execution of this function when InString is 'Turbo'. ▲

Table 15.3
Trace of for Loop When
InString Is 'Turbo'

I	InString[I]	TempString
5	'o'	'o'
4	'b'	'ob'
3	'r'	'obr'
2	'u'	'obru'
1	'T'	'obruT'

Figure 15.4
Function for Reversing
a String

```
function Reverse (InString : string) : string;
{Reverses the string stored in InString}

  var
    I               : Integer;         {loop-control variable}
    TempString  : string;              {temporary reversed string}

begin {Reverse}
  TempString := '';                    {Initialize TempString.}

  for I := Length(InString) downto 1 do
    TempString := Concat(TempString, InString[I]);

  Reverse := TempString              {Define result.}
end; {Reverse}
```

SYNTAX DISPLAY

Concat Function

Form: Concat(*string list*)
Example: Concat('Bo ', 'Diddly')
Interpretation: The string arguments in *string list* are joined together in the order in which they are listed.
Note: If the resulting string is longer than 255 characters, it is truncated after the 255th character.

String Search

When processing string data, we often need to locate a particular substring. For example, we might want to know if the string 'and ' appears in a sentence and, if so, where. If Target is a string of length four with contents 'and ', the statement

```
PosAnd := Pos(Target, Sentence)
```

assigns to PosAnd the starting position of the first occurrence of 'and ' in string Sentence. If the string 'Birds and bees fly all day.' is stored in Sentence, the value assigned to PosAnd is 7. If the string 'and ' is not in Sentence, the Pos function returns zero.

EXAMPLE 15.12 ▼

A compiler can determine the form of many statements by checking whether a statement begins with a reserved word. If leading blanks are removed from Statement and if Target is a string of length four with contents 'for ', the condition

```
Pos(Target, Statement) = 1
```

is true when `Statement` is a `for` statement.

The compiler can also extract the syntactic elements of each statement. For instance, a `for` statement may have the syntactic form

`for` *counter* `:=` *initial* `to` *final* `do` *statement*

The first two statements that follow use the `Pos` function to locate the strings `'for '` (contents of `Target1`) and `':='` (contents of `Target2`). The `if` statement copies the substring between these symbols into the string `Counter`.

```
PosFor := Pos(Target1, Statement);
PosAssign := Pos(Target2, Statement);
if (PosFor > 0) and (PosAssign > PosFor) then
  Counter := Copy(Statement, PosFor+4, PosAssign-PosFor-4)
```

Because the string `'for '` has four characters, the starting position of the *counter* is at position `PosFor+4`. The number of characters in the *counter* is determined by the expression `PosAssign-PosFor-4`. If the string `'for ID := 1 to N do X := X + 1'` is stored in `Statement`, then `PosFor` gets 1, `PosAssign` gets 8, and the contents of `Counter` are the string `'ID '` (length is 8-1-4, or 3).

PosFor   PosAssign   Counter

SYNTAX DISPLAY

Pos Function

Form: `Pos(`*pattern, source*`)`
Example: `Pos('you', 'Me/you')`
Interpretation: The string *source* is examined from left to right to determine the location of the first occurrence of the substring *pattern*. If *pattern* is found, the value returned is the position in *source* of the first character of *pattern*; otherwise, the value returned is zero.

Procedures Delete and Insert

Besides string-manipulation functions, Turbo Pascal has procedures to insert and delete substrings.

EXAMPLE 15.13 ▼

Assume that `Sentence` contains the string `'This is the example'` before the first procedure call. The procedure call statement

```
Delete (Sentence, 1, 5);
```

deletes five characters from string `Sentence`, starting at position 1. The new contents of `Sentence` become `'is the example'`.

If `Target` is the string of length four with contents `'the '`, the procedure call statement

```
Delete (Sentence, Pos(Target, Sentence), 4);
```

deletes the first occurrence of the string `'the '` from `Sentence`. The new contents of `Sentence` become `'is example'`. Finally, the statements

```
PosTarg := Pos(Target, Sentence);
if PosTarg > 0 then
  Delete (Sentence, PosTarg, Length(Target))
```

delete the first occurrence of string `Target` from `Sentence`, provided `Target` is found. If `Target` is the string `'ex'`, the new contents of `Sentence` become `'is ample'`. ▲

EXAMPLE 15.14 ▼

Assume that the contents of `Sentence` are the string `'is the stuff?'` and the contents of `NewString` are `'Where '`. The procedure call statement

```
Insert (NewString, Sentence, 1)
```

inserts the string `'Where '` at position 1 of string `Sentence`, changing its contents to `'Where is the stuff?'`.

   Assuming the contents of `Target` are `'stuff'` and the contents of `NewString` are `'*#%! '`, the statements

```
PosStuff := Pos(Target, Sentence);
if PosStuff > 0 then
  Insert (NewString, Sentence, PosStuff)
```

insert the string `'*#%! '` in front of the string `'stuff'` in `Sentence`. The new contents of `Sentence` become `'Where is the *#%! stuff'`. ▲

EXAMPLE 15.15 ▼

Procedure `Replace` in Fig. 15.5 replaces a specified target string (`Target`) in a source string (`Source`) with a new string (`Pattern`). It uses function `Pos` to locate `Target`, `Delete` to delete it, and `Insert` to insert `Pattern` in place of `Target`. An error message is displayed if `Target` is not found. ▲

SYNTAX DISPLAY

Delete Procedure

Form: `Delete` (*source, index, size*)
Example: `Delete ('He**llo', 3, 2)`
Interpretation: The next *size* characters are removed from string *source* starting with the character at position *index*. The parameter *source* must be a string, and *size* and *index* must be type `Integer`.

Figure 15.5
Procedure Replace

```
procedure Replace (Target, Pattern {input} : string;
                    var Source {input/output} : string);
{
   Replaces first string Target in Source with Pattern if
   found.
   Pre : Target, Pattern, and Source are defined.
   Post: Source is modified.
}
   var
     PosTarg : Integer;                    {position of Target}
begin {Replace}
   PosTarg := Pos(Target, Source);        {Locate Target.}
   if PosTarg > 0 then
     begin
        Delete (Source, PosTarg, Length(Target));
        Insert (Pattern, Source, PosTarg)
     end
   else
     WriteLn ('No replacement - ', Target, ' not found.')
end; {Replace}
```

Notes: If *index* is greater than Length (*source*), no characters are deleted. If *size* specifies more characters than remain, the rest of the string is deleted, beginning with position *index*.

SYNTAX DISPLAY

Insert Procedure

Form: Insert (*pattern*, *destination*, *index*)
Example: Insert ('bb', 'Buly', 3)
Interpretation: The string *pattern* is inserted before the character currently in position *index*. The parameters *pattern* and *destination* must be strings, and *index* must be type Integer.
Note: If the resulting string is longer than 255 characters, it is truncated after the 255th character.

Exercises for Section 15.3   **Self-Check**

1. Determine the result of the following procedure calls and function designators. Assume that the following string variables are type string[20] and that the initial contents of Temp1 are 'Abra' and of Temp2 are 'cadabra'.
   a. Magic := Concat(Temp1, Temp2)
   b. Length(Magic)

   c. `HisMagic := Copy(Magic, 1, 8)`
   d. `Delete (HisMagic, 4, 3)`
   e. `Insert (Temp1, HisMagic, 3)`
   f. `Pos(Temp2, Magic)`
   g. `Pos(Temp1, Magic)`
   h. `Val ('1.234', RealNum, Frror)`
   i. `Str (1.234 :3:1, RealStr)`
   j. `Val (Temp1, RealNum, Error)`
   k. `Str (0.00345 :3:1, RealStr)`

2. `Source`, `Target`, and `Destin` are three variables of type `string` with capacity 20. Assume that `Source` begins with a person's last name, followed by a comma and one space, and ends with the first name (i.e., *last name, first name*). Use `Pos` and `Copy` to store the first name in `Destin` and the last name in `Target`.

Programming

1. Write a function that will create a palindrome from any string. A palindrome is a string that reads the same backwards and forwards. Your function, given the string `'abc'`, should return `'abccba'`.
2. Write a procedure that reads an integer in a defined range (procedure inputs) into a string, converts it to integer, and if any error is made, requests a new integer. The procedure should return an in-range integer.

15.4   String Processing Illustrated

You have been using a text editor to create and edit Pascal programs. This fairly sophisticated program uses special commands to move the cursor around the screen and specify edit operations. Although you cannot develop such an editor yet, you can write a less sophisticated one.

CASE STUDY   Text Editor

PROBLEM ▼

Design and write an editor to perform some editing operations on a line of text. The editor should be able to locate a specified target string, delete a substring, insert a substring at a specified location, and replace one substring with another.

ANALYSIS ▼

We can use Turbo Pascal's string-manipulation functions and procedures to perform the editing operations relatively easily. We will write a program that enters a string and then processes the string as directed by edit commands.

Data Requirements

Problem Inputs

```
Source : string          {the source string}
Command : Char           {each edit command}
```

Problem Output

```
Source : string          {modified source string}
```

DESIGN ▼

Initial Algorithm

1. Read the string to be edited into `Source`.
2. `repeat`
     3. Read an edit command.
     4. Perform an edit operation.
   `until` done

Refinements and Program Structure

Step 4 is performed by procedure `DoEdit`, which calls the appropriate string operators to read any data strings and to perform the required operations. A portion of the structure chart for the text editor is shown in Fig. 15.6; the local variables and algorithm for procedure `DoEdit` follow.

Local Variables

```
OldStr : string   {substring to be found,
                     replaced, or deleted}
NewStr : string   {substring to be inserted}
Index : Integer   {index to the string Source}
```

Algorithm for DoEdit

1. `case Command of`
     `'D'`: Read the substring to be deleted and delete it.
     `'I'`: Read the substring to be inserted and its position
          and insert it.
     `'F'`: Read the substring to be found and print its position
          if found.

Figure 15.6
Structure Chart for Text Editor Program

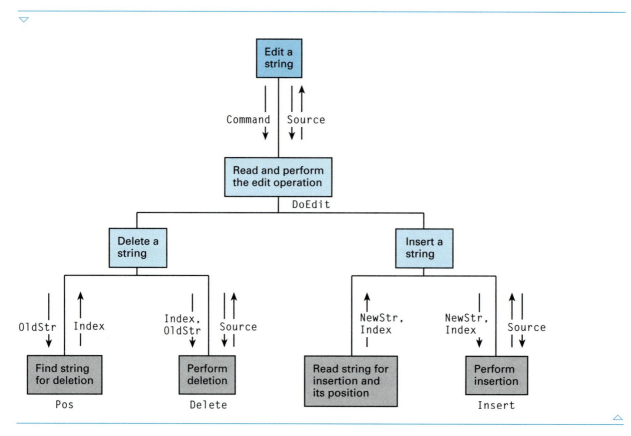

'R': Read the substring to be replaced and replace it with
a new substring.
end {case}

IMPLEMENTATION ▼

The complete program is shown in Fig. 15.7, along with a sample run.

Exercises for Section 15.4 **Self-Check**

1. What would be involved in adding a new command to the text editor that reverses the text 'Mary had' to become 'dah yraM'?
2. Draw the structure chart for replacing a string.

Figure 15.7
Text Editor Program and
Sample Run

Edit Window

```
program TextEdit;
{Performs text editing operations on a source string}

  const
    Sentinel = 'Q';        {sentinel command}

  var
    Source : string;                {the string being edited}
    Command : Char;                 {each edit command}

  {Insert procedure Replace.}   {See Fig. 15.5}

  procedure DoEdit (Command {input} : Char;
                        var Source {input/output} : string);
  {
    Performs the edit operation specified by Command.
    Pre : Command and Source are defined.
    Post: One or more data strings are read and
          Source is modified if Command is
          'D','I','F', or 'R'. If Command is 'Q',
          a message is displayed; otherwise, nothing
          is done.
  }
    var
      NewStr, OldStr : string;      {work strings}
      Index : Integer;              {index to string Source}

  begin {DoEdit}
    {Perform the operation.}
    case Command of
      'D' : begin {Delete}
              Write ('Delete what string? ');
              ReadLn (OldStr);
              Index := Pos(OldStr, Source);
              if Index > 0 then
                Delete (Source, Index, Length(OldStr))
              else
                begin
                  Write (OldStr);
                  WriteLn (' not found')
                end {if}
            end; {Delete}
      'I' : begin {Insert}
              Write ('Insert what string? ');
              ReadLn (NewStr);
              Write ('At what position? ');
              ReadLn (Index);
              Insert (NewStr, Source, Index)
            end; {Insert}
```

▷ ▷ ▷ ▷ ▷ ▷

```
             'F' : begin {Find}
                     Write ('Find what string? ');
                     ReadLn (OldStr);
                     Index := Pos(OldStr, Source);
                     if Index > 0 then
                       begin
                         Write (OldStr);
                         WriteLn (' found at position ', Index :3)
                       end
                     else
                       begin
                         Write (OldStr);
                         WriteLn (' not found')
                       end {if}
                 end; {Find}
           'R' : begin {Replace}
                     Write ('Replace old string? ');
                     ReadLn (OldStr);
                     Write ('With new string? ');
                     ReadLn (NewStr);
                     Replace (OldStr, NewStr, Source)
                 end; {Replace}
           'Q' : WriteLn ('Quitting text editor.')
       else
         WriteLn ('Invalid edit character')
       end {case}
     end; {DoEdit}

begin {TextEdit}
  {Read in the string to be edited.}
  WriteLn ('Enter the source string:');
  ReadLn (Source);

  {Perform each edit operation until done.}
  repeat
    {Get the operation symbol.}
    WriteLn;
    Write ('Enter D(Delete), I(Insert), ');
    Write ('F(Find), R(Replace), Q(Quit)> ');
    ReadLn (Command);
    Command := UpCase(Command);      {Convert to uppercase.}

    {Perform operation.}
    DoEdit (Command, Source);

    {Display latest string.}
    Write ('New source: ');
    WriteLn (Source)
  until Command = Sentinel
end. {TextEdit}
```

── ▷ ▷ ▷ ▷ ▷

Output Window

```
Enter the source string:
Mary had a cute little lamb.

Enter D(Delete), I(Insert), F(Find), R(Replace), Q(Quit)> f
Find what string? cute
cute found at position 12
New source: Mary had a cute little lamb.

Enter D(Delete), I(Insert), F(Find), R(Replace), Q(Quit)> i
Insert what string? very
At what position? 12
New source: Mary had a very cute little lamb.

Enter D(Delete), I(Insert), F(Find), R(Replace), Q(Quit)> R
Replace old string? lamb
With new string? lamb chop
New source: Mary had a very cute little lamb chop.

Enter D(Delete), I(Insert), F(Find), R(Replace), Q(Quit)> D
Delete what string? very cute little
New source: Mary had a lamb chop.

Enter D(Delete), I(Insert), F(Find), R(Replace), Q(Quit)> q
Quitting text editor.
New source: Mary had a lamb chop.
```

15.5   Common Programming Errors

Errors in Using Sets

Remember that a set variable, like any variable, must be initialized before it can be manipulated. It is tempting to assume that a set is empty and then to begin processing it without initializing it to the empty set, [], through an explicit assignment.

Many Pascal operators can be used with sets. The meaning of the operator changes when its operands are sets instead of numbers. Remember to use a unit set (a set of one element) when you insert or delete a set element. The set union operation in the expression

```
['A','E','O','U'] + 'I'          {incorrect set union}
```

is incorrect and should be rewritten as

```
['A','E','O','U'] + ['I']        {correct set union}
```

Because a set cannot be an operand of the standard `Read` or `Write` procedure, you must read in the elements of a set individually and insert them into an initially empty set using the set union operator. To print a set, you must test each value in the base type of a set for set membership. Only those values in the set should be printed.

Errors in Using Strings

Remember that the string operators provided by Turbo Pascal are not available in standard Pascal. Standard Pascal requires you to implement your own string abstract data type.

Carefully check the order of parameters when using the built-in operators. For function Pos and procedure Insert, the source string should be the second parameter, not the first.

Because strings are really arrays of characters, use the compiler directive {$R+} to detect any Range check errors.

CHAPTER REVIEW

1. The set data type stores a collection of elements of the same type (called the base type). Each value in the base type of a set either is a member of the set or is not. Unlike an array, a value can be saved only once in a set, and the set elements are unordered (e.g., [1,5,2,4] is the same set as [1,2,4,5]).

2. Use the set membership operator in to determine whether a particular value is a set element. The operators +, *, and - perform set union, set intersection, and set difference, respectively, when used with set operands. The relational operators = and <> test for set equality and inequality; the relational operators <= and >= test for subset and superset relationships.

3. Turbo Pascal provides several string operators to simplify the processing of textual data stored in variable-length strings. These include functions Length (return the length), Copy (extract a substring), Concat (join strings), and Pos (locate a substring) and procedures Insert (insert a substring) and Delete (delete a substring). Standard Pascal does not provide a variable-length string data type.

Summary of New Pascal Constructs

Construct	Effect
Set Type Declaration	

`type`
`   DigitSet = set of 0..9;`
 	
`var`
`   Digits, Primes : DigitSet;`
	Declares a set type DigitSet whose base type is the set of digits from 0 through 9. Digits and Primes are set variables of type DigitSet.

Set Assignment	

`Digits := [];`
`Primes := [2,3,5] + [7];`
`Digits := Digits + [1..3];`
`Digits := [0..9] - [1,3,5,7,9];`
 	
`Digits := [1,3,5,7,9] * Primes`
	Digits is the empty set.
	Primes is the set [2,3,5,7].
	Digits is the set [1,2,3].
	Digits is the set [0,2,4,6,8].
	Digits is the set [3,5,7].

Construct	Effect
Set Relations	
`Primes <= Digits`	True if `Primes` is a subset of `Digits`.
`Primes >= []`	Always True.
`Primes <> []`	True if `Primes` contains any element.
`[1,2,3] = [3,2,1]`	True because sets are unordered.
String Declaration	

`const Capacity = 10;`
`type StringType = string[Capacity];`
`var FirstName, LastName,`
`        TempName : StringType;`
	`FirstName`, `LastName`, and `TempName` are variable-length strings (string capacity is 10 characters)

String Assignment	

`FirstName := 'Daffy';`
`LastName := 'Duck';`
`TempName := LastName;`
	Saves `'Daffy'` in `FirstName` and `'Duck'` in `LastName` and `TempName`.

String Copy	
`TempName := Copy(FirstName, 1, 3);`	Copies `'Daf'` to `TempName`.
String Concatenation	

`TempName := Concat(FirstName,`
`                LastName);`
`TempName := FirstName + LastName;`
	Stores `'DaffyDuck'` in `TempName`.

String Search	

`Pos('Du', FirstName);`
`Pos('Du', LastName);`
`Pos('Du', TempName);`
	Returns 0 (`'Du'` not found).
	Returns 1 (`'Du'` found at 1).
	Returns 6 (`'Du'` found at 6).

String Deletion	
`Delete (TempName, 7, 2);`	Changes `TempName` to `'DaffyDk'`.
String Insertion	
`Insert ('uc', TempName, 7);`	Changes `TempName` to `'DaffyDuck'`.

Quick-Check Exercises

1. What is the universal set?
2. Which can have the most elements: a set union, an intersection, or a difference? Which of these operators is not commutative?
3. Can you have a set whose base type is `Integer` or `Char`? How about a subrange type with host type `Integer` or `Char`?
4. Does it make any difference in which order the elements of a set are inserted? Does it make any difference if an element is inserted more than once into the same set?
5. Given that `Set1` is `[1..3]`, what are the contents of the following sets?
   a. `Set2 := Set1 + [4,5,6];`
   b. `Set3 := Set1 - Set2;`
   c. `Set4 := Set3 + [4,7];`
   d. `Set5 := Set4 + [4,6];`
   e. `Set6 := Set5 * Set2;`
6. What is the advantage of storing a string in a variable of type `string` instead of using an array of characters?
7. Is it easier to compare two strings stored in variables of type `string` or in arrays of characters? Explain your answer.
8. Assuming S1, S2, and S3 are type `string`, what is the effect of the following statements when `Pos` returns a nonzero value?
   a. `S3 := Copy(S1, 1, 6);`
       `S1 := Concat(S3, S2);`
   b. `S3 := Copy(S2, 1, Pos(S1, S2) - 1);`
   c. `S3 := Copy(S2, Pos(S1, S2), Length(S2));`
   d. `S3 := Copy(S2, Pos(S1, S2), Length(S1));`
   e. `Delete (S2, Pos(S1, S2), Length(S1));`
   f. `Insert (S1, S2, Pos(S1, S2));`
9. Write a procedure to trim any trailing blank characters from a string by decreasing the length of the string until the last character is not a blank.

Answers to Quick-Check Exercises

1. The set containing all the values in the base type
2. The union of two sets. The set difference (operator `-`) is not commutative.
3. You cannot use `Integer` as a base type, but you can use `Char`. A subrange of `Integer` or `Char` can be the base type.
4. No; no
5. a. `[1..6]` b. `[]` c. `[4,7]` d. `[4,6,7]` e. `[4,6]`
6. The actual length is also stored. Turbo Pascal's string functions and procedures can be used to assist in processing the string data.
7. It is easier to compare two strings because you can use the relational operators. Two arrays can be compared element by element, but there may be some problems if the arrays don't contain the same number of elements.
8. a. The substring consisting of the first six characters in S1 is concatenated with S2; the result is stored in S1.
   b. The substring of S2 that precedes the first occurrence of S1 in S2 is assigned to S3.

    c.   The substring of S2 starting at the first occurrence of S1 in S2 is assigned to S3.

    d.   S1 is assigned to S3.

    e.   The first occurrence of S1 is deleted from S2.

    f.   S1 is inserted in S2 just before its first occurrence.

9.
```
procedure TrimString (var AString {input/output} :
                                        string);
  var
    Len : Integer;        {Length without trailing blanks}

begin {TrimString}
  Len := Length(AString);
  while (AString[Len] = ' ') and (Len > 1) do
    Len := Len - 1;

  {assert: non-blank reached or Len is 1}
  if AString[Len] = ' ' then
    AString := ''
  else
    AString := Copy(AString, 1, Len)
end; {TrimString}
```

Review Questions

1. Why may we be unable to declare a set whose base type is `Char` (in some versions of Pascal)?

2. Which of the following could be declared in Turbo Pascal as a set? Provide a set declaration for those that can and explain why not for those that cannot.
       a.   All integers
       b.   All integers from 50 to 80
       c.   All integers from 1900 to 2000
       d.   All real numbers from 0 to 1
       e.   All characters from A to Z
       f.   All Boolean values
       g.   The first 10 multiples of 9

3. Write the declarations for a set, `Oysters`, whose values are the months of the year (enumerated type `Month`). Initialize `Oysters` to the set of all months whose names contain the letter r. Write an assignment statement that inserts the month `May` in this set and deletes the month `September`.

4. The following `for` loop prints each member of a set whose elements are values of enumerated type `Day`. Write the declaration for set `TestSet`. Rewrite the loop as a `while` loop whose repetition condition is `TestSet <> []`. Use the set operator `-` to delete each set element after it is displayed.

```
for Today := Sunday to Saturday do
  if Today in TestSet then
    WriteDay (Today)
```

5. Provide the declarations for the following two sets. What are the intersection and the union of sets Vowel and Letter? What are the two set differences?

```
Vowel := ['Y', 'U', 'O', 'I'];
Letter := ['A' .. 'P'];
```

6. Given the statements

```
S2 := S1;
Delete (S2, 3, 5)
```

   what would be a sequence of statements that would put back into S2 what was deleted such that S2 = S1 again, assuming S2 can only be used once in an Insert procedure call?

7. Indicate whether each of the following identifiers is a procedure or function. Describe the type of result returned by each.

```
Length, Concat, Pos, Copy, Insert, Delete
```

8. Write the declarations and the statements for a program segment that first reads a data line into a variable of type StringType and stores all the symbols in the subrange '!'..'/' that appear in the string in a set Symbols1. Assume the ASCII character set and test each character in this subrange using function Pos to determine whether it appears in the string. If so, insert it in the set Symbols1. Next write a new search loop that scans the string, testing each character in the string for membership in the set ['!'..'/']. Insert each character that qualifies in set Symbols2. When you have finished, test whether Symbols1 and Symbols2 are identical sets.

Programming Projects

1. We have a group of ten people: Crissa, Neil, Patricia, Noel, Mary, Martin, Donald, John, Ruth, and Bill. Each person has a set of people to whom they tell secrets. Your task is to write a program that inputs the names of the people each person tells secrets to and determines everyone who will find out the secret, assuming Crissa knows it first. You will create two sets: people who know the secret and have told everyone to whom they tell secrets and people who know the secret but haven't told anyone yet. Initially the first set is empty and Crissa is in the second set. Your program will have a loop that selects a member of the second set, moves all the people that member tells secrets to into the second set only if they are not already in the first or second set, and moves the selected member to the first set. When the second set is empty, your program is complete.

2. Write a program that reads in a sequence of lines and displays a count of the total number of words in those lines and counts the number of words with one letter, two letters, and so on. Your program should include functions and procedures that correspond to the function and procedure headers that follow. Array element FreqTable[I] keeps track of the counts of words of length I.

```
procedure GetWord (Sentence {input} : string;
                    var Index {input/output} : Integer;
                    var AWord {output} : string);
{Return next word of Sentence found at or after Index.}

procedure TabOneWord (Aword{input} : string;
                var FreqTable {input/output} : ArrayType);
{Update FreqTable for cell corresponding to
 Length(AWord).}

procedure TabulateWords (var TestData {input} : Text;
                    var FreqTable {output} : ArrayType);
{
  Read file TestData and tabulate frequency of word
  lengths in array FreqTable.
  Calls: TabOneWord and GetWord.
}

function ArraySum (FreqTable : ArrayType) : Integer;
{Compute sum of word counts stored in FreqTable.}
```

3. ReadLn can read multiple numbers input on a single line as long as there are spaces between them. Unfortunately, they usually have commas between them instead. Write a procedure that can input five numbers into an array from user input, assuming they are all input on one line with commas and, possibly, extra spaces between them. Write a test program for your procedure and demonstrate its correct operation. *Hint:* Read the input into a string first.

4. Write a Pascal program to play the game TaxMan. In this game, a user plays against the computer with the object of accumulating the most points. The user selects a number from 1 to 40. If the number is still available, the user is credited with points equal to the number chosen and the computer is credited with points equivalent to the sum of the unclaimed factors of the number chosen. The user may not choose a number that has no factors. After a number is chosen, it and its factors are removed from the set of available numbers. The computer gets all unclaimed numbers added to its score when the game ends.

    To illustrate, consider the game played with the set of numbers 1 to 6. If the user selects 6, the computer gets all factors of 6, namely, 3, 2, 1, and the score is tied. Now only 4 and 5 are left to choose from; since the factors of 4 (2 and 1) have been removed from the set of available numbers and 5 has no factors other than itself and 1, the computer wins, 15 to 6. The user should have chosen 5 first, then 4, and then 6. Then the user would have won, 15 to 7.

5. Write a procedure that reads in an array of cards and stores it in an array of sets, one set for each suit. Use an enumerated type for the suits and one for the card face values. The data for each card will be presented in the form of a character representing the suit and a character representing the card face value ('2'..'9', 'T', 'J', 'Q', 'K', 'A').

6. Consider a hand of cards read in Programming Project 5 as a bridge hand and evaluate it. Award points for each card according to the following method:

Card Face Value	Points
2..10	0
jack	1
queen	2
king	3
ace	4

Also add one point for each suit that has only two cards, two points for each suit that has only one card, and three points for each suit that is missing.

7. Write a program that will read 400 characters into a 20 × 20 array. Afterward read in a character string of a maximum of 10 characters that will be used to search the "table" of characters. Indicate how many times the second string occurs in the 20 × 20 array. This should include horizontal, vertical, and right-diagonal occurrences. (Right-diagonal means going down and to the right for the search.)

8. Data compression is a common technique used to reduce the amount of data transmitted over a communications line. One way to compress data is to store a dictionary of common strings in an array. The compression program searches for the longest dictionary substring it can find at the beginning of the input string and outputs its subscript. If a dictionary match cannot be found, the program outputs the first character in the input itself. It then removes the substring matched or the unmatched character from the beginning of the input string and continues. Write a program that reads a dictionary of up to 100 substrings and several input strings and displays the compressed output strings.

9. Write a program to scan a line of characters containing an equation and calculate the result. Assume all operands are integers. Conduct tests to determine whether the equation is valid.

Valid operations are +, -, /, *, and ^, where +, -, /, and * have their typical functions and ^ indicates the value to its left is raised to the power of the operand to its right (which must be positive).

Numbers may be negative. All operations are done in left-to-right order (no operator precedence). For example,

```
2 + 3 ^ 2 + 36 * 1
```

would be

```
5 ^ 2 + 36 * 1 = 25 + 36 * 1 = 61 * 1 = 61
```

Use sets to verify the equations' operations, and ignore all blanks. Output should consist of an equal sign (=) and then the answer. If an equation is invalid, display the message ** INVALID **.

10. Rewrite Programming Project 9 to allow operands (including exponents) that are either integers or real numbers. You should read the characters of the operands one at a time and convert them to their equivalent numeric value.

CHAPTER SIXTEEN

External Data Structures: Files

access in random order
processing the elements of a data structure in arbitrary order

access in sequential order
processing all elements of a data structure starting with the first element and ending with the last element

This chapter covers the file data structure. Like arrays, files are ordered collections of elements of the same type. Because files are located in secondary memory (disk) rather than in main memory, they can be much larger than arrays. Moreover, the elements of an array can be accessed in arbitrary, or **random**, **order**; files in standard Pascal, in contrast, can be accessed only in **sequential order**. This means that file component 1, component 2, . . . , component $(N - 1)$ must be accessed before file component N.

Files should be familiar to you from your work on Chapter 8, where the files were *text files,* or files of characters. In this chapter, we will work with files whose components can be any simple or structured type. For example, we may have a file of integers or a file of records. These nontext files are called *binary files*.

The programs in Chapter 8 accessed text files sequentially. In Turbo Pascal, you can create direct-access files, where records can be accessed in any order. After introducing the file data type and discussing files composed of simple and structured components, we describe extensions to Pascal that allow a file to be accessed in random order, just like an array.

16.1 Text File ADT and Binary File ADT

Text File ADT

In Chapter 8, you learned about the structure of text files and the operations that can be performed on them. In this section, we will summarize this information as a formal specification for a text file abstract data type (see Table 16.1). This formal description will help us extend the text file data type to files that have other components besides characters.

Table 16.1
Specification for
Text File ADT

Structure

A text file is an ordered collection of characters from the Pascal character set stored on disk. The character <eoln> denotes the end of a line, and the character <eof> denotes the end of the file. The characters in the file are processed sequentially, starting with the first. A file location marker keeps track of the next character to be processed.

Operators
The descriptions of the operators use the following parameters:

> F is a file variable
> *file name* is a string
> *input list* is a list of simple variables possibly ending with a string variable
> *output list* is a list of simple variables, simple values, and strings

Assign (F, *file name*) Associates file F with the external file *file name*.
Reset (F) Opens file F for input (reading), placing the file location marker at the first character.
Rewrite (F) Opens file F for output (writing), placing the file location marker at the beginning of an empty file.
Read (F, *input list*) Reads data from file F into the variables specified in *input list*. If F is missing, it reads data from system file Input.
ReadLn (F, *input list*) Same as Read except that it advances the file location marker for file F to the start of the next line after performing the data entry.
Write (F, *output list*) Writes values in *output list* to file F. If F is missing, it writes to system file Output.
WriteLn (F, *output list*) Same as Write except that it writes an <eoln> to file F after all values.

EOF(F)   (function) Returns True if the <eof> is the next character in file F; otherwise, it returns False.

EOLN(F)   (function) Returns True if an <eoln> is the next character in file F; otherwise, it returns False.

Close (F)   Releases the disk file associated with file F. If the file is an output file, writes any values remaining in memory to the file and writes an <eof> character to the file.

Next we show how to use these operators with other file types. Three of these operators—ReadLn, WriteLn, and EOLN—can be used only with Text files because they process the <eoln> character, which cannot appear in other file types.

Declaring Binary Files

In addition to text files, we can declare new file types whose components are any type, simple or structured, except for another file type. Files with nontext components are binary files. A component of a **binary file** is stored on disk using the same binary form as it has in main memory.

binary file
a file whose components are
stored on disk in the same
form as in main memory

The declarations

```
type
   NumberFile = file of Integer;

   Book = record
             StockNum : Integer;
             Author,
             Title : string[20];
             Price : Real;
             Quantity : Integer
          end; {Book}

   BookFile = file of Book;

var
   Numbers : NumberFile;     {file with integer components}
   Books : BookFile;         {file with book components}
```

define a record type (Book), two file types (NumberFile and BookFile), and two file variables (Numbers and Books). File Numbers is a file with simple components (type Integer) and file Books is a file with structured components (record type Book).

Files Numbers and Books are binary files. File Numbers can contain a collection of integers. In Turbo Pascal, only integers in the range -32768 to 32767 can be stored in such a file. File Books can contain a collection of records of type Book.

File Type Declaration

Form: `type`
        file type = `file of` *component type*;

Example: `type`
```
        Item = record
                    ID : Integer;
                    Salary : Real
                end; {Item}

        ItemFile = file of Item;
```
Interpretation: A new type *file type* is declared whose components must be type *component type*. Any standard or previously declared data type, except for an object, another file type, or a structured type with a file type as one of its constituents, can be the component type.

Writing Information to a Binary File

How do we store information in a binary file? We must use procedure `Write` to store a variable or value of the same type as the file components. The statement

```
Write (Numbers, 1234)
```

writes the integer `1234` to binary file `Numbers` declared earlier. When we use `Write` with a binary file, the first parameter must be the file variable name and the second parameter must be a variable or value of the same type as the file components. We can write only one file component at a time. The statement

```
Write (Numbers, 1234, -999)    {invalid Write of 2 values}
```

is invalid because it attempts to write two integer values to file `Numbers`.

When writing an integer to binary file `Numbers`, Pascal copies its value from memory (internal storage) directly to disk (external storage). The same amount of memory—two bytes—is needed in both places. When Pascal writes an integer to a text file, the internal binary value is converted to a string of ASCII digit characters and the number of external bytes required depends on the length of this string. For example, the integer 1 requires a single byte of storage in a text file whereas the integer 16954 requires 5 bytes of storage in a text file (digit character 1, digit character 6, and so on). Both numbers require two bytes when stored in a binary file of integers.

We can write the internal binary form of a record variable directly to a binary file. If `MyBook` is a record variable (type `Book`) and `Books` is type `file of Book`, the statement

```
Write (Books, MyBook);
```

writes a new component to binary file `Books`. Recall that the statement

```
Write (Output, MyBook)    {invalid parameters for Write}
```

is invalid because `Output` is a text file (the screen) and Pascal does not allow us to write a record variable directly to a text file.

Reading Information from a Binary File

We retrieve file components in a similar manner. The statements

```
Read (Books, MyBook);
Read (Numbers, NextNum)
```

read the next component of a binary file (the first parameter) to the variable indicated by the second parameter. The binary image stored in the next file component is copied directly to the variable. The file location marker selects the file component to be read and is advanced to the next component after each `Read` operation.

Binary File ADT

We summarize all these points in the following specification for a binary file ADT (Table 16.2).

Table 16.2
Specification for Binary File ADT

Structure
A binary file is an ordered collection of simple or structured components that are all the same type. A binary file is terminated by an `<eof>` character. The components in a binary file are processed sequentially, starting with the first. A file location marker keeps track of the next component to be processed.

Operators
The descriptions of the operators use the following parameters:

F is a file variable
file name is a string
recvar is a variable of the same type as the components of file F

`Assign (F, `*file name*`)`   Associates file F with the external file *file name*.
`Reset (F)`   Opens file F for input (reading), placing the file location marker at the first character.
`Rewrite (F)`   Opens file F for output (writing), placing the file location marker at the beginning of an empty file.
`Read (F, `*recvar*`)`   Reads the next component from file F into *recvar* and advances the file location marker.
`Write (F, `*recvar*`)`   Writes the binary image of *recvar* as the next component of file F. If file F has simple components, a literal can be used in place of *recvar*.
`EOF(F)`   (function) Returns `True` if the `<eof>` is the next character in file F; otherwise, it returns `False`.
`Close (F)`   Releases the disk file associated with file F. If the file is an output file, writes any values remaining in the output buffer to the file and writes an `<eof>` character to the file.

1. If your computer stores a type `Real` value in memory in six bytes, how many bytes are required to store six real numbers in a binary file? Answer the same question for a text file in which each number is written using `WriteLn`, format specifier `:4:2`, and `<eoln>`, which requires two bytes. Are there any circumstances under which either of your answers might change?
2. Could both the binary file and the text file in Exercise 1 store all the same numbers? If not, provide some number that could be stored by one but not the other.
3. How many bytes are used to store each component of file `Books`?

16.2   Creating and Using Binary Files

Unlike a text file, a binary file cannot be created by using an editor program. The only way to create a binary file is by writing its components using a program. In this section, we show how to create a file with simple components and a file with structured components.

Creating and Using a File of Integers

Program `EchoFile` in Fig. 16.1 first creates and then echo prints file `Numbers` whose components are the integers from 1 to 1000. You can envision file `Numbers` as:

File `Numbers`

1	2	3	4	5	6	. . .	998	999	1000	`<eof>`

`EchoFile` begins by preparing file `Numbers` for output (the `Rewrite` statement). The `for` loop then creates a file of integer values, and the statement

`Write (Numbers, I);`   {Write each integer to Numbers.}

copies each value of `I` (1 to 1000) to file `Numbers`.

Next, file `Numbers` is closed and then prepared for input (the `Reset` statement). The `while` loop echo prints each value stored in `Numbers` until the end of file `Numbers` is reached (`EOF(Numbers)` is `True`). Within the loop, the statement

`Read (Numbers, NextInt);`   {Read next integer into NextInt.}

Figure 16.1
Program EchoFile

```
program EchoFile;

{Creates a file of integer values and echo prints it}

   const
     NumInt = 1000;              {number of integers in the file}

   type
     NumberFile = file of Integer;

   var
     Numbers : NumberFile;  {file of integers}
     I,                     {loop-control variable}
     NextInt : Integer;  {each integer read from file Numbers}
begin {EchoFile}
   Assign (Numbers, 'B:NUMBERS.DAT');
   Rewrite (Numbers);   {Initialize Numbers to an empty file.}

   {Create a file of integers.}
   for I := 1 to NumInt do
     Write (Numbers, I);   {Write each integer to Numbers.}

   {Echo print file Numbers.}
   Close (Numbers);
   Reset (Numbers);                {Prepare Numbers for input.}
   while not EOF(Numbers) do
     begin
       Read (Numbers, NextInt);   {Read next integer into
                                                    NextInt.}
       WriteLn (Output, NextInt :4)    {Display it.}
     end; {while}

   Close (Numbers)
end. {EchoFile}
```

reads the next file component (an integer value) into variable NextInt. The statement

```
WriteLn (Output, NextInt :4)                        {Display it.}
```

displays this value on a separate line of the screen (system file Output).

Creating a File of Records

Figure 16.2 creates a binary file, Inventory, that represents the inventory of a bookstore. Each file component is a record of type Book, because Inventory is declared as type BookFile (file of Book). The information saved

Figure 16.2
Creating a Book Store
Inventory File

Edit Window

```
program BookInventory;
{Creates a book file from keyboard data.}
  const
    StrLength = 20;                  {size of each string}
    Sentinel = 9999;                {sentinel stock number}

  type
    StockRange = 1111..9999;        {range of stock numbers}
    StringType = string[StrLength];
    Book = record
              StockNum : StockRange;
              Author,
              Title    : StringType;
              Price : Real;
              Quantity : Integer
           end;  {Book}
    BookFile = file of Book;

  var
    Inventory : BookFile;           {the book file}
    FileName : string[12];          {the file name}
    OneBook : Book;                 {each book}

  procedure ReadBook (var OneBook {output} : Book);
    {
     Reads a book from the keyboard into OneBook.
     Pre : None.
     Post: Data are read from the keyboard into each field of
           the record represented by parameter OneBook.
    }
    begin {ReadBook}
      with OneBook do
        begin
          Write ('Stock number> ');
          ReadLn (StockNum);
          if StockNum <> Sentinel then
            begin
              Write ('Author> ');
              ReadLn (Author);
              Write ('Title> ');
              ReadLn (Title);
              Write ('Price $');
              ReadLn (Price);
              Write ('Quantity> ');
              ReadLn (Quantity)
            end {if}
        end; {with}
      WriteLn
    end; {ReadBook}
```

▷ ▷ ▷ ▷ ▷ ▷

```
begin {BookInventory}
  Write ('Enter the inventory file name> ');
  ReadLn (FileName);
  Assign (Inventory, FileName);
  Rewrite (Inventory);          {Prepare Inventory for output.}

  {Read and copy each book until done.}
  WriteLn ('Enter the data requested for each book.');
  WriteLn ('Enter a stock number of 9999 when done.');
  ReadBook (OneBook);                   {Read first book.}
  while OneBook.StockNum <> Sentinel do
    begin
      Write (Inventory, OneBook); {Copy the book to Inventory.}
      ReadBook (OneBook)                {Read next book.}
    end; {while}

  Write (Inventory, OneBook);  {Write sentinel record to file.}

  WriteLn ('File Inventory completed.');
  Close (Inventory)
end. {BookInventory}
```

Output Window

```
Enter the inventory file name> INVEN.DAT
Enter the data requested for each book.
Enter a stock number of 9999 when done.
Stock Number> 1234
Author> Robert Ludlum
Title> The Parsifal Mosaic
Price $17.95
Quantity> 10

Stock Number> 7654
Author> Blaise Pascal
Title> Pascal Made Easy
Price $50.00
Quantity> 1

Stock Number> 9999
File Inventory completed.
```

in each component consists of a four-digit stock number, the book's author and title (strings), the price, and the quantity on hand.

The main program calls procedure ReadBook to enter the data for each book from the terminal into record variable OneBook. ReadBook first reads the book's stock number. If the stock number is not the sentinel, ReadBook calls procedure ReadLn to read the author and title strings. After OneBook is defined, the statement

```
Write (Inventory, OneBook);    {Copy the book to Inventory.}
```

copies it to file Inventory.

The binary file created when the program in Fig. 16.2 is run is shown next. The last record serves as a sentinel. The StockNum field (value is 9999) is the only field of the sentinel record that has its value defined.

File Inventory

1234	7654	9999	⌃
Robert Ludlum	Blaise Pascal	?	e
The Parsifal Mosaic	Pascal Made Easy	?	o
17.95	50.00	⋮	f
10	1	?	⌄

Array of Records and Files of Records

Program BookInventory stores a binary file of book records on disk. If you need to change the file contents, you first must read each record to be modified into main memory. For a file not overly large, you could store all its records in an array of records, update the array, and then write the modified array back to the file.

Reading the array data from a binary file is easier and more efficient than reading it from a text file. You can copy the binary image of each file record directly into its corresponding array element. If InvenArray is an array of records of type Book (up to MaxBook records), the following while loop reads the records of file Inventory into InvenArray:

```
Reset (Inventory);                      {Open the file for input.}
Next := 0;                              {InvenArray is empty.}
while not EOF(Inventory) and (Next < MaxBook) do
  begin
    Next := Next + 1;                   {Access next element.}
    Read (Inventory, InvenArray[Next])  {Store book in array.}
  end; {while}

if not EOF(Inventory) then
  WriteLn ('Warning - file too large for array.');
BookCount := Next;                      {Save count of books.}
Close (Inventory)
```

After modifying InvenArray, you should write its new contents to file Inventory, one record at a time. The next for loop accomplishes this:

```
Rewrite (Inventory);                {Open the file for output.}
for Next := 1 to BookCount do
  Write (Inventory, InvenArray[Next]);  {Write book to file.}

Close (Inventory)
```

Exercises for Section 16.2   *Self-Check*

1. Complete the following program. What does it do?

```
program Mystery;
  type
    NumberType = file of _____;

  var
    Data    :_____;
    OutData :_____;
    Next : Integer;

begin
  Assign (Data, 'DATA.DAT');
  Assign (OutData, 'OUT.DAT');
  _____(Data);
  _____(OutData);
  while not EOF(_____) do
    begin
      Read (_____, Next);
      if Next < 50 then
        begin
          Write (_____ , Next);
          WriteLn (_____, Next :2, ' failed exam')
        end {if}
    end; {while}

  Close (Data);
  Close (OutData)
end. {Mystery}
```

2. Why doesn't it matter that some of the fields of the sentinel record are not defined? Under what circumstances might this present a problem?
3. Write all the declarations necessary for a file whose components are student records, where each record consists of a student ID number and an array of five scores. Write a loop that reads each student's record from the file and displays the student's ID number and first score.

Programming

1. Write a procedure that resets file Inventory and displays each inventory record on the screen. Call procedure WriteBook to display each record.
2. Write procedure WriteBook.

16.3   File Merge

Like most data structures, a file frequently needs modification or updating after it has been created. You may want to modify one or more fields of an existing record, delete a record, insert a new record, or simply display the current field values for a record.

In the last section, we discussed reading the entire file into an array and then updating the array. This approach is not feasible if the file is very large or if we want to insert or delete some records. In these cases, the best approach is to create a new file whose records are based on the original file. To do this, we must read each record of the current file, perhaps modify it, and then write it to the new file.

file merge

a combination of two or more compatible files to form a new file that preserves the ordering of the records by key field

One common update operation is a file merge. In a **file merge**, two files of the same type are combined into a third file. If the records in the two original files are ordered according to a key field, the records in the new file must also be in order by key field. Recall that a record's *key field* contains a unique value that identifies the record.

CASE STUDY   **Merging Two Files**

PROBLEM ▼

Whenever it receives a new shipment of books, the bookstore prepares a file (Update) that describes the new shipment. To keep our inventory file (Inventory) up to date, we need a program to combine, or merge, the update file with the inventory file.

ANALYSIS ▼

We will assume that the records on both files are in order by stock number. We also reserve the largest stock number (9999) as a special sentinel value always found at the end of each file.

Our task is to create a third file (NewInven) from the data in the two existing files. If a stock number appears in only one of the files, then its corresponding record will be copied directly to NewInven. If a stock number appears in both files, then the data from file Update will be copied to NewInven, because that is the most recent information; however, the Quantity field of the record written to NewInven must be the sum of both Quantity fields (the quantity shipped plus the quantity on hand). The records in the new file must be in order by stock number.

Figure 16.3 illustrates the new file that results from merging two small sample files. For simplicity, only the Stock and Quantity fields of all three files are shown. The only stock numbers appearing on all three files are 4234 and

Figure 16.3
Sample File Merge

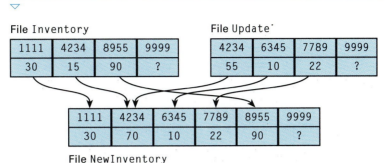

the sentinel stock number (9999). The original inventory file (`Inventory`) and the update file (`Update`) each contain four records (including the sentinel); the new inventory file (`NewInven`) contains six records (including the sentinel), in order by stock number. Records 1111 and 8955 are copied directly from file `Inventory`, records 6345 and 7789 are copied directly from file `Update`, and record 4234 is a combination of the data on files `Inventory` and `Update`.

The data requirements and the algorithm for a `Merge` procedure are described next. Because we are writing a procedure, the type declarations, which should appear in the main program, would be similar to those in Fig. 16.2. The main program should also declare three string variables to hold the external file names, read the external file names from the keyboard, and pass them to the merge procedure.

Data Requirements

Procedure Inputs

```
InvenName : string      {current inventory file name}
UpdateName : string     {update file name}
NewInvName : string     {new inventory file name}
```

Local Variables

```
Inventory : BookFile    {current inventory file}
Update : BookFile        {file of new books received}
NewInven : BookFile      {new inventory file}
InvenBook : Book         {current record from Inventory}
UpdateBook : Book        {current record from Update}
```

DESIGN ▼

Algorithm for File Merge

1. Prepare files `Inventory` and `Update` for input and file `NewInven` for output.

2. Read the first record from `Inventory` into `InvenBook` and from `Update` into `UpdateBook`.

3. Copy all records that appear in only one input file to `NewInven`. If a record appears in both input files, sum both `Quantity` values before copying record `UpdateBook` to `NewInven`.

Refinements and Program Structure

Step 3 compares each pair of records stored in `InvenBook` and `UpdateBook`. Because the records in file `NewInven` must be in order by stock number, the record with the smaller stock number is written to `NewInven`. Another record is then read from the file containing the record just written, and the comparison process is repeated. If the stock numbers of `UpdateBook` and `InvenBook` are the same (a record appears in both files), the new value of `UpdateBook.Quantity` is computed, the modified record is written to `NewInven`, and the next records are read from both input files.

Step 3 Refinement

3.1 `while` there are more records to read `do`
    3.2 `if InvenBook.StockNum < UpdateBook.StockNum then`
        3.3 Write `InvenBook` to `NewInven` and read the next record
            of `Inventory` into `InvenBook`.
      `else if InvenBook.StockNum > UpdateBook.StockNum then`
        3.4 Write `UpdateBook` to `NewInven` and read the next record
            of `Update` into `UpdateBook`.
      `else`
        3.5 Modify the `Quantity` field of `UpdateBook`, write
            `UpdateBook` to `NewInven`, and read the next record
            from `Inventory` and `Update`.
3.6 Write the sentinel record to `NewInven`.

Let's trace this refinement, assuming `InvenBook` and `UpdateBook` initially contain the first file records:

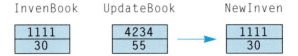

Because 1111 is less than 4234, record `InvenBook` is copied to file `NewInven` (Step 3.3), and the next record is read into `InvenBook`:

Now the stock numbers are equal, so the quantity fields are summed (Step 3.5), the new record with stock number 4234 is written to file `NewInven`, and the next records are read into `InvenBook` and `UpdateBook`:

InvenBook   UpdateBook   NewInven

8955		6345		1111	4234	6345
90		10		30	70	10

This time the record in UpdateBook is copied to NewInven (Step 3.4), the next record is read into UpdateBook, and the merge continues.

What happens when the end of one input file is reached? The stock number for the current record of that file will be 9999 (the maximum), so each record read from the other input file will be copied directly to file NewInven. When the ends of both input files are reached, the while loop is exited and the sentinel record is written to file NewInven (Step 3.6).

Procedure CopySmaller implements Step 3.2. The structure chart for the Merge procedure is shown in Fig. 16.4.

IMPLEMENTATION ▼

Procedure Merge is shown in Fig. 16.5. The only output displayed on the screen as a result of executing this procedure is the message File merge completed. After the procedure's execution, you may want to echo print file NewInven. To do so, reset file NewInven and then write individual fields of each record to the screen. When certain that file NewInven is correct, you can use an operating system command to rename it Inventory. You could then use the new file Inventory as the input inventory file and merge it with another Update file at a later time.

Figure 16.4
Structure Chart for
Procedure Merge

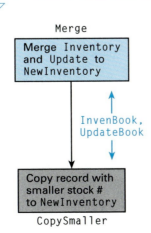

Figure 16.5
Procedures Merge and
CopySmaller

```
procedure CopySmaller (var InvenBook,
                           UpdateBook {input/output} : Book;
                       var Inventory {input}, Update {input},
                           NewInven {output} : BookFile);
begin {CopySmaller}
  if InvenBook.StockNum < UpdateBook.StockNum then
    begin {<}
      Write (NewInven, InvenBook);        {Copy InvenBook.}
      Read (Inventory, InvenBook)
    end {<}
  else if InvenBook.StockNum > UpdateBook.StockNum then
    begin {>}
      Write (NewInven, UpdateBook);       {Copy UpdateBook.}
      Read (Update, UpdateBook)
    end {>}
  else
    begin {=}
      UpdateBook.Quantity := UpdateBook.Quantity +
                              InvenBook.Quantity;
      Write (NewInven, UpdateBook);   {Copy new UpdateBook.}
      Read (Inventory, InvenBook);    {Read both records.}
      Read (Update, UpdateBook)
    end {=}
end;  {CopySmaller}

procedure Merge (InvenName, UpdateName, NewInvName
                                        {input} : string);
{
 Merges data on files Inventory and Update to file NewInven.
 Pre  : External names for 3 files are stored in parameters.
        Files Inventory and Update are existing files ordered
        by stock number, ending with a sentinel stock number.
 Post : Each record appearing in only Inventory or Update is
        copied to NewInven. If a stock number appears in
        both files, the Quantity fields are summed and the
        remaining fields are copied from Update. File NewInven
        is ordered by stock number and ends with the sentinel.
 Calls: CopySmaller
}
  var
    Inventory,             {old inventory file}
    Update,                {update file}
    NewInven : BookFile;   {new inventory file}
    InvenBook,             {current record of file Inventory}
    UpdateBook : Book;     {current record of file Update}

begin {Merge}
  {
   Prepare Inventory and Update for input,
   NewInven for output.
  }
```

```
Assign (Inventory, InvenName);
Assign (Update, UpdateName);
Assign (NewInven, NewInvName);
Reset (Inventory);  Reset (Update);  Rewrite (NewInven);

{Read the first record from Inventory and Update.}
Read (Inventory, InvenBook);
Read (Update, UpdateBook);
{
 Copy all records from file Inventory and Update
 to NewInven.
}
while (InvenBook.StockNum <> Sentinel) or
      (UpdateBook.StockNum <> Sentinel) do
   CopySmaller (InvenBook, UpdateBook, Inventory,
                Update, NewInven);

{Write the sentinel record to NewInven.}
Write (NewInven, InvenBook);

WriteLn ('File merge completed.');
Close (Inventory);
Close (Update);
Close (NewInven)
end; {Merge}
```

You can adapt the merge procedure to perform other update operations. For example, you could merge a file that represents the daily sales of all books (file Sales) with file Inventory to generate an updated inventory file at the end of each day. If the quantity field of each record in file Sales is subtracted from the quantity field of the corresponding record in file Inventory, the difference would represent the quantity remaining in stock. You could even delete records whose quantity fields became negative or zero by simply not copying such records to NewInven.

Program Style

Analysis of the Merge Procedure

Several questions arise about the merge procedure in Fig. 16.5. For example, what happens if an input file is empty or contains only the sentinel record? Because procedure Merge always reads at least one record, an execution error will occur if either input file is empty. If a file contains only the sentinel record, then only the sentinel record will be read from that file, and all the records in the other file will be copied directly to file NewInven. If both input files contain only the sentinel record, the while loop will be exited immediately, and only the sentinel record will be copied to file NewInven after loop exit.

▶▶▶▶▶▶

Finally, how efficient is the merge procedure if the end of one file is reached much sooner than the other? This imbalance would result in the stock number 9999 being repeatedly compared to the stock numbers on the file that is not yet finished. It would be more efficient to exit the `while` loop when the end of one file is reached, then copy all remaining records on the other file directly to file `NewInven`. This modification is left as an exercise at the end of this section.

TESTING ▼

To test the merge procedure, provide files that contain only the sentinel record as well as files with one or more actual records. Make sure that the merge procedure works properly regardless of which of the two input files has all its records processed first. Also make sure that there is exactly one sentinel record on the merged file.

Exercises for Section 16.3   *Self-Check*

1. In procedure `Merge`, what three assumptions are made about the two files that are merged? Must the two input files have the same number of records?
2. What happens if a record from one input file has the same stock number as a record from the other input file? What happens if one input file has two consecutive records with the same stock number?
3. What would happen if the `or` in the `while` condition in procedure `Merge` were changed to `and`?

Programming

1. Modify procedure `Merge`, assuming that its input files do not contain a sentinel record. In this case, there should not be a sentinel record on the merged file. Exit from the merge loop when the end of either file is reached and then copy the remaining records from the unfinished file.

16.4 Direct-Access Files (Optional)

When files are processed sequentially, each operation is performed on every file component and the components are processed in order, starting with the first. Sequential access is satisfactory whenever a file processing operation affects most of the components in a file. However, for processing only a few components in a large file, accessing every file component would be wasteful and time consuming.

direct access file
a file whose components can be accessed in arbitrary order

For this reason, Turbo Pascal, but not standard Pascal, provides operators that enable direct access to a binary file. A **direct access file** is one whose components can be accessed at any time, in any order. For this reason, direct access is also called random access and is analogous to storing a large array on disk. Turbo Pascal can use direct access to any binary file, provided that file has been opened for input (using `Reset`).

With direct access, we can intermix read and write operations on a file just as we can intermix retrieve and store operations in an array. With sequential access, in contrast, we can either read all the components of a file or write all its components, but we cannot write records to a file opened for input, or read records from a file opened for output.

Selecting a Record in a File

With sequential access, Turbo Pascal keeps track of the next record to process by automatically advancing the file location marker after each read or write operation. With direct access, the program must move the file location marker to the desired record before each read or write operation. To facilitate this process, Turbo Pascal numbers the file records in an increasing sequence, starting with 0 for the first file record.

If binary file `Inventory` (see Fig. 16.2) has been opened for input, the procedure call statement

```
Seek (Inventory, 9)
```

advances the file location marker for `Inventory` to record number 9. This is actually the tenth record, because the first record has record number 0.

Function `FileSize` returns the number of records in a binary file. For 20 records in file `Inventory` (record numbers 0 through 19), for example, the function designator `FileSize(Inventory)` returns 20.

EXAMPLE 16.1 ▼

Procedure `UpdateBook` in Fig. 16.6 updates the record of file `Inventory` selected by parameter `RecNum`. The condition

```
(RecNum >= 0) and (RecNum < FileSize(Inventory))
```

is true if `RecNum` is in range. The statement

```
Seek (Inventory, RecNum);
```

moves the file location marker to record number `RecNum` just before the `Read` operation and again just before the `Write` operation. It is necessary to execute this statement twice because the `Read` operation advances the file location marker to the next record (record `RecNum + 1`). ▲

SYNTAX DISPLAY

Seek Procedure

Form: Seek (*iofile, recnum*)
Example: Seek (Inventory, 10)
Interpretation: The file location marker for binary file *iofile* is moved to file component number *recnum,* where the first component has number 0.

Figure 16.6
Procedure UpdateBook

```
procedure UpdateBook (var Inventory {input/output} : BookFile;
                          RecNum,
                          Sales {input} : Integer);
{
  Updates record RecNum of file Inventory by subtracting the
  amount sold (Sales) from the Quantity field.
  Pre : Inventory is opened for input (using Reset)
        and RecNum and Sales are defined.
  Post: Quantity field of record RecNum is decremented by
        Sales.
}
  var
    OneBook : Book;         {record being updated}

begin {UpdateBook}
  if (RecNum >= 0) and (RecNum < FileSize(Inventory)) then
    begin
      Seek (Inventory, RecNum);        {Move to record RecNum.}
      Read (Inventory, OneBook);       {Read it.}
      OneBook.Quantity := OneBook.Quantity - Sales; {Update}
      Seek (Inventory, RecNum);        {Return to record RecNum.}
      Write (Inventory, OneBook)       {Write updated record.}
    end
  else
    WriteLn ('Record number is out of range.')
end; {UpdateBook}
```

Unpredictable results occur if the value of *recnum* is less than 0 or greater than *n* for a file of *n* components.

Note: The file *iofile* must have been opened for input using the Reset procedure prior to the first call to the Seek procedure.

SYNTAX DISPLAY

FileSize Function

Form: FileSize(*iofile*)

Example: FileSize(Inventory)

Interpretation: The FileSize function returns the number of components in binary file *iofile*.

Note: The file *iofile* must have been opened for input using the Reset procedure. FileSize is not part of standard Pascal.

Appending a Record to a File

In Turbo Pascal, the function designator FileSize(Inventory) returns the number of records in file Inventory. The statements

```
Seek (Inventory, FileSize(Inventory));
Write (Inventory, NewBook)
```

can be used to append a new record, `NewBook`, to the end of file `Inventory`. If there are *n* records in file `Inventory` (records 0 through *n* − 1), function `FileSize` returns *n*. Procedure `Seek` advances the file location marker to record number *n* or just past the last record in the current file. Procedure `Write` then writes `NewBook` to the end of the file.

Exercises for Section 16.4 ***Self-Check***

1. What happens if you omit the second `Seek` statement in Fig. 16.6?

Programming

1. Write a program fragment that prints the titles of every book in the inventory in the reverse order of that in the file.

16.5 Common Programming Errors

Always declare each binary file type and a file variable of that type, and be sure to prepare a binary file before attempting to read its records or write to it. Use `Assign` to associate the file variable with its corresponding external name, followed by `Reset` (for an input file) or `Rewrite` (for an output file). Don't forget to pass the file variable as the first of two parameters for each `Read` or `Write` operation; the second parameter must be a variable of the same type as the file components.

You can perform a number of operations with text files that you cannot perform with binary files. Because binary files are not segmented into lines, you cannot use the `EOLN` function or `ReadLn` and `WriteLn` procedures. Also, you cannot create or modify a binary file using an editor program. A binary file must be created by running a program before it can be used.

When using direct access to a binary file, open the file for input and use the `Seek` procedure to move the file location marker before every read and write operation. Remember that the first file component has number 0, not 1.

CHAPTER REVIEW

1. The file type `Text` is predefined. Its components are the Pascal characters and a special character, `<eoln>`. The `EOLN` function can test for an `<eoln>`, and the `WriteLn` statement places one in a text file.
2. You can declare and manipulate binary files whose components may be any simple or structured type (except for an object type or a structured type with a file type component).
3. Binary files have an advantage over `Text` files in that the binary image of a file component can be transferred directly between a variable in main memory and a binary file. The variable involved in the data transfer must be the same type (simple or structured) as the components of the binary file.

4. Turbo Pascal, but not standard Pascal, provides operators that permit direct access to binary files. With direct-access files, you can access the file components in arbitrary order and intermix read and write operations on the same file.

Summary of New Pascal Constructs

Construct	Effect
File-Type Declaration	

`type`
  `DigitFile = file of Integer;`
`var`
   `MoreDigits : DigitFile;`
	Declares a file type `DigitFile` whose components are integers. `MoreDigits` is a file of type `DigitFile`.

Seek Procedure	
`Seek (MoreDigits, 5)`	Positions the file location marker to the sixth component of binary file `MoreDigits`.
FileSize Function	
`FileSize(MoreDigits)`	Returns the number of components stored in binary file `MoreDigits`.

Quick-Check Exercises

1. What data types can be read from or written to a text file?
2. What data types can be read from or written to a binary file?
3. Binary and text files can be created using any standard text editor. True or false?
4. If we have a file of integers and each integer requires 2 bytes, how many bytes would be required to store 20 integers using a binary file? Would a text file require the same number, more, or less?
5. Comment on the correctness of this statement: It is more efficient to use a text file because the computer knows that each component is a single character that can be copied into a single byte of main memory; with a binary file, however, the size of the components may vary.
6. What limits the number of records that can be written to a file?
7. What limits the number of records that can be read from a file? How do you know when you have read them all?
8. What happens if the `Reset` operation is performed on a file that has just been created in a program? If the `Rewrite` operation is performed on the same file?
9. Assume you are merging two files with keys in the following sequence: file 1—112, 115, 222, 324, 999; file 2—111, 121, 132, 222, 444, 999. If 999 is the key of the sentinel record, what would be the sequence of keys in the merged file? What would be the result if the first two records of the second file were transposed?

10. What are the Seek commands to position the file location marker for file DirectFile to the first record in the file? The last record? After the last record?

Answers to Quick-Check Exercises

1. A string type or any of the standard data types (or a subrange thereof) except type Boolean can be read; any of the standard data types (or a subrange thereof) plus strings can be written.
2. The file's component type, which is any simple or structured type (except for an object) that does not have a file type as one of its constituents
3. True for text files, False for binary files
4. 40 bytes. Unless each integer can be written in two characters or less, the text file would require more bytes.
5. The statement is not correct. It is true that two binary files may have components of different sizes, but all the components of a particular file must be the same data type and the same size. This size can be determined from the type declarations. Because no data conversions are necessary when you use binary files, binary files are more efficient than text files.
6. The only limit is the available space on disk.
7. The number of records that were written to the file when it was created. Use the EOF function to test for the end-of-file mark.
8. Reset prepares the file for input so we can echo print it if we want to check the records that were written. Rewrite causes the data in the file to be lost.
9. The merged file would have the correct key sequence: 111, 112, 115, 121, 132, 222, 324, 444, 999. The merged file would have the incorrect key sequence: 112, 115, 121, 111, 132, 222, 324, 444, 999.
10. Seek (DirectFile, 0);
    Seek (DirectFile, FileSize(DirectFile) - 1)
    Seek (DirectFile, FileSize(DirectFile))

Review Questions

1. Given the following program fragment, why would the two numbers be readable in the future if a binary file is used and not if a text file is used?

   Write (OutFile, 1234);
   Write (OutFile, 5678)

2. What can always be said about the length of a binary file? Can the same be said about a text file?
3. Explain the difference between writing the integer 12345 to a binary file and to a text file. How many bytes of external storage would be needed for each file? Which operation would be faster?
4. Consider file EmpStat (type EmpFile) that contains records for up to 15 employees. The data for each employee consist of the employee's name (maximum length 20 characters), social security number (maximum length 11 characters), gross pay for the week (real), taxes deducted (real), and the net

pay (real) for the week. Write a program called `PayReport` that will create a text file `ReportFile` with the heading line

```
NAME      SOC-SEC-NUM     GROSS      TAXES      NET
```

followed by two blank lines, then the pertinent information under each column heading. `ReportFile` should contain up to 18 lines of information after `PayReport` is executed.

5. What are the characteristics of a binary file?

6. Imagine for a moment that you are a college professor who uses a computerized system to maintain student records. Write the type and variable declarations for a file that will consist of multiple records of type `StudentStats`. The statistics kept on each student are `GPA`, `Major`, `Address` (consisting of `Name`, `StreetAddress`, `City`, `State`, and `ZipCode`), and `ClassSchedule` (consisting of up to six records of `Class`, each containing `Description`, `Time`, and `Days` fields). Use whatever variable types are appropriate for each field.

7. What would happen if you opened a file using `Rewrite` prior to using `Seek` to retrieve a record from a direct access file?

8. Write a Boolean function that has as arguments a direct-access file of type `DataBase` and an `Integer` file component number. Your function should return `True` if the file component number is within range and `False` otherwise.

Programming Projects

1. Write a program to create a file of records, each containing a person's last name, first name, birth date, and sex. Create a new file of records containing only first names and sex. Also print out the complete name of every person whose last name begins with the letter A, C, F, or P through Z and who was born in a month beginning with the letter J.

2. Create separate text files for the salesmen and for the saleswomen in your furniture store. For each employee, include an employee number (four digits), a name, and a salary. Each file should be in order by employee number. Merge these two files into a third file (binary) that also has a gender field containing one of the values in the type (`Female`, `Male`). After the file merge operation, find the average salary for all employees. Then search the new file and print a list of all female employees earning more than the average salary and a separate list of all male employees earning more than the average salary. *Hint:* You will have to search the new file once for each list. Your program should include procedures corresponding to the following procedure headers:

```
procedure ReadOneRec (var DataFile {input} : Text;
                          Sex {input} : Gender;
                          var EmpRec {output} : EmployeeRec);
{
 Reads one employee record from text file DataFile and
 assigns Sex value to appropriate EmpRec field.
}

procedure MergeFile (var MaleFile, FemaleFile {input} :
                                                    Text;
                        var OutFile {output} : EmployeeFile);
```

```
{
 Merges the records from the two input files, adds gender
 field to the output record.
 Calls: ReadOneRec.
}

procedure FindAveSalary (var EmpFile {input} :
                                        EmployeeFile;
                         var Average {output} : Real);
{Computes average salary using all employee records}

procedure PrintHigh (Sex {input} : Gender;
                     var EmpFile {input} : EmployeeFile;
                     Average {input} : Real);
{
 Print gender-specific list of persons earning more than
 Average salary.
}
```

3. Write a procedure that will merge the contents of three sorted files by ID number and write the merged data to an output file. The parameters to the procedure will be the three input files and the one output file. The file records will be of the form

```
Data = record
        ID : Integer;
        Name : StringType;
        Salary : Real
      end; {Data}
```

Assume there is no sentinel record. Test your procedure with some sample data.

4. Cooking recipes can be stored on a computer and, with the use of files, quickly referenced.
   a. Write a procedure that will create a text file of recipes from information entered at the terminal. The format of the data to be stored is
      (1) recipe type (Dessert, Meat, etc.)
      (2) subtype (for Dessert, use Cake, Pie, or Brownies)
      (3) name (for cake, German Chocolate)
      (4) number of lines in the recipe to follow
      (5) the actual recipe
      Items 1–4 should be on separate lines.
   b. Write a procedure that will accept as parameters a file and a record of search parameters that will cause all recipes of a type, all recipes of a subtype, or a specific recipe to be written.

5. College football teams need a service to keep track of records and vital statistics. Write a program that will maintain this information in a file. An update file will be "posted" weekly against the master file of all team statistics to date, and all the records will be updated. All the information in both files will be stored in order by ID number. Each master record will contain the team's ID number; team name; number of games won, lost, and tied; total yards gained by the team's offense; total yards gained by the other teams against this one; total

points scored by this team; and total points scored by the other teams against this one.

For this program, use the master file `Teams` and update `Teams` from file `Weekly`. Write the updated information to a file called `NewTeams`. In addition, each record of the weekly file should be echo printed. At the completion of processing the files, write a message indicating the number of weekly scores processed, the team that scored the most points, and the team with the most offensive yardage for this week.

6. Write a program that takes a master file of college football information and prints out teams that match a specified set of search parameters. Some information you might want to print: all teams with a won/lost percentage in a certain range; all teams within a certain range of points scored or scored upon; all teams with a certain range of yardage gained or given up; all teams with a certain number of games won, tied, or lost. (*Note:* The won/lost percentage is calculated by dividing number of games won by total games played; ties count as half a game won.)

7. Write a program that updates a file of type `Inventory` (see Section 16.3). Your program should be able to modify an existing record, insert a new record, and delete an existing record. Assume that the update requests are in order by stock number and that they have the form

```
type
  ChangeKind = (Delete, Insert, Modify);
  UpdateReq = record
                case Change : ChangeKind of
                    Delete : (StockNumber : StockRange);
                    Insert : (NewBook : Book);
                    Modify : (ModBook : Book)
                end; {UpdateReq}
```

Each update request should be read from a binary file. Only the stock number appears in an update request for a deletion. The new book record is supplied for a request to insert a record or to modify an existing record. Your program should also print an error message for invalid requests, such as an attempt to delete a record that does not exist, an attempt to insert a new record with the same stock number as an existing record, or an attempt to modify a record that does not exist.

8. Redo Programming Project 7 as a menu-driven program using a direct-access file to save the inventory data. Assume that the `StockNumber` is used as the record number to access the inventory file. The subrange `StockRange` should be redefined to be `0..99` (to avoid having 1000 record positions that are never used in the inventory file). Support the following menu options: creating a blank file, inserting records, updating records, deleting records, displaying selected records, and displaying all active records.

Since records cannot be deleted physically from the direct-access inventory file, add a Boolean field (`DeletedRec`) to each inventory record. Deleting a record, then, would simply involve setting field `DeletedRec` to `True` and copying the modified record back to the inventory file. Likewise, adding a record would involve setting the `DeletedRec` field to `False`, in addition to assigning values to each of the other fields.

9. It is relatively easy to sort in memory, as we have seen. Sorting a disk file is called *external sorting*. One way to perform an external sort is to store each record's key and record number in an array, sort the array by key field using selection sort, read the file records in sorted order using Seek and the sorted record numbers, and then write them to a new sorted file. Write a procedure that performs an external sort on the following records, sorting on the integer value EmpNum, creating a new sorted file. Write a suitable test program for your procedure. Compare the number of bytes sorted in memory to the number of bytes in the entire file.

```
Employee = record
    EmpNum : Integer;
    Name, Street, City, State, Zip, Department : string
end;
```

CHAPTER SEVENTEEN

Pointers and
Linked Lists

In this chapter, we shift our attention from static structures, such as arrays and records, to dynamic data structures. Unlike static structures, in which the size of the data structure is established during compilation and remains unchanged throughout program execution, dynamic data structures expand and contract as a program executes. The particular dynamic data structure we will study is called a linked list. A *linked list* is a collection of elements (called *nodes*) that are records. Each node has a special field, called a pointer, that connects it to the next node in the list.

Linked list

Linked lists are extremely flexible. It is easy to add new information by creating a new node and inserting it between two existing nodes. It is also relatively easy to delete a node.

In this chapter, you will learn how to store information in linked lists and how to process this information. In Chapter 18, we will examine other examples of dynamic data structures, including stacks, queues, and binary trees.

17.1 Pointer Types and Pointers

The nodes in a linked list are joined by pointers. This section discusses what pointers are and how to use them.

Declaring Pointer Types and Pointer Variables

pointer variable (pointer)
a variable whose contents are
a memory cell address

We can declare pointer types in Pascal and then pointer variables that are pointer types. However, unlike other variables that may contain a particular value (or a collection of related values), **pointer variables** contain addresses or locations in memory. That is, we store the address of a particular data object (i.e., a record, array, or simple variable) in a pointer variable. For example, the declarations

```
type
  RealPointer = ^Real;

var
  P : RealPointer;
```

identify `RealPointer` as the name of a pointer type. We read `^Real` as "pointer to `Real`." The variable declaration specifies that `P` is a pointer variable of type `RealPointer` and allows us to store the *memory address* of a type `Real` variable in `P`.

SYNTAX DISPLAY

Pointer Type Declaration

Form: type *pointertype* = ^*datatype*;
Example: type RealPointer = ^Real;
Interpretation: Type *pointertype* is a data type whose values are memory cell addresses. A data element whose address is stored in a variable of type *pointertype* must be type *datatype*.

Allocating and Accessing New Storage Cells

The statement

```
New (P)
```

calls the Pascal procedure `New`, which allocates storage for a type `Real` value and places the address of this memory cell in pointer variable P. Once storage is allocated for the type `Real` value pointed to by P, we can store a value in that memory cell and manipulate it. **Dynamic allocation** is the process of allocating new storage during program execution.

dynamic allocation
the allocation of new storage during program execution

The actual memory address stored in pointer variable P is a number that has no meaning to us. Consequently, we represent the value of P by drawing an arrow to a memory cell:

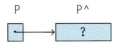

The ? in the memory cell with label P^ indicates that its contents are undefined just after `New (P)` is executed. In Pascal, the symbol P^ indicates the contents of the data area (memory cells) pointed to by P. The ^ (caret), called the *dereferencing operator,* follows the pointer name.

Pascal allocates storage at different times for the memory cells shown in the preceding diagram. Storage is allocated for pointer variable P during compilation when its variable declaration is reached. Storage is allocated for the cell with label P^ when the `New` statement is executed.

The data type of P determines the size and structure of the data area pointed to by P. Because P was declared as type `RealPointer` (i.e., type `RealPointer = ^Real`), P points to a memory area large enough to hold a `Real` value (four bytes).

The contents of a memory cell pointed to by P are processed just like any other type `Real` variable. The statement

```
P^ := 15.0
```

assigns 15.0 as the contents of the memory cell pointed to by P.

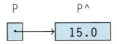

If `Val1` is a type `Real` variable, the statement

```
Val1 := P^ + 10.0
```

adds 10.0 and the contents of the cell pointed to by P and stores the sum (25.0) in `Val1`. The Boolean expression `Val1 <= P^` compares `Val1` to the contents of the cell pointed to by P, so its value is `False`. The statement

```
WriteLn ('The contents of cell pointed to by P are ', P^ :2:1)
```

displays the value of P^ as 15.0.

New Procedure

Form: New (*pointervar*)
Example: New (P)
Interpretation: Storage for a new data area is allocated, and the address of this data area is stored in pointer variable *pointervar*. If *pointervar* is type *pointertype,* the internal representation and size of the new data area are determined from the declaration for *pointertype*. Use *pointervar*^ to reference this data area.

Pointer Operations

Pointer variables do differ from variables of other types. A pointer variable can contain *only* a memory address. For the pointer variable P declared earlier (type ^Real), the following statements would be invalid because a type Integer or type Real value cannot be assigned to a pointer variable:

```
P := 1000;      {invalid assignment}
P := 15.5;      {invalid assignment}
```

The value (an address) of a pointer variable cannot be displayed, so the statement

```
WriteLn (P);    {invalid attempt to display an address}
```

would also be invalid.

If P and Q are both pointer variables of the same type, they can be manipulated with the assignment operator and the relational operators = and <>. For example, the *pointer assignment statement*

```
Q := P
```

copies the address stored in pointer variable P to pointer variable Q. As a result, both P and Q point to the same memory area, and we can reference the following cell using either P^ or Q^:

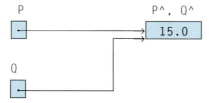

In this instance, the Boolean expression P = Q is True and P <> Q is False.

To summarize, the operators that can be used with pointer variables are :=, =, and <> and both operands must be pointer variables of the same type.

Pointers to Records

We can declare pointers to structured data types as well as to simple data types. Most commonly, we declare pointers to records or to objects. The declarations

```
type
  Electric = record
                Current : string[2];
                Volts : Integer
              end; {Node}

  EPointer = ^Electric;

var
  P, Q : EPointer;    {pointers to records of type Electric}
```

identify `EPointer` as a pointer type. A pointer variable of type `EPointer` points to a record of type `Electric` with two fields: `Current` and `Volts`.

Variables `P` and `Q` are pointer variables that can be used to point to records of type `Electric` (denoted by `P^` and `Q^`). The statement

```
New (P)
```

allocates storage for a record of type `Electric` and stores its memory address in pointer `P`. The data fields of record `P^` are initially undefined.

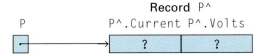

Recall that we used the field selector `Student.Name` to reference the `Name` field of record variable `Student`. We can also use a field selector to reference a field of a record pointed to by a pointer variable. For example, the field selector `P^.Current` references the `Current` field of the record pointed to by `P` (record `P^`). The assignment statements

```
P^.Current := 'AC';
P^.Volts := 115
```

define the fields of the record pointed to by `P` as shown here:

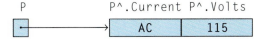

The statement

```
WriteLn (P^.Current, P^.Volts :4)
```

displays the data fields of the record pointed to by `P`. For the record in the preceding diagram, the statement displays the line

```
AC 115
```

The statement

```
New (Q)
```

stores the address of a new record of type `Electric` in pointer `Q`. The next statements copy the contents of the record pointed to by `P` (record `P^`) to the record pointed to by `Q` (record `Q^`), and change the `Volts` field of record `Q^`:

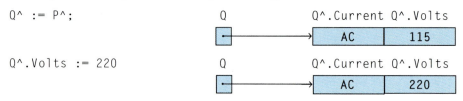

```
Q^ := P^;
```

```
Q^.Volts := 220
```

Finally the pointer assignment statement

```
Q := P
```

resets pointer `Q` to point to the same record as pointer `P`. The old record pointed to by `Q` still exists in memory but can no longer be accessed. Such a record is called an **orphan.**

orphan
a data area in memory that can't be accessed because its address is no longer stored in a pointer variable

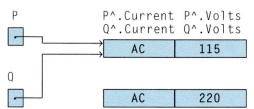

Exercises for Section 17.1 Self-Check

1. If P and Q are type `EPointer`, explain the effect of each valid assignment statement. Which are invalid?
   a. `P^.Current := 'CA'`   e. `P^.Volts := Q^ Volts`
   b. `P^ := Q^`   f. `P := Q`
   c. `P.Current := 'HT'`   g. `P^.Current := Q^.Volts`
   d. `P := 54`   h. `Q^ := P`

2. If A, B, and C are type `EPointer`, draw a diagram of pointers and memory cells after the following operations. Indicate any orphaned data areas.
   a. `New(A)`   d. `A := B`
   b. `New(B)`   e. `B := C`
   c. `New(C)`   f. `C := A`

Programming

1. For the following record type, write a program fragment that creates a collection of seven pointers, allocates memory for each pointer, and places the musical notes do, re, mi, fa, so, la, and ti in the data areas:

```
type
  MusicNote = record
                   Note : string[2]
                 end; {MusicNote}

  MusicNoteP = ^MusicNote;
```

17.2   Manipulating the Heap

heap

the area in main memory used
for the dynamic allocation of
storage

When New executes, where in memory is the new record stored? Pascal maintains a storage pool of available memory cells called a **heap** and allocates memory cells from this pool whenever procedure New is executed.

Effect of the New Statement on the Heap

If P is a pointer variable of type EPointer (declared in the last section), the statement

```
New (P);
```

allocates memory space for a record that stores two characters and an integer variable. The memory cells in this record are originally undefined (they retain whatever data were last stored in them), and the memory address of the first cell allocated is stored in P. Allocated cells are no longer considered part of the heap. The only way to reference allocated cells is through pointer variable P (for example, P^.Current or P^.Volts).

Figure 17.1 shows the pointer variable P and the heap before and after the execution of New (P). The *before* diagram shows pointer variable P as undefined before the execution of New (P). The *after* diagram shows P pointing to the first of four memory cells allocated for the new record (assuming that four memory cells can accommodate a record of type Electric). The cells still considered part of the heap are in gray.

For example, if the memory cells with addresses 1000 through 2000 were originally in the heap, after the execution of New (P) the memory cells with addresses 1000 through 1003 would no longer be part of the heap. The address 1000 would instead be stored in pointer variable P, and that cell would contain the first byte of P^.Current; memory cell 1002 would contain the first byte of P^.Volts.

Returning Cells to the Heap: The Dispose Procedure

The procedure call statement

```
Dispose (P);
```

returns the memory cells pointed to by P to the heap, restoring the heap to the state shown on the left of Fig. 17.1. At this point, the value of pointer variable P becomes undefined and the data formerly associated with P^ are

Figure 17.1
Heap Before and After
New (P)

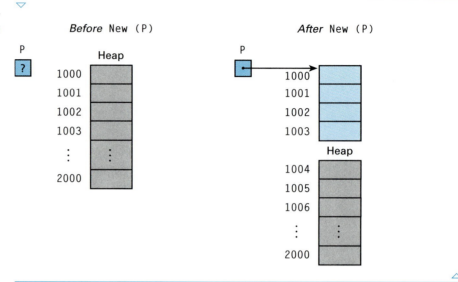

no longer accessible. The three cells that are returned to the heap can be reused later when another New statement is executed.

Often more than one pointer points to the same record. For that reason, be careful when you return the storage occupied by a record to the heap. If cells are reallocated after they are returned, errors may result if they are later referenced by another pointer that still points to them. Make sure you have no need for a particular record before you return the storage occupied by it.

SYNTAX DISPLAY

The Dispose Procedure

Form: Dispose (*pointervar*)
Example: Dispose (P)
Interpretation: The memory cells in the data area whose address is stored in pointer *pointervar* are returned to the heap. These cells can be reallocated when procedure New is called.

Exercise for Section 17.2   *Self-Check*

1.   In a program that is allocating memory space for temporary data items, what would be the consequences of failing to use Dispose when the data items are no longer needed?

17.3 Linked Lists

linked list
a connected group of dynamically allocated records

We can arrange groups of dynamically allocated records into a flexible data structure called a **linked list.** Linked lists are like chains of children's "pop beads," where each bead has a hole at one end and a plug at the other (see Fig. 17.2). We can connect the beads in the obvious way to form a chain and easily modify it. We can remove the color bead by disconnecting the two beads at both its ends and reattaching this pair of beads, add a new bead by connecting it to the bead at either end of the chain, or break the chain somewhere in the middle (between beads A and B) and insert a new bead by connecting one end to bead A and the other end to bead B. We show how to perform these operations to rearrange the records in a linked list next.

In this section, we use pointers to create linked lists. We can add a pointer field to a record and then build a linked list by connecting records with pointer fields. We call a record in a linked list a **node.**

node
an element of a linked list

Declaring Nodes

To declare a record type with a pointer field, we first declare a pointer type (NodePointer) and then a record type. To illustrate:

```
type
   NodePointer = ^Node;
   Node = record
             AWord : string[3];
             Count : Integer;
             Link : NodePointer
          end; {Node}

var
   P, Q, R : NodePointer;   {pointers to records of type Node}
```

A pointer variable of type NodePointer points to a record of type Node with three fields: AWord, Count, and Link. The first two fields store a string and an integer value; the third field, Link (type NodePointer), stores an address, as shown in the following diagram:

Figure 17.2
Children's Pop Beads in a Chain

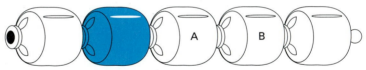

Pop bead   Chain of pop beads

Record of Type Node

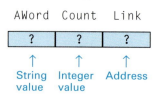

Notice that the type declaration for `NodePointer` refers to the identifier `Node`, which is not yet declared. The declaration of a pointer type is the *only* situation in which Pascal allows us to reference an undeclared identifier. The pointer type must be declared before any node that has a field of this type.

Connecting Nodes

The statements

```
New (P);
New (Q);
```

allocate storage for two records of type `Node`.

The assignment statements

```
P^.AWord := 'hat';   P^.Count := 2;
Q^.AWord := 'top';   Q^.Count := 3
```

define two fields of each node, as shown in Fig. 17.3. The `Link` fields are still undefined.

The statement

```
P^.Link := Q
```

stores the address of record `Q^` in the `Link` field of record `P^`, thereby connecting node `P^` to node `Q^` (see Fig. 17.4).

The `Link` field of the first node, `P^.Link`, points to the second node in the list and contains the same address as pointer `Q`. We can therefore use either field selector `Q^.AWord` or `P^.Link^.AWord` to access the `AWord` field of the second node in the list.

Figure 17.3
Nodes P^ and Q^

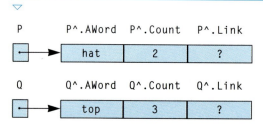

Figure 17.4
List with Two Elements

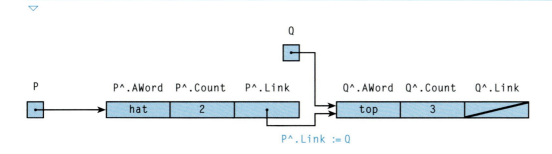

$$P^\wedge.\text{Link} := Q$$

We normally store a special pointer value, nil, in the pointer field of the last element in a list. We can use either of the following statements to accomplish this result. We usually represent the value nil by drawing a diagonal line in a pointer field:

```
Q^.Link := nil    |    P^.Link^.Link := nil
```

Inserting a Node in a List

To insert a new node between nodes P^ and Q^, we start with the statements

```
New (R);
R^.AWord := 'the';   R^.Count := 5;
```

They allocate and initialize a new node (R^), which is pointed to by pointer R. The statements

```
{1}    P^.Link := R;    {Connect node P^ to node R^.}
{2}    R^.Link := Q     {Connect node R^ to node Q^.}
```

assign new values to the Link fields of node P^ (statement {1}) and node R^ (statement {2}). Statement {1} connects node P^ to node R^; statement {2} connects node R^ to node Q^. Figure 17.5 shows the effect of these statements. The color arrows show the new values of the pointer fields; the gray arrow shows the old values.

Notice in Fig. 17.5 that we no longer need pointer variables Q and R to access the list nodes because we can reach each node by following a trail of pointers from pointer variable P. The first node (node P^) is called the **list head.** Table 17.1 shows some valid references to the list data, starting from the list head.

list head
the first node in a list

Figure 17.5
Inserting Node R^ in a List

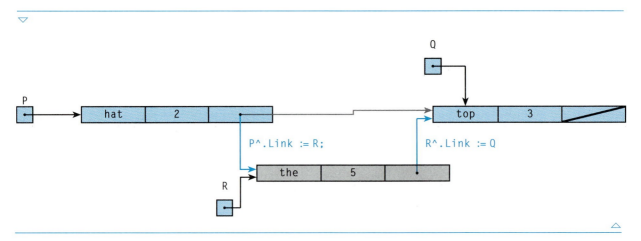

Table 17.1
References to List Nodes in
Fig. 17.5

Field Selector	Data Referenced
P^.AWord	hat
P^.Link	Link field of first node
P^.Link^.AWord	the
P^.Link^.Link	Link field of second node
P^.Link^.Link^.Count	3

Insertion at the Head of a List

Although we usually insert new data items at the end of a data structure, it is easier and more efficient to insert a new item at the head of a list. The following program fragment allocates a new node and inserts it at the head of the list pointed to by P. Pointer OldHead points to the original list head. After the insertion, P points to the new list head which is linked to the old list head, as shown in Fig. 17.6. The color arrows show the new values of the pointer fields; the gray arrow shows the old values.

```
OldHead := P;              {Save pointer to old list head.}
New (P);                   {Point P to a new node.}
P^.Link := OldHead   {Connect new list head to old list head.}
```

Insertion at the End of a List

Inserting an item at the end of a list is less efficient because we usually do not have a pointer to the last list element and so must follow the pointer trail

Figure 17.6
Insertion at the List Head

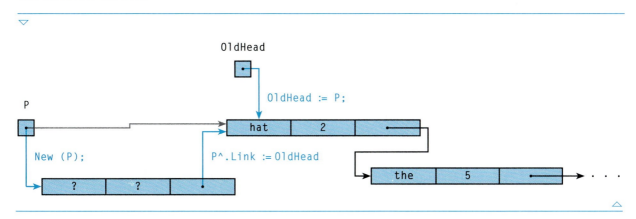

from the list head to the last list node and then perform the insertion. When Last is pointing to the last list node (Fig. 17.7), the statements

```
New (Last^.Link);        {Attach a new node to list end.}
Last^.Link^.Link := nil            {Mark new list end.}
```

connect a new node to the end of the list and set its Link field to nil.

Deleting a Node

To delete a node from a linked list, we simply change the Link field of the node that points to it (its *predecessor*). We want the predecessor to point to the node that follows the one being deleted (its *successor*). For example, to delete node R^ from the three-element list in Fig. 17.8, we change the Link field of node P^ to point to the successor of node R^. The statement

Figure 17.7
Insertion at the End of a List

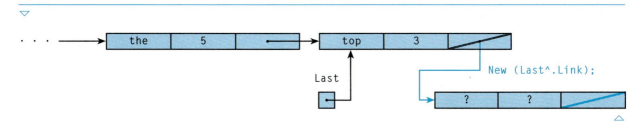

```
P^.Link := R^.Link;   {Bypass node R^.}
```

copies the address in the Link field of node R^ to the Link field of node P^, thereby deleting node R^ from the list. Then, we use the statements

```
R^.Link := nil;      {Disconnect R^ from its successor.}
Dispose (R)          {Return storage to the heap.}
```

to disconnect node R^ from the list and return its storage to the heap.

Traversing a List

In many list processing operations, we must process each node in the list in sequence, a procedure called **traversing a list.** We start at the list head and follow the trail of pointers.

One typical operation performed on most data structures is to display the data structure's contents. To display the contents of a list, we must display only the values of the information fields, not the link fields. Procedure PrintList in Fig. 17.9 displays the information fields of each node in the list shown in Fig. 17.8 (after the deletion). The procedure call statement

```
PrintList (P);
```

displays the output lines

```
hat 2
top 3
```

The while condition

```
Head <> nil
```

Figure 17.8
Deleting a List Node

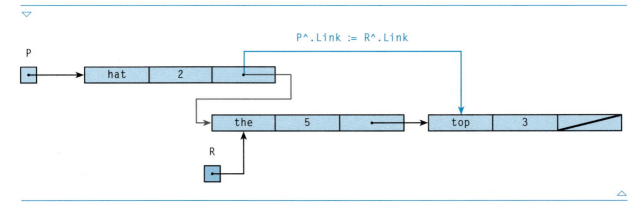

Figure 17.9
Procedure PrintList

```
procedure PrintList (Head {input} : ListPointer);
{
  Displays the list pointed to by Head.
  Pre : Head points to a list whose last node has a pointer
        field of nil.
  Post: The data fields of each list node are displayed and
        the last value of Head is nil.
}
begin {PrintList}
  {Traverse the list until the end is reached.}
  while Head <> nil do
    {invariant: No prior value of Head was nil.}
    begin
      Write (Head^.AWord);
      WriteLn (Head^.Count :2);
      Head := Head^.Link              {Advance to next node.}
    end {while}
end; {PrintList}
```

is common in loops that process lists. If the list to be displayed is empty, this condition is true initially and the loop body is skipped. If the list is not empty, the loop body executes and the last statement in the loop,

```
Head := Head^.Link       {Advance to next node.}
```

advances the pointer Head to the next list element, which is pointed to by the Link field of the current list element. After the last data value in the list is printed, this statement assigns the address nil to Head and loop exit occurs.

Because Head is a value parameter, a local copy of the pointer to the first list element is established when the procedure is entered. This local pointer is advanced, but the corresponding pointer in the calling program remains unchanged. What would happen to our list if Head was a variable parameter?

Program Style

Warning About Variable Parameters for Pointers

Consider the effect of parameter Head being a variable parameter instead of a value parameter. This would allow the procedure to change the corresponding actual parameter, regardless of our intentions. In PrintList and in many similar procedures, the last value assigned to the pointer parameter is nil. If Head is a variable parameter, the corresponding actual parameter would be set to `nil`, thereby disconnecting it from the list to which it pointed before the procedure call.

Passing a pointer as a value parameter protects that pointer from being changed by the procedure. However, you should realize that any changes made to other pointers in the list during the procedure's execution will remain.

Circular Lists and Two-Way Lists (Optional)

You can traverse a list in only one direction, and you can't move past the last element. To circumvent these restrictions, programmers use either circular or two-way lists.

Circular Lists

circular list

a list in which the last list node contains a pointer to the first list node

A **circular list** is one in which the last list node points back to the list head. In the following circular list, you can start anywhere in the list and still access all list elements:

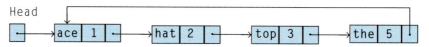

Two-Way Lists

two-way (doubly linked) list

a list in which each node has a pointer to its predecessor and successor

In a **two-way,** or **doubly linked, list,** each node has two pointers: one to the node's successor (`Right`) and one to the node's predecessor (`Left`). For the node `Next^` shown here,

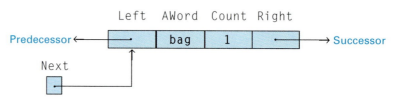

the statement

```
Next := Next^.Right
```

moves pointer `Next` to the successor node, and the statement

```
Next := Next^.Left
```

moves pointer `Next` to the predecessor node.

Exercises for Section 17.3 Self-Check

1. For the three-element list in Fig. 17.5, explain the effect of each fragment. Assume the list is restored to its initial state before each fragment executes.

```
a.  R^.Link := P                    f.  P^.Link := nil
b.  P^.Link := R                    g.  P^.Link := Q^.Link
c.  P := P^.Link                    h.  P^.Aword := R^.AWord
d.  P^.Count :=                     i.  P^.Link^.Link := nil
        P^.Link^.Link^.Count        j.  while P <> nil do
e.  New (Q^.Link);                        begin
    Q^.Link^.AWord := 'zzz';                P^.Count :=
    Q^.Link^.Count := 0;                            P^.Count + 1;
    Q^.Link^.Link := nil                    P := P^.Link
                                          end
```

2. How would you delete the node at the head of a list? How would you delete a node if you were given only a pointer to the node to be deleted and a pointer to the list head?

Programming

1. Write a function that finds the length of a list.
2. Write a fragment to advance pointer Last to the last node of a list whose head is P^. Then insert a new list node at the end of the list. Make sure you consider the special case of an initially empty list (P is nil).

17.4 Linked List ADT

A linked list can store any collection of records (e.g., a class of student records or a telephone directory) and its flexibility makes it an ideal data structure when insertions and deletions are frequent. In this section, we provide the specification for a linked list abstract data type (Table 17.2) and discuss how to implement some of its operators. We base our linked list ADT on the list ADT in Section 13.3.

Table 17.2
Specification for Linked
List Abstract Data Type

Structure
A linked list is a collection of elements, each with a key field that uniquely identifies it.

Operators
The descriptions of the operators use the following parameters:

    AnEntry (type Entry)
    Success (type Boolean)

Several operators use the Boolean parameter Success to indicate whether the operation succeeds (returns True) or fails (returns False).

Table 17.2
Specification for Linked
List Abstract Data Type
(continued)

`LinkList.Init` (constructor) Creates a linked list that is initially empty.

`LinkList.ReadList` Reads the entries from a text file and stores them in the linked list.

`LinkList.Insert (AnEntry, var Success)` Inserts a new entry at the beginning of the list.

`LinkList.Search (AnEntry, var Success)` Returns through `Success` an indication of whether the key in `AnEntry` is found.

`LinkList.Replace (AnEntry, var Success)` Replaces the entry with the same key as `AnEntry` with `AnEntry`.

`LinkList.Delete (AnEntry, var Success)` Deletes the entry with the same key as AnEntry.

`LinkList.Retrieve (var AnEntry, var Success)` Retrieves the entry with the same key as `AnEntry`.

`LinkList.GetCount` (function) Returns the count of entries in the list.

`LinkList.DisplayList` Displays all list entries.

`LinkList.Done` (destructor) Returns storage for all list entries.

Interface Section for Unit LinkListADT

The interface section (Fig. 17.10) follows from the specification given in Table 17.2. Each list node (record type `ListNode`) has an information part, `Info`, and a pointer field, `Link`. The information part has data type `Entry` that is declared in unit `EntryObjADT` (Fig. 13.6). A linked list object has only two data members: a pointer field, `Head`, that points to the first list node and an `Integer` field, `Count`, that keeps track of the number of nodes.

Compare the first data member for object `LinkList` with the first data member in object `List` (Fig. 13.9). In object `List`, the data member

```
Entries : EntryArray;  {array of entries}
```

is an array type housing all list elements; storage for the entire array of records is allocated during compilation. In contrast, object `LinkList` has the data member

```
Head : ListPointer;  {pointer to first node}
```

which points to the first list element. Storage is not allocated for the linked list nodes at compile time, but instead will be allocated as needed when new nodes are created during run time.

Object `LinkList` has three private methods: `DoSearch`, `DoDelete`, and `DoReplace`. We will discuss these methods when we implement methods `Search`, `Delete`, and `Replace`.

Figure 17.10
Interface Section for
LinkListADT

```
unit LinkListADT;

interface
  uses EntryObjADT;              {imports object type Entry}

type
  ListPointer = ^ListNode;
  ListNode = record
                Info : Entry;         {information part}
                Link : ListPointer    {connector to next node}
             end; {ListNode}

  LinkList = object
                constructor Init;
                procedure ReadList;
                procedure Insert (AnEntry : Entry;
                                       var Success : Boolean);
                procedure Search (AnEntry : Entry;
                                       var Success : Boolean);
                procedure Replace (AnEntry : Entry;
                                       var Success : Boolean);
                procedure Delete (AnEntry : Entry;
                                       var Success : Boolean);
                procedure Retrieve (var AnEntry : Entry;
                                       var Success : Boolean);
                function GetCount : Integer;
                procedure DisplayList;
                destructor Done;

             private
                Head : ListPointer;   {pointer to first node}
                Count : Integer;      {number of nodes}

                procedure DoSearch (First : ListPointer;
                                       AnEntry : Entry;
                                       var Success : Boolean);
                procedure DoReplace (var First : ListPointer;
                                       AnEntry : Entry;
                                       var Success : Boolean);
                procedure DoDelete (var First : ListPointer;
                                       AnEntry : Entry;
                                       var Success : Boolean);
             end; {LinkList}
```

Implementation Section for Unit LinkListADT

The implementation section contains the method declarations.

Init, ReadList, and Insert

For the object instance that is its recipient, `Init` (Fig. 17.11) sets the count of entries to `0` and the pointer field `Head` to `nil`.

The `while` loop in `ReadList` reads each entry's data (using method `Entry.ReadEntry`) and calls method `Insert` to store the data in a new node at the head of the linked list. Each entry is stored in the list in the reverse order from which it is read (i.e., the last entry read is stored in the list head).

Figure 17.11
Methods Init, ReadList,
and Insert

```
implementation

  constructor LinkList.Init;
  {
  Creates an initially empty list.
  pre : none
  post: Linked list with 0 elements is defined.
  }
  begin {Init}
    Count := 0;
    Head := nil
  end; {Init}

  procedure LinkList.ReadList;
  {
  Reads data records into a list.
  pre : Data file is a text file.
  post: Entries in data file are stored in the list.
  }
    var
      AnEntry : Entry;              {a new entry}
      InFile : Text;               {internal file variable}
      FileName : string;      {directory name of input file}
      Success : Boolean;      {flag}

  begin {ReadList}
    WriteLn ('Enter the data file name> ');
    ReadLn (FileName);
    Assign (InFile, FileName);
    Reset (InFile);                {Open the data file.}

    {Read each record and insert it in the list.}
    while not EOF(InFile) do
      begin
        AnEntry.ReadEntry (InFile, FileName); {Read entry.}
        Insert (AnEntry, Success)      {Insert it in the list.}
      end {while};

    Close (InFile)
  end; {ReadList}
```

▷ ▷ ▷ ▷ ▷ ▷

```
procedure LinkList.Insert (AnEntry : Entry;
                                var Success : Boolean);
{
 Inserts entry AnEntry into a list.
 pre : AnEntry is defined.
 post: Inserts AnEntry as the first list element and
       sets Success to True.
}
  var
    OldHead : ListPointer;      {pointer to old list head.}

begin {Insert}
  OldHead := Head;            {Save pointer to old head.}
  New (Head);                 {Point Head to a new node.}
  Head^.Info := AnEntry;      {Store new entry in new head.}
  Head^.Link := OldHead;      {Link new head to old head.}
  Count := Count + 1;         {Increase count of nodes.}
  Success := True
end; {Insert}
```

Method `Insert` places a new entry at the beginning of the list rather than the end because insertion at the beginning is easier. In `Insert`, the statements

```
OldHead := Head;             {Save pointer to old head.}
New (Head);                  {Point Head to a new node.}
Head^.Info := AnEntry;       {Store new entry in new head.}
Head^.Link := OldHead;       {Link new head to old head.}
```

store `AnEntry`'s data at the head of the list. The first statement stores the address of the current list head in `OldHead`, and the next two allocate a new head node and store `AnEntry` in it. The last statement connects the new list head to the rest of the list.

Figure 17.12 traces the insertion of the first two data records, assuming each data record contains a person's name and number. In each diagram, the color arrows show pointers that are changed by procedure `Insert`.

Search

We often use recursive algorithms to process linked data structures. A recursive search algorithm follows.

Algorithm for List Search

1. if the list is empty then
    Return with `Success` set to `False`.
  else if the first list node contains `AnEntry`'s key then
    Return with `Success` set to `True`.
  else
    Search the rest of the list.

Figure 17.12
Inserting the First Two
Data Records

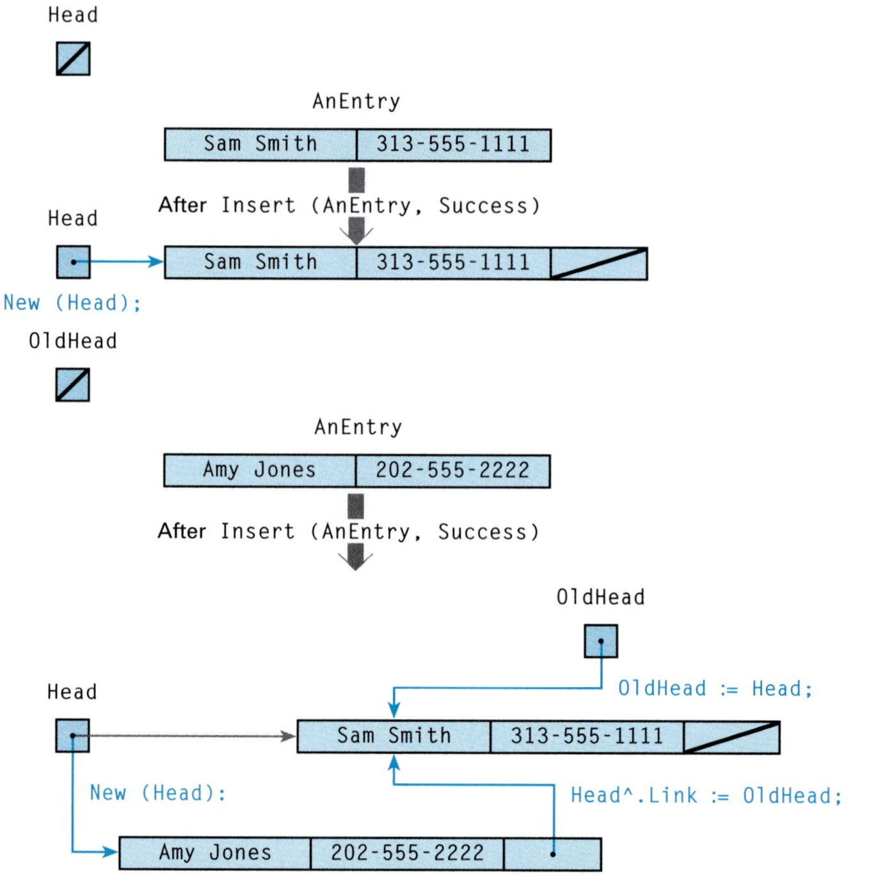

If the list is empty, the value of Success must be False. If the head of the list matches AnEntry, the value of Success must be True. Otherwise, the recursive step "Search the rest of the list" searches the list whose head is the second element of the previous list. This step causes the first element of successively smaller lists to be compared to AnEntry until the list being searched is empty (first stopping case—return False through Success) or its head matches AnEntry (second stopping case—return True through Success). Figure 17.13 traces the algorithm during an unsuccessful search, showing the list head (pointed to by First) for each recursive call.

Method Search (Fig. 17.14) calls private method DoSearch to start the search, passing the list head as the first parameter to DoSearch. Method

Figure 17.13
Search for AnEntry's Key

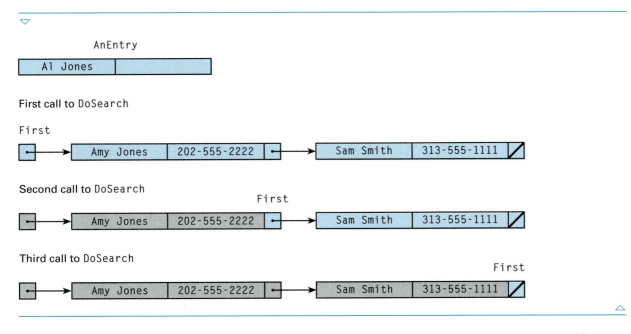

DoSearch implements the recursive search algorithm. In DoSearch, the condition AnEntry.EqualTo(First^.Info) compares the key field of AnEntry to the key field of the current list head. The statement

DoSearch (First^.Link, AnEntry, Success)

advances First to the second element of the current list, causing the rest of the list to be searched. The recursion stops as soon as a value is assigned to Success and, after unwinding from the recursion, that value is returned to the program that called Search.

Figure 17.14
Methods DoSearch
and Search

```
procedure LinkList.DoSearch (First {input} : ListPointer;
                             AnEntry {input} : Entry;
                             var Success {output} : Boolean);
{
 Performs recursive search.
 pre : First points to the head of the list being searched.
 post: If AnEntry's key is found, Success is set to True;
       otherwise, Success is set to False.
}
```

```
begin {DoSearch}
  if First = nil then
    Success := False
  else if AnEntry.EqualTo(First^.Info) then
    Success := True
  else
    DoSearch (First^.Link, AnEntry, Success)
end; {DoSearch}

procedure LinkList.Search (AnEntry {input} : Entry;
                             var Success {output} : Boolean);
{
 Calls DoSearch to search for AnEntry's key in the list.
 pre : AnEntry is defined.
 post: If AnEntry's key is found, Success is set to True;
       otherwise, Success is set to False.
}
begin {Search}
  DoSearch (Head, AnEntry, Success)
end; {Search}
```

Replace and Delete

Methods Replace (Fig. 17.15) and Delete (Fig. 17.16) are modeled after Search. Both methods call private methods (DoReplace or DoDelete) to compare the key of AnEntry to the first element of successively smaller lists. Because both recursive methods can modify the list, First is a variable parameter.

What happens when the current list head matches AnEntry's key? In DoReplace, the statement

Figure 17.15
Methods DoReplace
and Replace

```
procedure LinkList.DoReplace (var First {input/output} :
                                            ListPointer;
                              AnEntry {input} : Entry;
                              var Success {output} :
                                            Boolean);
{
 Performs recursive replacement.
 pre : First points to the head of the list being searched.
 post: Entry with same key as AnEntry is replaced and
       Success is True; otherwise, Success is False.
}
```

```
begin {DoReplace}
  if First = nil then
    Success := False
  else if AnEntry.EqualTo(First^.Info) then
    begin {found key}
      First^.Info := AnEntry;   {Replace item with AnEntry.}
      Success := True
    end {found key}
  else
    DoReplace (First^.Link, AnEntry, Success)
end; {DoReplace}

procedure LinkList.Replace (AnEntry {input} : Entry;
                                var Success {output} : Boolean);
{
 Substitutes AnEntry for the entry with matching key.
 pre : AnEntry is defined.
 post: Entry with same key as AnEntry is replaced and
       Success is True; otherwise, Success is False.
}
begin {Replace}
  DoReplace (Head, AnEntry, Success)
end; {Replace}
```

```
First^.Info := AnEntry;    {Replace item with AnEntry.}
```

replaces the data stored in the current list head with AnEntry. In DoDelete, the statement

```
First := First^.Link;              {Bypass old head.}
```

deletes the current list head, which is then returned to the heap (by Dispose). Both methods set Success to True, and procedure Delete decrements the data member Count.

Figure 17.16
Methods DoDelete
and Delete

```
procedure LinkList.DoDelete (var First {input/output} :
                                          ListPointer;
                             AnEntry {input} : Entry;
                             var Success {output} : Boolean);
{
 Performs recursive deletion.
 pre : First points to the head of the list being searched.
 post: If AnEntry is found, it is deleted and
       Success is True; otherwise, Success is False.
}
```

▷ ▷ ▷ ▷ ▷ ▷

```
var
   ToDelete : ListPointer; {pointer to node to delete.}

begin {DoDelete}
  if First = nil then
    Success := False
  else if AnEntry.EqualTo(First^.Info) then
    begin {found key}
      ToDelete := First;         {Delete list head.}
      First := First^.Link;        {Bypass old head.}
      ToDelete^.Link := nil;    {Disconnect old head.}
      Dispose (ToDelete);       {Return node to heap.}
      Success := True
    end {found key}
  else
    DoDelete (First^.Link, AnEntry, Success)
end; {DoDelete}

procedure LinkList.Delete (AnEntry : Entry;
                                var Success : Boolean);
{
 Deletes the entry with the same key as AnEntry.
 pre : AnEntry is defined.
 post: If AnEntry is found, it is deleted and
       Success is True; otherwise, Success is False.
}

begin {Delete}
  DoDelete (Head, AnEntry, Success);
  if Success then
    Count := Count - 1    {Decrement Count after deletion.}
end; {Delete}
```

△

Destructor Done

destructor

a method that returns storage for a dynamically allocated object

A dynamic object should have a special method called a **destructor** that returns all storage allocated to an object instance to the heap. If you create and use linked list L in a client program, you should send the message

L.Done

after you finish processing the linked list. This is analagous to closing a file after you finish reading it.

Figure 17.17 shows destructor Done. The steps in the while loop disconnect the current list head, return its storage to the heap, and advance Head to the next list element. Loop exit occurs when the list is empty (Head is nil).

Figure 17.17
Method Done

```
destructor  LinkList.Done;
{
 Returns storage for all list entries to heap.
 pre : Head points to a list.
 post: Count is 0 and all list storage is deallocated.
}
  var OldHead : ListPointer;    {Pointer to old list head}

begin {Done}
  while Head <> nil do
     {invariant : No prior value of Head was nil.}
     begin
        OldHead := Head;         {Save pointer to old head.}
        Head := Head^.Link;      {Advance Head down the list.}
        OldHead^.Link := nil;  {Disconnect old head.}
        Dispose (OldHead)        {Return storage.}
     end;   {while}

  Count := 0                     {List is empty.}
end;  {Done}

{Insert methods Retrieve, GetCount, DisplayList here.}

end. {LinkListADT}
```

Exercises for Section 17.4 *Self-Check*

1. Verify that method Insert works properly when the list being inserted into is an empty one. How does the nil pointer get stored in the Link field of the list element being inserted?

2. Assume a linked list contains the three strings 'Hat', 'Boy', 'Cat'. What successive lists are searched when method Search is called and the target key is 'Boy'? When the target key is 'Cup'?

3. Why it is easier to insert a new list element at the head of a list rather than the end? How would you perform an insertion at the end of a list for the list object declared in Fig. 17.10? Why is this an *O(N)* operation? How could you change the list object declaration so that insertion at the end of a list would be an *O*(1) operation?

4. How could a linked list be implemented using an array of records rather than pointers? How would you represent the links? How would you add new items? What are the disadvantages of this approach? How could you handle deletions to recover the array locations for future use?

Programming

1. Write methods `Retrieve`, `GetCount`, and `DisplayList`.
2. Write an iterative version of `Search`.
3. Write a recursive procedure to display the list in reverse order.

17.5   Common Programming Errors

Syntax Errors

Be sure to use the dereferencing operator ^ where it is needed. If `P` is a pointer variable, `P^.X` should be used to reference field `X` of the record pointed to by `P`.

The `New` and `Dispose` procedures allocate and deallocate storage, respectively. Both procedures require a parameter that is a pointer variable. `New (P)` is correct, while `New (P^)` is incorrect.

Run-Time Errors

Several run-time errors can occur when traversing linked data structures. For example, if pointer `Next` is supposed to point to each node in the linked list, make sure `Next` is initialized to point to the list head.

Watch out for infinite loops caused by failure to advance a pointer down a list. The `while` statement

```
while Next <> nil do
  Write (Next^.Data);
  Next := Next^.Link;
```

executes forever because the pointer assignment statement is not included in the loop body, so `Next` is not advanced down the list.

A run-time error can occur when the pointer `Next` is advanced too far down the list and `Next` takes on the value `nil`, indicating the end of the list. If pointer `Next` has the value `nil`, the `while` condition

```
while (Next <> nil) and (Next^.ID <> 9999) do
```

causes a run-time error on some systems because `Next^.ID` is undefined when `Next` is `nil`. The `while` condition should be rewritten as

```
while (Next^.Link <> nil) and (Next^.ID <> 9999) do
```

Problems with heap management can also cause run-time errors. If your program gets stuck in an infinite loop while you are creating a dynamic data structure, it could consume all memory cells on the storage heap. This situation leads to a `heap overflow` run-time error.

Similar problems can occur with recursive procedures. If a recursive procedure does not terminate, you can get a `stack overflow` error.

Make sure your program does not attempt to reference a list node after the node is returned to the heap. All pointers to a node being returned should be assigned new values so that the node can never be accessed unless it is reallocated.

Debugging Tips

It is difficult to debug programs that manipulate pointers, because the value of a pointer variable cannot be printed. If a pointer variable is displayed in the Watch window, it appears as a pair of hexadecimal numbers (*segment* : *offset*) that have little meaning to anyone other than a systems programmer. Consequently, you often will find it more informative to trace the execution of such a program by printing (or watching) an information field that uniquely identifies the list element being processed instead of the pointer itself.

When writing driver programs to test and debug list operators, you can create a small linked list by using the `New` statement to allocate several nodes and linking them into a list by using assignment statements (see Section 17.3). You also can use assignment statements to put information into the nodes, prior to linking them.

CHAPTER REVIEW

1. A pointer is a variable whose contents are a memory cell address. You can perform assignment and comparison operations on pointers, but you can't read or write pointer values.
2. The procedure call `New (P)` dynamically allocates storage for a memory area whose address is stored in pointer variable `P`. The data type of pointer `P` determines the structure of this data area, which is referenced as `P^`. The memory cells for this data area are taken from Pascal's heap. When the data area `P^` is no longer needed, use the procedure call `Dispose (P)` to return it to the storage heap.
3. If data area `P^` itself contains a pointer field, you can connect it to another like data area, thereby building a linked list. Linked lists are flexible data structures that shrink and expand as a program executes. It is relatively easy to insert and delete nodes of a linked list.
4. You can use object type `LinkList` declared in the linked list ADT in Section 17.4 to house a linked list. The methods of object `LinkList` are similar to those of the list ADT in Section 13.3 and include methods for performing search, insert, replace, and delete operations on a linked list, as well as reading records from a data file into a linked list and displaying the contents of a linked list.

Summary of New Pascal Constructs

Construct	Effect
Pointer Type Declaration	
| ```
type
  Pointer = ^Node;
  Node = record
    Info : Integer;
    Link : Pointer
  end; {Node}
``` | The type identifier `Pointer` is declared as a pointer to a record of type `Node`, where `Node` is a record type containing a field (`Link`) of type `Pointer`. |
| ```
var
  Head : Pointer;
``` | `Head` is a pointer variable of type `Pointer`. |
New Procedure	
`New (Head)`	A new record of type `Node` is allocated. This record is pointed to by `Head` and is referenced by `Head^`.
Dispose Procedure	
`Dispose (Head)`	The memory space occupied by the record `Head^` is returned to the storage pool.
Pointer Assignment	
`Head := Head^.Link`	The pointer `Head` is advanced to the next node in the dynamic data structure pointed to by `Head`.

Quick-Check Exercises

1. Procedure _____ allocates storage space for a data object that is referenced through a _____; procedure _____ returns the storage space to the _____.
2. What is the major advantage of using pointer representations of lists instead of using arrays to store listlike structures as we did in Chapter 13?
3. Assume a linked list object contains a pointer, `Rear`, to the last list element. Write the statements necessary to insert an element `NewItem` at the rear of the list instead of at the list head.
4. When an element is deleted from a linked list represented using pointers, it is automatically returned to the heap. True or false?
5. All pointers to a node that is returned to the heap are automatically reset to `nil` so they cannot reference the node returned to the heap. True or false?
6. Why would the following code fragment cause a run-time error? Assume `Link` is a pointer and `Data` is an integer. How could it be fixed?

```
while Head <> nil do
  Head := Head^.Link;
WriteLn ('Last data item in list is: ', Head^.Data);
```

7. If a linked list contains three elements with values `'Him'`, `'Her'`, and `'Its'` and H is a pointer to the list head, what is the effect of the following statements? Assume the data field is `Pronoun`, the link field is `Next`, and N and P are pointer variables.

```
N := H^.Next;
N^.Pronoun := 'She'
```

8. Answer Exercise 7 for the following segment:

```
P := H^.Next;
N := P^.Next;
P^.Next := N^.Next;
Dispose (N)
```

9. Answer Exercise 7 for the following segment:

```
N := H;
New (H);
H^.Pronoun := 'His';
H^.Next := N
```

10. When is it advantageous to use a linked-list data structure? When would an array be a better choice?

Answers to Quick-Check Exercises

1. New; pointer; `Dispose`; heap
2. Storage space is allocated as needed and not all at once.
3. ```
New (Rear^.Link);
Rear := Rear^.Link;
Rear^.Info := NewItem;
Rear^.Link := nil;
Count := Count + 1
```
4. False (`Dispose` must be called).
5. False
6. At loop exit, Head will be `nil`, so Head^.Data is invalid.

```
Last := nil;                    {Assume list is empty.}
while Head <> nil do
  begin
    Last := Head;               {Set Last to old Head.}
    Head := Head^.Link          {Advance Head.}
  end; {while}

if Last <> nil then
  WriteLn ('Last data item in list is: ', Last^.Data);
```

7. `'Her'` is replaced by `'She'`.
8. The third list element is deleted.
9. A new list node with value `'His'` is inserted at the front of the list.
10. When the number of elements is variable or insertions and deletions are frequent. When elements must be accessed randomly.
```

Review Questions

1. Define the term *linked list*. How are the list nodes connected? How many pointer variables would you need to access all nodes of a linked list with five nodes?

2. Why are recursive procedures often used for processing linked data structures?

3. Why is it more efficient to insert at the front of a list than at the end? What is the time in Big-O notation for insertion at the front of a list? At the end of a list? How can insertion at the end of a list be made more efficient?

4. If a linked list of data elements is in sorted order, could we perform a binary search on that list in $O(\log_2 N)$ time? Why or why not.

5. Give the missing type declarations and show the effect of each of the following statements. What does the fragment do?

    ```
    New (P);
    P^.Data := 'ABC';
    New (P^.Next);
    Q := P^.Next;
    Q^.Data := 'abc';
    Q^.Next := nil
    ```

Assume the following type declarations for Questions 6 through 9:

```
type
   StringType = string[10];
   ListPointer = ^Node;
   Node = record
             Name : StringType;
             Link : ListPointer
          end; {Node}

   HeadNode = record
                 Head : ListPointer;
                 NumItems : Integer
              end; {HeadNode}

var
   List : HeadNode;
```

6. Write a program segment that places the names Washington, Roosevelt, and Kennedy in successive elements of the linked list referenced by record List. Define List.NumItems accordingly.

7. Write an operator called DeleteLast that removes the last element from any list referenced by record List.

8. Write a procedure called CopyList that creates a linked list with new nodes that contain the same data as the linked list referenced by List.

9. Write a procedure to delete all nodes with Name field equal to Target (a parameter) from a linked list referenced by record List.

Programming Projects

1. Write a procedure that uses the selection sort strategy to create a sorted copy of a linked list, assuming the Entry object contains a method LessThan for comparing entries.

2. Write a linked-list merge procedure similar to the file merge procedure from Chapter 16 that creates a new sorted linked list by merging two linked lists that have been sorted using the procedure from Programming Project 1.

3. Modify Programming Project 1 at the end of Chapter 10 so that student grades are stored in a linked list rather than in an array of scores.

4. The singly linked list presented in this chapter makes it easy to process the list elements in order, but processing in reverse order is very difficult and time consuming. One solution is to use a two-way list (see Section 17.3). Create a new two-way list ADT based on the linked list ADT, and include a new procedure to display the list in reverse. Write a suitable test program for your ADT.

5. A polynomial can be represented as a linked list, where each node contains the coefficient and the exponent of a term of the polynomial. The polynomial $4x^3 + 3x^2 - 5$ would be represented as the following linked list:

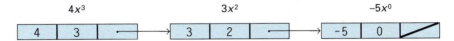

Write an abstract data type Polynomial that has operators for creating a polynomial, reading a polynomial, and adding and subtracting a pair of polynomials. Store the terms for each polynomial in decreasing order by exponent. *Hint:* To add or subtract two polynomials, traverse both lists. If a particular exponent value is present in either one, it also should be present in the result polynomial unless its coefficient is zero.

6. Each student in the university takes a different number of courses, so the registrar has decided to use a linked list to store each student's class schedule and an array of records to represent the whole student body. A portion of this data structure follows.

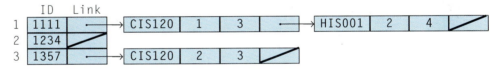

The records show that the first student (ID is 1111) is taking section 1 of CIS120 for 3 credits and section 2 of HIS001 for 4 credits; the second student (ID is 1234) is not enrolled, and so on. Write declarations for this data structure. Provide operators for creating the original array of student ID numbers, inserting a student's initial class schedule, adding a course, and dropping a course. Write a menu-driven program that uses these operators.

7. Many programs, including the Turbo Pascal environment, create multiple, overlapping windows on the screen. With overlapping windows comes the concept of a window being on top and a front-to-back ordering of windows. If windows are drawn from back to front, their appearance matches the expected results. Write a program that maintains a linked list of colored rectangles representing windows in front-to-back order. Your program should have a menu that allows the user to enter a letter for a rectangle, the color of the rectangle, and its screen location. Other menu options should allow the screen to be redrawn and any window to be moved to the top.

CHAPTER EIGHTEEN

Dynamic Data Structures

Linked lists are just one type of dynamic data structure. In this chapter, we introduce three others: stacks, queues, and binary search trees. We provide only a brief overview of these structures; you will cover them in more detail in advanced courses in computer science.

18.1 Stacks

A **stack** is a data structure in which only the top element can be accessed. To illustrate, the plates stored in the spring-loaded device in a buffet line perform like a stack. A customer always takes the top plate; when a plate is removed, the plate beneath it moves to the top.

The following diagram shows a stack of three characters. The letter C, the character at the top of the stack, is the only one we can access. We must remove C from the stack in order to access the symbol +. Removing a value from a stack is called **popping the stack,** and storing a data item in a stack is called **pushing** it onto the stack.

Stacks as Linked Lists

We can think of a stack as a linked list in which all insertions and deletions are performed at the list head. A list representation of the stack containing C, +, and 2 is

Top

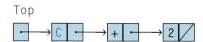

Pointer variable Top points to the list head. We can access only the character in node Top^, the letter C. Next we draw the stack after we push the symbol * onto it:

Top

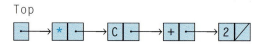

If we pop this stack, we retrieve the symbol * and restore the stack to its earlier state. A stack is called a **last-in, first-out (LIFO) structure** because the last element stored in a stack is always the first one removed.

Stack ADT

Table 18.1 provides a specification for a stack ADT. Besides operators Init, Push, and Pop, we include operators Retrieve and IsEmpty. Operator Retrieve accesses the top element on a stack without removing it. Operator IsEmpty determines whether a stack has any elements.

Table 18.1

Specification of Abstract Data Type Stack

Structure

A stack consists of a collection of elements all of the same data type (type StackData) and ordered by their placement on the stack. New elements are pushed onto the top of the stack. Only the element that was last pushed onto the stack can be popped or retrieved.

Operators

The following descriptions assume these parameters:

X (type StackData)
Success (type Boolean)

Stack.Init   (constructor) Creates an empty stack.
Stack.Push (X)   The value in X is placed on the top of the stack.
Stack.Pop (var X, var Success)   If the stack is not empty, the value at the top of the stack is removed, its value is placed in X, and Success is set to True. If the stack is empty, X is not defined and Success is set to False.
Stack.Retrieve (var X, var Success)   If the stack is not empty, the value at the top of the stack is copied into X, and Success is set to True. If the stack is empty, X is not defined and Success is set to False. In either case, the stack is not changed.
Stack.IsEmpty   (function) Returns True if the stack is empty; otherwise, returns False.
Stack.Done   (destructor) Returns storage for all stack entries.

Implementing a Stack ADT

The stack ADT is relatively easy to implement. Like a list, a stack node contains a data field, Info, that is type StackData (imported from Stack-DataADT) and a pointer field, Link. Object type Stack has a single data member, Top. Figure 18.1 shows the interface section for a stack ADT.

Figure 18.1

Interface Section for StackADT

```
unit StackADT;
{
  Contains declarations for object type Stack and its
  methods: Init, Push, Pop, Retrieve, IsEmpty.
}
interface
  uses StackDataADT;    {Import type StackData.}

  type
    StackPointer = ^StackNode;
    StackNode = record
                  Info : StackData;      {information part}
                  Link : StackPointer    {link to successor}
                end; {StackNode}
```

▷ ▷ ▷ ▷ ▷ ▷

```
Stack = object
        constructor Init;
        procedure Push (X : StackData);
        procedure Pop (var X : StackData;
                          var Success : Boolean);
        procedure Retrieve (var X : StackData;
                              var Success : Boolean);
        function IsEmpty : Boolean;
        destructor Done;

    private
      Top : StackPointer;      {top of stack pointer}
    end; {Stack}
```

Figure 18.2 shows the stack methods. Init and Push work just like linked list methods Init and Insert. In method Pop, the statements

```
X := Top^.Info;        {Copy value at top of stack into X.}
Top := Top^.Link;        {Reset pointer to top of stack.}
```

retrieve the data at the top of the stack (Top^.Info) and change pointer Top to point to the successor of the node at the top of the stack. Method Retrieve is left as an exercise.

Figure 18.2
Implementation Section for
StackADT

```
implementation

constructor Stack.Init;
{
  Creates an empty stack.
  Pre : None.
  Post: An empty stack is created.
}
begin {Init}
  Top := nil                {Set top-of-stack pointer to nil.}
end; {Init}

procedure Stack.Push (X {input} : StackData);
{
  Pushes X onto a stack.
  Pre : X is defined.
  Post: Top^.Info contains X.
}
  var OldTop : StackPointer; {pointer to old top of stack}

begin {Push}
  OldTop := Top;          {Save old top of stack.}
  New (Top);              {Allocate new node at top of stack.}
  Top^.Info := X;         {Store X in new node.}
  Top^.Link := OldTop     {Link new node to old stack.}
end; {Push}
```

▷ ▷ ▷ ▷ ▷

```
procedure Stack.Pop (var X {output} : StackData;
                     var Success {output} : Boolean);
{
  Pops the top of stack into X.
  Pre : Stack is defined.
  Post: Contents of X is data at top of stack, which is
        then removed from stack. Sets Success to indicate
        success (True) or failure (False) of pop operation.
}
  var
    OldTop : StackPointer;      {pointer to old top of stack}
begin {Pop}
  if Top = nil then
    Success := False
  else
    begin
      OldTop := Top;      {Save old top of stack.}
      X := Top^.Info;     {Copy value at top of stack into X.}
      Top := Top^.Link;   {Reset pointer to top of stack.}
      Dispose (OldTop);   {Return top node to the heap.}
      Success := True
    end {if}
end; {Pop}

function Stack.IsEmpty : Boolean;
{
  Pre : Stack is defined.
  Post: Returns True if stack is empty; otherwise, False.
}
begin {IsEmpty}
  IsEmpty := (Top = nil)
end; {IsEmpty}

  {Insert methods Retrieve and Done here.}

end. {StackADT}
```

Exercises for Section 18.1 *Self-Check*

1. Explain the difference between methods Pop and Retrieve.
2. Assume stack S is a stack of characters. Perform the following sequence of operations, then indicate the result of each operation and the new stack if it is changed. Rather than draw the stack each time, use the notation |2+C/ to represent a stack of four characters, where the last symbol on the right (/) is at the top of the stack.

```
S.Init;
S.Push ('$');
S.Push ('-');
S.Pop (NextCh, Success);
S.Retrieve (NextCh, Success);
Success := S.IsEmpty
```

3. It is helpful to include a field, `NumItems`, in object type `Stack` containing a count of the number of elements on the stack. What changes would be required to the type declaration and the stack operators if field `NumItems` were included?
4. How could a stack ADT be implemented using an array instead of a linked list? What are two disadvantages to this approach?

Programming

1. Implement method `Retrieve`.
2. Implement method `Done` that will empty a stack of all elements, freeing all memory used by the stack elements.
3. Write a method `CopyStack` that uses the stack operators to make a copy of an existing stack. The new stack will contain a duplicate of each node in the original stack. *Hint:* You will need to pop each node and store its data in a temporary stack.
4. Provide a declaration for a stack object assuming the stack data will be housed in an array instead of a linked list. Write methods `Push` and `Pop`.

18.2   Stack Applications

In Section 14.2, we showed how compilers use stacks to store procedure and function parameters. Compilers also use stacks for data storage while translating expressions. In general, we use stacks in a program to remember a sequence of data objects or actions in the reverse order from that in which they were encountered.

We examine two cases that use stacks. In the first, we use a stack to remember characters read in from a data line so they can be displayed in reverse order. In the second, we use a stack to store open parentheses read from an arithmetic expression so we can determine whether they are matched by corresponding closed parentheses.

CASE STUDY   Reversing a Data Line

Write a program that reads a data line and displays the characters in reverse order.

ANALYSIS ▼

We use a stack of characters as the primary data structure for this program. Push each data character onto the stack and then pop each character and display it. If the data line contains the word `house`, the character `e` will be stored at the top of the stack (see Figure 18.3). The letter `e` is the first letter popped and displayed, `s` is the next letter popped, and so on.

Figure 18.3
Pushing house onto a Stack

Data Requirements

Problem Input

each data character

Problem Output

each character on the stack

Program Variable

`S : Stack`

DESIGN

Initial Algorithm

1. Create an empty stack.
2. Push each data character onto the stack.
3. Pop each character from the stack and display it.

IMPLEMENTATION ▼

The program is shown in Fig. 18.4. Because S is a stack of characters, unit `StackDataADT` should contain the declaration

```
type
   StackData = Char;   {stack of characters}
```

The program calls method `Init` to create an empty stack S. The loop in procedure `FillStack` reads each character in the data line and pushes it onto the stack. The loop in procedure `DisplayStack` repeats until stack S is empty. During each repetition, it pops the top character and displays it.

Figure 18.4
Program PrintReverse

Edit Window

```
program PrintReverse;
{
  Reads a line of characters and displays it in reverse.
}

  uses StackADT, StackDataADT;
```

```
var
   S : Stack;          {stack of characters read}
procedure FillStack (var S {output} : Stack);
{
   Reads data characters and pushes them onto stack S.
   Pre : S is an empty stack.
   Post: S contains the data characters in reverse order.
}
   var
     NextCh : Char;              {next character}
begin {FillStack}
   Write ('Type a data line and press Enter> ');
   while not EOLN do
     begin
       Read (NextCh);
       S.Push (NextCh)    {Push next character on stack S.}
     end {while}
end; {FillStack}

procedure DisplayStack (var S {input/output} : Stack);
{
   Pops each character from stack S and displays it.
   Pre : Stack S is defined.
   Post: Stack S is empty and all characters are displayed.
}
   var
     Success : Boolean;
     NextCh : Char;              {each character from the stack}
begin {DisplayStack}
   while not S.IsEmpty do
     begin
       S.Pop (NextCh, Success);    {Pop next character off.}
       Write (NextCh)
     end; {while}
   WriteLn
end; {DisplayStack}

begin {PrintReverse}
   S.Init;
   FillStack (S);
   DisplayStack (S);
   S.Done
end. {PrintReverse}
```

Output Window

```
Type a data line and press Enter> house
esuoh
```

CASE STUDY

Checking for Balanced Parentheses

Another application of a stack is to determine whether the parentheses in an expression are balanced. For example, the expression

```
(a + b * (c / (d - e))) + (d / e)
1        2   3       321 1       1
```

has balanced parentheses. We can solve this problem without using a stack by ignoring all characters except the symbols (and). We start a counter at 1 and add 1 for each open parenthesis that follows another open parenthesis and subtract 1 for each closed parenthesis that follows another closed parenthesis. Because we are ignoring all other symbols, the parentheses being considered do not have to be consecutive characters. If the expression is balanced, the final count will be 1, and it will always be positive.

This task becomes more difficult if we expand our notion of parentheses to include braces and brackets. For example, the expression

```
(a + b * {c / [d - e]}) + (d / e)
```

is balanced, but the expression

```
(a + b * {c / [d - e}) + (d / e)
```

is not because the subexpression [d - e} is incorrect.

PROBLEM ▼

The set of open parenthesis symbols is {, [, and (. An expression is balanced if each subexpression that starts with the symbol { ends with the symbol }; the same is true for the symbol pairs [,] and (,). In other words, the unmatched open parenthesis nearest to each closed parenthesis must have the correct shape (e.g., if } is the closed parenthesis in question, the symbol { must be the nearest unmatched open parenthesis).

ANALYSIS ▼

Solving this problem without stacks would be fairly difficult, but with stacks it becomes easy. First, scan the expression from left to right, ignoring all characters except for parenthesis symbols (including braces and brackets). Push each open parenthesis symbol onto a stack of characters. For a closed parenthesis symbol, pop an open parenthesis from the stack and see whether it matches the closed parenthesis. If the symbols don't match or the stack is empty, there is an error in the expression. If they do match, continue the scan.

Data Requirements

Problem Input

```
Expression : string    {expression to be checked for
                        balanced parentheses}
```

Problem Output

The function result indicating whether the parentheses in `Expression` are balanced

Program Variables

```
ParenStack : Stack  {stack of open parentheses}
Balanced : Boolean  {flag indicating whether
                     parentheses are balanced}
NextCh : Char        {next character in Expression}
Index : Integer      {index of the next character}
OpenParen : Char     {open parenthesis at the top of the
                     stack}
CloseParen : Char    {closed parenthesis being matched}
```

DESIGN ▼

Initial Algorithm

1. Create an empty stack of characters.
2. Assume that the expression is balanced (`Balanced` is `True`).
3. `while` the expression is balanced and still in the expression `do`
   `begin`
   4. Get the next character in the expression.
   5. `if` the next character is an open parenthesis `then`
      6. Push it onto the stack.
      `else if` the next character is a closed parenthesis `then`
         `begin`
         7. Pop the top of the stack.
         8. `if` stack was empty or its top was incorrect `then`
             Set `Balanced` to `False`.
         `end {if}`
   `end {while}`
9. The expression is balanced if `Balanced` is `True` and the stack is empty.

The `if` statement in Step 5 tests each character in the expression, ignoring all characters except for open and closed parenthesis symbols. If the next character is an open parenthesis symbol, it is pushed onto the stack. If the next character is a closed parenthesis symbol, the nearest unmatched open parenthesis is retrieved (by popping the stack) and compared to the closed parenthesis (Steps 7 and 8). If the next character is not an open or closed parenthesis symbol, it is ignored.

IMPLEMENTATION ▼

Figure 18.5 shows a function that determines whether its input parameter (an expression) is balanced. The `if` statement in the `while` loop tests for open and closed parenthesis symbols. Each open parenthesis is pushed onto stack ParenStack. For each closed parenthesis, procedure Pop retrieves the nearest unmatched open parenthesis from the stack. If the stack is empty, Pop sets Balanced to False, causing the while loop exit. Otherwise, the case statement sets Balanced to indicate whether the character popped matches the current closed parenthesis symbol. After loop exit occurs, the function result is defined. It is true only when the expression is balanced and the stack is empty.

TESTING ▼

Write a driver program to test function IsBalanced. This program must import the type declaration for StackData (type is Char) from unit Stack-DataADT and object Stack (from unit StackADT). Be sure to use several balanced and unbalanced expressions to test IsBalanced, as well as an expression without parentheses.

....

Figure 18.5
Function IsBalanced

```
function IsBalanced (Expression : string) : Boolean;
{
  Determines whether Expression is balanced with respect
  to parentheses.
  Pre  : Expression is defined.
  Post : Returns True if Expression is balanced;
         otherwise, returns False.
  Imports: Stack, Push, Pop and IsEmpty from StackADT.
}
  var
    ParenStack : Stack;       {stack of open parentheses}
    NextCh,                   {next character in Expression}
    CloseParen,               {parenthesis to be matched}
    OpenParen : Char;         {open parenthesis at top of stack}
    Index : Integer;          {index to Expression}
    Balanced : Boolean;       {program flag}

begin {IsBalanced}
  ParenStack.Init;            {Create an empty stack.}
  Balanced := True;
  Index := 1;
```

▷ ▷ ▷ ▷ ▷ ▷

```
while Balanced and (Index <= Length(Expression)) do
  {invariant:
      All closed parentheses so far were matched and
      Index <= Length(Expression) + 1.
  }
  begin
    NextCh := Expression[Index];    {Access next character.}
    if NextCh in [ '(', '[', '{' ] then
       ParenStack.Push (NextCh)         {Push open parenthesis.}
    else if NextCh in [ ')', ']', '}' ] then
      begin {Matches open paren?}
        CloseParen := NextCh;
        {Get nearest unmatched open parenthesis.}
        ParenStack.Pop (OpenParen, Balanced);   {Pop stack.}
        if Balanced then
          {Check for match.}
          case CloseParen of
            ')' : Balanced := (OpenParen = '(' );
            ']' : Balanced := (OpenParen = '[' );
            '}' : Balanced := (OpenParen = '{' )
          end {case}
      end; {Matches open paren?}
    Index := Index + 1        {Access next character.}
  end; {while}

  {Define function result.}
  IsBalanced := Balanced and ParenStack.IsEmpty
end; {IsBalanced}
```

△

Exercises for Section 18.2 Self-Check

1. Trace the execution of function IsBalanced for each of the following
    expressions. Your trace should show the stack after each Push or Pop
    operation. Also show the values of Balanced, OpenParen, and Close-
    Paren after each parenthesis is processed.

    ```
    (a + b * {c / [d - e]}) + (d / e)
    (a + b * {c / [d - e}}) + (d / e)
    ```

Programming

1. Write a main program to test function IsBalanced.

18.3 Queues

queue
a data structure in which elements are inserted at one end and removed from the other end

A **queue** (pronounced "Q") is a listlike structure in which items are inserted
at one end and removed from the other end. In contrast, stack elements are
inserted and removed from the same end (the top of the stack).

first-in, first-out (FIFO) structure

a data structure in which the first element stored is the first to be removed

In a queue, the element that has been stored the longest is removed first, so a queue is called a **first-in, first-out (FIFO) structure.** A queue can be used to model a line of customers waiting at a checkout counter or a stream of jobs waiting to be printed by a printer.

Figure 18.6(a) shows a queue of three customers waiting for service at a bank. The name of the customer who has been waiting the longest is Mc-Mann (pointed to by Front); the name of the most recent arrival is Carson (pointed to by Rear). Customer Front^ will be the first one removed from the queue when a teller becomes available, and pointer Front will be reset to point to Wilson. Any new customers will be inserted after Carson in the queue, and pointer Rear will be adjusted accordingly. Figure 18.6(b) shows the queue after removing customer McMann, and Figure 18.6(c) shows the queue after inserting customer Perez.

Figure 18.6
Queue of Customers

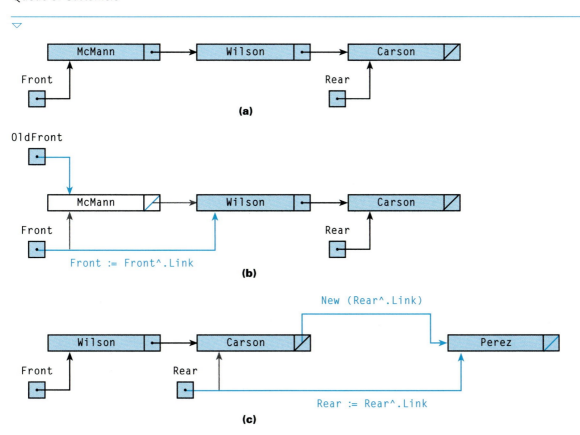

Queue ADT

Table 18.2 provides the specification for a queue ADT. We implement the queue ADT next.

Structure

A queue consists of a collection of elements all of the same data type and ordered according to time of arrival. The element that was inserted first is the only one that may be removed or examined. Elements are removed from the front of the queue and inserted at the rear of the queue.

Operators

The following descriptions assume these parameters:

El (type QueueData)
Success (type Boolean)

Queue.Init (constructor) Creates an empty queue.

Queue.Insert (El) The item in El is inserted at the rear of the queue.

Queue.Remove (var El, var Success) If the queue is not empty, the element at the front of the queue is removed and copied to El, and Success is set to True. If the queue is empty, El is not changed, and Success is set to False.

Queue.IsEmpty (function) Returns True if the queue is empty; otherwise, returns False.

Queue.GetSize (function) Returns the number of elements in the queue.

Queue.Done (destructor) Returns storage for all queue entries.

Implementing QueueADT

If we implement a queue as a linked list, removing elements from a queue is no different from removing them from a stack—the element at the front of the queue is removed next. Because new elements are inserted at the rear of the queue, however, we need a pointer to the last list element as well as the first. We can implement a queue as an object with two data members, Front and Rear. Pointer Front points to the node at the front of the queue, and pointer Rear points to the node at the rear of the queue. Because we might also want to know how many elements are in a queue, we will add a third data member, Size. Each queue node is a record with an information part and a link to the next queue node. Figure 18.7 shows the interface section for QueueADT.

Next we implement the queue methods. Init (Fig. 18.8) sets pointer fields Front and Rear to nil. If the queue is not empty, method Remove uses the statements

```
El := Front^.Info;              {Retrieve its data.}
Front := Front^.Link;      {Delete old first node.}
```

to retrieve the data stored in Front^.Info and reset Front to point to the successor of the node whose data is retrieved.

Figure 18.7
Interface Section for Unit
QueueADT

```
unit QueueADT;
{
   Contains declarations for object Queue and methods
   Init, Insert, Remove, and IsEmpty.
}

interface
   uses QueueDataADT;    {Import type QueueData.}

   type
      QueuePointer = ^QueueNode;
      QueueNode = record
                     Info : QueueData;      {information part}
                     Link : QueuePointer    {link to successor}
                  end; {QueueNode}

   Queue = object
              constructor Init;
              procedure Insert (El : QueueData);
              procedure Remove (var El : QueueData;
                                var Success : Boolean);
              function IsEmpty : Boolean;
              function GetSize : Integer;
              destructor Done;

           private
              Front,                  {pointer to front of Q}
              Rear : QueuePointer;    {pointer to rear of Q}
              Size : Integer;         {size of queue}
           end; {Queue}
```

Figure 18.8
Implementation Section for
Unit QueueADT

```
implementation

   constructor Queue.Init;
   {
      Creates an empty queue.
      Pre : None.
      Post: Initializes a queue of zero elements.
   }
   begin {Init}
      Front := nil;
      Rear  := nil;
      Size := 0
   end; {Init}

   procedure Queue.Remove (var El {output} : QueueData;
                           var Success {output} : Boolean);
```

```
{
  Removes the element at the front of the queue
  and copies it into El.
  Pre : The queue has been created.
  Post: If the queue is not empty, El contains its
        first element, Front points to new first element,
        and Success indicates success or failure.
}
  var
    OldFront : QueuePointer;       {temporary pointer}

begin {Remove}
  if Front = nil then
    Success := False               {Queue is empty.}
  else
    begin
      {Remove the element at the front of the queue.}
      OldFront := Front;   {Point OldFront to first node.}
      El := Front^.Info;                {Retrieve its data.}
      Front := Front^.Link;       {Delete old first node.}
      OldFront^.Link := nil;             {Disconnect it.}
      Dispose (OldFront);          {Deallocate storage.}
      Size := Size - 1;            {Decrement size of Q.}
      Success := True
    end {if}
end; {Remove}

procedure Queue.Insert (El {input} : QueueData);
{
 Inserts El in a queue.
 Pre : The queue has been created.
 Post: Inserts El in a new node and resets Rear to point
       to the new node. Also points Front to the new node
       if the queue has 1 element.
}
begin {Insert}
  if Rear = nil then
    begin {empty queue}
      New (Rear);                  {Point Rear to first node.}
      Front := Rear                {Point Front to first node.}
    end {empty queue}
  else
    begin {extend queue}
      New (Rear^.Link);   {Attach a node at end of queue.}
      Rear := Rear^.Link           {Point Rear to new node.}
    end; {extend queue}

  Rear^.Info := El;                {Define new node's data.}
  Rear^.Link := nil;
  Size := Size + 1                  {Increment size of Q.}
end; {Insert}

function Queue.IsEmpty : Boolean;
```

▷ ▷ ▷ ▷ ▷ ▷

```
   {
       Tests for an empty queue.
       Pre : Queue has been created.
       Post: Returns True if queue is empty; otherwise,
             returns False.
   }
   begin {IsEmpty}
     IsEmpty := (Front = nil)
   end; {IsEmpty}

   {Insert methods GetSize and Done here.}

end. {QueueADT}
```

If the queue is empty, method Insert allocates a new node and points Front and Rear to this node. Otherwise, the statements

```
New (Rear^.Link);    {Attach a node at end of queue.}
Rear := Rear^.Link         {Point Rear to new node.}
```

attach a new node to node Rear^ and reset Rear to point to the new node (Fig. 18.6c). Next, the statements

```
Rear^.Info := El;          {Define new node's data.}
Rear^.Link := nil;
```

store the data passed through parameter El in the new node and set its Link field to nil.

Exercises for Section 18.3   Self-Check

1. Redraw the queue in Fig. 18.6 after the insertion of customer Harris and the removal of one customer from the queue. Which customer is removed? How many customers are left? Show pointers First and Rear after each operation.
2. Trace the operation of procedures Insert and Remove as the operations in Question 1 are performed. Show before and after values for all pointers.
3. What changes would be made to method Insert to create a new method, RudeInsert, that inserts at the front of the queue rather than at the end?
4. In a circular queue, the node at the rear points to the node at the front of the queue (see circular lists in Section 17.3). Draw the queue in Fig. 18.6 as a circular queue with just one pointer field named Rear. Explain how you would access the queue element at the front of a circular queue.

Programming

1. Write methods Queue.GetSize and Queue.Done.

2. Add a new method, `Queue.Display`, that displays the data stored in a queue. Use method `QueueData.Display` to display each node's data.

3. Is it possible to simulate the operation of a queue using two stacks? Write an ADT for the queue object, assuming two stacks are used for storing the queue. What performance penalty do we pay for this implementation?

18.4 Binary Trees

leaf node
a binary tree node with no successors
root node
the first node in a binary tree
left subtree
the part of a tree pointed to by the left pointer of the root node
right subtree
the part of a tree pointed to by the right pointer of the root node

We can extend the concept of linked data structures to structures containing nodes with more than one pointer field. One such structure is a *binary tree* (or *tree*) whose nodes contain two pointer fields. Because one or both pointers can have the value `nil`, each node in a binary tree can have 0, 1, or 2 successor nodes.

Figure 18.9 shows two binary trees. For tree (a), each node stores a three-letter string. The nodes on the bottom of this tree have zero successors and are called **leaf nodes**; all other nodes have two successors. For tree (b), each node stores an integer. The nodes containing 40 and 45 have a single successor; all other nodes have no or two successors. A recursive definition of a binary tree is: A **binary tree** is either empty (no nodes) or it consists of a node, called the **root**, and two disjoint binary trees called its **left subtree** and **right subtree**, respectively.

In the definition for binary tree, the phrase *disjoint subtrees* means that a node cannot be in both a left and a right subtree of the same root node. For

Figure 18.9
Binary Trees

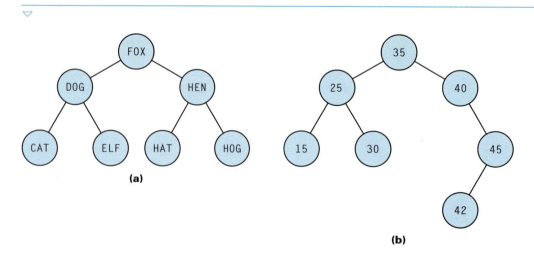

(a)

(b)

the trees shown in Fig. 18.9, the nodes containing FOX and 35 are the root nodes for each tree. The node containing DOG is the root of the left subtree of the tree whose root is FOX; the node containing CAT is the root of the left subtree of the tree whose root is DOG; the node containing CAT is a leaf node because both its subtrees are empty trees.

A binary tree resembles a family tree and the relationships among its members are described using the same terminology as for a family tree. In Fig. 18.9 the node containing HEN is the *parent* of the nodes containing HAT and HOG. Similarly, the nodes containing HAT and HOG are *siblings,* because they are both *children* of the same parent node. The root of a tree is an *ancestor* of all other nodes in the tree, and they in turn are *descendants* of the root node.

For simplicity, we did not show the pointer fields in Fig. 18.9. Be aware that each node has two pointer fields and that the nodes in (b) containing integers 45 and 42 are stored as follows.

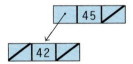

Binary Search Tree

In the rest of this chapter, we focus our attention on a particular kind of binary tree called a binary search tree. A binary search tree is a tree structure that stores data in such a way that they can be retrieved very efficiently. Every item stored in a binary search tree has a unique key.

A **binary search tree** is either empty or has the property that the item in its root has a larger key than each item in its left subtree and a smaller key than each item in its right subtree. Also, its left and right subtrees must be binary search trees.

The trees in Fig. 18.9 are examples of binary search trees; each node has a single data field that is its key. For tree (a), the string stored in every node is alphabetically larger than all strings in its left subtree and alphabetically smaller than all strings in its right subtree. For tree (b), the number stored in every node is larger than all numbers in its left subtree and smaller than all numbers in its right subtree. Notice that this must be true for every node in a binary search tree, not just the root node. For example, the number 40 must be larger than both numbers stored in its right subtree (45, 42).

Searching a Binary Search Tree

Next we explain how to search for an item in a binary search tree. To find a particular item, say E1, we compare E1's key to the root item's key. If E1's key is smaller, we know that E1 can only be in the left subtree so we search it. If E1's key is larger, we search the root's right subtree. We now write this recursive algorithm in pseudocode; the first two cases are stopping cases.

Algorithm for Searching a Binary Search Tree

1. `if` the tree is empty then
   The target key is not in the tree.
`else if` the target key is in the root item `then`
   The target key is found in the root item.
`else if` the target key is smaller than the root's key `then`
   Search the left subtree.
`else`
   Search the right subtree.

Figure 18.10 traces the search for 42 in a binary search tree containing integer keys. The pointer `Root` indicates the root node whose key is being compared to 42 at each step. The colored arrows show the search path. The search proceeds from the top (node 35) down to the node containing 42.

Building a Binary Search Tree

Before we can retrieve an item from a binary search tree, we must, of course, build the tree. This process requires that we read a collection of data items that is in no particular order and insert each one individually, making sure that the expanded tree is a binary search tree. A binary search tree builds from the root node down, so we must store the first data item in the root node. To store each subsequent data item, we must find its parent node in the tree, attach a new node to the parent, and then store that data item in the new node.

When inserting an item, we must search the existing tree to find that item's key or to locate its parent node. If our search is successful, the item's key is already in the tree, so we will not insert the item. (Duplicate keys are not allowed.) If unsuccessful, the search will terminate at the parent of the item. If the item's key is smaller than its parent's key, we attach a new node as the parent's left subtree and insert the item in this node. If the item's key is larger than its parent's key, we attach a new node as the parent's right subtree and insert the item in this node. The following recursive algorithm maintains the binary search tree property; the first two cases are stopping cases.

Algorithm for Insertion in a Binary Search Tree

1. `if` the tree is empty `then`
   Insert the new item in the tree's root node.
`else if` the root's key matches the new item's key `then`
   Skip insertion—duplicate key.
`else if` the new item's key is smaller than the root's key `then`
   Insert the new item in the root's left subtree.
`else`
   Insert the new item in the root's right subtree.

Figure 18.10
Searching for key 42

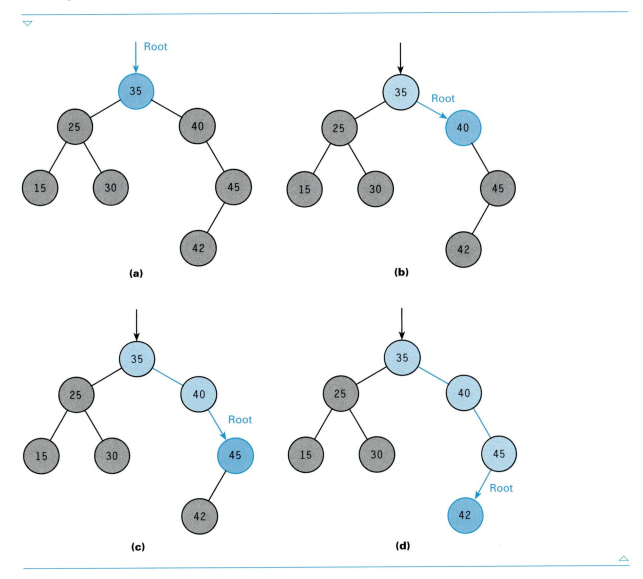

(a)

(b)

(c)

(d)

Figure 18.11 builds a tree from the list of keys: 40, 20, 10, 50, 65, 45, 30. The search path followed when inserting each key is shown in color.

The last node inserted (bottom right diagram) contains the key 30 and is inserted in the right subtree of node 20. Let's trace how this happens. Target key 30 is smaller than 40, so we insert 30 in the left subtree of node 40; this tree has 20 in its root. Target key 30 is greater than 20, so we insert 30 in the

Figure 18.11
Building a Binary Search Tree

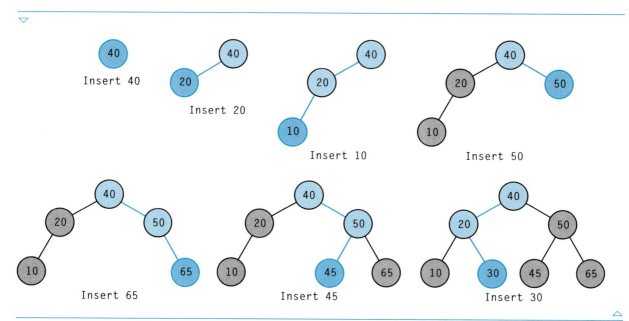

right subtree of node 20, an empty tree. Because node 20 has no right subtree, we allocate a new node and insert target 30 in it; the new node becomes the root of 20's right subtree.

Be aware that we would get a very different tree if we changed the order in which we inserted the keys. For example, if we inserted the keys in increasing order (10, 20, 30, . . .), each new key would be inserted in the right subtree of the previous key and all left pointers would be nil. The resulting tree would resemble a linked list. We will see later (Section 18.6) that the insertion order also affects search efficiency.

Displaying a Binary Search Tree

To display the contents of a binary search tree so that its items are listed in order by key value, use the next recursive algorithm.

Algorithm for Displaying a Binary Search Tree

1. if the tree is not empty then
    begin
    2. Display left subtree.
    3. Display root item.
    4. Display right subtree.
    end

For each node, the keys in its left subtree are displayed before the key in its root; the keys in its right subtree are displayed after the key in its root. Because the root key value lies between the key values in its left and right subtrees, the algorithm displays the items in order by key value as desired. Because the nodes' data components are displayed in order, this algorithm is also called an **inorder traversal.**

inorder traversal

displaying the items in a binary search tree in order by key value

Table 18.3 traces the sequence of calls generated by the display algorithm for the last tree in Fig. 18.11. Completing the sequence of calls for the last step shown, "Display right subtree of node 40.", is left as an exercise at the end of this section. The trace so far displays the item keys in the sequence: 10, 20, 30, 40.

Table 18.3
Trace of Tree Display
Algorithm

Display left subtree of node 40.

　Display left subtree of node 20.

　　Display left subtree of node 10.

　　　Tree is empty—return from displaying left subtree of node 10.

　　Display item with key 10.

　　Display right subtree of node 10.

　　　Tree is empty—return from displaying right subtree of node 10.

　　Return from displaying left subtree of node 20.

　Display item with key 20.

　Display right subtree of node 20.

　　Display left subtree of node 30.

　　　Tree is empty—return from displaying left subtree of node 30.

　　Display item with key 30.

　　Display right subtree of node 30.

　　　Tree is empty—return from displaying right subtree of node 30.

　　Return from displaying right subtree of node 20.

　Return from displaying left subtree of node 40.

Display item with key 40.

Display right subtree of node 40.

Exercises for Section 18.4 ***Self-Check***

1. Are the following trees binary search trees? Show the list of keys as they would be displayed by an inorder traversal of each tree. If these trees were binary search trees, what key values could be stored in the left subtree of the node containing key 50?

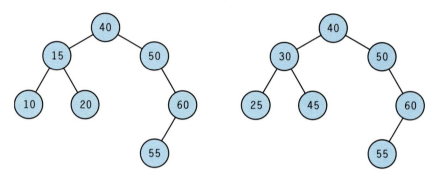

2. Complete the trace started in Table 18.3.
3. Show the binary search trees that would be created from the following lists of keys. Which tree do you think would be the most efficient to search? What can you say about the binary search tree formed in parts (b) and (c)? What can you say about the binary search tree formed in part (d)? How do you think searching it would compare to searching a linked list with the same keys?
   a. 25, 45, 15, 10, 60, 55, 12

   b. 25, 12, 55, 10, 15, 45, 60

   c. 25, 12, 10, 15, 55, 60, 45

   d. 10, 12, 15, 25, 45, 55, 60
4. What would be displayed by an inorder traversal of each tree in Question 3?

18.5 Binary Search Tree ADT

We now write the specification for a binary search tree abstract data type (Table 18.4). Besides the methods discussed so far (Search, Insert, and Display), we include a method, Retrieve, to return the tree item whose key matches a target key.

Structure
A binary search tree is a collection of elements (nodes) such that each has a unique key value and 0, 1, or 2 subtrees connected to it. The key value in each node of a binary search tree is larger than all key values in its left subtree and smaller than all key values in its right subtree.

Operators
The following descriptions assume these parameters:

El (type TreeData)
Success (type Boolean)

SearchTree.Init (constructor) Creates an empty binary search tree; must be called before any other operators.

SearchTree.Search (El, var Success) Searches a tree to find a node with the same key as El. If found, sets Success to True; otherwise, sets Success to False.

SearchTree.Insert (El, var Success) Inserts item El into the binary search tree and sets Success to True. If there is already an element with the same key as El, Success is set to False, and no insertion is performed.

SearchTree.Retrieve (var El, var Success) Retrieves through El the tree element with the same key as item El and sets Success to True. If there is no tree element with the same key as El, sets Success to False.

SearchTree.Display Displays the tree elements in order by key value.

SearchTree.Done (destructor) Returns storage for all tree entries.

Interface Section for Binary Search Tree ADT

The interface section for unit SearchTreeADT is shown in Fig. 18.12. Each binary search tree node contains a data field, Info, of type TreeData (imported from unit TreeDataADT) and two pointers, Left and Right, that connect it to its children:

Binary search tree node

Object type SearchTree contains a single pointer field, Root, that points to the root node of a tree.

Implementation Section for Binary Search Tree ADT

The implementation section contains the method declarations.

Figure 18.12

Interface Section for Unit
SearchTreeADT

```
unit SearchTreeADT;
{
  Contains object type SearchTree and its methods: Init,
  Search, Insert, Retrieve, and Display.
}
interface
  uses TreeDataADT;            {Import type TreeData and methods
                                    EqualTo, LessThan, DisplayItem.}
  type
    Branch = ^TreeNode;
    TreeNode = record
                    Info : TreeData;        {information part}
                    Left, Right : Branch  {subtree pointers}
                  end; {TreeNode}

  SearchTree = object
                    constructor Init;
                    procedure Search (El : TreeData;
                                          var Success : Boolean);
                    procedure Insert (El : TreeData;
                                          var Success : Boolean);
                    procedure Retrieve (var El : TreeData;
                                          var Success : Boolean);
                    procedure Display;
                    destructor Done;

                  private
                    Root : Branch;  {pointer to root node}
                    procedure DoSearch (ARoot : Branch;
                                          El : TreeData;
                                          var Success : Boolean);
                    procedure DoRetrieve (ARoot : Branch;
                                          var El : TreeData;
                                          var Success : Boolean);
                    procedure DoDisplay (ARoot : Branch;
                                          El : TreeData;
                                          var Success : Boolean);
                  end; {SearchTree}
```

Methods Init, Search, and Retrieve

We will start with methods Init and Search (Fig. 18.13). Init sets the Root
pointer of its object instance to nil. Method Search initiates a search for the
tree node with the same key as item El, the target item, by calling private
method DoSearch. Method DoSearch implements the recursive search algorithm illustrated in Fig. 18.10, beginning at the root of the tree to be
searched. Functions EqualTo and LessThan compare the keys of item El
and the root node in the obvious way (EqualTo tests for equality, LessThan
tests if El's key is less than the root's key). Both functions are methods for
object type TreeData.

Figure 18.13
Methods Init, Search, and
DoSearch

```
implementation

  constructor SearchTree.Init;
  {
    Creates an empty tree. Must be called first.
    Pre : None.
    Post: Root pointer is set to nil.
  }
  begin {Init}
    Root := nil
  end; {Init}

  procedure SearchTree.DoSearch (ARoot {input} : Branch;
                                 El {input} : TreeData;
                              var Success {output} : Boolean);
  {
    Searches for the item with same key as El in the
    subtree pointed to by ARoot.
    Pre : El and ARoot are defined.
    Post: If El's key is not found, Success is False;
          otherwise, Success is True.
  }
  begin {DoSearch}
    if ARoot = nil then
      Success := False                        {Tree is empty.}
    else if El.EqualTo(ARoot^.Info) then
      Success := True                         {Target is found.}
    else if El.LessThan(ARoot^.Info) then
      DoSearch (ARoot^.Left, El, Success)        {Search left.}
    else
      DoSearch (ARoot^.Right, El, Success)      {Search right.}
  end; {DoSearch}

  procedure SearchTree.Search (El {input} : TreeData;
                            var Success {output} : Boolean);
  {
    Searches for the item with same key as El in a binary
    search tree.
    Pre : The tree is defined.
    Post: If El's key is located, Success is True;
          otherwise, Success is False.
  }
  begin {Search}
    DoSearch (Root, El, Success) {Start search at tree root.}
  end; {Search}
```

Method `Retrieve` (see Programming Exercise 1 at the end of this section) returns the tree element with the same key as `El`. Its implementation would be similar to that of `Search`. When `DoRetrieve` (like `DoSearch`) locates `El`'s key, use the statements

```
El := ARoot^.Info;          {Return tree element with same key.}
Success := True                {Target is found and retrieved.}
```

to return the tree data through El (a variable parameter) and to indicate the result of the retrieval operation.

Method Insert

Method Insert is shown in Fig. 18.14. It calls private method DoInsert to perform the actual insertion, beginning at the root of the tree receiving the insertion message. Method DoInsert implements the insertion algorithm illustrated in Fig. 18.11.

In DoInsert if parameter ARoot is nil, the statements

```
New (ARoot);              {Connect ARoot to new node.}
ARoot^.Left := nil;          {Make new node a leaf.}
ARoot^.Right := nil;
ARoot^.Info := El;        {Insert El in node ARoot^.}
```

Figure 18.14

Methods DoInsert and Insert

```
procedure SearchTree.DoInsert (var ARoot {input/output} :
                                                    Branch;
                          El {input} : TreeData;
                          var Success {output} : Boolean);
{
  Inserts item El in the tree pointed to by ARoot.
  Pre : ARoot and El are defined.
  Post: If a node with same key as El is found, Success
        is set to False. If an empty tree is reached,
        points ARoot to a new node containing El and
        sets Success to True.
}
begin {DoInsert}
  {Check for empty tree.}
  if ARoot = nil then
    begin {Attach new node}
      New (ARoot);              {Connect ARoot to new node.}
      ARoot^.Left := nil;          {Make new node a leaf.}
      ARoot^.Right := nil;
      ARoot^.Info := El;        {Insert El in node ARoot^.}
      Success := True
    end {Attach new node}
  else if El.EqualTo(ARoot^.Info) then
    Success := False                        {Duplicate key.}
  else if El.LessThan(ARoot^.Info) then
    DoInsert (ARoot^.Left, El, Success)    {Insert left.}
  else
    DoInsert (ARoot^.Right, El, Success)   {Insert right.}
end; {DoInsert}
```

▷ ▷ ▷ ▷ ▷ ▷

```
procedure SearchTree.Insert (El {input} : TreeData;
                             var Success {output} : Boolean);
{
  Inserts item El into a binary search tree.
  Pre : El is defined and the tree is defined.
  Post: Success is True if the insertion is performed.
        If there is a node with the same key value as El,
        Success is False.
}
begin {Insert}
  DoInsert (Root, El, Success)
end; {Insert}
```

allocate a new tree node that is pointed to by ARoot and store El's data in it. The new node is a leaf node because its pointers are nil. The node that has ARoot as its left or right pointer is the parent of the new node. Figure 18.15 illustrates this for the insertion of 30 in a binary search tree. The right pointer of node 20 is nil before the insertion takes place.

Method Display

Method Display (Fig. 18.16) calls recursive method DoDisplay to display the tree items in order by key. Method DoDisplay calls method DisplayItem (part of object TreeData) to display each item.

Exercises for Section 18.5 ***Self-Check***

1. Explain the effect of the following program segment if MyTree is type SearchTree and TreeData is type Integer. Draw the tree built by the sequence of insertions. What values would be displayed?

Figure 18.15
Inserting a Node in a Tree

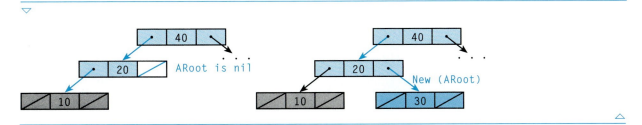

```
    begin
      MyTree.Init;
      MyTree.Insert (3000, Success);
      MyTree.Insert (2000, Success);
      MyTree.Insert (4000, Success);
      MyTree.Insert (5000, Success);
      MyTree.Insert (2500, Success);
      MyTree.Insert (6000, Success);
      MyTree.Search (2500, Success);
      MyTree.Search (1500, Success);
      TreeData := 6000;
      MyTree.Retrieve (TreeData, Success);
      MyTree.Display
    end.
```

2. Deleting an entry in a binary tree is more difficult than inserting one. Given any node that is to be deleted in a tree, what are the three cases for deletion and what must be done in each case? Be sure your approach preserves the binary search tree order.

Figure 18.16
Methods Display and
DoDisplay

```
procedure SearchTree.DoDisplay (ARoot {input} : Branch);
{
  Displays a binary search tree in key order.
  Pre : ARoot points to a binary search tree or is nil.
  Post: Displays each node in key order.
}
begin {DoDisplay}
  if ARoot <> nil then
    begin {recursive step}
      DoDisplay (ARoot^.Left);           {Display left subtree.}
      ARoot^.Info.DisplayItem;           {Display root item.}
      DoDisplay (ARoot^.Right)           {Display right subtree.}
    end {recursive step}
end; {DoDisplay}

procedure SearchTree.Display;
{
  Displays the elements of a binary search tree.
  Pre : Tree is the header node of a binary search tree.
  Post: Each element of the tree is displayed. The elements
        are displayed in ascending order by data value.
}
begin  {Display}
  DoDisplay (Root)
end; {Display}

{Insert methods Retrieve, DoRetrieve, and Done here.}

end. {SearchTreeADT}
```

Programming

1. Write methods `Retrieve`, `DoRetrieve`, and `Done`. For `Done`, use a recursive procedure that returns a node's left subtree to the heap, then its right subtree, and finally the node itself.
2. Write a method that reads a list of data items from a binary file into a binary search tree. Use method `Insert` to place each item where it belongs.

18.6 Efficiency of a Binary Search Tree

Searching a linked list for a target data value is an $O(N)$ process. In other words, the time required to search a list increases linearly with the size of the list. Searching a binary search tree can be a much more efficient process. If the left and right subtrees of every node are the exact same size, each move to the left or the right during a search eliminates the elements of the other subtree from the search process. Since they need not be searched, the number of nodes we do have to search is cut in half in each step. This is a *best-case analysis,* since, in reality, it is unlikely that a binary search tree will have exactly the same number of nodes in the left and right subtrees of each node. However, this best-case analysis is useful for showing the power of the binary search tree.

As an example, if N is 1023 it will require searching 10 trees (N = 1023, 511, 255, 127, 63, 31, 15, 7, 3, 1) to determine that a target is missing. It should require fewer than 10 probes to find a target that is in the tree. The number 1024 is a power of 2 (1024 is 2 raised to the power 10), so searching such a tree is an $O(\log_2 N)$ process ($\log_2 1024$ is 10). Keep in mind that not all binary search trees will have equal size left and right subtrees!

What difference does it make whether an algorithm is an $O(N)$ process or an $O(\log_2 N)$ process? Table 18.5 evaluates $\log_2 N$ for different values of N. A doubling of N causes $\log_2 N$ to increase by only 1. Since $\log_2 N$ increases much more slowly with $N,$ the performance of an $O(\log_2 N)$ algorithm is not as adversely affected by an increase in N.

Table 18.5
Values of N Versus $\log_2 N$

N	$\log_2 N$
32	5
64	6
128	7
256	8
512	9
1,024	10

Self-Check

1. Given the binary tree that follows, how many comparisons are needed to find each of the following keys or to determine that the key is not present? List the keys compared to the target for each search.
    a. 50   b. 55   c. 10   d. 65   e. 52   f. 48

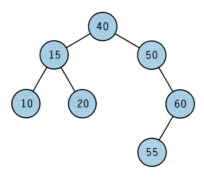

2. Why is it unlikely that a given binary tree will have exactly the name number of elements in the left and right subtrees of every node? For what numbers of nodes is this possible?
3. If the elements of a binary tree are inserted in order, what will the resulting tree look like? What is the Big-O notation for searching in this tree?
4. The binary search introduced in Chapter 14 also performed searches in $O(\log_2 N)$ time. Name two advantages of a binary tree over the binary search. Name one disadvantage.

18.7 Common Programming Errors

Because the procedures in this chapter manipulate pointer fields, you should review the errors described in Chapter 17. Make sure that recursive procedures do, in fact, terminate. Be careful when passing pointers to dynamic data structures as procedure parameters. If a pointer is passed as a variable parameter and is moved down the data structure, you might disconnect some nodes from the data structure.

CHAPTER REVIEW

1. A stack is a LIFO (last-in, first-out) structure in which all insertions (push operations) and deletions (pop operations) are done at the list head. Stacks have many varied uses in computer science including saving parameter lists for recursive modules and translating arithmetic expressions.

2. A queue is a FIFO (first-in, first-out) structure in which insertions are done at one end and deletions (removals) at the other. Queues are used to save lists of items waiting for the same resource (e.g., a printer).

3. A binary tree is a linked data structure in which each node has two pointer fields leading to the node's left and right subtrees. Each node in the tree belongs to either the left or right subtree of an ancestor node, but it cannot be in both subtrees of an ancestor node.

4. A binary search tree is a binary tree in which each node's key is greater than all keys in its left subtree and smaller than all keys in its right subtree. Searching for a key in a binary search tree is an $O(\log_2 N)$ process.

Quick-Check Exercises

1. If A, B, and C are inserted into a stack and a queue, what would be the order of removal for the stack? For the queue?

2. Often computers allow you to type characters ahead of the program's use of them. Should a stack or a queue be used to store these characters?

3. Write a program segment that removes the element just below the top of the stack. Use the stack operators.

4. Assume the left pointer of each node in the tree below is `nil`. Is it a binary search tree? What would be displayed by its inorder traversal? Write a sequence for inserting these keys that would create a binary search tree whose `nil` pointers were all at the lowest level. Is there more than one such sequence?

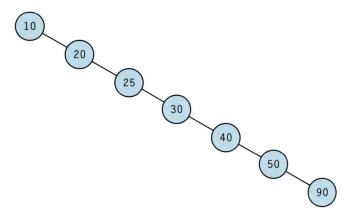

5. If a binary search tree has an inorder traversal of 1, 2, 3, 4, 5, 6, and the root node contains 3 and has 5 as the root of its right subtree, what do we know about the order that numbers were inserted in this tree?

6. A node in a binary search tree can have a maximum of two children. True or false?

7. What is the relationship between the left child, the right child, and their parent in a binary search tree? Between the right child and the parent? Between a parent and all descendants in its left subtree?

8. When is searching a binary search tree more efficient than searching an ordered linked list?

Answers to Quick-Check Exercises

1. For stack: C, B, A; for queue: A, B, C
2. Queue
3. ```
S.Pop (X, Success);
S.Pop (Y, Success);
S.Push (X);
```
4. Yes; 10, 20, 25, 30, 40, 50, 90; 30, 20, 10, 25, 50, 40, 90; yes
5. 3 was inserted first and 5 was inserted before 4 and 6.
6. True
7. Left child < parent < right child
   Parent > all its descendants
8. When the left and right subtrees of each node are similar in size

## Review Questions

1. Show the effects of each of the following operations on stack S and the parameters for Pop:

```
S.Init;
S.Push ('+');
S.Pop (X1, Success1);
S.Pop (X2, Success2);
S.Push ('(');
S.Push (')');
S.Pop (X3, Success3);
S.Pop (X4, Success4);
```

2. Write a stack operator that reverses the order of the top two stack elements if the stack has more than one element. Use Push and Pop.
3. Answer Question 1 for a queue Q of characters. Replace Push with Insert and Pop with Remove.
4. Write a queue operator MoveToRear that moves the element currently at the front of the queue to the rear of the queue. The element that was second in line will be at the front of the queue. Do this using operators Insert and Remove.
5. Write a queue operator MoveToFront that moves the element at the rear of the queue to the front of the queue. Do this using Insert and Remove.
6. Discuss the differences between a simple linked list and a binary tree. Consider such things as the number of pointer fields per node, search technique, and insertion algorithm.
7. How can you determine whether a binary tree node is a leaf?
8. Trace an inorder traversal of the following tree as it would be performed by method SearchTree.Display.
```

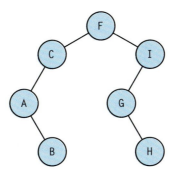

9. What happens when all the elements for a binary search tree are read and inserted in order? In reverse order? How does this affect the performance of programs that use the tree?

Programming Projects

1. Write a client program that uses the queue ADT to simulate a typical session for a bank teller. Change QueueData to represent a customer at a bank. Store the customer's name, the transaction type, and the amount in the customer record. After every five customers are processed, display the size of the queue and the names of the customers who are waiting.

    Your program should include procedures corresponding to the following procedure headers as part of your solution:

```
procedure WriteCust (OneCust {input} : Customer);
{Displays a single customer record}

procedure ReadCust (var OneCust {output} : Customer);
{Reads a single customer record from the keyboard}

procedure Arrive (var WaitingLine {input/output} : Queue;
                  var Success {output} : Boolean);
{
  Simulates the arrival of a single customer.
  Calls: ReadCust
}

procedure Depart (var WaitingLine {input/output} : Queue;
                  var Success {output} : Boolean);
{
  Simulates the departure of a single customer.
  Calls: WriteCust
}

procedure Show (WaitingLine {input} : Queue);
{
  Displays size and contents of the customer queue.
  Calls: WriteCust
}
```

2. Carry out Programming Project 1 using a stack instead of a queue.
3. Write a program to monitor the flow of an item into and out of a warehouse. The warehouse will have numerous deliveries and shipments for this item (a widget) during the time period covered. A shipment out is billed at 50% over the cost of a widget. Unfortunately, each shipment received may have a different cost associated with it. The firm's accountants have instituted a last-in, first-out system for filling orders. This means that the newest widgets are the first ones sent out to fill an order. This inventory system can be represented using a stack, with the Push procedure inserting a shipment received and the Pop procedure deleting a shipment out. Each data record will consist of the following items:

   S or O: shipment received or order to be sent
   Quantity: quantity received or shipped out
   Cost: cost per widget (for a shipment received only)
   Vendor: character string that names company sent to or received from

   Write the necessary procedures to store shipments received and to process orders. The output for an order will consist of the quantity and the total cost for all widgets in the order. *Hint:* Each widget price is 50% higher than its cost. The widgets used to fill an order may come from multiple shipments with different costs.
4. Redo Programming Project 3, this time assuming widgets are shipped using a first-in, first-out strategy. Use a queue to store the widget orders.
5. A *dequeue* might be described as a double-ended queue, that is, a structure in which elements can be inserted or removed from either end. Write a Turbo Pascal object that contains the declarations and methods for a dequeue.
6. The radix sorting algorithm uses an array of 10 queues (numbered 0 through 9) to simulate the operation of the old card-sorting machines. The algorithm requires one pass to be made for every digit of the numbers being sorted. For example, a list of three-digit numbers would require three passes through the list. During the first pass, the least significant digit (the ones digit) of each number is examined and the number is inserted at the rear of the queue whose subscript matches the digit. After all numbers have been processed, the elements of each queue, beginning with Queue[0], are copied one at a time to the end of an eleventh queue prior to beginning the next pass. The process is repeated for the next most significant digit (the tens digit) using the order of the numbers in the eleventh queue. The process is repeated for the next most significant digit (the hundreds digit). After the final pass, the eleventh queue will contain the numbers in sorted order. Write a program that implements radix sort using our QueueADT.
7. Use a binary search tree to maintain an airline passenger list. Each passenger record should contain the passenger name (record key), class (Economy, Business, FirstClass), and number of seats. The main program should be menu driven and allow the user to display the data for a particular passenger, display the entire list, create a list, insert a node, delete a node, and replace the data for a particular passenger. When deleting a node, simply change the number of assigned seats to zero and leave the passenger's node in the tree.

8. Save each word appearing in a block of text in a binary search tree. Also save the number of occurrences of each word and the line number for each occurrence. Use a stack for the line numbers. After all words have been processed, display each word in alphabetical order. Along with each word, display the number of occurrences and the line number for each occurrence.

9. The fastest binary tree is one which is as close to balanced as possible. However, there is no guarantee that elements will be inserted in the right order. It is possible to build a balanced binary tree if the elements to be inserted are in order in an array. Write a procedure and test program that, given a sorted array of elements, builds a balanced binary tree. Augment the binary search tree ADT to count the number of nodes that are searched to find an element and display the number of nodes that are searched to find each item in the tree. *Hint:* The root of the tree should be the middle (median) of the array; this project is easier to do if you use recursion.

10. Write a procedure that performs an inorder traversal of a binary tree without using recursion. It will be necessary to use a stack. Write a suitable test program for your procedure.

The Internet

network
a collection of computers that are linked together to share resources

Internet
a network of networks that links computers all over the world

As you learned in Chapter 1, a **network** is a collection of computers that are linked together to share resources. The **Internet** is a collection of networks that are linked together to form a very large network. It connects tens of thousands of computer networks all over the world in order to share information. These networks provide access for millions of people and, according to the Internet Society, the number of computers on the Internet is almost doubling every year.

The Internet has only recently become accessible to many people in their homes and offices, but the idea has been around for almost 30 years. In the late 1960s, the

ARPANET
the precursor to the Internet—
a network established by the
U.S. Department of Defense

United States Department of Defense Advanced Research Projects Agency began establishing a decentralized computer network known as **ARPANET**. Rather than there being one central distribution point, each computer on the network had the ability to pass information to or receive information from any other computer on the system. A network with this type of design can withstand damage to its individual pieces without the entire network's being damaged. From a defense standpoint, this is very important. The network and its information cannot be brought down by an attack to one or even more pieces of the network.

ARPANET linked government researchers, laboratory researchers, and academic researchers, but it was clear that there would be a demand to include more people. In response, the National Science Foundation funded the development of **NSFNET**, a network that connected networks at five supercomputer sites in the United States. Many colleges and universities connected to this network, expanding access to more members of the community. NSFNET was not just for those involved in research in computer science and the government but included anyone at the connected colleges and universities. ARPANET, NSFNET, and other networks eventually merged to create what is now known as the Internet. Millions of people all over the world use the Internet to exchange information. Anyone with a computer and a modem can connect to the Internet, and the number of users continues to increase at a tremendous rate.

NSFNET
a network developed by the
National Science Foundation
that is now part of the Internet

19.1   How the Internet Works

Packet-Switched Network

packet-switched
information is divided into
small pieces (packets) and
then sent across the network

The Internet is a **packet-switched** network. When data is sent across the network, it is first broken up into little pieces that are called packets. Each packet travels across the network separately; the pieces are put back together when they all reach their destination.

The advantage of a packet-switched network is that it allows several users to share just one communication line. Packets from many different data transmissions from many different people can travel along the same line without being slowed down by any one large piece of information. There are many different lines on the Internet that connect the various networks, so there is not just one route to each computer on the network but several routes.

The different routes are similar to the different roads that you may take to get to your local video store. If an accident or traffic jam is blocking your favorite route, you may choose a different route. In the same way, not all the packets from a single transmission will travel on the same line but will travel different routes that all eventually arrive at the same destination. As a packet travels along the route, it reaches machines (called **routers**) that switch the packet to an available line that will move it closer and closer until it reaches its final destination.

routers
special devices on a network
that guide packets from their
origin to their destination

Internet Protocols

In order to travel along these routes, each packet needs something like a roadmap to help it find the different routes from its origin to its destination. It would be very difficult to travel these routes without some directions. As the packet goes along the lines, the routers check out the information on its roadmap to help the packet along its way.

The creators of ARPANET recognized that many different types of computers would be connected to create this network and devised a way to allow them all to communicate. In order for the different types of computers to communicate and help the packets find their way, they must have a common language. The creators of ARPANET created the language of the Internet known as **Internet protocols**. Internet protocols are the set of rules that govern the exchange of information across the Internet and provide the roadmaps.

Internet protocols
the set of rules that governs the exchange of information across the Internet

TCP/IP

There are many layers of Internet protocols, but the most well-known are the **Internet Protocol** (**IP**) and the **Transmission Control Protocol** (**TCP**), often called TCP/IP, which is responsible for getting messages to their destination.

First, TCP breaks the message up into packets and gives it important information. This information includes identification of which message the packet belongs to and its position in the message. After the message is divided into packets, IP marks each packet with its address of origin and its destination address (Fig. 19.1).

As the packet travels along the Internet, routers use these addresses to decide the best route for the packet and pass the message closer to its destina-

Internet Protocol (IP)
the set of rules that governs the addressing of packets for travel across the Internet
Transmission Control Protocol (TCP)
the set of rules that governs the breaking up of a document into packets and the reassembly of the packets at the destination

Figure 19.1
Breaking a Message into Packets

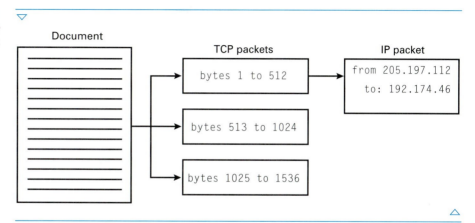

Figure 19.2
Different Routes for Message Packets

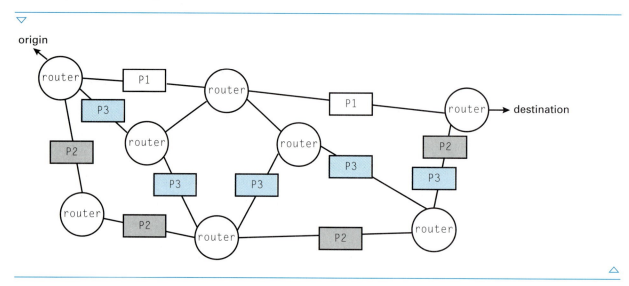

tion until it finally arrives. The route the packet takes is not decided when the packet is sent, but rather as the packet travels across the Internet and encounters different routers. When the packet reaches a router, the router makes a decision about where the packet should go next. If a particular route is closed for some reason, there are always alternative routes. Each packet in a transmission may travel a different route to get to the same destination (Fig. 19.2).

When the packets reach their destination, TCP reassembles the pieces of the message in the correct order. If the packets do not all reach their destination, TCP sends a message back to the machine that sent the original message and requests that the missing packet or packets be sent again.

IP Addressing

Getting the message to the correct destination relies heavily on a special method of identifying each computer. Each computer system and computer on the Internet has an **IP address** that uniquely identifies the particular machine. The IP address is a set of numbers separated by periods. For instance, the IP address for a computer in the Computer and Information Sciences Department at Temple University is 155.247.71.60.

These numbers are easily understood by the computer, but humans may have a little more trouble remembering addresses like these. Fortunately, each IP address corresponds to a name in the **domain name system**. For

IP address
the address of a computer on the Internet written in combinations of numbers and periods

domain name system
a convention for naming computers in words

domain name
the address of a computer on the Internet written in words

domain name system servers
devices that translate the domain names into IP addresses

instance, the corresponding **domain name** for the IP address 155.247.71.60 is joda.cis.temple.edu. We use the domain names when we are sending information across the Internet but the machines on the Internet use the numbers. The **domain name system servers** translate the names to numbers.

There are some naming conventions in the system that make it easier for us to remember and form names. For instance, because Temple University is a higher education institution, its domain name ends with edu. Some of the most common domain-name endings, or subdomains, include com for commercial organizations, gov for government organizations, org for nonprofit organizations, mil for military organizations, int for international organizations, and net for network organizations. The Internet Ad Hoc Committee recently created some additional subdomain names because there was such a limited number; the plan is to begin using these additional subdomain names sometime in 1997. The new subdomain names include store for merchants, web for web activities, arts for arts and cultural organizations, rec for recreation and entertainment organizations, info for information services, and nom for individuals. A list of subdomain names appears in Table 19.1.

The domain-name system works much like our postal-addressing system. In the postal-addressing system, the most specific information about you, your name, is listed first and the least specific, your city and state, is listed last. The subdomains listed in Table 19.1 are called top-level domains because they are very general. These high-level domains are at the end of the

Table 19.1
Subdomain Name Table

Domain Name	Description	Example
edu	Colleges and universities	Temple University
com	Commercial organizations	International Business Machines
gov	Government agencies	Library of Congress
org	Nonprofit organizations	Public television
mil	Military agencies	Army, Navy, etc.
net	Network service organizations	Inter Solutions Inc.
int	International organizations	NATO
store	Merchants	
web	Web activities	
arts	Arts and cultural organizations	
rec	Recreation and entertainment organizations	
info	Information organizations	
nom	Individuals	

domain name. More specific information comes first. For example, the name of a college or university (more specific information) precedes the general category of edu in a name—for instance, temple.edu. Even more specific would be the department within the college, Computer and Information Sciences. So the domain name for the network of the CIS department at Temple University is cis.temple.edu.

19.2   Internet Applications: E-mail, Telnet, and FTP

e-mail
the ability to send, receive, save, and reply to electronic mail messages over the Internet

Telnet
the ability to log onto many different computers on the Internet

FTP (File Transfer Protocol)
the Internet protocol that governs how files are sent along the Internet

World Wide Web
the portion of the Internet that allows easy access to documents in a uniform way

The Internet allows you to access and distribute information through many different services, each of which has a specific purpose. Some of the common services on the Internet are electronic mail (**e-mail**), **Telnet**, File Transfer Protocol (**FTP**), and the **World Wide Web**. There are many software programs that allow you to access each of these services, but no matter what software you use, its purpose remains the same. Most Internet service providers will give you the software necessary to use these basic services. We will describe e-mail, Telnet, and FTP briefly and then concentrate on the use of the World Wide Web.

E-mail

E-mail allows people on the Internet to communicate through the use of electronic messages. Messages sent to you are stored in your own personal file, and you can read them, reply to them, delete them after reading, or save them. You can also attach files to messages, send messages to multiple recipients, forward messages, and print messages. To send and receive e-mail messages, you need an e-mail program such as Pine or Eudora, as well as the e-mail address of the person to whom you wish to send a message.

E-mail is a fast and convenient way to communicate. Messages sent via the U.S. postal system usually take days to reach their destination, while messages sent electronically usually reach their destination in minutes. The message may be traveling to a computer on the same system, to a different state, or to a different country, but the transmission will still be very quick. Another advantage is that it does not cost any more to send electronic messages to distant destinations, to send larger messages, or to send messages to multiple recipients, although this could change.

synchronous
communication that takes place between two parties at the same time

asynchronous
communication that takes place between two parties at different times

When communicating by telephone, both parties must be available and willing to talk at the same time; this is known as **synchronous** communication. This means that responses are immediate. E-mail, however, is **asynchronous**, meaning that the parties communicating do not have to be available at the same time. The sender sends the message at his or her convenience and the recipient reads it at his or her convenience. Although there is a delay in response time with asynchronous communication, it can be a lot more convenient, especially in a global marketplace in which work schedules vary greatly.

Although e-mail is quick and convenient, it does have some disadvantages. One limitation is that it is very difficult to express tone in e-mail messages. There have been some attempts to combat this. WRITING A MESSAGE IN ALL CAPS CAN BE INTERPRETED AS YELLING. There are also many **emoticons** that have been developed to add tonal emphasis to a point. For example, :-) is a smiley face that is used to indicate that what was just written was a joke, of course. You may ;-) wink at a person or show him or her that you are sad :-(or shocked :-0. These emoticons help to clarify the tone of the message but do not overcome all the limitations.

E-mail is a lot less secure than communication by telephone or through the mail. Intercepting telephone messages without the help of the telephone company is very difficult to do. When sending mail through the U.S. postal system, it is easy to tell if the mail has been opened along the way, and it is illegal to tamper with anyone's mail in the U.S. postal system. Electronic mail, however, is not so secure. With e-mail, someone can read your messages and it will be imperceptible to you. Not only that, it has been ruled in the courts that system administrators in organizations have the right to read any and all e-mail at any time. It is very important to remember that e-mail is not private. Never send anything via e-mail that would make you uncomfortable if someone other than the recipient reads it.

Telnet

Telnet allows you to log onto other computers on the Internet to access their services. You may login to another computer system (called a **remote site** or **host**) from your computer system (called a **local site**) so that you can access information or run programs on the remote site.

There are two ways you may access a remote site. You may have access through a **full-privilege account** or a **guest account**. A full-privilege account requires a username and password for the remote system and generally allows more capabilities. A guest account allows you to login without a password or with a password that is made available to anyone who reaches the login screen. When using a guest account, you may have access to only certain applications and information at the remote site.

Some people have accounts both for business and for home and may telnet from one account to the other by using their username and password. This is an example of a full privilege account. Many systems, however, allow anyone to access their site to share resources by means of guest accounts.

To log onto a remote site, you need telnet software such as NCSA Telnet, Hytelnet, or EWAN. To connect to a site, you open a connection using your telnet software and the IP address or domain name of the computer system to which you wish to connect. Once you are connected to the remote system, you may see instructions for logging in, exiting, and terminating the connection in case of failure. You will receive information about how to login as a guest and what resources are available to you. Once you connect to the re-

---

emoticons
code symbols that express emotions or tone in e-mail messages

remote site or host
a computer system that you can connect to from your local computer system

local site
the computer system you are directly connected to

full-privilege account
an account with a user-id and password that enables you full access to a system

guest account
the ability to log on and access a system without having an account on that system

mote site, it is as if you are directly connected to that computer. You can access the same services as another user with the same privileges who is directly connected.

You can use telnet to search library catalogs, find weather information, access databases, and much more. For instance, you can connect to the library catalog at Harvard University, called HOLLIS (Harvard OnLine Library Information System), at the address `hollis.harvard.edu` to search the catalog. By telnetting to `pac.carl.org`, you can also connect to the CARL Corporation (Colorado Alliance of Research Libraries) to access more library catalogs, commercial databases, and community records. If you would like to find out the exact time according to the atomic clock in Boulder, Colorado, telnet to `india.colorado.edu 13`. If you are interested in your local weather report, the weather in Paris, a report on skiing conditions, or earthquake reports, telnet to the weather server at the University of Michigan's Department of Atmospheric, Oceanographic, and Space Sciences at `madlab.sprl.umich.edu 3000` (see Fig. 19.3). If you are researching recent legislation (1982–present), connect to the Library of Congress Information Service at `locis.loc.gov` and search its database.

Figure 19.3
Telnetting to University of Michigan Weather Server

▽

```
Give the command to open a telnet connection.
type telnet madlab.sprl.umich.edu 3000
-----------------------------------------------------------------------------
*                          University of Michigan                          *
*                          WEATHER UNDERGROUND                             *
-----------------------------------------------------------------------------
*                                                                          *
*                    comments: ldm@cirrus.sprl.umich.edu                   *
*                                                                          *
*  This information available on the web at http://www.wunderground.com and *
*       telnet rainmaker.wunderground.com                                  *
*       telnet downwind.sprl.umich.edu 3000                               *
*                                                                          *
* With Help from:  The National Science Foundation supported Unidata Project *
*                  University Corporation for Atmospheric Research         *
*                  Boulder, Colorado  80307-3000                          *
*                                                                          *
-----------------------------------------------------------------------------
*       This service is for educational and research purposes only.        *
*       Commercial, for-profit users should contact                        *
*       info@rainmaker.wunderground.com to acquire their own data feed.    *
-----------------------------------------------------------------------------
```

▷ ▷ ▷ ▷ ▷ ▷

Press Return for menu, or enter 3 letter forecast city code: <CR>

```
CITY FORECAST MENU
--------------------------------------------
1) Print forecast for selected city
2) Print climatic data for selected city
3) Display 3-letter city codes for a selected state
4) Display all 2-letter state codes
M) Return to main menu
X) Exit program
?) Help
Selection:3
```

Enter 2-letter state code: pa

```
----------------------
State   Code   City
----------------------
PA      PHL    Philadelphia
PA      LNS    Lancaster
PA      CXY    Harrisburg
PA      LBE    Latrobe
PA      AOO    Altoona
PA      JST    Johnstown
PA      RDG    Reading
PA      PIT    Pittsburgh
PA      ABE    Allentown
PA      UNV    State College
```
Press Return to continue, M to return to menu, X to exit: <CR>
```
PA      DUJ    Dubois
PA      IPT    Williamsport
PA      AVP    Scranton
PA      FKL    Franklin
PA      BFD    Bradford
PA      ERI    Erie
```

```
CITY FORECAST MENU
--------------------------------------------
1) Print forecast for selected city
2) Print climatic data for selected city
3) Display 3-letter city codes for a selected state
4) Display all 2-letter state codes
M) Return to main menu
X) Exit program
?) Help
Selection:1
```

Enter 3-letter city code: phl

```
Weather Conditions at 12 PM EDT on 1 AUG 97 for Philadelphia, PA.
Temp(F)        Humidity(%)    Wind(mph)    Pressure(in)   Weather
======================================================================
   82            42%          NORTH at 0   30.20          Mostly Cloudy
```

DELAWARE-PHILADELPHIA-
1030 AM EDT FRI AUG 1 1997

THIS AFTERNOON...SUNSHINE AND SOME HIGH CLOUDS. HIGH NEAR 90. WEST
WIND 5 TO 10 MPH.
TONIGHT...MOSTLY CLEAR. LOW 65 TO 70. LIGHT WEST WIND.
SATURDAY...PARTLY SUNNY. HIGH NEAR 90.

```
    ***********************
    State extended forecast
    ***********************
```

EXTENDED FORECAST...
SUNDAY...PARTLY CLOUDY WITH A CHANCE OF SHOWERS OR THUNDERSTORMS.
LOWS IN THE 60S. HIGHS NEAR 80 NORTH AND IN THE 80S ELSEWHERE.
MONDAY...PARTLY CLOUDY WITH A CHANCE OF SHOWERS AND THUNDERSTORMS...
MAINLY SOUTH. LOWS IN THE 60S. HIGHS IN THE MID 70S NORTH TO THE MID
80S SOUTH.
TUESDAY...PARTLY SUNNY. LOWS IN THE MID 50S NORTH TO THE MID 60S
SOUTHEAST. HIGHS IN THE LOW 70S NORTH TO THE LOW 80S SOUTHEAST.

The National Weather Service data is provided by the University of Michigan
Weather Underground project, National Science Foundation-funded Unidata project,
and Alden Electronics, Inc., and is for non-commercial use only.

```
    CITY FORECAST MENU
    -----------------------------------------
    1) Print forecast for selected city
    2) Print climatic data for selected city
    3) Display 3-letter city codes for a selected state
    4) Display all 2-letter state codes
    M) Return to main menu
    X) Exit program
    ?) Help
    Selection:X
--------------------------------------------------------------------
*                        BLUE-SKIES!                              *
*                                                                 *
*   The BLUE-SKIES program offers users relatively fast access to *
*   literally hundreds of real-time weather and environmental images. *
*                                                                 *
*   For more information, see the Blue-Skies information under    *
*   the "?) Answers to all your questions" option on the main menu *
*   of the Weather Underground.                                   *
--------------------------------------------------------------------
```

A lot of information is located on the Internet and is accessible by telnet. Finding that information could be very difficult. Fortunately, many people have voluntarily collected lists of telnet sites, included them in guidebooks, and made them available on the Internet. In the next section, we will find out how to locate some of the lists and download them using FTP.

FTP

Although telnet allows you access to view a lot of very valuable information and applications, it does not allow you to transfer them to your own computer to save and use at a later date. If you want to locate some books you saw in the Harvard Library Catalog, you may want to save their descriptions, print them, and take the information to the local library. Fortunately, there is a way to transfer files between computers on the Internet. The method for doing this is called File Transfer Protocol, or **FTP**.

FTP (File Transfer Protocol) the Internet protocol that governs how files are sent along the Internet

To transfer files from one Internet computer to another, you will need an FTP program and the domain name or address of the Internet computer you wish to transfer a file to or from. You will also need to know where the file is located on that particular site. The files at FTP sites, called archives, are arranged in directories. In order to find a particular file, it is helpful to know the directory path where the file is located. Often, when you are given information about a particular FTP site, you are also given information about the directory or directories in which you can find useful files.

You use the FTP program to make a connection between the two computers. After the connection is made, you work your way through the directory path to the files you are looking for; then you may transfer files to and from your computer and the remote computer. There are many different FTP programs that vary greatly in their interface and ease of use. With the increased emphasis on graphical user interfaces, there are quite a few FTP programs that make the traversing of directories and the transferring of files as easy as clicking a button or dragging a filename across the screen. On some systems you may have to use commands such as `dir` or `ls` to get a listing of the files and directories at a particular location, `cd` to change to a different directory, and `get` to copy a file from the remote system to your local computer.

anonymous FTP sites FTP sites that allow access to users who do not have accounts for that site

Many places on the Internet are set up as **anonymous FTP sites**. An anonymous FTP site allows anyone access to the files on that site without needing an account on that system. An anonymous FTP site is similar to a telnet guest account because you do not have full access to the files on that computer system. You can access publicly available files and you may copy files from the remote system, but you usually do not have the privilege of transferring files to the remote system. Another similarity is that you do not need a special username and password because you do not have an account. In most cases, the username for an anonymous FTP site is `anonymous` and the password is your e-mail address. You should never use your actual password as the password for an anonymous FTP site because the site is not secure.

Anonymous FTP sites contain all sorts of files, including text, program, and graphics files. You can find text files that contain anything from a collection of Dave Letterman's top 10 lists to modern translations of Chaucer's Canterbury Tales and the source code for this book. You can also find application files that include games, software updates, utility programs, and just about anything else you might be looking for. You can transfer all types of files using your FTP application.

Many Internet reference books include lists of commonly used FTP sites and what is available on those sites. There are also lists of FTP sites that are available on the Internet at anonymous FTP sites. One such site is at the National Chiao Tung University in Taiwan at tp.edu.tw. Follow the directory path to /documents/internet/guides/ftp-list for a list of anonymous FTP sites. Another site is located at the Massachusetts Institute of Technology at the address rtfm.mit.edu. The FTP sites are compiled in files that are located in the directory /pub/usenet/alt.answers/ftp-list/sitelist (see Fig. 19.4). If you load theses file into a word-processing program, you can search the list for keywords and find many interesting and useful sites. Another useful source of FTP sites is word of mouth. Keep your ears open.

Although there are many lists and many people to give you advice, it can still be difficult to find exactly what you are looking for. Fortunately, there is

Figure 19.4

Connecting to an Anonymous FTP Site at MIT

▽

```
type ftp rtfm.mit.edu
once connected, you will be prompted for a username
type anonymous
when prompted for a password,
type your email address
to change to the directory pub/usenet/alt.answers/ftp-list/sitelist,
type cd pub/usenet/alt.answers/ftp-list/sitelist
once you are at the correct directory you can transfer the files,
type get part1
this will transfer the file named part1 to your computer
to get all the files at once,
type mget part*
as each file is displayed, type y to transfer them.
```

△

Archie
a system that allows you to search for files stored on other FTP sites

a system called **Archie** that allows you to search for files that are located at anonymous FTP sites. You can use Archie, AnArchie, or other Archie searching programs to search by file name or search for keywords in the descriptions of files. Archie servers will search for the file and tell you on what computer and in which directory you can find the files that match your search criteria.

19.3 The World Wide Web

The World Wide Web (WWW) was introduced in 1989 and although the newest application of the Internet, it is already the most popular feature. The WWW was developed at CERN (the European Laboratory for Particle Physics), which was interested in creating an effective and uniform way of accessing all the information on the Internet. It combines individual tools such as e-mail, telnet, FTP, and Archie into one integrated system with a common, easy-to-use interface. You can use the WWW to send, view, retrieve, and search for information. Not only does the Web provide easy access to information on the Internet, it also has the advantage of linking that information to other pieces of closely related information through its use of hypertext and hypermedia.

Hypertext and Hypermedia

links
connections that allow a user to access related documents while reading another document
hypertext
documents that contain connections or links to other documents
hypermedia
hypertext that includes links to sound, graphics, and video

One of the most important features of the WWW is that it contains connections (or **links**) to other places on the Web that contain information related to the subject you are currently investigating. The links to the connections are made through **hypertext** or **hypermedia**. Hypertext allows you to connect text in one document to text in other documents. If you are reading about gardening and you come across a section on vegetable gardening, using hypertext, you would select the words 'vegetable gardening', which would link you to additional documents related to vegetable gardening. You may see information on organic vegetable gardening, container vegetable gardening, or specific vegetables. If you select one of those hypertext links, the text you now see will contain more links that allow you to connect to other related topics. You may continue selecting links to give yourself a tour of vegetable gardening, container gardening, related topics, or you may choose to return to your original topic of gardening.

Hypermedia is hypertext with flash. It allows you to make connections not only to text but also to graphics, video, and sound. For instance, if you are interested in a new compact disc by your favorite band, you may select a link to a sound clip from its latest album, a video clip from its latest video, a picture of the band, or the itinerary for its upcoming tour.

Web Browser

web browser
software that allows you to display and view WWW documents

download
sending files from an FTP site or WWW server to a user's computer

In order to access the WWW, you need to have a program called a **web browser**. The browser is used to display the text (most display graphics as well) and to activate the links. As mentioned earlier, the web allows you to use all the Internet tools with just one program, so web browsers also allow you to **download** files using FTP, to send mail, and to visit telnet sites.

There are two types of browsers: text browsers and graphical browsers. Graphical browsers are more popular because they are very easy to use and can display images and video (hypermedia). Text browsers only show text (hypertext) but are generally much faster. One of the most commonly used text browsers is a program called Lynx. Some of the more common graphical browsers are Mosaic, Netscape, and Internet Explorer.

The sophistication and friendliness of the graphical web browsers have helped the WWW to gain so much popularity. These browsers present the information in a useful format and one with which we are familiar. When you view the web through a graphical browser, it looks very much like a newspaper, magazine, or book. Since we are familiar with this format, browsing through the web and finding information is very easy. Information on the WWW is divided into units called pages just as in newspapers, magazines, and books.

HTTP and HTML

There are many different web browsers but, like other Internet tools, they must all conform to the same protocol so that any machine on the Internet can access information and make information available through the WWW interface. The protocol for the WWW is called Hypertext Transfer Protocol (**HTTP**). This protocol allows machines to send and receive hypertext and hypermedia information.

HTTP (Hypertext Transfer Protocol)
the Internet protocol that governs the transmission of hypertext and hypermedia documents

HTML (Hypertext Mark-up Language)
a language used to create and format WWW pages or documents

tags
a formatting code used in an HTML document

In addition to the protocol for sending and receiving WWW documents, there is also a common language for writing and displaying those documents called Hypertext Mark-up Language (**HTML**). HTML is used to create and format pages on the web. An HTML document is an ASCII text document that contains information about formatting. HTML documents are formatted using **tags** that control the placement and size of images, text, headings, borders, links, and much more. We will learn more about HTML tags in the section about writing simple WWW pages.

Connecting to the WWW

In order to access information on the WWW, you need a web browser and you need to know where the WWW documents are located. The location of a document, link, or service on the WWW is referred to as its Uniform Resource Locator (URL) or address. A URL has two parts: the first part identifies the ser-

Figure 19.5

Connecting to the
Addison Wesley Longman
Home Page Using
Netscape Navigator

Type `http://www.awl.com` in the `Go To` field of Netscape's Navigator

vice being used and the second part represents the address of the machine on which the information is located. For example, if you wish to view the Addison Wesley Longman home pages, the URL `http://www.awl.com` will get you there. The `http` part says that you wish to connect to the HTTP server so that you may view HTML documents. The `www.awl.com` part is the domain name of the machine where the HTML documents are located. Using your browser, type in the URL and you will be connected to the HTTP sever at Addison Wesley Longman. Once connected, you will be able to view their HTML documents. URLs usually start with `http` to indicate that you wish to use the service that reads HTML documents but they may also start with `ftp`, `telnet`, or `mailto`, depending on which service you are using.

Another helpful feature of a web browser is the ability to mark certain sites with a **bookmark**. Bookmarks allow you to return to a site without having to type in the address or go through links. Browsers generally have menu options for adding, deleting, or connecting to a bookmarked site. Once you get to the Addison Wesley Longman pages, you may want to add a bookmark in your browser.

bookmark

a site whose URL is saved so that you can easily return to it at a later date

Figure 19.6
The Addison Wesley
Longman Home Page

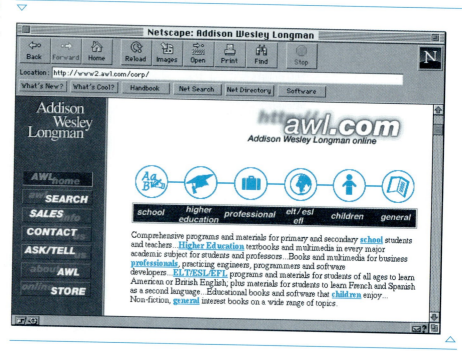

Once you are connected, you will see a hypermedia document that contains general information about Addison Wesley Longman and some links to related information (Fig. 19.6). You may select the links by clicking on them with your mouse. Hypertext links usually appear in a color that is different from the standard text and are usually underlined. In Fig. 19.6, the standard text is black and the hypertext links are in color and underlined. Many of the images (icons) are also links. There is no rule for distinguishing which icons are links and which are just images but as you use the web, you will begin to get a feel for it.

On the page shown in Fig. 19.6, you may select the link that connects to books suitable for higher education by using the mouse to click on the highlighted words 'higher education', or the image of the mortarboard. When you select the link, the page shown in Fig. 19.7 will load.

If you select the link to Computer and Engineering by clicking on the text or the image above the text, the page shown in Fig. 19.8 will load.

Type in Koffman in the window labeled Quick Search: and click the search button. You will get the page shown in Fig. 19.9

Select Turbo Pascal, Fifth Edition (Fig. 19.10).

You will see a brief description of the book and some information that is helpful for ordering.

Figure 19.7
Addison Wesley Longman
Higher Education Page

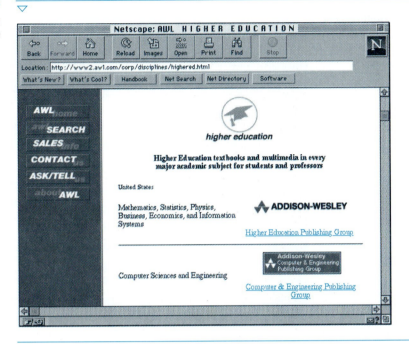

Figure 19.8
The Addison Wesley
Longman Computer and
Engineering Home Page

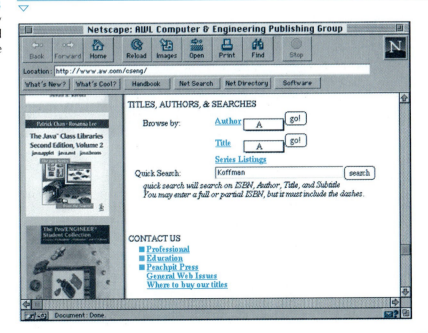

Figure 19.9
Books Authored or
Coauthored by Koffman

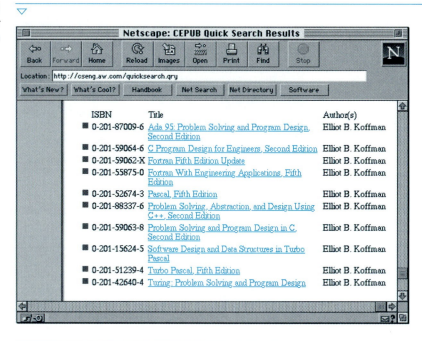

Figure 19.10
Addison Wesley Longman
Koffman Turbo Pascal
Book, Fifth Edition

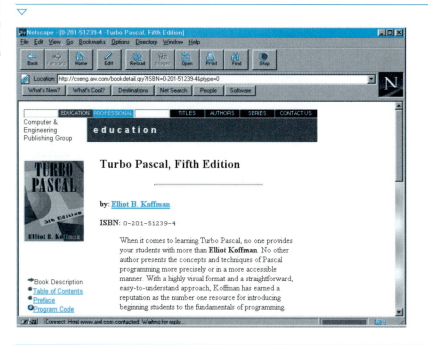

Figure 19.11
List of Turbo Pascal, 5th
Edition Files Available for
FTP

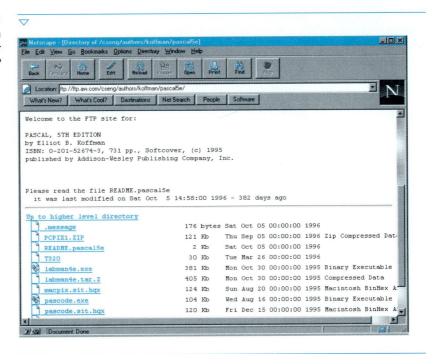

Most of the links on these pages are to other HTML documents, but these are not the only links that are available. These pages allow you to link to mail, telnet, and FTP, all with the same interface. For example, there is a link to `Program Code` for the Turbo Pascal book (see Fig. 19.10) that brings you to an FTP site for downloading sample programs. Because the WWW has all the Internet services together, the FTP site looks similar to other WWW pages (Fig. 19.11). Notice that the URL for this site begins with 'ftp'. To download a file, just click on it and it will be transferred to your computer (Fig. 19.12). Mail and telnet work just as easily as FTP on the WWW. Find a link to an e-mail address, click on it, compose a quick message, and send the message. Find a telnet link and browse through it with the click of a button. The integration of all these services with one common interface is one of the most important features of the WWW.

Searching the WWW

If you know the address of a particular site, it is easy to get there by typing the URL in your browser. If you do not know the URL for a site, but you do know which site you wish to get to, you can often guess by using the domain name conventions and the name of the organization you wish to connect to. Try fig-

Figure 19.12

Downloading a File Using
FTP on the WWW

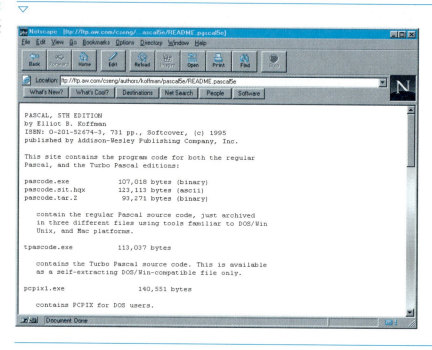

uring out the name for the *New York Times* newspaper, a commercial organization. You are correct if you guessed `http://www.nytimes.com`. Even if you
don't know an address, usually you can make a pretty good guess.

If you want to find something on the WWW but don't know where to find
it, then the problem is more difficult to solve. The WWW is so large that it can
be overwhelming. A good place to look for help is at the bookstore. There you
will find many guides that list sites by category and provide their URLs. There
are also many online guides to the WWW. These guides provide catalogues of
WWW sites and their contents. One such guide is the WWW Virtual Library
(`http://info.cern.ch/hypertext/DataSources/bySubject/Overview.`
`html`), which is maintained by CERN.

The WWW is so large and is growing so rapidly, however, that no one
guide can keep up with it all. Fortunately, there are services on the WWW
that are set up to help in just this situation.

If you do not know a particular site but are interested in finding information on a particular topic, you can use one of the many **search engines** on
the WWW. These search engines search the pages for you and return URLs
based on your search criteria. To find what you need, connect to one of
these engines, enter a few keywords, click a button, and wait a minute or
two for the results. These search engines allow you to do very sophisticated
Boolean searches so that you can find exactly what you are looking for. Most
of the search engines also rank the results based on how many of the key-

search engines
Internet WWW server that
processes users' requests to
search the WWW for HTML
documents on particular subjects

Table 19.2
Common Search Engines
and Their URLs

Altavista	`http://www.altavista.com`
Excite	`http://www.excite.com`
Infoseek	`http://www.guide.infoseek.com`
Lycos	`http://www.lycos.com`
Metacrawler	`http://www.metacrawler.com`
Webcrawler	`http://www.webcrawler.com`
Yahoo	`http://www.yahoo.com`

words were found in the documents. Each of the search engines is a little bit different and may return different results with the same search criteria. Use a few of them to start and then pick your favorite (see Table 19.2).

Figure 19.13 depicts a sample search for online WWW guides using the Metacrawler search engine at `http://www.metacrawler.com`. Metacrawler polls other search engines and returns the top 10 choices from each of them. The results are then ranked according to the number of keywords that appeared in each document (see Fig. 19.14).

Figure 19.13
Searching the WWW for
Online Guides Using
Metacrawler

▽

Connect to metacrawler.
Enter keywords for the search `World Wide Web Online Guides Subject`.
Click the `Search` button.

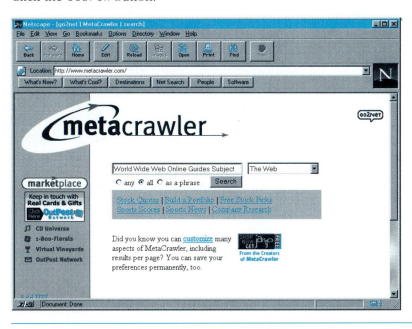

Figure 19.14
Search Results with
Rankings

Select Virtual Online.

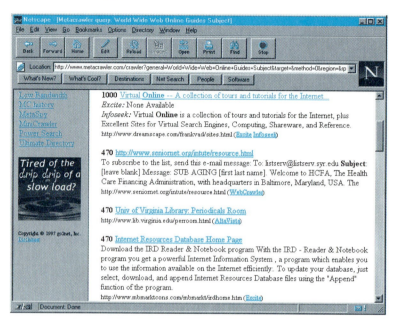

Figure 19.15
Virtual Online's List of
Internet Guides

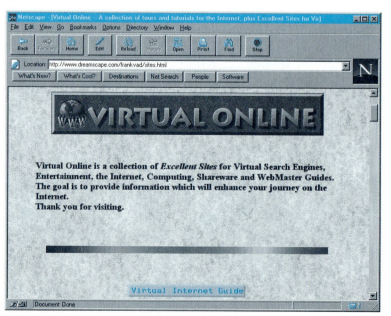

More About Browsers

WWW browsers can do even more than link to hypertext and hypermedia documents, FTP sites, telnet sites, and mail. You can also use most browsers to save the text information on a page, copy an image, keep a list of URLs of frequently visited sites, keep a history of sites you have visited, move backward and forward through links you have visited, print WWW pages, and much more. Explore the options that are made available through the menu on your web browser.

Writing Your Own Web Page Using HTML

A web page is written in HTML. The page is simply a text document with special formatting commands that tell web browsers how the information on it should be displayed. To write your own web page, all you need is a text editor, some knowledge of HTML tags, and a browser so that you can view your finished product. We will discuss some of the basic tags in this section and write a simple web page.

HTML Tags

All tags in HTML appear in < >. HTML is not case sensitive, so you can write the tags any way you would like. It is a good idea to develop a convention that clearly separates tags from the rest of the text. One good method is to write tags in all uppercase.

Many formatting tags require that you both begin and end the tag. They begin with <TAG> and end with </TAG>. The / indicates that the formatting does not apply to the next part of the text.

Each HTML document should begin with the tag <HTML> and end with the tag </HTML>. HTML documents are divided into two sections: the head and the body. The head contains the title of the page and the body contains the contents of the page. The head should start with the tag <HEAD> and end with the tag </HEAD>. Inside the head is the title. The title appears at the top of the window in your browser. The beginning tag for title is <TITLE>; it ends with </TITLE>. Every HTML document must have a title.

The body of your document should begin with the tag <BODY> and end with </BODY>. Inside the body you will have many formatting tags. You must use tags to specify all formatting, including text size, style, alignment, and even carriage returns (see Table 19.3).

There are many other tags, including tags for creating tables and lists, inserting images, changing background and text colors, creating background images, and creating links. There are many books on writing HTML docu-

Table 19.3
HTML Formatting Tags

Start Tag	End Tag	Result
`<H#>`	`</H#>`	Creates a heading that appears on a line by itself; H1 is the largest heading and H6 is the smallest
` `	none	Inserts a carriage return so that the text moves to the next line
`<P>`	none	Inserts a carriage return and then a blank line
`<HR>`	none	Inserts a horizontal line
`<B>`	`</B>`	Bold text
`<U>`	`</U>`	Underlined text
`<I>`	`</I>`	Italicized text
`<EM>`	`</EM>`	Emphasized text—browser specific
`<CENTER>`	`</CENTER>`	Centers text

ments and many online guides. You can use your WWW search engines to find HTML guides that will help you with the features just listed and many more.

Creating Links in HTML Documents

As mentioned earlier, one of the most important features of the WWW is that it allows you to link your page to other pages on the WWW. You can link to documents anywhere on the WWW. To link to documents on another machine, all you need to know is the URL for that document. If you want to link to a document that is on the same machine as your page, all you need to know is the name of the file and the directory in which it is located. You can also link to a specific point within any page.

When you create a link in HTML, you specify the document you wish to link to, and the text (or image) that the user will click when they wish to connect to the document. Here is an example.

EXAMPLE 19.1: Connecting to a Document on Another Machine ▼

To create a link to the Addison-Wesley home pages, type the following:

```
<A HREF ="http://www.awl.com/">Addison-Wesley Home Page</A>
```

This tells the location of the web page (*http://www.awl.com*) and the text that will appear on the page to indicate the link (Addison-Wesley Home Page). On your web page, you will see the words 'Addison-Wesley Home Page' underlined and highlighted in the link color. You can click this text to connect to the Addison-Wesley site on the WWW.   ▲

Creating an HTML Document

1. Use a text editor or word processor to type something like the following sample HTML document.

```
<HTML>
<HEAD>
<TITLE>Robin Koffman's Homepage</TITLE>
</HEAD>

<BODY>
<H1><CENTER>Welcome to Robin's Homepage!!!</CENTER>
<CENTER>Read this page to learn a little about HTML.</CENTER></H1>
<HR>
<H2>HTML tags</H2>
HTML tags are enclosed in <>. <p>
Each tag identifies how the text that follows it will appear on the page.<p>
To end a particular format, the tag with a / before it is sometimes used.

<H3>Examples</H3>
<H4>Document Sections</H4>
Each HTML document should begin with the HTML tag and end with /HTML.<BR>
The HEAD of the document contains the TITLE.<BR>
The TITLE of the document appears at the top of the window in your WWW browser.<BR>
The BODY follows the HEAD and contains all the information on the page.<BR>

<H4>Headers and Paragraphs</H4>
H with a number after it stands for header and size.
<H1>H1 is the largest</H1> and <H6>H6 is the smallest</H6>
All headers are displayed on a line by themselves.<BR>

HR will give you a line across the screen like this. <HR>
The HR tag does not have /HR to end it.<BR>
Extra spaces, tabs, and carriage returns are ignored in HTML.<BR>
To get extra spaces, tabs, or carriage returns, you must use special tags.<BR>
Creating spaces and tabs can be done using tables.<BR>
<BR>BR moves the text to the next line.<BR>
P inserts a carriage return and then a blank line before the next text.<P>
The HR, BR, and P tags do not have /HR, /BR, and /P to end them<P>

<H4>Text Styles</H4>
<B>B will give you bold text </B><BR>
<U>U will give you underlined text </U><BR>
<CENTER>CENTER will center your text </CENTER>
<EM>EM indicates emphasis - on netscape, emphasized text is written in italics
</EM><BR>
<I>I will give you italicized text</I>
```

```
<H4>Links</H4>
To link to the Addison-Wesley Home Page, click here --->
<A HREF = "http://www.awl.com/" > Addison-Wesley Home Page</A>
<P>
To link to a nice HTML guide, click here --->
<A HREF = "http://www.ncsa.uiuc.edu/General/Internet/WWW/HTMLPrimerAll.html">
Beginner's Guide to HTML</A>

</BODY>
</HTML>
```

2. Save the document you typed as a text file. If you are using a sophisticated word processor, you will have to specify that you wish to save the
file as a text file. WWW browsers will read only text files, so this is an
important step. The file can have any name but should end with `.html`
to indicate that it is an HTML document.

3. To view the document in its WWW format, use your browser to open
the file you just saved. To do this in Netscape, choose Open File from
the File menu. You will see your document formatted as it would appear on the WWW (Fig. 19.16).

For other people to view the document, the file must be loaded onto an
HTTP server. Most Internet providers allow you to load your WWW pages onto
their server. Once it is loaded, anyone on the WWW can visit your home page.

Figure 19.16
Robin's Home Page

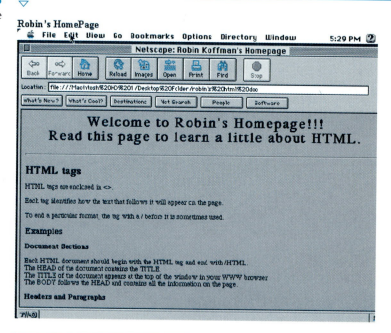

19.4 Etiquette, Security, and Accuracy

When the Internet first started, it was used by a very small community whose members had similar goals. This community developed a culture to which most people naturally adapted. As the resources of the Internet grow and the number of users increases, the community of users becomes more diverse. The Internet now is used by researchers, students, consumers, and sellers. There is no longer one unifying goal that helps define the culture. With the growth and diversification of the Internet, the potential for disagreement grows as well.

Etiquette

Just as with other kinds of communication, you should show respect on the Internet. Because the Internet is so large and diverse, it is hard to know exactly what the rules are. Fortunately, even if you don't know the rules, common sense and courtesy will go a long way.

acceptable use policies
policies used by personnel on an organization's computer system

netiquette
codes of etiquette for a particular system

Many organizations do have rules that are spelled out in **acceptable use policies**. These policies contain codes of etiquette or '**netiquette**' for a particular system. There is no acceptable use policy for the entire Internet and policies for different systems vary. It is a good idea to check with your service provider or university to learn its policy.

Here are some guidelines that are often included in acceptable use policies:

Your account is for your own use. You should not give your password to anyone else.

Follow copyright rules for software.

When writing papers, it is important to cite electronic sources. Using electronic information and presenting it as your own is plagiarism.

E-mail chain letters are forbidden on many systems and can result in termination of your account.

Be polite in all correspondence and use appropriate language. Try to make your tone as clear as possible by using emoticons.

Send mail only to people you know or have had contact with. Do not send unsolicited mail.

Do not send or download extremely large files. This may disrupt the use of the system.

Access only those computers that welcome you.

Security

As mentioned earlier, communication on the Internet is not very secure. As messages travel across the Internet in packets, these packets pass through many computers on the way to their final destination. Anybody who has access to one of these machines and the knowledge to do it can put the packets together and find out what was sent.

As the Internet is used more and more for business, the issue of security will have to be dealt with. You would not want to send any private information such as credit card numbers over the Internet if they can be intercepted at various points along the way. Many people are working to make the sending of sensitive information more secure. One such way is to use programs that put the information into a special format that can be read only by the sender and the recipient. These programs scramble the message on the way out (**encoding**) and then unscramble the message at the destination (**decoding**). No information on the Internet is secure unless it has been encoded.

E-mail is not secure either because it also travels across the Internet in packets that pass through many computers. Not only that, system administrators are legally entitled to read any and all files on a system. Many systems also make backups of files so even if you have erased a file on your account, the file may still be accessible somewhere.

encoding

changing a message so that it cannot be read during travel to its destination

decoding

making a coded message readable after it reaches its destination

Accuracy

The Internet can be a wonderful resource for researching almost any topic. However, it is important to read any document on the Internet critically. Because there are not many rules and nobody oversees the content, a lot of information on the Internet is inaccurate. Publishing on the Internet is so easy that almost anyone can do it and say anything he or she pleases. There is no guarantee that the information is current or accurate, so don't believe everything you read.

Turbo Pascal's Integrated Environment

In this appendix, we discuss the Turbo Pascal 7.0 programming environment and the MS-DOS (Microsoft Disk Operating System). All of the programs in the book will also run if you use Turbo Pascal with Microsoft Windows. However, you must insert the line

```
uses WinCrt;
```

just after the program statement.

A.1 The Turbo Pascal Integrated Environment

All Main menu items have menus of their own from which you can choose other tasks to perform or make changes in the way Turbo Pascal will compile your programs and link together previously compiled units. If a menu item is followed by ellipses (. . .), choosing that item causes a dialog box to be displayed. Choosing an item followed by an arrowhead causes another menu to pop up. Unmarked commands are performed as soon as they are selected. Each Main menu item is described below.

The **File menu** provides the user with DOS file manipulation capabilities.

New   Creates a new file in a new Edit window.
Open...   Opens an existing file in an Edit window.
Save   Saves the file displayed in the active Edit window.
Save as...   Saves file in the active window using a new filename.
Save all   Saves all modified files.
Change dir...   Chooses new default directory.
Print   Prints contents of active Edit window on system printer.
Printer setup...   Chooses printer filter to use for printing.
DOS shell   Exits to DOS. Type exit at DOS prompt to return.
Exit   Exits Turbo Pascal.

The **Edit menu** undoes mistakes and manages the Clipboard.

Edit	
Undo	Alt-BkSp
Redo	
Cut	Shift-Del
Copy	Ctrl-Ins
Paste	Shift-Ins
Clear	Ctrl-Del
Show clipboard	

`Undo`   Undoes previous editor operation.

`Redo`   Redoes previous undone editor operation.

`Cut`   Moves selected block of text from Edit window to Clipboard.

`Copy`   Copies selected text from Edit window to Clipboard.

`Paste`   Moves selected text from Clipboard to Edit window.

`Clear`   Deletes selected text from Edit window or Clipboard.

`Show Clipboard`   Opens Clipboard window and makes it active.

The **Search menu** handles searching operations during editing.

Search
Find...
Replace...
Search again
Go to line number...
Show last compiler error
Find error...
Find procedure...

`Find...`   Allows user to search for text string in active Edit window.

`Replace...`   Allows user to search for and replace a text string.

`Search again`   Repeats last Find or Replace operation.

`Go to line number...`   Moves cursor to a specified line number.

`Show last compiler error`   Moves cursor to position of last error.

`Find error...`   Moves cursor to position of last run-time error.

`Find procedure...`   Searches for procedure or function header.

The **Run menu** manages program execution.

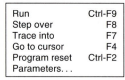

Run	
Run	Ctrl-F9
Step over	F8
Trace into	F7
Go to cursor	F4
Program reset	Ctrl-F2
Parameters...	

`Run`   Executes the current program.

`Step over`   Executes next statement stepping over functions and procedures.

`Trace into`   Executes next statement.

`Go to cursor`   Executes program, stops at Edit cursor position.

`Program reset`   Restarts debugging session, releases all program resources.

`Parameters...`   Sets command-line parameters passed to program.

The **Compile menu** handles program and unit compilation.

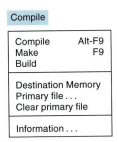

`Compile` Compiles source file displayed in active Edit window.

`Make` Compiles files that have been modified since last compile.

`Build` Recompiles source file and all imported files.

`Destination` Specifies whether source file is compiled to memory or disk.

`Primary file...` Specifies file that is focus of Make and Build.

`Clear primary file` Clears previously set primary file.

`Information...` Displays status of program and system memory usage.

The **Debug menu** manages program debugging facilities.

`Breakpoints` Allows user to set, view, and edit breakpoints.

`Call stack` Displays active subprogram calls.

`Register` Opens the Register window.

`Watch` Opens the Watch window.

`Output` Opens the Output window.

`User screen` Switches to full-screen user output.

`Evaluate/modify...` Allows expression evaluation or variable modification.

`Add watch...` Inserts a watch expression into the Watch window.

`Add breakpoint...` Adds a program breakpoint.

The **Tools menu** allows the user to run utility programs.

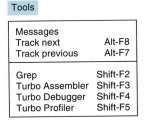

`Messages` Opens the tool Message window.

`Track next` Goes to next line.

`Track previous` Goes to previous line.

`Grep`
`Turbo Assembler`
`Turbo Debugger` } User-installed tools.
`Turbo Profiler`

The **Options menu** allows the user to set integrated environment controls.

Options

Compiler...
Memory sizes...
Linker...
Debugger...
Directories...
Tools...

Environment   ▶

Open...
Save
Save as...

Compiler...   Allows user to set compiler directive defaults.
Memory sizes...   Allows user to specify default stack and heap sizes for compiled programs.
Linker...   Allows user to set linker options.
Debugger...   Allows user to set debugger options.
Directories...   Allows user to specify paths for units, include files, and object files.
Tools...   Allows user to create or change tool menu entries.
Environment   Allows user to change editor, mouse, and color.
Open...   Loads previously saved options file.
Save...   Saves current options settings in an options file.
Save as...   Saves current options settings under new filename.

The **Window menu** provides window management capabilities from keyboard.

Window

Tile
Cascade
Close all
Refresh display

Size/Move   Ctrl-F5
Zoom   F5
Next   F6
Previous   Shift-F6
Close   Alt-F3

List...   Alt-0

Tile   Arranges desktop windows so they do not overlap.
Cascade   Arranges desktop windows with overlap.
Close all   Closes all windows and clears all history lists.
Refresh display   Redraws the desktop.
Size/Move   Changes size or position of window.
Zoom   Switches from full-screen to reduced window sizes.
Next   Makes next window the active window.
Previous   Makes the previously active window the active window.
Close   Closes the active window.
List...   Shows a list of all active windows.

The **Help menu** manages the online Help system.

Help

Contents
Index   Shift-F1
Topic search   Ctrl-F1
Previous topic   Alt-F1
Using help
Files...

Compiler directives
Reserved words
Standard units
Turbo Pascal Language
Error messages

About...

Contents   Displays table of contents for online Help.
Index   Displays index for online Help.
Topic search   Allows user to select a topic for online Help.
Previous topic   Redisplays last-viewed Help screen.
Using help   Instructions on how to use online Help.
Files...   Adds or deletes installed Help files.
Compiler directives   Display help on compiler directives.
Reserved words   Displays reserved words.

Standard units   Displays list of Turbo Pascal units.

Turbo Pascal Language   Shows help on Turbo Pascal Language.

Error messages   Displays error message help.

About...   Shows Turbo Pascal version and copyright information.

The Edit Local Menu

There is one additional menu in the Turbo Pascal integrated environment called the Edit Local menu. This menu is displayed any time the mouse cursor is inside an Edit window and the right mouse button is clicked. The menu items are described below.

Cut	Shift-Del
Copy	Ctrl-Ins
Paste	Shift-Ins
Clear	Ctrl-Del
Open file at cursor	
Topic Search	Ctrl-F1
Toggle breakpoint	Ctrl-F8
Go to cursor	F4
Evaluate/modify...	Ctrl-F4
Add watch...	Ctrl-F7
Options...	

Cut   Moves selected block of text from Edit window to Clipboard.

Copy   Copies selected block of text from Edit window to Clipboard.

Paste   Copies selected text from Clipboard to Edit window.

Clear   Deletes selected text from Edit window or Clipboard.

Open file at cursor   Opens the file indicated by the Edit cursor.

Topic Search   Displays Help for topic under Edit cursor.

Toggle breakpoint   Enables or disables breakpoint at Edit cursor.

Go to cursor   Executes program, stops at Edit cursor position.

Evaluate/modify...   Evaluates an expression or modifies a variable.

Add watch...   Inserts a watch expression in the Watch window.

Options...   Allows user to specify editor option settings.

A.2 Windows and Dialog Boxes

The Turbo Pascal integrated environment makes extensive use of windows and dialog boxes in its user interface. Windows are screen areas that can be moved, resized, overlapped, opened, and closed. Dialog boxes are movable screen areas that contain fields that allow options to be viewed and set. Unlike windows, which remain on the desktop even when they are not active, dialog boxes are usually removed from the desktop once their options have been set.

Windows

Turbo Pascal uses several types of windows. Most have the features shown in Fig. A.1. Edit windows are opened by the Open or New command in the File menu. Many other windows are opened by a Window menu command. You can have a number of windows open in the Turbo Pascal environment, but only one window is active at any one time. Most menu commands apply only to the active window. Turbo Pascal places a double-lined border around the active window. To activate a window, place your mouse cursor on the window and click the left button, or press the F6 key (Next window) repeatedly until the double-lined border appears around the window, or hold down the Alt key and type the number of the window (e.g., press Alt-3 for window 3).

To close the active window, press Alt-F3 or position your mouse cursor on the window's close box and click the left mouse button. To change the size of the window or its location, use the Window menu Size/Move command or your mouse. To move a window, position the mouse cursor on the

Figure A.1
A Typical Window

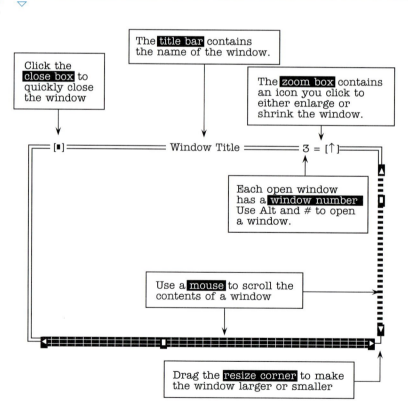

Click the close box to quickly close the window

The title bar contains the name of the window.

The zoom box contains an icon you click to either enlarge or shrink the window.

Window Title

Each open window has a window number Use Alt and # to open a window.

Use a mouse to scroll the contents of a window

Drag the resize corner to make the window larger or smaller

window title bar and drag it (click and then hold the left mouse button while you move the mouse cursor) to the desired desktop position. The window will follow the mouse cursor. To resize a window, position the mouse cursor on the lower right corner and drag the corner until the window becomes the desired size.

If a window has been resized, you can expand it to occupy the full screen by pressing the F5 key. Pressing the F5 key a second time shrinks the window back to its reduced size. You can also achieve the same effect by positioning your mouse cursor on the zoom box and clicking the left button.

You can scroll the text that appears inside a window horizontally or vertically by using the appropriate scroll bars on the sides of the window. Position the mouse cursor on one of the scroll bar arrowheads and press and hold the left button to scroll the window in the desired direction. You can also position the mouse cursor on the scroll bar box, press the left button, and drag it to some other point in the scroll bar. The text will be quickly positioned to that relative point in the window. If you do not have a mouse, use the cursor arrow keys to scroll the window text.

Dialog Boxes

A dialog box provides a convenient means of viewing and setting multiple command options. A typical dialog box appears in Fig. A.2. Five basic types of controls may be present in a dialog box: radio buttons, check boxes, action buttons, input field boxes, and list boxes.

You can mark as many check boxes as you want in a dialog box. An X will appear when you activate a check box. You can mark only one radio button active in each group of radio buttons shown in a dialog box. To change the activation status of either a check box or a radio button, position the mouse cursor over the box or button and click the left mouse button. If you are not using a mouse, use the Tab key to select the desired check box or radio button and then press the Spacebar.

Figure A.2
Typical Turbo Pascal
Dialog Box

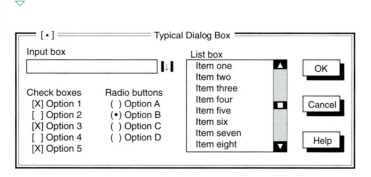

Action buttons are activated either by using your mouse or by using the Tab and Enter keys. The dialog box shown in Fig. A.2 has three action buttons: OK, Cancel, and Help. If you activate OK, the dialog box is closed and the command is executed. If you activate Cancel (or press the Esc key), the dialog box is closed and the command is not executed. Activating the Help button causes temporary exit to an appropriate Help screen.

Input field boxes require you to enter the appropriate text from the keyboard. If a box containing an arrow follows the input field box, a history list is associated with the input field. To access the history list, use your mouse and click on the arrow box or use the Down arrow key. Then you can enter text from the history list to the input field by using your mouse or the cursor keys to highlight and select the desired text. You can edit history list items before you make a selection.

You can make selections from a list box by using your mouse and the scroll bar or by using the cursor keys to highlight the desired item. Use the Enter key or the left mouse button to select the highlighted item.

A.3   Using the Turbo Pascal Editor

The Turbo Pascal editor is invoked when you open an Edit window. The editor allows you to create new programs or to change existing ones. Turbo Pascal 7.0 allows you to have several Edit windows displayed on the desktop at once. The editor uses special commands shown in Fig. A.3 for moving the cursor in the Edit window, inserting text, deleting text, and searching for text.

You can press one of the four arrow keys to move the Edit cursor, or move the mouse cursor to the desired character and click the left mouse button. Several commands are also available for faster and more convenient movement in the Edit window. Pressing the Home key moves the cursor to column 1 of the current line. Pressing the End key moves the cursor to the last position in the current line. Typing Ctrl-Home or Ctrl-End moves the cursor to the top or bottom, respectively, of the Edit window.

As a program file grows larger, it may become too big to appear on the screen all at once. To move back to a previous page of text, press the PgUp key. To move ahead to the next page of text, press the PgDn key. To move the cursor to the beginning or end of the file, type Ctrl-PgUp or Ctrl-PgDn, respectively. You can also use your mouse and the Edit window scroll bars to display any portion of your program.

Block Operations

Several operations can be performed on an entire section of a file, called a block. Before performing any block operation, you must first designate a particular section of your program or file as a block. To use your mouse to mark a block of text, click the left button and drag the mouse cursor over the desired text. Release the left button when the entire block appears in inverse video.

Figure A.3
Turbo Pascal Editor
Commands

▽

Cursor Movements

Character left	←	or	^S
Character right	→	or	^D
Word left	^←	or	^A
Word right	^→	or	^F
Line up	↑	or	^E
Line down	↓	or	^X
Scroll up	^W		
Scroll down	^Z		
Page up	PgUp	or	^R
Page down	PgDn	or	^C
To beginning of line	Home	or	^QS
To end of line	End	or	^QD
To top of window	^Home	or	^QE
To bottom of window	^End	or	^QX
To top of file	^PgUp	or	^QR
To end of file	^PgDn	or	^QC
To beginning of block	^QB		
To end of block	^QK		
To last cursor position	^QP		
To last error position	^QW		

Insert and Delete

Insert mode on/off	Ins	or	^V
Insert line	^N		
Insert compiler directives	^OO		
Delete line	^Y		
Delete to end of line	^QY		
Delete word right of cursor	^T		
Delete char under cursor	Del	or	^G
Delete char left of cursor	BkSp	or	^H

Block Commands

Mark block	Shift-arrow (↑, ↓, →, ←)
Mark block begin	^KB
Mark block end	^KK

Mark single word	^KT		
Mark single line	^KL		
Hide/display block	^KH		
Copy block	^KC		
Move block	^KV		
Delete block	^KY	or	^Del
Read block from disk	^KR		
Write block to disk	^KW		
Cut to clipboard	Shift-Del		
Copy to clipboard	^Ins		
Paste from clipboard	Shift-Ins		
Print block	^KP		
Block indent	^KI		
Block unindent	^KU		

Miscellaneous Editing Commands

Abort operation	Esc		
Autoindent on/off	^OI		
Control char prefix	^P		
Pair braces forward	^Q[		
Pair braces backward	^Q]		
Find	^QF		
Find and replace	^QA		
Find place marker	^Qn		
Repeat last search	^L		
Restore line	^QL		
Save and edit	F2		
Set place marker	^Kn		
Tab	Tab	or	^I
Tab mode	^OT		
Language help	^F1		
Invoke Main menu	F10		
Load file	F3		
Optimal fill on/off	^OF		
Unindent on/off	^OU		
Close window	Alt-F3		

Note: ^ means to hold the Ctrl key prior to typing the next key; n means any integer number.

△

Using the Clipboard

You can use the Edit menu to copy and move blocks of text. You do this by marking the desired block of text and then copying the marked block of text to the Clipboard, using the Copy command from the Edit menu. Next, you position the Edit cursor at the location in the active window where the Clipboard text is to be copied. Now you can copy the Clipboard text by using the Paste command from the Edit menu.

A.4   Some MS-DOS Commands

A principal function of the disk operating system is the maintenance of disk files. Before you can save a file on a new disk, you must *format the disk* (using the command FORMAT). Make sure you do not attempt to format drive C.

You can use the DIR command to see what files are currently on the disk. Each file name is listed in the *disk directory*. Once you know the files on a disk, you can delete a file (using the command ERASE), duplicate a file (using the command COPY), rename a file (using the command RENAME), or display a file on the screen or printer (using the command TYPE). Table A.1 describes each of these commands.

Table A.1
MS-DOS Commands

Command	Effect
CD C:\BP	Makes subdirectory BP on disk drive C the active directory.
COPY B:AFILE.XYZ B:PAYDAY.TXT	Makes a duplicate copy of file AFILE.XYZ on disk drive B. The new file has the name PAYDAY.TXT, and its contents are identical to those of the original file.
DIR	Displays the files in the active directory.
DIR B:	Displays the directory for the disk in drive B.
ERASE B:AFILE.XYZ	Removes file AFILE.XYZ from disk B and frees up the storage allocated to it for use by other files.
FORMAT B:	Formats the disk on drive B so it can be used for storage of files.
RENAME B:AFILE.XYZ PAYDAY.TXT	Changes the name of AFILE.XYZ on disk B to PAYDAY.TXT.
TYPE B:APROG.PAS	Displays the file B:APROG.PAS on the screen.
TYPE B:APROG.PAS >PRN	Prints the file B:APROG.PAS.

Reserved Words, Standard Identifiers, Operators, Units, Functions, Procedures, and Compiler Directives

Reserved Words and Standard Directives

Reserved words are integral parts of Turbo Pascal. They cannot be redefined and must not be declared as user-defined identifiers.

and	exports	mod	shr
asm	file	nil	string
array	for	not	then
begin	function	object	to
case	goto	of	type
const	if	or	unit
constructor	implementation	packed	until
destructor	in	procedure	uses
div	inherited	program	var
do	inline	record	while
downto	interface	repeat	with
else	label	set	xor
end	library	shl	

The following are Turbo Pascal's standard directives. Unlike reserved words, you may redefine them, but we do not advise this.

absolute	far	near	virtual
assembler	forward	private	
external	interrupt	public	

private and public act as reserved words within object type declarations, but are otherwise treated as directives.

Selected Standard Identifiers

Turbo Pascal defines a number of standard identifiers for predefined types, constants, variables, procedures, and functions. Any standard identifier may be redefined but it will mean loss of the facility offered by that identifier and may lead to confusion.

```
Units
  Crt, Dos, Graph, Overlay, Printer, System

Constants
  False, True, MaxInt, MaxLongInt

Types
  Boolean, Char, Text, Integer, ShortInt, LongInt, Byte,
  Word, Real, Single, Double, Extended, Comp

Files
  Input, Output

Functions
  Abs, ArcTan, Chr, Cos, Concat, Copy, EOF, EOLN, Exp,
  FileSize, Frac, Int, IOResult, Ln, Length, Odd, Ord, Pi, Pos,
  Pred, Random, Round, Sin, Sqr, Sqrt, Succ, Trunc, Upcase

Procedures
  Assign, Close, Delete, Dispose, Erase, Exit, Halt, Insert,
  New, Randomize, Read, ReadLn, Reset, Rewrite, Seek, Str,
  Val, Write, WriteLn
```

Operators

Table B.1 summarizes all the operators of Turbo Pascal. The operators are grouped in order of descending precedence. If the Operand Type and Result Type columns contain `Integer`, `Real`, the result type is `Real` unless both operands are integers. *Scalar types* are all ordinal and `Real` data types.

Table B.1
Table of Operators

Operator	Operation	Operand Type(s)	Result Type
+ unary	Sign identity	`Integer, Real`	Same as operand
– unary	Sign inversion	`Integer, Real`	Same as operand
@	Operand address	Variable reference or procedure or function identifier	Pointer
`not`	Negation	`Integer, Boolean`	Same as operand
`*`	Multiplication	`Integer, Real`	`Integer, Real`
	Set intersection	Any set type	Same as operand
`/`	Division	`Integer, Real`	`Real`
`div`	Integer division	`Integer`	`Integer`
`mod`	Modulus (remainder)	`Integer`	`Integer`
`and`	Arithmetical and	`Integer`	`Integer`
	Logical and	`Boolean`	`Boolean`
`shl`	Shift left	`Integer`	`Integer`
`shr`	Shift right	`Integer`	`Integer`
`+`	Addition	`Integer, Real`	`Integer, Real`
	Concatenation	`string` or `Char`	`string`
	Set union	Any set type	Same as operand

Operator	**Operation**	**Operand Type(s)**	**Result Type**
–	Subtraction	`Integer, Real`	`Integer, Real`
	Set difference	Any set type	Same as operand
`or`	Arithmetical or	`Integer`	`Integer`
	Logical or	`Boolean`	`Boolean`
`xor`	Arithmetical xor	`Integer`	`Integer`
	Logical xor	`Boolean`	`Boolean`
`=`	Equality	Any scalar type	`Boolean`
		string	`Boolean`
		Any set type	`Boolean`
		Any pointer type	`Boolean`
`<>`	Inequality	Any scalar type	`Boolean`
		string	`Boolean`
		Any set type	`Boolean`
		Any pointer type	`Boolean`
`>=`	Set inclusion	Any set type	`Boolean`
	Greater than or equal	Any scalar type	`Boolean`
		string	`Boolean`
`<=`	Set inclusion	Any set type	`Boolean`
	Less than or equal	Any scalar type	`Boolean`
		string	`Boolean`
`>`	Greater than	Any scalar type	`Boolean`
		string	`Boolean`
`<`	Less than	Any scalar type	`Boolean`
		string	`Boolean`
`in`	Set membership	The first operand may be of any ordinal type, the second must be a set of elements of that type.	`Boolean`

Table B.1
Table of Operators
(*Cont.*)

Units

Turbo Pascal is distributed with several predefined units, similar to those that you might define yourself, containing a large number of additional constants, types, functions, and procedures. Some of these predefined units are described in Table B.2. All but the `Graph` unit are stored in the file `TURBO.TPL`. The details of the contents of each unit are described in the *Borland Pascal Reference Guide* and also in the on-line help facility provided in the Turbo Pascal integrated environment.

Table B.2
Table of Standard Units

Unit	**Description**
`Crt`	Contains routines that allow you full control over the PC's screen display, keyboard, and sound
`Dos`	Supports several DOS functions, including date-and-time control, directory search, and program execution

Unit	Description
Graph	Stored in the file GRAPH.TPU, contains a library of 50 graphics routines and device-independent graphics support for several display devices
Overlay	Contains the Turbo Pascal unit overlay management routines, which allow units to be swapped between main memory and disk storage during program execution
Printer	Provides easy access to a printer connected to your computer system by declaring a Text file Lst and associating it with the DOS device LPT1
System	Contains run-time support routines for all standard identifiers and is used automatically by any program or unit, without requiring a reference in a uses statement

Functions

Some of the predefined functions of Turbo Pascal appear in Table B.3. The functions following the dotted line are not part of standard Pascal.

Function	Returns
Abs(num)	Integer or real absolute value of its integer or real argument.
ArcTan(num)	Angle whose tangent is num. The result is expressed in radians.
Chr(num)	Character with ordinal number corresponding to the integer num.
Cos(num)	Cosine of real angle num, expressed in radians.
EOF(fil)	Boolean value indicating end of file status of file variable fil.
EOLN(fil)	Boolean value indicating end of line status of Text file fil.
Exp(num)	Value of *e* (2.71828) raised to the power indicated by its real argument.
Ln(num)	Logarithm base *e* of its real argument.
Odd(num)	True if its integer argument is an odd number; False if not.
Ord(ordinal)	Ordinal number corresponding to its ordinal type argument.
Pred(ordinal)	Predecessor of its ordinal type argument.
Round(num)	Closest integer to its real argument.
Sin(num)	Sine of real angle num, expressed in radians.
Sqr(num)	Square of its integer or real argument.
Sqrt(num)	Real number representing the positive square root of its integer or real argument.
Succ(ordinal)	Successor of its ordinal type argument.
Trunc(num)	Integer part of its real argument.

Table B.3	Function	Returns
Table of Functions (*Cont.*)	Concat(st1, st2,...,stN)	String formed by concatenating its argument strings in the order in which they appear.
	Copy(st, pos, num)	Substring of st starting at position pos and consisting of num characters.
	FileSize(fil)	Number of components contained in its file argument.
	Frac(num)	Fractional part of its real argument num.
	High(arg)	If argument is an open array, returns the largest subscript value relative to 0 as the smallest subscript. If argument is an ordinal type, returns the largest value for that type.
	Int(num)	Real number representing the whole number part of its real argument.
	IOResult	Number of input/output error (returns 0 if no input/output error has occurred since previous call).
	Length(st)	Number of characters in its string argument st.
	Low(arg)	Returns the smallest value for its ordinal type argument.
	New(ptype, constructor)	A pointer to object storage is allocated on the heap.
	Pi	Approximation to Pi (3.1415926536).
	Pos(subst, st)	Starting position in st of first occurrence of the string contained in subst (returns 0 if subst does not appear in st).
	Random or Random(int)	Real random number between 0.0 and 1.0 if no argument given; if integer argument is given, returns random integer greater than or equal to 0 and less than int. The procedure Randomize should be called prior to the first reference to Random.
	UpCase(ch)	Uppercase equivalent of Char argument ch, if one exists.

Procedures

Some of the predefined procedures of Turbo Pascal appear in Table B.4. The procedures following the dotted line are not part of standard Pascal.

Table B.4	Procedure	Effect
Table of Procedures	Dispose (p)	Returns dynamic storage pointed to by pointer variable p to heap.
	New (p)	Creates new dynamic variable and sets pointer variable p to point to its memory location.
	Read (f, variables)	Reads data from file f to satisfy the list variables. If f is not a Text file, only one component can

Table B.4	**Procedure**	**Effect**
Table of Procedures *(Cont.)*		be read at a time. If f is not specified, data are read from file Input (the keyboard).
	ReadLn (f, variables)	Reads data from Text file f to satisfy the list of variables; skips any characters at the end of the last line read.
	Reset (f)	Opens file f for input and sets the file-position pointer to the beginning.
	Rewrite (f)	Prepares file f for output and sets the file-position pointer to the beginning. Prior file contents are lost.
	Write (f, outputs)	Writes data in the order specified by outputs to file f. If f is not a Text file, only one component may be written at a time. If f is not specified, data are written to Output (the screen).
	WriteLn (f, outputs)	Writes data in order specified by outputs to Text file f; writes end-of-line marker after the data.
	Assign (f, st)	Assigns name of external file contained in the string expression st to file variable f.
	Close (f)	Closes file f.
	Delete (st, pos, num)	Removes substring of string st starting at position pos and consisting of num characters.
	Dispose (p, destructor);	If called with a destructor as second argument, Dispose can be used to return object storage to heap.
	Erase (f)	Erases external file associated with file variable f from disk.
	Exit	Halts execution of current block and returns control to the calling block.
	Halt	Stops program execution and returns control to the operating system.
	Insert (obj, targ, pos)	Inserts string obj into string targ starting at position pos in targ.
	New (p, constructor)	If called with a constructor as second argument, New can be used to allocate and initialize heap storage for an object.
	Randomize	Initializes the built-in random-number generator with a random value derived from the system clock.
	Seek (f, recnum)	Moves file-position pointer for file f to component number indicated by LongInt argument recnum.
	Str (numval, st)	Converts numeric value of numval to string stored in st. Form of st is specified by format part of numval.
	Val (st, num, code)	If successful, converts string st to an integer or real value as determined by the type of num and code is set to 0. If not successful, code will be set to the position of first offending character in st.

Compiler Directives

A Turbo Pascal compiler directive consists of an opening curly brace ({) followed by a dollar sign, followed by the option name (one or more letters), followed by the option value (+ or –) or parameters affecting the compilation of the program or unit, and is terminated by a closing curly brace (}). Spaces are not allowed before a dollar sign or between the option name and option value. At least one space must separate the option name from a parameter. Examples of several compiler directives appear below.

```
{$B-}
{$R+}
{$B-, $R+, $D-}        {3 compiler directives}
```

A plus sign as the value of a compiler option enables it (makes it active), and a minus sign value disables the option (makes it passive). The compiler directive

```
{$I INCLUDE.PAS}
```

includes the source code from file `INCLUDE.PAS` during compilation.

Table B.5
Compiler Option
Directives

Directive	Default	Effect
Align Data	{$A+}	Align variables on word boundaries.
Boolean Evaluation	{$B-}	Use short-circuit evaluation of Boolean expressions.
Debug Information	{$D+}	Generate debug information during compilation. Usually used with {$L+}.
Emulation	{$E+}	Links floating-point run-time library, which emulates the 80x87 numeric coprocessor.
Force Far Call	{$F-}	Allow Turbo Pascal to choose near or far call model for function and procedure calls, based on program context.
Generate 286 Instructions	{$G-}	Do not use any special 80286 processor instructions during code generation.
Input/Output Checking	{$I+}	Enables automatic generation of code to check the result of an input/output procedure call.
Local Symbol Information	{$L+}	Generate local symbol information during compilation. Must be used with {$D+}.
Numeric Processing	{$N-}	Perform all real-type calculations by calling the TP run-time library routines and not the actual 80x87 routines.
Overlay Code Generation	{$O-}	Disables overlay code generation.
Open Parameters	{$P-}	Disallows use of open string or array as declarations for function or procedure formal parameters.

Table B.5	Directive	Default	Effect
Compiler Option Directives (*Cont.*)	Overflow Checking	{$Q-}	Disables generation of code to check for integer overflow during arithmetic operations. {$Q+} is often used with {$R+}.
	Range Checking	{$R-}	Disables generation of code to check for range-checking and object initialization violations.
	Stack-Overflow Checking	{$S+}	Enables generation of code at beginning of each procedure or function, which checks for enough stack space to meet local data needs of subprogram.
	Typed @ Operator	{$T-}	Disables pointer type checking for @ result value.
	Var-String Checking	{$V+}	Enables strict type checking for string variables passed to var parameters.
	Extended Syntax	{$X+}	Enables support for special Turbo Pascal function and string capabilities.
	Symbol Reference Information	{$Y+}	Enables generation of symbol reference information.

Turbo Pascal Syntax Diagrams

program

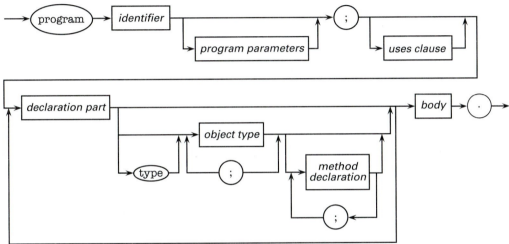

program parameters

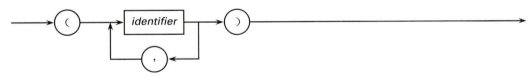

body

uses clause

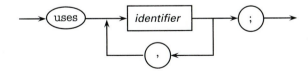

unit

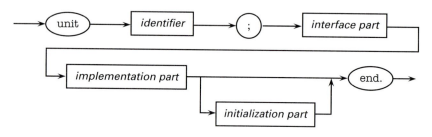

implementation part

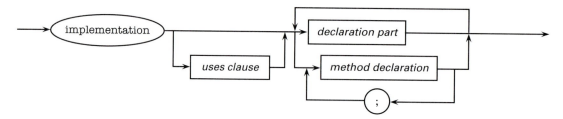

interface part

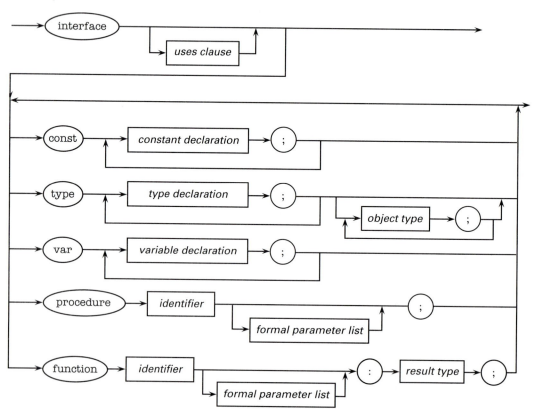

initialization part

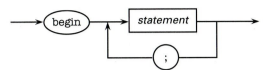

declaration part

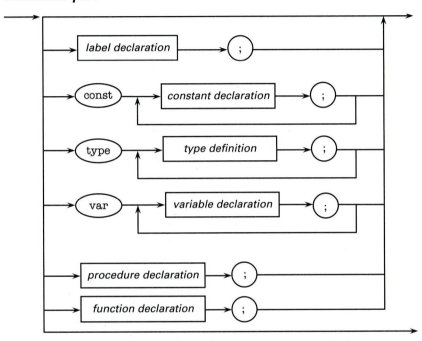

label declaration

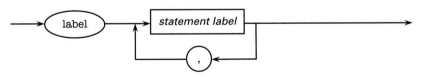

constant definition

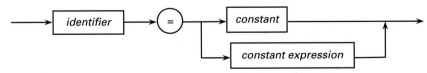

type definition

variable declaration

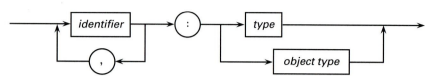

statement label

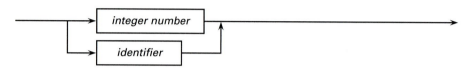

constant

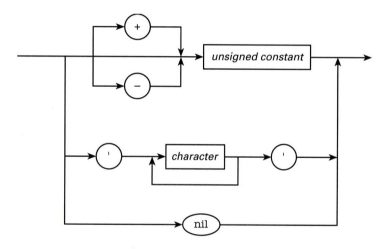

unsigned constant

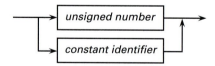

identifier

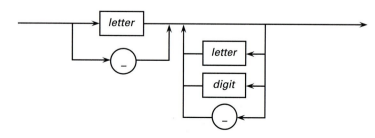

function declaration

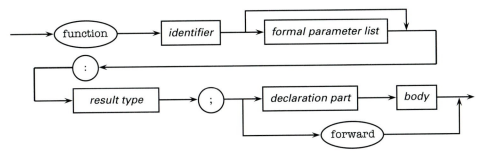

result type

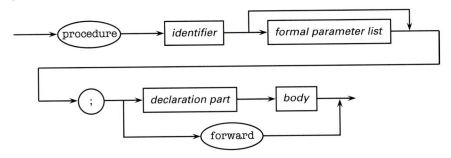

procedure declaration

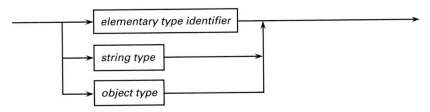

formal parameter list

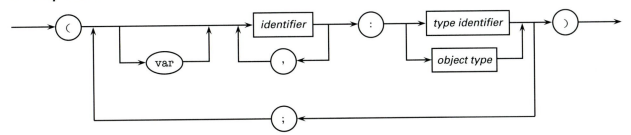

type

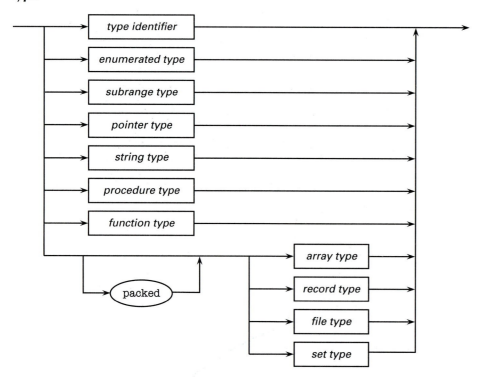

enumerated type

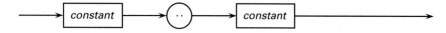

subrange type

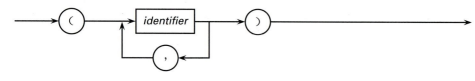

string type

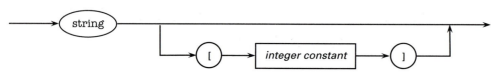

pointer type

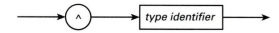

procedure type

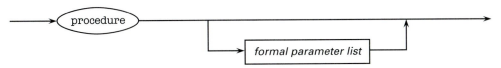

function type

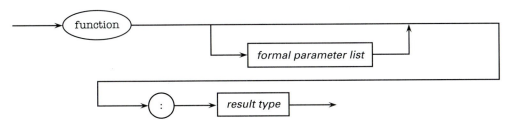

array type

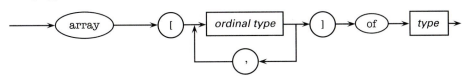

record type

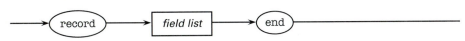

field list

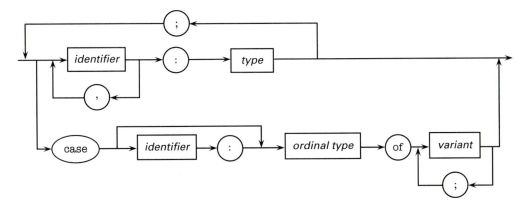

variant

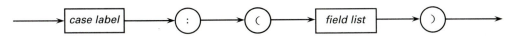

file type

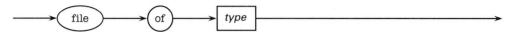

set type

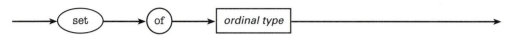

compound statement

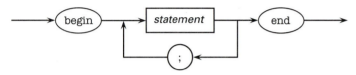

statement

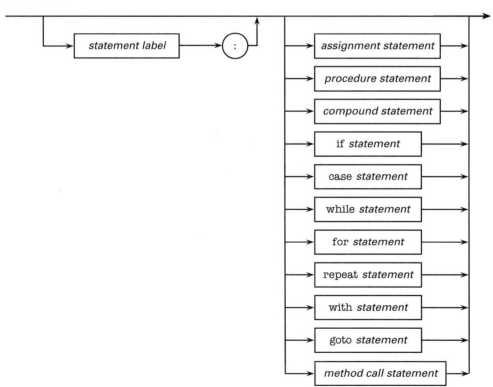

assignment statement

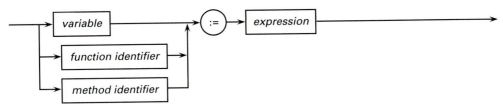

procedure call statement

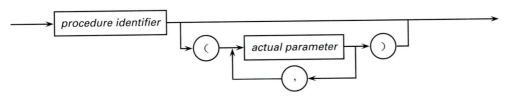

if statement

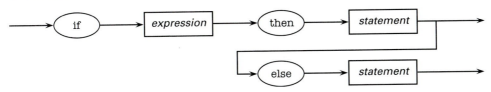

while statement

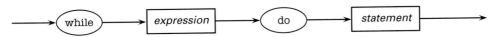

for statement

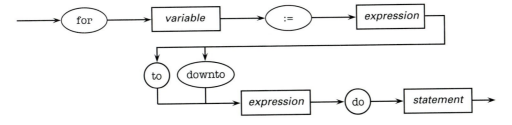

case statement

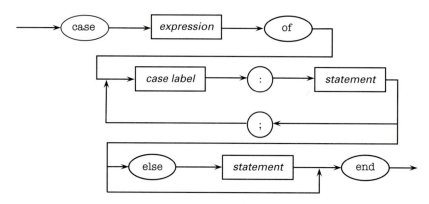

case label

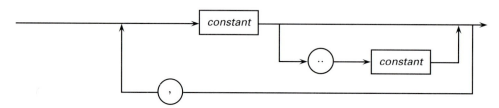

repeat statement

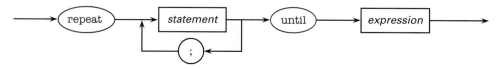

with statement

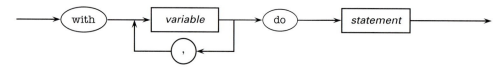

goto statement

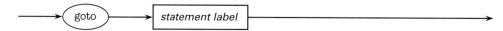

actual parameter

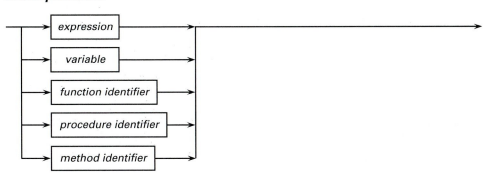

expression

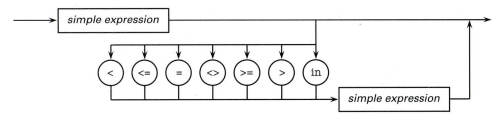

simple expression

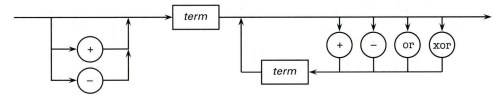

term

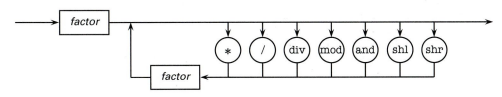

factor

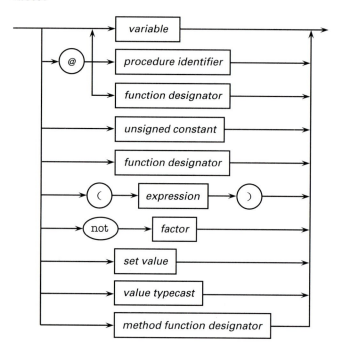

function designator

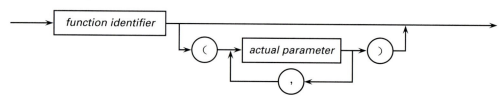

set value

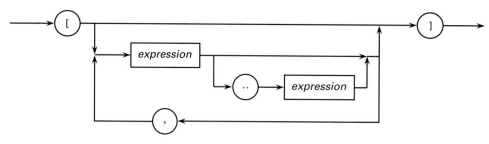

value typecast

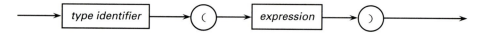

variable

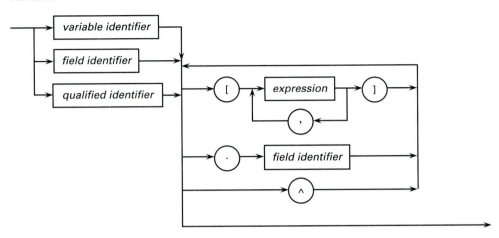

qualified identifier

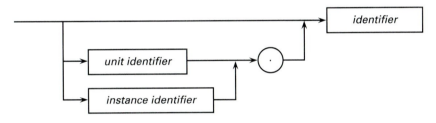

unsigned number

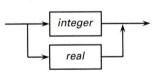

signed number

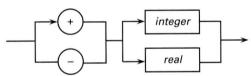

integer

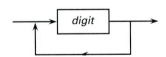

real

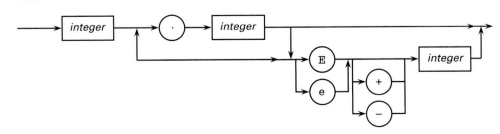

object type

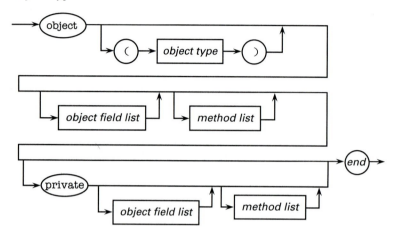

object field list

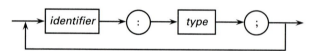

method list

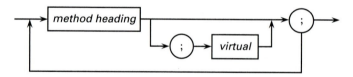

method heading

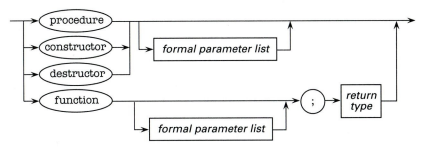

method declaration

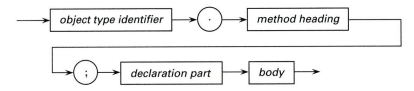

method call statement

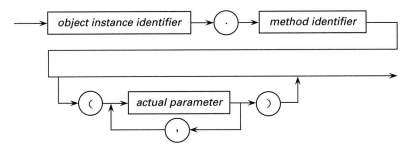

method function designator

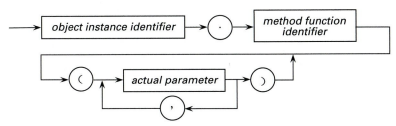

ASCII Character Set

Table D.1 contains the character codes from 0 to 127 for Turbo Pascal. On most computer systems, only the codes from 32 (blank or space) to 126 (symbol ~) have printable characters. The other codes represent the non-printable control characters. The IBM PC implementation of Turbo Pascal provides printable symbols for the nonprintable codes as well.

Table D.1

Table of ASCII Characters

Code	Char	Code	Char	Code	Char	Code	Char
0	^@ NUL	32	□	64	@	96	`
1	^A SOH	33	!	65	A	97	a
2	^B STX	34	"	66	B	98	b
3	^C ETX	35	#	67	C	99	c
4	^D EOT	36	$	68	D	100	d
5	^E ENQ	37	%	69	E	101	e
6	^F ACK	38	&	70	F	102	f
7	^G BEL	39	'	71	G	103	g
8	^H BS	40	(	72	H	104	h
9	^I HT	41	)	73	I	105	i
10	^J LF	42	*	74	J	106	j
11	^K VT	43	+	75	K	107	k
12	^L FF	44	,	76	L	108	l
13	^M CR	45	–	77	M	109	m
14	^N SO	46	.	78	N	110	n
15	^O SI	47	/	79	O	111	o
16	^P DLE	48	0	80	P	112	p
17	^Q DC1	49	1	81	Q	113	q
18	^R DC2	50	2	82	R	114	r
19	^S DC3	51	3	83	S	115	s
20	^T DC4	52	4	84	T	116	t
21	^U NAK	53	5	85	U	117	u
22	^V SYN	54	6	86	V	118	v
23	^W ETB	55	7	87	W	119	w
24	^X CAN	56	8	88	X	120	x
25	^Y EM	57	9	89	Y	121	y
26	^Z SUB	58	:	90	Z	122	z
27	^[ESC	59	;	91	[	123	{
28	^\ FS	60	<	92	\	124		
29	^] GS	61	=	93	]	125	}
30	^^ RS	62	>	94	^	126	~
31	^_ US	63	?	95	_	127	DEL

A P P E N D I X   E

Reference Guide to Turbo Pascal Constructs

Construct	Page	Example
Unit heading	399	`unit GradeSetADT;`
Public part	398	`interface`
Type declaration	319	`  type`
set type	626	`    GradeSet = set of 'A'..'Z';`
Function heading	278	`    function ValidGrade (NextCh : Char) : Boolean;`
Comment	58	`    {Returns True if NextCh is a valid grade.}`
Procedure heading	263	`    procedure PrintSet (InSet {input} : GradeSet);`
Comment	58	`    {Displays set Inset.}`
Private part	399	`implementation`
Function declaration	278	`    function ValidGrade (Next Ch : Char) : Boolean;`
		`    begin {ValidGrade}`
Boolean assignment	146	`      ValidGrade :=`
Set operatior in	630	`              NextCh in ['A'..'F', 'I', 'P', 'W']`
End of function	278	`    end; {ValidGrade}`
Procedure declaration	263	`    procedure PrintSet (InSet {input} : GradeSet);`
Local variable	252	`      var NextCh : Char;        {loop-control variable}`
		`    begin {PrintSet}`
for statement	215	`      for Next Ch := 'A' to 'Z' do`
if statement	151	`        if Next Ch in InSet then`
Write procedure	50	`          Write (NextCh);`
WriteLn procedure	50	`      WriteLn`
End of procedure	263	`    end; {printSet}`
End of unit	399	`end. {GradeSetADT}`
Program heading	39	`program Guide;`
Multiline comment	58	`{`
		`  This program shows examples of`
		`  Pascal constructs.`
		`}`
uses statement	390	`uses GradeSet ADT;`
Constant declaration	41	`const`
Integer	44	`  StrLength = 20;`
Character	44	`  Blank = ' ';`

Construct	Page	Example
String	44	`School = 'Temple University';`
Real	44	`DeansList = 3.5;`
		`Probation = 1.0;`
Type declaration	319	`type`
Subrange	320	`StudentIndex = 1..100;`
Enumerated	325	`College = (Business, Arts, Science, General);`
String	465	`String20 = string[StrLength];`
Record	511	`StuData = record`
		`           Name : String20;`
		`           GPA : Real;`
		`           InCollege : College`
		`        end; {StuData}`
Pointer	688	`ClassPointer = ^Student;`
List node	695	`Student = record`
		`           Info : StuData;          {data field}`
		`           Next : ClassPointer     {pointer}`
		`        end; {Student}`
Array	429	`MajorArray = array [StudentIndex] of College;`
File	662	`StuFile = file of StuData;`
Variable declaration	45	`var`
Record	511	`CurStu : StuData;             {input - student data}`
Set	626	`Grades : GradeSet;            {allowable grades}`
Text file	349	`InFile : Text;                {input - text file}`
File	661	`OutFile : StuFile;            {output - binary file}`
Pointer	695	`ClassList : ClassPointer;     {list of classes}`
Array	428	`Major : MajorArray;           {array of majors}`
Character	42	`NextCh : Char;                {input - character}`
Integer	41	`CountProb : Integer;          {counter}`
String	43	`LastName : String20;          {last name}`
Program body	37	`begin {Guide}`
WriteLn procedure	50	`WriteLn ('Registration for ', School);`
Assignment	46	`CountProb := 0;                  {initialize counter.}`
with statement	516	`with CurStu do`
Compound statement	140	`begin                        {Define fields of CurStu.}`
String assignment	48	`Name := 'Jackson, Michael Bad';`
Display prompt	50	`Write ('Enter GPA> ');`
ReadLn procedure	52	`ReadLn (GPA);`
Enumerated assign	326	`InCollege := Arts`
		`end; {with}`
case statement with	179	`case CurStu.InCollege of`
field selector as	177	`Business : WriteLn ('Business major');`
case selector		`Arts     : WriteLn ('Arts major');`
		`Science  : WriteLn ('Science major');`
		`General  : WriteLn ('General major');`
		`end; {case}`

Construct	Page	Example

Nested if
Embedded apostrophe
	167
	79
		`if CurStu.GPA > DeansList then`
		`  WriteLn ('  On the Dean''s List')`
		`else if CurStu.GPA > Probation then`
		`  WriteLn ('Satisfactory progress')`
		`else`
		`  begin`

Format a string
Increment counter
	73
	196
		`    WriteLn ('On Probation' :21);`
		`    CountProb := CountProb + 1`
		`end; {nested if}`

Assign array element
Assign procedure
Open file for input
Set assignment
	430
	356
	356
	627
		`Major[1] := CurStu.InCollege;`
		`Assign (InFile, 'InFile.TXT');`
		`Reset (InFile);`
		`Grades := [];                    {null set}`

while statement with
    end-of-file test
repeat statement
Read text file
Convert to uppercase
Function designator
Set union
End-of-line test
ReadLn with text file
	196
	358
	223
	351
	317
	97
	631
	361
	353
		`while not EOF(InFile) do`
		`  begin`
		`    repeat`
		`      Read (InFile, NextCh);        {Get character.}`
		`      NextCh := UpCase(NextCh);`
		`      if ValidGrade(NextCh) then`
		`        Grades := Grades + [Next Ch]`
		`    until EOLN(InFile);`
		`    ReadLn (InFile)                {Skip end-of-line.}`
		`  end; {while}`

Procedure call	109	`PrintSet (Grades);`

Assign procedure
Open file for output
Write binary file
Close procedure
	356
	357
	662
	358
		`Assign (OutFile, 'OutFile.Bin');`
		`Rewrite (OutFile);`
		`Write (OutFile, CurStu);          {Write 1st record.}`
		`Close (InFile);   Close (OutFile);`

Open file for input
Read binary file
Extract substring
    before first comma
Compare strings
	356
	663
	640
	643
	465
		`Reset (OutFile);`
		`Read (OutFile, CurStu);          {Read 1st record.}`
		`LastName := Copy(CurStu.Name, 1,`
		`             Pos (',', CurStu.Name) - 1);`
		`if LastName <> 'Jackson' then`
		`  WriteLn ('Jackson is not #1');`

New procedure
Record assign to node
Allocate second node
String assignment
Assign to second node
Pointer assignment
	690
	696
	696
	48
	698
	690
		`New (ClassList);                {Allocate 1st list node.}`
		`ClassList^.Info := CurStu;`
		`New (ClassList^.Next);          {Connect 2nd node.}`
		`CurStu.Name := 'Pascal, Turbo';`
		`ClassList^.Next^.Info := CurStu;`
		`ClassList^.Next^.Next := nil;   {end of list}`

Construct	Page	Example
List traversal	700	```while ClassList <> nil do```
		```begin```
Display node data	701	```WriteLn (ClassList^.Info.Name);```
Advance pointer	701	```ClassList := ClassList^.Next```
		```end {while}```
Program end	37	```end. {Guide}```

Answers to Odd-Numbered Self-Check Exercises

CHAPTER 1

Section 1.1
1. Software

Section 1.2
1. Cell 0: `75.625`
   Cell 2: `0.005`
   Cell 999: `75.62`
3. Bit, byte, memory cell, main memory, secondary memory

Section 1.3
1. Since computers don't think, they don't check the correctness of your thoughts. If there is a logic error, only you can determine whether the answer makes sense. It is better to catch errors prior to entering the program into the computer.

Section 1.4
1. Add A, B, and C. Store result in X.
   Divide Y by Z. Store result in X.
   Subtract B from C and then add A. Store result in D.
   Add 1 to Z. Store result in Z.

Section 1.5
1. Source program, compiler, editor

Section 1.6
1.
```
program Hello;

begin
   WriteLn ('Hi There');
   WriteLn ('My name is Donna');
   WriteLn ('Bye')
end.
```

CHAPTER 2

Section 2.1
1. Problem requirements, analysis, design, implementation, testing, operation and maintenance

Section 2.2
1. Algorithm with refinements:
   1. Read the fabric size in square yards.
   2. Convert the fabric size to square meters.

2.1 The fabric size in square meters is the result of
   dividing the fabric size in square yards by 1.196.
3. Display the fabric size in square meters.

Section 2.3

1. Declaration section and program body.
3. Reserved words: `end, program, begin, const`
   Standard identifiers: `ReadLn`
   Valid identifiers: `ReadLn, Bill, Rate, Start, XYZ123, ThisIsALongOne`
   Invalid identifiers: `Sue's, 123XYZ, Y=Z, Prog#2, 'MaxScores'`

Section 2.4

1. a. `0.0103`   `1234500`   `123450`
   b. `1.3E+3`   `1.2345E+2`   `4.26E-3`
3. Because the value of pi will not change during program execution

Section 2.5

1. `Enter two integers>`
   `M = 10`
   `N = 10`
3. a. Valid, `8.5` is stored in R   f. Valid, value of C is stored in S
   b. Valid, `10` is stored in I   g. Invalid
   c. Invalid   h. Valid, value of I is stored in R
   d. Invalid   i. Invalid
   e. Invalid   j. Valid, 10 plus value of I is stored in R

Section 2.6

1. `{This is a comment?}`
   `(* How about this one {it seems like a comment} doesn't it *)`
3. `program Small;`

```
    var
       X, Y, Z : Real;

    begin
       Y := 15.0;
       Z := -Y + 3.5;
       X := Y + Z;
       WriteLn (X, Y, Z)
    end.
```

The first statement says that the name of the program is `Small`. The reserved word
`var` indicates that variable declarations follow. The next line declares and reserves
space in memory for three variables (X, Y, Z) of type `Real`. The `begin` line indicates that executable code follows. The first assignment statement sets the variable
Y to the value `15.0`. The next statement sets the variable Z to negative Y plus
`3.5`, which is `11.5`. The next statement displays the values of X, Y, and Z (`3.5`,
`15.0`, and `-11.5`, respectively). The last line indicates the end of the program.

Section 2.7

1. a. `22 div 7 = 3`   `7 div 22 = 0`   `22 mod 7 = 1`   `7 mod 22 = 7`
   b. `16 div 15 = 1`   `15 div 16 = 0`   `16 mod 15 = 1`   `15 mod 16 = 15`
   c. `23 div 3 = 7`   `3 div 23 = 0`   `23 mod 3 = 2`   `3 mod 23 = 3`
   d. `16 div -4 = -4`   `-4 div 16 = 0`   `16 mod -4 = 0`   `-4 mod 16 = -4`

3.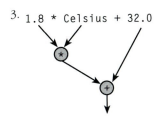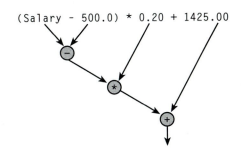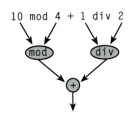

Value of last expression is 2

5. a. `White` is 2.5.   c. `Orange` is 0.   e. `Lime` is 2.
   b. `Green` is 1.0.   d. `Blue` is -3.0.   f. `Purple` is 0.6666....

Section 2.8

# denotes a blank space.

1. `#-99#Bottles`
   `#-99#####-99`

3. `#####1#1#####1`
   `###10#10###10`
   `##100#100##100`
   `#1000#1000#1000`

CHAPTER 3

Section 3.1

1. Problem inputs: `Hours : Real`   `{number of hours worked}`
                   `Rate  : Real`   `{hourly rate of pay}`
   Problem output: `Gross : Real`   `{gross salary}`
   Algorithm
      1. Read hours worked and rate of pay.
      2. Compute gross salary.
      3. Print gross salary.

3. The algorithm needs to read separately the number of hours to be paid at the normal hourly rate (`RegHours`) and hours to be paid at overtime rate (`OTHours`); the formula used to compute gross salary also would need to be modified.

Section 3.2

1. a. `Sqrt(U + V) * Sqr(W)`
   b. `Y * Ln(X)`
   c. `Sqrt((X - Y) * Sqr(X - Y))`
   d. `Abs((X * Y) - (W / Z))`

Section 3.3

1. The design phase

Section 3.4

1. The code for `PrintM` would have to be duplicated twice if the program did not use procedures.

Section 3.5

1. Procedure parameters are used to pass information between the separate modules of a program and between the main program and its modules. Parameters simplify

the use of a procedure by many different calling procedures or other programs. Procedures with parameters are building blocks for constructing larger programs.

Section 3.6

1. Because there is more discrepancy of the vertical pixel count than horizontal from system to system, the head radius is based on `GetMaxY` to prevent the picture from falling off the bottom of the screen.
3. `Rectangle (X1 + 55, Y1 + 30, X5 - 55, Y5 - 25); {left window}`
   `Rectangle (X6 + 55, Y1 + 30, X3 - 55, Y5 - 25); {right window}`

CHAPTER 4

Section 4.2

1. a. Incorrect—and has a higher precedence than <.
   b. Correct
3. a. `True`   b. `True`   c. `True`   d. `False`   e. `True`

Section 4.3

1. a. Not less
   b. Greater than

Section 4.4

1. `A23B, A1c`
3. Change the first box with element *Letter* to

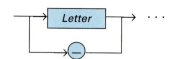

Section 4.5

1. ```
{correct if statement}
if X > Y then
   begin
      X := X + 10.0;
      WriteLn ('X Bigger')
   end
else
   WriteLn ('X Smaller');
WriteLn ('Y is ', Y);
```
3. `Y` would be printed only when `X` is not greater than `Y`.
5. The `if` statement, expression, simple expression, term, factor, variable, statement, and assignment statement syntax diagrams would be used to validate this `if` statement.

## Section 4.6

1. Step 4 Refinement (revised)
   4.1 Net gets `Gross`
   4.2 `if` there are union dues `then`
        Net gets `Gross - Dues`

3. Initial Algorithm for circular or square pizza:

   1. Read in the pizza's size, price, and shape.
   2. Compute the pizza's area.
   3. Compute the pizza's unit price.
   4. Display the unit price and area.
```

Algorithm Refinements for Steps 2 and 3:

Step 2 Refinement
    2.1 if shape is round then
        2.2 Compute area for pizza with diameter Size.
            2.2.1 Assign Size / 2 to Radius.
            2.2.2 Assign Pi * Radius * Radius to Area.
    else
        2.3 Compute area for pizza with side Size.
            2.3.1 Assign Size * Size to Area.

Step 3 Refinement
    3.1 Assign Price / Area to UnitPrice.

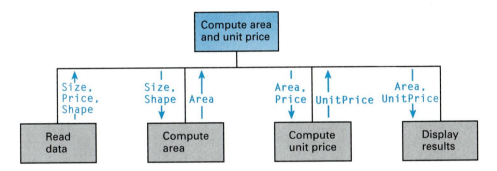

Area is not used by the first subproblem (Read data). It is computed in the second (Compute area) and is passed out so that the third subproblem (Compute unit price) can use it as an input for further computing. Area is an input to the fourth subproblem (Display results). Because Display writes the results to the screen, the value of Area is a program output (output for program user).

Section 4.7

1. Hours = 41, Rate = 2.25

Section 4.8

1.

Statement Part	Salary	Tax	Effect
	13500.00	?	
if Salary < 0.0			13500.00 < 0.00 is False.
else if Salary < 1500.00			13500.00 < 1500.00 is False.
else if Salary < 3000.00			13500.00 < 3000.00 is False.
else if Salary < 5000.00			13500.00 < 5000.00 is False.
else if Salary < 8000.00			13500.00 < 8000.00 is False.
else if Salary <= 15000.00			13500.00 <= 15000.00 is True.
Tax := (Salary - 8000.00)			Evaluates to 5500.00.
* 0.25			Evaluates to 1375.00.
+ 1425.00		2800.00	Tax is 2800.00.

3. a. True with and without short-circuit evaluation
   b. True with short-circuit evaluation; a division by zero error results without short-circuit evaluation.

Section 4.9

```
1. if X = 2 then
     WriteLn ('Snake Eyes!')
   else if (X = 7) or (X = 11) then
     WriteLn ('Win!')
   else
     WriteLn ('Try again.');
```
3. Most of our examples in Section 4.8 contained nested if statements using conditions requiring the comparison of Real expressions, which are not valid as case selectors.

CHAPTER 5

Section 5.1

1. The loop will be executed three times.
   Output: 9
          81
         6561
         3
3. The loop will execute forever if the last statement in the loop body is omitted.

Section 5.2

1. 1
   5
   25
   125
3. Exponential, X raised to the Y power

Section 5.3

1. 0
3. Trace of program in Fig. 5.6:

Statement	InitBal	Balance	Bill	Effect
`ReadLn (InitBal)`	150.00	?	?	Enter start balance
`Balance := InitBal;`		150.00		Initialize Balance
`while Balance >= 0.0 do`				150.00 >= 0.0 is true
`ReadLn (Bill);`			25.00	Enter first bill
`if Balance >= Bill then`				150.00 >= 25.00 is true
`WriteLn ('Issue check..`				Pay the bill
`Balance := Balance - Bill`		125.00		Reduce Balance
`while Balance >= 0.0 do`				125.00 >= 0.0 is true
`ReadLn (Bill)`			30.00	Enter second bill
`if Balance >= Bill then`				125.00 >= 30.00 is true
`WriteLn ('Issue check..`				Pay the bill
`Balance := Balance - Bill`		95.00		Reduce Balance
`while Balance >= 0.0 do`				95.00 >= 0.0 is true
`ReadLn (Bill)`			50.00	Enter third bill
`if Balance >= Bill then`				95.00 >= 50.00 is true
`WriteLn ('Issue check..`				Pay the bill
`Balance := Balance - Bill`		45.00		Reduce Balance
`while Balance >= 0.0 do`				45.00 >= 0.0 is true
`ReadLn (Bill)`			75.00	Enter fourth bill
`if Balance >= Bill then`				45.00 >= 75.00 is false
`WriteLn ('No check ...`				Display Balance

Statement	InitBal	Balance	Bill	*Effect*
`Balance := Balance - Bill`		-30.00		Reduce Balance
`while Balance >= 0.0 do`				-30.00 >= 0.0 is false, exit loop
`WriteLn ('Insufficient ...')`				Display final message

Section 5.4

1. This is necessary to ensure that the columns will line up. They can do so only if a column width is specified for every output value.

3.
```
program SumScores;
{Accumulates the sum of exam scores}

   const
      Sentinel = -1;         {sentinel value}

   var
      Score,                 {input - each exam score}
      Sum : Integer;         {output - sum of scores}
      SentRead: Boolean;     {flag to terminate loop}

begin {SumScores}
   {Accumulate the sum.}
   Sum := 0;
   SentRead := False;
   WriteLn ('When done, enter ', Sentinel, ' to stop.');
   Write ('Enter the first score> ');
   ReadLn (Score);
   SentRead := (Score = Sentinel);
   while not SentRead do
      begin
         Sum := Sum + Score;
         Write ('Enter the next score> ');
         ReadLn (Score);
         SentRead := (Score = Sentinel)
      end; {while}

   {Display the sum.}
   WriteLn;
   WriteLn ('Sum of exam scores is ', Sum :1)
end. {SumScores}
```

Section 5.5

1.

Program Statement	I	J	*Effect*
	?	?	
`J := 10`		10	Sets J to 10.
`for I := 1 to 5 do`	1		Initializes I to 1.
`  WriteLn (I, J)`			Displays 1 and 10.
`  J := J - 2`		8	Assigns 10 - 2 to J.
increment and test I	2		2 <= 5 is true.
`  WriteLn (I, J)`			Displays 2 and 8.
`  J := J - 2`		6	Assigns 8 - 2 to J.

```
increment and test I     3        3 <= 5 is true.
   WriteLn (I, J)                  Displays 3 and 6.
   J := J - 2            4        Assigns 6 - 2 to J.
increment and test I     4        4 <= 5 is true.
   WriteLn (I, J)                  Displays 4 and 4.
   J := J - 2            2        Assigns 4 - 2 to J.
increment and test I     5        5 <= 5 is true.
   WriteLn (I, J)                  Displays 5 and 2.
   J := J - 2            0        Assigns 2 - 2 to J.
increment and test I     5        Exits loop.
```

3. a. `for Celsius := -10 to 10 do`
   b. `for Celsius := 100 downto 1 do`
   c. `for Celsius := 15 to 50 do`
   d. `for Celsius := 50 downto -75 do`

Section 5.6

1. a. `(X > Y) or (X = 15)`
   b. `(X > Y) and (Z <> 7.5)`
   c. `(X = 15) and ((Z <> 7.5) or (X > Y))`
   d. `not Flag and (X <> 15.7)`
   e. `Flag or (X > 8)`
3. A `repeat-until` loop may be used instead of a `while` loop when the loop body must be executed at least once.

Section 5.7

1. a.
```
*
**
***
****
*****
```
   b.
```
***
***
***
***
***
```

Section 5.8

1.
```
while Count <= N do
   begin
      WriteLn ('Count = ', Count);
      Sum := Sum + Count;
      Count := Count + 1;
      WriteLn ('Sum = ', Sum)
   end;
```

CHAPTER 6

Section 6.1

1. a. `321`   b. `54321` is displayed.   c. `5`
   d. `M` should be declared on the same level that procedure `Down` is called from, be it the main program or another procedure. It must be assignment compatible with integers.

Section 6.2
1.

Statement	X	Y	Z	Temp	*Effect*
Shuffle (X, Y, Z);	5	7	2	?	
Temp := X;				5	Temp gets 5 from X
X := Y;	7				X gets 7 from Y
Y := Z;		2			Y gets 2 from Z
Z := Temp			5		Z gets 5 from Temp

3. Inputs: W, X
   Outputs: Y, Z

Section 6.3
1.

Actual Parameter	*Formal Parameter*	*Parameter Kind*
M	A	Integer, value
MaxInt	B	Integer, value
Y	C	Real, variable
X	D	Real, variable
Next	E	Char, variable
35	A	Integer, value
M * 10	B	Integer, value
Y	C	Real, variable
X	D	Real, variable
Next	E	Char, variable

3. a. Type Real of Z does not correspond to type Integer of formal parameter X.
   b. Correct
   c. Correct
   d. Type Integer of M does not correspond to type Real of variable formal parameter A.
   e. 35.0 and 15.0 cannot correspond to variable parameters. Type Real of actual parameter X does not correspond with type Integer of formal parameter X.
   f. Correct
   g. Parameter names A and B have not been declared in the main program. Type Real of actual parameter X does not correspond with type Integer of formal parameter X.
   h. Correct
   i. Expressions (X + Y) and (Y - Z) cannot correspond to a variable parameter.
   j. Type Real of actual parameter X does not correspond with type Integer of formal parameter X.
   k. Four actual parameters are one too many for three formal parameters.
   l. Correct

Section 6.4
1. You is local to Proc1; therefore it can be referenced only within the block of Proc1, not outside.
   Because Proc1 is declared before Proc2
3. a. Parameter X is set to 5.5; global variable Y is set to 6.6; identifiers M, N, and You are undeclared.

   b. Global variables X and Y are set to 5.5 and 6.6, respectively; identifiers M, N, and You are undeclared.

5. Pi is a global constant. A is a global procedure. F is also a global procedure, but it cannot be called by procedures A or D, which are declared before it. The scope of parameter X and local variables B and C declared in procedure A is the block for A, including procedure D. The scope of procedure D is the block for A. This means it can be called only by A or by itself. The scope of parameter S and local constant Star is procedure D. The scope of parameters X and Y and local variable D declared in procedure F is the block for F.

Section 6.5

1. Functions allow us to simplify numeric computation, since they directly relate to the mathematical view of a function. Also, a well-written function avoids side effects, simplifying program verification.
3. a. Function Hypot squares its arguments and returns the square root of their sum as its value.
   b. C := Hypot(A, B)

Section 6.6

1. ComputeSum contains calls to Write and ReadLn.
3. Main program data area   PrintSumAve data area

Section 6.8

1. Mystery(4, 3) → 4 * Mystery(4, 2) →
   4 * (4 * Mystery(4, 1)) → 4 * (4 * (4)) = 64
   Mystery computes the value of M^N.

CHAPTER 7

Section 7.1

1. The result is 1000.0. Cancellation error implies the number cannot be represented to this accuracy.

Section 7.2

1. a. True and True is True.
   b. True or True is True.
   c. True and False is False.
   d. True or False is True.

Section 7.3

1. ASCII values are shown.
   65 < 97 is True.   48 <> 0 is True.
   65 <> 97 is True.   48 <= 48 is True.
   90 > 65 is True.   51 <= 57 is True.
   90 > 97 is False.   57 <= 65 is True.

Section 7.4

1. a. 1 b. False c. True d. 1
3.
```
Ch := 'A';
   while Ch <= 'Z' do
      begin
         WriteLn (Ch, Ord(Ch));
         Ch := Succ(Ch)
      end;
```

Section 7.5

1. The invalid subranges are e, f, g, h, and i.

Section 7.6

1. a. OK
   b. Out of range
   c. OK
   d. J > 0
   e. Invalid type
   f. OK
   g. Invalid type

Section 7.7

1. a. 1
   b. 4
   c. False
   d. Thursday
   e. Invalid
   f. 5
   g. Wednesday
   h. True
   i. Undefined
   j. 6

CHAPTER 8

Section 8.1

1. a. An airline reservation program would probably be best implemented as an interactive task, because booking an airplane seat is often done by seeing what's available and then reducing the list of possibilities to a single choice by asking the client about his or her preferences before actually booking the seat.
   b. The task of printing student transcripts could be done as a batch processing task, since the program input could reasonably be stored and the output printed without additional information from the program user.
3. The <eoln> characters indicate when a line should end and the next begin.

Section 8.2

1. InFile is the input file, the screen is the output file, and InFile is tested by function EOLN:

```
Assign (InFile, 'MYDATA.TXT');
Reset (InFile);
while not EOLN(InFile) do
   begin
      Read (InFile, Next);
      Write (Next)
   end; {while}
```

Section 8.3

1. a. Trailing blanks after a name would be copied as part of the employee's name by procedure CopyLine and would not be encountered by the ReadLn statement in procedure ProcessEmp. Trailing blanks after a value read into Rate

would cause `CopyLine` to read a blank name and would cause the error described next.

b. Blank lines processed by `CopyLine` would have the effect of having no name
printed if encountered by `CopyLine` and would potentially cause a run-time
error if encountered by the `ReadLn` statement in `ProcessEmp` (if a name
data line were encountered while looking for a numeric data value to read).

CHAPTER 9

Section 9.1

1. Specification, analysis, and design (to analyst); implementation (to librarian).

Section 9.2

1. The procedure's directory location must be known, along with a precise desrip-
tion of its interface.

Section 9.3

1. A blue window in the middle of the screen appears with the following text in
white. User-entered data are also shown.

```
Enter C for check, D for deposit >C
```


```
Enter Amount $25.00
```

Section 9.4

1. Procedures are called by other modules, some of which the programmer may be
unaware of. Changing procedure parameters would require changes to all programs that use the procedure.

Section 9.5

1.

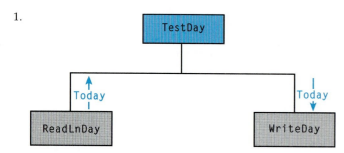

Section 9.6

1. When the procedure is part of the code to be debugged. When the procedure is
known to work correctly

Section 9.7

1. Test data used during white box testing are designed to exercise every logic path
within a given code segment or procedure. A procedure interface error would not
be discovered until after the procedure has become part of a larger module or
complete program and has been called at least once.

Section 9.8

1. a. {invariant:
       InRange = False and no N has been read satisfying
       the condition MinN <= N <= MaxN.
   }
   {assert:
     MinN <= N <= MaxN, or,
     MinN > MaxN and N is not defined.
   }

   b. Add the following assertion after the if-then-else statement:

   {assert:
     MinN <= MaxN and an in-range value for N has not been
     entered; or MinN > MaxN and it is not possible to
     enter a value of N in the interval MinN..MaxN.
   }

3. The loop invariant must be true after each loop repetition. Number > 0 would conflict with the assertion made following the loop that Number is 0.

Section 9.9

1. The user cannot override the code that is already within the system, while a computer programmer can create loopholes in that code to cover unscrupulous acts.

CHAPTER 10

Section 10.1

1. type
       XArray = array [1..3] of Real;

   var
     X : XArray;
     Y, X3 : Real;

3. Five memory cells are allocated for type Char data after the variable declaration.
5. a. type
         RealArray = array [Boolean] of Real;

      var
        N : RealArray;
   b. type
         IntArray = array ['A'..'F'] of Integer;

      var
        N : IntArray;
   c. type
         BoolArray = array [Char] of Boolean;

      var
        Flags : BoolArray;
   d. Invalid array
   e. type
         RealArray = array [Char] of Real;

```
var
   X : RealArray;
```

f. Invalid array

g. type
```
      Day = (Sun, Mon, Tue, Wed, Thu, Fri, Sat);
      RealArray = array [Day] of Real;
```

```
   var
      Y : RealArray;
```

Section 10.2

1. The initial contents of array X are:

[1]	[2]	[3]	[4]	[5]	[6]	[7]	[8]
16.0	12.0	6.0	8.0	2.5	12.0	14.0	-54.5

Statement	*Effect*
I := 3;	Initializes array subscript I to 3.
X[I] := X[I] + 10.0;	Increases value in X[3] to 16.0.
X[I - 1] := X[2 * I - 1];	Assigns value in X[5], 2.5, to X[2].
X[I + 1] := X[2*I] + X[2*I + 1]	Assigns sum of values in X[6] and X[7] to X[4], 26.0.
for I := 5 to 7 do	Shifts values up one array element. Sets X[5] to 12.0, X[6] to
X[I] := X[I + 1];	14.0, and X[7] to -54.5.
for I := 3 downto 1 do	Shifts values down one array element. Sets X[4] to 16.0, X[3] to
X[I + 1] := X[I];	2.5, and X[2] to 16.0.

The final contents of array X are:

[1]	[2]	[3]	[4]	[5]	[6]	[7]	[8]
16.0	16.0	2.5	16.0	12.0	14.0	-54.5	-54.5

Section 10.3

1. It is better to pass the entire array of data rather than individual elements if several elements of the array are being manipulated by a procedure.
3. I is equal to MaxSize if both arrays are the same; I is equal to 3 if the third elements do not match; I is equal to MaxSize if only the last elements do not match.

Section 10.4

1. The condition (ClassLength < ClassSize) in the while loop evaluates to False; therefore, the loop containing EnterInt is exited.
3. If (TempScore = Sentinel), we do not want the Sentinel value to be included in the array. If (ClassLength = ClassSize), the array is full, so there is no room to insert the next data value, even if it is valid.

Section 10.5

1. a. ClassLength is returned as the position of the match.
   b. The position of the first match is returned.
3. To sort in descending order, replace the > with a < in the comparison statement of function FindMin (Fig. 10.17). Also, rename FindMin to FindMax, FindMin's variable MinIndex to MaxIndex, and SelectSort's variable IndexOfMin to IndexOfMax.

Section 10.6

1. a. N * N times; O(N²).
   b. N * 2 times; O(N).
   c. N + (N-1) + ⋯ + 2 + 1 times; O(N²)

Section 10.7

1. Change ReadCode by adding a local Char variable InCode and replace the Read with:

```
begin
  Read (InCode);
  Code[InCode]:= NextLetter
end;
```

CHAPTER 11

Section 11.1

1. a. 20
   b. WriteLn (Matrix[3,4])
   c. 11
   d. Offset = 4 × (i - 1) + (j - 1)

Section 11.2

1. a. All the quarters for person 1.
      Sales[1, Fall], Sales[1, Winter], Sales[1, Spring], Sales[1, Summer]
   b. The Spring quarters for the first 5 people.
      Sales[1, Spring], Sales[2, Spring], Sales[3, Spring], Sales[4, Spring], Sales[5, Spring]
   c. The Fall quarter for the first 5 people, followed by the Winter quarter for the first 5 people, and so on.

Section 11.3

1. An array of this type can hold 420 elements (6 × 10 × 7):

```
type
  LetterRange = 'A'..'F';
  NumberRange = 1..10;
  Day = (Sun, Mon, Tue, Wed, Thu, Fri, Sat);
  AnArray = array [LetterRange, NumberRange, Day] of Real.
```

3. The array would be stored as follows:

```
[1, Main, Freshman]      {all elements for course 1}
  . . .
[1, Main, Senior]
[1, Ambler, Freshman]
  . . .
[1, Ambler, Senior]
  . . .
  . . .
[1, Montco, Freshman]
  . . .
[1, Montco, Senior]
```
All elements for course 2.
```
  . . .
```
All elements for course 50.

CHAPTER 12

Section 12.1

```
1. const
     StrLength = 20;
   type
     StringType = string[StrLength];
     Part = record
                PartNum : Integer;
                Name : StringType;
                Quantity : Integer;
                Price : Real
            end; {Part}
```

Section 12.2

1. This program segment prints the statistics for Exam1, copies the contents of Exam1 into Exam2 (type ExamStats), modifies the High field of Exam2, and finally prints new statistics for Exam2.

Section 12.3

1. If with is used, we could refer to the record member Second directly, conflicting with the existing definition of Second.

Section 12.4

1. a. The letter e
   b. Invalid
   c. Invalid
   d. Jones, Sally
   e. Invalid
   f. The letter A
   g. Invalid
   h. Invalid

Section 12.5

1. NewAddress must be type Address.

Section 12.6

1. Married: 22 bytes
   Divorced: 6 bytes
   Single: 1 byte

CHAPTER 13

Section 13.1

1. a. Real data type operators: := , +, -, *, /, = , <>, <, >, <= , >=
      Real data type standard functions: Abs, ArcTan, Cos, Exp, Ln, Round, Sin, Sqr, Sqrt, Trunc

   b. Char data type operators: := , = , <>, <, >, <= , >=
      Char data type standard functions: Ord, Pred, Succ

   c. Boolean data type operators: := , = , <>, <, >, <= , >= , not, or, and
      Boolean data type standard functions: Ord, Pred, Succ
3. Initializes two data objects and checks whether their key values are the same. It displays the key values: Jennie Moss*****Jackie Moss.

Data type `Entry` is required for `MyEmp` and `YourEmp`, and data type `string` for `Name1` and `Name2`.

Section 13.2

1. The object's method member implementation must be qualified by the object's name, and, inside each method, data member names are not qualified. For a record type declared as an ADT, a record must be passed to each operator and used to qualify each data member (field) inside the operator.
3. Private data members prevent inadvertent or intentional bypassing of the object methods by direct access to the variables. Private method members allow the creation of procedures and functions that can be used only by other member procedures and functions.

Section 13.3

1. a. `MyDirectory.ReadList`. Reads the entries from a text file and stores them in the list.
   b. Not invalid. Retrieves the entry with the same key as `AnEntry`.
   c. `MyDirectory.Insert (AnEntry, Success)`. Inserts `AnEntry` at the end of the list if the list is not full.
   d. `MyDirectory.Init`. Creates a list that is initially empty.
   e. Not invalid. Deletes an entry in the list with key `'Silly Sam'`.
3. Yes. The code works with or without the use of `Self`. It saves execution time, since it does not have to call method member `GetCount`.

Section 13.4

1. a. `MyRectangle := MySquare;`
      `MySquare.Display`
      Assigns `MySquare` object instance to its ancestor `MyRectangle` object instance; displays the square object.
   b. Not invalid. Assigns `MySquare` object instance to its ancestor and displays the `Rectangle` object.
   c. `MySquare.Init (5.5)`. Creates an instance of a `Square` object.
   d. `MyFigure := MySquare;`
      `MyFigure.Display;`
      `MySquare.Display`
      Assigns `MySquare` object instance to its ancestor `MyFigure` object instance and first displays the `Figure` object and then the `Square` object.
3. No, it would not. `List` maintains a list of `Entry` objects and is not an expanded or specialized `Entry` object.

CHAPTER 14

Section 14.1

1.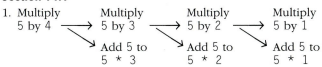

3. The output of the program is 4 3 2 2 3 4.

Section 14.2

1. The actual parameter in the recursive call `Reverse (N-1)` is an expression and must therefore correspond to a formal parameter that is a value parameter.

3.
```
                                                              Result
   Multiply (5, 4)     M| 5              N| 4                    ?
   Multiply (5, 3)     M| 5, 5           N| 4, 3                 ?
   Multiply (5, 2)     M| 5, 5, 5        N| 4, 3, 2             ?
   Multiply (5, 1)     M| 5, 5, 5, 5     N| 4, 3, 2, 1          ?
   Return from (5, 1)  M| 5, 5, 5        N| 4, 3, 2             5
   Return from (5, 2)  M| 5, 5           N| 4, 3               10
   Return from (5, 3)  M| 5              N| 4                  15
   Return from (5, 4)  M|                N|                    20
```

Section 14.3

1. The output of the program: 3. Function `Puzzle` computes log (base 2) of N or the number of times N can be divided by 2.
3. The resulting Fibonacci number would be the next Fibonacci number in the series, that is, `Fibonacci(n)` = `Fibonacci(n+1)`. This results in the series 1, 2, 3, 5, 8, 13, 21, 34 . . . as opposed to the original series 1, 1, 2, 3, 5, 8, 13, 21, 34. . . .

Section 14.4

1. Trace of recursive function `Equal`:
   Call `Equal` with N = 3. X[3] <> Y[3], return false.
3. Function `Mystery` returns the largest value in an array.
   Trace of function `Mystery`:

   Call `Mystery` with N = 3.
     Call `Mystery` with N = 2.
       Call `Mystery` with N = 1.
         Mystery := X [1]; (1).
         Return from third call.
       Mystery := X [2]; (15).
       Return from second call.
     Mystery := Temp; (15).
     Return from first call. Answer is 15.

Section 14.5

1.

Call Number	First	Last	Middle
1	1	9	5
2	1	4	2
3	3	4	3
4	4	4	4

Thus the `Target` of 40 is found at index position 4.

Section 14.6

1. Problems generated from "Move three disks from peg B to peg A":

   1. Move two disks from peg B to peg C.
      1.1 Move one disk from peg B to peg A.
      1.2 Move disk 2 from peg B to peg C.
      1.3 Move one disk from peg A to peg C.
   2. Move disk 3 from peg B to peg A.
   3. Move two disks from peg C to peg A.
      3.1 Move one disk from peg C to peg B.
      3.2 Move disk 2 from peg C to peg A.
      3.3 Move one disk from peg B to peg A.

Problems generated from "Move three disks from peg A to peg C":

1. Move two disks from peg A to peg B.
    1.1 Move one disk from peg A to peg C.
    1.2 Move disk 2 from peg A to peg B.
    1.3 Move one disk from peg C to peg B.
2. Move disk 3 from peg A to C.
3. Move two disks from peg B to C.
    3.1 Move one disk from peg B to peg A.
    3.2 Move disk 2 from peg B to peg C.
    3.3 Move one disk from peg A to peg C.

CHAPTER 15

Section 15.1

1. a. Valid: 1, 2, 3, 4, 5
   b. Valid: '1', '2', '3', '4', '5'
   c. Invalid
   d. Valid: '1', '3', 'A', 'B', 'C'
   e. Valid: 1, 10, 500, 501

Section 15.2

1. a. [1, 3, 4, 5, 6, 7]   g. [1, 2, 3, 5, 7]
   b. [1, 2, 3, 5, 7]   h. [2]
   c. [1, 2, 3, 4, 5, 6, 7]   i. []
   d. True   j. True
   e. True   k. False
   f. False   l. True

Section 15.3

1. a. Magic is 'Abracadabra'.
   b. 11
   c. HisMagic is 'Abracada'.
   d. HisMagic is 'Abrda'.
   e. HisMagic is 'AbAbrarda'.
   f. 5
   g. 1
   h. RealNum is 1.234, Error is 0.
   i. RealStr is '1.2'.
   j. Invalid. RealNum will be undefined, and Error will be 1, indicating an error in the source string at position one.
   k. RealStr is '0.0'.

Section 15.4

1. In procedure DoEdit, add a new case label 'V' for text reversal ('R' is already taken). Call procedure Reverse from Fig. 15.4.

CHAPTER 16

Section 16.1

1. In a binary file, 36 bytes are required to store six type Real numbers.

    In a text file, 4 bytes are required to store each Real number formatted with :4:2. If each number is followed by an <eoln>, there are 6 bytes per line or 36 bytes in total.

There are no circumstances in which the storage capacity required to store six type `Real` numbers in a binary file will change. However, this is not true for the text file. The storage capacity will increase if any numbers require more than a field width of four. This will be the case for a real number larger than 9.99 or any negative number.

3. Assuming that six bytes are required for type `Real` and two bytes are required for type `Integer`, then 50 bytes are required to store one component of file `Books` (2 + 20 + 20 + 6 + 2).

Section 16.2

1. The program reads a collection of numbers from `Data` and writes each number less than fifty to `OutData` and displays it on the output screen with the message `'failed.'`

```
program Mystery;
  type
    NumberType = file of Integer;
  var
    Data : NumberType;
    OutData : NumberType;
    Next : Integer;
begin
  Assign (Data, 'DATA.DAT');
  Assign (OutData, 'OUT.DAT');
  Reset (Data);
  Rewrite (OutData);

  while not EOF(Data) do
    begin
      Read (Data, Next);
      if Next < 50 then
        begin
          Write (OutData, Next);
          WriteLn (Output, Next :2, ' failed')
        end {if}
    end; {while}

  Close (Data);
  Close (OutData)
end. {Mystery}
```

3.
```
type
    ScoreArray = array [1..5] of Integer;
    Student = record
                ID : Integer;
                Scores : ScoreArray
              end;

    StudentFile = File of Student;
  var
    StuFile : StudentFile;
    NextStu : Student;

  begin
    Reset (StuFile);
    while not EOF(StuFile) do
```

```
begin
   Read (StuFile, NextStu);
   WriteLn (Output, NextStu, ID, NextStu, Scores[1])
end; {while}
```

Section 16.3

1. The file types are the same, all records are in order by stock number in each file, and both files have a sentinel record at the end. The input files need not have the same number of records.
3. The merge would complete when the end of either file was reached, without transferring the remaining records in the other file.

Section 16.4

1. If the second Seek statement is omitted, then the modified inventory record will be written immediately after the original inventory record, overwriting the record that is there.

CHAPTER 17

Section 17.1

1. a. The string 'CA' is stored in the Current field of the record pointed to by P.
   b. The record pointed to by Q is copied into the record pointed to by P.
   c. Invalid, should be written as P^.Current := 'HT'
   d. Invalid, P cannot be assigned an integer
   e. Copies the Volts field of record Q^ to record P^.
   f. Assigns P to point to the same record as pointer Q.
   g. Invalid, the Current field cannot be assigned an integer.
   h. Invalid, should be written as Q := P or Q^ := P^.

Section 17.2

1. The memory is not returned to the heap, so it is unavailable for other programs and/or operations that could use it.

Section 17.3

1. a. Assigns the Link field of the record pointed to by R to point to the same node as P. Node Q^ is deleted from this new circular list of two nodes.
   b. Assigns the Link field of the record pointed to by P to point to the node pointed to by R. The list is unchanged.
   c. Assigns P to point to the record pointed to by P's Link field (node R^). The original first list node is deleted from the list.
   d. Assigns the Count field of the record pointed to by P to the same value of the Count field of the record pointed to by Q (P's Count field is assigned the value of 3).
   e. Creates a new node and stores its address in the Link field of the record pointed to by Q. Initializes the fields of the newly created node to 'zzz', 0, and nil for AWord, Count, and Link. Thus a new node is added to the end of the linked list.
   f. Assigns nil to the Link field of the record pointed to by P, thereby denoting that this node is the last (as well as the first) node in the list.
   g. Causes the Link field of the record pointed to by P to point to the same node as the Link field of the record pointed to by Q, nil.
   h. Copies the AWord field from the record pointed to by R to the AWord field that P points to, 'the'.

i. Assigns the Link field of the record pointed to by R to nil by following the chain of pointers starting from P. Node Q^ is deleted.

j. Traverses the list, incrementing the Count field of each node by one until all nodes have been processed.

Section 17.4

1. Method Insert does indeed work properly for an empty list. The nil pointer gets stored in the Link field of the node being inserted by copying the old value of the list head (which was stored in OldHead) into the Link field.

3. It is easier to insert a new element at the head of the list because it is pointed to by Head, whereas there is no pointer to the end of the list.

   To insert at the end of a list, we would have to traverse the list starting at the head until we reach a nil pointer value in the Link field. We would then allocate a new node, initialize its data fields, connect it to the node whose Link field was nil, and store the nil pointer in the Link field of the newly created node.

   This is an O(N) operation because a traversal requires that we examine N nodes.

   To make the insertion at the end of a list an O(1) operation, we need to add a second pointer to the end of the list, say Tail, as a data member for the List object.

CHAPTER 18

Section 18.1

1. The Pop method removes and returns the element from the top of the stack, providing that the stack is not empty. Method Retrieve returns the element at the top of the stack, providing that the stack is not empty, without affecting the state of the stack.

3. The necessary changes to the type declarations are:
   a. Add data member NumItems, which should be type Integer.
   b. Add a new header for a method that returns the value that NumItems contains.

   The necessary changes to the methods are:
   a. Initialize NumItems to zero in constructor Init.
   b. Increment NumItems by one in method Push.
   c. Decrement NumItems by one in method Pop, only if the stack is nonempty.

Section 18.2

1. First expression:

Stack	OpenParen	CloseParen	Balanced
(			
({			
({[			
({	[	]	True
(	{	}	True
empty	(	)	True
(			
empty	(	)	True

Second expression:

Stack	OpenParen	CloseParen	Balanced
(			
({			
({[			
({	[	}	False

Section 18.3

1.

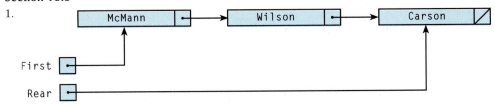

After insertion: Rear points to node following Carson.

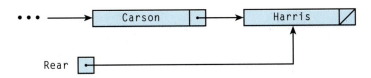

After removal of McMann, First points to Wilson.

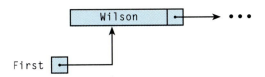

Customer McMann is the customer removed. There are three customers left.

3.
```
procedure Queue.RudeInsert (El : QueueData);
   var
      OldFront : QueuePointer;

begin {RudeInsert}
   if Front = NIL then
      begin {empty queue}
         New (Front);
         Rear := Front
      end {empty queue}
   else
      begin {extend queue}
         OldFront := Front; {Save old Front.}
         New (Front);          {Allocate node for rude person.}
         Front^.Link := OldFront {Connect to old queue.}
      end; {extend queue}

   Front^.Info := El;
   Size := Size + 1
end; {RudeInsert}
```

Section 18.4

1. The first tree is a binary search tree whereas the second is not.

   Inorder traversal of first tree:

```
    10, 15, 20, 40, 50, 55, 60
```
Inorder traversal of second tree:
```
    25, 30, 45, 40, 50, 55, 60
```

In the left subtree of the node containing 50, one would expect to find key values that are less than 50.

3. a.
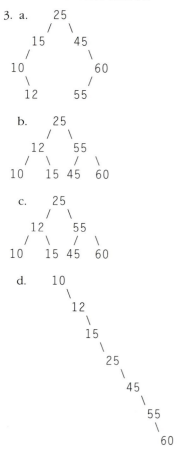

b.
```
      25
     /  \
   12    55
  / \   / \
10  15 45  60
```

c.
```
      25
     /  \
   12    55
  / \   / \
10  15 45  60
```

d.
```
      10
        \
         12
           \
            15
              \
               25
                 \
                  45
                    \
                     55
                       \
                        60
```

Trees (b) and (c) are the most efficient to search.

The binary search trees in (b) and (c) are full binary search trees. Every node, except the leaves, has a left and a right subtree. Searching the tree is an $O(\log N)$ process.

For the binary search tree in (d), each node has an empty left subtree. Searching (d) is an $O(N)$ process just as in searching a linked list with the same keys.

Section 18.5

1. `MyTree.Init;`
   Creates an empty binary search tree by setting the data member `Root` to `nil`.
   `MyTree.Insert (3000, Success);`
   Inserts 3000 into the binary search tree returning `True` in `Success`. This is the root since it is the first value inserted.

`MyTree.Insert (2000, Success);`
Inserts 2000, in the left subtree of the node containing 3000, into the binary search tree returning `True` in `Success`.

`MyTree.Insert (4000, Success);`
Inserts 4000, in the right subtree of the node containing 3000, into the binary search tree returning `True` in `Success`.

`MyTree.Insert (5000, Success);`
Inserts 5000, in the right subtree of the node containing 4000, into the binary search tree returning `True` in `Success`.

`MyTree.Insert (2500, Success);`
Inserts 2500, in the right subtree of the node containing 2000, into the binary search tree returning `True` in `Success`.

`MyTree.Insert (6000, Success);`
Inserts 6000, in the right subtree of the node containing 5000, into the binary search tree returning `True` in `Success`.

`MyTree.Search (2500, Success);`
Searches the binary search tree for the key value of 2500. Takes the left subtree of the node containing 3000 (since 2500 < 3000), and then the right subtree of the node containing 2000 (since 2500 > 2000). `Success` is `True`, indicating that the search key was found.

`MyTree.Search (1500, Success);`
Searches the binary search tree for the key value of 1500. Takes the two left subtrees of the nodes containing 3000 and 2000, respectively. `Success` is `False` (since the left subtree of the node containing 2000 is `nil`), indicating that the search key was not found.

`MyTree.Retrieve (TreeData, Success);`
Searches the binary search tree for the key value of 6000 (value of `TreeData`). Searches the right subtrees of the nodes containing 3000, 4000, and 5000, respectively. `Success` is `True`, indicating that the key value was found, and returns this element of the tree in `TreeData`.

`MyTree.Display;`
Displays the binary search tree in key order.

The tree built by the sequence of insertions is:

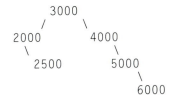

```
        3000
       /    \
   2000      4000
      \         \
       2500      5000
                    \
                     6000
```

The values displayed are:
`2000, 2500, 3000, 4000, 5000, 6000`

Section 18.6

1. Excluding the pointer comparisons (testing for `nil`):
   a. With a target key of 50, two comparisons are necessary to find the target:

Key	Result	Subtree taken
40	40 < 50	Right
50	50 = 50	None

b. With a target key of 55, four comparisons are necessary to find the target:

Key	Result	Subtree taken
40	40 < 55	Right
50	50 < 55	Right
60	60 > 55	Left
55	55 = 55	None

c. With a target key of 10, three comparisons are necessary to find the target:

Key	Result	Subtree taken
40	40 > 10	Left
15	15 > 10	Left
10	10 = 10	None

d. With a target key of 65, three comparisons are necessary to determine that 65 is not present:

Key	Result	Subtree taken
40	40 < 65	Right
50	50 < 65	Right
60	60 < 65	None

e. With a target key of 52, four comparisons are necessary to determine that 52 is not present:

Key	Result	Subtree taken
40	40 < 52	Right
50	50 < 52	Right
60	60 > 52	Left
55	55 > 52	None

f. With a target key of 48, three comparisons are necessary to determine that 48 is not present:

Key	Result	Subtree taken
40	40 < 48	Right
50	50 > 48	None

3. There will be no left subtree for each node, only a right subtree. The Big-O notation for searching a tree like this is O(N).

Index

Note: A boldface page number indicates that the term is defined on that page.

Index for Chapter 19

Credits

The screenshot of the Netscape homepage, Figure 19.5, was reproduced with permission.

Copyright 1996 Netscape Communications Corp. Used with permission. All Rights Reserved. This electronic file or page may not be reprinted or copied without the express written permission of Netscape.

Netscape Communications Corporation has not authorized, sponsored, or endorsed, or approved this publication and is not responsible for its content. Netscape and the Netscape Communications Corporate Logos, are trademarks and trade names of Netscape Communications Corporation. All other product names and/or logos are trademarks of their respective owners.

The screenshot of MetaCrawler, Figure 19.13, was reproduced with permission from go2net, Inc.